READER IN PUBLIC OPINION AND COMMUNICATION

Reader in

PUBLIC OPINION

and

COMMUNICATION

ENLARGED EDITION

Edited by Bernard Berelson and Morris Janowitz

The Free Press of Glencoe

A DIVISION OF THE CROWELL-COLLIER PUBLISHING COMPANY

CONTENTS

INTRODUCTION

Conditions of modern life have increasingly called attention to the importance of public opinion and communication. Growing secularization has meant that more and more areas of life are open to opinion rather than divine law and to communication rather than revelation. Growing industrialization has not only extended literacy; in addition, it has provided the technical facilities for mass communication. Urbanization has not only brought large audiences together but it has also created the need for communication within and between audiences, among many diverse social groups. The development of democratic processes has widened the public whose opinions count and has increased the social and political responsibilities of the communication media. The importance of public opinion and communication is clear.

It is so clear that study of the field has increased in recent years. The events of World War I and the subsequent concern over the pervasive effects of "propaganda" mark the initial acceleration of interest. Basic changes in public opinion during the depression and the monopoly market in opinion and communication under totalitarian governments helped to stimulate research in the field. Commercial interest in audience research and in opinion polling contributed certain techniques which could be applied to other problems. Research in the field was accelerated during World War II by demands for studies on the effect of communications upon military personnel, adjustment to army life and attitudes toward military leaders, enemy propaganda, and civilian morale. After the war this growing interest led to the establishment of additional university centers for the study of public opinion and communication by the methods of social science. Together with the continuing activities of industry and government, they now represent a large scale research enterprise.

All of this activity has produced volumes of theoretical speculation and formulation as well as other volumes of empirical research. As yet, however, there is no single volume which adequately synthesizes and collates the available concepts and propositions in the field. In the absence of such a volume we have attempted to prepare the next best thing—a collection of readings representative of the best work in the field.

This volume is designed primarily for the advanced student in the field and in the neighboring social sciences. We hope it will also be useful to practitioners in the field, to teachers, and to research workers in public opinion and communication.

The scope of the volume is best defined by its table of contents. Because of space requirements we were not able to include material directly concerned with research techniques in the field although we have made a conscious effort to represent some major techniques in our substantive selections. Nor were we able to include material on certain interesting yet peripheral or subordinate areas such as non-verbal communication or the history of the media. (In these cases, however, we have included brief bibliographies.) Throughout the volume we have attempted to represent the distinctive contributions made by students of various fields—sociology, psychology, political science, history, economics, anthropology, law, journalism, librarianship—as well as to represent what might be called various schools of thought within the field.

The major criterion of selection was the quality of the contribution. The contribution could be made as a theoretical or conceptual analysis (as in Cooley or Mead), as an addition to substantive knowledge (as in Nixon or Herzog), or as an illustration of the application of research methods to substantive problems (as in Warner-Henry or Asheim). Again, contributions were selected as overviews of a field of interest (as in Lazarsfeld on audience research) or as studies of particular aspects of the field (as in Kornhauser or White). Since it would be impossible to "cover" the field of public opinion and communication within the limits of this volume, no attempt was made to do so. However, we do hope that despite the difficulty of selection, we have succeeded in representing the major streams of interest and modes of thought now active in the field. (Accessibility of the item in other sources was only a minor consideration in our selection; it came into play only in those few cases in which selection could not be made on other grounds.)

The brief introductions to each section of the Reader are intended primarily to explain the bases of selection operating in each particular instance. We have also included a selected bibliography of additional readings for each section of the outline.

We wish to express our gratitude to the members of the advisory board for their diligent and thoughtful work on the problems of organization and selection. The final composition of the Reader has benefited greatly from their advice. Of course, they bear no responsibility for the finished volume.

Our grateful thanks go to the authors of the items for their permission to reprint. Formal acknowledgments and citations are presented in connection with each selection.

Finally, we wish to express our gratitude to Jeremiah Kaplan, editor of The Free Press, for his interest and cooperation in this undertaking as well as for other publications of social science interest.

Bernard Berelson
Morris Janowitz

University of Chicago
January, 1950

READER IN PUBLIC OPINION AND COMMUNICATION

1

THEORY OF PUBLIC OPINION

There is no generally accepted theory of public opinion, nor even a generally recognized attempt at the formulation of such a theory, in the sense of a body of inter-related propositions of high generality and explanatory power. But there are a series of writings from various standpoints within the social sciences—political science, psychology, sociology—which provide not only clarifying definitions and classifications but also insightful observations about the functioning of public opinion in modern society.

Contrary to popular notions and even to the ideas of some practitioners in the field, the study of public opinion did not spring full-panoplied from the brow of George Gallup in the 1930's. Political theorists had always given consideration to the problems of public opinion, even though they did not always call it by that term. A summary statement of the development of the concept and of the treatment it receives in political theory is contained in the essay by Palmer. This historical review serves to introduce a series of writings by political theorists of the 19th and early 20th centuries who began to give the field its modern definition (represented here by Thompson and Lowell). They were concerned with such themes as the relationship between the development of public opinion and population trends; the influence of industrialization, urbanization, and democratization upon the growth and character of public opinion; the moral implications of broadening the opinion base through education and suffrage; the relationship of public opinion to the procedures of democratic government; the role of opinion in theories of political power. In them we find not only conceptualization and problem-statement but also an emphasis upon the empirical analysis of opinion phenomena.

This trend, carried forward after World War I by American students of public opinion, led into the technical advances of the 1930's and 1940's—which, incidentally, served to distract attention from theoretical problems in an over-attention upon methodological concerns. Indicative of one theoretical approach is the selection from Lasswell which applies principles of dynamic psychology to the area of politics, in an analysis of broad symbols

1

of identification. Another approach, based upon the social psychology of Mead, is represented by the selection from Blumer. Finally, the article by Katz illustrates an attempt to translate theoretical concerns into empirical research operations, thus typifying efforts to bring research and theory into a relationship of mutual enrichment instead of the antagonism which characterizes much of the literature of the field. The tendency to use theory in the statement of researchable problems and to build theory on the foundation of empirical results is now becoming characteristic of the best work in the field.

Paul A. Palmer

THE CONCEPT OF PUBLIC OPINION
IN POLITICAL THEORY

Historians of political theory have given us full accounts, in general treatises and in monographs, of such doctrines as nationalism, *raison d'etat*, sovereignty, and natural law; but they have, for the most part, ignored the concept of public opinion. The general histories contain only incidental references to it, and special studies have been rare. American scholars, with but few exceptions, appear to believe that the treatises of Lowell and of Lippmann are at once the first and the last word on the subject. It is time to dispel this parochial, unhistorical illusion.

As a matter of fact, the roots of the concept lie deep in the past. There was, it is true, no explicit formulation of it prior to the eighteenth century and no systematic treatment of it prior to the nineteenth; but in earlier writings one finds anticipations and approximations of modern theorizing about public opinion. The problem of the many to hold an opinion about and to pass judgment upon political issues engaged the attention of the Greeks. Of Plato one may say, with Laski, that he "denied the value of any general public opinion." It is significant that Lippmann takes the famous cave analogy of Book VII of the *Republic* as the text of his skeptical *Public Opinion*. Aristotle appraised more highly the political competence of the masses. The principle that the multitude should be supreme contains "an element of truth." "Hence," continues Aristotle, "the many are better judges than a single man of music and poetry; for some understand one part and some another; and among them they understand the whole. . . . The knowledge of a house is not limited to the builder only; the user, or, in other words, the master, of the house will even be a better judge than the builder, just as the pilot will judge better of a rudder than a carpenter, and the guest will judge better of a feast than the cook."

Reprinted from *Essays in History and Political Theory in Honor of Charles Howard McIlwain*, (1936), pp. 230-257, by permission of the publisher. (Copyright, 1936, by The President and Fellows of Harvard College.)

Certain phrases and ideas in the political and juristic vocabulary of the Romans and in the writings of the medieval period are likewise related to some aspects of the modern concept of public opinion. Roman authors of the classical period had little respect for the *vulgus*. Inscribed in bold letters around the walls of the reading room of the *Institut für Zeitungskunde* at the University of Berlin is this line from Cicero's oration in behalf of Quintus Roscius: "*Sic est vulgus: ex veritate pauca, ex opinione multa aestimat.*" The phrase "*opinio publica,*" moreover, is found in both classical and medieval Latin; but the context shows that it was without the political connotation of "public opinion" (or "*opinion publique,*" or "*öffentliche Meinung*"). More closely related to the modern view of public opinion as the basis of law is the *consensus populi* of the Roman and medieval jurists, but those who employed the phrase did not discuss its implications in any detail. Of medieval origin is the proverb "*Vox populi, vox Dei.*" It is found in the writings of Alcuin and of William of Malmesbury. Machiavelli referred to it in the *Discorsi*. "Not without reason," he wrote in Chapter LXIII, Book I, "is the voice of the people compared to the voice of God." Since the latter part of the eighteenth century, indeed, it has been quoted, approvingly or otherwise, in almost every discussion of the source and competence of public opinion.

Tributes to the power of opinion became increasingly frequent in the seventeenth and eighteenth centuries. Blaise Pascal hailed opinion as "Queen of the World," a phrase which the physiocrats and the *philosophes* quoted time and time again. "People cry out against the *philosophes,*" wrote Voltaire; "they are justified in doing so, for if opinion is the Queen of the World, the *philosophes* govern this queen." Hobbes declared that, in a sense, "they say truly and properly that say the world is governed by opinion." In the *Essay concerning Human Understanding* Locke distinguished three classes of laws: the divine law, the civil law, and "the law of opinion or reputation." Hume argued brilliantly that all governments, however despotic, are based upon opinion.

Thus by the middle of the eighteenth century there was general recognition of the strength and of the divine, mysterious origin and validity of opinion. Rousseau, as Lord Acton observed, applied the theory of popular infallibility to the state. In his first discussion of the *volonté générale* he came to the conclusion that the "most general will is also the most just and that the voice of people is the voice of God." In the *Social Contract* he pays tribute to the power of opinion. We find in the first chapter the suggestion that even a despotism rests upon the opinion of the subjects. "He believes himself to be a master of others who is none the less more of a slave than they"—a statement on which a passage in *Emile* may serve as a commentary: "Despotic rule is servile even when it is based on opinion; for you depend on the prejudices of those whom you rule through prejudices. In order to conduct them as you wish, you must conduct yourself as they wish." Indeed, whatever the form of government, the most fundamental of all laws is that of opinion. Political, civil, and criminal laws are all based upon it. Again, in his last important political treatise, *Considérations sur le gouvernement de Pologne* (1772), he enforces the point that "Whoever makes it his business to give laws to a people must know how to sway opinions and through them govern the passions of men."

More significant, however, than these characterizations of the power of opinion is the fact that first among influential political theorists Rousseau made use of the phrase "public opinion" *(l'opinion publique)* and thus laid the basis for further development of the concept. It is, of course, obvious that his "general will" is closely related to modern definitions and appraisals of public opinion. Rousseau himself, however, does not indicate specifically the relation of public opinion to the general will and to law. What he seems to say is that law (civil, criminal, or political) is effective only if it is based on wholesome customs and an enlightened opinion. With reference to the institution of a censorial tribunal he declares: "Just as the declaration of the general will is made by the law, the declaration of public judgment is made by the censorial tribunal. Public opinion is the sort of law of which the censor is the minister." Stating that public opinion is not subject to coercion, he refers, in a footnote, to a more detailed discussion of the relation between law and public opinion in his *Lettre à M. d'Alembert* (1762). Therein, describing the evils which would arise from the establishment of a theatre in Geneva, he argues that no laws could prevent the corruption which such an institution would cause. The government can influence morals *(moeurs)* only through public opinion *(l'opinion publique)*. It cannot influence or direct public opinion by law or any instrument of coercion. The tribunal of the marshals of France, instituted in 1651 for the purpose of adjudicating quarrels which might lead to duels, failed precisely because it embodied an attempt to subdue public opinion by a show of force. "Opinion, Queen of the World, is not subject to the power of kings; they are themselves its first slaves."

Another Genevan, Jacques Necker, first discussed in detail the nature and significance of public opinion as a factor in statecraft. "More than anyone else," he justly declared, "I have called attention in my various works to the rule of public opinion and its increasing power." It is not difficult to account for Necker's insistent emphasis on public opinion as a political force. As finance minister he was forced to wrestle with the problem of public credit; and public credit, as he repeatedly remarked, depends on the opinion which actual and potential holders of government securities entertain with respect to the stability and integrity of the government. Such opinion, the opinion of the *bourgeoisie*, constitutes public opinion as Necker interprets the phrase. The rise of public opinion and the recognition of its importance were closely connected, as Lord Acton keenly observed, with the rise of the national debt. Necker also frequented the *salons,* and in particular the one presided over by his charming wife, and had occasion to feel the influence which that institution exerted in affairs of state. He remarked that during the reigns of Louis XV and Louis XVI the courtiers and even the ministers would have risked displeasing the royal family in preference to exposing themselves to an unwelcome reception in the leading *salons* of Paris. Thus Necker saw in the increasing power, self-consciousness, and articulateness of the *bourgeoisie* the basis and significance of public opinion.

"This public opinion," he wrote in his first important publication, "strengthens or weakens all human institutions." "Only fools, pure theorists, or apprentices in moral philosophy fail to take public opinion into account in their political undertakings." Particularly in France has it attained complete supremacy. "It is thus that most foreigners . . . have difficulty in forming a just idea of the authority exercised in France by public opinion; they have difficulty in understanding the nature of an invisible power which, without treasures, without a bodyguard, and without an army gives laws to the city, to the court, and even to the palaces of kings."

The nature and the force of public opinion, in Necker's view, vary according to the form of government. In a despotism public opinion does not exist. In a republic men cherish the independence of their individual opinions to such an extent that it is difficult for anything like a public opinion to arise. Within a democracy public opinion has no distinctive character. It is most effective and wholesome in its operation under a limited monarchy, with its gradations of rank and social classes, as in the France of the *ancien régime* or in the British constitutional system. In such circumstances public opinion is at once stronger and more enlightened than the law. It may be regarded as a tribunal before which all statesmen must render their accounts and which must be enlightened by publicity if its judgments are to be correct. It is the principal safeguard against abuse of political authority.

Apart from the discussion of public opinion in the writings of Necker (which cover the period from 1773 to 1804), there was, so far as I have been able to discover, no explicit, detailed analysis of the concept in French during the era of the Revolution and the Empire. It is true that the phrase *"opinion publique,"* partly no doubt as a result of Necker's frequent use of it, became a catch-word or slogan, and that references to it abound in the ephemeral political literature of the period. The general assumptions embodied in these brief and incidental treatments are the already familiar ones that public opinion is created by and follows the writings of the enlightened few; that it is a potent social and political force, "Queen of the World," which brings on revolution, makes and unmakes statesmen; and that it is the chief check on the holders of power. Evidence of the respect paid to it by revolutionary leaders is seen in the fact that they consecrated one of the *sans-culottides,* the five days rounding out the republican year, to Opinion.

The first discussions of public opinion in German constitute one element of the influence of the French Revolution on German thought. Almost without exception the writers who concerned themselves with the subject acknowledged their indebtedness to the ideas current in revolutionary France. They recognized that the phrase *"öffentlich Meinung"* which they employed as the equivalent of *"opinion publique"* was a novel one, and they viewed the concept connected with it as an outgrowth of the great Revolution.

Several of these early discussions of public opinion may be singled out for special mention. A suggestive inquiry into the nature and competence of public opinion is to be found in C. M. Wieland's famous *Gespräche unter vier Augen* (1799). Wieland, whom Gooch calls the "German Voltaire" and "perhaps the most representative figure of the *Aufklärung,*" devotes the ninth of his dialogues to this subject; and allows the participants, Egbert and Sinibald, to come to the conclusion that henceforth, as a consequence of the French Revolution, governments can no longer exist without respecting public opinion. The essay "On Public Opinion" by the philosopher Christian Garve presents a more detailed analysis of the concept. "From France," he writes in the opening paragraph, "whence so much both good and evil has been brought to us, are derived both the concept and the phrase 'public opinion.'" What is public opinion? "Public opinion as interpreted by those who first used this expression and by those French writers who are clearest on the subject is the agreement of many or of the majority of the citizens of a state with respect to judgments which every single individual has arrived at as a result of his own reflection or of his practical knowledge of a given matter." Garve goes on to appraise the validity of *"Vox populi, vox Dei,"* and to conclude that public opinion is particularly competent to deal with general principles. A more ambitious attempt to relate the concept of public opinion to a general theory of the state is found in the work of another philosopher, Jakob Fries, entitled *Philosophische Rechtslehre und Kritik aller positiven Gesetzgebung* (1803). In public opinion Fries finds the basis for the rule of law within the state.

Worthy of more extended comment is the evaluation of public opinion in the most important German contribution to political theory in the first part of the nineteenth century, Hegel's *Grundlinien der Philosophie des Rechts.* Public opinion, according to Hegel, is essentially contradictory in character. Thus it deserves at once to be respected and despised. It should be respected for the essential principles which it embodies. It should be despised with respect to its outward expression. "In public opinion truth and falsehood exist together. It is the task of the great man to find the truth in it. For he is indeed the great man who tells his age what it wishes and means and carries it out. He realizes the inwardness and essential nature of his time; and he who does not know how to despise public opinion in some of its manifestations will never bring anything great into being."

The first detailed discussion of public opinion in English is from the pen of Jeremy Bentham. Throughout his writings he insisted upon the importance of public opinion as an instrument of social control; and in his more specifically political treatises, compiled after 1814, he regarded the free expression of public opinion as the chief safeguard against misrule and as the characteristic mark of a democratic state.

It is noteworthy that Bentham used the phrase "public opinion" quite consciously, albeit somewhat hesitantly. Always precise in his terminology, he took pains to indicate wherein the expression failed to convey his exact meaning. The word "opinion," he observed, is unhappy in that it does not connote an influence on action; and the phrase "public opinion" may be employed only in deference to common usage.

In his earlier writings, *An Introduction to the Principles of Morals and Legislation* (1789) and *The Theory of Legislation* (1802), Bentham is concerned with public opinion as an instrument of social control—or, in his own words, as a "sanction." "There are," Bentham states, "four distinguishable sources from which pleasure and pain are in use to flow: considered separately, they may be termed the *physical,* the *political,* the *moral,* and the *religious:* and inasmuch as the pleasures and pains belonging to each of them are capable of giving a binding force to any law or rule of conduct, they may all of them be termed sanctions." The moral or popular sanction issues from "such chance persons in the community as the party in question may happen in the course of his life to have concern with, according to each man's spontaneous disposition, and not according to any settled or concerted rule." Elsewhere Bentham comments that the moral sanction may also be called the "sanction of public opinion." The legislator cannot ignore public opinion. It should be "his object to increase the force of this motive and to regulate its intensity." "His greatest difficulty will be in conciliating the public opinion, in correcting it when erroneous, and in giving it that bent which shall be most favorable to produce obedience to his mandates." In his *Essay on Political Tactics,* written in 1789, Bentham considers more fully the relation between public opinion and legislation. As a safeguard against abuse of power, he demands publicity for all official acts; and in an enlightened public opinion he sees a tribunal which "unites all the wisdom and all the justice of the nation." We should love publicity for the enemies it makes: "the malefactor, who seeks to escape the notice of the judge; the tyrant, who seeks to stifle public opinion, whilst he fears to hear its voice; the timid or indolent man, who complains of the general incapacity in order to screen his own."

When in later life Bentham began to explore the broader fields of political science and political theory, he displayed the same respect for public opinion as a remedy for misrule. He had, moreover, become a firm believer in a democracy, partly as a result of his association with James Mill; and he developed his theory of public opinion as an integral part of a democratic theory of the state. In the *Securities against Misrule adapted to a Mohammedan State* and in the *Constitutional Code,* he described the nature and functions of what he called the "public opinion tribunal." "To a representative democracy," he declares in the introduction to the *Code,* "this unofficial, unpaid, and incorruptible judicatory is an instrument of support; and in regard to it, the object and endeavour will be to maximize the rectitude of the decisions given by it . . . To every other form of government, it is by correspondent causes rendered an object of terror and anxiety, though the magnitude of its power is universally acknowledged among them." "Public opinion," he states by way of definition, "may be considered as a system of law emanating from the body of the people . . . To the pernicious exercise of the power of government it is the only check; to the beneficial an indispensable supplement. Even at the present stage in the career of civilization, its dictates coincide, on most points, with those of the *greatest happiness* principle; on some, however, it still deviates from them; but as its deviations have all along been less and less numerous, and less wide, sooner or later they will cease to be discernible, aberration will vanish, coincidence will be complete." The most important factor in the formation and expression of public opinion is in the newspaper press. "In this instrument may be seen not only an appropriate organ of the public opinion tribunal, but the only regularly and constantly acting one."

Thus by the end of the first quarter of the nineteenth century the concept of public opinion had entered the main current of political theory. All who concerned themselves with it agreed that it was a phenomenon of great force and significance in political life. Profound disagreement arose, however, as to the virtue and competence of public opinion. Generally speaking, supporters of democracy and of liberal institutions praised public opinion as the voice of the enlightened middle class, as a safeguard against misrule, and as an agent of progress. Critics of democracy and of certain aspects of representative government were skeptical as to its competence, and urged the necessity of limiting the scope of its activity. Discussions from both points of view, especially after 1840, displayed an increasing recognition of the daily press as a factor in the formation and expression of public opinion.

The contrasting views of public opinion were clearly stated, in Hegelian fashion, by Friedrich Ancillon in his *Vermittlung der Extreme in den Mein-*

ungen (1828). As a thesis (*Satz*) he defines the liberal doctrine as follows: "Public opinion is more than ever before the principal power in the political world, and it must light the path of governments as a guiding star, and be followed by them. In all political affairs, and especially in the matter of legislation, it must be interrogated and heeded." As the antithesis (*Gegensatz*) he sets forth the conservative doctrine: "Public opinion is a false, fluctuating, transitory illusion, a usurped authority. Far from being the vital principle of states, it leads them along false paths, and exposes them to continual disturbances." Discussions of public opinion embodying the point of view epitomized in Ancillon's *Satz* may be found in the writings of Karl Rosenkranz, W. A. R. MacKinnon, Henry Thomas Buckle, Charles Dollfus, Karl Biedermann, and J. C. Bluntschli. Friedrich Julius Stahl, David Urquhart, Sir Henry Maine, and Rudolf Gneist were among those who emphasized the limitations and defects of public opinion.

Some writers, however, approached the problem in a more objective, comprehensive fashion. Carl von Gersdorf in his *Uber den Begriff und das Wesen der öffentlichen Meinung* (1846), the most detailed analysis of public opinion in the first part of the nineteenth century, traced the historical evolution of public opinion, distinguished the issues with which it is competent to deal, and defined its relation to law and to sovereignty. Sir George Cornewall Lewis, in an *Essay on the Influence of Authority in Matters of Opinion* (1849), ably supported the thesis that public opinion is better qualified to point to the existence of political evils than to provide remedies for them; and he criticized the newspaper press as an organ of public opinion. Franz von Holtzendorff, in his *Wesen und Werth der öffentlichen Meinung* (1879), concerned himself with the competence of public opinion, and analyzed closely the nature and influence of the newspaper press. Alexis de Tocqueville and James Bryce, the latter in an exhaustive fashion, described the operation and peculiar characteristics of public opinion in a democratic state. A. V. Dicey and Wilhelm Bauer wrote detailed accounts of the historical foundation and development of public opinion. In a rather formalistic treatise A. Lawrence Lowell clarified the concept with clear-cut definitions.

The exact relation of public opinion to law and to sovereignty, discussed incidentally by some of the writers mentioned in the preceding paragraph, was analyzed more carefully by several political theorists. Sovereignty, according to John Taylor, is "an intellectual political being. In Britain it is parliamentary, in America national. Public opinion ought to rule according to our policy; parliamentary according to hers." In John Austin's view public (or, as he puts it, "general") opinion is not sovereign. It cannot be, for its source is indeterminate; sovereignty must be exercised by a "determinate superior." In his *Manual of Political Ethics* (1838), Francis Lieber suggests in rather obscure fashion that public opinion is one way in which sovereignty manifests itself, and maintains that the relation between law and public opinion is so close as to approach identity. What has come to be perhaps the prevailing view of the matter was stated by D. G. Ritchie. Public opinion is the political sovereign. "The problem of good government is the problem of the proper relation between the legal and political sovereign." Esmein's analysis leads him to the same conclusion. According to W. W. Willoughby, the theory of sovereignty implicit in Lieber's definition of public opinion is invalid. Following Austin, Willoughby denies that public opinion can be called sovereign. Public opinion is an extra-legal force, and sovereignty is a legal concept. As such, it inheres in bodies which have the legal power of expressing the will of the state. "Behind those persons we do not as publicists or jurists need to look . . . We leave to the sociologist or practical politician the examination of the nature and force of public opinion."

Since the latter part of the nineteenth century, as a matter of fact, political theorists have drawn heavily on the contributions of sociology and social psychology. Following Gabriel Tarde, Graham Wallas, and Arthur Christensen, they have studied the non-rational, emotional factors at work in the formation and expression of public opinion. A. F. Bentley called attention to group activity as a factor in the formation process. In his study of social causation Bentley criticizes severely the concept of public opinion developed by Dicey in the latter's *Law and Public Opinion*. Dicey "owed us in this book . . . a quantitative analysis of public opinion in terms of the different elements of the population which expressed themselves through it. He owed us an investigation of the exact things really wanted under the cover of the 'opinion' by each group of the people, with time and place and circumstance all taken up into the center of the statement. In other words, he owed us a social dissection . . . and not a rhapsody." The fact is that nearly all works on political science "either indulge in some wise and vague observation, or else make a frank admission of ignorance," with respect to public opinion. The solution of the problem is to be found in the recognition of public opinion as a phenomenon of the group process. "There is no public opinion . . . not activity reflecting or representing the activity of a group or set of groups." This suggestion that public opinion can be analyzed and measured in terms of the groups contributing to its formation has inspired much discussion and research during the past two decades, particularly in the United States.

The experience of the World War intensified the tendency to emphasize the non-rational forces involved in the formation or manipulation of public opinion, and it promoted a deep and widespread skepticism as to the validity of democratic theory in general and the competence of public opinion in particular. The recent writings of Walter Lippmann, Ferdinand

Tönnies, and Wilhelm Bauer, despite their differing emphasis and point of view, are all illustrative of this trend. Lippmann's works embody a powerful attack on the traditional theory of democracy and its postulate of the "omnicompetent citizen." Tonnies' analysis, unlike that of Lippmann, is based upon an interpretation of the political experience of several nations and upon a full consideration of the historical background. It is in his description of the behavior of the various nations during the World War that he stressed the non-rational, emotional character of public opinion. Dr. Bauer, in his historical survey of public opinion, is likewise impressed by the manipulation of opinion during the World War, especially as practiced by the enemies of the Central Powers; and, citing Tarde and Wallas, he regards public opinion as an emotional force which statesmen must endeavor to control.

Some critics of the traditional democratic theory of public opinion, moreover, have attacked the phrase "public opinion" itself as vague or misleading. At a round table meeting devoted to the "Measurement of Public Opinion," a group of American political scientists found themselves unable to agree on a definition of public opinion. "It was decided, therefore, that the round table might do well to consider the problem of measuring opinion, especially relating to political matters, and avoid the use of the term public opinion if possible." In a study entitled *Quantitative Methods in Politics* (New York, 1928), S. A. Rice argues that "attitudes" is to be preferred to "public opinion," since the latter phrase connotes too much of a "rational and conscious element in the actual motivation." A tendency to avoid the phrase *"öffentliche Meinung"* has likewise asserted itself in recent German sociological and political treatises.

It remains to be seen whether such a tendency will introduce a larger measure of clarity into the consideration of the problem. In any case, it may be suggested that political scientists will not be able to dispense with the phrase "public opinion" altogether so long as it is current in popular usage. If politicians and statesmen continue to use the term in state papers and addresses, the political scientist must seek to explain what it is they have in mind. The natural scientist may perfectly well coin his own esoteric terms or reduce all his findings to a mathematical formula; but the social scientist, who finds his material in the acts and speech of the general run of humanity, cannot hope fully to transcend the language of common experience.

Whatever terminology he may employ, the political scientist should find in the application of the comparative method a basis for the fuller understanding of the nature of public opinion. Before he attempts to make generalizations concerning it, he should try to acquaint himself with its sources and activity in various nations with respect to various matters. Pioneer work of this sort has already been done. Hermann Oncken, the historian, has stressed the necessity of employing the comparative method; and Ferdinand Tönnies, albeit with his sense of objectivity somewhat dulled by the experience of the War, has made some use of it. Lord Bryce, in his *Modern Democracies* (1921), offered the best illustration of this approach to the problem. He clearly outlined the contrasting characteristics of public opinion in France, Switzerland, the United States, and other democratic countries. His application of the method is doubtless rather too impressionistic to be wholly satisfactory, but it does indicate the line which future studies may follow.

If the political scientist should broaden his study of public opinion to include more than one country, he should also deepen it to include more than matters of contemporary interest. He should, in other words, try to set the problem in its historical perspective. Here, too, he will find that work has already been done. Bauer has traced the evolution of public opinion through various historical epochs, and there have been innumerable studies of the activity of public opinion in particular periods with respect to various political issues. In such historical studies, both general and special, the political scientist may find much that is relevant to his purpose.

Finally, it may be urged that the historian, in his turn, may profit from a study of the contributions made by political scientists, sociologists, and social psychologists. From such conceptual treatment he may gain suggestive hints as to the means of interpreting historical phenomena in which public opinion plays an important part. Specifically, the historian should learn to question the assumption, which too often he uncritically accepts, that the press is the only organ through which public opinion is influenced and expressed. More specifically, he should attempt to discover whether, in given instances, the press actually makes or simply expresses public opinion. In his study of diplomacy, he must try to see to what extent governments themselves shape the public opinion which they profess to obey. By throwing light on such problems, the historian may show the way to a deeper analytical and conceptual treatment on the part of his brethren in political science and sociology. In short, the study of public opinion is preeminently one which demands the continuous cooperation of all who are seeking to understand the activities of man as a social and political animal.

George Carslake Thompson

THE EVALUATION

OF PUBLIC OPINION

In considering its place in our Constitution we have been speaking of public opinion as if it were one and indivisible. But in fact when one course from among several possible courses has to be chosen in reference to a matter which concerns a number of people, it often happens that a controversy ensues. People may disagree about the facts; or, agreeing about the facts, they may differ in their calculations; or, agreeing in the calculation that a certain course will attain one object at the sacrifice of another, they may differ in their estimation of the relative worth of these objects; and this last element of difference may spring from any one of an infinite series of sources, ranging from mere differences of personal sentiment or interest up to the most general and fundamental differences of thought and principle. Consultation may do much to bring about an agreement as to what is practicable in many instances, but in others the conflict of opinions will remain irreconcilable, and then the course finally adopted will be adopted without the consent and against the will of some of the persons concerned. This is true of any body of people associated together, but if they form a *State* then the power of determining upon the course to be adopted and of constraining the acquiescence even of those who dislike or disapprove it must reside somewhere, and it is this power which writers on jurisprudence call sovereignty.

It must be remembered that "public opinion", "the will of the nation," and phrases of that kind are really nothing but metaphors, for thought and will are attributes of a single mind, and "the public" or "the nation" are aggregates of many minds.

One of Mr. Galton's typical portraits, formed by super-imposing the portraits of a number of individuals, in which the individual peculiarities are eliminated and the features which are common to the type come out,

Reprinted from *Public Opinion and Lord Beaconsfield* (1886), pp. 29-37, by permission of the publisher. (Copyright, 1886, by Macmillan Co.)

is in some respects an analogue of "public opinion." But this method assumes a general conformity of type among the individuals who are grouped together, and if we attempt too wide a generalization, or if we have to deal with diverse, still more with conflicting, types, the method breaks down. To get at any satisfactory result we must group burglars with burglars and philanthropists with philanthropists. Under circumstances such as those with which we have to deal, where the discrepancies are great and numerous, we cannot reduce public opinion to one type, but we can reduce it to a limited number of types.

With regard to the expression "the national will" the case is somewhat different. The national will must always be one, however fierce may be the internal dissensions. The psychological analogy seems to hold good, for will is the expression of the final impulse after all the motives have had play. The national will, then, is that which would be the will of the sovereign if sovereignty were vested in a single man. Apart from the occasional use of the phrase as applied to the people in distinction from, or in opposition to, their government, the phrase always has an implied reference to this hypothetical autocrat, with his mind made up and acting accordingly. And though he may vacillate, at any one moment he must will one thing. How he makes up his mind is the question to which an account of the constitution of any country is the answer, and how the imaginary being who stands for the will of England made up his mind in the particular case we are considering is the question which we must try to solve. We shall see him torn, as it were, by conflicting motives, and if we can gauge the strength of each legitimate motive, we may be able to judge by the course actually pursued whether there were any bye motives operating.

The opinion which is politically predominant, or in other words sovereign, is a matter which can be definitely ascertained by reference to the course which the State actually follows. But that is not what we mean when we speak of the "predominant" or "preponderating" opinion. By such phrases as these, we mean the same thing which men have in their minds when they talk of the true, or the real opinion of the country, and it is another question whether this is actually sovereign or not. If the constitution of a state insures that power shall be exercised according to the preponderating public opinion, we say shortly that in such a state public opinion is sovereign. We conceive of the persons who contribute to the predominating public opinion as forming a quasicorporate body, and we need not stop to consider the metaphysical problem, whether sovereignty is vested for the time being in these shifting and indeterminate individuals, or in the officials who are intrusted with the actual exercise of power.

The question now arises, "What criterion have we which will enable us, amid conflicting counsels, to say where the weight of opinion lies?" Public opinion being manifold, we want some calculus by which to distinguish that particular opinion which preponderates.

So far as public opinion is organized on some such form as Parliament, the preponderating opinion can of course be easily ascertained. But all organization or machinery is imperfect, and though Parliament professedly exists as the reflex of the country's opinion, and derives its authority from that fact, yet there are occasions when it is felt that the true opinion of the country is something distinct from that of Parliament. How then is this true opinion to be ascertained?

But it may be questioned whether the problem suggested is one which, in the nature of things, admits of a complete and satisfactory solution even in theory, irrespective of imperfections in the machinery through which, as a matter of practical politics, the attempt must be made to give effect to the best approximation attainable. May not some of the factors of the weight of public opinion be ultimately incommensurate? For instance, a small number of great philosophers and statesmen might be opposed to a large number of ignorant persons. In such a case could anything be said more than some such account of the matter as this?—"Here is so much opinion of such a kind on one side, and so much more opinion of such another kind on the other side." On the other hand if the numbers on each side were even approximately equal, there would be no difficulty in pronouncing that the opinion of the philosophers preponderated. Thus, although cases may occur where we must confess ourselves baffled, there are others—and these are practically the most numerous and important— where the difficulty does not appear to be insuperable.

We want to know then, what the considerations are which we should consciously or unconsciously apply, if, as unprejudiced observers, with the facts fully before us, we were pronouncing on the relative weight of competing opinions.

In the first place we should find that we need not bring into the competition every minute variety of opinion which could possibly be discovered. As has already been observed, opinion though manifold may be practically treated as grouped according to certain types. Therefore we need not go the full length of the maxim, "*Quot homines tot sententiæ.*" Again, as it is not every singular or obscure crotchet, neither is it every passing flash of like or dislike, which must be taken into the account; an opinion must have a certain *persistence* as well as a certain *volume,* to entitle it to rank as "public opinion" at all. Volume (or the number of persons among whom the opinion is *diffused*), and persistence in duration, are quantitative elements of opinion. These go some way to measuring its importance; but not the whole way, for there are qualitative elements which must be regarded too. We recognize that a few men who hold a definite opinion *earnestly* and on *rational grounds* will outweigh a greater number who merely entertain a slight preference which they cannot explain for something vague and general.

The words "on rational grounds" suggest a difficulty. It may be said the phrase is merely a veil for the meaning "on grounds with which the person who used it agrees." Are we entitled to pronounce that to be the most reasonable opinion which seems to us to be so? A man could only answer "yes" on the assumption that he was possessed of a perfectly normal mind. After all, it seems to be the same difficulty which presents itself when an ultimate objective standard is sought in any department of inquiry into human conduct, from ethics down to taste;—the difficulty which Aristotle sought to get over by the introduction of the "wise man." The desideratum seems to be to eliminate everything of the nature of "personal equation."

There are, as we said above, three main causes which may lead to a difference of opinion between men in politics; firstly, differences in the views of facts; secondly, differences in the estimation of the best means for attaining desired ends; and thirdly, differences in the appraisement of various ends. The phrase "on rational grounds" then means, with regard to differences about facts, an opinion which rests on some basis of evidence; as to the estimate of the best means for securing desired ends, it means a carefully reasoned view which has the support of appropriate analogies; and with regard to the appraisement of ends, the phrase indicates that the end on which political action is based is one which reasonable men recognize as affording an appropriate motive.

For the purpose of weighing individual opinions we should take into account the opportunities the individuals have had of informing themselves of the facts, and the manner in which they have drawn their conclusions. And so before the principle of majority or diffusion can be accepted in estimating the weight of public opinion, there are two scrutinies that must be applied to it. First, it must be considered whether the majority is determined by any question of class interest. Next, we must endeavor to distinguish between cases where the volume of an opinion consists in the unanimity of a number of uninstructed people, who all take their political creed on trust from a similar source; and cases where there is a real consensus of many minds of differing types who have reasoned their way to the same conclusion. Where we have a consensus which shows itself, when tried by either of these scrutinies, *independent*, it carries an authority of a far higher degree than that which is due to its mere numbers. We should expect to find the *best* public opinion in the verdict of such a consensus, when confirmed by the weight of numbers, and when held with such intensity and persistence as to preclude the notion that the reasons which led men to it were frivolous or transient.

Thus there are four principal characteristics which, it seems, should be taken into account in the evaluation of public opinion:—diffusion, persistence, intensity, and reasonableness. One very important element of reasonableness is *elaboration,* which term may be used to denote either on the one hand *definiteness with regard to practical action,* or on the other the degree to which the opinion in question results from a thought-out political theory; let us say *theoretical completeness.*

If we classify opinions according to their definiteness with regard to practical action we can distinguish these three ascending stages:

1st. A general preference.

2nd. A wish for a particular end or course of action.

3rd. A belief as to the best practical means for achieving those particular ends which are desired.

Or, to put the same thing in another light, when we enumerate the different factors of public opinion which appeared during the discussion on the Eastern question, we find that they group themselves as answers to the three following questions:

1. What is the kind of political action which I like generally to see England engaged in?

2. What are the considerations in connection with the Eastern question which strike me as important?

3. What do I think the English government had better do, looking at matters all round?

If we denote the answers to these questions respectively as biases, notions, and policies, we get three words, answering to the three ascending stages of definiteness, by which we can class such opinions as had volume and persistence enough to rank as public. In terms of this nomenclature, then, a policy is the most definite form which anything diffused enough to count as public opinion assumes. It is not merely an approval of a certain sort of conduct, or a desire for a particular end. It is all this, together with a conception of certain means as the best practicable for attaining that particular end which is regarded as most important, having regard to all the surrounding circumstances. Out-of-door public opinion can hardly strike out a policy for itself. It must have the assurance that the means are practicable from some one whose position implies that he has the opportunity of knowing the facts. A policy implies a notion, or in most cases a group of notions, which may be regarded as its factors, and also a belief that all the material circumstances have been taken into account. Policies, at least for the most part, are mutually exclusive.

It is otherwise when we descend a stage in the order of definiteness, and come to notions; for several ends can be desired at the same time, and in fact one man will probably hold several allied notions, nay, one man may consistently hold notions which are factors of different policies, and two men who have adopted different policies may entertain a notion in common —they may both recognize the end as desirable, but one may give it the first place, and the other think it should give way to something which he considers of greater importance. Thus, though a policy implies a notion, the converse is not the case; for a notion may have existed in a man's mind without leading him to adopt a policy at all; it may be because he has not advanced from the conception of ends to that of means, or perhaps, because he considers he has not all the factors of the problem before him, or again, because he may fail to decide which notion should weigh for most among several which commend themselves to him, but which point to different policies.

If we turn for a moment to the consideration of the specific factors of English public opinion about the Eastern question of 1876, and make a list of the "notions" which can be distinguished, arranged in such a way as to exhibit what may be called the continuity of public opinion, we shall be struck with the fact that the transition from any one notion to the next on the list is not violent. If a man holds one he will be very likely to hold the next too; and yet when we pass over several steps, a divergence becomes apparent, and presently perhaps we come to a notion which is the direct negation of that with which we began. Thus some of these notions are mutually exclusive, while others of them can exist simultaneously in the same mind, and many of them are so nearly allied that they most probably will be held together. Arranged in this way the notions fall naturally into groups which we may call "views," for they seem to answer to the views one or other of which actual men would entertain; actual men, that is to say, as distinguished from the ideal politician whom it is convenient to imagine for purposes of analysis, whose mind takes in one notion, and one notion only. The views seem to occupy an intermediate position between the policies and the notions.

We notice that subjectively the notions are of two kinds. In the first place there are those which positively lead men to approve policies and to adopt views, and in the second place there are apologetic notions which are called in argumentatively to reinforce and defend a foregone conclusion.

The conviction of the importance of a particular end, or the desire for a particular course of action, while they are confined to small knots or individual thinkers, lack that volume which entitles them to rank as public opinion at all. But such ideas industriously preached with favoring circumstances often gather volume (if losing something of their elaboration), till they fairly rank as notions or as policies in the sense we have given to these terms. They are the germs which falling on fruitful soil will grow to something which may move the world, or falling on stony ground may perish. Mr. Freeman long looked upon himself, as he said, as one preaching in the wilderness, but his anti-Turkish doctrine became a view of mighty power. Mr. Grant Duff's nostrum for solving the Eastern question by enthroning the Duke and Duchess of Edinburgh at Constantinople never became a policy.

We have no precise numerical test of the volume necessary to constitute an opinion public, nor need we look for numerical accuracy on such
a point. But there are two indications that will serve with tolerable precision.

In the first place, is the matter mentioned by candidates in their election addresses and in "Parliament out of session"?—not, of course, here
or there only, but would an omission be remarked upon as unsatisfactory?
The other test is, has the matter passed from the magazines to the newspapers? Is it a common subject for leading articles, and do a good many
people write to editors about it? If these conditions are answered, it may
be said broadly that there is enough of volume to constitute the opinion in
question public.

Turning now to those elements of public opinion which we distinguish
as biases, it seems that a bias may be either a popular instinctive judgment
embodying a generalization more or less consciously made from the moral
sentiments or from the proclivities to which politics afford a field, or again,
that it may be one of those moral sentiments or proclivities themselves in
a simple instinctive form.

If the analysis is pushed far enough, it may be said that in the last
resort all political opinion (except what is the outcome of mere self-interest) must ultimately rest upon *instincts;* that is upon moral sentiments
of approval or reprobation, and upon emotional proclivities of like or dislike. Upon this instinctive basis political judgments are founded of greater
or less generality. The political philosopher seeks maxims applicable to the
whole course of history; the statesman, contemplating one particular group
of states, arrives at his maxims of international law; the ordinary citizen
has a general conception, perhaps a little vague, as to the sort of way in
which he desires his own country to act.

Thus we recognize the second of the two directions in which, as we
observed, political opinion is capable of elaboration. In distinguishing policies, notions, and biases, we considered one of these, that is definiteness, or
elaboration in the direction of practical action, having regard to the actual
circumstances of the time and place. We now note that in the other, that
is in the direction of elaboration with reference to theoretical completeness,
we can go upwards from the popular instinctive like or dislike to the highest generalization of political philosophy.

It may be broadly laid down that the diffusion of opinion varies inversely with its elaboration, either in the direction of practical definiteness,
or of theoretical completeness. Widely diffused complete political theories
are hardly to be looked for. But the popular instinct and instinctive judgments seem to be diffused enough to count as effective public opinion, and
it is these which constitute that kind of public opinion which we propose
to distinguish as biases.

A. Lawrence Lowell

THE NATURE OF PUBLIC OPINION

"Vox Populi may be Vox Dei, but very little attention shows that there has never been any agreement as to what Vox means or as to what Populus means." In spite of endless discussions about democracy, this remark of Sir Henry Maine is still so far true that no other excuse is needed for studying the conceptions which lie at the very base of popular government. In doing so one must distinguish the form from the substance; for the world of politics is full of forms in which the spirit is dead—mere shams, but sometimes not recognized as such even by the chief actors, sometimes deceiving the outside multitude, sometimes no longer misleading anyone. Shams are, indeed, not without value. Political shams have done for English government what fictions have done for English law. They have promoted growth without revolutionary change. But while shams play an important part in political evolution, they are snares for the political philosopher who fails to see through them, who ascribes to the forms a meaning that they do not really possess. Popular government may in substance exist under the form of a monarchy, and an autocratic despotism can be set up without destroying the forms of democracy. If we look through the forms to observe the vital forces behind them; if we fix our attention, not on the procedure, the extent of the franchise, the machinery of elections, and such outward things, but on the essence of the matter, popular government, in one important aspect at least, may be said to consist of the control of political affairs by public opinion. In this book, therefore, an attempt is made to analyze public opinion in order to determine its nature, the conditions under which it can exist, the subjects to which it can apply, the methods by which it can be faithfully expressed, and the regulation under a popular government of affairs to which it is not directly applicable.

Each of the two words that make up the expression "public opinion"

Reprinted from *Public Opinion and Popular Government*, 1913, pp. 3-15, by permission of the publisher. (Copyright, 1913, by Longmans, Green and Co.)

is significant, and each of them may be examined by itself. To fulfil the requirement an opinion must be public, and it must be really an opinion. Let us begin with the first of these qualities.

If two highwaymen meet a belated traveller on a dark road and propose to relieve him of his watch and wallet, it would clearly be an abuse of terms to say that in the assemblage on that lonely spot there was a public opinion in favor of a redistribution of property. Nor would it make any difference, for this purpose, whether there were two highwaymen and one traveller, or one robber and two victims. The absurdity in such a case of speaking about the duty of the minority to submit to the verdict of public opinion is self-evident; and it is not due to the fact that the three men on the road form part of a larger community, or that they are subject to the jurisdiction of a common government. The expression would be quite as inappropriate if no organized state existed; on a savage island, for example, where two cannibals were greedy to devour one shipwrecked mariner. In short the three men in each of the cases supposed do not form a community that is capable of a public opinion on the question involved. May this not be equally true under an organized government, among people that are for certain purposes a community?

To take an illustration nearer home. At the time of the Reconstruction that followed the American Civil War the question whether public opinion in a southern state was, or was not, in favor of extending the suffrage to the negroes could not in any true sense be said to depend on which of the two races had a slight numerical majority. One opinion may have been public or general in regard to the whites, the other public or general in regard to the negroes, but neither opinion was public or general in regard to the whole population. Examples of this kind could be multiplied indefinitely. They can be found in Ireland, in Austria-Hungary, in Turkey, in India, in any country where the cleavage of race, religion, or politics is sharp and deep enough to cut the community into fragments too far apart for an accord on fundamental matters. When the Mohammedans spread the faith of Islam by the sword, could the question whether public opinion in a conquered country favored Christianity or Mohammedanism be said to depend on a small preponderance in numbers of the Christians or the followers of the Prophet; and were the minority under any obligation to surrender their creed? The government was entirely in the hands of the Mussulmans, but would it be rational to assert that if they numbered ninety-nine thousand against one hundred thousand Christians public opinion in the country was against them, whereas if they were to massacre two thousand of the Christians public opinion would then be on their side? Likewise in Bohemia at the present day, where the Germans and the Czechs are struggling for supremacy, would there not be an obvious fallacy in claiming that whichever race could show a bare majority would have the support of public opinion in requiring its own language to be taught to all the children in the schools.

In all these instances an opinion cannot be public or general with respect to both elements in the state. For that purpose they are as distinct as if they belonged to different commonwealths. You may count heads, you may break heads, you may impose uniformity by force; but on the matters at stake the two elements do not form a community capable of an opinion that is in any rational sense public or general. As Mr. Bryce points out, a great deal of confusion arises from using the term sometimes to mean everybody's views, that is, the aggregate of all that is thought, and sometimes the views of the majority. If we are to employ the term in a sense that is significant for government, that imports any obligation moral or political on the part of the minority, surely enough has been said to show that the opinion of a mere majority does not by itself always suffice. Something more is clearly needed.

But if the opinion of a majority does not of itself constitute a public opinion, it is equally certain that unanimity is not required. To confine the term to cases where there is no dissent would deprive it of all value and would be equivalent to saying that it rarely, if ever, exists. Moreover, unanimous opinion is of no importance for our purpose, because it is perfectly sure to be effective in any form of government, however despotic, and it is, therefore, of no particular interest in the study of democracy. Legislation by unanimity was actually tried in the kingdom of Poland, where each member of the assembly had the right of *liberum veto* on any measure, and it prevented progress, fostered violence, and spelled failure. The Polish system has been lauded as the acme of liberty, but in fact it was directly opposed to the fundamental principle of modern popular government; that is, the conduct of public affairs in accord with a public opinion which is general, although not universal, and which implies under certain conditions a duty on the part of the minority to submit.

If then unanimity is not necessary to public opinion and a majority is not enough, where shall we seek the essential elements of its existence? A suggestion much in point may be found in the speculations of the most ingenious political philosopher of the eighteenth century. In his *Contrat Social* Rousseau attempts to prove that in becoming a member of a state the natural man may remain perfectly free and continue to obey only his own will. He tells us that in forming a state men desire to enforce the common will of all the members; and he takes as the basis of all political action this common will, which is nearly akin to our idea of public opinion. Now, in order to reconcile the absolute freedom of every citizen to obey only his own volition, with the passing of laws in every civilized state against opposition, he says that when the assembled people are consulted on any measure, their votes express, not their personal wishes upon the subject, but their opinions in regard to the common will, and thus the defeated minority have not had their desires thwarted, but have simply been mistaken in their views about the common will. All men, he insists, want to give effect to this common will, which becomes, therefore, the universal will of everyone and is always carried out.

Though stated in a somewhat fanciful way, the theory contains a highly important truth, which may be clothed in a more modern dress. A body of men are politically capable of a public opinion only so far as they are agreed upon the ends and aims of government and upon the principles by which those ends shall be attained. They must be united, also, about the means whereby the action of the government is to be determined, in a conviction, for example, that the views of a majority—or it may be some other portion of their numbers—ought to prevail; and a political community as a whole is capable of public opinion only when this is true of the great bulk of the citizens. Such an assumption was implied, though usually not expressed in all theories of the Social Compact; and, indeed, it is involved in all theories that base rightful government upon the consent of the governed, for the consent required is not a universal approval by all the people of every measure enacted, but a consensus in regard to the legitimate character of the ruling authority and its right to decide the questions that arise.

The power of the courts in America to hold statutes unconstitutional furnishes an illustration of this doctrine. It rests upon a distinction between those things that may be done by ordinary legislative procedure and those that may not; the theory being that in the case of the former the people have consented to abide by the decision of the majority as expressed by their representatives, whereas in the case of matters not placed by the constitution within the competence of the legislature, the people as a whole have given no such consent. With regard to these they have agreed to abide only by a decree uttered in more solemn forms, or by the determination of something greater than a mere majority. The court, therefore, in holding a statute unconstitutional, is in effect deciding that it is not within the range of acts to which the whole people have given their consent; so that while the opinion in favor of the act may be an opinion of the majority of the voters, it is not a public opinion of the community, because it is not one where the people as a whole are united in a conviction that the views of the majority, at least as expressed through the ordinary channels, ought to prevail.

We have seen that in some countries the population has contained, and for that matter still contains, distinct elements which are sharply at odds upon the vital political questions of the day. In such a case the discordant forces may be violent enough to preclude a general consent that the opinion of the majority ought to prevail; but this is not always true. If they are not, the assumption which lies at the foundation of popular government remains unimpaired. If they are, the forms of democracy may still be in operation, although their meaning is essentially altered. It may be worth while to dwell on this contrast a moment because it makes clear the difference between true public opinion and the opinion of a majority.

Leaving out of account those doctrines whereby political authority is traced to a direct supernatural origin, government among men is commonly based in theory either on consent or on force, and in fact each of these factors plays a larger or smaller part in every civilized country. So far as the preponderating opinion is one which the minority does not share, but which it feels ought, as the opinion of the majority, to be carried out, the government is conducted by a true public opinion or by consent. So far as the preponderating opinion is one the execution of which the minority would resist by force if it could do so successfully, the government is based upon force. At times it may be necessary to give effect to an opinion of the majority against the violent resistance, or through the reluctant submission, of the minority. A violent resistance may involve the suppression of an armed insurrection or civil war. But even when there is no resort to actual force it remains true that in any case where the minority does not concede the right of the majority to decide, submission is yielded only to obviously superior strength; and obedience is the result of compulsion, not of public opinion. The power to carry out its will under such conditions must to some extent be inherent in every government. Habitual criminals are held in check by force everywhere. But in many nations at the present day there are great masses of well-intentioned citizens who do not admit the right of the majority to rule. These persons and the political parties in which they group themselves are termed irreconcilable, and when we speak of public opinion in that country we cannot include them. So far as they are concerned there can be no general or public opinion.

Let us be perfectly clear upon this point. The presence of irreconcilables does not mean that the government is illegitimate, or that it is not justified in enforcing its will upon the reluctant minority. That will depend upon other considerations. The use of force may be unavoidable if any settled government is to be upheld, if civic order is to be maintained. But it does mean that the fundamental assumption of popular government, the control of political affairs by an opinion which is truly public, is set aside. Florence may, or may not, have been justified in disfranchising her noble families, but Freeman was certainly right in his opinion that by so doing she lost her right to be called a democracy,—that is, a government by all the people,—and it makes little difference for this purpose whether a part of the body politic is formally excluded from any share in public affairs or overawed by force into submission.

One more remark must be made before quitting the subject of the relation of public opinion to the opinion of the majority. The late Gabriel Tarde, with his habitual keen insight, insisted on the importance of the intensity of belief as a factor in the spread of opinions. There is a common impression that public opinion depends upon and is measured by the mere number of persons to be found on each side of a question; but this is far from accurate. If forty-nine per cent of a community feel very strongly on one side, and fifty-one per cent are lukewarmly on the other, the former opinion has the greater public force behind it and is certain to prevail ultimately if it does not at once. The ideas of people who possess the greatest knowledge of a subject are also of more weight than those of an equal number of ignorant persons. If, for example, all the physicians, backed by all other educated men, are confident that an impure water supply causes typhoid fever, while the rest of the people are mildly incredulous, it can hardly be said that public opinion is opposed to that notion. One man who holds his belief tenaciously counts for as much as several men who hold theirs weakly, because he is more aggressive, and thereby compels and overawes others into apparent agreement with him, or at least into silence and inaction. This is, perhaps, especially true of moral questions. It is not improbable that a large part of the accepted moral code is maintained by the earnestness of a minority, while more than half of the community is indifferent or unconvinced. In short, public opinion is not strictly the opinion of the numerical majority, and no form of its expression measures the mere majority, for individual views are always to some extent weighed as well as counted. Without attempting to consider how the weight attaching to intensity and intelligence can be accurately gauged, it is enough for our purpose to point out that when we speak of the opinion of a majority we mean, not the numerical, but the effective majority.

No doubt differences in the intensity of belief explain some sudden transformations in politics and in ethical standards, many people holding their views with so little conviction that they are ready to follow in the wake of any strong leader in thought or action. On the other hand they explain in part also cases where a law is enacted readily but enforced with difficulty; for the law may be carried through by a comparatively small body of very earnest men, who produce a disproportionate effect by the heat of their conviction; while the bulk of the people are apathetic and unwilling to support the effort required to overcome a steady passive resistance to the enforcement of the law.

The problem of intensity of belief is connected, moreover, with the fact that different ways of ascertaining the popular will may give different results, in accordance with the larger or smaller proportion of the indifferent who are gathered in to vote. But this is a matter that belongs properly to a later discussion of the methods of expressing public opinion. We are dealing here only with its essential nature.

To sum up what has been said in this chapter: public opinion to be worthy of the name, to be the proper motive force in a democracy, must be really public; and popular government is based upon the assumption of a public opinion of that kind. In order that it may be public a majority is not enough, and unanimity is not required, but the opinion must be such that while the minority may not share it, they feel bound, by conviction not by fear, to accept it; and if democracy is complete the submission of the minority must be given ungrudgingly. An essential difference between government by public opinion as thus defined and by the bare will of a selfish majority has been well expressed by President Hadley. After saying that laws imposed by a majority on a reluctant minority are commonly inoperative, he adds, "It cannot be too often repeated that those opinions which a man is prepared to maintain at another's cost, but not at his own, count for little in forming the general sentiment of a community, or in producing any effective public movement."

Harold D. Lasswell

NATIONS AND CLASSES:
THE SYMBOLS OF IDENTIFICATION

When Ernst Werner Techow, Erwin Kern, and Hermann Fischer assassinated Walther Rathenau in 1922, they invoked the name of the Fatherland, the monarchy, the spirit of Potsdam. When Friedrich Adler shot the Austrian Prime Minister in 1916, he said it was not because he desired publicity, or because he enjoyed the pleasure of murdering his fellow man, but because the working classes required it. When Pilsudski and Stalin robbed banks in the years before 1917, they said it was not because they needed money and adventure for themselves, but because the overthrow of czarism and the liberation of the oppressed working masses of the world demanded it. When the Paris commune was drowned in blood, it was because the interests of "patriotism" and of "civilization" required it. The millions who struggled from 1914 to 1918 in the thin zones which surrounded the Central Powers were fighting for "God," "country," "civilization," "humanity," "international law," "a war to end war," and a "lasting peace."

The role of these justifying symbols in politics is one of the principal topics of analytic inquiry. With which acts are particular symbols connected? How are the justifying symbols grouped geographically throughout the world? How are they related to one another and to the whole context of political change? The embittered paranoiac who slays the first passer-by whom he suspects of turning destructive rays upon him is of mediocre interest to the student of politics, though a paranoiac like Gorgulov who kills the President of France as the "enemy" of his people becomes relevant on account of the target of his act and the accompanying verbalizations. The person who views himself as representative of a larger unity has widened the configuration against which his act is to be con-

Reprinted from *World Politics and Personal Insecurity: A Contribution to Political Psychiatry* (1935), pp. 29-51 by permission of the author and the publisher. (Copyright, 1935, by McGraw-Hill.)

strued. To be of greatest interest to us, the act of demolishing another must be enshrined in justifications. The muscle movements must occur in a context of verbal legitimacy. There must be evidence of the process of self-justification by referring to entities larger than the self, another contribution to the voluminous chapter of human history entitled "The Story of Man and His Justifications."

A satisfactory geography of politics would chart the symbols which men invoke to justify their pretensions, and disclose the nature of the acts with which each symbol is affiliated.[1] Our usual maps show the world of "states," but the world of politics is richer, including acts justified in the name of churches, races, nationalities, tribes, classes, and dynasties. From the study of psychological areas we can often surmise the nature of coming changes in the activity and organization areas. Particularistic expressions in the old Dual Monarchy presaged the approaching end of the state and no doubt the spread of class symbols in the contemporary world is the precursor of drastic changes of boundary lines.

If we look with fresh naïveté at the distribution of persons who use common identifying symbols, many anomalies appear. How does it happen that a man living by Lake Michigan identifies himself with a name that includes the population of New York, a thousand miles east, and of San Diego, several thousand miles west, and yet excludes the population of Winnipeg and Toronto? How does he come to associate himself with the "poor white trash" of the South, and not with the farmers of Alberta; or with the blacks of Georgia, and not with the whites of Quebec?

The relationship between geographical features and symbols seems fast and loose. Australians occupy a continent and the whites, at least, have a unifying term, but the Europeans, Asiatics, Africans, North and South Americans, who occupy continents, are split into parochial groups. Those who live in the Mississippi River Valley call themselves by one inclusive name, but those who are settled in the valley of the Danube use many names. Most of the inhabitants of the principal Japanese islands have a common term, but the North Irelanders are distinct from the South Irelanders.

Symbols do not unite all those who live on the great highlands or in the great lowlands of the earth. If the Italian peninsula is, in a fashion,

---

[1] Concerning the theory of the symbol in the logical, psychological, and sociopolitical sense, see E. Cassirer, *Philosophie der symbolischen Formen*, 2 vols., Berlin, 1923-1925; C. I. Lewis, *The Mind and World Order*, New York, 1929; A. N. Whitehead, *Symbolism, Its Meaning and Effect*, Cambridge, Mass., 1928; Charles W. Morris, *Six Theories of Mind*, Chicago, 1932; C. K. Ogden and I. A. Richards, *The Meaning of Meaning*, New York, 1925; the forthcoming posthumous publications of George Herbert Mead; Charles E. Merriam, *The Making of Citizens*, Chicago, 1931; Isidor Ginsburg, "National Symbolism," Chap. 17 in Paul Kosok, *Modern Germany*, Chicago, 1933; John F. Markey, *The Symbolic Process and Its Integration in Children*, New York, 1928.

unified, the Scandinavian peninsula is disunited. Geographical zones which are defined by deciduous or coniferous forests, or by characteristic temperature, rainfall, or barometric ranges, do not neatly coincide with areas of identification.

The relations are discrepant even between such highly organized areas as states and the zones of common national sentiment. The German organization area does not now include Alsace and Lorraine, Eupen and Malmédy, Upper Silesia and the corridor, or Austria; Magyars are to be found in the organization area of Roumania, Yugoslavia, and Czechoslovakia; Bulgarians live in Macedonia, Thrace, and the Dobruja; Ukrainians are in Polish Galicia, Roumanian Bukovina, and Bessarabia; Arabs are in French Syria, British Palestine, and elsewhere; Greeks appear in Cyprus, the Dodecanese, and Constantinople. Self-assertive minorities are found within the empires of Great Britain, France, the Netherlands, Japan, Portugal, and the United States.

If we examine the relation between areas of sentiment and of organization, on the one hand, and areas of special activity on the other, instances of noncongruence multiply. The iron and steel manufacturing districts of South Chicago, northern Ohio, and Alabama, together with the Lake Superior ore deposits and various coal and limestone areas, are all included within the United States; but the industrial region of the Rhineland is split between two antagonistic states and nationalities.

The symbols referred to thus far have historically been connected with geographical locations. Another powerful body of symbols has fixed upon some nonspatial characteristic. Most portentous of these is the "proletariat," in whose name various working-class districts of the world are being mobilized to reject the authority of those who use the symbols of "nationalism" or "individualism," and to accept the authority of those who invoke the new verbalism. Even here curious discrepancies reveal themselves, since many of the active proletarians turn out to be lawyers, university graduates, publicists, sons of middle-class or upper-class families, and many of the inactive proletarians prove to be serfs or wage earners in the Southern black belt, in South African mines, or on Caribbean fruit plantations.

No doubt our hypothetically naïve observer would innocently ask why so much stress is put on "place" words or "economic" words as unifying symbols. The wonder grows if one remembers that the number of words which can be used to distinguish one person from another is unlimited. All the curly-haired people might be united in curly-haired consciousness versus all the straight-haired people; all the dry-skinned people might be united against the oily-skinned people; but words about propinquity and tradition and economic standing have thus far outcompeted physical words in the rivalry for human loyalty.

If one took seriously the task of guiding the sentimentalization of likenesses and differences, it would doubtless be essential to sift out very complex types and to christen them appropriately. The world might with some justification be united into those who are thin, leptosomic in physique, schizoid in temperament, and disposed to schizophrenia, and into those who are plumpish, pyknic in physique, manic-depressive in temperament, and disposed to manic depressive psychoses. Dr. Ernst Kretschmer, since he invented this modern synthesis, could be the George Washington of this division [2] and wars could be fought over whether the leptosomes are right in calling him leptosomic, or whether the pyknics are right in calling him pyknic. Dr. Carl Jung has done much to create an "introvert" and "extravert" consciousness in mankind, yet the introverts and extraverts are not yet demanding self-determination.[3]

Now this purely schematic consideration of potentialities in human relations may emancipate some of us personally from automatic loyalty to the particular symbolisms which we have incorporated into our personality. Such formalism, however, is far removed from the state of the circumambient world, where specific national and class differences are taken with so much seriousness. For better or worse we are embedded in historical configurations which are characterized by the existence of a large number of comprehensive symbols in the name of which people die or kill. In examining these phenomena, we may in some respects be guided by the results of intensive personality studies which have disclosed so much about the dynamics of the process of identification itself.

We know that the components of behavior which are prominent in the early history of the organism, but which are modified as unacceptable to the environment, persist within the adult structure. They display themselves in crassest form during the regressive manifestations of severe mental disease, when the later integrations break up and the earlier coordinations are freed. Such adults may be unable to control their elementary excretions, or to masticate food, or to utter more than primitive cries and sounds. Training does not abolish the earlier action formations of the biopsychic structure but stylizes them in various conventional ways. However, this stylization in the form of appropriate language, gesture, and dress never entirely succeeds; the elementary components secure partial expression as socially irrelevant physiological tensions, as peculiar mannerisms and stereotyped movements, as verbal slips, as forgetting, as embarrassment, as tones of elation or depression. We know that the personality in relation to another personality is reacting with an organism which has been modified in consequence of its whole history in human relations, and that these

[2] See *Physique and Character*, New York, 1925.

[3] *Psychological Types*, New York, 1924. For the growth of the identification symbolism, reference might be made to Dow Thompson, *A Mind That Was Different*, Harlow Publishing Co., Oklahoma City, 1931.

modifications are comparatively unstable. What we call being civilized consists in using the "appropriate" patterns for the gratification of the elementary and the complicated impulse structures which are activated in particular situations. Only the special student of personality can hope to discern much of the meaning of slight deviations from the conventional, and he can be reasonably sure of his interpretations only when he has an opportunity to examine the personality under specialized conditions.

To say that the organism reacts as an organism means specifically what it says: the organism performs complicated acts of integration whose elementary components are sucking and spitting, biting, swallowing, striking, scratching, tearing, shoving, touching and rubbing, injecting or rejecting genital organs, looking, presenting for inspection, holding, expelling from the mouth, from intestinal, urethral, and genital tracts, running away, covering and throwing the body. Behavior consists of inordinately complex ways of disposing of such activations. With developed personalities, activity components are stylized in relation to the immediate situations in such ways that the simple acts which are initiated in any situation create tensions which are disposed of smoothly and for the most part indirectly.

We may grasp the hand of the person next to us according to the accepted forms of the social situation, smiling genially; yet repressed hostilities may be expressed in moods of slight depression or constraint, in some speech blocking as one repeats the conventional verbal forms, or in such bodily symptoms as localized skin irritations. The significance of these various formations as compromises between impulses to attack the other person and impulses to inhibit overt hostility can only become manifest when the individual learns how to employ the free-fantasy technique of exposing his reactive structure.[4]

Now what is it that happens when one person becomes emotionally bound to the symbol of another, or to the symbol of the collectivity? An emotional attachment occurs when the symbol of the other is taken as one means of gratifying the affectionate (the libidinal) impulses which are not permitted to exhaust themselves in direct and primitive ways upon the object. Strictly speaking, the symbol of the aspect of the self which is taken by the self to be characterized by an "external" reference secures the libidinal charge.

The emotional relations which are directly relevant to our field of discourse arise in the perception of similarities between an object and ourselves (by partial identification[5]). The necessary prerequisite is the presence of aim-inhibited impulses which are available for redirection

[4] See my *Psychopathology and Politics*, Chaps. 2 and 3, Chicago, 1930.

[5] The identification dynamisms are summarized in S. Freud, *Group Psychology and the Analysis of the Ego*, Chap. 7, London, 1922.

toward substitute symbols. We identify with others (a process which is not necessarily accompanied by acute self-awareness) by perceiving that they are from the same college, the same town, the same country; that they admire the same politicians, scientists, or teachers; that they exercise the same skills; that they resemble our past attachments, and so on through an incalculably vast list of possibilities.

The emotional relation to the other is not necessarily positive; we do not invariably remodel ourselves by taking over some feature of his personality pattern. We may react negatively by identifying him with some aspect of our own personality which we deplore as weak or disreputable. In this case we reject the proffered pattern and release profoundly destructive impulses.

Quite often persons are related to the same object (as viewed by a specified observer) without a common externalized symbol of the object, and without a common symbol of all those who are identified with the object. I may be impressed by a stranger whom I see walking alone in the Bois de Boulogne, but my subjective symbol of the stranger may not be related to a name which I could use as an external symbol of the man, or to a symbol of the other people who, unknown to me, have also partially identified with him. This relationship of the man and the several people who have no externalized symbols of him or of one another is one which we shall call *multiple identification*. This condition is highly potential for the more complex identification relationships. The transition to *counteridentification* may be very quickly managed when the multiply identified discover one another and develop external symbols of one another and of the person to whom they occupy a common relation. We may learn that the lone stranger in the Bois de Boulogne is Dr. X, who has new theories of stopping disease through irradiation, and we may be disposed to accept and propagate his methods. The disciples of a political sage or the associates of an active agitator may be bound by the ties of counteridentification.[6]

Of great political relevance is *mutual identification*, whose distinguishing mark is the inclusion of persons within the field of reference of the symbol who are beyond the face-to-face experience of any one person. The term "American" includes persons who are dead and gone and those who are geographically remote, and thus beyond the primary experience of those identified with the word. Interlapping identifications among persons in relation to this symbol make such mutual identifications possible.

Some politically significant reference symbols have comparatively circumscribed fields of allusion, like "Gandhi," but others are extremely difficult to characterize. No very circumscribed aspect of the world can be

---

[6] *Identification* is to be distinguished from *affiliation*, in which the conscious components are preponderant.

chosen as the reference frame for the "United States"; historically it is by no means certain when sufficient identifications had arisen to constitute a relationship for which a separate name was relevant. "Americans" is a word that does not apply to all who fall within the organization area called the United States of America, for one excludes those who reside within the legal jurisdiction without becoming psychologically organized toward the unifying symbol.

The early subjective life of the infant appears without sharp references to the surrounding objects in the environment. There is no evidence that ego references are clearly separated from environmental references. This imprecise relationship between the ego and its surroundings is recaptured in the sense of cosmic participation so characteristic of states of deep psychic regression. Those who emerge from them can often recount that they felt at one with the sun, the moon, and the stars, that they seemed to occupy the heavens and the earth, being indistinguishable from them, and aware of no boundary between the "I" and the "cosmos." Such mental states can be temporarily achieved by means of drugs, brain concussions, and spiritual exercises.

The environment of the infant and child is teeming with words of ambiguous reference, which take on positive or negative significance long before there is enough contact with reality either to define their frames of reference, or to distinguish those whose frames of reference are wholly indeterminate. As an "adult" the individual continues to respond to these articulations in many childish and juvenile ways, very often imputing some special and even awesome significance to them. Such words are "law and order," "patriotism," "a gentleman and a soldier," "truth," "justice," "honor," "good," "bad," "loyalty," "duty," "Germans," "French," "Negroes," "national hero," "good citizens," "national interest," "king," "constitution"; but these words do not stand alone in primitive concentrations of irrelevant affect. The whole of our vocabulary, plus our non-verbal symbols, is caught in the mesh of early structuralizations of this kind, so that the inner meaning of our symbols is never revealed except through the technique of free fantasy.

Identification with any particular symbol by any person at any phase of his career line initiates a complex process of symbol elaboration. All the earlier loves tend to be reactivated in relation to the new symbol. The individual who late in life experiences "conversion" and becomes an "American" or a "Czech" or a "Lithuanian" or a "Communist" or a "Socialist" or a "Catholic" reads into this symbol the loves and hopes of his entire personality. His elaborations of the symbol will depend upon the forms of expression with which his personality has been equipped through aptitude and training. If he belongs to those who require large emotional responses from the environment, and if he has a facile technique for the oral or written production of language, he may fill the auditoriums of his vicinity with rhetoric and the printing presses with poetry and prose. When the Dreyfus affair in France awakened the Jewish self-consciousness of Theodor Herzl, he quickly expressed himself in lectures, plays, essays, and programs for the recovery of a national home. These symbol elaborations were also determined by the patterns formed for the glorification of a collective symbol of identification within the culture to which he had been exposed. Hence a "Jewish nation" at such a time and place seemed to Herzl to demand immediate statehood.

The displacement of the infantile, childish, and juvenile affects upon symbols of ambiguous reference has led to the creation of remarkable monuments to human vanity. Nations, classes, tribes, and churches have been treated as collective symbols in the name of which the individual may indulge his elementary urges for supreme power, for omniscience, for amorality, for security.[7]

The examination of such symbol structures became one of the interesting exercises of the eighteenth century intellectuals as the clashes among organization areas broadened into clashes among "nations." One of the studies of the day was an *Essay on National Pride,* by Dr. J. G. Zimmerman, physician to His Britannic Majesty at Hanover, and a minor literary light.[8] His book appeared two years after the beginning of the Seven Years' War, and he commented shrewdly that "Newton will often be called an almanac maker, and Montesquieu a blockhead, while the French and English struggle with all their power for the mastery of the American trade." The principal part of his essay classifies illustrations of national and tribal symbolism, taken from the history and ethnology of the period. He comments upon "the Greenlander, who laps with his dog in the same platter" and holds himself superior to the Danish invader. "Ask the Carribee Indians who live at the mouth of the Orinoque, from what nation they derive their origin; they answer 'Why, we only are men.'" He repeats the Indian fable of the nation of hunchbacks who derided and scorned the straight backs. "The inhabitants of the Ladrones believe that their language is the only one in the world, and therefore that all the other nations on the earth are dumb." He notes that "the vanity of mankind has ever filled the immense vacuity beyond the authentic memorials of the origin of every

---

[7] The developmental formula of the political personality has been stated as follows:

$$p\} \ d\} \ r = P$$

The symbol p represents private motives, d displacement on to public objects, r rationalization in terms of public interest; P signifies the political man. The d and the r are mainly derived from the contact of the personality with secondary group symbols. See my *Psychopathology and Politics,* pp. 261-263, Chicago, 1930.

[8] First Edition, Zurich, 1758. English by Samuel H. Wilcocke, New York. Printed by M. L. and W. A. Davis for H. Caritat, Bookseller and Librarian, 1799. See my "Two Forgotten Studies in Political Psychology," *American Political Science Review,* 19 (1925):707-717.

nation with fabulous history, at pleasing removing their antiquity to the remotest ages, in order to proportionally increase its luster." He cites "the yet uncivilized inhabitants of Paraguay" who "give to the moon the endearing appellation of mother; and when their parent is eclipsed, they run out of their huts with the greatest activity, and making the most hideous lamentations, they shoot a vast number of arrows into the air in order to defend the moon from the dogs who attack her." Observing that men prefer the diet to which they are accustomed, the Doctor pungently adds, "The love of our country is little more, in many cases, than the love of an ass for his manger."

The prominence of physical features has prompted innumerable attempts to elaborate the superior claims of collective symbols by imputing special significance to bodily characteristics. It was formerly held that the "inferior races" had "ugly" features, such as slant eyes, large noses, flat noses, thick lips. The Japanese soon presented a special problem here, because they showed as much industrial and fighting ability as many Europeans; but they thought the large eyes and aquiline noses of the West were ugly. The growing recognition of the influence of suggestion on forms of aesthetic taste renders such comparisons of relative "beauty" rather ludicrous. Pigmentation of the skin has also been a focus of "superiority-inferiority" claims, but investigation has revealed that pigmentation scarcely correlates with any agreed index of "capacity."

At the First Universal Congress of Races inventories were made of the bodily details which had been chosen by various people to rationalize their superiority claims. These covered a wide gamut, including pigmentation of the hair, pigmentation of the iris, the pattern of the hair sectioned transversely, the nasal index, the cephalic index, the geometric variations in the form of the cranium or the face, the amount of hemoglobin in the blood, the rapidity of the pulse, "vital capacity," muscular strength, quantity of urine, weight, height, variation in the respiration of civilized and noncivilized women, shape of the female sex organs, shape of the breasts, distribution of fat on women's hips, protrusion of the lower jaw, convolution of the ears, depth and carrying power of the voice, resistance to disease, quantity of water in the tissues, and weight of the brain.[9] Much skepticism prevails among scientists on all efforts to relate somatic differences to general ideas about supremacy.[10]

[9] Gustav Spiller edited the *Papers on Inter-racial Problems* of the *Universal Races Congress,* London, 1911.

[10] See Jean Finot, *Le préjugé des races,* Paris, 1905; F. H. Hankins, *The Racial Basis of Civilization,* New York, 1926; Franz Boas, *Anthropology and Modern Life,* New York, 1928; Friedrich Hertz, *Race and Civilization,* New York, 1928. The principal result of the general intelligence-testing movement has been to expose subtle cultural differences. See T. R. Garth, *Race Psychology: A Study of Racial Mental Differences,* New York, 1931.

Each symbol of identification is elaborated according to the patterns already existing in the culture for symbols of that class. There are thus preformed praise patterns of symbol and practice available for application to the new symbol. Since our Western European culture was so long dominated by the symbolism of Christianity, the rising national and proletarian movements, quite without premeditation, look over the Christian patterns. A classical instance of this is the famous procession at the first session of the Legislative Assembly in France in the autumn of 1791, when twelve elderly patriarchs went in search of the Book of the Constitution.

They came back, having at their head the archivist Camus, who, holding up the Book with his two hands and resting it on his breast, carried with slow and measured tread the new Blessed Sacrament of the French. All the deputies arose and bared their heads. Camus, with meditative mien, kept his eyes lowered.[11]

Writers on many of our contemporary symbols of identification have recently become acutely aware of these connections. It is frequently noted how the principal symbol is endowed with godlike attributes, the collective mission is idealized, an elaborate ritualism is evolved about a banner, pledges of unswerving fidelity are taken ("I pledge allegiance to my flag . . ."), holidays (holy days) are observed, the veneration of statues, pictures, and shrines increases, a body of official doctrines is reverently reiterated and stoutly defended, learned commentators elaborate the subtleties of the official ideology, and devices of popularization are exploited to reach every stratum of the supporting community and to proselyte among the unconverted.[12]

The modern phenomenon of nationalism represents a complicated synthesis of religious, cultural, state, democratic, and allied patterns. Once partly integrated around a particular symbol each new configuration diffused as a culture complex, eliciting fresh acts of identification from some, and provoking decisive acts of rejection from others. Affirmation aroused counteraffirmation, and the outcome of the dialectic was to insure the propagation of the general pattern, subject to profound differentiations in detail.

Since the possession of a distinctive language came to be regarded as one of the details essential to the status of the fully developed national symbol, language revivals became inseparable from the early history of most nationalistic movements. Restrictions of any kind upon the use of the vernacular in schools, universities, law courts, legislatures, forums, churches, or markets were bitterly resented. Intellectuals expanded the national vo-

[11] A. Mathiez, *Les origines des cultes révolutionnaires*, Paris, 1904, p. 27.

[12] Religion and nationalism is extensively discussed in the works of Carlton J. H. Hayes, Hans Kohn, and Charles E. Merriam previously referred to. For religion and proletarianism, see Werner Sombart, and also Waldemar Gurian, *Bolshevism; Theory and Practice*, New York, 1932.

cabulary as well as the national literature. In Finland the vernacular was fashioned into a literary vehicle on a par with Swedish; in Bohemia the Czech language supplanted the foreign literary speech, which was German; in Albania the nationalists remodeled the crude vernacular into a literary medium. In Greece the artificial "pure" Greek was launched, but failed, the popular "demotike" winning out. Among the Vlachs in Macedonia a national movement got under way with the revival of the vernacular, Roumanian, which the Greeks failed to suppress. In Roumania the spread of nationalism went hand in hand with the expansion of the national tongue. In Hungary the vernacular was modified into a phonetic language that supplanted German as the polite medium. In Norway the Norse dialects were modified into Landsmaal, which has been recognized as co-official with Riksmaal or Dano-Norwegian. Similar processes occurred in Iceland, Ireland, Lithuania, Poland, Ukrainia, Armenia, Wales, Scotland, Flemish Belgium, French Canada, Palestine, and some other communities.[13]

The general objects of collective effort on behalf of the collective symbol are thus profoundly affected by the patterns conceived to be appropriate in the culture to symbols of this class. Identification with the collective symbol likewise involves identification with many, if not all, of these status symbols, and the discrepancy between the existing position of the collective symbol and the patterns deemed appropriate to the class defines the objectives of concerted effort.

The remodeling of the personality through identification varies from minor changes in vocabulary to profound redefinitions of career, in which individuals devote themselves to the performance of specialized functions in the collective enterprise. They may become devoted missionaries of the cause, exhorting in public and private, or they may carry on the detailed work of administering central office routine, collecting information, soliciting funds, distributing material. The professional revolutionary is one of the most prominent examples of full-time devotion to the expression of the claims of a collective symbol.

The adaptive processes which are initiated in identification modify the relation of the symbol to other symbols in the lives of the persons affected; these other symbols are both "public" and "private" and their interconnections may be infinitely complex. The symbol of the local merchants' association may be reenforced to strengthen the symbol of the nation; but this process of redefinition may involve the inclusion of certain commercial policy demands into the national symbol. This latter process, by means of which special and private demands are legitimized in terms of the more

[13] See Carl D. Buck, "Language and the Sentiment of Nationality," *American Political Science Review*, 10 (1916):44-69. G. S. H. Rossouw traced the rise of Afrikander in South Africa in *Nationalism and Language*, University of Chicago, 1922, Ph. D. dissertation, and reviewed the literature.

inclusive symbol, adds greatly to the acceptability of the latter. A central core of allusion is sustained and redefined in terms of "tactical" or "strategical" considerations. Personalities display prodigious skill in justifying private goals in terms of master symbols; insofar as this process is unconscious, it is rationalization; insofar as it is conscious, it is justification.

The relation between symbols of identification and of demand, which have just been indicated, may be amplified by noticing the relations between symbols of identification and of expectation. Identification with collective symbols usually modifies the outlook of the person on the future of the world. Expectations are generated about the benevolent implications of future history for cherished aspirations. The result is over-optimism about the future status of the master symbol. Over-optimism about the future may lead to direct action under very unfavorable circumstances. The tragic consequences of the March action in the year 1921 in Germany were partly ascribable to the unduly sanguine expectations of recent converts to the left proletarian cause. Recent converts to a master symbol are notoriously prone to overestimate the future. Conversion experiences come as solutions of acute conflicts between strong tendency systems within the personality, and the convert is not infrequently driven to impulsive acts of expiation for the hostilities which were so long directed against the newly introjected symbol. The redefinition of future expectations is in part due to the relatively exclusive preoccupation of the individual with the fate of the master symbol. The whole meaning of history is sharpened into some simplified struggle between Good and Evil, bourgeois and proletarian, oppressor and oppressed. The future derives its portentous quality from the fact that it alone can disclose the fate of the contending symbols.

Symbols of identification, demand, and expectation reciprocally influence one another, and interplay with changes in the division of labor. Optimism and devotion may affect the work rate and the birth rate, modifying the value hierarchy. The development of power machinery may cheapen production and lead to the expansion of the market. Demands which are serviceable in extending the market may be redefined in terms of the master symbols of nation or state. Such dynamic interrelations between "material" and "ideological" continue to redefine areas of activity, sentiment, and organization.

From the foregoing it is evident that the spread of any master identifying symbol depends upon the connections among details of great apparent diversity. The success of any symbol in competition with other symbols depends upon frequency of exposure in forms capable of eliciting favorable response, and upon presentation at times when the readjustive possibilities of the population are high. The level of general reactivity is itself modified by many changes in the material and symbolic configuration of specific persons, and any process of diffusion, once under way, reacts with each new aspect of the continually shifting context in which it operates. The study of the historical spread of symbols and practices has clarified many conditions which facilitate the process,[14] and the use of psychoanalysis has disclosed significant intrapsychic connections of which we were formerly unaware. In particular, psychoanalysis provides an infinitely enriched conception of all that is implied in those unconscious receptivities which, spontaneously aligned in the direction of dominating personalities, constitute the interlapping matrices through which symbols radiate with special rapidity and intensity throughout society.

All research confirms the importance of exposing the specific sequence through which symbol clusters pass. When did a national symbol of identification become associated with demands to oust foreigners from jobs in the army and the bureaucracy? When did sensitiveness to being ruled by executives of foreign origin develop? When did it cease to be good form to speak a foreign tongue? When did it become socially necessary to patronize native art? When did it become imperative to "buy Chinese" or "sell Chinese?" When did it become socially advisable to name children after political heroes? When did it become disloyal to accept favors in return for exercising an official duty? [15]

Recent social science has undertaken to follow and to explain the speedy diffusion of nationalism since the later years of the eighteenth century.[16] In the foreground appears the rapid application of modern technology to production, profoundly altering the life situation of many members of the community. Perceiving new possibilities of profit, self-selected enterprisers took the initiative in demanding many modifications in traditional ways of life, clashing with the symbols and practices favorable to

[14] Cultural anthropologists have contributed to our knowledge of the dynamics of diffusion. See Edward Sapir, *Time Perspective in Aboriginal American Culture*, Memoir 90, pp. 30 ff., Canada, Geological Survey, 1916; Edward Sapir, "Custom," *Encyclopedia of the Social Sciences;* Roland B. Dixon, *Building of Cultures*, pp. 59ff., New York, 1928; Leslie Spier, "The Sun Dance of the Plains Indians: Its Development and Diffusion," *Anthropological Papers of the American Museum of Natural History*, Vol. 16, Part 7, especially pp. 501 ff., New York, 1921; Paul Radin, "A Sketch of the Peyote Cult of the Winnebago: A Study in Borrowing," *Journal of Religious Psychology*, 7 (1914): 1-22.

[15] See the studies in the history of patriotism by Roberto Michels and Carlton J. H. Hayes; the Civic Training Series edited by Charles E. Merriam; Charles A. Beard and G. H. E. Smith, *The Idea of National Interest; An Analytical Study in American Foreign Policy*, New York, 1934.

[16] In addition to the literature previously cited, see Friedrich Hertz, "Wesen und Werden der Nation," *Nation und Nationalität*, Erg.- Bd., *Jahrbuch für Soziologie*, Karlsruhe, 1927; H. O. Ziegler, *Die Moderne Nation, Ein Beitrag zur politischen Soziologie*, Tübingen, 1931; R. Johannet, *Le principe des nationalités*, Paris, 1923; *Verhandlungen des zweiten deutschen Soziologentages vom 20. bis 22. Oktober, 1912, in Berlin*, Tübingen, 1913; Otto Bauer, *Die Nationalitätenfrage und die Sozialdemokratie*, Vienna, 1924; Karl Renner, *Der Kampf der österreichischen Nationen um den Staat*, 2 vols., Vienna, 1902; Karl Renner, *Der nationale Streit um die Aemter und die Sozialdemokratie*, Vienna, 1908; Koppel S. Pinson, *Bibliographical Introduction to Nationalism* (announced); and various books of Harry Elmer Barnes.

the landed property group. Finding themselves in organization areas where decision making was a restricted privilege, needing ways and means of rendering themselves effective at the centers of dominance, they responded positively to symbols of protest and plan which were circulated by specialized verbalizers. Gradually the ideology of the ruling élite was called into question in the name of mankind as a whole. Democratic language assisted in mobilizing the animosities of the "underprivileged" in mass action which finally altered the methods of élite recruitment and the language of justification. Where members of the bourgeoisie got control of the government, as in France, they transformed their earlier antistate orientation into a pro-state and pro-governmental ideology. Nationalism became henceforth a means of nullifying proletarian challenges from within, and of fostering the power of the state in the world balance. Where the bourgeoisie was particularly weak, and an older social formation needed military support from the masses to defend itself from invasion, the older élite exploited as much as possible of the place-, time-, and tradition-bound symbolism at hand. In Prussia the bourgeoisie never succeeded in capturing the language of nationalism from the monarchy and the feudality that rallied to repulse the French.

In the competition of merely local enterprises with one another, merely local differences are emphasized; hence effective nationalism could not appear until the expansion of the market made possible the concentrating of strong initiative in the hands of enterprisers who were situated at the principal metropoles.

The upper bourgeoisie at the chief marketing centers were receptive to the elaborated symbols of nationalism as they were developed by orators, journalists, poets, novelists, essayists, and systematists. The ideological incorporation of the lesser centers and the back country into the policy of the bourgeois state spread from the centers of dominance by means of the propagation of literacy and by the expansion of such secondary means of incessant stimulation as the press. The expansion of capitalist enterprise tended to promote the active widening of the marketing area for certain goods, like textiles, and, later, iron and steel products. The result was to facilitate the growth of a world-marketing area, which in turn set up many dialectical processes in the form of local opposition to foreign competition. These acute localistic reactions created groups which were favorably disposed toward new local nationalistic expressions. We notice the discovery of local identities throughout Europe, and beyond, as the nineteenth century wore on. The multiplication of state organization areas at the end of the World War is one of the residues of this process.

The emergence in an old organization area of a new élite which speaks in the name of the proletariat challenges the official symbolism of the ruling élites elsewhere. Unity of action would seem to be advantageous among these various élites in the face of the new threat, but intercapitalistic conflicts are still fostered by the importance of safeguarding foreign economic outlets and of uniting the community around nationalistic symbols; there is also a general tendency to doubt the immediate acuteness of the crisis.[17]

The calculation of pecuniary advantage is a highly "rational" process; yet the social patterns which permit this rational process to go on must be sustained by an irrational consensus. Hence the tension between the rational and the traditional is peculiarly high under capitalism, which requires consensus, yet fosters the rational analysis of every acquired symbol and practice. The rationalism of capitalism has rendered it peculiarly dependent for positive values, ethical imperatives, and unifying goal symbols upon its legacies from previous cultures. The vestiges of primitive folk culture *(Gemeinschaft)* have been drags upon the completely ruthless application of the principle of calculated pecuniary advantage in The Great Society.[18] The insecurities arising from the changes in the material environment have been augmented by the stresses arising from the decline in potency of the older religious symbols and practices. Nationalism and proletarianism are secularized alternatives to the surviving religious patterns, answering to the need of personalities to restabilize themselves in a mobile world.

The emergence of the last world-revolutionary pattern has intensified appeals to parochialism in the postwar world.[19] The older middle-class formations have revivified the national symbols at the expense of class or world symbols, and supplied blood, money, and applause to programs which have been designed to curb the "alien" and "radical" elements in the community. German Nationalism Socialism relies on the older middle classes. If proletarian strategists can devise ways and means of disintegrating the loyalties of the middle classes, proletarian struggles might in time of advancing economic distress eventuate successfully, short of the demoralization involved in prolonged or unsuccessful war.

[17] Many of the economic aspects of nationalism are well handled in Waldemar Mitscherlich, *Nationalismus: Die Geschichte einer Idee*, Leipzig, 1929; R. G. Hawtrey, *Economic Aspects of Sovereignty*, London, 1930; Walter Sulzbach, *Nationales Gemeinschaftsgefühl und wirtschaftliches Interesse*, Leipzig, 1929; József Eötvös, *Der Einfluss der herrschenden Ideen des 19 Jahrhunderts auf den staat* (from Hungarian), Leipzig, 1854; and in the writings of Bukharin, Lenin, and other historical materialists.

[18] The relations between *Gemeinschaft* and *Gesellschaft*, first extensively developed by Ferdinand Tönnies, are carefully restated in Hans Freyer, *Soziologie als Wirklichkeitswissenschaft*, pp. 230-252, Leipzig and Berlin, 1930.

[19] See Helen Martin, *Nationalism and Children's Books* (University of Chicago Ph. D. dissertation, 1934), which applies a rigorous technique to the study of the factors affecting the diffusion of children's books throughout the world.

Herbert Blumer

THE MASS, THE PUBLIC,
AND PUBLIC OPINION

We are selecting the term *mass* to denote an elementary and spontaneous collective grouping which, in many respects, is like the crowd but
fundamentally different from it in other ways. *The mass is represented
by people who participate in mass behavior,* such as those who are excited
by some national event, those who share in a land boom, those who are
interested in a murder trial which is reported in the press, or those who
participate in some large migration.

DISTINGUISHABLE FEATURES OF THE MASS: So conceived, the mass has a
number of distinguishable features. *First,* its membership may come from
all walks of life, and from all distinguishable social strata; it may include
people of different class position, of different vocation, of different cultural
attainment, and of different wealth. One can recognize this in the case of
the mass of people who follow a murder trial. *Secondly,* the mass is an
anonymous group, or more exactly, is composed of anonymous individuals.
Third, there exists little interaction or change of experience between the
members of the mass. They are usually physically separated from one
another, and, being anonymous, do not have the opportunity to mill as do
the members of the crowd. *Fourth,* the mass is very loosely organized and
is not able to act with the concertedness or unity that marks the crowd.

THE RÔLE OF INDIVIDUALS IN THE MASS: The fact that the mass consists
of individuals belonging to a wide variety of local groups and cultures is
important. For it signifies that the object of interest which gains the attention of those who form the mass is something which lies on the outside of
the local cultures and groups; and therefore, that this object of interest is
not defined or explained in terms of the understandings or rules of these
local groups. The object of mass interest can be thought of as attracting

Reprinted from *New Outline of the Principles of Sociology* (1946), edited by Alfred
McClung Lee, pp. 185-93, by permission of the author and the publisher. (Copyright,
1946, by Barnes and Noble.)

the attention of people away from their local cultures and spheres of life and turning it toward a wider universe, toward areas which are not defined or covered by rules, regulations, or expectations. In this sense the mass can be viewed as constituted by detached and alienated individuals who face objects or areas of life which are interesting, but which are also puzzling and not easy to understand and order. Consequently, before such objects, the members of the mass are likely to be confused and uncertain in their actions. Further, in not being able to communicate with each other, except in limited and imperfect ways, the members of the mass are forced to act separately, as individuals.

SOCIETY AND THE MASS: From this brief characterization it can be seen that the mass is devoid of the features of a society or a community. It has no social organization, no body of custom and tradition, no established set of rules or rituals, no organized group of sentiments, no structure of status rôles, and no established leadership. It merely consists of an aggregation of individuals who are separate, detached, anonymous, and thus, homogeneous as far as mass behavior is concerned. It can be seen, further, that the behavior of the mass, just because it is not made by preëstablished rule or expectation, is spontaneous, indigenous, and elementary. In these respects, the mass is a great deal like the crowd.

In other respects, there is an important difference. It has already been noted that the mass does not mill or interact as the crowd does. Instead, the individuals are separated from one another and unknown to one another. This fact means that the individual in the mass, instead of being stripped of his self awareness is, on the other hand apt to be rather acutely self-conscious. Instead of acting in response to the suggestions and excited stimulation of those with whom he is in rapport, he acts in response to the object that has gained his attention and on the basis of the impulses that are aroused by it.

NATURE OF MASS BEHAVIOR: This raises the question as to how the mass behaves. The answer is in terms of each individual's seeking to answer his own needs. The form of mass behavior, paradoxically, is laid down by individual lines of activity and not by concerted action. These individual activities are primarily in the form of selections—such as the selection of a new dentifrice, a book, a play, a party platform, a new fashion, a philosophy, or a gospel—selections which are made in response to the vague impulses and feelings which are awakened by the object of mass interest. Mass behavior, even though a congeries of individual lines of action, may become of momentous significance. If these lines converge, the influence of the mass may be enormous, as is shown by the far-reaching effects on institutions ensuing from shifts in the selective interest of the mass. A political party may be disorganized or a commercial institution wrecked by such shifts in interest or taste.

When mass behavior becomes organized as into a movement, it ceases to be mass behavior, but becomes societal in nature. Its whole nature changes in acquiring a structure, a program, a defining culture, traditions, prescribed rules, an in-group attitude, and a we-consciousness. It is for this reason that we have appropriately limited it to the forms of behavior which have been described.

INCREASING IMPORTANCE OF MASS BEHAVIOR: Under conditions of modern urban and industrial life, mass behavior has emerged in increasing magnitude and importance. This is due primarily to the operation of factors which have detached people from their local cultures and local group settings. Migration, changes of residence, newspapers, motion pictures, the radio, education—all have operated to detach individuals from customary moorings and thrust them into a new and wider world. In the face of this world, individuals have had to make adjustments on the basis of largely unaided selections. The convergence of their selections has made the mass a potent influence. At times, its behavior comes to approximate that of a crowd, especially under conditions of excitement. At such times it is likely to be influenced by excited appeals as these appear in the press or over the radio—appeals that play upon primitive impulses, antipathies, and traditional hatreds. This should not obscure the fact that the mass may behave without such crowd-like frenzy. It may be much more influenced by an artist or a writer who happens to sense the vague feelings of the mass and to give expression and articulation to them.

INSTANCES OF MASS BEHAVIOR: In order to make clearer the nature of the mass and of mass behavior, a brief consideration can be given to a few instances. Gold rushes and land rushes illustrate many of the features of mass behavior. The people who participate in them usually come from a wide variety of backgrounds; together they constitute a heterogeneous assemblage. Thus, those who engaged in the Klondike Rush or the Oklahoma Land Boom came from different localities and areas. In the rush, each individual (or at best, family) had his own goal or objective, so that between the participants there was a minimum of coöperation and very little feeling of allegiance or loyalty. Each was trying to get ahead of the other, and each had to take care of himself. Once the rush is under way, there is little discipline, and no organization to enforce order. Under such conditions it is easy to see how a rush turns into a stampede or a panic.

MASS ADVERTISING: Some further appreciation of the nature of mass behavior is yielded by a brief treatment of mass advertising. In such advertising, the appeal has to be addressed to the anonymous individual. The relation between the advertisement and the prospective purchaser is a direct one—there is no organization or leadership which can deliver, so to speak, the body of purchasers to the seller. Instead, each individual acts upon the basis of his own selection. The purchasers are a heterogeneous group coming from many communities and walks of life; as members of the mass, however, because of their anonymity, they are homogeneous or essentially alike.

PROLETARIAN MASSES: What are sometimes spoken of as the proletarian masses illustrate other features of the mass. They represent a large population with little organization or effective communication. Such people usually have been wrested loose from a stable group life. They are usually disturbed, even though it be only in the form of vague hopes or new tastes and interests. Consequently, there is a lot of groping in their behavior—an uncertain process of selection among objects and ideas that come to their attention.

NATURE OF THE PUBLIC: We shall consider the public as the remaining elementary collective grouping. The term *public* is used to refer to a group of people (a) who are confronted by an issue, (b) who are divided in their ideas as to how to meet the issue, and (c) who engage in discussion over the issue. As such, it is to be distinguished from a public in the sense of a national people, as when one speaks of the public of the United States, and also from a *following*, as in the instance of the "public" of a motion picture star. The presence of an issue, of discussion, and of a collective opinion is the mark of the public.

THE PUBLIC AS A GROUP: We refer to the public as an elementary and spontaneous collective grouping because it comes into existence not as a result of design, but as a natural response to a certain kind of situation. That the public does not exist as an established group and that its behavior is not prescribed by traditions or cultural patterns is indicated by the very fact that its existence centers on the presence of an issue. As issues vary, so do the corresponding publics. And the fact that an issue exists signifies the presence of a situation which cannot be met on the basis of a cultural rule but which must be met by a collective decision arrived at through a process of discussion. In this sense, the public is a grouping that is natural and not conventional, one that is spontaneous and not preëstablished.

CHARACTERISTIC FEATURES OF THE PUBLIC: This elementary and natural character of the public can be better appreciated by noticing that the public, like the crowd and the mass, is lacking in the characteristic features of a society. The existence of an issue means that the group has to act; yet there are no understandings, definitions, or rules prescribing what that action should be. If there were, there would be, of course, no issue. It is in this sense that we can speak of the public as having no culture—no traditions to dictate what its action shall be. Further, since a public comes into existence only with an issue it does not have the form or organization of a society. In it, people do not have fixed status rôles. Nor does the public have any we-feeling or consciousness of its identity. Instead, the public is a kind of amorphous group whose size and membership varies with the issue; instead of having its activity prescribed, it is engaged in an effort to arrive at an act, and therefore forced to *create* its action.

The peculiarity of the public is that it is marked by disagreement and hence by *discussion* as to what should be done. This fact has a number of implications. For one thing, it indicates that the interaction that occurs in the public is markedly different from that which takes place in the crowd. A crowd mills, develops rapport, and reaches a unanimity unmarred by disagreement. The public interacts on the basis of interpretation, enters into dispute, and consequently is characterized by conflict relations. Correspondingly, individuals in the public are likely to have their self-consciousness intensified and their critical powers heightened instead of losing self-awareness and critical ability as occurs in the crowd. In the public, arguments are advanced, are criticized, and are met by counter-arguments. The interaction, therefore, makes for opposition instead of the mutual support and unanimity that mark the crowd.

Another point of interest is that this discussion, which is based on difference, places some premium on facts and makes for rational consideration. While, as we shall see, the interaction may fall short by far of realizing these characteristics, the tendency is in their direction. The crowd means that rumor and spectacular suggestion predominate; but the presence of opposition and disagreement in the public means that contentions are challenged and become subject to criticism. In the face of attack that threatens to undermine their character, such contentions have to be bolstered or revised in the face of criticisms that cannot be ignored. Since facts can maintain their validity, they come to be valued; and since the discussion is argumentative, rational considerations come to occupy a rôle of some importance.

BEHAVIOR PATTERNS OF THE PUBLIC: Now we can consider the question as to how a public acts. This question is interesting, particularly because the public does not act like a society, a crowd, or the mass. A society manages to act by following a prescribed rule or consensus; a crowd, by developing rapport; and the mass, by the convergence of individual selections. But the public faces, in a sense, the dilemma of how to become a unit when it is actually divided, of how to act concertedly when there is a disagreement as to what the action should be. The public acquires its particular type of unity and manages to act by arriving at a collective decision or by developing a collective opinion. It becomes necessary to consider now the nature of public opinion and the manner of its formation.

PUBLIC OPINION: Public opinion should be viewed as a collective product. As such, it is not a unanimous opinion with which everyone in the public agrees, nor is it necessarily the opinion of a majority. Being a collective opinion it may be (and usually is) different from the opinion of any of the groups in the public. It can be thought of, perhaps, as a composite opinion formed out of the several opinions that are held in the public; or better, as the central tendency set by•the striving among these separate opinions and, consequently, as being shaped by the relative strength and play of opposition among them. In this process, the opinion of some minority group may exert a much greater influence in the shaping of the collective opinion than does the view of a majority group. Being a collective product, public opinion does represent the entire public as it is being mobilized to act on the issue, and as such, does enable concerted action which is not necessarily based on consensus, rapport, or chance alignment of individual choices. Public opinion is always moving toward a decision even though it never is unanimous.

THE UNIVERSE OF DISCOURSE: The formation of public opinion occurs through the give and take of discussion. Argument and counter-argument become the means by which it is shaped. For this process of discussion to go on, it is essential for the public to have what has been called a "universe of discourse"—the possession of a common language or the ability to agree on the meaning of fundamental terms. Unless they can understand one another, discussion and argumentation are not only fruitless, but impossible. Public discussion today, particularly on certain national issues, is likely to be hampered by the absence of a universe of discourse. Further, if the groups or parties in the public adopt dogmatic and sectarian positions, public discussion comes to a standstill; for such sectarian attitudes are tantamount to a refusal to adopt the point of view of one another and to alter one's own position in the face of attack or criticism. The formation of public opinion implies that people share one another's experience and are willing to make compromises and concessions. It is only in this way that the public, divided as it is, can come to act as a unit.

INTEREST GROUPS: The public, ordinarily, is made up of interest groups and a more detached and disinterested spectator-like body. The issue which creates the public is usually set by contesting interest groups. These interest groups have an immediate private concern in the way the issue is met and, therefore, they endeavor to win to their position the support and allegiance of the outside disinterested groups. This puts the disinterested group, as Lippmann has pointed out, in the position of arbiter and judge. It is their alignment which determines, usually, which of the competing schemes is likely to enter most freely into the final action. This strategic and decisive place held by those not identified with the immediate interest groups means that public discussion is carried on primarily among them. The interest groups endeavor to shape and set the opinions of these relatively disinterested people.

Viewed in this way, one can understand the varying quality of public opinion, and also the use of means of influence such as propaganda, which subvert intelligent public discussion. A given public opinion is likely to be anywhere between a highly emotional and prejudiced point of view and a highly intelligent and thoughtful opinion. In other words, public discussion may be carried on different levels, with different degrees of thoroughness and limitation. The efforts made by interest groups to shape public opinion may be primarily attempts to arouse or set emotional attitudes and to provide misinformation. It is this feature which has led many students of public opinion to deny its rational character and to emphasize instead, its emotional and unreasoned nature. One must recognize, however, that the very process of controversial discussion forces a certain amount of rational consideration and that, consequently, the resulting collective opinion has a certain rational character. The fact that contentions have to be defended and justified and opposing contentions criticized and shown to be untenable, involves evaluation, weighing, and judgment. Perhaps it would be accurate to say that public opinion is rational, but need not be intelligent.

THE RÔLE OF PUBLIC DISCUSSION: It is clear that the quality of public opinion depends to a large extent on the effectiveness of public discussion. In turn, this effectiveness depends on the availability and flexibility of the agencies of public communication, such as the press, the radio, and public meetings. Basic to their effective use is the possibility of free discussion. If certain of the contending views are barred from gaining presentation to the disinterested public or suffer some discrimination as to the possibility of being argued before them, then, correspondingly, there is interference with effective public discussion.

As mentioned above, the concerns of interest groups readily lead them to efforts to manipulate public opinion. This is particularly true today, when public issues are many and the opportunities for thorough discussion are limited. This setting has been conducive to the employment, in increasing degree, of "propaganda"; today most students of public opinion find that their chief concern is the study of propaganda.

Daniel Katz

THREE CRITERIA:
KNOWLEDGE, CONVICTION, AND SIGNIFICANCE

About fifty years ago William James wrote in prophetic vein: "Messrs. Dar-win and Galton have set the example of circulars of questions sent out by the hundred to those supposed able to reply. The custom has spread, and it will be well for us in the next generation if such circulars be not ranked among the common pests of life. Meanwhile information grows, and results emerge." [1]

In his phrase "those supposed able to reply" James recognized the basic problem in opinion research which is the major concern of these few pages. For the competence of people in answering various types of questions and the evaluation of their answers lie at the heart of any questionnaire method whether it be a written personality inventory or an oral interview. Recent criticisms by Hugh Johnson and Robert Moses of the Gallup polls have pro-duced a popular awareness of this problem—long a matter of concern in the field of psychological and social science. In this field attempts have been made to insure reliability in the answers of respondents by questioning only for limited purposes. For example, in devising methods for measuring attitudes, L. L. Thurstone restricted his conception of attitude to feelings of like or dislike for social symbols. [2] He realized that this area of feeling-tone toward words such as the Catholic Church or the Democratic Party could be tapped much more readily and reliably through the questionnaire tech-nique than could other psychological areas. In social surveys, moreover, it is an accepted practice to pre-test attitudinal material to insure the ex-clusion of questions which can not be answered meaningfully by respon-

Reprinted from The Public Opinion Quarterly, Vol. IV (1940), pp. 277-284, by permis-sion of the author and the publisher. (Copyright, 1940, by the Princeton University Press.)

[1] William James, Principles of Psychology. New York: Henry Holt, 1890, Vol. I, p. 194.

[2] L. L. Thurstone, "Attitudes Can Be Measured," American Journal of Sociology, 1928, 33, 529-554.

dents. And this practice implies more qualitative analysis than do the trial runs of the polls.

In evaluating the public opinion polls three criteria are of interest to the social scientist: (1) Do people know enough about the questions asked to give reliable and meaningful answers? (2) Do people have convictions upon the subject so that there is real stability to their answers? (3) Assuming that answers can be obtained with a satisfactory degree of reliability, are the questions themselves of any genuine significance for social science?

These three criteria of *knowledge, conviction* and *significance* can be more profitably applied to the polls if we first analyze the psychological areas to which questions have been directed. These psychological areas are of four types: (1) motives or reasons why; (2) affect, or feelings of favor or disfavor toward social symbols, for example, the emotional reactions of rejection or approval which the term New Deal arouses in many people; (3) ideas and opinions about public and social issues; and (4) ideas and opinions about personal problems.

Perhaps the most important area is that of motives. Here the polls can make no great contribution, for the questionnaire method tells us relatively little of the real reasons back of behavior. Only in special instances do people have sufficient insight to report accurately about their motivation. An individual's account of his motives, nonetheless, is useful as a rationalized statement of his purposes. Though it does not indicate his underlying motive, it may well indicate the goal toward which he is moving.[3] In fairness to the polls, moreover, it should be noted that they have wisely refrained from asking many questions about motives. They can be criticized for this omission, but not very justly, since no one method of social investigation can cover all the areas of study.

In the area of feeling toward symbols fall the real bread-and-butter questions of the polls—the political preferences of the voting public. Political party names and the names of the leading contestants in a final election are labels which evoke an emotional (more properly an effective) response of like or dislike. In this general area the three criteria of knowledge, conviction, and significance are met in a highly satisfactory manner. The only knowledge necessary is familiarity with the symbol or label. Knowledge of the party platform or of its historical background is not necessary to indicate preference for it. We do not go to a public opinion poll to find out about what a party has to offer the country. Conviction is guaranteed by the emotional coloring of the political symbols. The significance for social science of the numerous miniature elections of the polls is perhaps more debatable. We will know in time how people vote on election day and

[3] A neat account of this point is furnished in Sorel's demonstration of the reenforcing effect of social myths or ideologies in dramatizing the aspirations of popular movements. Cf. G. Sorel, *Reflections On Violence*. New York: B. W. Huebsch, 1914.

the pre-knowledge is more valuable practically than scientifically. But the trends in voting preference during the campaign which the polls furnish can be analyzed in relation to objective events and in relation to income, age and other groupings of the voting population.

The great contribution of the polls to social research comes in this area of feeling-tone. They have established once and for all a point which laboratory experiments and social surveys had failed to clinch, namely that the questionnaire technique can give highly reliable and highly valid results in revealing people's feelings toward social symbols. By accurate predictions of elections the polls have made it incontrovertible that people will respond in actual social situations as they do when responding to an oral or written questionnaire, provided that the situation is similar and in this general affective area.[4]

The popular writer seems to think in blanket terms. Because he is impressed by the success of the polls in election prediction he will generalize this success to all the questions asked by the polls. Or impressed by some questionable finding on a public issue he will damn the polls completely. Neither alternative is correct. By their accurate prediction of election returns the polls have justified the questionnaire method for sampling affective responses to social symbols.

In the third and fourth areas of ideas on personal and public issues and attitudes toward social action it is essential to apply the criteria of knowledge, conviction and significance very strictly. If people lack a minimum knowledge of such issues as balancing the budget or amending the Wagner Act, then their answers will be a function of elements in the questioning method other than the real meaning of the question which is posed for them. This may not necessarily appear in a reliability coefficient of the sample, but it will be there nevertheless.

The American Institute of Public Opinion and *Fortune* pretest their questions to avoid phrasing which will be unintelligible to the public and to avoid issues unknown to the man on the street. The findings of the American Institute on this score are interpreted by its own representatives as evidence of their errors in the past in assuming a higher level of knowledge on pressing public questions than the average man possesses. They report, for example, that many people are ignorant of the various Cabinet officers and their functions, of reciprocal trade treaties, of the Dies Committee, of the National Labor Relations Board, of the meaning of the phrase "balancing the budget." For instance, 52 per cent of a representative sample frankly admitted that they did not know what a reciprocal trade treaty is; 31 per cent gave incorrect definitions; 9 per cent doubtful ones; and only 8 per cent were able to define the term correctly, even though every doubt was resolved in favor of the respondents.

[4] D. Katz and H. Cantril, "Public Opinion Polls," *Sociometry*, 1937, 1, 155-179.

On the whole, the treatment of public issues in the Institute and *Fortune* polls has not been ideal from the point of view of asking clear and meaningful questions. In an effort to obtain newsworthy information the poll directors have shot at their testing staff the political questions of the moment. The testing staff frequently finds these questions are not intelligible to the man on the street. The result is some compromise either on issues or on wording which does not remove the basic difficulty in the type of question asked. This difficulty is the symbolization of issues in political or technical terms. There is a failure to grasp the point of view of the average citizen and to interpret the question as he would come to grips with it. The lack of knowledge of the American public about public affairs is not as anti-democratic in implication as it may appear at first glance. The man on the street may be able to give meaningful answers to important questions if they are stated for him in his own language and in terms of his own thinking rather than in terms of the mental world of the politician and journalist.

Poll questions have suffered, too, from their remoteness from the individual's life and so have failed to meet the criterion of conviction. In other words, on many of the issues which the polls have sampled people have not held strong attitudes. For example, after the first few months of the present war American participation seems to the average man to be fairly remote and consequently his answer to the Gallup question about our entering the war may not reflect a stable attitude. Since it is a remote issue he does not hold the opinion strongly and his opinion may change quickly under the impact of objective events. Evidence of the unreality to the American people of American participation in the war is furnished in a study by the Princeton Public Opinion Research Project which shows that people in families containing members of draft age are no more opposed to our participation than people less personally affected.

A genuine source of error in interpreting the poll returns on public questions, then, is the assumption of a crystallized public opinion when none in fact exists. To have some measure of this factor the polls have been reporting the number of people who say they have no opinion on the issue in question. Yet this report is not wholly satisfactory because it remains to be established that the no-opinion vote is a valuable measure of the degree to which opinion on a measure has crystallized.

Moreover, even the amount of the no-opinion vote is lost sight of in the newspaper account of the Gallup release. This misinterpretation is due in part to the fact that Gallup discards the no-opinion answers before computing the percentage of people answering "yes" or "no." The percentage of affirmative replies reported is not a proportion of the total sample but of the total number of people who have opinions.

An instance of how this leads to false inferences appeared in the impression created in January 1939 that the American people were overwhelmingly in favor of the Dies Committee and the continuation of its activities. At that time Gallup asked: "Have you heard or read about the Dies Committee for investigating un-American activities?" Thirty-nine per cent said they had never heard of it. Those who had heard of it were then asked: "Do you think its findings have been important enough so that the investigations should be continued?" Twenty-two per cent had no opinion. Of those who had an opinion 74 per cent were in favor of continuing the committee and 26 per cent were opposed. The inference drawn by many people, however, was that three-fourths of the American public wanted the committee maintained.[5] As a matter of fact only 34 per cent of the group sampled were favorably disposed toward the Dies Committee and 66 per cent had either never heard of it, had no opinion, or were opposed to it. Now the American Institute is technically not at fault in that its releases contain all of the above information, but its method of expressing percentages is open to criticism since its releases are intended for popular consumption and not for scientific journals.

In addition to the no-opinion device, the American Institute of Public Opinion has employed the "filtering question" to rule out meaningless answers and to detect the degree to which opinion has crystallized. The filtering question asks the respondent if he has heard or is acquainted with the terms in the main question. If he has not, his opinion is not requested on the issue, but a count is made of respondents like himself who have little knowledge of the issue. In the questions on the Dies Committee the opening inquiry about having read or heard about the committee constituted a "filtering question."

Still another way of discovering the crystallization of public opinion is the scale technique employed by the *Fortune* surveys. The scale technique admits of shades of opinion instead of the yes-no dichotomy of the Gallup poll. With a scale technique the type of distribution of opinion furnishes some insight into the degree of superficiality of the answers of respondents. When people are convinced of the correctness of their views the distribution of opinion is generally not a normal one. It is either U-shaped or badly skewed to one side or other. The U-shaped curve indicates that people fall into opposed camps and the skewed curve that a majority agree in taking a decided stand.

The major difficulty of the polls has been their inability to distinguish between problems which the respondent regards as his own and problems which he regards as public issues. Part of the difficulty is inherent in the nature of the situation. A question of public policy may often involve the individual in a direct personal manner, but if it has not been personalized

[5] Britt and Menefee suggest that this was the inference drawn by many Congressmen. Cf. S. H. Britt and S. C. Menefee, *Public Opinion Quarterly*, 1939, 3, 449-457.

for him in advance he will conceive of it as concerning that impersonal social structure called "Government" and as having no close interest for him. For example, Gallup has asked: "Do you think every labor union should be required to take out a license (permit) from the United States government?"; and the *Fortune* survey has inquired: "Should the U.S. try to develop its own industries to the point where it does not have to buy any products from foreign countries?" Until the implications of these questions are made personal and explicit to people, many of them will have no real conviction in their answers. On the other hand, a question which might seem on the surface as purely personal may (because of the individual's awareness that others think as he does) be considered by the respondent as the government's business as well as his own.

The trouble has been that the polls have often assumed that because a problem is of practical importance or of political interest, therefore there is a public opinion on the problem which can be measured. This assumption is based upon a misunderstanding of the nature of public opinion. Public opinion does not automatically arise because there is a problem, present or potential, for the nation or some considerable portion of it. It is true that a few generations ago this was actually the case for the community in rural America. Then, if a problem arose, it implied an objective situation confronting all members of the community and a public opinion soon developed. But today when people live in large groups, the presence of a problem is often not accompanied by a series of objective events which involve considerable numbers of people in a direct manner. People are not often compelled by the external situation to take a stand upon the problem. They may admit when the question arises that it is a problem for the impersonal agency of government but they do not feel it as their own problem. To make them take a stand on an issue (and, of course, the right stand) we have developed to an elaborate extent, techniques of molding opinion through the media of mass impression manipulated by pressure groups.

Modern public opinion is thus of two types: common attitudes aroused by the impact of an objective event, sufficiently broad to affect in a direct manner large numbers within the population (for example a depression); or common attitudes aroused by the pressure of an intensive propaganda campaign. The first type of opinion is like the old type of community opinion but in our day and age it is much less common than opinion created by agencies of symbol manipulation. The inference is clear that when the polls ask questions about issues which have not been brought home to the people, either through events affecting them or propaganda enlisting their support, the results can not be interpreted as indicative of public opinion.

A few examples of such poll questions follow: "Do you think the Federal government should give money to states to help local schools?" "Should state governments transfer more of their powers to the Federal government?" "Should legal picketing be limited to one or two pickets, or should the number be unlimited?" "Should the government appropriate money to build a new U.S. merchant fleet?" "Do you think the attitude of the Roosevelt administration toward the electric power companies has been too severe?" "Would you favor having Congress set aside six million dollars each for the Republican and Democratic parties once every four years, so that the parties would not have to collect campaign funds from individuals and corporations, in return for which they would sometimes be expected to give favors?"

To these and similar questions might be added the polling for presidential nominees long before the state primaries were under way, when many of the names of the candidates meant little as symbols of policy, program or personality type. The objection is not to the use of questions on which there is no crystallized public opinion but to the interpretation placed upon the answers to these questions as representing the public opinion of the nation.

That the man on the street is not altogether unaware of this situation appears in the results of the polls themselves. The great majority of the American people are opposed to our entrance into the European War. Yet, when Gallup asked in September 1939 if we are going to be drawn into the war, 56 per cent of those who had an opinion answered in the affirmative. Now there is a real contradiction here, for it is as if people said, "No, we don't want war but public opinion is for it." What may really be involved is the tacit recognition by people that they will go along with their fellows and conform when the propaganda agencies go to work. This is not so much to say that any public opinion can be foisted on the people from above, as it is to emphasize that people tend to fall in line rather than take the chance of being black-listed as nonconformers.

Granted, however, that the polls give reliable reports of crystallized public opinion on certain issues, the social scientist may still be critical of the significance of these findings for his science. Have the most significant questions been asked to describe the public mind? Has an issue been thoroughly explored in all of its psychological implications with a battery of related questions? On studies of trends in opinion have the proper precautions been taken to hold constant the questioning process, the questions asked and the samples taken? Do other measures exist such as an index of propaganda to which opinion trends can be related?

These and similar questions can well be raised by the student of social science. Categorical answers are not so easily supplied. The limitations of the polls as commercial agencies dependent for their very life upon the news value of their results must be recognized. Straw votes in an election campaign are news but the thorough exploration of attitudes on many important questions may often be regarded as dull by the copy desk. This is the point at which the Gallup and *Fortune* polls depart most widely from traditional attitudinal studies in social science. The social scientist sets up his survey as an experiment to test a hypothesis or to gather data in so comprehensive a fashion that it will furnish hypotheses. In the polls taken by the American Institute many unrelated questions are asked and they are not devised to test hypotheses and advance the science of public opinion. The *Fortune* surveys, however, are now being more thorough in their exploration of issues and are devoting a complete ballot to a series of questions on the same problem. Their satisfaction with this procedure promises to result in deeper and more consistent probing. The American Institute is also likely to move in this direction in the future.

It should be remembered that an instrument must be evaluated with reference to other available devices. And from this point of view the polls of public opinion immediately take on stature. Our other sources for this type of information on the whole have been and are meager as compared with the polls. Most psychological investigations of attitudes have been based not upon a random sample of the population but upon a sample of the universe of college sophomores. Federal and state censuses of the population, of unemployment, etc., have concentrated upon objective information and have neglected the psychological aspects of human beings. The historian and the sociologist have often had to be content with studies which deal with secondary sources of data. They consult newspaper files, the popular songs of the period, the best sellers of the day, to get at what the polls will give the future historian more directly.

In fine, public opinion polls should be evaluated in a discriminating fashion. They are not going to revolutionize social science, but neither will they be negligible instruments for social science. It is common to reject a method because it does not give us all the answers. There has hardly been a mathematical tool or a methodological instrument devised for social and psychological research which has not drawn criticism because it could not give the whole story. It is similar with the polls. They have definite limitations but they are still a valuable asset to the student of society. They are not adequate to explore all the problems in public opinion and social psychology. No single instrument is. They are most adequate in measuring affect toward social symbols and they have made their greatest contribution in this field. In the area of opinions and attitudes they are decidedly useful, but here they must be interpreted with the greatest caution and supplemented wherever possible by other methods.

2

FORMATION OF PUBLIC OPINION

Because of technical and practical considerations, more research atten-tion has been paid to descriptions of opinions than to analyses of the forma-tion and development of opinion. Studies in the former category were not only more feasible technically but also easier to support financially. Ac-cordingly, there is now available a whole inventory of opinions toward a wide range of topics held by various social and political groups in the United States and other countries. The findings of such studies have had their value for the instruction of scholars, the decisions of policy makers, and the enlightenment of the general public. However, they have been of limited usefulness for problems in the formation of opinion and for this reason no simply descriptive studies have been included here.

But the literature does contain certain examples of substantive and methodological contributions to the basic question of why people hold the opinions they do. First, there is the speculation of the insightful observer mentally exploring the psychological processes of opinion formation, rep-resented here in the selection from Lippmann. The later accumulation of a body of opinion data made it possible to carry out sophisticated analyses of some personal determinants of opinion, as demonstrated in Kornhauser's contribution on the relationship of opinion to "class" factors. After public opinion polling had provided a body of answers to standardized opinion questions, it became possible to chart the trends in the gross development of opinions and relate them to external political and military events, as illustrated in the study by Cantril. Criticism of such studies as "superficial" or "static" led to attempts to conduct research on opinion formation with the concepts and techniques of dynamic psychology. Thus case studies were collected by Bettelheim and Janowitz in an effort to explain under-lying attitudes toward ethnic relations by means of such deeper person-ality characteristics as anxiety and subjective deprivation. The problems of opinion formation have also been attacked by means of repeated interview-ing and observation of the same people, a technique which can be consid-ered as an attempt to combine the advantages of the sample survey with *intensive case studies; the selection from* The People's Choice *illustrates the application of this procedure to the temporal development of opinion.*

Despite these advances, however, the field has yet to produce a rigorous investigation of the determinative influence of several factors upon opinion formation—personal characteristics, external events, communication content, personal associations, formal group memberships—simultaneously and in combination, as they occur in reality. Such studies would require the use of several research procedures, some of which would have to be devised for the purpose.

Walter Lippmann

STEREOTYPES

Each of us lives and works on a small part of the earth's surface, moves in a small circle, and of these acquaintances knows only a few intimately. Of any public event that has wide effects we see at best only a phase and an aspect. This is as true of the eminent insiders who draft treaties, make laws, and issue orders, as it is of those who have treaties framed for them, laws promulgated to them, orders given at them. Inevitably our opinions cover a bigger space, a longer reach of time, a greater number of things, than we can directly observe. They have, therefore, to be pieced together out of what others have reported and what we can imagine.

Yet even the eyewitness does not bring back a naïve picture of the scene.[1] For experience seems to show that he himself brings something to the scene which later he takes away from it, that oftener than not what he imagines to be the account of an event is really a tranfiguration of it. Few facts in consciousness seem to be merely given. Most facts in consciousness seem to be partly made. A report is the joint product of the knower and known, in which the rôle of the observer is always selective and usually

Reprinted from *Public Opinion* (1922), pp. 59-70, by permission of the author and the publisher. (Copyright, 1922, by Macmillan Co.)

[1] *E.g. cf.* Edmond Locard, *L'Enquête Criminelle et les Méthodes Scientifiques.* A great deal of interesting material has been gathered in late years on the credibility of the witness, which shows, as an able reviewer of Dr. Locard's book says in *The Times* (London) Literary Supplement (August 18, 1921), that credibility varies as to classes of witnesses and classes of events, and also as to type of perception. Thus, perception of touch, odor, and taste have low evidential value. Our hearing is defective and arbitrary when it judges the sources and direction of sound, and in listening to the talk of other people "words which are not heard will be supplied by the witness in all good faith. He will have a theory of the purport of the conversation, and will arrange the sounds he heard to fit it." Even visual perceptions are liable to great error, as in identification, recognition, judgment of distance, estimates of numbers, for example, the size of a crowd. In the untrained observer the sense of time is highly variable. All these original weaknesses are complicated by tricks of memory, and the incessant creative quality of the imagination. *Cf.* also Sherrington, *The Integrative Action of the Nervous System*, pp. 318-327.

The late Professor Hugo Münsterberg wrote a popular book on this subject called *On the Witness Stand.*

61

creative. The facts we see depend on where we are placed, and the habits of our eyes.

An unfamiliar scene is like the baby's world, "one great, blooming, buzzing confusion." [2] This is the way, says Mr. John Dewey,[3] that any new thing strikes an adult, so far as the thing is really new and strange. "Foreign languages that we do not understand always seem jibberings, babblings, in which it is impossible to fix a definite, clearcut, individualized group of sounds. The countryman in the crowded street, the landlubber at sea, the ignoramus in sport at a contest between experts in a complicated game, are further instances. Put an inexperienced man in a factory, and at first the work seems to him a meaningless medley. All strangers of another race proverbially look alike to the visiting stranger. Only gross differences of size or color are perceived by an outsider in a flock of sheep, each of which is perfectly individualized to the shepherd. A diffusive blur and an indiscriminately shifting suction characterize what we do not understand. The problem of the acquisition of meaning by things, or (stated in another way) of forming habits of simple apprehension, is thus the problem of introducing (1) *definiteness* and *distinction* and (2) *consistency* or *stability* of meaning into what is otherwise vague and wavering."

But the kind of definiteness and consistency introduced depends upon who introduces them. In a later passage [4] Dewey gives an example of how differently an experienced layman and a chemist might define the word metal. "Smoothness, hardness, glossiness, and brilliancy, heavy weight for its size . . . the serviceable properties of capacity for being hammered and pulled without breaking, of being softened by heat and hardened by cold, of retaining the shape and form given, of resistance to pressure and decay, would probably be included" in the layman's definition. But the chemist would likely as not ignore these esthetic and utilitarian qualities, and define a metal as "any chemical element that enters into combination with oxygen so as to form a base."

For the most part we do not first see, and then define, we define first and then see. In the great blooming, buzzing confusion of the outer world we pick out what our culture has already defined for us, and we tend to perceive that which we have picked out in the form stereotyped for us by our culture. Of the great men who assembled at Paris to settle the affairs of mankind, how many were there who were able to see much of the Europe about them, rather than their commitments about Europe? Could anyone have penetrated the mind of M. Clemenceau, would he have found there images of the Europe of 1919, or a great sediment of stereotyped ideas accumulated and hardened in a long and pugnacious existence? Did

[2] Wm. James, *Principles of Psychology*, Vol. I, p. 488.
[3] John Dewey, *How We Think*, p. 121.
[4] *Op. cit.*, p. 133.

he see the Germans of 1919, or the German type as he had learned to see it since 1871? He saw the type, and among the reports that came to him from Germany, he took to heart those reports, and, it seems, those only, which fitted the type that was in his mind. If a junker blustered, that was an authentic German; if a labor leader confessed the guilt of the empire, he was not an authentic German.

At a Congress of Psychology in Göttingen an interesting experiment was made with a crowd of presumably trained observers.[5]

"Not far from the hall in which the Congress was sitting there was a public fête with a masked ball. Suddenly the door of the hall was thrown open and a clown rushed in madly pursued by a negro, revolver in hand. They stopped in the middle of the room fighting; the clown fell, the negro leapt upon him, fired, and then both rushed out of the hall. The whole incident hardly lasted twenty seconds.

"The President asked those present to write immediately a report since there was sure to be a judicial inquiry. Forty reports were sent in. Only one had less than 20% of mistakes in regard to the principal facts; fourteen had 20% to 40% of mistakes; twelve from 40% to 50%; thirteen more than 50%. Moreover in twenty-four accounts 10% of the details were pure inventions and this proportion was exceeded in ten accounts and diminished in six. Briefly a quarter of the accounts were false.

"It goes without saying that the whole scene had been arranged and even photographed in advance. The ten false reports may then be relegated to the category of tales and legends; twenty-four accounts are half legendary, and six have a value approximating to exact evidence."

Thus out of forty trained observers writing a responsible account of a scene that had just happened before their eyes, more than a majority saw a scene that had not taken place. What then did they see? One would suppose it was easier to tell what had occurred, than to invent something which had not occurred. They saw their stereotype of such a brawl. All of them had in the course of their lives acquired a series of images of brawls, and these images flickered before their eyes. In one man these images displaced less than 20% of the actual scene, in thirteen men more than half. In thirty-four out of the forty observers the stereotypes preëmpted at least one-tenth of the scene.

A distinguished art critic said [6] that "what with the almost numberless shapes assumed by an object. . . . What with our insensitiveness and inattention, things scarcely would have for us features and outlines so determined and clear that we could recall them at will, but for the stereotyped shapes art has lent them." The truth is even broader than that, for the stereotyped shapes lent to the world come not merely from art, in the sense of painting and sculpture and literature, but from our moral codes and

[5] A von Gennep, *La formation des légendes*, pp. 158-159. Cited F. van Langenhove, *The Growth of a Legend*, pp. 120-122.

[6] Bernard Berenson, *The Central Italian Painters of the Renaissance*, pp. 60, *et seq.*

our social philosophies and our political agitations as well. Substitute in the following passage of Mr. Berenson's, the words 'politics,' 'business,' and 'society,' for the word 'art' and the sentences will be no less true: ". . . unless years devoted to the study of all schools of art have taught us also to see with our own eyes, we soon fall into the habit of moulding whatever we look at into the forms borrowed from the one art with which we are acquainted. There is our standard of artistic reality. Let anyone give us shapes and colors which we cannot instantly match in our paltry stock of hackneyed forms and tints, and we shake our heads at his failure to reproduce things as we know they certainly are, or we accuse him of insincerity."

Mr. Berenson speaks of our displeasure when a painter "does not visualize objects exactly as we do," and of the difficulty of appreciating the art of the Middle Ages because since then "our manner of visualizing forms has changed in a thousand ways." [7] He goes on to show how in regard to the human figure we have been taught to see what we do see. "Created by Donatello and Masaccio, and sanctioned by the Humanists, the new canon of the human figure, the new cast of features . . . presented to the ruling classes of that time the type of human being most likely to win the day in the combat of human forces. . . . Who had the power to break through this new standard of vision and, out of the chaos of things, to select shapes more definitely expressive of reality than those fixed by men of genius? No one had such power. People had perforce to see things in that way and in no other, and to see only the shapes depicted, to love only the ideals presented. . . ." [8]

If we cannot fully understand the acts of other people, until we know what they think they know, then in order to do justice we have to appraise not only the information which has been at their disposal, but the minds through which they have filtered it. For the accepted types, the current patterns, the standard versions, intercept information on its way to consciousness. Americanization, for example, is superficially at least the substitution of American for European stereotypes. Thus the peasant who might see his landlord as if he were the lord of the manor, his employer as he saw the local magnate, is taught by Americanization to see the landlord and employer according to American standards. This constitutes a change of mind, which is, in effect, when the inoculation succeeds, a

---

[7] *Cf.* also his comment on *Dante's Visual Images, and his Early Illustrators* in *The Study and Criticism of Italian Art* (First Series), p. 13. "We cannot help dressing Virgil as a Roman, and giving him a 'Classical profile' and 'statuesque carriage,' but Dante's visual image of Virgil was probably no less mediaeval, no more based on a critical reconstruction of antiquity, than his entire conception of the Roman poet. Fourteenth Century illustrators make Virgil look like a mediaeval scholar, dressed in cap and gown, and there is no reason why Dante's visual image of him should have been other than this."

[8] *The Central Italian Painters*, pp. 66-67.

change of vision. His eyes see differently. One kindly gentlewoman has confessed that the stereotypes are of such overwhelming importance, that when hers are not indulged, she at least is unable to accept the brotherhood of man and the fatherhood of God: "we are strangely affected by the clothes we wear. Garments create a mental and social atmosphere. What can be hoped for the Americanism of a man who insists on employing a London tailor? One's very food affects his Americanism. What kind of American consciousness can grow in the atmosphere of sauerkraut and Limburger cheese? Or what can you expect of the Americanism of the man whose breath always reeks of garlic?" [9]

This lady might well have been the patron of a pageant which a friend of mine once attended. It was called the Melting Pot, and it was given on the Fourth of July in an automobile town where many foreign-born workers are employed. In the center of the baseball park at second base stood a huge wooden and canvas pot. There were flights of steps up to the rim on two sides. After the audience had settled itself, and the band had played, a procession came through an opening at one side of the field. It was made up of men of all the foreign nationalities employed in the factories. They wore their native costumes, they were singing their national songs; they danced their folk dances, and carried the banners of all Europe. The master of ceremonies was the principal of the grade school dressed as Uncle Sam. He led them to the pot. He directed them up the steps to the rim, and inside. He called them out again on the other side. They came, dressed in derby hats, coats, pants, vest, stiff collar and polka-dot tie, undoubtedly, said my friend, each with an Eversharp pencil in his pocket, and all singing the Star-Spangled Banner.

To the promoters of this pageant, and probably to most of the actors, it seemed as if they had managed to express the most intimate difficulty to friendly association between the older peoples of America and the newer. The contradiction of their stereotypes interfered with the full recognition of their common humanity. The people who change their names know this. They mean to change themselves, and the attitude of strangers toward them.

There is, of course, some connection between the scene outside and the mind through which we watch it, just as there are some long-haired men and short-haired women in radical gatherings. But to the hurried observer a slight connection is enough. If there are two bobbed heads and four beards in the audience, it will be a bobbed and bearded audience to the reporter who knows beforehand that such gatherings are composed of people with these tastes in the management of their hair. There is a connection between our vision and the facts, but it is often a strange connection. A man has rarely looked at a landscape, let us say, except to

[9] Cited by Mr. Edward Hale Bierstadt, *New Republic,* June 1, 1921, p. 21.

examine its possibilities for division into building lots, but he has seen a number of landscapes hanging in the parlor. And from them he has learned to think of a landscape as a rosy sunset, or as a country road with a church steeple and a silver moon. One day he goes to the country, and for hours he does not see a single landscape. Then the sun goes down looking rosy. At once he recognizes a landscape and exclaims that it is beautiful. But two days later, when he tries to recall what he saw, the odds are that he will remember chiefly some landscape in a parlor.

Unless he has been drunk or dreaming or insane he did see a sunset, but he saw in it, and above all remembers from it, more of what the oil painting taught him to observe, than what an impressionist painter, for example, or a cultivated Japanese would have seen and taken away with him. And the Japanese and the painter in turn will have seen and remembered more of the form they had learned, unless they happen to be the very rare people who find fresh sight for mankind. In untrained observation we pick recognizable signs out of the environment. The signs stand for ideas, and these ideas we fill out with our stock of images. We do not so much see this man and that subject; rather we notice that the thing is man or sunset, and then see chiefly what our mind is already full of on those subjects.

There is economy in this. For the attempt to see all things freshly and in detail, rather than as types and generalities, is exhausting, and among busy affairs practically out of the question. In a circle of friends, and in relation to close associates or competitors, there is no shortcut through, and no substitute for, an individualized understanding. Those whom we love and admire most are the men and women whose consciousness is peopled thickly with persons rather than with types, who know us rather than the classification into which we might fit. For even without phrasing it to ourselves, we feel intuitively that all classification is in relation to some purpose not necessarily our own; that between two human beings no association has final dignity in which each does not take the other as an end in himself. There is a taint on any contact between two people which does not affirm as an axiom the personal inviolability of both.

But modern life is hurried and multifarious, above all physical distance separates men who are often in vital contact with each other, such as employer and employee, official and voter. There is neither time nor opportunity for intimate acquaintance. Instead we notice a trait which marks a well known type, and fill in the rest of the picture by means of the stereotypes we carry about in our heads. He is an agitator. That much we notice, or are told. Well, an agitator is this sort of person, and so *he* is this sort of person. He is an intellectual. He is a plutocrat. He is a foreigner. He is a "South European." He is from Back Bay. He is a Harvard Man.

How different from the statement: he is a Yale Man. He is a regular
fellow. He is a West Pointer. He is an old army sergeant. He is a Greenwich
Villager: what don't we know about him then, and about her? He is an
international banker. He is from Main Street.

The subtlest and most pervasive of all influences are those which create
and maintain the repertory of stereotypes. We are told about the world
before we see it. We imagine most things before we experience them. And
those preconceptions, unless education has made us acutely aware, govern
deeply the whole process of perception. They mark out certain objects as
familiar or strange, emphasizing the difference, so that the slightly familiar
is seen as very familiar, and the somewhat strange as sharply alien. They
are aroused by small signs, which may vary from a true index to a vague
analogy. Aroused, they flood fresh vision with older images, and project
into the world what has been resurrected in memory. Were there no
practical uniformities in the environment, there would be no economy and
only error in the human habit of accepting foresight for sight. But there
are uniformities sufficiently accurate, and the need of economizing attention
is so inevitable, that the abandonment of all stereotypes for a whole
innocent approach to experience would impoverish human life.

What matters is the character of the stereotypes, and the gullibility
with which we employ them. And these in the end depend upon those
inclusive patterns which constitute our philosophy of life. If in that
philosophy we assume that the world is codified according to a code which
we possess, we are likely to make our reports of what is going on describe
a world run by our code. But if our philosophy tells us that each man is
only a small part of the world, that his intelligence catches at best only
phases and aspects in a coarse net of ideas, then, when we use our stereotypes, we tend to know that they are only stereotypes, to hold them lightly,
to modify them gladly. We tend, also, to realize more and more clearly
when our ideas started, where they started, how they came to us, why we
accepted them. All useful history is antiseptic in this fashion. It enables
us to know what fairy tale, what school book, what tradition, what novel,
play, picture, phrase, planted one preconception in this mind, another in
that mind.

Those who wish to censor art do not at least underestimate this influence. They generally misunderstand it, and almost always they are ab-
surdly bent on preventing other people from discovering anything not
sanctioned by them. But at any rate, like Plato in his argument about the
poets, they feel vaguely that the types acquired through fiction tend to be
imposed on reality. Thus there can be little doubt that the moving picture
is steadily building up imagery which is then evoked by the words people
read in their newspapers. In the whole experience of the race there has

been no aid to visualization comparable to the cinema. If a Florentine wished to visualize the saints, he could go to the frescoes in his church, where he might see a vision of saints standardized for his time by Giotto. If an Athenian wished to visualize the gods he went to the temples. But the number of objects which were pictured was not great. And in the East, where the spirit of the second commandment was widely accepted, the portraiture of concrete things was even more meager, and for that reason perhaps the faculty of practical decision was by so much reduced. In the western world, however, during the last few centuries there has been an enormous increase in the volume and scope of secular description, the word picture, the narrative, the illustrated narrative, and finally the moving picture and, perhaps, the talking picture.

Photographs have the kind of authority over imagination to-day, which the printed word had yesterday, and the spoken word before that. They seem utterly real. They come, we imagine, directly to us without human meddling, and they are the most effortless food for the mind conceivable. Any description in words, or even any inert picture, requires an effort of memory before a picture exists in the mind. But on the screen the whole process of observing, describing, reporting, and then imagining, has been accomplished for you. Without more trouble than is needed to stay awake the result which your imagination is always aiming at is reeled off on the screen. The shadowy idea becomes vivid; your hazy notion, let us say, of the Ku Klux Klan, thanks to Mr. Griffiths, takes vivid shape when you see *The Birth of a Nation.* Historically it may be the wrong shape, morally it may be a pernicious shape, but it is a shape, and I doubt whether anyone who has seen the film and does not know more about the Ku Klux Klan than Mr. Griffiths, will ever hear the name again without seeing those white horsemen.

And so when we speak of the mind of a group of people, of the French mind, the militarist mind, the bolshevik mind, we are liable to serious confusion unless we agree to separate the instinctive equipment from the stereotypes, and the formulae which play so decisive a part in building up the mental world to which the native character is adapted and responds. Failure to make this distinction accounts for oceans of loose talk about collective minds, national souls, and race psychology. To be sure a stereotype may be so consistently and authoritatively transmitted in each generation from parent to child that it seems almost like a biological fact. In some respects, we may indeed have become, as Mr. Wallas says,[10] biologically parasitic upon our social heritage. But certainly there is not the least scientific evidence which would enable anyone to argue that men are born with the political habits of the country in which they are born. In so far

[10] Graham Wallas, *Our Social Heritage,* p. 17.

as political habits are alike in a nation, the first places to look for an explanation are the nursery, the school, the church, not in that limbo inhabited by Group Minds and National Souls. Until you have thoroughly failed to see tradition being handed on from parents, teachers, priests, and uncles, it is a solecism of the worst order to ascribe political differences to the germ plasm.

It is possible to generalize tentatively and with a decent humility about comparative differences within the same category of education and experience. Yet even this is a tricky enterprise. For almost no two experiences are exactly alike, not even of two children in the same household. The older son never does have the experience of being the younger. And therefore, until we are able to discount the difference in nurture, we must withhold judgment about differences of nature. As well judge the productivity of two soils by comparing their yield before you know which is in Labrador and which is in Iowa, whether they have been cultivated and enriched, exhausted, or allowed to run wild.

Arthur W. Kornhauser

ANALYSIS OF "CLASS" STRUCTURE
OF CONTEMPORARY AMERICAN SOCIETY:
PSYCHOLOGICAL BASES OF CLASS DIVISIONS

Is our contemporary American society composed of "classes"? Does the population fall into several broad social groups holding opposed viewpoints and values? Or is it rather true, as so often dogmatically declared, that in America there are no classes, there are only the artificial class antagonisms stirred up by alien agitators and political demagogues? Answers to these questions turn in part upon what is meant by "class" and in part upon the facts.

Evidence on Class Attitudes from
Psychological Studies

Evidence of the kind needed is still extremely scarce and fragmentary. Nevertheless it represents an important beginning in the effort to establish reliable and objective bases for conclusions about contemporary social classes. What is wanted is evidence that goes beyond individual opinions, beyond formal demands of organized groups, beyond formulations of class positions by official spokesmen. These are so frequently propagandist statements, off-hand superficialities, euphemisms, intentional or unintentional distortions of underlying attitudes, or views of unrepresentative persons, that it becomes impossible to know what credence they deserve.

More direct and revealing evidence is sometimes secured in election returns—either in public or private organizations. Occasionally, too, objective and quantitative reports of other behavior are available—labor turnover figures, for example, or circulation records for "radical" publications. All such data, to be useful for the purposes here considered, must be

Reprinted from *Industrial Conflict: A Psychological Interpretation* (1939), pp. 230-250, by permission of the author and the publisher. (Copyright, 1939, by the Society for the Psychological Study of Social Issues.)

broken down by income or occupational groups—a requirement only infrequently met. Tendencies have been found, in typical studies of this sort, for poorer economic groups to be more favorable to change [1] and for lower paid and less skilled workers to have higher rates of voluntary turnover.[2]

The type of evidence of greatest significance is that contributed by surveys and special studies of public attitudes. These investigations, principally by psychologists, avoid much of the subjective bias and unsupported conclusions characteristic of writing in this field. Here, in recent years, is at least a start toward carefully collected data from which conclusions may be drawn about classes. It represents a significant step beyond mere assertion and counter-assertion by "experts" of conflicting conviction.

The data from attitude studies will be considered in their bearing on four aspects of the general problem: (a) How different are the broad income and occupational groups in their stands on social and political issues? (b) How different are they in their feelings of satisfaction or discontent? (c) What are some of the significant factors other than income and occupation related to attitude differences of the kind mentioned in (a)? (d) Where do cleavages occur among groups in the income scale and in occupational classifications—or is there no breaking into distinct classes?

Class Differences in Attitudes
On Social and Political Issues

That large differences do exist between income and occupational groups in their opinions on important issues of the day can no longer be denied even by those least willing to admit the fact. The split of opinion on various New Deal measures and other current issues has become increasingly apparent. Typical evidence on this point is summarized in the following tables.

Studies of public attitudes which supply this evidence are relatively new. They are essentially nothing more than refinements and extensions of

[1] See H. F. Gosnell, *Machine Politics: Chicago Model* (Chicago: University of Chicago Press, 1937); J. A. Neprash, *The Brookhart Campaigns in Iowa 1920-1926: A Study in the Motivation of Political Attitudes* (New York: Columbia University, 1932); S. A. Rice, *Quantitative Methods in Politics* (New York: Knopf, 1928); R. S. and H. M. Lynd, *Middletown in Transition*, p. 359 (New York: Harcourt, 1937); R. J. Dangerfield and R. H. Flynn, "Voter Motivation in the 1936 Oklahoma Primary," *Southwestern Social Science Quarterly* (1936), 17, 97-105; W. F. Ogburn and D. Peterson, "Political Thought of Social Classes," *Political Science Quarterly* (1916), 31, 300-317.

[2] See S. H. Slichter, *The Turnover of Factory Labor* (New York: Appleton, 1919); P. F. Brissenden, *Labor Turnover in Industry* (New York: Macmillan, 1922); A. Bezanson, *et al.*, *Four Years of Labor Mobility: A Study of Labor Turnover in a Group of Selected Plants in Philadelphia*, 1921-1924 (Philadelphia: University of Pennsylvania Press, 1925).

older straw-vote techniques. Opinions are sought concerning all sorts of timely issues in contrast to straw votes only on candidates, etc. In the better surveys, too, far more care is given than formerly to proper asking of questions and especially to securing of more representative samples of the population. The two large-scale, continuous polls of opinion on a national scale are those by the American Institute of Public Opinion [3] (headed by Dr. George Gallup) and those by *Fortune* magazine.[4] On a more restricted set of issues, similar work has been conducted by the Psychological Corporation.[5] In addition a large number of special studies are completed in this field each year—for publications, business firms, political and industrial groups, and for pure research purposes.[6] Naturally not all the studies live up to adequately high standards in their procedures, grave errors of sampling being particularly common. Consequently each set of findings needs to be critically examined before the conclusions are accepted.[7] The results used in Tables I, II, III, have been chosen as representative of the most reliable studies. For present purposes no attempt will be made to go back of them.

In all these examples from quite independent sources, marked differences in opinions are seen to be correlated with the objective differences in income and occupation. The less favored economic groups incline decidedly more, as expected, toward social change in the "liberal" or "radical" direction and toward forces supposedly making for such change. The questions for which large differences are found pertain especially to the

[3] For brief description of the work of this organization see: American Institute of Public Opinion, *The New Science of Public Opinion Measurement* (New York, 1938—issued by the Institute); G. Gallup and C. Robinson, "American Institute of Public Opinion—Surveys, 1935-1938," *Public Opinion Quarterly* (1938), 2, 373-398; D. Katz and H. Cantril, "Public Opinion Polls," *Sociometry* (1937), I, 155-179.

[4] These survey results appear quarterly in *Fortune* magazine; for notes on procedure see *Fortune*, October, 1935, p. 58, and October, 1936, p. 224. Also see D. Katz and H. Cantril, *op. cit.*

[5] See "The Psychological Corporation, A Study of Public Relations and Social Attitudes," *Journal of Applied Psychology* (1937), 21, 589-602.

[6] The one special study of which a great deal of use is made in the following pages will be referred to as the Chicago Attitude Survey. This study was conducted in 1937 by Arthur W. Korhnauser; the results have not yet been published in full. A preliminary part of the study is reported in the *Public Opinion Quarterly* (1938), 2, 260-268, and a brief abstract of a later report appears in the *Psychological Bulletin* (1938), 35, 663. The Chicago study was aimed in large part at the central problem of this chapter—the relation between people's economic position and their attitudes on some broad social-political issues. Some 2000 adults were interviewed in their homes in an effort to secure a representative sample of different sections of the population. An additional 2000 persons were reached in order to obtain samples of specially chosen occupational groups. In all instances responses were given to a formal set of questions, so that the results could be used in simple statistical comparisons.

[7] Thus one large-scale study, in many respects excellent, depended for its sample upon the persons chosen in a hit-and-miss fashion by scores of untrained and unsupervised members of the National League of Women Voters, scattered through many states.

distribution of wealth and income, the control of industry, the encouragement of strong labor unions, the approval of Roosevelt and the New Deal.
The results may be interpreted as reflections of general dissatisfaction and
desire for remedial change on the part of persons least happily adjusted
under existing conditions.

There is some suggestion in these and other similar findings that the
recent trend has been toward a drawing apart of the upper and lower
economic groupings. This is indicated particularly by the decreasing percentage at the upper income level favorable to Roosevelt and the New

TABLE I—Popularity of President Roosevelt by Income Classes

PER CENT FOR ROOSEVELT[8]

American Institute of Public Opinion Polls[9]	Upper Income	Middle Income	Lower Income
1936 Election	42	59	76
November, 1938	28	49	73

Fortune Polls[10]	Prosperous	Upper Middle	Lower Middle	Poor
July, 1938	39	53	62	75

	Family Income			
Chicago Attitude Survey[11]	Over $5000	$2000-5000	$1000-2000	Under $1000
1936 Election	46	67	79	81

	Type of Neighborhood			
Lynd *Middletown* Analysis[12]	Business Class	Largely Business Class but Mixed	Largely Working Class but Mixed	Working Class
1936 Election	47	53	65	69

[8] The percentage figures are not strictly comparable for the different reports listed,
since there were variations in the form of question, in the divisions of the population,
and in the computations of per cents. In all instances in this and subsequent tables
(where the data permitted) per cents are based on "for" and "against" responses, omitting "undecided" or qualified answers. Most of the percentage figures from *Fortune* have
been recalculated in this way.

[9] From release dated November 20, 1938. The first row shows per cent who actually
voted for Roosevelt in 1936. The November, 1938, figures are based on the question: "If
you were voting today, would you vote for or against Roosevelt?" The middle income
group contains "almost half of the total voting population."

[10] *Fortune*, July, 1938, pp. 36-37. "Is your present feeling toward President Roosevelt one of general approval or disapproval?" The income groups are divided as follows:
prosperous, 10 per cent; upper middle, 30 per cent; lower middle, 40 per cent; poor,
20 per cent.

[11] Unpublished. Men were asked in 1937 whom they had voted for in the 1936
election.

[12] R. S. and H. M. Lynd, *Middletown in Transition* (New York: Harcourt, 1937),
p. 359.

TABLE II—Class Differences on Illustrative Public Questions

American Institute of Public Opinion Polls	Upper Income	Middle Income	Lower Income
(1) Like to see Roosevelt administration more liberal or more conservative?[13]			
% "More Liberal"	10	22	48
(2) Increase government spending?[14]			
% Yes	23	32	57

Fortune Surveys	Prosperous	Upper Middle	Lower Middle	Poor
(1) Approve Roosevelt's attitude toward business?[15]				
% Yes	31	43	54	66
(2) Governmental redistribution of wealth?[16]				
% For vs. against	23	(figures not given)		60

| Psychological Corporation | Income Groups | | | |
	A	B	C	D
(1) Government control of business?[17]				
% For more vs. less	15	27	40	57
(2) Government helping or hurting business?[18]				
% Believe "helping"	32	47	67	78
(3) Expand Supreme Court?[19]				
% Yes	17	25	37	50

| Chicago Attitude Survey (May–July 1937) | Income Groups | | | |
	A	B	C	D
(1) In favor of New Deal?[20]				
% Yes	38	66	79	83
(2) In favor of strong labor unions?[21]				
% Yes	28	56	75	84
(3) Government ownership of big industries?[22]				
% Yes	5	19	31	57
(4) In labor disputes, side with workers, employers, or neither?[23]				
% "With workers"	15	40	57	63
(5) Governmental redistribution of wealth and income?[24]				
% For	38	55	72	81

[13] Release of June 28, 1938. The full question was: "During the next two years would you like to see the Roosevelt administration be more liberal or more conservative?"

[14] Release of June 16, 1938. The full question asked: "Do you think government spending should be increased to help get business out of its present slump?"

[15] *Fortune*, July, 1938, p. 37. "On the whole, do you approve or disapprove of President Roosevelt's attitude toward big business?"

[16] *Fortune*, October, 1937, p. 150. "Is a third of the nation underprivileged, and should the government take from the rich to give to that third?" Percentages have been recalculated omitting ambiguous and qualified answers.

[17] From a privately circulated report by the Psychological Corporation: *A Study of Monopoly*, November, 1938. The question was: "Should there be more or less government control of business?" The income groups, from A to D, contain respectively 10 per cent, 30 per cent, 40 per cent, and 20 per cent of the population. Percentages have been recalculated, omitting "Don't know" answers (also on the following questions).

[18] Same source as preceding. "Do you believe that the present government is helping or hurting business?"

[19] From report by the Psychological Corporation: *A Study of Public Relations*, No-

A few examples of occupational differences are shown in Table III.

TABLE III—Occupational Differences on Illustrative Public Questions [25]

Occupational Groups (men)	Voted for Roosevelt in 1936 % For	In Favor of New Deal % Yes	In Favor of Strong Labor Unions % Yes	Government Ownership % For	Side With Workers, Employers, or Neither % "Worker"	Redistribution of Wealth % For
Major business executives	32	23	26	0	7	31
Engineers (professional)	39	34	21	6	22	42
Minor business executives and small owners	55	52	38	14	23	51
Office workers	60	68	46	21	38	54
Skilled manual workers	77	77	73	35	62	72
Unskilled and semi-skilled manual workers	82	83	82	38	58	73

Deal.[26] How far this is a temporary, and how far a long-run tendency cannot at present be soundly judged. In fact, all the measurements of this kind are so new, and hence so largely confined to depression years, that one can only guess what they may reveal through periods of greater prosperity. Almost certainly the differences in percentages would diminish in "good times," but it seems probable that the essential features of the relations will not be profoundly altered.

It is revealing to compare with the foregoing data the results for certain other questions which show little difference among occupational or income groups. In Table IV are assembled a number of questions in answer to which relatively small differences occurred among economic groups.

Several distinct explanations are involved in accounting for the comparatively small differences shown in this table. In one set of questions the nature of the wording is probably the predominant factor. Thus it is noticeable that the American Institute question on labor unions, couched in very general terms which invite assent, is responded to almost equally favorably at upper and lower income levels. The question asked in Chicago, specifying "strong unions to which almost all workers would belong,"

vember, 1937. "Do you believe the United States Supreme Court should have six new judges?"

[20] From unpublished report. "In general, are you in favor of the New Deal (the policies of President Roosevelt and his advisers)?"

[21] "Are you in favor of strong labor unions to which almost all workers would belong?"

[22] "Would you like to see the government own and run the big industries of the country?"

[23] "In disputes between working people and employers do you usually side with the workers, the employers, or neither?"

[24] "Do you believe the government should aim at making people's wealth and income more nearly equal?"

[25] Based on data from the Chicago Attitude Survey of 1937.

[26] See first two rows of figures in Table I.

shows a very sharp falling off in approval as the income scale is ascended (See Table II). Similarly the *Fortune* question on whether liberals should unite shows less variation by classes than might be expected primarily because of the vague and shifty meaning of "liberal"—as further evidence obtained in the same survey clearly indicated. In certain other questions, like those of the Psychological Corporation on the effects of big business and the Chicago question on government letting business alone, the wording calls for difficult evaluative judgments which apparently do not represent general directions of feeling about economic affairs, as do questions like those in Table II. Still other questions, illustrated by the two on Roosevelt's rearmament and international policies, are by their nature ones where class differences would be unlikely to appear in the present-day nationalistic world. Nevertheless, *questions of this kind, which afford little opportunity for class differences to be measured, have been used at times as the basis for unwarranted conclusions concerning the absence of significant attitude differences among economic groups.*

The remaining four questions of Table IV can reasonably be interpreted in a quite different manner. The *Fortune* question on inheritance probably reflects, at the low income levels, the wide-spread hope for a "lucky break," whether it be winning the sweepstakes or inheriting a fortune from a lost uncle. In part it doubtless mirrors, too, the irresistibly attractive American tradition of unlimited individual opportunity to make one's pile and thereby provide richly for one's family. If each individual feels that he may be the lucky or successful one, why not preserve untrammeled freedom to pass our riches to those who survive us? The other three questions more directly express this general viewpoint. Even the poorest group overwhelmingly accepts the belief that their children will rise to a higher level, that there is no working class. A clear majority go so far, in answer to the *Fortune* question, as to assert that "any young man with thrift, ability, and ambition has the opportunity to rise in the world, own his own home, and earn $5000 or more a year."

These last mentioned results are in striking contrast to the large differences observed for many questions earlier considered. People at lower income levels, it appears, differ markedly from those better off, in their feelings about the distribution of wealth and influence, the control of economic affairs, and the desirability of changes in a "New Deal" direction. But they cling devotedly to the American belief in individual opportunity. They expect either themselves or their children to "get ahead." Thus important contrasts in class attitudes on deep-cutting questions of public policy exist side by side with rather general rejection by individuals of any feeling that they are permanent members of a "class."

TABLE IV—Illustrative Questions Showing Relatively Slight Differences among Classes

American Institute of Public Opinion Polls	Upper and Middle Income (Not Separated)			Lower Income
(1) In favor of labor unions?[27]				
% Yes	74			81

Fortune Surveys	Prosperous	Upper Middle	Lower Middle	Poor
(1) Roosevelt's international policy?[28]				
% For	71	76	77	80
(2) Roosevelt's rearmament policy?[29]				
% For	80	80	84	85
(3) Should liberals of all parties unite?[30]				
% "Good idea" vs. "Bad idea"	53	59	70	72
(4) What limit on amount inherited?[31]				
% "No limit"	68	61	60	57
5) Opportunity for young man to rise and earn $5000?[32]				
% Yes or "Yes, if lucky"	70	67	62	54

	Income Groups			
Psychological Corporation	A	B	C	D
(1) Large corporations do more good than harm?[33]				
% "More good"	92	88	86	83
(2) Big companies do more than small to lower prices?[34]				
% "Big companies do more"	93	92	85	81

	Income Groups			
Chicago Attitude Survey	A	B	C	D
(1) Should government let business alone?[35]				
% Yes	86	74	70	66
(2) No "working class" in America?[36]				
% Agreeing	78	71	70	64
(3) Believe children will be better off than you?[37]				
% Yes	86	91	88	86

[27] Release of July 4, 1937. "Are you in favor of labor unions?"

[28] *Fortune*, July, 1938, pp. 36-37. "On the whole, do you approve or disapprove of President Roosevelt's international policy?"

[29] *Fortune*, July, 1938, pp. 36-37. "On the whole, do you approve of President Roosevelt's rearmament policy?"

[30] *Fortune*, November, 1938, p. 74. "In a fireside talk President Roosevelt proposed that old party lines be disregarded and that the liberals of all parties unite to support liberal candidates for Congress. Do you think this is a good or bad idea?"

[31] *Fortune*, October, 1936, p. 56. "How much money do you think any one person should be allowed to inherit?"

[32] *Fortune*, January, 1937, p. 86. "Do you think that today any young man with thrift, ability, and ambition has the opportunity to rise in the world, own his own home, and earn $5000 or more a year?"

[33] The Psychological Corporation, *A Study of Monopoly*, November, 1938. "Do you think that large companies like these (six of the largest corporations mentioned by name) do more *good than harm* or more *harm than good?*"

[34] Same source. "In general, do the big companies or the small companies do more to make things cheaper, that is, reduce the price of goods?"

[35] Unpublished. The question was: "Do you think the government should let the business system alone as far as possible?"

[36] "Do you think the following idea is true: 'In America there is no "working class." Working people and their children can rise to better positions; they do not have to remain ordinary workers'?"

[37] "Do you believe the chances are good that your children will have a higher position and be better off than you are?"

Additional Significant Factors Related to
Attitude Differences

The purpose of this section is to stress the fact that an explanation of social attitudes with emphasis solely on income and occupation factors is necessarily distorted. For a rounded understanding it is essential that the effect of other influences be recognized which cut athwart the socio-economic grouping. These other factors account for important divergent opinions within each class and for certain similarities of opinion between classes.

First, there are the broad social group influences—the effects of nationality, geographic section, size of community, religion, and race. Conclusions on these matters are at present based far more on casual experience than on scientific studies. Nevertheless, there can be no question that the more extreme variations among these influences do profoundly affect opinions on public issues. Persons born and reared in countries as different as, say, Russia, Japan, and England, almost inevitably will have contrasting attitudes on many social questions. Limiting the discussion to present-day America, tendencies are frequently noted for members of particular racial, religious, or nationality groups to have characteristic attitudes somewhat independent of the persons' economic status and different from the attitudes of their fellow citizens at the same income level. These tendencies are probably restricted to a rather limited range of issues, however, and obviously there is a great amount of overlapping of opinions from group to group even on those questions where the groups as a whole diverge most widely.

A number of attitude measurement studies have added bits of evidence to the practical knowledge of politicians and social observers concerning these group influences. Almost all the studies, however, deal with specially selected groups like college students, rather than with samples of adults in general. Moreover, little or no attempt is usually made to exclude the effect of economic level when comparing religious, national, and racial groups. While the results are consequently difficult to interpret, they do point to genuine effects independent of the income and occupational determinants.[38]

A few examples of findings will be given from opinion surveys of recent years, wherever effort was made to sample the adult population as a whole. Results of this kind are still fragmentary and insufficient to justify final conclusions. On the whole, the differences on broad political and economic questions among the groups now considered appear to be de-

---

[38] A number of these investigations are summarized in G. Murphy, L. B. Murphy, and T. M. Newcomb, *Experimental Social Psychology* (New York: Harper, 1937).

cidedly less than those earlier noted among, income and occupational classes. The illustrations below represent the larger variations; on most issues the differences are far less.

As one example, a few figures are given which show significant differences between Negroes and white population at low income levels. In the Chicago survey of attitudes, the Negroes varied little from the white respondents at the same income level with respect to public issues. The largest difference was in answer to the question: Do you think that working people in general get fair treatment and fair play? The comparable percentages of men saying "Yes" are: White, 30 per cent; Negro, 11 per cent. On questions of labor unionism and government ownership the Negroes are very slightly more favorable (more "radical") than corresponding white groups. Figures for the entire nation, secured from time to time in the *Fortune* surveys, are in part similar, in part conflicting. Attitudes of the Southern rural and small-town Negro can scarcely be expected to agree with those of his Chicago cousin. On a question concerning fair treatment of labor, however, the Negro-white comparison by *Fortune* gives results similar to those for Chicago. Of the whites 36 per cent, and of the Negroes 18 per cent, say labor is fairly rather than unfairly treated.[39] The question: "Has Roosevelt too much power?" received 39 per cent "yes" responses from whites against 24 per cent by Negroes.[40] But *Fortune* found Negroes much closer to upper-class whites on a number of other questions. For example: "Do you believe that the government should allow a man who has investments worth over a million dollars to keep them, subject only to present taxes?" Of the low income white group 33 per cent said "Yes"; of the Negroes, 70 per cent; of the prosperous white class, 77 per cent.[41] Similarly with a question of whether corporation officials are paid too much—save that here the Negroes actually outdo the prosperous white group in their approval of present or larger salaries. A parallel question in Chicago, however, shows that the Negroes there object to the large salaries as commonly as do the lower income white groups.

More briefly, a few findings on other groups are as follows: In the Chicago sample, Protestants as a group are rather consistently more conservative on the questions asked (New Deal, unionism, distribution of wealth, etc.) at each income level than are Catholics, Jews, and those saying "no religion." Native born are somewhat more conservative on a number of questions than are the foreign born. In the nation-wide inquiries by Gallup, *Fortune*, and others, regional differences and rural-urban differences often appear. Thus the American Institute of Public Opinion

[39] *Fortune*, October, 1935, p. 164. "Do you believe that in general labor is fairly or unfairly treated in this country today?"
[40] *Fortune*, July, 1938, pp. 74-76.
[41] *Fortune*, July, 1935, p. 66.

reports a recent 47 per cent for Roosevelt in New England against 64 per cent in the South; [42] a farm vote 53 per cent favorable, compared to 66 per cent in cities over 500,000; Southern farm voters 72 per cent favorable; Midwest farm voters 47 per cent. Similar differences are revealed on many specific public issues.

All these findings serve to emphasize the complexity of the group influences affecting social attitudes. The group influences are only in part those imposed by conditions of income and occupation. Economic classes can hardly be subjectively homogeneous when each broad income or occupational division of the population includes men of diverse race, religion, national origin, regional, and community interests—with each of these ties exercising a significant, even if secondary, hold upon the individual's purposes and upon his beliefs concerning appropriate means for fulfilling these purposes. *A simple, automatic "economic determinism" of social opinion is psychologically pure fiction.* While the actual amount of influence exerted by the various noneconomic affiliations remains a problem for research, the *fact* of such influence is undeniable.

Remaining, now, are the more personal variables affecting social attitudes—the many respects in which the individuals within the social groupings vary among themselves. Here come the objective differences of sex, age, education, etc., and the more subtle variations in temperament, personal motivations, and subjective feelings of adjustment.

Among adults differences in sex, age, and schooling appear to have some, but very limited, relation to opinions on broad social issues, within groups of uniform income. The Chicago data indicate significant relations on particular issues and for some income ranges, but surprisingly slight variations for the findings as a whole. Illustrative of the relations found are these: At the lower income levels, women are definitely less favorable to unions than are men (e.g., 69 per cent *versus* 84 per cent "in favor of strong labor unions to which almost all workers would belong"; at the next higher income level ($1000 to $2000) the corresponding figures are 59 per cent for women *versus* 75 per cent for men). Analyses by age and schooling reveal no *uniform* tendencies. At the high income level the older men are slightly more conservative on a number of issues, but this is not true at other income levels. In the matter of education, those having only elementary schooling tend to be more conservative among the well-to-do, but tend in the liberal or radical direction among those with smaller incomes. Additional schooling, that is, appears to make for greater moderation in one's "class" attitudes.

With respect to all these and similar relations, the important point here

[42] The pairs of percentages are taken, in order, from releases of the American Institute of Public Opinion of the following dates: December 4, 1938; January 8, 1939; October 8, 1938.

is simply this: that the objective personal data, while less closely and consistently related to opinions than is economic status, do also have a significant bearing upon the particular attitudes held. These factors, like the noneconomic group influences previously considered, help account for the nonuniformity of opinion within homogeneous socio-economic groups.

Quite apart from the indications of any quantitative research results, it is clear that powerful, and in some measure peculiar, influences do operate upon each individual as he develops his personal adjustments and his social orientation within the family, the play group, the school, church, and place of employment. Intensive study of individual cases, as well as everyday observation, often reveals the molding of attitudes by specific personal experiences—domination by parents, contact with other races, a love affair, failure on a job, and so on indefinitely. *These personal determinants of attitudes constitute additional reasons why persons living under given "class" conditions may develop views quite contrary to those of their fellows.*

One important reflection of the personal variations is the satisfaction or dissatisfaction people express concerning their status, opportunities, and enjoyment of life. How far are these individual feelings of adjustment related to attitudes on public issues? Is personal discontent associated with desire to change political and economic conditions? A major aim of the Chicago attitude investigation was to throw light on these questions. To do this, responses on the personal satisfaction questions were studied in relation to responses on the objective social policy questions. Broadly stated, it is found that within the several income and occupational groups persons who express dissatisfaction with their work, their status, and opportunities, differ markedly from those better satisfied. This is especially true at the higher income levels and in those instances where the particular point of dissatisfaction is understandably related to the social issue in question.

These relations may be briefly illustrated as follows:

One question asked whether the person was in favor of strong labor unions. A personal satisfaction question in another part of the blank asked: "Do you feel that your children (or those of your friends and neighbors) have as much opportunity as they should have?" It turns out that among the people who are satisfied about their children's opportunity, 53 per cent are favorable to unions; of those dissatisfied, 77 per cent are favorable. On government ownership the contrast is more striking: 44 per cent of the dissatisfied as against 17 per cent of the satisfied vote "yes." Other satisfaction questions such as: "Do you like the kind of work you do?" are significantly but less closely related to most of the social opinion questions.

Still more important, however, is the contrast in these relations from one income level to another. To cite only one example: Government owner-ship is favored, among those with incomes under $1000, almost equally by the personally satisfied and those dissatisfied (55 per cent and 61 per cent respectively); at the $1000 to $2000 level, the dissatisfied are almost *twice* as likely as the satisfied to be for government ownership (42 per cent and 22 per cent respectively); among those over $2000 the dissatisfied are favorable *five times* as often as the satisfied (35 per cent and 7 per cent respectively). On this and a number of other issues, the personally dis-satisfied at the upper income levels tend to hold views approaching those more commonly held by the economically less favored. The comparisons suggest the generalization that while at the upper levels it tends to be the personally unadjusted or discontented who are liberal or radical, at the lower income levels *personal* dissatisfaction is secondary as an influence.

In summary, now, the following statement appears justified concerning the various factors related to differences in the broad politico-economic attitudes of the type considered here. The evidence points clearly to large and important attitude differences between income classes. Similar, but to some extent independent, differences occur between occupational groups. The study indicates equally clearly that within the homogeneous economic groupings, opinions on particular social issues are significantly associated with differences in other factors such as sex, age, schooling, race, foreign birth, religion, etc. Within the economic groups, moreover, important differ-ences in social attitudes are found to be correlated with the feelings of satisfaction or discontent expressed by individuals in response to questions concerning their personal status and opportunities. Altogether, then, a survey of available material serves to emphasize the central importance both of direct economic determinants of opinion and also of the noneco-nomic, personal factors.

Hadley Cantril

TRENDS OF OPINION DURING WORLD WAR II:
SOME GUIDES TO INTERPRETATION

Our understanding of man's social behavior will improve only in so far as we are able to study this behavior concretely and to test principles that may be derived from the experimental laboratory in everyday-life situations. The outbreak of World War II was taken as a significant, if horrible, emergent situation that would present the social scientist with a challenge of his up-to-the-now understanding and enable him to accumulate more data to help him in his self-appointed task of figuring out why men behave as they do. Therefore, at the beginning of this war, the Office of Public Opinion Research undertook to follow some of the reactions of American public opinion to the exciting and tragic events which everyone knew in a vague way were bound to occur in the next few years.[1]

This article has two purposes. The first is to make data embodied in the accompanying trend charts available to persons who may have some interest in or use for the material before time can be found to analyze it in detail along with additional data accumulated during the war years. Much of this material was available only to the White House and to certain government officials at the time it was collected. When the opportunity arises, I hope a much more complete account of the reaction of American opinion during World War II can be prepared. In the meantime, some of the basic trends given here may be of use to those social scientists or other persons who are interested in the study of opinion over a period of time, who are more specifically concerned with World War II, or who would like to have on record the potential use of opinion surveys as guides to or reflections of official policy.[2]

Reprinted from *The Public Opinion Quarterly*, Vol. XII (Spring, 1948), pp. 30-44, by permission of the author and the publisher. (Copyright, 1948, by the Princeton University Press.)

[1] This study was made possible first by a Rockefeller Foundation grant, and later by other private funds.

[2] Charts 1 and 2 represent U.S. opinion before Pearl Harbor; two additional charts were presented in the original article.

I should once more like to express my indebtedness to George Gallup and the staff

Secondly, anyone studying survey data with the purpose of understanding opinion and its determinants will see in the accompanying trend charts reflections of certain psychological principles that can be derived from experimental data and from controlled studies of everyday life, as well as from results obtained via public opinion polls. Since my own interest in public opinion is chiefly that of a person labeled a "social psychologist," it may be of some help to persons in other fields if a psychologist indicates what seem to him to be some of the psychological principles or useful higher-order abstractions which the combined data of psychology, including these trend charts, allow us to formulate at this stage of the development of our young science.

Collection of Trend Data

The material on which the trend charts are based was all obtained through surveys of stratified samples of the adult U.S. population. The great advantages public opinion survey data have over most other kinds of intelligence information used for the interpretation of public opinion are: (1) identical questions are asked (2) of a representative sample of the adult population (3) at approximately the same time.

The data obtained from the outbreak of the war through 1942 were gathered for this Office through the facilities of the American Institute of Public Opinion. The charts also include all points obtained by the American Institute where AIPO questions were worded identically to those used by this Office.

In 1943 the Office set up its own nation-wide interviewing facilities to undertake special research tasks. Most of the points on the trend charts obtained subsequent to the end of 1942 are based on data obtained through this organization, known as the Research Council, Inc. To make sure that the sample used in our own surveys was comparable to that of the Institute, a number of questions were deliberately repeated simultaneously via both mechanisms. Entirely comparable results were obtained.[3] The minimum sample used by the Institute during this period was 3000 cases. The minimum sample used by the Research Council was 1200 cases. The Research Council sample was given a test in the election of 1944 where the outcome

---

of the American Institute of Public Opinion for their cooperation in this study and permission to use their data. I am also most grateful to Gerard B. Lambert for his support of our work during the last three years of the war. Working with Jerry Lambert during some of the war years and later discussing opinion formation with Adelbert Ames, Jr., of the Hanover Institute have been stimulating experiences. I have also profited by discussions of the principles listed with Andie Knutson and Albert Hastorf.

[3] See Cantril, H., "Do Different Polls Get the Same Results?", *Public Opinion Quarterly*, 9, No. 1 (1945), 61-69.

of the election was predicted with an error of one half of one per cent.[4]

The dates indicated in all the charts are the dates on which ballots were sent out from Princeton. This means that the opinions represented are the opinions of a representative sample of the adult American population during the subsequent week or ten days of the time specifically plotted.

A few events are included at the top of each chart as reference points. Those who want to examine the relation of events to opinion more carefully will necessarily have to compile their own detailed list of events which space makes impossible here. These may be obtained from any newspaper that has complete coverage of domestic and foreign events or more conveniently from some periodical such as *Current History* which contains a monthly index of events.

Although events as such are obviously of the utmost importance as determinants of opinion, just as obviously events are by no means the only determinants of opinion. The context in which events occur must always be borne in mind. No implication is made here that there is any necessary direct causal relationship between events and opinion although such relationships, when the context of opinion is analyzed, are by no means denied.

In the interest of clarity, it has been necessary on all except one question (the pre-Pearl Harbor question concerning which side would win the war) to leave out the trend of "no opinion" percentages and, generally, to confine the charts to only one of the alternatives presented.

It is impossible to spell out in any brief space the many relationships between opinions and events and between one opinion and another that can be seen by a careful inspection of the accompanying charts. Nevertheless, the material gathered should afford the future historian a great deal more insight on what the war meant to the people back home than historians have had of any previous conflict in world history. Obviously, historical speculation of how people felt during the American, French, or Russian Revolutions, during the Civil War, or during any other specified historical period would have been narrowed if it had been possible during those periods to accumulate data which had the reliability of current polling material.

Since funds for this undertaking were necessarily limited and since an investment of around $100 was represented each time a question was asked, the major task was that of selecting questions and timing their use in a way to secure the maximum value over an unpredictable period of time. Obviously, a question that made sense one week might be completely irrelevant or nonsensical the next week. Historians of the future will no

[4] See Katz, D., "The Polls and the 1944 Election," *Public Opinion Quarterly*, 8, No. 4 (1944), 468-487.

doubt wonder why many questions were not posed to the American people during the war. Frequently, hindsight showed that some significant trends had been missed and that it was now too late to begin picking them up.

Questions on Wartime Opinion

The questions on which the trend charts are based were phrased as follows:

CHART 1.

1. *Which side do you think will win the war—England, or Germany and Italy?*
2. *Do you think the United States will go into the war in Europe sometime before it is over, or do you think we will stay out of the war?*

CHART 2.

1. *Which of these two things do you think is the more important for the United States to try to do—to keep out of war ourselves, or to help England win even at the risk of getting into the war?*
2. *If the question of the United States going to war against Germany and Italy came up for a national vote within the next 2 or 3 weeks, would you vote to go into the war or to stay out of the war?*
3. *Do you think the United States should declare war on Germany and Italy and send our army and navy abroad to fight?*
4. *Do you think it was a mistake for the United States to enter the last World War?*
5. *Do you think the United States should risk war with Japan, if necessary, in order to keep Japan from taking the Dutch East Indies and Singapore?*

Psychological Interpretation of Opinions

When we analyze opinions relating to wartime phenomena, as well as others, we find that an opinion, like an attitude, can best be understood if it is regarded as a particular variety of perception. The basic principles concerning the nature of perception also hold for the nature of opinion. By an "opinion" we generally refer to an attitude which has been or often is expressed by an individual. The psychology of "opinion" is therefore the same as the psychology of "attitudes." Both are rooted in the psychology of perception.

The principles worked out here may seem to be quite self-evident. Some of them are expressed in the second person. For experience is yours alone and the validity of any psychological formulation must be tested

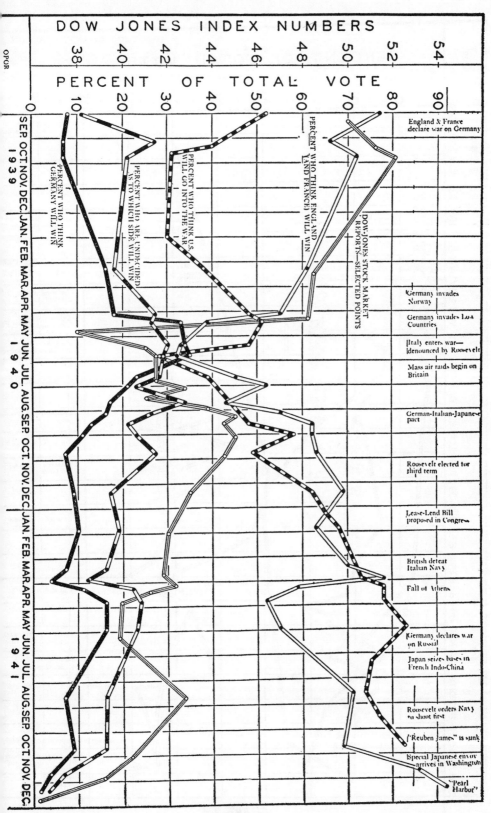

CHART 1

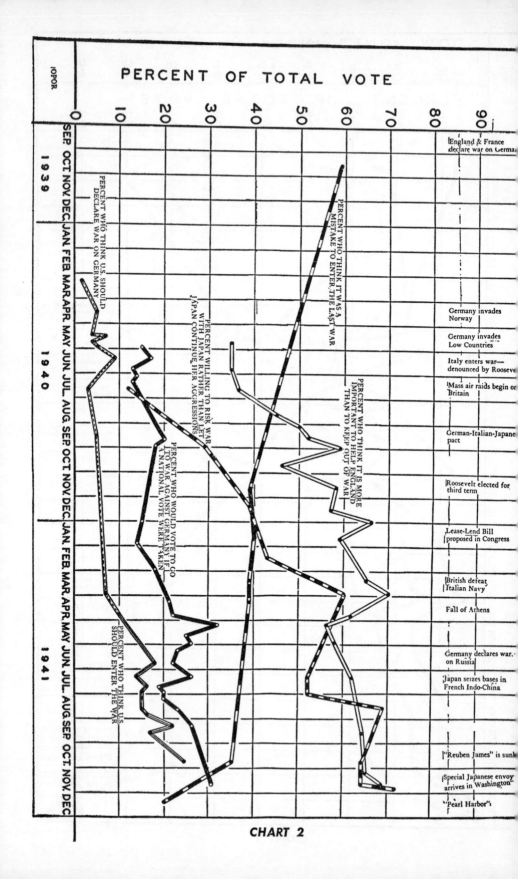

CHART 2

finally in your own experience. A few concrete applications of the principles are indicated.[5]

1. An opinion is formed when, and only when, you face a frustrating situation where a judgment is required on which you must base action that will help you carry out a purpose.

It is therefore unreasonable to expect that all people will have opinions on the same problems. Since the specific purposes that affect social behavior are largely determined by the membership and reference group identifications acquired, questions used on surveys and data obtained from representative samples of the total adult population must be studied with this fact always clearly in mind.

2. An opinion is built up from past experience as a guide to purposive action.

The *raison d'être* of any opinion can only be understood when we learn what the past experiences of an individual are and how these are tied to his purposes. Since it is impossible at best to acquire a complete developmental history of any individual and since the polling mechanism must usually and deliberately rule out the possibility of elaborate depth interviewing as impracticable, questionnaires must be designed and analyzed in terms of the best probable hunches that may get at indicators of experiences (i.e. occupation, education, church attendance) which may at least give some insights into the nature of past experience and its functional significance to the respondent.

3. An opinion is based chiefly on unconscious cues which are mustered together and integrated when their relevance in forming a value-judgment for purposive action is aroused by some situation.

Since the basic purposes behind our behavior are apt to be so poorly understood by us, and since our value-judgments are generally made so swiftly and unconsciously, the "reasons" people give for their expressed opinions can at best be regarded as only partial.

4. Knowledge and rational thought serve the function of bringing into the process of value-judgment (opinion formation) more cues to be weighed.

5. Knowledge must not be confused with understanding. Understanding, as distinguished from knowledge, means that knowledge has been put to some concrete test in purposive action.

It cannot therefore be expected that "information" or "knowledge" as such will have any consistent or uniform effect on opinion. "Knowledge" is useful only in so far as it is functionally related to purpose. Public opinion studies must therefore aim at understanding when and why knowledge be-

[5] In 1944 when analyzing Charts 1 and 2, I made note of "Some Laws of Public Opinion" in *Gauging Public Opinion*, Princeton University Press, 1944, ch. 16. The present principles are not supplements or additions to the seventeen "laws" previously indicated, but may be regarded as higher-order generalizations which include the laws previously indicated.

comes functional. Mere cataloguings of relationships between "information" and opinion are apt to be misleading.

6. *Opinion is not changed or modified unless or until (1) your purposes change, or (2) your actions have demonstrated to you that your previous opinions are poor guides to effective action in achieving some purpose.*

An understanding of shifts of opinions with events or situations can therefore be obtained only in so far as the significance of the event or situation to purposive activity is understood.

7. *Whether or not an opinion will actually help you carry out a purpose can only be tested by action in concrete situations. If you, yourself, are not the direct participant in the action, you may still, if less reliably, test your opinions by observing the effectiveness of the actions of others whose purposes you believe you share and understand.*

8. *Opinions, upon which concrete judgment and actions are based, often appear to go counter to opinions abstractly held since the latter are purely intellectual data that either call for no concrete action or offer no possibility of concrete action.*

Even though opinion may be fairly uniform concerning a given topic, such as the role the United States should play in international affairs, the public may often be properly described as "apathetic" to the problem, since people see few if any ways in which they can act concretely to implement purpose as reflected by opinion. The functional role played by institutions such as local governments, the church, or the United Nations in the lives of individuals can only be concretely understood when the possibilities they provide for specific action on the part of the individual are known.

9. *Opinions which have not been tested by action are apt to be meaningless in concreteness, poor guides to future actions, and unreliable as the basis of predicting behavior.*

You may "believe in" abstractions such as "democracy," "freedom," or "Christianity" but nevertheless frequently act in undemocratic, repressive or unchristian ways in concrete situations where your hunch is that your own purposes will be thwarted by the behavior of others.

10. *When the reliability of an opinion as a guide for purposive action is confirmed by concrete action, you experience a sense of surety as a psychological co-product. On the other hand, a feeling of insecurity accompanies a prognosis for action which is not confirmed by concrete action.*

11. *Surety also results when cues built up from past experience supplement each other; lack of surety results when cues conflict with each other. When an individual has conflicting specific purposes, he inevitably acquires conflicting opinions which are subjectively accompanied by a feeling of lack of surety, of frustration.*

12. At critical times, opinions may be described as relatively "unstructured" and people are found to be relatively "suggestible" because former standards and cues are unable to provide reliable guides for purposive action in new and emergent situations.

It is during such periods as these that the ability of older leaders is tested and, if it proves inadequate as it often does, that new leaders are likely to emerge. Perhaps the most important role of any leader is to provide the value-judgments necessary to interpret new and emergent situations in such a way that this new perception will appear to people as plausible and as having a high chance of serving as a guide to effective action, thus resolving frustrations created by the inadequacy of previous understandings. The confidence in any leader depends upon his ability to demonstrate his capacity to make effective value-judgments. The popularity of a leader is likely to be particularly high when he has taken some action which resolves frustration by giving the impression that the action will help achieve the desired goals.

13. Opinions occur within a context of expectancy. If you are a human being, plugged in to concrete social life with its constant flux and change, the opinions you have now serve to connect the past with the future in terms of concrete action.

14. Expectancies must not be confused with predictions. Predictions are more in the nature of abstract intellectual judgments not necessarily taken into account in determining your present action. Predictions become expectancies when you adjust your present behavior in terms of what you think will be the effect of such adjustment on the carrying out of your purposes.

"Predictions" will be most meaningful, then, in areas of "expectancy"— that is, when a person has related the possibility of a future occurrence to his own situation. Public opinion questions which ask people to predict the outcome of elections, the probability of a depression, etc. should therefore first determine whether or not a future occurrence is regarded as an "expectancy," that is, as a probable future occurrence that is being taken into account in an individual's *present* adjustments.

15. Opinion is affected by events only when those events are perceived as having some personal significance in terms of aiding or hindering the carrying out of your purposes.

Events which may be of great "historical" importance or which may be reported in banner headlines are by no means always those that affect opinion except as they may help to build up a context for interpretation and for the plausibility of future judgments.

16. The intensity with which an opinion is held is dependent upon the importance of the purpose the opinion serves. You are by no means always conscious of the purposes to which your opinions are casually related. In fact, you are by no means always conscious of your purposes.

Studies of the intensity of opinion will have more than descriptive value only in so far as poll administrators can obtain some information of the particular hierarchy of purposes held by particular respondents.

17. Most opinions, as compared with non-social perceptions, are felt with relatively high intensity since opinions, unlike some other perceptions, usually involve the purposes of other people and the relationship of their purposes to yours.

Since the purposes of other people may be seen as potential threats or aids to the carrying out of your own purposes, when we are studying intensities of opinion it is essential to determine group identifications and gather all information possible concerning group loyalties and what individuals regard as the major threats to the achievement of their purposes.

18. Your opinions are "accurate" or "right" in proportion as they take into account all factors relevant to the successful carrying out of purposes.

In so far as your opinions do not include the purposes of all other human beings who might be affected by your actions, these opinions will in the long run prove "inaccurate" or "wrong." It seems not unlikely that it is for this reason that nearly every great religious prophet used as a cornerstone for his teaching a precept almost identical to the Golden Rule of Christianity.

19. Over any long historical period, opinions may be expected to become more "accurate" as men learn through frustration and experience to include in their perceptions the purposes of others.

In this connection, technological developments such as methods of communication, production, or warfare that increase the interdependence of human beings will eventually build up in men perceptions (opinions) adequate to accommodate the uses of technology to serve their own purposes. Increasing interdependence due to technological advances will force the inclusion of the purposes of more and more people into our perception. This also means that over the long haul, abstractions such as "race," "class," "nationality," "capital vs. labor," etc. are bound to break down since the perception of men as members of an abstract grouping goes counter to the perception of other human beings *qua* human beings.

20. Opinion cannot be explained or fully understood in terms of correlation relationships only. Higher-order abstractions are necessary. Especially necessary for the understanding of opinions is an understanding of the purposes of human beings and their capacities for making value-judgments.

This is one of the most compelling reasons to supplement survey data with more complete case studies, and insights thus gained should wherever possible be subjected to laboratory tests as checks of any higher-order abstractions used as "explanations." [6]

Conclusion

Historians and other social scientists may find in the data provided by public opinion studies a new and useful body of information to aid them in interpretation. The social psychologist, on the other hand, is likely to be working in a vacuum if he does not actively seek the aid of the historian, the economist, the ethnologist, or the sociologist in his own search for the determinants of opinion.

And it is, of course, the special responsibility of the psychologist to seek out by a variety of methods those relationships that are causal and to try to point out to his colleagues in other areas the interplay of the psychological processes characteristic of man *irrespective of* the time or place in which a man lives. Otherwise, the psychologist has only himself to blame if oversimplified abstractions (such as lists of instincts or needs, typologies of one sort or another, or certain Freudian concepts) are appealed to by those who depend on the psychologist for their assumptions concerning human nature.

[6] For a more inclusive formulation of the principles indicated here, see Cantril, H., *Understanding Man's Social Behavior: Preliminary Notes,* Office of Public Opinion Research, Princeton, N. J., 1947.

Bruno Bettelheim and Morris Janowitz

ETHNIC TOLERANCE: A FUNCTION OF SOCIAL AND PERSONAL CONTROL

In this study of ethnic intolerance [1] we attempt to throw light on the principles of group hostility in general and on ethnic hostility as a special subtype.

The four main hypotheses that the research sought to test were based on sociological theory and dynamic psychology. They were: (1) hostility toward out-groups is a function of the hostile individual's feeling that he has suffered deprivations in the past; (2) such hostility toward out-groups is a function of the hostile individual's anxiety in anticipation of future tasks; (3) the individual blames out-groups for his failure at mastery and projects undesirable characteristics denied in himself upon members of the out-group because of inadequate personal and social controls which favor irrational discharge and evasion rather than rational action; (4) ethnic intolerance can be viewed in terms of the individual's position within the social structure either statically or dynamically. It was assumed that ethnic intolerance was related more to the individual's dynamic movement within the structure of society than to his position at a particular moment. No claim is made that these hypotheses are universally applicable, but they seemed useful in understanding hostility in modern industrialized communities.

A major premise of the study was that persons who believe they have undergone deprivations are disposed to ethnic intolerance. It seemed plausible to study ex-soldiers, since they had suffered deprivations in varying degrees and might be especially responsive to the appeal of intolerance. A random sample of one hundred and fifty male war veterans,

Reprinted from *The American Journal of Sociology*, Vol. LV (1949), pp. 137-145, by permission of the authors and the publisher. (Copyright, 1949, by *The American Journal of Sociology*.)

[1] This paper summarizes parts of a study of the ethnic attitudes of Chicago veterans of World War II, entitled *The Dynamics of Prejudice* (New York: Harper and Brothers, 1950).

all residents of Chicago, was studied. Former officers were eliminated from study, since their experiences were at variance with those of enlisted men and since most of them came from social and economic backgrounds which differed from those of enlisted men. Hence the sample tended more adequately to represent the economic lower and lower-middle classes. Members of those major ethnic groups toward which hostility is projected were not included, that is, Negroes, Jews, Chinese, Japanese, and Mexicans.

The data were obtained through intensive interviews in which free associations were always encouraged. The interviewers were psychiatrically trained social workers, experienced in public opinion surveying. The wide range of personal data sought and the special problems of building rapport before gathering data on ethnic attitudes required long interviews which took from four to seven hours and in several cases were carried on in two sessions. The veterans were offered ample opportunity to express personal views on many issues and to recount their wartime experiences before ethnic minorities were mentioned.

On the basis of an exploratory study we found it necessary to distinguish four types of veterans with respect to their ethnic attitudes. For the sake of brevity, only the four types of anti-Semite are mentioned, but a parallel classification as regards anti-Negro attitudes was also developed. These four types of anti-Semite were designated as *intensely anti-Semitic, outspoken anti-Semitic, stereotyped anti-Semitic,* and *tolerant* toward Jews and were characterized as follows: (1) The *intensely anti-Semitic* veteran was spontaneously outspoken in expressing a preference for restrictive action against the Jews even before the subject was raised. (2) The *outspoken anti-Semitic* man revealed no spontaneous preference for restrictive action against the Jews. Instead, outspoken hostility toward the Jews emerged only toward the end of the interview when he was directly questioned. As in the case of the intensely anti-Semitic veteran, his thinking contained a wide range of unfavorable stereotypes. (3) The *stereotyped anti-Semitic* man expressed no preference for hostile or restrictive action against the Jews even when questioned directly. Instead, he merely expressed a variety of stereotyped notions about the Jews, including some which were not necessarily unfavorable from his point of view. (4) The *tolerant* veteran revealed no elaborately stereotyped beliefs about the Jews (among the statements of even the most tolerant veterans isolated stereotypes might from time to time be found). Moreover, not even when questioned directly did he advocate restrictive action against the Jews.

The interview situation was so constructed that the responses to questions would permit a clear discrimination among these four types of ethnic intolerance. The first portion of the interview was designed to offer the men an opportunity for spontaneous expression of hostility against minorities without bringing this subject to their attention. In a second portion, especially in connection with Army experiences, ample opportunity was offered to display stereotyped thinking by asking, for example, who the "gold-brickers" or troublemakers had been. Only the last portion contained direct questions on ethnic minorities. There the stimuli "Negro" and "Jew" were introduced to determine which men were consistently tolerant. First it was asked what kinds of soldiers they made, next what the subject thought of social and economic association with them, and then what his views were on possible changes in the current patterns of inter-ethnic relations.[2] Table I shows the distribution of degrees of intolerance.

TABLE I—Distribution of Intolerance

	Anti-Semitic		Anti-Negro	
	No.	Per Cent	No.	Per Cent
Tolerant	61	41	12	8
Stereotyped	42	28	40	27
Outspoken	41	27	74	49
Intense	6	4	24	16
Total	150	100	150	100

We tried to determine whether the men's social and economic history could account for their ethnic intolerance. Among the characteristics studied were age, education, religion, political affiliation, income, and social status. But the data indicate that—subject to certain limitations—these factors of themselves do not seem to account for differences in the degree or nature of intolerance.

Table II, for example, shows that no statistically significant relation exists between income and socioeconomic status, on the one hand, and intensity of anti-Semitism, on the other.[3] The same was true for such other categories as education, age, and religious affiliation. Which newspaper, magazine, or radio program the men favored was also unrelated to the intensity of ethnic hostility. The pattern of anti-Negro distribution was similar.

Social mobility.—The picture changes, however, if a static concept of social status is replaced by the dynamic concept of social mobility. It was possible to gather precise data on the social mobility of one hundred and thirty veterans. They were rated as having experienced downward mobility or upward mobility if they had moved at least one grade up or down on the Alba Edward's socioeconomic scale when compared with their previous civilian employment.

Table III shows that ethnic hostility was most highly concentrated in the downwardly mobile group, while the pattern was *significantly* reversed

[2] The full methodological and statistical details of the procedure will be found in *The Dynamics of Prejudice.*

[3] Where a significant difference is reported, it is at least at the 0.01 confidence limit.

TABLE II—Correlates of Anti-Semitism

Total Cases	Tolerant (61) (Per Cent)	Stereotyped (42) (Per Cent)	Outspoken and Intense (47) (Per Cent)	Total (150) (Per Cent)	No.
Age:					
Under 28	44	27	29	100	94
29-36	34	30	36	100	56
Education:					
Did not complete high school	35	31	34	100	65
Completed high school	39	28	33	100	46
Some college or more	51	23	26	100	39
Religion:*					
Catholic	40	28	32	100	103
Protestant	48	25	27	100	33
No present religious denomination	33	33	33	100	12
Current salary:					
Up to $2,500	39	33	28	100	59
$2,500 to $3,000	39	24	37	100	43
$3,000 and over	43	18	39	100	28
Not applicable	45	35	20	100	20
Socioeconomic status:					
Top four groups	42	24	34	100	70
Semiskilled and unskilled	38	33	29	100	80

* Two cases of Greek Orthodox not included.

TABLE III—Intolerance and Mobility

	Downward Mobility		No Mobility		Upward Mobility		Total	
	No.	Per Cent	No.	Per Cent	No.	Per Cent	No.	Per Cent
Anti-Semitic:								
Tolerant	2	11	25	37	22	50	49	38
Stereotyped	3	17	26	38	8	18	37	28
Outspoken and intense	13	72	17	25	14	32	44	34
Anti-Negro:								
Tolerant and stereotyped	5	28	18	26	22	50	45	34
Outspoken	5	28	40	59	17	39	62	48
Intense	8	44	10	15	5	11	23	18
Total	18	..	68	..	44	..	130	..

for those who had risen in their social position. Those who had experienced no change presented a picture somewhat in the middle; the relationship between ethnic intolerance and social mobility (as defined in this study) was also present when educational level was held constant.

The group which was static showed the highest concentration of stereotyped opinions—that is, they were "middle-of-the-roaders" with regard to anti-Semitism. Over 70 per cent of the stereotyped anti-Semites were found in this middle category. This illuminates the relation between mobility and intolerance. On the other hand, the no-mobility group was most generally in the outspokenly anti-Negro category. This supplies another crude index of the limits of intolerance toward minority groups in a northern urban industrial community. In the case of the Jew the social norms were most likely to produce merely stereotyped thinking, while it was correspondingly "normal" to be outspoken in one's hostility toward the Negro.

In view of the association between upward social mobility and tolerance, the few cases (14) who displayed both upward mobility and were outspokenly anti-Semitic warrant special attention. The actual income gains associated with upward mobility reveal that the men who were both outspokenly anti-Semitic and upwardly mobile tended to be considerably more mobile than the others. This may be tentatively explained by the fact that sharp upward mobility is likely to be associated with marked aggressiveness in general. The data, particularly on those in the group downwardly mobile, suggest that to understand intolerance it is less important to concentrate on the social and economic background of the individual than to investigate the character of his social mobility.

Feeling of deprivation.—Whatever their social and economic life-histories had been, all the men interviewed had one common experience—the Army. Reactions to comparable wartime deprivations thus afforded a unique opportunity to examine the hypothesis that the individual who suffers deprivation tries to restore his integration and self-control by the expression of hostility, one form of which may be ethnic hostility. But here a sharp distinction must be introduced between *actual* deprivations experienced and his *feelings* of deprivation. Whether the men reacted favorably to Army life primarily because they experienced relief from the insecurities of civilian life was also pertinent.

Army experiences which involved *objective* deprivations were found not related to differential degrees of ethnic intolerance (combat versus noncombat service, wounds, length of service, etc.). On the other hand, a clear association emerged between the display of *feelings* of deprivation and outspoken or intense anti-Semitic and anti-Negro attitudes.

On the basis of a content analysis it was found that it was possible to make reliable decisions as to whether the veterans (1) accepted it in a matter-of-fact way, (2) were embittered about Army life, or (3) were attached to it or gratified by it. The overwhelming majority of those who were tolerant, regardless of the specific content of their wartime experiences, had an attitude of acceptance toward Army life, while the intolerant veteran presented a completely reversed picture (see Table IV). The latter were overwhelmingly embittered by Army life. In addition, those who declared themselves particularly attached to Army life displayed a high concentration of intolerance.

TABLE IV—Acceptance of Army

	Tolerant		Stereotyped		Outspoken and Intense		Total	
	No.	Per Cent	No.	Per Cent	No.	Per Cent	No.	Per Cent
Accepted Army life	44	81	21	64	6	17	71	58
Embittered toward Army life	6	11	7	21	20	56	33	27
Attached to or gratified by Army life	4	8	5	15	10	27	19	15
Total	54	..	33	..	36	..	123	..

The judging of one's war experiences as depriving or not is a function of the individual's total personality and of the adequacy of his adjustive mechanisms. The interview records of those who seemed gratified by Army life revealed that they were also the men who described themselves as economically and socially deprived before induction; they seem to have been poorly adjusted to civilian society and to have found gratification and release in the particular adventure and comradeship of Army life.

Controls for tolerance.—There seems little doubt that frustrating social experiences and the inability to integrate them account to a large degree for those aggressions which are vented in ethnic hostility. While our investigation could not ascertain which particular experiences accounted for the men's frustration, it permitted us to ascertain their readiness to submit in general to the existing controls by society. If, by and large, they accepted social institutions, it seems reasonable to assume that such acceptance implied a willingness to control their own aggressive tendencies for the sake of society. Or, oversimplifying complex emotional tendencies, one might say that those men who felt that society fulfilled its task in protecting them against unavoidable frustrations were also those who, in return, were willing to come to terms with society by controlling their aggressive tendencies as society demands. Hence, the hypothesis correlating the men's acceptance or rejection of society with their ethnic attitudes had to be tested. The Army is only one of many social institutions. The postulated association between intolerance and the rejection of social controls, which was central in terms of this study, had to be investigated for a number of other institutions as well.

Control, technically speaking, is the ability to store tension internally or to discharge it in socially constructive action rather than in unwarranted hostile action. The predominant mechanisms of control which a person uses for dealing with inner tensions are among the most important elements characterizing his personality. Each of these mechanisms of control is more or less adequate for containing a particular type of aggression generated in the individual by anxiety. These controls or restraints remain adequate only if the level of tension does not become overpowering, thereby creating unmasterable anxiety. It will not suffice to investigate the association between control and tolerance in general; it is necessary to discriminate between tolerance as it relates to three types of control over hostile tendencies: (1) external or social control, (2) superego or conscience control, and (3) rational self-control or ego control.

Religion may serve as the prototype of an institution, the acceptance of, or submission to, which was found to be related to tolerance. Unquestioning acceptance of religious values indicates that the individual tends to rely on a type of control in which he is guided by traditional and nonrational external social forces. In contrast, control is exercised not by the minister or the priest but originates within the person, although such inner control may have come initially from their teachings. If the moral teachings of the church are accepted by the individual not through fear of damnation or of societal disapproval but because he considers them absolute standards of behavior independent of external threats of approval, then we say that the individual has "internalized" these moral precepts. They have become an internal control, but a control which is still only partially conscious and only partly rational. Such control is exercised over the individual by his "conscience," or, technically speaking, by his superego.

Markedly different from *external* control through outside institutions and from *superego* control, which also depends for its effectiveness on props in the external world (such as parental images or institutionalized religion), is the rational control of irrational tendencies which forces them into consciousness and then deals with them along purely rational lines. The latter may be termed "ego control." In actuality, the three types of control are nearly always coexistent, and in each individual case control will depend in varying degrees on all three—external, superego, and ego control. In the men studied, wherever control was present it was overwhelmingly the result of a combination of external and superego control, with the first being dominant. Only few men were also motivated by ego control, and in even fewer was ego control dominant over superego or external control. Hence a study of external, i.e., societal, control was the only one which promised to permit insight into the correlation between acceptance of, or submission to, social control and ethnic intolerance for this particular group.

The analysis of religious attitudes indicated that veterans who had stable religious convictions tended to be the more tolerant. When the political party system was viewed as another norm-setting institution, a similar relationship of at least partial acceptance or consensus with this basic institution was found to be associated with tolerance. Whether the veteran was Democratic or Republican was in no way indicative of his attitude toward minorities. But the veteran who rejected or condemned both parties ("they are both crooks") tended to be the most hostile toward minorities.

Thus not only greater stability in societal status but the very existence of stable religious and political affiliations as well proved to be correlated with tolerance. These phenomena are indicative of the tolerant individual's relatively greater control over his instinctual tendencies, controls which are strong enough to prevent immediate discharge of tension in asocial action. Such delay in the discharge of tension permits its canalization into socially more acceptable outlets.

To explore more fully this relationship between tolerance and control, the responses to other symbols of societal authority which signify *external* control of the individual were also investigated. Two groups of institutions were analyzed separately. The first group, that of Army control through discipline and officers' authority, is discussed below. The second group was composed of significant representatives of civilian authority to which the men were relatively subject at the time of the interview.

Four institutions were singled out as being most relevant. They were: (1) the administration of veterans' affairs; (2) the political party system; (3) the federal government; and (4) the economic system, as defined by the subjects themselves.

The veterans' views of each of these institutions were quite complex and in some respects ambivalent. Nevertheless, it was possible to analyze attitudes toward them on a continuum of acceptance, rejection, or intermediate.

When acceptance or rejection of the four representative institutions was compared with the degree of anti-Semitism (Table V), it appeared

TABLE V—Attitudes toward the Jew and toward Controlling Institutions

Attitude Toward Controlling Institutions	Tolerant		Stereotyped		Outspoken and Intense		Total	
	No.	Per Cent	No.	Per Cent	No.	Per Cent	No.	Per Cent
Acceptance	41	67	20	48	11	23	72	48
Intermediate	15	25	17	40	13	28	45	30
Rejection	5	8	5	12	23	49	33	22
Total	61	..	42	..	47	..	150	..

that only an insignificant percentage of the tolerant men rejected them, while nearly half the outspoken and intense anti-Semites did so. This is in marked contrast, for example, to studies of certain types of college students, in whom radical rejection of authority is combined with liberalism toward minority groups.

Controls, it may be said, are not internalized by merely accepting society. On the contrary, general attitudes of accepting existing society and its institutions are the result of previous internalization of societal values as personally transmitted by parents, teachers, and peers. Hence the acceptance of individuals who are representatives of societal values should have been more closely related to internal control than the acceptance of discipline in general, which is more characteristic of external control. Attitudes toward officers seem suitable gauges for the individual's attitudes toward control. Incidentally, most of the men evaluated their officers on the basis of personal quality, their moral authority, and not on the basis of their punitive power.

The tolerant veteran appeared able to maintain better relations with his officers; he was more willing to accept the authority and discipline of the Army as represented by them. In general, his attitude was reasonable. When queried as to how the fellows in their outfits got along with the officers, tolerant veterans were significantly more prone to claim they got along well than were the intolerant men.

In the case of the Negro (Table VI), societal controls exercise a restraining influence only on what would be classified as violent, as "intense," intolerance. Violence is generally disapproved of by the controlling institutions, while they approve, if not enforce, stereotyped and outspoken attitudes. The men who were strongly influenced by external controls were, in the majority, stereotyped and outspoken but not intense in their intolerance toward Negroes, as the present data show.

TABLE VI—Attitudes toward the Negro and toward Controlling Institutions

Attitude Toward Controlling Institutions	Tolerant		Stereotyped		Outspoken		Intense		Total	
	No.	Per Cent	No.	Per Cent	No.	Per Cent	No.	Per Cent	No.	Per Cent
Acceptance	9	75	19	48	38	51	6	25	72	48
Intermediate	2	17	16	40	23	31	4	17	45	30
Rejection	1	8	5	12	13	18	14	58	33	22
Total	12	..	40	..	74	..	24	..	150	..

The division between those who rejected and those who accepted external control came between outspoken and intense attitudes toward Negroes. To score "high" on the index of rejection for the four controlling institutions meant that an individual was likely to fall in the intensely anti-Negro category. Thus acceptance of external controls not only was inadequate in conditioning men to be tolerant of the Negroes but was not even enough to prevent them from holding outspoken views in that regard. It served only to restrain demands for violence.

Stereotyped thinking.—Precisely because most of the men in the sample based their restraint of aggressive tendencies on societal controls rather than on inner integration, some aggression remained uncontrolled. This the men needed to explain to themselves—and to others. For an explanation they fell back again on what society, or rather their associates, provided in the way of a justification for minority aggression. It has already been mentioned that most of the men voiced their ethnic attitudes in terms of stereotypes. The use of these stereotypes reveals a further influence—if not control—by society on ethnic attitudes and should therefore at least be mentioned.

One of the hypotheses of this study is that intolerance is a function of anxiety, frustration, and deprivation, while the intolerant person's accusations are ways to justify his aggression. While the rationalizations for this intolerance must permit a minimum of reality testing, they will also condition the ways in which hostile feelings are discharged.

All intolerant veterans avoided reality testing to some degree, and each of them made statements about minorities which showed that they neglected the individual's uniquely personal characteristics—in short, they used stereotypes. As was to be expected, those who were only moderately biased retained more ability to test reality. They were more able to evaluate correctly the individuals whom they met, but they clung to stereotyped thinking about the rest of the discriminated group. In this way it remained possible to retain the stereotyped attitudes which permitted discharge of hostility despite actual experiences to the contrary. Such a limited amount of reality testing did not seem to be available to strongly biased individuals.

Because the intolerant person's rationalizations are closely, although not obviously, connected with his reasons for intolerance, he must take care to protect them. On the other hand, they also reveal the nature of the anxieties which underlie them.

An examination of the five most frequent Negro and five most frequent Jewish stereotypes reveals strikingly different results, each set of which presents a more or less integrated pattern (see Tables VII and VIII). The composite pattern of stereotypes about Jews does not stress personally "obnoxious" characteristics. In the main, they are represented in terms of a powerful, well-organized group which, by inference, threatens the subject.

TABLE VII—Stereotypes Characterizing Jews

Stereotype	No. of Veterans Mentioning Stereotypes
They are clannish; they help one another	37
They have the money	26
They control everything (or have an urge to control everything); they are running the country	24
They use underhanded or sharp business methods	24
They do not work; they do not do manual labor	19

On the other hand, the stereotypes about the Negro stress the individual, personally "offensive" characteristics of the Negro. As the stereotypes of the group characteristics of Jews implied a threat to the values and

TABLE VIII—Stereotypes Characterizing Negroes

Stereotype	No. of Veterans Mentioning Stereotypes
They are sloppy, dirty, filthy	53
They depreciate property	33
They are taking over; they are forcing out the whites	25
They are lazy; they are slackers in work	22
They are ignorant; have low intelligence	18
They have low character; they are immoral and dishonest	18

well-being of the intolerant white, so, too, those about the Negro were used to describe a conception of the Negro as a threat, particularly because the Negro was "forcing out the whites."

A comparison of the distribution of stereotypes applied to Jews and Negroes, as indicated by this enumeration, with those used by the National Socialists in Germany permits certain observations. In Germany the whole of the stereotypes, which in the United States were divided between Jews and Negroes, were applied to the Jews. Thus in the United States, where two or more ethnic minorities are available, a tendency emerges to separate the stereotypes into two sets and to assign each of them to one minority group. One of these two sets indicates feelings of being anxious because of one minority's (the Jews') assumed power of overwhelming control. The other set of stereotypes shows feelings of anxiety because of the second minority's (the Negroes') assumed ability to permit itself the enjoyment of primitive, socially unacceptable forms of gratification. Thus, of two minority groups which differ in physical characteristics, such as skin color, the minority showing greater physical difference is used for projecting anxieties associated with dirtiness and sex desires. Conversely, the minority whose physical characteristics are more similar to those of the majority become a symbol for anxieties concerning overpowering control. If we apply the frame of reference of dynamic psychology to these observations, then these stereotypes permit further emphasis on the relation between tolerance and control. The individual who has achieved an integration or an inner balance between superego demands and instinctual, asocial strivings does not need to externalize either of them in a vain effort to establish a control that he does not possess. The intolerant man who cannot control his superego demands or instinctual drives projects them upon ethnic minorities as if, by fighting them in this way or by at least discharging excessive tension, he seeks to regain control over unconscious tendencies.

Actual experiences later in life, once the personality has been formed, seem relatively incapable of breaking down this delusional mechanism. Questioning revealed, for example, that although Army experience threw the men into new and varied contacts with Jews and frequently with Negroes, the stereotypes applied to the service of Jews and Negroes in the Army proved largely an extension of the conceptions of civilian life into Army experiences.

It seems reasonable to assume that as long as anxiety and insecurity persist as a root of intolerance, the effort to dispel stereotypes by rational propaganda is at best a half-measure. On an individual level only greater personal integration combined with social and economic security seems to offer hope for better interethnic relations. Moreover, those who accept social controls are the more tolerant men, while they are also, relatively speaking, less tolerant of the Negro because Negro discrimination is more obviously condoned, both publicly and privately. This should lead, among other things, to additional efforts to change social practice in ways that will tangibly demonstrate that ethnic discrimination is contrary to the mores of society, a conviction which was very weak even among the more tolerant men.

Paul F. Lazarsfeld, Bernard Berelson, and Hazel Gaudet

TIME OF FINAL DECISION

All during an election campaign, people can make up their minds. Many traditional party voters, however, know far in advance of the campaign for whom they will vote. It might be possible now to forecast the party for which Southerners will vote in 1960, although the issue and candidates will not be known for fifteen years. Others decide during a particular term of office whether they will support the incumbent and his party at the next election. Many know in May, even before candidates are nominated, how they will vote in November.

Interviews with the panel permitted us to distinguish three kinds of voters classified according to the time when they made their *final vote decision*—the decision which they followed throughout the rest of the campaign and in the voting booth.

"*May Voters*": These pre-campaign deciders knew in May, at our first interview, how they would vote, maintained their choice throughout the campaign, and actually voted for that choice in November. Their votes had been finally determined by May.

"*June-to-August Voters*": These people settled upon a candidate during the convention period (our August interview was the first interview after both conventions), maintained their choice throughout the rest of the campaign, and actually voted for that choice in November. Their votes were finally determined in June, July or August.

"*September-to-November Voters*": These people did not definitely make up their minds until the last few months of the campaign, some of them not until Election Day itself. Their votes were finally determined only in September, October or November.

What were the significant differences among these groups of people? Why did some people make up their minds before the campaign began,

Reprinted with minor editorial adaptations from *The People's Choice: How the Voter Makes Up His Mind in a Presidential Campaign* (1944), pp. 52-61; 65-69, by permission of the authors and the publisher. (Copyright, 1948, by the Columbia University Press.)

106

others during the first months of the campaign, and still others not until the end of the campaign?

The analysis of this chapter develops two major factors influencing the time of final decision. First, the people whose decision was delayed had *less interest* in the election. Second, those who made their choice in the late days of the campaign were people subject to *more cross-pressures.* By "cross-pressures" we mean the conflicts and inconsistencies among the factors which influence vote decision. Some of these factors in the environment of the voter may influence him toward the Republicans while others may operate in favor of the Democrats. In other words, cross-pressures upon the voter drive him in opposite directions.

Interest and Time of Decision

The more interested people were in the election, the sooner they definitely decided how they would vote. Almost two-thirds of the voters with great interest had already made up their minds by May; but considerably less than half of the voters with less interest in the election had made up their minds by May. Only one-eighth of the greatly interested waited until the late period of the campaign before finally deciding how they would vote; twice as many of the less interested delayed their decision until that period.

The general tendency for late decision among the less interested held for both parties. But on each level of interest, the Democrats tended to decide later than the Republicans.

Certain other manifestations of interest also wane in the group whose decision is postponed until the later stages of a campaign. At one point respondents were asked whether they were "very anxious" to see their candidate elected, whether it was "not terribly important" although "I would like to see my candidate elected," or whether "it doesn't make much difference."

The particular persons who were "very anxious" to have their candidate win were those who decided on their vote early in the campaign. The same reasons which impelled them to choose a candidate early in the game and stick with him also served to make them quite concerned about his election. The people who were not particularly concerned about the outcome of the election were those who decided late in the campaign. They felt that nothing much was at stake and waited for happenstance or friends to make up their minds for them. As the campaign moved on, the respondents who answered "don't know" were also saying in effect "don't care."

The campaign managers were thus continuously faced with the task of propagandizing not only a steadily shrinking segment of the electorate but also a segment whose interest in and concern with the election also steadily shrank. By the end of the campaign, the managers were exerting their greatest efforts to catch the few votes of the least interested and least involved persons.

Cross-Pressures and Time of Decision

We have indicated that there were a number of factors differentiating Republican and Democratic voters. Each of these factors could be considered a "pressure" upon final vote decision. We found the Protestant vote allied to the Republicans and the Catholic vote more strongly Democratic. We found that individuals on the higher socio-economic status levels tended to vote Republican and their poorer neighbors to vote Democratic. In other words, a vote decision can be considered the net effect of a variety of pressures.

Now what if these individual factors work in opposite directions? Suppose an individual is *both* prosperous and Catholic? How will he make up his mind? Or suppose he belongs to the Protestant faith and lives in a poor section of the community? Which of the conflicting influences will win out? People who are subject to contradictory and opposing influences of this kind are said to be under cross-pressures.

The more evenly balanced these opposing pressures were, the longer the voter delayed in making up his mind. We shall use six instances of cross-pressures to show their effect in delaying the time of decision. The first three cases involve personal characteristics of the voter; the next two, relationships between the voter and other people around him; and the last, the voter's basic political attitudes.

(1) *Religion and Socio-Economic Status Level:* The first cross-pressure we have already mentioned. Protestants on lower socio-economic status levels (C— & D) and Catholics on upper socio-economic status levels (A, B, & C+) were subject to this cross-pressure.

(2) *Occupation and Identification:* In the November interview respondents were asked with what groups in the community they identified themselves—big business, small business, labor, etc. While most people identified themselves with the class to which they would have been assigned by occupation, some semi-skilled and unskilled workers tended to think of themselves as belonging with the business class and a few white-collar people thought of themselves as belonging with labor. Since the business group ordinarily supported one party and the labor group the other, a cross-pressure was set up between the voter's objective occupation and his subjective identification.

(3) *1936 Vote and 1940 Vote:* Most of the people—but again not all of them—voted for the same party in both presidential elections. The voters who changed between the 1936 and the 1940 elections—primarily made up

of persons who had voted for Roosevelt in 1936 but were for Willkie in 1940—could be regarded as having something of a tradition to overcome. Their way was psychologically more obstructed than that of the people who voted consistently for the same party in all recent elections.

(4) *The Voter and His Family:* As we shall see, the American family maintains considerable political solidarity, with all adult members voting the same way. But sometimes other members of the respondent's family disagreed with him and oftener other members of the family were undecided. In either case, the respondent was under a cross-pressure between the views of two members of the family or between his own ideas and those of at least one other member of his family.

(5) *The Voter and His Associates:* Friends as well as family create a political environment which may be congenial or hostile. In the October interviews, respondents were asked whether they had noticed changes in vote intention on the part of people around them. Republicans who noted a trend toward Willkie and Democrats who were aware mainly of changes toward Roosevelt were in a congenial situation. What they saw going on around them coincided with their own preferences. But the few who noticed trends towards the opposition party were subjected thereby to conflicting pressures from their associates.

(6) *1940 Vote Intention and Attitude Toward Business and Government:* And, finally, cross-pressures may exist between a person's vote intention and his attitude on a basic issue of the election. In the October interview, respondents were questioned on their attitudes toward one such issue: they were asked whether they considered it more important for a president to have experience in business or in government. Most people with Republican vote intentions wanted a president with business experience and most people who intended to vote Democratic preferred government experience in their candidate. There were, however, some respondents whose attitude and vote intention were conflicting—Republicans who wanted government experience in their presidential candidate and Democrats who thought business experience was more important. These deviates, then, were subject to a certain amount of cross-pressure.

Whatever the source of the conflicting pressures, whether from social status or class identification, from voting traditions or the attitudes of associates, the consistent result was to delay the voter's final decision. The voters who were subject to cross-pressures on their vote decided later than the voters for whom the various factors reinforced one another. And of all the cross-pressures which we have identified the single most effective one in delaying vote decision was the lack of complete agreement within the family.

Why did people subject to cross-pressures delay their final decisions as to how they should vote? In the first place, it was difficult for them to make up their minds simply because they had good reasons for voting for both candidates. Sometimes such reasons were so completely balanced that the decision had to be referred to a third factor for settlement. The doubt as to which was the better course—to vote Republican or to vote Democratic—combined with the process of self-argument caused the delay in the final vote decision of such people.

In the second place, some of the people subject to cross-pressures delayed their final vote decisions because they were waiting for events to resolve the conflicting pressures. In the case of conflicting personal characteristics, such resolution was hardly possible but in other cases a reconciliation of conflicting interests might be anticipated. A person might hope that during the campaign he could convince other members of his family, or even more, he might give the family every chance to bring him around to their way of thinking. And the family often does just that. Or, again, he might wait for events in the campaign to provide him with a basis for making up his mind. Although there is a tendency toward consistency in attitudes, sometimes the contradiction was not resolved and the voter actually went to the polls with the cross-pressures still in operation.

Such conflicting pressures make voters "fair game" for the campaign managers of both parties, for they have a foot in each party. They are subject to factors which influence them to vote Republican and others, perhaps equally strong, which influence them to vote Democratic.

From this particular point of view, the heavy campaigning of both parties at the end of the campaign is a good investment for both sides— to the extent to which it can be effective at all. We will recall that the people who make up their minds last are those who think the election will affect them least. It may be, then, that explicit attempts by the candidates and their managers to prove to them that the election *will* make a difference to them would be more effective than any amount of continued argumentation of the issues as such. One hypothesis is that the person or the party that convinces the hesitant voter of the importance of the election to him personally—in terms of what he concretely wants—can have his vote.

The Types of Changes

People delayed their final vote decisions either because they did not have enough interest in the election to push through to a definite choice or because the selection of a candidate put them in a difficult situation, containing elements favorable to both sides. But the process of delay did not work identically for all of them. Some people were "Don't Know's" until sometime during the campaign and then definitely decided on their vote. Others decided early in the campaign for one of the candidates, then had a period of doubt when they became undecided or even went over to the other side, and finally came back to the original choice. Still others changed from one particular party to the other. In short, the people who did not make up their minds until some time during the campaign proper differed in the ways in which they came to their final vote decision. In this sense, the three main kinds of changers were the following (the figures are percentages of the voters as a whole):

28% Crystallizers: They are people who had no vote intention in May but later acquired one; they went from "Don't Know" to Republican (14%) or from "Don't Know" to Democrat (14%).

15% Waverers: They are people who started out with a vote intention, then fell away from it (either to "Don't Know" or to the other party) and later returned to their original choice. Most of them went from a party to "Don't Know" and then back to the original party (11%: Republicans, 5.5%; Democrats, 5.5%), and others from a party to the other party and then back to the first party (4%: Republicans, 1%; Democrats, 3%).

8% Party Changers: They are people who started out with a vote intention and later changed to the other party, finally voting for it. They went from Republican to Democrat (2%) or from Democrat to Republican (6%).

We might note now, for use later, that all the changes of the crystallizers and most of the waverers involved only one of the parties; the other part of the change was a "Don't Know" opinion. On the other hand, all the party changers and some of the waverers were at one time or another in the camp of each party; their changes involved allegiance to both parties at different times. In other words, 39% of the changes made by the voters involved only one party and only 12% of them involved both parties. Or, adding the constants from May to November, the vote intentions of 88% of all the voters were limited to one party and the vote intentions of only 12% of the voters took in both parties, at one time or another.

Of the waverers who left their original choice for indecision, fully 82% returned to it as the more congenial home. But those who wandered away to the other party did not return so readily; only 32% came back to the party of their first choice. If a person leaves his party for indecision he almost always returns to it later, but if he leaves it for the opposition, he seldom returns to it.

As the campaign wore on, what kinds of changers were still left to be convinced, once and for all?

The three kinds of changers—the crystallizers, the waverers, and the party changers—all came to their final decision sometime after May, but not all at the same time. Actually, the crystallizers decided much earlier than the others; 68% had settled their vote by August as against only 48% of the party changers and 46% of the waverers.

But the waverers—the people who left the party of their original choice but later came back and voted for it—comprise a special group because as we noted above, there were two different kinds of waverers. There were those who wavered only to indecision and there were those who wavered all the way to the other party. The "distance" of the wavering is significant both for time of final decision and, as we shall see, for the roles of interest and cross-pressures. The indecision waverers definitely decided much earlier than the party waverers (57% by August as against 14%). If, then, we divide the changers into two groups—the one-party changers (crystallizers and indecision waverers) and the two-party changers (the straight party changers and the party waverers)—we find that the people who intended sometime during the campaign to vote for both parties took much longer to reach a final vote decision than those who varied only between one of the parties and indecision. Almost two-thirds of the two-party changers did not definitely decide until the last period of the campaign; almost two-thirds of the one-party changers definitely decided by August. As the campaign went into its last weeks, the people who were still to make up their minds, relatively speaking, were those who had been in the camp of the opposition earlier.

What were the roles of interest in the election and cross-pressures in voting background for these groups of voters who had arrived at their final vote decision in different ways? Did these two influential factors differentiate such voters?

The story is clear. There was a steady decrease of interest and a steady increase of cross-pressures from constants to one-party changers to two-party changers. The people who changed their position during the campaign but never enough to move into both parties stood between the constants and the two-party people. In other words, the more interest and the fewer conflicting pressures a person had, the more he tended to decide once and for all early in the game and never change his mind thereafter. If a person had somewhat less interest and somewhat more cross-pressures, then he tended to doubt longer and oftener than the constants but he slid back only to a tentative "don't know" and never far enough to get into the other camp. Only those people who had much less interest and many more conflicting pressures actually vacillated between the two parties.

That tells the story of the two-party changers: they were the people who were torn in both directions and who did not have enough interest in the election to cut through the conflicting pressures upon them and come to a deliberate and definite decision. Instead, they drifted along during the campaign, drifting into both parties. They not only delayed longer than any other group of voters in making their final vote decision but when they did make it, as we shall see, they were as likely as not to be swayed by someone in their immediate environment. These people, who in a sense were the only ones of the entire electorate to make a complete change during the campaign were: the least interested in the election; the least concerned about its outcome; the least attentive to political material in the formal media of communication; the last to settle upon a vote decision; and the most likely to be persuaded, finally, by a personal contact, not an "issue" of the election.

In short, the party changers—relatively, the people whose votes still remained to be definitely determined during the last stages of the campaign, the people who could swing an election during those last days— were, so to speak, available to the person who saw them last before Election Day. The notion that the people who switch parties during the campaign are mainly the reasoned, thoughtful, conscientious people who were convinced by the issues of the election is just plain wrong. Actually, they were mainly just the opposite.

3

IMPACT OF PUBLIC OPINION
UPON PUBLIC POLICY

*In the preceding section we were concerned with problems in the forma-
tion of public opinion, i.e., how opinions come to be what they are. In this
section we are concerned not with the "causes" of opinion but with its
consequences. Our central consideration here has to do with the ways in
which public opinion is, or should be, applied in the determination of
public policy. Does the legislative process follow the dictates of public
opinion, and should it? Under what conditions is public opinion more and
less appropriate as a guide for public action? In what sense does public
opinion form the basis of legislation, decree, law?*

*A broad historical analysis of the inter-relations between law and public
opinion is contained in the selection from Dicey's classical work in that
field. The long-range perspective of this study is supplemented by a detailed case study of the shifts in public opinion during the debate over a
single legislative event (Cantwell). Finally there is the question of whether
public opinion polls do a service or disservice to the democratic process
(Ranney). As soon as it became possible to provide a picture of public
opinion toward various political issues—the absence of which Bryce had
noted years before—the question was raised of the extent to which opinion
polls supply adequate guideposts for legislative action in a democratic
society. It is to the complex political problems involved in the practical expression and application of public opinion that the Ranney article addresses
itself.*

A. V. Dicey

THE RELATION BETWEEN LAW
AND PUBLIC OPINION

My aim in these lectures is to exhibit the close dependence of legislation, and even of the absence of legislation, in England during the nineteenth century upon the varying currents of public opinion.

The fact of this dependence will be assumed by most students with even too great readiness. We are all of us so accustomed to endow public opinion with a mysterious or almost supernatural power, that we neglect to examine what it is that we mean by public opinion, to measure the true limits of its authority, and to ascertain the mode of its operation. Surprise may indeed be felt, not at the statement that law depends upon opinion, but at this assertion being limited to England, and to England during the last century. The limitation, however, is intentional, and admits of full justification.

True indeed it is that the existence and the alteration of human institutions must, in a sense, always and everywhere depend upon the beliefs or feelings, or, in other words, upon the opinion of the society in which such institutions flourish.

"As force," writes Hume, "is always on the side of the governed, the governors have nothing to support them but opinion. It is, therefore, on opinion only that government is founded; and this maxim extends to the most despotic and most military governments, as well as to the most free and most popular. The Soldan of Egypt, or the Emperor of Rome, might drive his harmless subjects, like brute beasts, against their sentiments and inclination; but he must, at least, have led his mamelukes, or praetorian bands, like men, by their opinion."

And so true is this observation that the authority even of a Southern planter over his slaves rested at bottom upon the opinion of the Negroes

Reprinted from *Lectures on The Relation of Law and Public Opinion in England During the Nineteenth Century* (1914), pp. 1-7, by permission of the publisher. (Copyright, 1914, by Macmillan Co.)

whom he at his pleasure flogged or killed. Their combined physical force exceeded the planter's own personal strength, and the strength of the few whites who might be expected to stand by him. The blacks obeyed the slave-owner from the opinion, whether well or ill founded, that in the long run they would in a contest with their masters have the worst of the fight; and even more from that habit of submission which, though enforced by the occasional punishment of rebels, was grounded upon a number of complicated sentiments, such, for example, as admiration for superior ability and courage, or gratitude for kindness, which cannot by any fair analysis be reduced to a mere form of fear, but constitutes a kind of prevalent moral atmosphere. The whites, in short, ruled in virtue of the opinion, entertained by their slaves no less than themselves, that the slave-owners possessed qualities which gave them the might, and even the right, to be masters. With the rightness or wrongness of this conviction we are not here in any way concerned. Its existence is adduced only as a proof that, even in the most extreme case conceivable, Hume's doctrine holds good, and the opinion of the governed is the real foundation of all government.

But, though obedience to law must of necessity be enforced by opinion of some sort, and Hume's paradox thus turns out to be a truism, this statement does not involve the admission that the law of every country is itself the result of what we mean by "public opinion." This term, when used in reference to legislation, is merely a short way of describing the belief or conviction prevalent in a given society that particular laws are beneficial, and therefore ought to be maintained, or repealed in accordance with the opinion or wishes of its inhabitants. Now this assertion, though it is, if properly understood, true with regard to England at the present day, is clearly not true of all countries, at all times, and indeed has not always been true even of England.

For, in the first place, there exist many communities in which public opinion—if by that term be meant speculative views held by the mass of the people as to the alteration or improvement of their institutions—can hardly be said to have any existence. The members of such societies are influenced by habit rather than by thought. Their mode of life is determined by customary rules, which may indeed have originated in the necessities of a given social condition, or even in speculative doctrines entertained by ancient law-givers, but which, whatever be their origin, assuredly owe their continuance to use and wont. It is, in truth, only under the peculiar conditions of an advanced civilisation that opinion dictates legislative change. In many Eastern countries, opinion—which is better described as traditional or instinctive feeling—has for ages been, in general, hostile to change and favourable to the maintenance of inherited habits. There, as in the West, opinion, in a very wide sense of that word, rules; but such aversion to change as for ages keeps a society within the limits of traditional action, is a very different thing from the public opinion which in the England of the nineteenth and twentieth centuries has demanded constant improvements in the law of the land.

It is possible, in the second place, to point to realms where laws and institutions have been altered or revolutionised in deference to opinion, but where the beliefs which have guided legislative reform have not been what we mean in England by "public" opinion. They have been, not ideas entertained by the inhabitants of a country, or by the greater part thereof, but convictions held by a small number of men, or even by a single individual who happened to be placed in a position of commanding authority. We must, indeed, remember that no ruler, however powerful, can stand completely alone, and that the despots who have caused or guided revolutions have been influenced by the opinion, if not of their own country, yet of their generation. But it may be asserted with substantial truth that Peter the Great laid the foundation of Russian power without much deference to the opinion of Russia, and that modern Prussia was created by Frederick the Great, who certainly drew his ideas of good government from other than Prussian sources. It was not, then, the public opinion of the Russian people or the public opinion of the Prussians, but the convictions of a single man which in each case moulded the laws and institutions of a powerful country. At this moment legislation in British India is the work of a body of English specialists who follow to a great extent the current of English opinion. They are, indeed, it is to be hoped, guided far more by their own experience and by their practical knowledge of India, than by English sentiment; but Anglo-Indian officials though they may not always obey the transitory feelings of the English public, certainly do not represent Indian public opinion.

In the third place, the law of a country may fail, for a time, to represent public opinion owing to the lack of any legislative organ which adequately responds to the sentiment of the age. A portion, at least, of that accumulation of abuses, which was the cause of the occasion of the French Revolution, may fairly be ascribed to the want of any legislative body possessing both the power and the will to carry out reforms which had long been demanded by the intelligence of the French nation. Some critics may, it is true, deny that a legislative organ was lacking: a French king held in his hands under the *ancient régime* an authority nearly approaching to sovereign power, and an enlightened despot might, it has been suggested, have conferred upon the country all the benefits promised by the Revolution. But the power of the French Crown was practically more limited than modern critics always perceive, whilst the circumstances no less than the character of Louis XV and Louis XVI disqualified these monarchs for performing the part of enlightened despots. The "Parliaments," again, which assuredly possessed some legislative power, might, it has been argued, have reformed the laws and institutions of the country. But the Parliaments were after all Courts, not legislatures, and represented the prejudices of lawyers, not the aspirations of reformers; Frenchmen, zealous for the removal of abuses, looked, as a matter of fact, with more hope to the action of the king than to the legislation of Parliaments which represented the antiquated conservatism of a past age. The want, then, of a legislative organ was in France a check upon the influence of public opinion. Nor can it be denied that even in England defective legislative machinery has at times lessened the immediate influence of opinion. The chief cause, no doubt, of the arrest of almost every kind of reform during the latest years of the eighteenth and the earlier part of the nineteenth century, was a state of feeling so hostile to revolution that it forbade the most salutary innovations. But "legislative stagnation," as it has been termed, lasted in England for at least ten or twenty years beyond the date when it ought naturally to have come to an end; and it can hardly be disputed that this delay in the improvement of English institutions was due in part to the defects of the unreformed Parliament—that is, to the non-existence of a satisfactory legislative organ.

Frank V. Cantwell

PUBLIC OPINION
AND THE LEGISLATIVE PROCESS

The rôle played by public opinion in a democracy, particularly as it affects the legislative process, has long been a subject for speculation by political scientists. The advent of controlled quota sampling permits of the study of this important relationship in measurable terms. The object of the present discussion is to trace the interaction of public opinion and the executive and legislative branches of government as they have dealt with a single public question—reorganization of the Supreme Court, as presented to Congress for consideration by President Roosevelt on February 5, 1937. Enlargement of the Supreme Court from nine to fifteen members was the most controversial feature of the general reorganization of the federal judiciary proposed by the President, aimed at speeding up the process of clearing cases through the federal court system, and making the system more "representative" of the wishes of the people.

The debate on enlargement of the Supreme Court provides a useful and interesting case study for several reasons. The case as a public issue has a definite beginning and end, ranging from the proposal of the judiciary reform bill by the President on February 5 to the death of Senator Joseph T. Robinson on July 14, 1937. As it was debated by public and legislators, the issue was a relatively clear-cut one, uncomplicated by side issues or utterly foreign events that might have influenced the course of either legislators or the public. Finally, and of decided importance, the American Institute of Public Opinion made weekly measurements of opinion toward the proposal during the entire period that reorganization of the Court was a public question. This permits the correlation of reliable opinion samplings with events in the debate and the observation of their relationship.

Reprinted from *The American Political Science Review,* Vol. LV (1946), pp. 924-35, by permission of the author and the publisher. (Copyright, 1946, by The American Political Science Association.)

From this observation it is hoped to throw light on several specific questions: (1) What is the general nature of the relationship between the public and its legislators? (2) What are the forces at work which determine the direction that public opinion will take in a debate of this type? (3) Is there a noticeable tendency on the part of legislators to follow the guidance of public opinion, and if so, to what extent do legislators take their lead from the public? (4) To what extent do legislators attempt to swing opinion to their way of thinking? (5) Are there any phases of the relationship between the public and legislators that might be improved so as to make it more effective in approaching the process of deciding public policy?

From accounts of the Court debate as carried in the *New York Times,* the following short outline of leading developments in the debate has been prepared:

Chronological Listing of Events in the Court Debate

February 5—President Roosevelt sends message to Congress recommending reorganization of the federal judiciary, including increasing the membership of the Supreme Court from nine to fifteen members. President reported "calm and confident," reflecting his conviction that he has a huge popular mandate for what he is doing. Message creates shock throughout country.

March 1—The Supreme Court upholds Congressional resolution abrogating payments in gold. Decision is of aid to New Deal.

March 4—President Roosevelt, in Democratic Victory Dinner speech, calls for party loyalty on the Supreme Court issue.

March 8—The President, in a fireside chat, assures Americans that, in proposing reorganization of the Court, he is seeking to protect them from the Court's usurpations.

March 9—Homer Cummings, Attorney-General, opens Administration arguments before Senate Judiciary Committee, saying the bill will restore the governmental machinery to its proper balance.

March 22—Senator Burton K. Wheeler opens opposition arguments before Senate Judiciary Committee and reads a statement from Chief Justice Charles E. Hughes saying enlargement of the Court is "unnecessary." Statement is said to have the approval of Justices Brandeis and Van Devanter.

March 29—The Supreme Court reverses Adkins v. Children's Hospital decision and holds constitutional minimum wage law of the state of Washington. Adkins case specifically overruled by 5-4 decision. Decision opens way for federal minimum wage legislation.

April 12—In handing down decisions in four specific cases, the Supreme Court upholds the National Labor Relations Act (Wagner Act). Decision in chief case is 5-4.

April 28—Senators Hatch, McCarran, and O'Mahoney, members of the Senate Judiciary Committee previously uncommitted on Supreme Court Bill, announce opposition on basis of testimony offered before the Committee.

May 10—Washington reports say that Justices Brandeis and Van Devanter will retire from Court in June.

May 18—Justice Willis Van Devanter, 78, retires.

May 24—The Supreme Court upholds the Social Security Act in ruling on three cases, two by 5-4 decisions.

June 14—The Senate Judiciary Committee reports unfavorably to the Senate on the Court bill, terming the proposal "a needless, futile, and utterly dangerous abandonment of constitutional principle." Vote is 10-8 against proposal.

July 14—Senator Joseph T. Robinson, majority leader of the Senate, dies suddenly. Supreme Court Bill will be abandoned.

Two questions were asked weekly by the Gallup Poll during the debate. The first question was asked during the period from February 15 to April 5, and reads: "Are you in favor of President Roosevelt's proposal regarding the Supreme Court?" The second question covers the period from April 12 to June 7, and reads: "Should Congress pass the President's Supreme Court plan?" In both questions, the Supreme Court plan was stated to be "President Roosevelt's." Possibly the use of the President's name might have introduced a bias, although throughout the debate, in the newspapers, on the radio, and in the halls of Congress, the plan was also identified with the President. In view of this very common identification, the possibility of such a bias is minimized. In any event, any tendency toward bias would not affect the validity of the figures as used in this study, since a bias would be constant.

Phase One of the Debate. The initial period in the debate extends from the introduction of the President's proposal on February 5 until the week immediately preceding the two speeches made by the President. In this early period public attitudes toward the proposal divided equally, 45 per cent of the people expressing approval of the proposal, and 45 per cent expressing disapproval, with 10 per cent in the "no opinion" category. These figures are from the Gallup Poll taken during the week of February 15. At approximately the same time, the *New York Times* reported that an informal poll of senators made by *Times* reporters showed that 32 senators were on record as favoring the proposal, 28 as against the proposal, while 35 remained uncommitted. Thus, while 90 per cent of the public had put themselves on record as favoring or disapproving the proposal, only 63 per cent of the senators had taken a definite stand. One week later, on February 17, the *Times* news columns carried this statement from a Washington staff member: "Conservative Democrats . . . especially those in the Senate, gagged at the proposals. . . . Many of them maintained a prudent silence, waiting to see how the cat of public opinion would jump."

In this first stage of the debate, newspapers and radio commentators began to take definite stands on the proposals, and senators and other public figures began to make statements setting forth their positions. Senator Norris declared against the bill; former Governor Alf Landon, who had carried the Republican standard in the presidential election a few months earlier, came out against the proposal; Senator Champ Clark declared against the scheme; and Senators Glass and Wheeler denounced it. The only figure of magnitude to raise his voice in favor of the proposal was Senator La Follette. In the face of this cumulation of official opinion against the proposal, public opinion began to turn against the plan, and by March 1 the Gallup Poll reported that the anti-proposal vote had grown to 48 per cent, while the pro-proposal vote had slumped to 41 per cent— a difference of 7 percentage points. The President and his advisers became aware that public sentiment was turning away from the proposal.

As early as February 15, the *Times* reported that Attorney-General Cummings and Senator Sherman Minton were planning to make appeals for public support of the plan. The *Times* news columns said: "The frank object of all these appeals is to induce the backers of the President to send telegrams and letters to their senators and representatives to offset the thousands received at the Capitol in the last few days in opposition to his sweeping plan for remaking the Supreme Court with more liberal-minded men." On February 19, the *Times* said: "On the showing of in-formal polls that the Administration's judiciary reform bill may hang on the decision of less than a dozen senators, President Roosevelt and the forces identified with him, particularly organized labor, intensified their efforts to insure its passage as a prerequisite to further New Deal legisla-tion. . . . The opposition strategists in the Senate . . . were . . . making preparations for one of the stiffest legislative battles of recent years. They were making no particular effort to dig into the dwindling reservoir of unpledged senators, leaving that to the weight of the letters and telegrams still coming in from all parts of the country." Phase One of the debate may be summarized by saying that the President introduced the proposal with the hope that public opinion, which had given him a handsome victory in November, would provide the pressure necessary to push the proposal through Congress. This public pressure was not forthcoming, and the public had become increasingly hostile. Opposition senators were bid-ing their time as they watched public opinion swing behind them. So far as the Administration was concerned, a counter-attack was necessary to win back public favor to the proposal.

Phase Two. The second phase of the debate may be entitled the Ad-ministration drive for public support. The outstanding development during this phase was the entry of the President directly into the discussion. With opinion turning away from the proposal, it became obvious that use of the most powerful weapon in the New Deal arsenal was indicated—a personal appeal from the President. Consequently, the President made two speeches to the nation within five days, an address at the Democratic Victory Dinner on March 4 and a fireside chat on March 8. The *New York Times* reported the fireside chat in these words: "He had no intention of packing the Court with 'spineless puppets.' He simply proposed to return the Court to its 'rightful and historic place' and save the Constitution from 'hardening of the arteries'." On the morning following the fireside chat, Attorney-General Cummings opened the Administration case before the Senate Judiciary Committee, saying that the proposal would restore the governmental machinery to its proper balance. The Gallup Poll for the week of March 1 immediately registered the impact of the President's speeches. The anti-proposal vote fell to 47 per cent and in two weeks dropped precipitately to 41 per cent, the lowest point reached by the No vote at any stage of the debate. On the other hand, the pro-proposal vote began a climb that was to last until March 29, rising from 41 to 45 per cent during the month. Success had apparently crowned the effort of the Administration to win the favor of public opinion, for the Yes vote now held a slim margin over the No vote. However, as will be seen, this margin was to prove far from decisive.

Phase Three. On March 22, the opposition forces swung back into action as Senator Burton Wheeler, chief of the anti-court reorganization forces, opened the opposition arguments before the Senate Judiciary Committee. As the first opposition witness, Senator Wheeler read a statement from Chief Justice Charles E. Hughes saying enlargement of the Court was "unnecessary"; and the statement was said to have the approval of Justices Brandeis and Van Devanter. During that week the No vote turned again and began a steady climb upward which was to mount almost steadily until the proposal was finally killed. Evidently, opposition arguments before the Judiciary Committee were sufficiently convincing to solidify the No vote, the constant strength of the oppositionists among the public from this date onward is shown.

Phase Four. The turning point in the debate was reached on March 29. On that day, the Supreme Court handed down a decision reversing an earlier decision in the Adkins v. Children's Hospital case. The effect was to hold constitutional the minimum wage law of the state of Washington, thus paving the way for federal minimum wage legislation, one of the chief objectives of the New Deal. The effect on public opinion of the switch by the Supreme Court was nothing short of profound. The Yes vote, or those in favor of reorganization, began a sharp slump from which it never fully recovered. In terms of percentages, the Yes vote dropped from a high of 45 per cent in the week before the reversed decision in the Adkins case to a low of 31 per cent on May 17. It is safe to say that the Administration lost its case before the public on the day when the Supreme Court did its famous about-face. It is to be noted, however, that the Yes vote which became estranged from the proposal did not shift into the No group, but fell into indecision and became allied with the No Opinion group. The growth of the No Opinion group almost matches, point for point, the decline in the Yes group. This phenomenon will be enlarged upon below.

From the beginning of Phase Two onward, the Senate Judiciary Committee had been holding extensive hearings at which educators, farm and labor leaders, women's group leaders, and the representatives of almost every special interest group in the nation appeared and presented their case. To what extent the members of the Judiciary Committee were "holding off" from presenting the bill for a formal test on the Senate floor is difficult to tell with exactness. During this period, opinion was in a state of flux, and the Judiciary Committee served a valuable function by permitting opinion to crystallize. Some evidence of political maneuvering to take advantage of a favorable climate of opinion is revealed in a charge made by Senators Wheeler and Van Nuys on April 3, five days after the Supreme Court handed down the decision in the Adkins case. The *New York Times* reported the two Senators as charging Attorney-General Cummings with a "gag" attempt, based on reports that Mr. Cummings had hinted that he would like to see the Judiciary Committee bring the hearings to a close. The *Times* reported the Senators as saying: "There is no doubt the Attorney-General would like to close public hearings on this issue. . . . Hundreds of American citizens, holding responsible positions at the bar, in universities, and in the molding of public opinion have asked to be heard . . . it is the duty of the Senate Judiciary Committee to continue these hearings until every cross-section of public opinion has been given an opportunity to present its views." Senator Wheeler was astute enough to realize that the tide of opinion was running against the proposal, and that time was playing into the hands of the opposition, just as Mr. Cummings knew that time was playing against the Administration. The two opposition Senators realized the impact of the Supreme Court decision of March 29 on the public and were willing to continue the hearings of the Judiciary Committee until such time as the increased opposition they expected from the public should have an opportunity to register itself through witnesses at the hearings and through senatorial channels of sounding opinion. The Judiciary Committee did continue its hearings, and reports continued to furnish the bulk of newspaper and radio accounts of the reorganization debate. The incident is illustrative of the dependence that both sides placed upon the pressure of public opinion to furnish the force needed to carry the day. Opponents and proponents alike realized that without the backing of public opinion they were lost, and were anxiously trying to win opinion to their side, while waiting for opinion to crystallize sufficiently so that a clear-cut case of public support would be forthcoming.

On April 12, with the No vote holding a six per cent margin over the Yes vote, the Supreme Court handed down a decision upholding the National Labor Relations Act in rulings on four specific cases. In the chief case, the decision was five to four in favor of the act. Strangely enough, the effect of this decision on public opinion was the reverse of that in the Adkins case. The No vote went down slightly while the Yes vote mounted slightly. This reversal of opinion can be traced to the fact that the Administration immediately made capital of the two successive favorable decisions of the Court, following a series of reverses for the New Deal—maintaining that the two decisions proved the point that the Court was actually composed of human beings who were subject to error and could see the error of their ways. The Administration raised its famous cry that Court decisions rested on whether a Justice came down heads or tails, which indicated the need for a larger Court membership. This argument, although it had an immediate effect, was not powerful enough to change the trend of opinion, and the following week (April 19) the No vote rose three percentage points, while the Yes vote sank two points.

Phase Five. The next development of note in the debate occurred on May 10, when reports from Washington circled the country to the effect that Justices Brandeis and Van Devanter intended to retire from the Court in June. The effect of this report was to increase public indecision, which had been mounting steadily from the introduction of the proposal, and after the report had gained credence the No Opinion group stood at a high of 25 per cent on May 17. It is worth pausing to note the state of opinion at this time.

TABLE I—Shift in Vote on Court Reorganization, February 15-May 17 [1]

	February 15	May 17	Difference
Yes, favor reorganization	45%	31%	−14%
No, oppose reorganization	45%	44%	− 1%
No opinion	10%	25%	+15%

Table I shows that the opposition group had held its own, despite sharp dips. The Yes group, proponents of reorganization had lost a total of 14 percentage points; the No Opinion group had risen from 10 per cent to 25 per cent; and the table shows that those who lost faith in their position did not feel powerfully enough affected to jump into the opposite camp, but that their reaction was to fall into a state of indecision. The gain for the No Opinion group represents the total defection from both the Yes and No groups. In other words, the public was still not clear upon a course of action, although the number of Yes people who were growing increasingly doubtful of their position was very much larger than the respective No group. The importance of this observation lies in the assumption that members of the Senate were idling along, waiting for a popular reaction. This was not to be forthcoming, since the people were becoming in-

[1] February 15 represents roughly the introduction of the proposal. May 17 is representative of the period following circulation of reports that Justices Brandeis and Van Devanter would retire in June.

creasingly indecisive. But for the next event unfolding on May 18, it is difficult to say how long this deadlock between the people and their legislators, each waiting for the other to act, might have lasted.

Phase Six. The deadlock was broken on the date mentioned with announcement of the retirement from the Supreme Court of Justice Willis Van Devanter at the age of seventy-eight. This announcement immediately cleared the atmosphere, and both opponents and proponents of the court reorganization proposal were enabled to make up their minds definitely. Opinion had at last crystallized. The retirement of Justice Van Devanter meant that the President would be able to appoint to the Court a Justice more in sympathy with New Deal objectives. In turn, this appointment, together with the recent "liberalization" of the Court in the Adkins and Wagner Act decisions, meant that for all practical purposes the Court had been reorganized. De facto reorganization apparently was satisfactory to the public, and the No vote rose quickly until on June 7 opponents of court reorganization had 50 per cent of the public behind them, while only 35 per cent favored reorganization. The No Opinion vote sank rapidly from 25 per cent on May 17 to 15 per cent on June 7.

Table II shows that after the retirement of Justice Van Devanter, opinion crystallized more rapidly in the direction of opposition to the proposal than in favor of it. A total defection of 10 per cent of those originally favoring reorganization can be noted, five per cent of these people switching their vote into opposition, while five per cent were unable to come to a decision and moved into the No Opinion group.

TABLE II—Shift in Vote on Court Reorganization, February 15-June 7

	February 5	June 7	Difference
Yes, favor reorganization	45%	35%	−10%
No, oppose reorganization	45%	50%	+ 5%
No opinion	10%	15%	+ 5%

This evident satisfaction of the people with the changed court situation came as a great relief to legislators, who were now able to deal with the delicate problem of de jure court reorganization. On June 14, with the battle of public opinion decided, and with opinion firmly behind it, the Senate Judiciary Committee reported unfavorably (ten to eight) to the Senate on the Judiciary Reorganization Bill, terming the measure "a needless, futile, and utterly dangerous abandonment of constitutional principle." Reorganization of the Court was no longer a public issue; and whatever lingering inclination there might have been on the part of the Administration to press for court reform in the face of public opposition was dissipated by the death on July 14 of Senator Joseph T. Robinson, majority leader of the Senate, who had thrown all of his strength into the fray on behalf of the proposal.

Having examined in some detail the interplay between public opinion and events in the court debate, it is now possible to form conclusions as to the general nature of the relationship between the public and its legislators as they deal jointly with a public question. In many respects, the debate on the Court is typical of the problems which present themselves for solution in our democracy. For this reason, the conclusions which follow have been cast in such a form that they may be applied to understanding the nature of any similar debate on a public question. At the same time, it must be borne in mind that so many diverse factors operate while a question runs its public course that these conclusions have applicability only in so far as the phenomena at work in a given situation are taken into consideration. Further study of the type of relationship under consideration will permit the understanding with considerable exactness of how public opinion and the legislative process affect each other. This, in turn, will enable the public and legislators to operate together at full efficiency; for it is undeniable that national questions must be solved by the joint action of the people and their elected legislative representatives.

1. *Legislators display an inclination to "wait on" public opinion to shape itself before dealing formally with questions.* This does not mean that senators were content merely to follow the lead of public opinion, for many made an effort to mold opinion to their way of thinking through radio addresses and personal appearances. It does mean that the great majority of senators were keenly aware of the existence of public opinion and hesitant to take action so long as its final direction was not absolutely certain. Although many senators committed themselves publicly during the course of the debate, at no time did either side show determination to force a showdown on the floor of the Senate, such hesitation seeming to stem from the uncertain condition of public opinion, which never registered above 50 per cent either for or against the proposal.

The function of the Senate Judiciary Committee as a sounding board is interesting. As long as any doubt remained about public sentiment toward the bill, the committee remained in session, and only when it was perfectly plain that public support for the proposal would not be forthcoming did it make its unfavorable report. During the extended period of public hearings, an amazing array of witnesses appeared before the committee and every possible type of argument for and against the proposal was brought forth. Doubtless this varied array of witnesses gave to the senators valuable clues as to public feeling on the proposal, and it was on the basis of testimony offered before the committee that Senators Hatch, McCarran, and

O'Mahoney announced their opposition to the bill. The most useful function of the committee seems to have been to hold in abeyance the necessity of making a formal decision while senators waited in the hope that public opinion would develop in a decisive direction and render unnecessary a decision on the Senate floor.

2. *Events played a more important rôle than Congress or the President in shaping the direction of public opinion.* The six leading determinants of opinion in the debate were: (1) the President's Victory Dinner speech and fireside chat on the fourth and eighth of March; (2) the opening of the Administration case before the Senate Judiciary Committee on March 9; (3) the opening of opposition arguments against the proposal before the committee on March 22; (4) the decision of the Supreme Court overruling an earlier decision in the Adkins v. Children's Hospital case on March 29, which paved the way for federal minimum wage legislation and broke the succession of anti-New Deal decisions handed down by the Court; (5) Washington reports, beginning on May 10, that Justices Brandeis and Van Devanter were planning to retire; and (6) the retirement on May 18 of Justice Van Devanter.

Of these six steps in the downfall of the Court proposal, three were attempts by government officials (the President and senators) to mobilize opinion in a particular direction. The other three were events in the sense of being unanticipated happenings beyond the province of either proponents or opponents of the proposal. While the President's speeches and the arguments given before the Senate Judiciary Committee affected public opinion measurably, they were incapable of affecting it decisively. The major event in opinion-determination was the decision of the Court in the Adkins case. From the time of this decision, the public Yes vote dropped off steadily, while the No vote rose. The second most important step in opinion-determination was the retirement of Justice Van Devanter, with the effect of crystallizing opinion which had been drifting into indecision as the debate wore on. As Cantril has said, "opinion is generally determined more by events than by words—unless those words are themselves interpreted as an 'event'." [2]

3. *Public opinion cannot propose a course of action, and a healthy public opinion requires leadership.* Throughout the course of the debate, as shown by the accompanying data, public opinion was responsive to political moves and events. At no time was there observable any great spontaneous movement of opinion in a direction which would have indicated to legislators the necessity for taking a particular course of action that would have broken the deadlock. It is characteristic of public opinion that it cannot generate a proposal or series of proposals serving to satisfy its needs. Public opinion can indicate very powerfully the general area of

[2] Hadley Cantril, *Gauging Public Opinion* (Princeton, 1944), p. 226.

its needs, but it remains for an individual or group of individuals to come forward with specific proposals toward which opinion can display approval or disapproval. We have seen how, during the course of the debate, the public support that fell away from both the Yes and No sides of the discussion tended to gather in the No Opinion category, where it remained in a state of indecision awaiting some new determining factor that would move it once more into the realm of decision. Those legislators who waited in the hope that public opinion would show them the way were waiting in vain. Public opinion in a democracy responds to leadership, and needs the stimulus of leadership in order to crystallize one way or the other on specific proposals. Legislators are perfectly correct in sounding opinion so that they may determine whether or not they are moving in a direction calculated to meet popular needs. It is completely fallacious for legislators to wait on public opinion to tell them what to do, because public opinion waits on leadership to supply the grist of fact and suggestion so that it can fulfill its function, which is the acceptance or rejection of proposals. In a sentence, when faced with a specific problem, public opinion will respond to proposals, but cannot generate them; generation of proposals is the function of the legislators.

John C. Ranney

DO THE POLLS SERVE
DEMOCRACY?

Most of the current controversy over public opinion polls has centered about the question of their accuracy: the reliability of the sample taken, the impartiality of the sponsorship, the honesty of the interviewer and the interviewed, the fairness of the questions, the measurement of intensities or gradations of feeling, and the validity of the analysis or interpretation.[1] These are all, admittedly, important questions; but they tend to ignore or to beg one which is both more important and more theoretical: Assuming that the polls were to attain a miraculously perfect and unchallengeable accuracy, would they, even then, contribute significantly to the working of democracy?

One's first inclination is to take it for granted that the answer is "Yes." No principle, in democratic theory, has been more fundamental than the belief that political decisions ought to be made by the people as a whole or in accordance with their desires.[2] Yet no principle, in democratic practice, has proved more difficult of precise application. In theory, even when doubts are entertained as to the rationality, the objectivity, and the capacity of the ordinary citizen, modern democratic writers have continued to find the essence of democracy in popular participation in policy-making.[3] But

Reprinted from *The Public Opinion Quarterly*, Vol. X (1946), pp. 249-60, by permission of the author and the publisher. (Copyright, 1946, by Princeton University Press.)

[1] See, for example, in recent issues of the *Public Opinion Quarterly* (Vol. 9), Edward L. Bernays, "Attitude Polls—Servants or Masters?" pp. 264-268b (Fall, 1945); Gordon M. Connelly, "Now Let's Look at the Real Problem: Validity," pp. 51-60 (Spring, 1945); Leo P. Crespi, "The Cheater Problem in Polling," pp. 431-445 (Winter, 1945-46); and the symposium, "The Discussion Goes On," pp. 403-410 (Winter, 1945-46).

[2] I do not intend to imply, of course, that this is the whole of democratic theory.

[3] For some recent statements on this subject, see Carl L. Becker, *Modern Democracy* (New Haven, 1941), p. 7; James Bryce, *Modern Democracies* (New York, 1924), Vol. 1, p. 20; Francis Coker, *Recent Political Thought* (New York and London, 1934), p. 293; Carl J. Friedrich, *The New Belief in the Common Man* (Boston, 1942), pp. 31, 221; Harold J. Laski, "Democracy," *Encyclopaedia of the Social Sciences* (New York, 1932), Vol. 3, pp. 80, 84; John D. Lewis, "The Elements of Democracy," *American*

in practice, it has long been apparent that our electoral system, as a reflection of popular wishes and as a channel for popular activity, leaves a good deal to be desired.

Various improvements have been suggested, ranging from the initiative and the referendum to proportional or functional representation. But none of these devices, except by placing an intolerable strain on the voter, has solved the problem of how to reflect simultaneously the great diversity of his interests and attitudes on different issues.[4] The result, under our present system, is that even if one assumes that the voter does anything more than choose between the personalities of rival candidates, an election approximates what has been called "plebiscitary democracy." It is a way of approving or disapproving in the most general terms the policies of the party or individual in office and of renewing or transferring this exceedingly vague mandate for the coming term of office.[5]

Such a check and consultation is much better than none at all. Notwithstanding its resemblance to some of the dictatorial plebiscites, it permits, in a free society, the expression of at least the major discontents. But consultations which are so sweeping and which occur at such rare intervals are only the thinnest caricature of the democratic belief that the health of the community depends upon the personal, active, and continuous political participation of the body of its citizens.

It is here that the polls are supposed to make their great contribution. By separating the issues from one another, by stating them simply and clearly, and by covering the electorate completely and continuously, they avoid the most obvious obscurities, strains, and distortions of the older procedures. If to these virtues one might add unchallengeable accuracy, the well-known dream of Bryce would be realized: the will of the majority of the citizens could be ascertained at all times; representative assemblies and elaborate voting machinery would be unnecessary and obsolete.[6]

Political Science Review, Vol. 34, p. 469 (June, 1940); A. D. Lindsay, *The Modern Democratic State* (London, New York, Toronto, 1943), Vol. 1, pp. 267-268; Charles E. Merriam, *The New Democracy and the New Despotism* (New York, 1939), pp. 11-12; Francis Graham Wilson, *The Elements of Modern Politics* (New York and London, 1936), pp. 189-190, 247.

[4] John Dickinson, "Democratic Realities and the Democratic Dogma," *American Political Science Review*, Vol. 24, p. 300 (May, 1930); Pendleton Herring, *The Politics of Democracy* (New York, 1940), p. 329; E. E. Schattschneider, *Party Government* (New York, 1942), p. 33. For the weaknesses of such devices as the initiative and referendum, see Harold F. Gosnell, "The Polls and Other Mechanisms of Democracy," *Public Opinion Quarterly*, Vol. 4, p. 225 (June, 1940); A. Lawrence Lowell, *Public Opinion and Popular Government* (New York, 1913), pp. 152-235; William B. Munro, "Initiative and Referendum," *Encyclopaedia of the Social Sciences*, Vol. 4, pp. 50-52.

[5] The electoral system is, of course, supplemented by the interpretive work of the pressure groups, and they provide an important instrument for popular political action. But it is obvious that many of them are at least as much concerned with misrepresenting or flouting public opinion on individual issues as with representing it.

[6] *The American Commonwealth* (New York, 1920), Vol. 2, p. 262.

Not everyone has rejoiced over this possibility. Anyone who agrees with Hamilton, for example, that the people are turbulent and changing, seldom judging or determining right, is hardly likely to welcome a device to make the voice of the people (which decidedly is not the voice of God) more audible than ever.[7] Nor is this attitude likely to surprise or disturb the genuine democrat.

What should disturb him, however, is the fact that there are many people who consider themselves good democrats and who nevertheless consider the polls a menace to democracy. The objections of this second group deserve more systematic attention than they have yet received.[8]

The first and most frequent of these objections is that the polls destroy political courage and leadership. Every adequate government, it is maintained, requires these qualities in its officials. They can exist, however, only where there is freedom and flexibility and where the statesman is not bound, either in form or in fact, by rigid instructions from the voters. The government official, whether Congressman or administrator, has access to information which is beyond the reach of the ordinary voter, and he has something more than the ordinary voter's leisure in which to consider it. To subject his judgment to the ill-informed and hasty judgment of the electorate is to commit the political crime of rendering a decision before considering the evidence on which it ought to be based. It is true that the polls have no official standing and cannot bind any office-holder. But, the charge runs, the official who wants to keep his job will abandon his duty of analyzing and judging proposed policies in favor of the simpler, and safer, device of deciding as the polls tell him to decide.[9]

So far as the legislator is concerned, there are several weaknesses in this argument. Simply as a matter of fact, it would be extremely difficult to show that the polls have had a decisive effect in determining the voting habits of any substantial number of representatives.[10] It is one of the

[7] See, for example, Col. O. R. McGuire, "The U.S. Constitution and Ten Shekels of Silver," *Public Opinion Quarterly*, Vol. 4, pp. 232-235 (June, 1940).

[8] In this discussion I am not taking up the question of the accuracy of the polls, since the principle at issue is really one of whether even an accurate poll is a desirable thing in a democracy.

[9] For a concise statement of this position, see Eric F. Goldman, "Poll on the Polls," *Public Opinion Quarterly*, Vol. 8, pp. 461-467 (Winter, 1944-45), and the literature there cited.

[10] More Congressmen would be influenced by the polls, and the argument strengthened, if there were more general confidence in their accuracy and if the returns were published by Congressional districts. For evidence of the influence of polls on legislators, see L. E. Gleeck, "96 Congressmen Make Up Their Minds," *Public Opinion Quarterly*, Vol. 4, pp. 3-24 (March, 1940); George W. Hartman, "Judgments of State Legislators Concerning Public Opinion," *Journal of Social Psychology*, Vol. 21, pp. 105-114 (February, 1945); Martin Kriesberg, "What Congressmen and Administrators Think of the Polls," *Public Opinion Quarterly*, Vol. 9, pp. 333-337 (Fall, 1945); George F. Lewis, Jr., "The Congressmen Look at the Polls," *Ibid.*, Vol. 4, pp. 229-231 (June, 1940).

dubious advantages of the American system that it is extremely difficult to allocate responsibility; and even in those cases in which responsibility can be fixed, the ordinary voter is only too likely to be ignorant of the voting record of his representative. The average Congressman on the average issue need not worry too much about the opinion of his constituents in the mass. What he does need to worry about is the opinion of specific organizations and individuals inside his constituency, especially the political machines and the organized pressure groups. Any Congressman who is concerned with political realities knows that it is more important to appease a well-disciplined minority, which can deliver the votes on election day, than to gratify an unorganized and casual majority, the intensity of whose convictions and the efficacy of whose action is far less likely to be decisive. If the polls exert any influence at all, therefore, they tend to moderate or deflate rather than to reinforce the special pressures already influencing legislators.[11]

The absence of scientific methods for measuring opinion, moreover, has never prevented politicians from trying to guess what it is. The representative, if such there be, who follows the polls slavishly would have his ear well to the ground under any circumstances. It is hard to see how democracy is undermined or its moral fibre destroyed simply by providing him with more reliable methods of judgment. It can hardly be urged that so long as a representative is going to vote according to public opinion anyway, the more distorted his picture of it, the better. Nor would it be easy to show that, among those restrained by the polls, the idealists seriously outnumber those who would otherwise follow the dictates of selfish and limited interests.

Finally, it should be remembered that public opinion is not so definite and rigid as the argument implies. In some instances, changes have been both rapid and extreme, and political leaders have often been in a strategic position to influence or shape it. In addition, men of intelligence and foresight who understand the probable effects of an unfortunate policy or the misconceptions on which it is based can anticipate the ultimate revulsion of public feeling and act accordingly. Voters, it should be remembered, do not always show great tolerance for the Congressman who excuses his own past mistakes with the plea that most of the electorate, at the time, shared his way of thinking.

Although the argument concerning the destruction of leadership is usually made with the legislator in mind, it actually has somewhat more factual strength in the case of the policy-making administrator. Surveys indicate that he is more likely to pay attention to the results of the polls, and he is also more likely to have expert or specialized personal knowledge

[11] The opposite assumption is the basis for the *New York Times'* frequently quoted criticism of the polls, November 13, 1936, p. 22.

as an alternative basis for decision.[12] There is a possibility, at least, that his interest in the polls may indicate a tendency to subordinate his own well-informed judgment to the opinion of the electorate; and there is a further possibility that he may become so dependent upon it that he will take no action at all when that opinion is confused or divided or simply non-existent.

On the other hand, the administrator is, if anything, subject to even greater and more numerous pressures than is the Congressman. For him, therefore, the polls may be even more important as a basis for resisting minority pressures in the public interest. Moreover, like the legislator, he has considerable power to influence public opinion, although his methods are somewhat different; and a precise knowledge of what that opinion is can be an important help in enlightening or changing it.

The factual basis, or lack of basis, for the argument that the polls destroy leadership is less important, however, than two of the argument's theoretical implications.

The first of these is that government officials, whether legislators or administrators, constitute something of an expert body, possessing unusual intelligence, information, and skill, and that to this body the voter, because of his personal inadequacy, should delegate his power.

This argument, however, proves too much. If expertness is to be the criterion for the right to participate in government, the ordinary Congressman would himself have difficulty in qualifying.[13] Even the policy-making administrator, in an age of increasingly voluminous and technical legislation, is likely to be an expert only in the most attenuated sense of the term.[14] To be sure, both he and the legislator must make use of the knowledge and experience of the expert, especially in determining the technical means to achieve broader and predetermined objectives. But when it comes to determining the objectives themselves—and it is with objectives rather than with means that the polls are primarily concerned— the democratic theorist who would free leaders from the restraint of a less well-informed public opinion is, consciously or unconsciously, on the road to what, since the days of Plato, has been the radically undemocratic position of urging rule by some elite.

The second theoretical implication is the even stranger one that ignorance of what the people want and feel is a positive advantage in a

[12] Kriesberg, *op. cit.* The polls, it should be noted, are generally concerned with broader matters of policy rather than with the technical matters in regard to which the expert has the greatest competence.

[13] John Dewey, *The Public and Its Problems* (New York, 1927), p. 124; Herman Finer, *The Theory and Practice of Modern Government* (New York, 1934), pp. 100-101.

[14] It is difficult to make a simple generalization on this subject because of the great variety of levels and types of administrative activity. But the quality of mind of the policy-making administrator is fundamentally different from that of the true expert, whose field of competence is necessarily quite restricted.

democracy. Yet few defenses of democracy have been more persuasive than the one which insists that democracy alone provides the government with adequate information about the desires and attitudes of the people and that, even if these prove to be ignorant or irrational, it is only on the basis of such information that a government can act intelligently. Legislation cannot be separated from the practical problem of administration and enforcement; and it is of fundamental importance, in framing and administering laws with intelligence, to understand, as one of the vital factors in the situation, the state of public feeling.[15] This is not to say that opinion is the only factor to be considered. It is saying that it is an essential element in the rational analysis of any political situation. People will not refrain from having opinions and acting upon them simply because they are not asked what they are. Yet statesmen, whether legislators or administrators, are unlikely to have direct personal knowledge of these feelings; and the weaknesses of elections, the press, and other methods of identifying them have been obvious for decades. Here, therefore, if anywhere, the polls, far from being a menace to democracy, give substance and meaning to what has always, in theory, been one of its outstanding advantages.[16]

In short, so far as this first set of criticisms is concerned, the polls are neither, in fact, so destructive of leadership and courage as critics suggest nor, in theory, so incompatible with the traditional meaning of democracy. On the contrary, the unstated assumptions of the critics tend logically to a conclusion which is itself basically undemocratic.

A second set of charges is remarkable for the way in which it parallels Hamilton's way of thinking for purposes which are quite un-Hamiltonian. Its authors agree that the intelligence and judgment of the people is to be distrusted—not because of their radicalism, however, but because of their conservatism and complacency. Far from being a source of turbulence and unrest and a menace to private property and traditional ways of doing things, the people are so conventional and so contented with things as they are that they constitute a formidable brake upon progress, slow to see the need for drastic social changes and slow to take the necessary steps, always doing too little and always doing it too late. Public opinion polls, by giving publicity to these attitudes, increase their force. In addition, the attention and deference paid them intensify both the complacency of the people and their confidence in their own mystical rightness. What the people need, however, is to develop some realization of their own short-

15 Ernest Barker, *Reflections on Government* (London, 1942), pp. 74-75, 199, 230; John Dewey, *op cit.*, pp. 206-208; George Gallup and Saul Forbes Rae, *The Pulse of Democracy* (New York, 1940), p. 265; A. D. Lindsay, *op. cit.*, pp. 144, 269-270, 274.
16 The use already made of the polls by such governmental agencies as the Department of Agriculture indicates their value in making this theoretical advantage of democracy into a real one. See Friedrich, *op. cit.*, pp. 117, 217-221.

comings and some willingness to leave to the expert those matters of which he alone can judge.[17]

Here, as in the case of the first set of criticisms, it would be difficult to prove that the people are actually more conservative than their representatives. Some observers, in fact, contend that the polls have repeatedly shown the people to be far readier than Congress to accept progressive ideas.[18] But even if the people proved, as a regular matter, to be a hindrance to progress, certain theoretical difficulties would remain. It is undoubtedly true that the process of modern government is too technical and complex to be directed in detail by the ordinary citizen and that the skill and knowledge of the expert must be tapped in a responsible fashion. Yet this argument is too easily confused with the very different argument that the "responsible" expert must be given the power to introduce, according to his own judgment, drastic social changes. There is, to begin with, a certain lack of logic in an argument which speaks of ultimate responsibility to the public while maintaining that "trained intelligence" must none the less be free to introduce the drastic changes which the uninformed public is not prepared to accept. And the more one tries to avoid this dilemma by limiting responsibility to the voter in favor of government by disinterested, wise, and public-spirited elite, the more the criticism becomes one, not of the polls as a hindrance to the operation of democracy, but of democracy as a hindrance to progress.

The defense of democracy, which is as old as Aristotle, does not need to be elaborated here.[19] But it is essential to point out, as Plato himself came to recognize, that no government, however well intentioned, can force a community to move in directions in which it does not want to move, or to move much more rapidly than it would otherwise move, without resorting to instruments of force and tyranny which are incompatible with both the spirit and the practice of democracy.[20]

The third, and by far the most valid, criticism which can be made of the polls is that they represent a fundamental misconception of the nature of democracy. Bryce's picture of a society in which the will of the majority of the citizens would be ascertainable at all times is neither a very profound nor a very realistic picture of democratic society. Democracy is not simply the ascertaining and the applying of a "will of the people"—a somewhat mystical entity existing in and of itself, independent, unified, and complete.[21]

[17] Robert S. Lynd, "Democracy in Reverse," *Public Opinion Quarterly*, Vol. 4, pp. 218-220 (June, 1940). See also Lindsay, *op. cit.*, p. 234.

[18] William A. Lydgate, *What America Thinks* (New York, 1944), pp. 2-8.

[19] For a further discussion of this subject, see Friedrich, *op. cit.*, pp. 41, 217-218, 220-221; John D. Lewis, *op. cit.*; Lindsay, *op. cit.*, pp. 268-277.

[20] Dewey, *op. cit.*, p. 208; Dickinson, *op. cit.*, pp. 301-304; Laski, *op. cit.*, p. 84; John Stuart Mill, *Considerations on Representative Government* (New York, 1862), pp. 55-80.

[21] Dickinson, *op. cit.*, pp. 288-289; John D. Lewis, *op. cit.*, p. 471.

It is the whole long process by which the people and their agents inform themselves, discuss, make compromises, and finally arrive at a decision.[22]

The people are not the only element in this process, and they are not necessarily the agent which is best suited to each part of the task. In general, the executive and the administrative services are best fitted to see policy as a whole and to prepare a coherent program as well as to handle the technical details of legislation. The legislature provides a forum in which the different interests within the country can confront one another in a regularized way, as the people cannot, and acquire something of the mutual understanding and comprehensive outlook which is essential for the satisfactory adjustment of interests. The people themselves, finally, can express better than any other agency what it is they need and want.

None of these functions, it is true, belongs exclusively to any one agency, nor can any be separated rigidly from the others. The process of discussion and adjustment is a continuous one, carried on on all levels. There is a constant interweaving and interpenetration of talk and action subject to no precise demarcation but in which it is none the less essential that each agency refrain from functions which are beyond its competence.[23] In this process the operation of the polls may be positively harmful, not in interfering with "government by experts" as more frequently charged, but in emphasizing the content of the opinion rather than the way in which it is formed and in focusing attention on the divergency of opinion rather than upon the process of adjusting and integrating it.

To say this is not to urge a restriction on popular participation but to emphasize its real nature and function. Popular participation in government is thin and meaningless if it is nothing more than the registering of an opinion. It becomes meaningful to the extent that the opinion is itself the product of information, discussion, and practical political action. There is something not only pathetic but indicative of a basic weakness in the polls' conception of democracy in the stories of those who tell interviewers they could give a "better answer" to the questions if only they had time to read up a bit or think things over. It is precisely this reading up and thinking over which are the essence of political participation and which make politics an educational experience, developing the character and capacity of the citizens.[24]

The polls, however, except as their publication tends to stimulate

22 Barker, *op. cit.*, pp. 36, 67; C. Delisle Burns, *Democracy* (London, 1929), p. 90; Dickinson, *op. cit.*, pp. 291-292; Friedrich, *Constitutional Government and Democracy* (Boston, 1941), p. 255; Lindsay, *The Essentials of Democracy* (Philadelphia, 1929).

23 Barker, *op. cit.*, pp. 43-44; Dickinson, *op. cit.*, p. 301; Finer, *op. cit.*, pp. 99-101, 369; Friedrich, *Constitutional Government*, pp. 255, 415; John D. Lewis, *op. cit.*, pp. 469-470; Merriam, *op. cit.*, pp. 120-121; Mill, *op. cit.*, pp. 115-116.

24 To some, this is the greatest justification of democracy. Burns, *op. cit.*, pp. 7, 71-72, 88-89; Coker, *op. cit.*, p. 294; Dewey, *op. cit.*, pp. 206-208; Mill, *op. cit.*, pp. 69-80, 170; Alexis de Tocqueville, *Democracy in America* (New York, 1838), p. 232.

political interest, play almost no part in this process. They make it possible for the people to express their attitude toward specific proposals and even to indicate the intensity of their feeling on the subject; and they can distinguish the attitudes of different social and economic groups from one another. But they provide no mechanism on the popular level for promoting discussion, for reconciling and adjusting conflicting sectional, class, or group interests, or for working out a coherent and comprehensive legislative program.

In fact, far less perfect instruments for discovering the "will" of the voters are often much more effective in arousing popular participation. The initiative and the referendum, for all their weaknesses, stir opponents and advocates of measures to unusual activity and stimulate a large proportion of the voters, rather than a small selected sample, to consider and discuss the issues.[25] Similarly, the privately-conducted British Peace Ballot proved to be an educational experience for the entire British people.[26] Even the much maligned *Literary Digest* Poll performed a greater service in arousing thought and discussion than did its more accurate competitors.

In short, the polls are not concerned with, and provide no remedy for, the gravest weaknesses in the democratic process. If one thinks of democracy in practical terms of discussion and political activity rather than of a disembodied "will," the great need is to get rid of the obstacles to popular education, information, debate, judgment, and enforcement of responsibility. To do this, there must be a multiple effort directed against a multiplicity of evils. To mention only a few of these, the political education in most of our schools, handicapped as they are by conventional schoolboards and the fear of controversy, is wretchedly inadequate. In too many cities the sources of information are insufficient, the news itself distorted, and the free competition of ideas seriously restricted.[27] In general, our facilities for discussion—clubs, unions, pressure organizations, forums, round-tables, and the radio—provide no adequate successor to the town meeting in the sense of active and responsible personal participation.[28] More fundamentally, the

[25] Edwin A. Cottrell, "Twenty-Five Years of Direct Legislation in California," *Public Opinion Quarterly*, Vol. 3, pp. 30-45 (January, 1939). For a different opinion, see Waldo Schumacher, "Thirty Years of People's Rule in Oregon," *Political Science Quarterly*, Vol. 47, pp. 242-258 (June, 1932).

[26] Dame Adelaide Livingstone, *The Peace Ballot* (London, 1935), pp. 19-29.

[27] The development of the one-newspaper pattern is particularly unfortunate. Oswald Garrison Villard, *The Disappearing Daily* (New York, 1944), pp. 3, 5, 10-12. See also Morris L. Ernst, *The First Freedom* (New York, 1946), xii and *passim* for a survey not only of the newspaper but of book publishing, the radio, and the motion picture.

[28] On the need for new devices for discussion, see Harwood L. Childs, *An Introduction to Public Opinion* (New York, 1940), p. 137; Coker, *op. cit.*, p. 373; Harold D. Lasswell, *Democracy through Public Opinion* (Menasha, Wisconsin, 1941), pp. 80-95; Merriam, *On the Agenda of Democracy* (Cambridge, 1941), pp. 21-22; Joseph R. Starr, "Political Parties and Public Opinion," *Public Opinion Quarterly*, Vol. 3, pp. 436-448

undemocratic character of much of our economic and social life is a real hindrance to the growth of political democracy.

Moreover, even if our political education were magnificent, the channels of information completely clear, the facilities for discussion abundant, and the spirit of democracy universal, the obscurity and confusion in our political system, resulting from its checks and balances and its lack of party discipline, would make it almost impossible for the ordinary voter to understand what is going on, to pass judgment intelligently, and to place responsibility. Yet any government in which the people are to share must at a minimum be comprehensible. Obscurity and anonymity kill democracy. These defects, however, are present in our government, and about them the polls can do very little.

The chief advantage of the polls is that, in an age of increasing strain upon traditional democratic procedures, they have made a constructive technical contribution by reflecting sensitively and flexibly the currents of public feelings, by making this information available to political leaders in a way which is neither rigid nor mandatory, and by testing the claims of special interests to represent the desires of the people as a whole. These are services performed by no other agency, and they should not be underestimated.

But if, in a democracy, the health of the community depends upon the personal, active, and continuous political participation of the body of its citizens, this contribution is a limited and even a minor one. Even when used with the greatest accuracy and intelligence, the polls cannot achieve any fundamental improvement until our political system itself is simplified, until the lines of responsibility are clarified, and until devices are discovered for increasing the direct participation of the people, not simply in the registration of their aims, but in the deliberative procedure which is the real heart of democracy.

(July, 1939). For a more optimistic picture, see Friedlich, *Constitutional Government*, p. 546.

4

THEORY OF COMMUNICATION

*T*heoretical analysis of the communication process emerges in some form whenever social scientists seek to describe society in its broad dimensions. The crucial pervasiveness of communication activities, evident in the functioning of the simplest and most primitive social organizations, is particularly apparent in the industrialized, urbanized, secularized mass society.

Contributions to a theory of communication have been made by workers in various fields—philosophy, sociology, anthropology, political science, psychology—and any unified theory (or theories) developing out of the current emphasis upon empirical work will have to take account of varied analyses. In the conceptualization of the communication process, one theoretical position (illustrated here in the selection from Cooley) sees the process as the binding force in organized society. This overall view of the social function of communication is followed by a selection from Mead dealing in detail with the specific psychological mechanisms at the basis of the individual's capacity to communicate with himself as well as with others. The articles by Sapir and Park are further examples of theoretical positions concerned with the integrating and disintegrating effects of communication upon organized group life.

Somewhat in contrast to these writers are the selections from Lasswell and Hovland which typify efforts to delimit and define the theoretical aspects of communication into formulations which can be subjected to empirical research. In developing his theories of political influence, Lasswell has constructed a political formulation of the communication process which is abbreviated in his widely known formula, "Who says what to whom, with what effect?" His selection presents a set of categories for analyzing the communication process which has had wide influence on recent research. The application of the learning theory of modern psychology to the problem of communication effects is illustrated in the Hovland article.

Charles H. Cooley

THE SIGNIFICANCE OF COMMUNICATION

By Communication is here meant the mechanism through which human relations exist and develop—all the symbols of the mind, together with the means of conveying them through space and preserving them in time. It includes the expression of the face, attitude and gesture, the tones of the voice, words, writing, printing, railways, telegraphs, telephones, and whatever else may be the latest achievement in the conquest of space and time. All these taken together, in the intricacy of their actual combination, make up an organic whole corresponding to the organic whole of human thought; and everything in the way of mental growth has an external existence therein. The more closely we consider this mechanism the more intimate will appear its relation to the inner life of mankind, and nothing will more help us to understand the latter than such consideration.

There is no sharp line between the means of communication and the rest of the external world. In a sense all objects and actions are symbols of the mind, and nearly anything may be used as a sign—as I may signify the moon or a squirrel to a child by merely pointing at it, or by imitating with the voice the chatter of the one or drawing an outline of the other. But there is also, almost from the first, a conventional development of communication, springing out of spontaneous signs but soon losing evident connection with them, a system of standard symbols existing for the mere purpose of conveying thought; and it is this we have chiefly to consider.

Without communication the mind does not develop a true human nature, but remains in an abnormal and nondescript state neither human nor properly brutal. This is movingly illustrated by the case of Helen Keller, who, as all the world knows, was cut off at *eighteen months* from the cheerful ways of men by the loss of sight and hearing; and did not renew the connection until she was nearly *seven years* old. Although her mind was

Reprinted from *Social Organization* (1909), pp. 61-65; 80-103, by permission of the publisher. (Copyright, 1909, by Charles Scribner's Sons; 1937, by Elsie Jones Cooley.)

not wholly isolated during this period, since she retained the use of a considerable number of signs learned during infancy, yet her impulses were crude and uncontrolled, and her thought so unconnected that she afterward remembered almost nothing that occurred before the awakening which took place toward the close of her seventh year.

The story of that awakening, as told by her teacher, gives as vivid a picture as we need have of the significance to the individual mind of the general fact and idea of communication. For weeks Miss Sullivan had been spelling words into her hand which Helen had repeated and associated with objects; but she had not yet grasped the idea of language in general, the fact that everything had a name, and that through names she could share her own experiences with others, and learn theirs—the idea that there is *fellowship in thought*. This came quite suddenly.

"This morning," writes her teacher, "while she was washing, she wanted to know the name for water. . . . I spelled w-a-t-e-r and thought no more about it until after breakfast. Then it occurred to me that with the help of this new word I might succeed in straightening out the mug-milk difficulty [a confusion of ideas previously discussed]. We went out into the pump-house and I made Helen hold her mug under the pump while I pumped. As the cold water gushed forth filling the mug I spelled w-a-t-e-r in Helen's free hand. The word coming so close upon the sensation of cold water rushing over her hand seemed to startle her. She dropped the mug and stood as one transfixed. A new light came into her face. She spelled water several times. Then she dropped on the ground and asked for its name, and pointed to the pump and the trellis, and suddenly turning round she asked for my name. I spelled 'teacher.' Just then the nurse brought Helen's little sister into the pump-house, and Helen spelled 'baby' and pointed to the nurse. All the way back to the house she was highly excited, and learned the name of every object she touched, so that in a few hours she had added thirty new words to her vocabulary."

The following day Miss Sullivan writes, "Helen got up this morning like a radiant fairy. She has flitted from object to object, asking the name of everything and kissing me for very gladness." And four days later, "Everything must have a name now. . . . She drops the signs and pantomine she used before, so soon as she has words to supply their place, and the acquirement of a new word affords her the liveliest pleasure. And we notice that her face grows more expressive each day."[1]

This experience is a type of what happens more gradually to all of us: it is through communication that we get our higher development. The faces and conversation of our associates; books, letters, travel, arts, and the like, by awakening thought and feeling and guiding them in certain channels, supply the stimulus and framework for all our growth.

In the same way, if we take a larger view and consider the life of a social group, we see that communication, including its organization into literature, art, and institutions, is truly the outside or visible structure of thought, as much cause as effect of the inside or conscious life of men.

[1] *The Story of My Life*, pp. 316, 317.

All is one growth: the symbols, the traditions, the institutions are projected from the mind, to be sure, but in the very instant of their projection, and thereafter, they react upon it, and in a sense control it, stimulating, developing, and fixing certain thoughts at the expense of others to which no awakening suggestion comes. By the aid of this structure the individual is a member not only of a family, a class, and a state, but of a larger whole reaching back to prehistoric men whose thought has gone to build it up. In this whole he lives as in an element, drawing from it the materials of his growth and adding to it whatever constructive thought he may express.

Thus the system of communication is a tool, a progressive invention, whose improvements react upon mankind and alter the life of every individual and institution. A study of these improvements is one of the best ways by which to approach an understanding of the mental and social changes that are bound up with them; because it gives a tangible framework for our ideas—just as one who wished to grasp the organic character of industry and commerce might well begin with a study of the railway system and of the amount and kind of commodities it carries, proceeding thence to the more abstract transactions of finance.

And when we come to the modern era, especially, we can understand nothing rightly unless we perceive the manner in which the revolution in communication has made a new world for us. So in the pages that follow I shall aim to show what the growth of intercourse implies in the way of social development, inquiring particularly into the effect of recent changes.

Modern Communication: Enlargement and Animation

The changes that have taken place since the beginning of the nineteenth century are such as to constitute a new epoch in communication, and in the whole system of society. They deserve, therefore, careful consideration, not so much in their mechanical aspect, which is familiar to every one, as in their operation upon the larger mind.

If one were to analyze the mechanism of intercourse, he might, perhaps, distinguish four factors that mainly contribute to its efficiency, namely:

Expressiveness, or the range of ideas and feelings it is competent to carry.

Permanence of record, or the overcoming of time.

Swiftness, or the overcoming of space.

Diffusion, or access to all classes of men.

Now while gains have no doubt been made in expressiveness, as in the enlargement of our vocabulary to embrace the ideas of modern science; and even in permanence of record, for scientific and other special purposes; yet certainly the long steps of recent times have been made in the direction of swiftness and diffusion. For most purposes our speech is no better than in the age of Elizabeth, if so good; but what facility we have gained in the application of it! The cheapening of printing, permitting an inundation of popular books, magazines and newspapers, has been supplemented by the rise of the modern postal system and the conquest of distance by railroads, telegraphs and telephones. And along with these extensions of the spoken or written word have come new arts of reproduction, such as photography, photo-engraving, phonography and the like—of greater social import than we realize—by which new kinds of impression from the visible or audible world may be fixed and disseminated.

It is not too much to say that these changes are the basis, from a mechanical standpoint, of nearly everything that is characteristic in the psychology of modern life. In a general way they mean the expansion of human nature, that is to say, of its power to express itself in social wholes. They make it possible for society to be organized more and more on the higher faculties of man, on intelligence and sympathy, rather than on authority, caste, and routine. They mean freedom, outlook, indefinite possibility. The public consciousness, instead of being confined as regards its more active phases to local groups, extends by even steps with that give-and-take of suggestions that the new intercourse makes possible, until wide nations, and finally the world itself, may be included in one lively mental whole.

The general character of this change is well expressed by the two words *enlargement* and *animation*. Social contacts are extended in space and quickened in time, and in the same degree the mental unity they imply becomes wider and more alert. The individual is broadened by coming into relation with a larger and more various life, and he is kept stirred up, sometimes to excess, by the multitude of changing suggestions which this life brings to him.

From whatever point of view we study modern society to compare it with the past or to forecast the future, we ought to keep at least a sub-consciousness of this radical change in mechanism, without allowing for which nothing else can be understood.

In the United States, for instance, at the close of the eighteenth century, public consciousness of any active kind was confined to small localities. Travel was slow, uncomfortable and costly, and people undertaking a considerable journey often made their wills beforehand. The newspapers, appearing weekly in the larger towns, were entirely lacking in what we should call news; and the number of letters sent during a year in all the thirteen states was much less than that now handled by the New York office in a single day. People are far more alive to-day to what is going on in China, if it happens to interest them, than they were then to events a hundred miles away. The isolation of even large towns from the rest of the world, and the consequent introversion of men's minds upon local concerns, was something we can hardly conceive. In the country "the environment of the farm was the neighborhood; the environment of the village was the encircling farms and the local tradition; . . . few conventions assembled for discussion and common action; educational centres did not radiate the shock of a new intellectual life to every hamlet; federations and unions did not bind men, near and remote, into that fellowship that makes one composite type of many human sorts. It was an age of sects, intolerant from lack of acquaintance." [2]

The change to the present régime of railroads, telegraphs, daily papers, telephones and the rest has involved a revolution in every phase of life; in commerce, in politics, in education, even in mere sociability and gossip —this revolution always consisting in an enlargement and quickening of the kind of life in question.

Probably there is nothing in this new mechanism quite so pervasive and characteristic as the daily newspaper, which is as vehemently praised as it is abused, and in both cases with good reason. What a strange practice it is, when you think of it, that a man should sit down to his breakfast table and, instead of conversing with his wife, and children, hold before his face a sort of screen on which is inscribed a world-wide gossip!

The essential function of the newspaper is, of course, to serve as a bulletin of important news and a medium for the interchange of ideas, through the printing of interviews, letters, speeches and editorial comment. In this way it is indispensable to the organization of the public mind.

The bulk of its matter, however, is best described by the phase organized gossip. This sort of intercourse that people formerly carried on at cross-road stores or over the back fence, has now attained the dignity of print and an imposing system. That we absorb a flood of this does not necessarily mean that our minds are degenerate, but merely that we are gratifying an old appetite in a new way. Henry James speaks with a severity natural to literary sensibility of "the ubiquitous newspaper face, with its mere monstrosity and deformity of feature, and the vast open mouth, adjusted as to the chatter of Bedlam, that flings the flood-gates of vulgarity farther back [in America] than anywhere else on earth." [3] But after all is it any more vulgar than the older kind of gossip? No doubt it seems worse for venturing to share with literature the use of the printed word.

That the bulk of the contents of the newspaper is of the nature of gossip may be seen by noting three traits which together seem to make a fair definition of that word. It is copious, designed to occupy, without exerting, the mind. It consists mostly of personalities and appeals to superficial emotion. It is untrustworthy—except upon a few matters of moment which the public are likely to follow up and verify. These traits any one

[2] W. L. Anderson, *The Country Town*, pp. 209, 210.
[3] "The Manners of American Women," *Harper's Bazar*, May, 1907.

who is curious may substantiate by a study of his own morning journal.

There is a better and a worse side to this enlargement of gossip. On the former we may reckon the fact that it promotes a widespread sociability and sense of community; we know that people all over the country are laughing at the same jokes or thrilling with the same mild excitement over the foot-ball game, and we absorb a conviction that they are good fellows much like ourselves. It also tends powerfully, through the fear of publicity, to enforce a popular, somewhat vulgar, but sound and human standard of morality. On the other hand it fosters superficiality and commonplace in every sphere of thought and feeling, and is, of course, the antithesis of literature and of all high or fine spiritual achievement. It stands for diffusion as opposed to distinction.

In politics communication makes possible public opinion, which, when organized, is democracy. The whole growth of this, and of the popular education and enlightenment that go with it, is immediately dependent upon the telegraph, the newspaper and the fast mail, for there can be no popular mind upon questions of the day, over wide areas, except as the people are promptly informed of such questions and are enabled to exchange views regarding them.

Our government, under the Constitution, was not originally a democracy, and was not intended to be so by the men that framed it. It was expected to be a representative republic, the people choosing men of character and wisdom, who would proceed to the capital, inform themselves there upon current questions, and deliberate and decide regarding them. That the people might think and act more directly was not foreseen. The Constitution is not democratic in spirit, and, as Mr. Bryce has noted,[4] might under different conditions have become the basis of an aristocratic system.

That any system could have held even the original thirteen states in firm union without the advent of modern communication is very doubtful. Political philosophy, from Plato to Montesquieu, had taught that free states must be small, and Frederick the Great is said to have ridiculed the idea of one extending from Maine to Georgia. "A large empire," says Montesquieu, "supposes a despotic authority in the person who governs. It is necessary that the quickness of the prince's resolutions should supply the distance of the places they are sent to."[5]

Democracy has arisen here, as it seems to be arising everywhere in the civilized world, not, chiefly, because of changes in the formal constitution, but as the outcome of conditions which make it natural for the people to have and to express a consciousness regarding questions of the day. It is said by those who know China that while that country was at war with

---

[4] *The American Commonwealth,* chap. 26.
[5] *The Spirit of Laws,* book viii, chap. 19.

Japan the majority of the Chinese were unaware that a war was in progress. Such ignorance makes the sway of public opinion impossible; and, conversely, it seems likely that no state, having a vigorous people, can long escape that sway except by repressing the interchange of thought. When the people have information and discussion they will have a will, and this must sooner or later get hold of the institutions of society.

One is often impressed with the thought that there ought to be some wider name for the modern movement than democracy, some name which should more distinctly suggest the enlargement and quickening of the general mind, of which the formal rule of the people is only one among many manifestations. The current of new life that is sweeping with augmenting force through the older structures of society, now carrying them away, now leaving them outwardly undisturbed, has no adequate name.

Popular education is an inseparable part of all this: the individual must have at least those arts of reading and writing without which he can hardly be a vital member of the new organism. And that further development of education, rapidly becoming a conscious aim of modern society, which strives to give to every person a special training in preparation for whatever function he may have aptitude for, is also a phase of the freer and more flexible organization of mental energy. The same enlargement runs through all life, including fashion and other trivial or fugitive kinds of intercourse. And the widest phase of all, upon whose momentousness I need not dwell, is that rise of an international consciousness, in literature, in science and, finally, in politics, which holds out a trustworthy promise of the indefinite enlargement of justice and amity.

This unification of life by a freer course of thought is not only contemporaneous, overcoming space, but also historical, bringing the past into the present, and making every notable achievement of the race a possible factor in its current life—as when, by skilful reproduction the work of a mediæval painter is brought home to people dwelling five hundred years later on the other side of the globe. Our time is one of "large discourse, looking before and after."

There are remarkable possibilities in this diffusive vigor. Never, certainly, were great masses of men so rapidly rising to higher levels as now. There are the same facilities for disseminating improvement in mind and manners as in material devices; and the new communication has spread like morning light over the world, awakening, enlightening, enlarging, and filling with expectation. Human nature desires the good, when it once perceives it, and in all that is easily understood and imitated great headway is making.

Nor is there, as I shall try to show later, any good reason to think that the conditions are permanently unfavorable to the rise of special and select types of excellence. The same facility of communication which animates millions with the emulation of common models, also makes it easy for more discriminating minds to unite in small groups. The general fact is that human nature is set free; in time it will no doubt justify its freedom.

The enlargement affects not only thought but feeling, favoring the growth of a sense of common humanity, of moral unity, between nations, races and classes. Among members of a communicating whole feeling may not always be friendly, but it must be, in a sense, sympathetic, involving some consciousness of the other's point of view. Even the animosities of modern nations are of a human and imaginative sort, not the blind animal hostility of a more primitive age. They are resentments, and resentment, as Charles Lamb says, is of the family of love.

The relations between persons or communities that are without mutual understanding are necessarily on a low plane. There may be indifference, or a blind anger due to interference or there may be a good-natured tolerance; but there is no consciousness of a common nature to warm up the kindly sentiments. A really human fellow-feeling was anciently confined within the tribe, men outside not being felt as members of a common whole. The alien was commonly treated as a more or less useful or dangerous animal—destroyed, despoiled or enslaved. Even in these days we care little about people whose life is not brought home to us by some kind of sympathetic contact. We may read statistics of the miserable life of the Italians and Jews in New York and Chicago; of bad housing, sweatshops and tuberculosis; but we care little more about them than we do about the sufferers from the Black Death, unless their life is realized to us in some human way, either by personal contact, or by pictures and imaginative description.

And we are getting this at the present time. The resources of modern communication are used in stimulating and gratifying our interest in every phase of human life. Russians, Japanese, Filipinos, fishermen, miners, millionaires, criminals, tramps and opium-eaters are brought home to us. The press well understands that nothing human is alien to us if it is only made comprehensible.

With a mind enlarged and supplied by such training, the man of to-day inclines to look for a common nature everywhere, and to demand that the whole world shall be brought under the sway of common principles of kindness and justice. He wants to see international strife allayed—in such a way, however, as not to prevent the expansion of capable races and the survival of better types; he wishes the friction of classes reduced and each interest fairly treated—but without checking individuality and enterprise. There was never so general an eagerness that righteousness should prevail; the chief matter of dispute is upon the principles under which it may be established.

The work of communication in enlarging human nature is partly immediate, through facilitating contact, but even more it is indirect, through favoring the increase of intelligence, the decline of mechanical and arbitrary forms of organization, and the rise of a more humane type of society. History may be regarded as a record of the struggle of man to realize his aspirations through organization; and the new communication is an efficient tool for this purpose. Assuming that the human heart and conscience, restricted only by the difficulties of organization, is the arbiter of what institutions are to become, we may expect the facility of intercourse to be the starting-point of an era of moral progress.

George Herbert Mead

THOUGHT, COMMUNICATION, AND
THE SIGNIFICANT SYMBOL

We have contended that there is no particular faculty of imitation in the sense that the sound or the sight of another's response is itself a stimulus to carry out the same reaction, but rather that if there is already present in the individual an action like the action of another, then there is a situation which makes imitation possible. What is necessary now to carry through that imitation is that the conduct and the gesture of the individual which calls out a response in the other should also tend to call out the same response in himself. In the dog-fight this is not present: the attitude in the one dog does not tend to call out the same attitude in the other. In some respects that actually may occur in the case of two boxers. The man who makes a feint is calling out a certain blow from his opponent, and that act of his own does have that meaning to him, that is, he has in some sense initiated the same act in himself. It does not go clear through, but he has stirred up the centers in his central nervous system which would lead to his making the same blow that his opponent is led to make, so that he calls out in himself, or tends to call out, the same response which he calls out in the other. There you have the basis for so-called imitation. Such is the process which is so widely recognized at present in manners of speech, of dress, and of attitudes.

We are more or less unconsciously seeing ourselves as others see us. We are unconsciously addressing ourselves as others address us; in the same way as the sparrow takes up the note of the canary we pick up the dialects about us. Of course, there must be these particular responses in our own mechanism. We are calling out in the other person something we are calling out in ourselves, so that unconsciously we take over these attitudes. We are unconsciously putting ourselves in the place of others and

Reprinted from *Mind, Self, and Society* (1934), pp. 68-75, by permission of the editor, Charles Morris, and the publisher. (Copyright, 1934, by The University of Chicago Press.)

acting as others act. I want simply to isolate the general mechanism here, because it is of very fundamental importance in the development of what we call self-consciousness and the appearance of the self. We are, especially through the use of the vocal gestures, continually arousing in ourselves those responses which we call out in other persons, so that we are taking the attitudes of the other persons into our own conduct. The critical importance of language in the development of human experience lies in this fact that the stimulus is one that can react upon the speaking individual as it reacts upon the other.

A behaviorist, such as Watson, holds that all of our thinking is vocalization. In thinking we are simply starting to use certain words. That is in a sense true. However, Watson does not take into account all that is involved here, namely, that these stimuli are the essential elements in elaborate social processes and carry with them the value of those social processes. The vocal process as such has this great importance, and it is fair to assume that the vocal process, together with the intelligence and thought that go with it, is not simply a playing of particular vocal elements against each other. Such a view neglects the social context of language.[1]

The importance, then, of the vocal stimulus lies in this fact that the individual can hear what he says and in hearing what he says is tending to respond as the other person responds. When we speak now of this response on the part of the individual to the others we come back to the situation of asking some person to do something. We ordinarily express that by saying that one knows what he is asking you to do. Take the illustration of asking someone to do something, and then doing it one's self. Perhaps the person addressed does not hear you or acts slowly, and then you carry the action out yourself. You find in yourself, in this way, the same tendency which you are asking the other individual to carry out. Your request stirred up in you that same response which you stirred up in the other individual. How difficult it is to show someone else how to do something which you know how to do yourself! The slowness of the response makes it hard to restrain yourself from doing what you are teaching.

[1] Gestures, if carried back to the matrix from which they spring, are always found to inhere in or involve a larger social act of which they are phases. In dealing with communication we have first to recognize its earliest origins in the unconscious conversation of gestures. Conscious communication—conscious conversation of gestures—arises when gestures become signs, that is, when they come to carry for the individuals making them and the individuals responding to them, definite meanings or significations in terms of the subsequent behavior of the individuals making them; so that, by serving as prior indications, to the individuals responding to them, of the subsequent behavior of the individuals making them, they make possible the mutual adjustment of the various individual components of the social act to one another, and also, by calling forth in the individuals making them the same responses implicitly that they call forth explicitly in the individuals to whom they are made, they render possible the rise of self-consciousness in connection with this mutual adjustment.

You have aroused the same response in yourself as you arouse in the other individual.

In seeking for an explanation of this, we ordinarily assume a certain group of centers in the nervous system which are connected with each other, and which express themselves in the action. If we try to find in a central nervous system something that answers to our word "chair," what we should find would be presumably simply an organization of a whole group of possible reactions so connected that if one starts in one direction one will carry out one process, if in another direction one will carry out another process. The chair is primarily what one sits down in. It is a physical object at a distance. One may move toward an object at a distance and then enter upon the process of sitting down when one reaches it. There is a stimulus which excites certain paths which cause the individual to go toward that object and to sit down. Those centers are in some degree physical. There is, it is to be noted, an influence of the later act on the earlier act. The later process which is to go on has already been initiated and that later process has its influence on the earlier process (the one that takes place before this process, already initiated, can be completed). Now, such an organization of a great group of nervous elements as will lead to conduct with reference to the objects about us is what one would find in the central nervous system answering to what we call an object. The complications are very great, but the central nervous system has an almost infinite number of elements in it, and they can be organized not only in spatial connection with each other, but also from a temporal standpoint. In virtue of this last fact, our conduct is made up of a series of steps which follow each other, and the later steps may be already started and influence the earlier ones. The thing we are going to do is playing back on what we are doing now. That organization in the neural elements in reference to what we call a physical object would be what we call a conceptual object stated in terms of the central nervous system.

In rough fashion it is the initiation of such a set of organized sets of responses that answers to what we call the idea or concept of a thing. If one asked what the idea of a dog is, and tried to find that idea in the central nervous system, one would find a whole group of responses which are more or less connected together by definite paths so that when one uses the term "dog" he does tend to call out this group of responses. A dog is a possible playmate, a possible enemy, one's own property or somebody else's. There is a whole series of possible responses. There are certain types of these responses which are in all of us, and there are others which vary with the individuals, but there is always an organization of the responses which can be called out by the term "dog." So if one is speaking of a dog to another person he is arousing in himself this set of responses which he is arousing in the other individual.

It is, of course, the relationship of this symbol, this vocal gesture, to such a set of responses in the individual himself as well as in the other that makes of that vocal gesture what I call a significant symbol. A symbol does tend to call out in the individual a group of reactions such as it calls out in the other, but there is something further that is involved in its being a significant symbol: this response within one's self to such a word as "chair," or "dog," is one which is a stimulus to the individual as well as a response. This is what, of course, is involved in what we term the meaning of a thing, or its significance.[2] We often act with reference to objects in what we call an intelligent fashion, although we can act without the meaning of the object being present in our experience. One can start to dress for dinner, as they tell of the absent-minded college professor, and find himself in his pajamas in bed. A certain process of undressing was started and carried out mechanically; he did not recognize the meaning of what he was doing. He intended to go to dinner and found he had gone to bed. The meaning involved in his action was not present. The steps in this case were all intelligent steps which controlled his conduct with reference to later action, but he did not think about what he was doing. The later action was not a stimulus to his response, but just carried itself out when it was once started.

When we speak of the meaning of what we are doing we are making the response itself that we are on the point of carrying out a stimulus to our action. It becomes a stimulus to a later stage of action which is to take place from the point of view of this particular response. In the case of the boxer the blow that he is starting to direct toward his opponent is to call out a certain response which will open up the guard of his opponent so that he can strike. The meaning is a stimulus for the preparation of the real blow he expects to deliver. The response which he calls out in himself (the guarding reaction) is the stimulus to him to strike where an opening is given. This action which he has initiated already in himself thus becomes

---

[2] The inclusion of the matrix or complex of attitudes and responses constituting any given social situation or act, within the experience of any one of the individuals implicated in that situation or act (the inclusion within his experience of his attitudes toward other individuals, of their responses to his attitudes toward them, of their attitudes toward him, and of his responses to these attitudes) in all that an *idea* amounts to; or at any rate is the only basis for its occurrence or existence "in the mind" of the given individual.

In the case of the unconscious conversation of gestures, or in the case of the process of communication carried on by means of it, none of the individuals participating in it is conscious of the meaning of the conversation—that meaning does not appear in the experience of any one of the separate individuals involved in the conversation or carrying it on; whereas, in the case of the conscious conversation of gestures, or in the case of the process of communication carried on by means of it, each of the individuals participating in it is conscious of the meaning of the conversation, precisely because that meaning does appear in his experience, and because such appearance is what consciousness of that meaning implies.

a stimulus for his later response. He knows what his opponent is going to do, since the guarding movement is one which is already aroused, and becomes a stimulus to strike where the opening is given. The meaning would not have been present in his conduct unless it became a stimulus to strike where the favorable opening appears.

Such is the difference between intelligent conduct on the part of animals and what we call a reflective individual.[3] We say the animal does not think. He does not put himself in a position for which he is responsible; he does not put himself in the place of the other person and say, in effect, "He will act in such a way and I will act in this way." If the individual can act in this way, and the attitude which he calls out in himself can become a stimulus to him for another act, we have meaningful conduct. Where the response of the other person is called out and becomes a stimulus to control his action, then he has the meaning of the other person's act in his own experience. That is the general mechanism of what we term "thought," for in order that thought may exist there must be symbols, vocal gestures generally, which arouse in the individual himself the response which he is calling out in the other, and such that from the point of view of that response he is able to direct his later conduct. It involves not only communication in the sense in which birds and animals communicate with each other, but also an arousal in the individual himself of the response which he is calling out in the other individual, a taking of the rôle of the other, a tendency to act as the other person acts. One participates in the same process the other person is carrying out and controls his action with reference to that participation. It is that which constitutes the meaning of an object, namely, the common response in one's self as well as in the other person, which becomes, in turn, a stimulus to one's self.

If you conceive of the mind as just a sort of conscious substance in which there are certain impressions and states, and hold that one of those states is a universal, then a word becomes purely arbitrary—it is just a symbol.[4] You can then take words and pronounce them backwards, as

---

[3] For the nature of animal conduct see "Concerning Animal Perception," *Psychological Review*, XIV (1907), 383 ff.

[4] Müller attempts to put the values of thought into language; but this attempt is fallacious, because language has those values only as the most effective mechanism of thought merely because it carries the conscious or significant conversation of gestures to its highest and most perfect development. There must be some sort of an implicit attitude (that is, a response which is initiated without being fully carried out) in the organism making the gesture—an attitude which answers to the overt response to the gesture on the part of another individual, and which corresponds to the attitude called forth or aroused in this other organism by the gesture—if thought is to develop in the organism making the gesture. And it is the central nervous system which provides the mechanism for such implicit attitudes or responses.

The identification of language with reason is in one sense an absurdity, but in another sense it is valid. It is valid, namely, in the sense that the process of language brings the total social act into the experience of the given individual as himself involved in the

children do; there seems to be absolute freedom of arrangement and language seems to be an entirely mechanical thing that lies outside of the process of intelligence. If you recognize that language is, however, just a part of a co-operative process, that part which does lead to an adjustment to the response of the other so that the whole activity can go on, then language has only a limited range of arbitrariness. If you are talking to another person you are, perhaps, able to scent the change in his attitude by something that would not strike a third person at all. You may know his mannerism, and that becomes a gesture to you, a part of the response of the individual. There is a certain range possible within the gesture as to what is to serve as the symbol. We may say that a whole set of separate symbols with one meaning are acceptable; but they always are gestures, that is, they are always parts of the act of the individual which reveal what he is going to do to the other person so that when the person utilizes the clue he calls out in himself the attitude of the other. Language is not ever arbitrary in the sense of simply denoting a bare state of consciousness by a word. What particular part of one's act will serve to direct co-operative activity is more or less arbitrary. Different phases of the act may do it. What seems unimportant in itself may be highly important in revealing what the attitude is. In that sense one can speak of the gesture itself as unimportant, but it is of great importance as to what the gesture is going to reveal. This is seen in the difference between the purely intellectual character of the symbol and its emotional character. A poet depends upon the latter; for him language is rich and full of values which we, perhaps, utterly ignore. In trying to express a message in something less than ten words, we merely want to convey a certain meaning, while the poet is dealing with what is really living tissue, the emotional throb in the expression itself. There is, then, a great range in our use of language; but whatever phase of this range is used is a part of a social process, and it is always that part by means of which we affect ourselves as we affect others and mediate the social situation through this understanding of what we are saying. That is fundamental for any language; if it is going to be language one has to understand what he is saying, has to affect himself as he affects others.

act, and thus makes the process of reason possible. But though the process of reason is and must be carried on in terms of the process of language—in terms, that is, of words —it is not simply constituted by the latter.

Edward Sapir

COMMUNICATION

It is obvious that for the building up of society, its units and subdivisions, and the understandings which prevail between its members some processes of communication are needed. While we often speak of society as though it were a static structure defined by tradition, it is, in the more intimate sense, nothing of the kind, but a highly intricate network of partial or complete understandings between the members of organizational units of every degree of size and complexity, ranging from a pair of lovers or a family to a league of nations or that ever increasing portion of humanity which can be reached by the press through all its transnational ramifications. It is only apparently a static sum of social institutions; actually it is being reanimated or creatively reaffirmed from day to day by particular acts of a communicative nature which obtain among individuals participating in it. Thus the Republican party cannot be said to exist as such, but only to the extent that its tradition is being constantly added to and upheld by such simple acts of communication as that John Doe votes the Republican ticket, thereby communicating a certain kind of message, or that a half dozen individuals meet at a certain time and place, formally or informally, in order to communicate ideas to one another and eventually to decide what points of national interest, real or supposed, are to be allowed to come up many months later for discussion in a gathering of members of the party. The Republican party as a historic entity is merely abstracted from thousands upon thousands of such single acts of communication, which have in common certain persistent features of reference. If we extend this example into every conceivable field in which communication has a place we soon realize that every cultural pattern and every single act of social behavior involve communication in either an explicit or an implicit sense.

One may conveniently distinguish between certain fundamental tech-

Reprinted from *Encyclopedia of the Social Sciences,* edited by Edwin R. Seligman, Vol. IV (1931), pp. 78-80, by permission of the publisher. (Copyright, 1931, by the Macmillan Co.)

niques, or primary processes, which are communicative in character and certain secondary techniques which facilitate the process of communication. The distinction is perhaps of no great psychological importance but has a very real historical and sociological significance, inasmuch as the fundamental processes are common to all mankind, while the secondary techniques emerge only at relatively sophisticated levels of civilization. Among the primary communicative processes of society may be mentioned: language; gesture, in its widest sense; the imitation of overt behavior; and a large and ill defined group of implicit processes which grow out of overt behavior and which may be rather vaguely referred to as "social suggestion."

Language is the most explicit type of communicative behavior that we know of. It need not here be defined beyond pointing out that it consists in every case known to us of an absolutely complete referential apparatus of phonetic symbols which have the property of locating every known social referent, including all the recognized data of perception which the society that it serves carries in its tradition. Language is the communicative process par excellence in every known society, and it is exceedingly important to observe that whatever may be the shortcomings of a primitive society judged from the vantage point of civilization its language inevitably forms as sure, complete and potentially creative an apparatus of referential symbolism as the most sophisticated language that we know of. What this means for a theory of communication is that the mechanics of significant understanding between human beings are as sure and complex and rich in overtones in one society as in another, primitive or sophisticated.

Gesture includes much more than the manipulation of the hands and other visible and movable parts of the organism. Intonations of the voice may register attitudes and feelings quite as significantly as the clenched fist, the wave of the hand, the shrugging of the shoulders or the lifting of the eyebrows. The field of gesture interplays constantly with that of language proper, but there are many facts of a psychological and historical order which show that there are subtle yet firm lines of demarcation between them. Thus, to give but one example, the consistent message delivered by language symbolism in the narrow sense, whether by speech or by writing, may flatly contradict the message communicated by the synchronous system of gestures, consisting of movements of the hands and head, intonations of the voice and breathing symbolisms. The former system may be entirely conscious, the latter entirely unconscious. Linguistic, as opposed to gesture, communication tends to be the official and socially accredited one; hence one may intuitively interpret the relatively unconscious symbolisms of gesture as psychologically more significant in a given context than the words actually used. In such cases as these we have a conflict between explicit and implicit communications in the growth of the individual's social experience.

The primary condition for the consolidation of society is the imitation of overt behavior. Such imitation, while not communicative in intent, has always the retroactive value of a communication, for in the process of falling in with the ways of society one in effect acquiesces in the meanings that inhere in these ways. When one learns to go to church, for instance, because other members of the community set the pace for this kind of activity, it is as though a communication had been received and acted upon. It is the function of language to articulate and rationalize the full content of these informal communications in the growth of the individual's social experience.

Even less directly communicative in character than overt behavior and its imitation is "social suggestion" as the sum total of new acts and new meanings that are implicitly made possible by these types of social behavior. Thus, the particular method of revolting against the habit of church going in a given society, while contradictory, on the surface, of the conventional meanings of that society, may nevertheless receive all its social significance from hundreds of existing prior communications that belong to the culture of the group as a whole. The importance of the unformulated and unverbalized communications of society is so great that one who is not intuitively familiar with them is likely to be baffled by the significance of certain kinds of behavior, even if he is thoroughly aware of their external forms and of the verbal symbols that accompany them. It is largely the function of the artist to make articulate these more subtle intentions of society.

Communicative processes do not merely apply to society as such; they are indefinitely varied as to form and meaning for the various types of personal relationships into which society resolves itself. Thus, a fixed type of conduct or a linguistic symbol has not by any means necessarily the same communicative significance within the confines of the family, among the members of an economic group and in the nation at large. Generally speaking, the smaller the circle and the more complex the understandings already arrived at within it, the more economical can the act of communication afford to become. A single word passed between members of an intimate group, in spite of its apparent vagueness and ambiguity, may constitute a far more precise communication than volumes of carefully prepared correspondence interchanged between two governments.

There seem to be three main classes of techniques which have for their object the facilitation of the primary communicative processes of society. These may be referred to as: language transfers; symbolisms arising from special technical situations; and the creation of physical conditions favorable for the communicative act. Of language transfers the best known example is writing. The Morse telegraph code is another example. These and many other communicative techniques have this in common, that while they are overtly not at all like one another their organization is based on the primary symbolic organization which has arisen in the domain of speech. Psychologically, therefore, they extend the communicative character of speech to situations in which for one reason or another speech is not possible.

In the more special class of communicative symbolism one cannot make a word to word translation, as it were, back to speech but can only paraphrase in speech the intent of the communication. Here belong such symbolic systems as wigwagging, the use of railroad lights, bugle calls in the army and smoke signals. It is interesting to observe that while they are late in developing in the history of society they are very much less complex in structure than language itself. They are of value partly in helping out a situation where neither language nor any form of language transfer can be applied, partly where it is desired to encourage the automatic nature of the desired response. Thus, because language is extraordinarily rich in meaning it sometimes becomes a little annoying or even dangerous to rely upon it where only a simple this or that, or yes or no, is expected to be the response.

The importance of extending the physical conditions allowing for communication is obvious. The railroad, the telegraph, the telephone, the radio and the airplane are among the best examples. It is to be noted that such instruments as the railroad and the radio are not communicative in character as such; they become so only because they facilitate the presentation of types of stimuli which act as symbols of communication or which contain implications of communicative significance. Thus, a telephone is of no use unless the party at the other end understands the language of the person calling up. Again, the fact that a railroad runs me to a certain point is of no real communicative importance unless there are fixed bonds of interest which connect me with the inhabitants of the place. The failure to bear in mind these obvious points has tended to make some writers exaggerate the importance of the spread in modern times of such inventions as the railroad and the telephone.

The history of civilization has been marked by a progressive increase in the radius of communication. In a typically primitive society communication is reserved for the members of the tribe and at best a small number of surrounding tribes with whom relations are intermittent rather than continuous and who act as a kind of buffer between the significant psychological world—the world of one's own tribal culture—and the great unknown or unreal that lies beyond. Today, in our own civilization, the appearance of a new fashion in Paris is linked by a series of rapid and necessary events with the appearance of the same fashion in such distant places as Berlin, London, New York, San Francisco and Yokohama. The underlying reason for this remarkable change in the radius and rapidity of communication is the gradual diffusion of cultural traits or, in other words, of meaningful cultural reactions. Among the various types of cultural diffusion that of language itself is of paramount importance. Secondary technical devices making for ease of communication are also, of course, of great importance.

The multiplication of far-reaching techniques of communication has two important results. In the first place, it increases the sheer radius of communication, so that for certain purposes the whole civilized world is made the psychological equivalent of a primitive tribe. In the second place, it lessens the importance of mere geographical contiguity. Owing to the technical nature of these sophisticated communicative devices, parts of the world that are geographically remote may, in terms of behavior, be actually much closer to one another than adjoining regions, which, from the historical standpoint, are supposed to share a larger body of common understandings. This means, of course, a tendency to remap the world both sociologically and psychologically. Even now it is possible to say that the scattered "scientific world" is a social unity which has no clear cut geographical location. Further, the world of urban understanding in America contrasts rather sharply with the rural world. The weakening of the geographical factor in social organization must in the long run profoundly modify our attitude toward the meaning of personal relations and of social classes and even nationalities.

The increasing ease of communication is purchased at a price, for it is becoming increasingly difficult to keep an intended communication within the desired bounds. A humble example of this new problem is the inadvisability of making certain kinds of statement on the telephone. Another example is the insidious cheapening of literary and artistic values due to the foreseen and economically advantageous "widening of the appeal." All effects which demand a certain intimacy of understanding tend to become difficult and are therefore avoided. It is a question whether the obvious increase of overt communication is not constantly being corrected, as it were, by the creation of new obstacles to communication. The fear of being too easily understood may, in many cases, be more aptly defined as the fear of being understood by too many—so many, indeed, as to endanger the psychological reality of the image of the enlarged self confronting the not-self.

On the whole, however, it is rather the obstacles to communication that are felt as annoying or ominous. The most important of these obstacles in the modern world is undoubtedly the great diversity of languages. The enormous amount of energy put into the task of translation implies a passionate desire to make as light of the language difficulty as possible. In the long run it seems almost unavoidable that the civilized world will adopt some one language of intercommunication, say English or Esperanto, which can be set aside for denotive purposes pure and simple.

Robert E. Park

REFLECTIONS ON COMMUNICATION
AND CULTURE

COMMUNICATION AND COMPETITION: What does communication do and how does it function in the cultural process? It seems to do several different things. Communication creates, or makes possible at least, that consensus and understanding among the individual components of a social group which eventually gives it and them the character not merely of society but of a cultural unit. It spins a web of custom and mutual expectation which binds together social entities as diverse as the family group, a labor organization, or the haggling participants in a village market. Communication maintains the concert necessary to enable them to function; each in its several ways.

Family group or labor organization, every form of society except the most transient, has a life-history and a tradition. It is by communication that this tradition is transmitted. It is in this way that the continuity of common enterprises and social institutions is maintained, not merely from day to day, but from generation to generation. Thus, the function of communication seems to be to maintain the unity and integrity of the social group in its two dimensions—space and time. It is in recognition of this fact that John Dewey has said: "Society not only continues to exist by transmission, by communication, but may fairly be said to exist in transmission, in communication."

Implicit in Dewey's statement, however, is a conception of society that is not generally nor everywhere accepted, since it seems to identify the social with the moral order. By so doing it limits the term "social" to those relations of individuals that are personal, customary, and moral.

"When individuals use one another to get results, without reference to their emotional or intellectual disposition and consent," says Dewey, they are involved in relations that are not social. To make the matter clear, he

Reprinted from *The American Journal of Sociology*, Vol. XLIV (1939), pp. 191-205, by permission of the publisher. (Copyright, 1939, by *The American Journal of Sociology*.)

adds, "So far as the relations of parent and child, teacher and pupil, remain upon this level, they form no true social group, no matter how closely their respective activities touch one another."

It is obvious, however, that communication, if it is the typical social process, is not the only form of interaction that goes on among the individual units of a social group. "We are compelled to recognize," he admits, "that even within the most social group there are many relations which are not yet social"—not social, at any rate, in the sense in which he uses the term. Competition, for example, performs a social function of a somewhat different sort, but one that is at least comparable to that of communication. The economic order in society seems to be very largely a by-product of competition. In any case, competition is, as Cooley observes, "the very heart of the economic process." What we ordinarily designate as economic competition, however, is not competition in the Malthusian sense of that term in which it is identical with the struggle for existence. Economic competition is always competition that is controlled and regulated to some extent by convention, understanding, and law.

The investigations of plant and animal ecologists have discovered that even where competition is free and unrestricted, as it is in the so-called plant and animal communities, there exists among creatures living in the same habitat a kind of natural economy. What characterizes this economy is a division of labor and an unconscious co-operation of competing organisms. Wherever in nature competition or the struggle for existence brings about a stable organization among competing individuals, it is because they have achieved in some form or another a division of labor and some form of conscious or unconscious co-operation. In such case the competing species or individual, each occupying the particular niche in which it fits, will have created an environment in which all can live together under conditions where each could not live separately. This natural economy of plant and animals is called symbiosis.

Man's relation to other men is, to a very much larger extent than has hitherto been recognized, symbiotic rather than social, in the sense in which Dewey uses that term. Competition among plants and animals tends to bring about an orderly distribution as well as a mutual adaptation of the species living together in a common habitat. Competition among human beings has brought about, or at any rate helped to bring about, not merely a territorial, but an occupational distribution of races and peoples. Incidentally, it has brought about that inevitable division of labor which is fundamental to every permanent form of society from the family to the nation.

If the struggle for existence, as Darwin conceived it, was a determining factor in producing that diversity of living types described in the *Origin of the Species,* then economic competition, the struggle for a livelihood, seems to have been a decisive factor in bringing about among human beings a comparable occupational diversity. But this division of labor wherever it exists in human society is limited by custom; and custom is a product of communication.

As a matter of fact, competition and communication operate everywhere within the same local habitat and within the same community, but in relative independence of each other. The area of competition and of the symbiotic relationship is, however, invariably wider and more inclusive than the area of those intimate, personal, and moral relations initiated by communication. Commerce invariably expands more widely and rapidly than linguistic or cultural understanding. It is, it seems, this cultural lag that makes most of our political and cultural problems. But the main point is that communication, where it exists, invariably modifies and qualifies competition, and the cultural order imposes limitations on the symbiotic.

Most of you will perhaps recall Sumner's description of primitive society, a territory occupied by little scattered ethnocentric groups, each the focus and center of a little world in which all members are bound together in ties of mutual understanding and loyalty.

Outside of these little tribal and familial units, on the other hand, men live in relation with one another not unlike those in which they live with the plants and animals, that is to say, in a kind of symbiosis, very little modified by mutual understanding or agreements of any sort. Under these circumstances the fundamental social and economic order is enforced and maintained by competition, but competition modified and controlled to an ever increasing degree by custom, convention, and law.

As a matter of fact, society everywhere exhibits two fundamental forms of organization—the familial and the communal. Familial society seems to have had its source in the interest and in the urge of individuals, not merely to live as individuals but to perpetuate the race. Thus the family seems to rest, finally, on an instinctive basis. Communal society, on the other hand, has arisen out of the need of the individuals to survive as individuals. Under these conditions men have come together, not in response to some gregarious impulse comparable with the sexual instinct, but for the more pragmatic and intelligible reason that they are useful to one another.

In spite of the changes which time and civilization have wrought in the existing social order, man lives as he always has, in two worlds—the little world of family and the great world of commerce and politics. In the little world the order which predominates is intimate, personal, and moral. In the larger world man is free to pursue his individual interests in his own individual way, relatively uninhibited by the expectations and claims which, in a more intimate social order, the interests of others might impose upon him. In the family it is communication and the personal influences which communication mediates that are the source and principle of order. In the world of commerce, and to a less degree in politics, it is competition in the more sublimated form of conflict and rivalry, which imposes such order as exists.

What all this suggests, though not perhaps so obviously as I should like, is that competition and communication, although they perform divergent and unco-ordinated social functions, nevertheless in the actual life of society they supplement and complete each other.

Competition seems to be the principle of individuation in the life of the person and of society. Under the influence of this principle the individual adapts and accommodates himself, not merely to the human habitat but to the occupational organization of the society of which he is a member. He follows the vocation and does the thing he can, rather than the thing he might like to do. Communication, on the other hand, operates primarily as an integrating and socializing principle.

It is true, of course, that when new forms of communication have brought about more intimate associations among individuals or peoples who have been culturally isolated, the first consequence may be to intensify competition. Furthermore, under the influence of communication, competition tends to assume a new character. It becomes conflict. In that case the struggle for existence is likely to be intensified by fears, animosities, and jealousies, which the presence of the competitor and the knowledge of his purposes arouse. Under such circumstances a competitor becomes an enemy.

On the other hand, it is always possible to come to terms with an enemy whom one knows and with whom one can communicate, and, in the long run, greater intimacy inevitably brings with it a more profound understanding, the result of which is to humanize social relations and to substitute a moral order for one that is fundamentally symbiotic rather than social, always in the restricted sense of that term.

DIFFUSION: Communication, whether it takes place through the medium of gesture, articulate speech, or conventional symbols of any sort whatever, always involves, it seems to me, an interpretation of the attitude or intent of the person whose word or gesture supplied the stimulus. What anything means to anyone at any time is substantially what it means, has meant, or will mean, to someone else. Communication is a process or form of interaction that is interpersonal, i.e., social in the narrower sense. The process is complete only when it results in some sort of understanding. In other words, communication is never merely a case of ·stimulus and response in the sense in which those terms are used in individual psychology. It is rather expression, interpretation, and response.

In some cases, in most cases perhaps, and particularly where the persons involved are *en rapport,* the response of individual A to an expressive action of individual B is likely to be immediate and well-nigh automatic. This is obviously so in the case of hypnotic suggestion, and particularly so under the condition of what is called "isolated rapport," where the subject responds to the suggestion of the hypnotizer and to those of no one else.

We must conceive individuals in society as living constantly enveloped in an atmosphere of subconscious suggestion. In this atmosphere they are constantly responsive, not merely to the overt acts but to the moods and the presence of other persons, in somewhat the same way that they are to the weather. What we call the fluctuations of public opinion, public sentiment, and fashion, are, in fact, a kind of social weather. These changes in the social weather evoke changes in internal tensions of persons who are *en rapport:* changes are so subtle that they amount to a kind of clairvoyance. It is only in moments of abstraction that this condition of clairvoyance is interrupted and then only partially. A suggestion is, of course, not a mere stimulus, but a stimulus that is interpreted as an expression of a wish or an attitude. The literature of hypnotism indicates how subtle suggestions may be and how responsive under certain conditions individuals may be to them.

Sometimes, to be sure, the sense and meaning of the behavior and language of those about us are obscure; this sets us thinking, and leaves us sometimes with a sense of frustration and confusion. At other times it arouses us, not to definite action, but to vague emotional protest or inarticulate opposition. This emotional expression of unrest, multiplied and intensified by the reflex influence of mind on mind, may take the form finally of a social brain storm like dancing mania of the Middle Ages or the commercial panic of 1929. Under more normal conditions unrest may express itself in social agitation or in the less violent form of discussion and debate.

These are some of the manifold ways in which communication operating within the limits of an existing culture group changes, directly and indirectly, the pattern of cultural life. If I merely refer to these manifestations here in passing it is because a fuller discussion of them would involve problems of collective behavior which are so diverse and manifold that they have become the subject of special discipline of the social sciences.

The cultural process ordinarily presents itself in two dimensions or aspects which are intimately bound up with and determined by the conditions under which communication inevitably takes place. They are: diffusion and acculturation.

As communication takes place between persons, it is necessarily involved in all the complexities incident to the transmission of a stimulus from the source *a quo* to a terminus *ad quem*—i.e., from a person of whose mind it is an expression to the person in whose mind it finds a response. The obvious conditions which facilitate or obstruct these processes are mainly physical and in modern times they have been progressively over- come by means of technical devices like the alphabet, printing-press, radio, etc.

The less obvious obstacles to effective communication are the difficulties that grow out of differences of language, tradition, experience, and interest. By interest in this instance I mean what Thomas refers to as the "run of attention." Everywhere and always, certain interests, persons, or events are in the focus of attention; certain things are in fashion. Whatever has importance and prestige at the moment has power to direct for a time the currents of public opinion, even if it does not change, in the long run, the trend of events. All these things are factors in communication and either facilitate or make difficult the transmission of news from one country to another. The manner in which news circulates is typical of one way in which cultural diffusion takes place.

Discussions of the deficiencies of the press often proceed on the implicit assumption that the communication of news from one cultural area to another—from the Orient to the Occident, for example, or from Berlin to New York—is an operation as simple as the transportation of a commodity like bricks. One can, of course, transport words across cultural marches, but the interpretations which they receive on two sides of a political or cultural boundary will depend upon the context which their different interpreters bring to them. That context, in turn, will depend rather more upon the past experience and present temper of the people to whom the words are addressed than upon either the art of the good will of the persons who report them.

Foreign correspondents know, as no one who has not had the experi- ence, how difficult it is under ordinary circumstances to make the public read foreign news. They know, also, how much more difficult it is to make events happening beyond his horizon intelligible to the average man in the street. In general, news circulates widely in every direction in pro- portion as it is interesting and intelligible. In that respect it is not unlike any other cultural item, the oil cans of the Standard Oil Company or the Singer sewing-machine for example, which are now possibly the most widely dispersed of all our modern cultural artifacts.

Each and every artifact or item of news inevitably tends to reach the places where it will be appreciated and understood. Cultural traits are assimilated only as they are understood, and they are understood only as they are assimilated. This does not mean that a cultural artifact or an item of news will have everywhere the same meaning; quite the contrary. But the different meanings they do have in different places will tend to converge, as diffusion is succeeded by acculturation.

It is extraordinary to what extent and with what rapidity news tends to reach the minds of those to whom its message, if intelligible, is important. On the other hand, just as important, if less remarkable, is the difficulty of communicating a message that is neither important nor intelligible to the persons to whom it is addressed. This latter is a problem of the schools, particularly the problem of rote learning.

Thirty-three years ago the conclusion of the Russian-Japanese War made news that I suspect circulated farther and more rapidly than any other report of events had ever traveled before. One heard echoes of it in regions as far apart as the mountain fastnesses of Tibet and the forests of Central Africa. It was news that a nation of colored people had defeated and conquered a nation of white people. The same item of news might travel further and with greater speed today, but it would not have the same importance. The question of how and why and under what circumstances news circulates is an important one and deserves more attention than has yet been given to it.

It is a familiar observation of students of the cultural process that artifacts, the traits of a material culture, are more easily diffused and more rapidly assimilated than similar items of a nonmaterial culture—political institutions and religious practices, for example. That is no more than to say that trade expands, on the whole, more rapidly than religion. But that, too, depends upon circumstances. Consider, for example, the sudden rapid diffusion in the modern world of communism.

One reason the terms of a material culture are so widely diffused and assimilated is because their uses are obvious and their values, whatever they be, are rational and secular. One needs no rite or ceremony to initiate him into mysteries involved in the use of a wheelbarrow or rifle. When the first plow was introduced into South Africa, an old chief who was invited to be present and see the demonstration recognized its value at once. He said, "This is a great thing the white man has brought us." Then after some reflection he added: "It is worth as much as ten wives."

What we call civilization, as distinguished from culture, is largely composed of such artifacts and technical devices as can be diffused without undermining the existing social institutions and without impairing the ability of a people to act collectively, that is to say, consistently and in concert. Institutions seem to exist primarily to facilitate collective action, and anything that involves a society rather than the individuals of which that society is composed is hard to export. Diffusion takes place more easily when the social unity is relaxed.

It is no secret, I suppose, that there is invariably an intimate and indissoluble relation between commerce and the news. The centers of trade are invariably the centers of news; the centers to which the news inevitably comes and from whence it is diffused, first to the local community and then, according to its interests and importance, to the ends of the earth.

During this diffusion a process of selection necessarily takes place. Some news items travel further and more rapidly than others. This is true even when all or most of the physical obstacles to communication have been overcome. The reason of course is simple enough. It is bound up with the inevitably egocentric character of human beings and the ethnocentric character of human relations generally. An event is important only as we believe we can do something about it. It loses importance in proportion as the possibility of doing that something seems more remote. An earthquake in China assumes, in view of our incorrigible provincialism, less importance than a funeral in our village. This is an example of what is meant by social distance, which is the term in which sociologists seek to conceptualize and, in some sense, measure personal relations and personal intimacies. Importance is ultimately a personal matter; a matter of social distance.

The principle involved in the circulation of news is not different from that involved in the cultural process of diffusion, wherever it takes place. Individuals and societies assimilate most readily, as I have said, what is at once interesting and intelligible.

ACCULTURATION: If the market place is the center from which news is disseminated and cultural influences are diffused, it is, likewise, the center in which old ideas go into the crucible and new ideas emerge. The market place, where men gather to dicker and chaffer, is in the very nature of things a kind of forum where men of diverse interests and different minds are engaged in peaceful controversy, trying to come to terms about values and prices; trying, also, by a process that is fundamentally dialectical, to explore the different meanings things have for men of different interests; seeking to reach understandings based rather more on reason and rather less on tradition and the prejudices which custom has sanctioned, if not sanctified. It is for this reason that the great metropolitan cities—Rome, London, and Paris—cities to which peoples come and go from the four ends of the earth, are in a perpetual ferment of enlightenment; are continually involved—to use a German expression, in an *Aufklärung*. Under such conditions the historical process is quickened, and acculturation, the mutual interpenetration of minds and cultures, goes forward at a rapid pace.

When peoples of different races and divergent cultures seek to live together within the limits of the same local economy, they are likely to live for a time in relations which I have described as symbiotic rather than social, using that term in this connection as Dewey and others have used it, namely, as identical with cultural. They live, in short, in physical contiguity, but in more or less complete moral isolation, a situation which corresponds in effect if not in fact, to Sumner's description of primitive society.

This has been and still is the situation of some of those little religious sects like the Mennonites, which have from time to time sought refuge in the United States and elsewhere, settling on the frontiers of European civilization, where they might hope to live in something like tribal isolation—untrammeled and uncorrupted by intercourse with a Gentile world.

It was to preserve this isolation that some of Pennsylvania's "plain people," the Amish, protested against a gift of $112,000 of P.W.A. funds which the government was pressing upon them for new schoolhouses. New schools, in this case, involved the use of busses, to which the "plain people" were opposed. They believed, also, and no doubt quite correctly, that intimate association of Amish children with the mixed population of a consolidated school to whom Amish folkways would certainly seem quaint, would undermine the discipline and the sacred solidarity of Amish society.

This situation, in which peoples occupying the same territory live in a moral isolation more or less complete, was historically, so long as they lived in the seclusion of their religious community, the situation of a more sophisticated people than the Amish, namely, the Jews. It has been, to a less extent, the situation of every immigrant people which has for any reason sought to find a place in the economic order of an established society and at the same time maintain a cultural tradition that was alien to it.

Inevitably, however, in the natural course, under modern conditions of life, both the immigrant and the sectarian seek to escape from this isolation in order that they may participate more actively in the social life of the people about them. It is then, if not earlier, that they become aware of the social distance that sets them apart from the members of the dominant cultural group. Under these circumstances acculturation becomes involved in and part of the struggle of immigrants and sectarians alike for status. Everything that marks them as strangers—manners, accent, habits of speech and thought—makes this struggle difficult. The cultural conflict which then ensues—whether openly manifested or merely sensed—tends, as conflict invariably does, to heighten self-consciousness in members of both cultural groups, in those who are classed as aliens and in those who count themselves native.

However, anything that intensifies self-consciousness and stimulates introspection inevitably brings to the surface and into clear consciousness sentiments and attitudes that otherwise would escape rational criticism and interpretation. Otherwise they would probably, as the psychoanalysts tell us, continue active in the dark backgrounds of consciousness. They would still function as part of that "vital secret" to which William James refers in his essay *A Certain Blindness in Human Beings*—a secret of which each of us is profoundly conscious because it is the substance of one's own self-consciousness and of one's individual point of view—but for which we look in vain to others for sympathy and understanding. But conflict, and particularly cultural conflict, in so far as it brings into the light of understanding impulses and attitudes of which we would otherwise remain unconscious, inevitably increases our knowledge not merely of ourselves but of our fellows, since the attitudes and sentiments which we find in ourselves we are able to appreciate and understand, no matter how indirectly expressed, when we find them in the minds of others.

Acculturation, if we conceive it in radical fashion, may be said to begin with the intimate associations and understandings that grow up in the family between mother and child and somewhat later with other members of the family. But while mothers are necessarily, and under all ordinary circumstances, profoundly interested and responsive to their children, it is notorious that they do not always understand them.

The situation differs, but not greatly, with other members of the family —notably with the relations between husband and wife. Men are naturally and instinctively interested in and attracted by women, particularly strange women, but they often find them difficult to understand. In fact men have felt in the past and still feel in some obscure way, I suspect, that women, no matter how interesting, are not quite human in the sense and to the degree that this is true of themselves.

If this is not true to the same extent today that it once was, it is because men and women, in the family and outside of it, live in more intimate association with one another than they formerly did. They still have their separate worlds, but they get together as they formerly did not. They speak the same language. But this is true also of parents and children. Both understand each other better than they once did.

Men and women have learned a great deal about one another from experience, but they have learned more—in the sense of understanding one another and in the ability to communicate—from literature and the arts. In fact it is just the function of literature and the arts and of what are described in academic circles as the humanities to give us this intimate personal and inside knowledge of each other which makes social life more amiable and collective action possible.

I am, perhaps, wrong in describing the intimate associations which family life permits and enforces as if they were part and parcel of the cultural process. That may seem to be employing a term in a context which is so foreign to it as to destroy its original meaning. I am not sure, however, that this is quite true. At any rate, in the family in which husband and wife are of different racial stocks, with different cultural heritages, the process of acculturation—and acculturation in the sense in which it is familiar to students—takes place more obviously and more effectively than it does elsewhere. It is this fact and not its biological consequences which gives recent studies of race mixture and interracial marriage, like the studies of Romanzo Adams in Hawaii, a significance they would not otherwise have. It is in the life-histories of mixed bloods whose origin ordinarily imposes upon them the task of assimilating the heritages of two divergent cultures, that the process and consequences of acculturation are most obvious and open to investigation. The reason is that the man of mixed blood is a "marginal man," so called, that is, the man who lives in two worlds but is not quite at home in either.

❉   ❉   ❉

In conclusion, I shall revert to the distinction with which I started—the distinction between language and forms of communication which are referential, as a scientific description, and language and forms of communication which are symbolic and expressive, as in literature and the fine arts. It seems clear that the function of news is definitely referential. If it does not have the status in science of a classified fact, it is at least indispensable to government and to business. On the other hand, the function of art and of the cinema is, on the whole, in spite of the use that has been made of it for educational purposes, definitely symbolic, and as such it profoundly influences sentiment and attitudes even when it does not make any real contribution to knowledge.

Harold D. Lasswell

THE THEORY OF
POLITICAL PROPAGANDA

Propaganda is the management of collective attitudes by the manipulation of significant symbols. The word attitude is taken to mean a tendency to act according to certain patterns of valuation. The existence of an attitude is not a direct datum of experience, but an inference from signs which have a conventionalized significance. We say that the voters of a certain ward resent a negro candidate, and in so doing we have compactly summarized the tendency of a particular group to act toward a particular object in a specific context. The valuational patterns upon which this inference is founded may be primitive gestures of the face and body, or more sophisticated gestures of the pen and voice. Taken together, these objects which have a standard meaning in a group are called significant symbols. The elevated eyebrow, the clenched fist, the sharp voice, the pungent phrase, have their references established within the web of a particular culture. Such significant symbols are paraphernalia employed in expressing the attitudes, and they are also capable of being employed to reaffirm or redefine attitudes. Thus, significant symbols have both an expressive and a propagandist function in public life.

The idea of a "collective attitude" is not that of a super-organic, extra-natural entity. Collective phenomena have too often been treated as if they were on a plane apart from individual action. Confusion has arisen principally because students have been slow to invent a word able to bear the connotation of uniformity without also implying a biological or metaphysical unity. The anthropologists have introduced the notion of a pattern to designate the standard uniformities of conduct at a given time and place, and this is the sense of the word here intended. Thus the collective attitude, as a pattern, is a distribution of individual acts and

Reprinted from *The American Political Science Review*, Vol. XXI (1927), pp. 627-30, by permission of the author and the publisher. (Copyright, 1927, by the American Political Science Association.)

not an indwelling spirit which has achieved transitory realization in the rough, coarse facts of the world of sense.

Collective attitudes are amenable to many modes of alteration. They may be shattered before an onslaught of violent intimidation or disintegrated by economic coercion. They may be reaffirmed in the muscular regimentation of drill. But their arrangement and rearrangement occurs principally under the impetus of significant symbols; and the technique of using significant symbols for this purpose is propaganda.

Propaganda as a word is closely allied in popular and technical usage with certain others. It must be distinguished from education. We need a name for the processes by which techniques are inculcated—techniques of spelling, letter-forming, adding, piano-playing, and lathe-handling. If this be education, we are free to apply the term propaganda to the creation of valuational dispositions or attitudes.

The deliberative attitude is capable of being separated from the propagandist attitude. Deliberation implies the search for the solution of a besetting problem with no desire to prejudice a particular solution in advance. The propagandist is very much concerned about how a specific solution is to be evoked and "put over." And though the most subtle propaganda closely resembles disinterested deliberation, there is no difficulty in distinguishing the extremes.

What is the relation between propaganda and the changing of opinions through psychiatric interviews? Such an interview is an intensive approach to the individual by means of which the interviewer gains access to the individual's private stock of meanings and becomes capable of exploiting them rather than the standard meanings of the groups of which the individual is a member. The intimate, continuing relationship which is set up under quasi-clinical conditions is quite beyond the reach of the propagandist, who must restrict himself to dealing with the individual as a standard member of some groups or sub-groups which he differentiates upon the basis of extrinsic evidence.

Propagandas may be classified upon the basis of many possible criteria. Some are carried on by organizations like the Anti-Cigarette League which have a definite and restricted objective; others are conducted by organizations, like most civic associations, which have a rather general and diffused purpose. This objective may be revolutionary or counter-revolutionary, reformist or counter-reformist, depending upon whether or not a sweeping institutional change is involved. Propaganda may be carried on by organizations which rely almost exclusively upon it or which use it as an auxiliary implement among several means of social control. Some propagandas are essentially temporary, like the boosters' club for a favorite son, or comparatively permanent. Some propagandas are intra-group, in the sense that they exist to consolidate an existing attitude and not, like the extra-group propagandas, to assume the additional burden of proselyting. There are propagandas which are manned by those who hope to reap direct, tangible, and substantial gains from them; others are staffed by those who are content with a remote, intangible, and rather imprecise advantage to themselves. Some are run by men who make it their life work, and others are handled by amateurs. Some depend upon a central or skeleton staff and others rely upon widespread and catholic associations. One propaganda group may flourish in secret and another may invite publicity.

Besides all these conceivable and often valuable distinctions, propagandas may be conveniently divided according to the object toward which it is proposed to modify or crystallize an attitude. Some propagandas exist to organize an attitude toward a person, like Mr. Coolidge or Mr. Smith; others to organize an attitude toward a group, like the Japanese or the workers; others to organize an attitude toward a policy or institution, like free trade or parliamentary government; and still others to organize an attitude toward a mode of personal participation, like buying war bonds or joining the marines. No propaganda fits tightly into its category of major emphasis, and it must be remembered that pigeon-holes are invented to serve convenience and not to satisfy yearnings for the immortal and the immutable.

If we state the strategy of propaganda in cultural terms, we may say that it involves the presentation of an object in a culture in such a manner that certain cultural attitudes will be organized toward it. The problem of the propagandist is to intensify the attitudes favorable to his purpose, to reverse the attitudes hostile to it, and to attract the indifferent, or, at the worst, to prevent them from assuming a hostile bent.

Every cultural group has its vested values. These may include the ownership of property or the possession of claims to ceremonial deference. An object toward which it is hoped to arouse hostility must be presented as a menace to as many of these values as possible. There are always ambitious hopes of increasing values, and the object must be made to appear as the stumbling block to their realization. There are patterns of right and wrong, and the object must be made to flout the good. There are standards of propriety, and the object must appear ridiculous and gauche. If the plan is to draw out positive attitudes toward an object, it must be presented, not as a menace and an obstruction, nor as despicable or absurd, but as a protector of our values, a champion of our dreams, and a model of virtue and propriety.

Propaganda objects must be chosen with extreme care. The primary objects are usually quite distinct. Thus war propaganda involves the enemy, the ally, and the neutral. It involves leaders on both sides and the support of certain policies and institutions. It implies the control of attitudes toward various forms of participation—enlistment, bond buying, and strenuous exertion. These, and similar objects, are conspicuously entangled in the context of the total situation, and the propagandist can easily see that he must deal with them. But some are contingently and not primarily implicated. They are important in the sense that unless precautions are taken attention may be inconveniently diverted to them. The accumulating unrest of a nation may be turned by social revolutionaries into an outburst against the government which distracts the hostility of the community from the enemy, and breakdown ensues. War propaganda must therefore include the social revolutionist as an object of hostility, and all propaganda must be conceived with sufficient scope to embrace these contingent objects.

The strategy of propaganda, which has been phrased in cultural terms, can readily be described in the language of stimulus-response. Translated into this vocabulary, which is especially intelligible to some, the propagandist may be said to be concerned with the multiplication of those stimuli which are best calculated to evoke the desired responses, and with the nullification of those stimuli which are likely to instigate the undesired responses. Putting the same thing into terms of social suggestion, the problem of the propagandist is to multiply all the suggestions favorable to the attitudes which he wishes to produce and strengthen, and to restrict all suggestions which are unfavorable to them. In this sense of the word, suggestion is not used as it is in individual psychology to mean the acceptance of an idea without reflection; it refers to cultural material with a recognizable meaning.

Whatever form of words helps to ignite the imagination of the practical manipulator of attitudes is the most valuable one. Terminological difficulties disappear when we turn from the problem of choosing propaganda matter to discuss the specific carriers of propaganda material. The form in which the significant symbols are embodied to reach the public may be spoken, written, pictorial, or musical, and the number of stimulus carriers is infinite. If the propagandist identifies himself imaginatively with the life of his subjects in a particular situation, he is able to explore several channels of approach. Consider, for a moment, the people who ride the street cars. They may be reached by placards posted inside the car, by posters on the billboards along the track, by newspapers which they read, by conversations which they overhear, by leaflets which are openly or surreptitiously slipped into their hands, by street demonstrations at halting places, and no doubt by other means. Of these possible occasions there are no end. People walk along the streets or ride in automobiles, trams, and subways, elevated trains, boats, electrical or steam railways; they congregate in theatres, churches, lecture halls, eating places, athletic parks, concert rooms, barber shops and beauty parlors, coffee-houses and drug stores; people work in offices, warehouses, mills, factories, and conveyances. An inspection of the life patterns of any community reveals•the web of mobility routes and congregating centres through which interested fact and opinion may be disseminated.

Propaganda rose to transitory importance in the past whenever a social system based upon the sanctions of antiquity was broken up by a tyrant. The ever-present function of propaganda in modern life is in large measure attributable to the social disorganization which has been precipitated by the rapid advent of technological changes. Impersonality has supplanted personal loyalty to leaders. Literacy and the physical channels of communication have quickened the connection between those who rule and the ruled. Conventions have arisen which favor the ventilation of opinions and the taking of votes. Most of that which formerly could be done by violence and intimidation must now be done by argument and persuasion. Democracy has proclaimed the dictatorship of palaver, and the technique of dictating to the dictator is named propaganda.

Carl I. Hovland

SOCIAL COMMUNICATION

Communication as an *art* has had a very long history. The writer, the orator, the public relations counsellor, and the advertiser have been leading practitioners of this art. Communication as a field of scientific inquiry, on the other hand, has been of fairly recent origin. Within the last decade or so, however, there has developed the promise of a genuine science of communication—a systematic attempt to formulate in rigorous fashion the principles by which information is transmitted and opinions and attitudes formed.

The development of this new field has been at least in part a response to the growing urgency of the problem. In industry the increasing concentration of control has widened the gap between workers and management and the feeling has arisen on both sides of the need for more effective intercommunications. The different frames of reference of management and of the worker have intensified this problem. The next speaker on the program will discuss this topic in connection with labor-management studies.

In our national life the same gap between lawmaker and citizen exists. Formal means of intercommunication have helped somewhat. The radio has brought the political leader closer to the voter and the public opinion poll has brought the views of the citizens more closely to the attention of the lawmaker. But there is still felt by many the lack of more effective intercommunication to replace the lost intimacy of the town meeting in the early days of our democracy.

On the international scene the same lack of communication appears. I recently heard one of our important United Nations officials say, "If only we could communicate with the Russians." There is here not the problem of physical communication, but of psychological communication, not a language barrier alone but ideological barriers to communication.

Reprinted from the *Proceedings of the American Philosophical Society*, Vol. 92, No. 5 (1948), pp. 371-75, by permission of the author and the publisher. (Copyright, 1948, by the American Philosophical Society.)

The problem of communications is made more challenging by the fact that it is not an area for an isolated specialist. Adequate understanding of the problems of this field depends on a wider variety of talent and range of specialization than almost any other problem in the social sciences. A real science of communication will require the cooperation of both the practitioner and the scientist. Thus the newspaper editor, the radio broadcaster, the movie producer, as well as the psychologist, the sociologist, the anthropologist, and the political scientist have important roles to perform.[1]

Numerous definitions of the term "communication" have been given but for purposes of the present discussion I should like to define communication as the process by which an individual (the communicator) transmits stimuli (usually verbal symbols) to modify the behavior of other individuals (communicatees).

This definition thus defines the research task as being the analysis of four factors: (1) the *communicator* who transmits the communication; (2) the *stimuli* transmitted by the communicator; (3) the *individuals* who respond to the communication; (4) the *responses* made to the communication by the communicatee. In addition, we must analyze the *laws* and *principles* relating the above elements.

Numerous studies have been made of the communicator and how his characteristics affect the response of those receiving the communication.[2] In this category belong such important problems as the effect of communications in which the true communicator is not revealed, and the effectiveness of appeals made by the communicator in person compared with those in which the message is transmitted through radio, motion pictures or other media.

Analysis of the second factor, the stimuli, has been the most thoroughly studied. In fact when mention is made of communication analysis, or of institutes of communication, which are springing up on all sides, this is the aspect usually meant. With the growing complexity of our civilization just knowing what material is being transmitted is a gigantic and important task. Analysis of the material transmitted through the various channels of communication has required the development of precise quantitative techniques. The study of the stimuli transmitted by the communicator employs the familiar technique of *content analysis.* Just before the war and during the war work on this problem made rapid strides. The studies of Lasswell, Kris, and Speier on analysis of enemy propaganda through newspapers, radio, and movies constitute good examples of the developments of the last

[1] This is well illustrated in the diversity of contributors to the recent symposium: Communication and social action, Yeager, W. H., and W. E. Utterback, ed., *Annals Amer. Acad. Pol. and Soc. Sci. 250,* 1947.

[2] *Cf., e.g.,* Smith, B. L., The political communication specialist of our times, pp. 31-73, in Smith, B. L., H. D. Lasswell, and R. D. Casey, *Propaganda, communication, and public opinion,* Princeton Univ. Press, 1946.

few years in this area. These methods provide analysis in terms of the subject matter of a communication, its thematic content, type of symbolization, kinds of rhetorical devices used, syntactical characteristics, etc.[3] Without the thorough description made possible by these new and more precise methods of describing the content aspect of the stimuli the task of formulating principles and generalizations would be most difficult.

Because the stimuli used in communication are primarily verbal symbols it is important to understand the role of language in communication. Recent developments in the analysis of language and the field of semantics promise important application to the science of communication.[4] The analysis of this problem requires taking into account not only the differences between the languages of different nations but the equally critical problem of the differences in language between groups within our own society— e. g., between the scientist and the layman or between labor and management.

Scientific studies of the material transmitted try to be objective and uninterested in the *values* of the material transmitted. So it is at this point that research must be supplemented by studies of other groups—of the regulation of communication, the maintenance of a free press, and the variety of topics surveyed by the Commission on Freedom of the Press.[5] Here the philosopher, the student of government, and the lawyer, all have a significant place. Research can provide them with objective data basic to their analysis particularly in connection with evaluating the effect of various communication policies.

We now turn to the third of our problems—the analysis of the individual who receives the communication. Here we have the core of the problem of individual psychology. What are the motives of the individuals, what are their capacities, how do their predispositions influence the way in which they react to various stimuli presented? While psychology is most concerned with these problems, other adjacent disciplines have made significant contributions to our understanding. Psychiatry and psychoanalysis have contributed to the analysis of the complex motives of the individual. Anthropological research in our own culture has shown us how the dominant motives and patterns of an individual can be predicted from factors such as his occupation and social class. Thus important information about the individual to be affected by the communication is furnished by census-type data. Just knowing that an individual is twenty-one years of age, wealthy, and has a high intelligence test score permits us to make

[3] Lasswell, H. D., Describing the contents of communications, pp. 74-94, in Smith, B. L., H. D. Lasswell, and R. D. Casey, *op. cit.*

[4] *Cf. e.g.*, Johnson, W., *People in quandaries; the semantics of personal adjustment,* N. Y., Harper's, 1946.

[5] Chafee, Z., *Government and mass communication,* 2 v., Univ. of Chicago Press, 1947.

highly significant predictions of the individual's motives, habits, and capacity to learn, which are extremely relevant to the type of communication used. Procedures derived from clinical psychology and first-hand knowledge of the individual permit still better prediction. This field appears very promising for future developments in our understanding of communication. Studies of other cultures and other national patterns is an integral part of this problem. Better understanding of the countries of Eastern Europe, for example, and consequent better communication with them requires extensive research on the predispositions of individuals in various cultures of the world. Work on this problem is now being begun at a number of centers.

The fourth facet of analysis is that of responses to communication. Some aspects of this problem are much more developed than others. One of the simplest responses is that of attention to the communication. Studies of what readers have noticed in communication and what they have read, for example, in the daily newspapers, are relatively numerous. Within the last few years there have been increasingly frequent attempts to relate simple responses, like reading behavior, to the characteristics of the individual responding. Such studies relate readership to sex, educational level, age group, etc.

Similarly a great deal of research on the response side has been done in the field of radio. But here the primary emphasis has been on the responses of listening and enjoyment. Devices for recording of responses of like or dislike have been of some assistance in this phase of the problem.[6] Only recently have there been corresponding studies of the effectiveness of radio in influencing opinion and in transmitting information.[7] Much the same has been true of the large amount of research that has gone into the analysis of response to the movies. The emphasis has been on what do people like. This has been the aspect that has had the great commercial backing. The beginnings of interest in other directions were shown in the Payne Fund studies on the effects of the movies on a wide variety of phases of social behavior.[8] The work which we did during the war on the analysis of the effectiveness of the films prepared by the Army to give soldiers the background of the war and our participation in it may also be mentioned.[9] Here the responses studied were in terms of the amount of information

[6] Hallonquist, T., and E. A. Suchman, Listening to the listener, pp. 265-334, in *Radio research, 1943-1945*, Lazarsfeld, P. F., and F. N. Stanton, ed., N. Y., Duell, Sloan, and Pearce, 1944.

[7] Cf., e.g., Wilson, E. C., The effectiveness of documentary broadcasts, *Public Opin. Quart. 12:* 19-29, 1948.

[8] Charters, W. W., *Motion pictures and youth: a summary*, N. Y., Macmillan, 1933.

[9] *Experiments on mass communications*, by Hovland, Lumsdaine, and Sheffield, Princeton University Press, 1949.

received, the opinions which were changed, and the effect of changes in information and opinion on motivation.

The analysis of response to communication has been enormously facilitated by recent improvements in technique. Public opinion methods have made rapid strides as will be seen from the papers presented this afternoon. But these methods do not suffice for the many aspects to be covered. Intensive interview methods are needed on many phases of the problem. For some phases of the problem adaptations of clinical procedures will probably prove essential to understand fully the total impact of communication. Another aspect of the problem requiring much further work is that of relating the different types of responses made to communication. This includes study of how changes in opinion and verbal statement are related to other phases of behavior like social action. This brings in the fascinating problem of how to change the way an individual perceives a problem and how changes in his perception affect his other actions.

Our research task also includes the formulation of principles and laws relating the stimuli, the individual, and the response. Here we are immediately stuck by the wide generality of the problem. We find that the principles needed for an understanding of communication are the very ones needed for an understanding of other aspects of behavior all the way from psychological warfare to individual psychotherapy in a face-to-face situation. We are thus at once benefited by the years of basic work that have gone into analysis of psychological behavior and its change, and at the same time confronted anew in changed form with the many large unsolved problems of human relations.

We are, of course, benefited in the search for principles by the years of experience of practitioners of the communication art. Let us survey briefly these contributions.

The field of education has made significant contributions. On the problems of how to transmit factual information, for example, the work of the last twenty years has been very enlightening. But even more significant problems exist in the field of communication of values and attitudes. Here we are largely in unknown territory, with a strong realization on the part of educators of the magnitude of the problem and its importance but with little dependable information at hand.

Another important source of hypotheses is the work which has been done on discussion groups. From wide practical experience a number of excellent books have been written on how to conduct discussion groups, strategic and tactical procedures, and the like.[10] Few of these recommendations have been put to experimental test but there are contained in these books numerous important ideas which should be evaluated.

[10] *Cf.*, *e.g.*, Elliott, H. S., *The process of group thinking*, N. Y., Association Press, 1928.

Some systematic work directed toward study of discussion groups was done by our research group during the war to determine the type of leadership which is most effective and the effectiveness of various types of presentation. Extensive studies of the effectiveness of group discussion were carried out during the war by the late Kurt Lewin and his associates.[11] Their studies indicated that group discussion followed by a group decision to carry out some particular social action, like eating less white bread, or trying out meat substitutes, was more effective than lectures and individual decision. This research raises a large number of important questions for research as to the factors responsible for the alleged effectiveness of group decision, such as the interrelationships between the members of the group, the personality characteristics of those who are and are not influenced by the group pressures, and the like. Such research should greatly clarify our understanding of the interrelationships of the individual and the group in communication. Other significant work is being planned in the analysis of conference discussions and their effectiveness in various situations.

Work on psychotherapy has been of value as a source of hypotheses. This represents an important form of communication—of the face-to-face variety. From the extensive work on this problem many hypotheses have developed which if confirmed should be applicable to mass communication as well. Let me quote a single example. It has long been a belief on the part of many psychotherapists that decisions reached independently by the client or patient are apt to be more influential and lasting than those suggested by the therapist. Some work has been done along this line for individual psychotherapy. How about this generalization at the mass communication level? Is it more effective to present evidence for the point being communicated without drawing the implied conclusion and letting the communicatee draw the conclusion? Or is it better to present the evidence and also draw the conclusion for the reader or hearer? Preliminary work we have underway seems to indicate that an important variable is the intelligence of the individual or group addressed. With the more intelligent members of the audience the effects may be more lasting when they participated in the decision process but with less intelligent members the correct conclusion may not always be seen and grasped without being made explicitly by the communication.

Advertising wisdom yields a number of important hypotheses. Where systematic results are available they have considerable significance because of the fact that the objective of the communication is usually clearly defined. This is in contrast to certain other areas where people are eager to communicate but it is extremely difficult to define what they are trying to

[11] Lewin, K., Forces behind food habits and methods of change, pp. 35-65, in The problem of changing food habits, *Bull. Nat. Res. Council*, No. 108, Oct. 1943.

communicate so that one can make any adequate evaluation of the success of the effort.

There are a number of important limitations, however, to work in advertising as a source of principles of communication.

The first is the fact that many of the results are kept confidential because of their commercial value. A second difficulty is the complexity of the situation in which research is carried on. Organizations frequently have simultaneous radio, newspaper, magazine, and poster advertising with complex temporal relations which make it difficult to attribute results to specifiable causes. Thirdly, the research has been done primarily without reference to theoretical systematization so that it is difficult to generalize the results to new situations. Results are most frequently of the type that ad A produces more sales than ad B, but without any systematic account of the respects in which the two ads were the same and in which they were different.

Lastly, important ideas have come from analysis of problems of communication in industry. The importance of this problem was clearly shown by the early studies of Mayo [12] and others. A book like that of Chester Barnard [13] on leadership has a large number of significant hypotheses as to the role of communications, the formal and informal channels which exist within an organization and the barriers to more effective communication up and down the lines of organization and across them. Systematic work is being begun on the problem of communication within management, between management and the worker, and between management and the public.

The problem confronting us currently is not then lack of ideas and hypotheses. These as we have seen are available on every side. What are primarily lacking are two things: (1) lack of a comprehensive theoretical structure to embrace the diverse ideas and hunches from the various fields and (2) systematic experimental work to check and verify or refute the hypotheses obtaining.

In systematizing the field the work which has been done on the psychology of learning has proved of enormous help. This is not unexpected when we stop to consider that communication is essentially that phase of learning in which the conditions for learning are set up by another individual, the communicator. Thus all teaching is communicating.

As a result of the intimate relationship of communication to learning we have a quite sizeable body of principles already available to guide us in the development of a science of communication. We know the elements

[12] Mayo, E., *The human problems of an industrial civilization*, N. Y., Macmillan, 1933.

[13] Barnard, C. I., *The functions of the executive*, Harvard Univ. Press, 1938.

which are most relevant to analysis of this process—stimuli, responses, motives, and rewards. We know something about the conditions under which new habits are required. We know what happens when the four elements are appropriately timed and what happens when they are not.

These principles tie together a lot of the hunches derived from some of the practical groups mentioned earlier. But they also tend to make us skeptical of some of the theories advanced by some communicators. Let me cite one example.

Many advertisers assert that any communication will be effective if it is repeated frequently enough. Psychological theory, on the other hand, stresses the fact that repetition will only be effective when the proper combinations of the other elements of motive, reward, and response are observed. Without a response leading to satisfaction not learning, but "unlearning" should occur. At the superficial level we could say that many repetitions will strengthen the desired behavior but the strengthening is not the result of repetition alone.

This approach of the advertiser to the problem of communication is illustrated in the story in today's *New York Times* concerning a planned campaign to eliminate race prejudice.

An aggressive national advertising campaign utilizing virtually every type of medium reaching the public, with the objective of "making racial prejudice as unpopular as B.O." will be carried on by the Advertising Council, Inc., it was announced yesterday.

During a press conference prior to the announcement of the campaign, Lee Bristol, vice president of Bristol-Myers and campaign coordinator, said: "Every means of advertising which could probably be useful will be mobilized in this fight against prejudice. Some of the best brains in the advertising profession have donated their time and talent to the design of striking posters and eloquent statements of the American creed. Through business facilities we will use advertising in newspapers, magazines, over the air, in outdoor display panels, and subway car cards."

Discussing the program, Edward Royal, council campaign manager, said it would be pushed strongly in the South. "We know that there is some support in the South already," Mr. Royal asserted. "We intend to hit the South as hard and as often as we can and feel reasonably certain that much of our material will be run in Southern newspapers and other media consistently." [14]

The objective is a worthy one and communication media may have an important role in attacking this problem, but I am sure you will feel from Mr. Wirth's paper later in the program that some important elements of the problem have not been sufficiently taken into account. However, if the copy for the campaign is adequately keyed to important personal motives, repetition will increase the chances of an individual's being exposed to the communication.

[14] *New York Times* for Feb. 6, 1948.

I have stressed the role of psychological theory. Equally important is the development of sociological and anthropological theories concerning communications. The way in which communication is transmitted in various types of social structure is an obvious example where the individual and the group are interdependent. Even more significant is the fact that understanding of the reward system for individuals is only possible in the light of the structure of the individual's society, and that sociological and anthropological analyses of what gets rewarded and what gets punished in the society as a whole, and more particularly in the subgroups of the society, has a most important function.

This brief survey has, I hope, shown that within the last decade there have been developed the basic materials needed to support an all-out offensive in developing a science of communication. The improved techniques for the analysis of the content of communication, the recent improvement in methods of studying the behavior elicited by communication, and the availability of both accumulated experience and some systematic theory make it possible to set up more critical observation and experiments. It appears quite likely that we shall witness substantial progress within the next years on this important new frontier.

5

COMMUNICATION MEDIA:
STRUCTURE AND CONTROL

Organization and Management

*T*he facts on the structure and control of the mass media of communication are many and varied. We have not represented them here because they are continuously changing, because they are readily available in standard sources, and because we have preferred to devote space to studies involving the correlation and interpretation of the facts. Thus the selections in this section were not chosen to present a simple description of the structure and control of the media but were rather chosen as significant contributions to the method of control analysis or as significant attacks on special substantive problems.

Analysis of quantitative data on control structure is exemplified in Nixon's study of the concentration of newspaper ownership, one of the central problems in this area. White's selection on radio deals with institutional self-regulation, the typical industry procedure to guarantee its acceptance of social responsibility. Finally, systematic analysis of the factors involved in determining policy for the mass media is represented in Horton's case study of a major decision in the development of television.

There are some important aspects of the structure and control of the mass media which are not represented here. Given space, we would have included selections dealing with the role of pressure groups, the impact of advertising, and the characteristics and functioning of media personnel. And given appropriate material, we would have included studies of relatively neglected problems in this area, such as the relationship between control structure and communication content and the remote yet powerful influence of the audience back upon the determination of communication content.

Raymond B. Nixon

CONCENTRATION AND ABSENTEEISM IN
DAILY NEWSPAPER OWNERSHIP

Concentration of ownership among American dailies has been proceeding for some fifty-five years, following in the wake of far more sweeping mergers and consolidations in business and industry at large. As one result, the number of English-language dailies of general circulation in the United States is today the lowest since 1891, though total daily circulation is the highest on record.

Total daily circulation has climbed from the beginning, with only a few easily explained slumps. The number of dailies, on the other hand, reached a peak of 2,600 in 1909 and since that time has been going down almost as steadily as circulation has been going up. Allowing for local combinations (two or more dailies in the same city with a common owner) and chains (two or more dailies in different cities under the same ultimate control), the present maximum number of daily ownerships does not exceed 1,300.

Several significant studies have been made in recent years of the growth of both one-publisher communities and daily chains.[1] So far as this writer can determine, however, no one has attempted a state-by-state analysis of

Reprinted with minor adaptations from *Journalism Quarterly*, Vol. XXII (1945), pp. 97-114, by permission of the author and the publisher. (Copyright, 1945, by The American Association of Schools and Departments of Journalism and The American Association of Teachers of Journalism.)

[1] See Paul Neurath, "One-Publisher Communities: Factors Influencing Trend," *Journalism Quarterly*, XXI: 230-42 (Sept., 1944), and William Weinfeld, "The Growth of Daily Newspaper Chains in the United States," *Journalism Quarterly*, XIII: 357-80 (Dec., 1936). Both contain extensive references to earlier important studies. Neurath finds that "the trend toward one-publisher communities in the sense that the marginal papers disappear or that all papers in the community are published by the same publisher" is observable from about 1890. Weinfeld points out that the oldest of the existing chains, the Scripps-Howard Newspapers, also dates to 1890, although the first chain was formed in 1878.

These earlier studies, like the present one, have been concerned only with daily newspapers. A similar trend toward one-newspaper places in the weekly field (from

local ownership concentration on the basis of circulation. While the best studies of chains have considered circulation, they too are incomplete in that they fail to distinguish between chain papers that are locally owned and those that are absentee-owned. Yet the degree of absenteeism is obviously important in discussing chains, just as circulation figures are essential in understanding any type of ownership situation.

The first purpose of this study, therefore, has been to bring earlier findings up to date and to supplement them with information on the extent of concentration and absenteeism in daily ownership.[2]

Since both of these trends have been attributed primarily to economic causes, a second purpose has been to discover what, if any, economic effects may be setting counter-forces in motion. For if economic factors are fundamental, as they no doubt will be so long as the press remains free, it is to such forces that we must look for a hint of things to come.

The trend toward fewer and larger units of production in American newspaper publishing made rapid headway following World War I. Between the two war years of 1918 and 1944, the total number of all dailies declined 19.4 per cent, while their total circulation went up 60.4 per cent. The number of Sunday papers declined less, showing a loss of only 4.5 per cent, but the increase in Sunday circulation was even more remarkable—136.3 per cent. It was in the first four years following the war (1919-22) that "the number and circulation of chain newspapers grew as never before."[3]

From 1930 through 1944, detailed records of daily suspensions and mergers are available. In this period, total daily circulation rose from 39,425,615 to 45,954,838, a gain of 16.8 per cent, whereas the number of dailies fell from 1,944 to 1,744, a loss of 10.2 per cent. Actually the gross rate of disappearance in these fifteen years was 29.6 per cent, for 576 dailies suspended publication. But the establishment of new papers, mostly short-lived affairs in the smaller cities, cut the net loss down to 200 (Table I).

Of the 576 "disappearing dailies," 276 suspended outright, 165 were merged with other papers and dropped, and 135 were reduced in frequency to tri-weekly, semi-weekly or weekly. That mergers have been going on for

66.1 per cent in 1900 to 86.5 per cent in 1930) is described by Willey and Weinfeld, "The Country Weekly and the Emergence of "One-Newspaper Places.'" *Journalism Quarterly*, XI- 250 (Sept., 1934). There also are many chains of weeklies, but apparently they have never been tabulated.

[2] Figures on the number of dailies and their circulation from 1918 through 1944 are taken from the annual compilations of *Editor & Publisher,* as noted in the accompanying tables; for earlier years, acknowledgement is made to tabulations in the Appendix to A. M. Lee, *The Daily Newspaper in America* (New York: 1937). Information concerning local combinations and chain and absentee ownerships not recorded by *Editor & Publisher* has been obtained from newspaper publishers, editors and many others. However, they are in no way responsible for the writer's interpretations and conclusions.

[3] Weinfeld, *op. cit.,* p. 362.

many decades is indicated by the 449 hyphenated names in the 1945 *Editor & Publisher* directory.[4] The names of a much larger number have disappeared entirely through suspensions.

TABLE I—Suspensions of English-Language Daily Newspapers of General Circulation in the United States, 1930-1947 *

Year	Outright Suspension	Merged and Dropped	Daily to Weekly, etc.	Total Suspensions	Total Dailies Dec. 31	Circulation September 30
1929**	...	...	...	...	1,944	39,425,615
1930	22	14	2	38	1,942	39,589,172
1931	26	19	7	52	1,923	38,761,187
1932	22	20	6	48	1,913	36,407,297
1933	23	15	7	45	1,911	35,175,238
1934	18	5	8	31	1,929	36,709,010
1935	11	6	4	21	1,950	38,155,540
1936	15	6	4	25	1,989	40,292,266
1937	22	17	12	51	1,993	41,418,730
1938	24	16	12	52	1,936	39,571,839
1939	30	7	24	61	1,888	39,670,682
1940	21	8	12	41	1,878	41,131,611
1941	19	10	9	38	1,857	42,080,391
1942	34	15	31	80	1,787	43,374,850
1943	9	9	10	28	1,754	44,392,829
1944	5	2	3	10	1,744	45,954,838
1945	3	5	2	10	1,749	48,384,188
1946	11	5	5	21	1,763	50,927,505
1947	21	3	8	32	1,769	51,673,276
	336	182	166	684		

Net Loss in Number of Dailies in 18-Year Period, 175
Gain in Total Circulation, 12,247,661

* The figures for suspensions are compiled from records kept by the American Newspaper Publishers Association; the total number of dailies and the total circulation each year are taken from the "Ready Reckoner" in *Editor & Publisher International Year Book Numbers*, 1930-1947.

** No detailed record of suspensions was kept until 1930.

Along with suspensions and mergers have come the consolidation of once competing papers into local combinations that continue publication under a single owner. In 1930 there were 89 single-owner cities with such combinations; at the end of 1944 and on March 1, 1945, there were 161. Of these, 159 are cities having two-paper combinations; one (Minneapolis) has three papers with a common ownership; and another (Springfield, Mass.) has four papers with the same publisher. In 13 other cities the only two existing dailies have entered into partial combinations (joint printing or advertising arrangements) which place their business offices on a non-competitive basis. This makes 174 cities in which the full or partial combination of all local dailies potentially eliminates competition. There are

4 There were 441 such hyphenated names in the 1940 directory, according to George L. Bird, "Newspaper Monopoly and Political Independence." *Journalism Quarterly*, XVII: 209 (Sept., 1940).

23 other combinations in competitive cities, making a grand total of 197. The total in 1930 was 144.

Compared with the earlier tabulations by A. M. Lee,[5] this new tabulation reveals that the total number of cities with daily newspapers went up from 1,402 in 1930 to 1,460 in 1937 and now has come down to 1,394. On the other hand, the number of one-daily cities increased steadily from 1,002 (71.4 per cent) in 1930 to 1,103 (79.1 per cent) in 1945. The total number of all non-competitive cities jumped from 1,114 (79.4 per cent) in 1930 to 1,277 (91.6 per cent) in 1945.

Perhaps the most amazing fact is that daily newspaper competition, certainly in the full economic meaning of the word, has been eliminated from all but 117 American cities. Ten entire states now have no local competition whatever.

A similar tabulation, not published here, shows that only 37 of the nation's 413 Sunday-newspaper cities have local competition; 22 entire states have no competitive Sunday papers.

On a circulation basis, however, the picture differs considerably. Only 40.2 per cent of the total daily circulation is non-competitive, as compared with 91.6 per cent of the total daily cities. On Sundays 34.9 per cent of the circulation is non-competitive, as against 91 per cent of the total Sunday-paper cities. The reason for this, of course, is that daily and Sunday circulations are concentrated most heavily in the larger cities, where competition still remains and probably will continue to flourish.

Even in the one-daily cities there are certain ameliorative factors. In the first place, the majority of one-daily communities are small cities which obviously could not give decent support to more than one such paper. Then, too, some of them have competition from a strong local weekly or an independent radio station.[6] Most important of all, modern communication and transportation mean that even the small-city daily often has competi-

---

[5] "The Basic Newspaper Pattern," *Annals of the American Academy of Political and Social Science*, CCXIX: 46 (Jan., 1942). Assuming that Dr. Lee counted as two or more cities certain areas which the writer counted as only one city (such as Rock Island-Moline, Ill., and the boroughs of Greater New York), the number of daily newspaper cities today is almost exactly the same as in 1945.

The writer recognizes, of course, that certain cities listed as "competitive" have two or more newspapers under separate ownerships but with almost identical social and political policies. Moreover, there may be understandings between the publishers of some such papers which reduce economic competition almost to the vanishing point.

[6] "If radio stations and newspapers are taken together, 36 per cent of the communities have more than one medium of communication," says Paul F. Lazarsfeld, "The Daily Newspaper and Its Competitors," *Annals of the American Academy of Political and Social Science*, CCXIX: 41 (Jan., 1942). Of course "about 25 per cent of all radio stations are majority owned by newspaper interests." A survey by the writer in the state of Georgia, where 92 per cent of the daily cities are without local daily competition, shows that non-competitive cities are reduced to 82.8 per cent when competing weeklies and independent radio stations are counted.

tion on important local stories, as well as in national news and advertising, from some nearby big-city daily. With 700 magazines circulating an aggregate of 140,000,000 copies an issue, and with 30,000,000 families listening an average of five hours a day to the radio,[7] no single medium of communication in the United States can be said to enjoy a complete "monopoly."

In explaining suspensions, mergers and combinations, publishers point out that they are due to seemingly "inexorable" economic trends. Among these they cite such factors as the loss of advertising revenue to radio, the preference of advertisers for fewer media with larger circulations and the increased cost of machinery, newsprint, labor, taxes and nearly every other item of the newspaper's expenses. For many papers it has been, as Nelson Poynter says, a case of "death or consolidation."[8]

One may agree with this statement and still point out that most of the suspensions and mergers represent the elimination of a weak paper by a strong paper, and that the survivor in nearly every instance has been made stronger by its inheritance of a non-competitive field.[9]

The same is true of combinations of two or more dailies which continue publication under a single publisher. Commenting in 1943 on this type of consolidation, Arthur Robb, then editor of *Editor & Publisher*, attributed it frankly [10] to the desire of publishers to effect savings in plant investment

TABLE II—Population Analysis of All Daily Newspaper Cities, March 1, 1945

Population Group	Total Daily Cities	One- Daily Cities	Other 1-Owner Cities	Partial Merger Cities	Total Non-com- petitive	Total Compet- itive
Less than 10,000	547	523	9	..	532	14
10,000-25,000	474	409	45	..	454	21
25,000-50,000	182	117	45	3	165	16
50,000-100,000	94	34	40	6	80	15
100,000-200,000	51	15	12	4	31	20
200,000-300,000	17	4	6	..	11	6
300,000-400,000	12	1	3	..	4	8
400,000-500,000	3	..	1	..	..	3
500,000-1,000,000	9	..	..	..	..	9
1,000,000 or over	5	..	..	..	..	5
Totals	1,394	1,103	161	13	1,277	117

and operation and to eliminate competition in the sale of advertising and circulation. Heavy and expensive newspaper machinery is so well constructed, he pointed out, that two papers a day can be printed in the same

[7] Lazarsfeld, *op. cit.*, p. 32.

[8] "The Economic Problems of the Press and the Changing Newspaper," *Annals of the American Academy of Political and Social Science*, CCXIX: 85 (Jan., 1942).

[9] Clyde H. Knox, "The Newspaper Outlook for 1944," address delivered before the Missouri Press Association, Nov. 5, 1943. Privately printed, Kansas City.

[10] "Shop Talk at Thirty," *Editor & Publisher*, Oct. 30, 1943, p. 48.

plant with little increased allowance for depreciation. In addition to this, one advertising sales force, one accounting department and one circulation system can operate almost as cheaply for two papers as for one.

Defending the elimination of competition, Mr. Robb said that in competitive situations the leading newspaper often made it difficult for its competitors by cutting rates and going after volume both in circulation and in advertising. Unable to fight it out on a rate basis, the weaker paper frequently "went haywire" by offering expensive premiums to get circulation and by giving all sorts of free publicity and bonuses to sell advertising. "Each newspaper did its best to convince prospective customers that the other fellow was not worthy of patronage, and too often both succeeded in that destructive course." Advertisers also took advantage of the situation, which made it easy for a store or combination of stores to attempt "whipsawing tactics, playing one newspaper against the other." So far as the elimination of such practices is concerned, most observers probably would agree with Mr. Robb that the results of combinations have been desirable.

Nearly all the published criticisms of one-publisher communities have been based not on economic but on socio-political grounds. "It is unquestionably within the power of the publisher of the only daily paper or papers in a city to determine how completely and how accurately the news of the day—local, state, national and international—shall be presented to his readers," wrote Dr. Willard G. Bleyer [11] in 1934. *Editor & Publisher*,[12] while holding that the majority of non-competitive ownerships have been conscious of their responsibilities, added editorially in 1938: "The danger remains that freedom for minority expression will be curtailed . . ."

It is obviously to meet such objections as these that the owners of some local combinations, like those of certain chains, operate two or more papers with different editorial policies. In a situation like that of the Cleveland *News* and *Plain Dealer*, where there is a long tradition of independence, the public apparently accepts such an arrangement in good faith. In other cities the response seems to have been less favorable, perhaps because, as one editor explained it to me, "the editorials in one of the papers lack sincerity, or can be suspected of lacking sincerity."

The "partial-combination" plan is a more recent innovation by which most of the economic advantages of joint operation may be obtained without incurring the editorial disadvantages. Here two existing papers merge their business facilities, in part or in whole, while leaving ownership and editorial autonomy to separate publishers. Beginning with the Albuquerque (N.M.) *Journal* and *Tribune* in February, 1933, eight of these partial

[11] "Freedom of the Press and the New Deal," *Journalism Quarterly*, XI: (March, 1934).
[12] Dec. 31, 1938, p. 20.

combinations have set up separate corporations and printing establishments to print both papers. The other five at present have only joint business arrangements, confined in some instances to the combination selling of advertising.

The formula varies, but in the joint-printing cities (Albuquerque, Chattanooga, El Paso, Evansville, Nashville, Topeka, Tulsa and Tucson) "all circulation and advertising revenues go into a common pool. All expenses except editorial expenses are paid from this pool, and the surplus is distributed between the publishers of the rival newspapers according to a previously negotiated ratio." [13]

The publishers who have entered into such arrangements are "enthusiastic for the results, without exception." Letters to the writer from editors in all the partial-combination cities disclose that they are equally enthusiastic. All assert that editorial independence has been maintained. Indeed, several say that, since joint operation lessens advertising pressure, editorial independence actually has been increased.

"One cannot have editorial independence unless he has economic independence," one editor wrote. "Joint operation gives us that."

In two instances it was intimated that a city would have only one daily but for the partial combination, inasmuch as one of the papers had been losing money steadily before the business merger was effected.

The only discordant note came from one of the older editors, who, although expressing the opinion that joint business operations had not interfered with editorial independence, added:

> It is my conviction that this editorial and news independence will not continue and that in the end . . . readers will have poorer papers than they would have if we were entirely individual . . . I think it is inevitable that the ownership will eventually influence the editorial pages to its way of thinking and that it will be impossible to maintain independent editorial policies.

On the economic side, however, the vote of both publishers and editors in favor of joint operation is unanimous. The best evidence that the savings are "substantial throughout" [14] is found in the fact that *there is apparently no case on record of two papers which have come together—in a combination or partial combination—ever going back to separate operation.*

Although the term "newspaper chain" means simply two or more newspapers in different cities with the same ownership or control, most critics seem to imply that chain ownership is the same as absentee ownership.

---

[13] Poynter, *op. cit.*, p. 85.

[14] These words are taken from the letter to the writer by the general manager of a morning and evening combination. Commenting on it, Professor Charles L. Allen points out that a merger or combination sometimes entails an additional outlay for such items as severance pay, scrapping of old machinery and buying of new, etc. He agrees, however, that in most instances the cost of operation is lowered "almost immediately."

For example, it has been said that the chain "applies national formulae to local situations to which they are never quite adequate," and that the chain "changes the character of the newspaper . . . to a purely commercial organization and instrumentality . . ." [15]

Yet the home paper of a chain may be just as much a part of the community as if its owner had no papers elsewhere. Conversely, a paper may have no connection with a chain and still have an owner, either resident or absentee, whose only interest is "purely commercial."

That generalizations are extremely dangerous is indicated by the fact that four of the eight papers ranked by Kingsbury and Hart in 1934 as "leaders in ethical journalism" were chain papers.[16] Most readers of this article doubtless also could name "absentee-owned papers" which would rank exceedingly high by any standard of measurement. The writer is not concerned here with the ethical implications of either chain or absentee ownership, but merely with its relative extent.

There are some two-daily chains in which neither paper justly can be classified as "absentee-owned." For example, the Chicago *Tribune* owns all the stock of the New York *Daily News*. One of the two owners of the papers, Colonel Robert A. McCormick, lives in Chicago and runs the *Tribune*. The other, Captain James M. Patterson, lives in New York and runs the *Daily News*. It would be difficult to prove that there is any significant degree of "absentee control" on either of these papers. The same is true of several other two-city chains, notably that of the Cowles brothers in Minneapolis and Des Moines and that of J. David Stern in the neighboring cities of Camden and Philadelphia.

In still other situations it is impractical to classify any member of a chain as the "home paper." For instance, William Randolph Hearst is not the resident editor of any of his papers in California, where he lives, and the business headquarters of the organization are in New York. Consequently, it seems proper to regard all papers of this chain as absentee-owned and also as owned "outside the state."

The Speidel-McCraken interests in Wyoming present another special problem. Tracy S. McCraken is resident publisher of the two papers in Cheyenne, where the Speidel Newspapers, Inc., own at least 50 per cent of the stock. However, Mr. McCraken is the largest stockholder and president of four other papers outside Cheyenne. Although he asserts that "where one has partners like mine the question of control never rises," all six of these papers fall in the absentee-owned class under the rule followed here.

[15] Quoted by Curtis D. MacDougall, *Newsroom Problems and Policies* (New York: 1941), pp. 16-17.

[16] Susan M. Kingsbury, Hornell Hart and Associates, "Measuring the Ethics of American Newspapers," *Journalism Quarterly*, XI: 300 (Sept., 1934).

The rule is that, irrespective of the amount of local autonomy which may exist, a paper is classified as "absentee-owned" whenever the ultimate ownership or control appears beyond any reasonable doubt to lie outside the city of publication.

On the basis of this definition, 297 or 17 per cent of the English-language dailies of general circulation in the United States as of March 1, 1945, are absentee-owned. The circulation of these papers is 12,755,791 or 27.7 per cent of the total circulation. On Sundays the relative number of absentee-owned papers is 25.2 per cent, while the relative circulation is 31.5 per cent.

The total number of all chain dailies as of March 1, 1945, is 370 (21.2 per cent of the total).[17] This figure is obtained by subtracting 16 individual ownerships from the number of absentee-owned papers and adding the 89 "home-papers" of the various chains. In contrast, the number of chain dailies identified by William Weinfeld [18] for 1935 was 328 or 16.8 per cent of the total number of papers in that year. On Sundays the relative number of chain papers is now 32.9 per cent against 25.3 per cent in 1935, while the total circulation today is 53.8 per cent as compared with 25.3 per cent in 1935.

In spite of this slight increase during the last ten years, relative chain circulation is still below its 1930 peak of 43.4 per cent daily and 54.1 per cent Sunday. In fact, the proportion of chain circulation to total circulation has remained at almost exactly the same point for the last fifteen years. The number of chain papers has increased, but the average circulation has decreased.

The average chain also has grown smaller in number of papers. Weinfeld in 1935 listed 63 chains with an average of 5.1 papers each, while the tabulation for 1945 shows 76 chains with an average of 4.8 papers each. Of the 52 chains which are on both lists, 16 have grown smaller, losing an average of 2.8 papers each; 13 have grown larger, gaining an average of 2.4 papers each; and 23 have remained the same size.

A comparison of the 1935 and 1945 lists reveals likewise that there has been a tendency away from large national chains toward state and regional chains, or chains of only a few large papers. At present 44 of the 76 chains

[17] These are the writer's own figures, as explained in Table IV. The list of daily chains in *Editor & Publisher International Year Book Number* for 1945, p. 180, contains only 51 chains with 289 papers when one chain of technical dailies, three now defunct chains (so far as *dailies* are concerned) and the subsidiary chains of the Copley newspapers are omitted. Correspondence with the former editor of *Editor & Publisher* indicates that it is the policy of the magazine to list only *acknowledged* chains and combinations. For example, the *Year Book* never listed the four dailies owned by the International Paper Company in the South, although the ownership was described by Arthur Robb in his excellent history of chains in the *Golden Jubilee Number* of July 21, 1934, p. 232. The recent sale of all the International Paper Company's dailies has eliminated this chain.

[18] *Op. cit.*, p. 379.

(57.8 per cent) are confined to one state, and 255 (67.6 per cent) of the 370 chain dailies are located in the state in which their ownership is located.

Although none of the earlier studies of chains has divided papers on this basis, some further comparisons are possible. For example, the two national chains which in 1935 were largest in number of dailies have both declined, Hearst from 26 to 17 papers and Scripps-Howard from 23 to 18. The Frank E. Gannett chain, which was third largest in 1935, has grown from 16 to 17 papers (14 in New York, two in adjoining states, only one at any distance). These are highly concentrated in location and enjoy a large degree of local autonomy.

Hearst, McCormick-Patterson and Scripps-Howard still lead in total daily circulation, in the order named, but Hearst has lost ground and Scripps-Howard has gained only slightly. The chain which has gained most in circulation, McCormick-Patterson, is concentrated entirely in two cities and has one of its two owners as resident publisher each city.

The implications of all this are clear: daily chain ownership has been becoming more *intensive* and less *extensive* in its concentration. Indeed, when one encounters a situation like that of the Marlboro-Hudson (Mass.) chain, where the two papers are located in cities only five miles apart and sell their advertising only in combination, it is almost a toss-up as to whether it should be classified as a chain or as a local combination.

It remains to be determined whether the more extensive national chains have declined because they had reached that still unknown point at which the advantages of chain operation fail to compensate for the disadvantages of absentee ownership. Perhaps the owners merely have been too busy looking after their present properties during these years of depression and war to give much thought to expansion. The chains experienced their greatest growth after World War I and may expand similarly after World War II. The time seems to have passed, however, when a Hearst would seek to further his presidential ambitions through personally directed papers located in every section of the country. Present-day conditions seem to favor a more intensive type of ownership concentration, in which absenteeism is less of a factor.

Since the national chains seem to be at a standstill and the still growing state and regional chains appear to be becoming more and more intensive in their concentration, let us take another look at the local combinations. Here the trend is unbroken. The critics who have pointed out the dangers to a sound public opinion seem to have had little effect. But what of the effect of the combinations themselves on the newspaper's chief source of revenue: the advertiser?

One complaint sometimes heard is that the savings effected by the selling of advertising in combination have benefited only the newspapers.

To check its validity, an examination was made of the advertising rates of 97 non-competitive combinations formed between 1927 and 1942, before and after the consolidation took place. In 43 instances the new combined rate of the two papers was lower than the sum of the old individual rates; in 31 cases it was the same; and in 23 it was higher. While it is entirely possible that the old rates were too low, as a result of cutthroat competition, the fact remains that 54 out of 97 combinations apparently resulted in no financial benefits to the advertiser.

Even more striking is an analysis made by the American Association of Advertising Agencies for all dailies whose rates were reported in 1941 by *Standard Rate and Data Service* (Table III). This comparison, broken down into 19 population groups to eliminate unfairness, shows that the milline rates for 211 pairs of papers sold in enforced combination averaged higher, in every population group but the four largest, than the milline rates of 1,334 papers sold independently.

The effect of combinations to which advertisers object most strenuously, however, is not the higher milline rate but the "enforced combination rate." This means that the advertiser is forced to buy space in both papers of the combination in order to advertise in one. The growing prevalence of this practice is shown by the "Ready Reckoner" in the 1945 *Editor & Publisher Year Book*, which reveals that an advertiser who wishes to use the total

TABLE III—Comparison of Milline Rates of Independent Newspapers With Those of Papers Having Optional or Enforced Combinations *

| Circulation Group | Advertising Sold Independently | | | Sold in Combination | |
	Morning	Evening	Morning & Evening**	Optional	Enforced
Under 1,200	...	23.00(19)	23.00(19)	...	...
1,200-1,799	17.22(3)	15.24(50)	15.35(53)	...	...
1,800-2,699	13.57(9)	11.30(105)	11.48(114)	...	...
2,700-3,999	9.99(22)	8.93(245)	9.02(267)	...	9.94(9)
4,000-5,999	7.70(22)	7.53(265)	7.55(287)	...	8.35(7)
6,000-8,999	6.26(14)	6.38(160)	6.37(174)	...	7.56(10)
9,000-13,499	5.24(11)	5.22(95)	5.22(106)	...	5.95(30)
13,500-19,999	4.23(8)	4.30(74)	4.29(82)	...	4.81(35)
20,000-29,999	3.62(14)	3.72(36)	3.69(50)	...	4.19(29)
30,000-44,999	3.31(10)	3.09(44)	3.13(54)	3.93(2)	3.64(25)
45,000-67,499	2.33(11)	2.65(22)	2.54(33)	2.97(4)	2.87(22)
67,500-99,999	2.26(4)	2.40(16)	2.37(20)	2.17(1)	2.54(12)
100,000-149,999	2.09(16)	2.38(13)	2.22(29)	1.90(1)	2.24(7)
150,000-219,999	2.53(1)	1.96(16)	2.00(17)	2.05(2)	1.95(7)
220,000-329,999	1.90(7)	1.87(8)	1.89(15)	1.98(1)	1.63(4)
330,000-499,999	1.73(4)	1.51(6)	1.60(10)	...	1.44(2)
500,000-749,999	1.22(1)	1.57(1)	1.40(2)	...	.96(1)
750,000-1,124,999	.99(1)	...	.99(1)	...	...
Over 1,125,000	.85(1)	...	.85(1)	...	...

* From analysis of American Association of Advertising Agencies, based upon rates reported in *Standard Rate & Data Service* for 1941. Used by permission.

** Average and number of all daily newspapers shown in two preceding columns combined.

18,059,252 morning circulation of the nation now must buy an additional 6,262,324 in evening circulation, while the advertiser who wishes to use the total of 27,895,586 evening circulation must buy an additional 6,073,865 in morning circulation. Thus, the cost of a campaign in all morning papers is increased by 44.6 per cent, and that of a campaign in all evening papers by 13.7 per cent.

Of 50 two-paper combinations in 135 cities with 100,000 or more A.B.C. circulation, 21 pairs in 1943 had enforced combination rates for both national and local advertising; 21 pairs had such rates but not local advertising; 7 pairs had only optional combination rates; and 1 pair had no combination rate. Only five combinations in cities without competing newspapers did not have an enforced combination rate, either national or local, or both.[19]

To check the attitude of national advertisers toward the enforced combination rate, executives of thirty of the largest agencies in the country were asked for a confidential opinion. Nineteen replied. Although a few qualified their answers in some way, all indicated that they regard the enforced combination as "undesirable."

They contend that it increases the cost to the advertiser on a per-reader basis even more than the rates themselves imply, for there is inevitably overlapping in the circulation of two papers in the same city.

"The important point," wrote the head of one large New York agency, "is that the advertiser's cost in the market usually rises considerably. For example, the average advertiser in Nashville used to spend thirteen or fourteen cents a line. Now this cost is thirty cents. We used to place campaigns in Minneapolis at about twenty-five cents a line. Now this cost is sixty cents. Most of these situations follow the same pattern."

Some products have "limited market opportunities," another executive contended. For these the enforced combination makes it impossible to buy "the type of circulation and coverage which is required for a given advertising problem."

To this the publishers reply that for advertised products there is usually no such thing as a "limited local market." It is therefore to the national advertiser's advantage, they say, to have an enforced combination which gives him greater coverage and more frequency than he ordinarily would buy.

It is more difficult to evaluate the reactions of local advertisers to the enforced combination, since the rate is not applied to them so uniformly. Even where the combination rate is listed as enforced locally, exceptions often are made for certain classes of advertising or inducements are offered to lessen opposition. However, of 16 department-store advertising managers

[19] Figures compiled from a study of *Market and Newspaper Statistics*, Vol. 12-A, published by the American Association of Advertising Agencies (New York: 1943).

n 10 single-combination newspaper cities who were asked for an opinion, only one who had had any direct experience with a fully enforced local combination rate regarded it as "desirable."

Comments from department store executives included these:

"The enforced combination rates . . . create a monopoly, and a monopoly by the newspaper is one of the worst things that can happen."

"Sometimes it is not desirable to advertise merchandise in two papers, especially when shipments . . . sell out almost as soon as one ad has appeared. When a clearance is announced, it is to our disadvantage to run the ad more than one time."

"We have had better results preparing new copy for each paper."

Because of objections such as these, at least two non-competitive cities (Mobile, Ala., and Madison, Wis.) which had enforced combination rates in 1943 have now gone back to lower individual rates, with the combination optional. In Mobile each paper in the combination lists an individual rate almost as high as the combination rate, but in Madison the individual rates are virtually the same as before the two papers went into their partial merger.[20]

Unless readjustments of this kind continue to be made, and unless postwar expansion brings a reversal of the trend toward one-publisher communities, it is possible that those who have been urging governmental action to maintain multiple outlets of news and opinion may find their ranks reinforced by an unexpected ally: the newspaper advertiser.

Regulation of the purely business aspects of journalism by a governmental commission, in the same way that public utilities are regulated, may be more imminent than we realize. Two straws in the wind are the suit against the Associated Press and the Federal Communications Commission's hearing on newspaper ownership of radio stations. Another is the federal court decision whereby fifteen New York department stores and their trade association were fined $5,000 each in the spring of 1943 on a charge of conspiracy to withhold advertising from the New York *Times*.[21]

This latter decision, hailed by many as a victory for the press, may turn out to be otherwise. For if advertisers can be fined for combining to withhold advertising, the courts are almost certain to hold, sooner or later, that newspapers which combine to raise advertising or circulation rates also should be subject to legal authority.

"Freedom of the press" hardly would prove effective as a defense. As

[20] The Madison situation is one of the most interesting of all the partial combinations. Here the two afternoon papers, keen editorial rivals, have worked out an exchange of *non-voting* stock whereby each paper owns a half interest in the other, although all the *voting* stock of each paper is held by the original separate owners. As noted above, the papers at first adopted an enforced combination rate but now have abandoned it. A further point of interest is that one of the papers is a chain daily.

[21] *Editor & Publisher*, April 17, 1943, p. 11.

Dr. Fred S. Siebert has pointed out,[22] the decisions of a liberal Supreme Court in recent years have placed the American newspaper "in possession of greater freedom to gather, publish and comment on the news than ever before in its history." At the same time, the courts have shown increasing reluctance "to extend the meaning of the constitutional guarantees of freedom of the press to cover social and economic regulations."

If the economic forces that lead to mergers and combinations are "inexorable," what can the individual publisher do to forestall such regulation?

These suggestions should be prefaced by an admission that certain possible events may render them less urgent. The perfection of cheaper methods of printing, such as photolithography without typesetting, may multiply local channels of opinion and advertising to such an extent that the cries of "monopoly" will subside. Furthermore, the postwar development of FM broadcasting, television and facsimile may prove just as effective as cheaper printing in providing new competitive media through which "truth and falsehood may grapple."

But if these things do not come in time, what can the publisher do?

First of all, he can dedicate his paper as never before to the principles of intelligent and objective reporting, giving all sides a fair hearing in the news columns and confining the views of the owner to the editorial page. Even here, as several recent writers have suggested,[23] the owner-publisher, particularly of a combination or chain, should reign as a "constitutional monarch," with the active editor as "prime minister." If the publisher cannot get down from his throne and mingle with the people, then the editor should. He should keep the people on his side by putting their interests first.

Second, he can demonstrate to the advertiser as well as to the reader that the benefits of consolidation are not solely on the publisher's side of the ledger. With this in view, some reconsideration of the enforced combination rate might be in order. It seems difficult if not impossible to answer completely the argument that "compelling national advertisers to use combination papers which local advertisers may use individually is discriminatory."

Third, if the publisher is in a community where consolidation has not been effected but merely seems inevitable, he can consider whether the joint printing plan is not more desirable, certainly from the public's point of view, than a complete merger or combination.

[22] "Legal Developments Affecting the Press," *Annals of the American Academy of Political and Social Science*, CCXIX (Jan., 1942).

[23] Notably Wilson Harris in *The Daily Press* (Cambridge England: 1943) and Robert Lasch in "For a Free Press," *Atlantic Monthly*, CLXXIV: 1: 39-44 (July, 1944).

Above all, the American press must find ways of adapting itself to changing economic conditions without losing its editorial vitality and independence. As a result of suspensions and consolidations, the daily newspaper admittedly has gained greater economic stability than ever before. We must make certain that this stability does not bring with it editorial rigidity and sterility.

Llewellyn White

THE AMERICAN RADIO:
TOWARD SELF-REGULATION

It often has been remarked that the radio broadcasting industry operates under a poorly defined charter. Possibly it would be more accurate to say that it operates under no charter. A study of the public and private utterances of those most directly connected with broadcasting reveals (1) that the attitudes of individuals changed sharply as the industry developed and (2) that at no period in this quarter-century of development have the industry's spokesmen been able to agree on a precise definition of the broadcasters' responsibilities.

Probably changing attitudes were inevitable in a changing industry. Certainly, much of what was said in the 1920's was a natural expression of the groping for guidance in a new field the outlines of which were then clearly visible to no one. It will serve no useful purpose to recall here that David Sarnoff, in 1922, envisioned radio as a "public service" comparable to the free library or that delegates to Secretary Hoover's First Radio Conference in the same year voted to outlaw all direct advertising. Advertising was not at the time an issue.

Nor is it remarkable that the broadcasters should have come, in time, to depend for their revenues upon the "evil" which they had once banished by resolution; the remarkable thing is that the shift of emphasis was so thoroughgoing that twenty years later Mark Woods, president of the American Broadcasting Company, could say unblushingly [1] that "we are selling time for one specific reason, and that is to sell goods." And what makes it remarkable is that Woods, who was not an advertising man, nonetheless spoke the vernacular of the advertising man. Like the beleaguered Czechs of ancient Bohemia, the broadcasters had cried out for

Reprinted from *The American Radio* (1947), pp. 68-85, by permission of the author and the publisher. (Copyright, 1947, by The University of Chicago Press.)

[1] In a colloquy with Commissioner Clifford J. Durr during F.C.C. hearings leading to separation of the National Broadcasting Company's Red and Blue networks.

208

succor. Like the Hapsburgs, the advertising men who came to rescue remained to rule. And, like many a philosophical Slav, the broadcasters accepted the conquerer's tongue.

The point is significant because the advertising people brought to broadcasting not only their language but also their mores and standards. One may criticize the broadcasters for accepting them, but he could hardly accuse the broadcasters of failing to live up to them. For example, there is nothing immoral in an advertising man's admission that his primary purpose is to sell goods. So that, if we weigh Woods' words as the words of an advertising practitioner and still find them shocking, then the indictment will have to cover all advertising men, as well as a majority of the broadcasters. Perhaps it should also cover those educational and eleemosynary bodies that talked a good deal about "rescuing" radio in the twenties but did very little; a Congress that did not heed the broadcasters' plea for help; and a listening public that responded to it with contributions of dimes and half-dollars.

As has been noted, the American Society of Composers, Authors, and Publishers was as alert to the possibilities of radio broadcasting as Westinghouse's Dr. Frank Conrad. It had long been the practice of A.S.C.A.P. to exact royalties for copyrighted music sung or played upon the stage or etched on phonograph records. The application of this royalty principle to broadcasting seemed altogether reasonable. To many a broadcaster struggling along on a shoestring, it was a move fraught with peril. A number of midwestern broadcasters organized an informal committee of correspondence, and on April 25, 1923, met in Chicago to form a society for mutual aid, which they styled the "National Association of Broadcasters." The idea of a trade-association to resist the inroads of well-organized groups like A.S.C.A.P. (and government, since the conscientious Secretary of Commerce was believed to be getting increasingly "stuffy" about licenses to use already overworked frequencies) gained nation-wide favor; and on October 11 a second meeting was held in New York, at which time the membership base was broadened to include broadcasters from all parts of the country.

Organized resistance to A.S.C.A.P. was less successful than organized resistance to Hoover, but for six years these two relatively specific items constituted the agenda. There is not one word in the literature of N.A.B. or in the transcripts of its proceedings from 1923 to 1929 to indicate that a yearning for self-regulation played any part in its councils until the passage of the Radio Act of 1927 made government regulation an unpleasant reality. Not until March 25, 1929, did N.A.B. get around to writing its first "Code of Ethics," an admirable, if somewhat sketchy, document which was commended to the attention of all broadcasters by the newly appointed Federal Radio Commission.

Briefly, it proscribed the broadcasting of anything which would be barred from the mails as "fraudulent, deceptive, or obscene" and of "any matter which would commonly be regarded as offensive"; warned members to be wary of the claims of advertisers and their products; forbade statements derogatory to competing broadcasters, sponsors, or products; and provided for investigation of violations of these restrictions.

The N.A.B. of this period was still essentially an association of broadcasters. Half-a-dozen advertising agencies that had begun to manifest interest in the new medium sent "observers" to the N.A.B. sessions, as did the American Association of Advertising Agencies (A.A.A.A.) and the Association of National Advertisers (A.N.A.). At the 1929 convention some of these "observers" ventured to suggest to the broadcasters that they include in their Code a set of advertising standards comparable to those which the advertisers had applied in the other media. The station-owners and managers were still concerned about how much straight commercialism the public would stand for, and they wrote provisions so much more drastic than anything the advertising men had had in mind that the latter prevailed on the broadcasters to circulate them quietly among the N.A.B. members rather than make them public along with the Code. This "Standard of Commercial Practice," which any present-day radio listener will recognize as a collector's item, provided:

1. There should be a "decided difference" between what might be broadcast before 6:00 P.M. and what might be broadcast after that hour. The time before 6:00 P.M. was declared to be included in the "business day," and it was decided that "part at least" of it might be devoted to "programs of a business nature." After 6:00 "time is for recreation and relaxation; therefore commercial programs should be of the good-will type."

2. Commercial announcements, "as the term is generally understood," should not be broadcast between 7:00 and 11:00 P.M.

3. "The client's business and product should be mentioned sufficiently to insure an adequate return on his investment, but never to the extent that it loses listeners to the station."

The 1929 Code was reviewed at the annual N.A.B. meeting in 1931, but certain changes that had been tactfully suggested by the F.R.C. were tabled. Not until 1935 did the standing Code Committee produce a new instrument, and then the clamor was for something that would subdue the "unethical" fly-by-night stations that were springing up over the land. Clause 6 of the 1929 Code, the only one referring to the functions of the government's regulatory agency, was dropped. Three new clauses sought to bulwark the positions of the "ethical" advertisers and station-owners.

The new Code lasted two years and pleased no one. Some independent broadcasters regarded it as simply a watered-down version of the 1929 instrument and blamed the networks for the watering-down. Network representatives spoke bitterly (albeit in private) of the "downward pull" of the "lowest common denominator." Members [2] of N.A.B. observed the Code to the extent that it pleased them. There were no penalties for flouting it.

Even so, many broadcasters felt that the diluted standards were too confining. In 1937 this latter element took over the direction of N.A.B., reorganized it, and publicly dedicated the industry to a simple five-point program:

1. Find a solution for the music-copyright problem.

2. Resist efforts of the International Allied Printing Trades Council to saddle a tax on radio time sales.

3. "Eliminate certain practices and policies" reflected in programs and commercial announcements which had had "an adverse effect on the industry."

4. Promote the wider use of radio as an advertising medium.

5. Prevent "unfavorable" legislation.

In February, 1938, N.A.B. installed its first full-time paid president, Neville Miller, former mayor of Louisville. But the industry needed more than a "front" and a "practical" program. The networks were in the throes of monopoly hearings before the F.C.C. In the course of these hearings, President Sarnoff had stated:

"The fate of broadcasting in other nations and the attacks on democracy throughout the world clearly indicate the necessity of finding a democratic solution for the problems of the American system of broadcasting—a solution which on the one hand will enable us fully to meet the social obligations of radio and on the other will protect our traditional freedoms. I would therefore like to take this opportunity to advocate to the broadcasting industry that it establish a voluntary system of self-regulation in its field of public service, and that it take the necessary steps to make that self-regulation effective."

Miller promptly appointed a new code committee to produce the sort of charter that radio had ignored or resisted for more than fifteen years. Before the committee had finished its deliberations, however, the war had precipitated a showdown in the field of international broadcasting. World Wide, the National Broadcasting Company, the Columbia Broadcasting System, General Electric, Westinghouse, and Crosley were sending to Europe and Latin America by short wave pretty much what they pleased. In May, 1939, the Federal Communications Commission drew up a tentative statement of principles. In hearings lasting into the summer, N.A.B. successfully combated this first attempt of the government to sketch the barest outlines of program standards. This offending statement of principles, shelved in favor of laissez faire until the Coordinators of Information and

---

[2] At no time has N.A.B. embraced all broadcasters; as of the close of 1946, some three hundred stations were not members.

Inter-American Affairs took over short-wave broadcasting early in 1942, read:

"A licensee of an international broadcast station shall render only an international broadcast service which will reflect the culture of this country and which will promote international goodwill, understanding and cooperation. Any program solely intended for and directed to an audience in the continental United States does not meet the requirements for this service."

To the advertising agencies then completely dominating the industry, and especially the networks,[3] the outlook seemed unpromising, if not downright alarming. If the F.C.C. could say that domestic programs would not pass muster abroad, might it not soon conclude that they were not adequate at home either?

Moreover, there was the war. Father Coughlin had shown how explosive the isolationist-interventionist feud could be on the air. Had not the time come to call a halt to controversy altogether, curb this violator of the first tenet of advertising: "Don't upset anybody"?

Could the broadcasters, who, after all, had offered no protest when the advertisers moved in to an extent that they had never dared to do in the press, be counted on to "take a stand"?

The answer was of course "No"; and the advertising men and their friends in the networks proceeded to write a "Code To End Codes," but only after a battle in which wiser voices, including that of Edward Klauber, executive vice-president of C.B.S., were silenced. Klauber had taken a "good" code to what has ever since been referred to by those who believe in good codes as "the Atlantic City fiasco."

The "Standards of Practice of the National Association of Broadcasters," made public on July 11, 1939, is worthy of the closest scrutiny and analysis by students of mass communication, advertising, and psychology. In some two hundred words, it placed "crime-does-not-pay" and cowman breakfast-food serials for children in the context of "character development." "Education" was dismissed in five lines, "Religion" in four. "News" was to be "fair" and "accurate." "Commercial programs and length of commercial copy" came straight from the A.A.A.A. handbook; the 7:00–11:00 P.M. "recreation period" of a decade earlier was to have up to 20-odd minutes of "plugs"[4]—more if in the form of "participation programs, announcement programs, musical clocks, shoppers' guides," or "local programs." But the chef d'œuvre was the section on "Controversial Public Issues." In some three hundred and fifty of the most carefully weighed words in the

[3] The agencies were delivering 87 per cent of the chains' business—the shows being agency-conceived, the scripts agency-written, the talent agency-picked and rehearsed, the finished "package" even accompanied by a convenient check list of the optional stations that the broadcasters were to "plug in."

[4] If the 4-hour segment were cut into 5-minute periods, the figure would be 40 minutes for "plugs."

history of advertising double-talk the drafters made certain that broadcasters would eschew controversy as a plague-ridden orphan, feared by all, unwanted by the makers of soap and cigarettes.

That the advertising men were not altogether undetected and unopposed in their designs is perhaps indicated by an editorial in the August–September issue of *Education by Radio*, bulletin of the National Committee on Education by Radio:

"Early in 1939, the National Association of Broadcasters, trade association for the industry, appointed a committee to prepare a code which would constitute at once on instrument of self-regulation for the industry and a protection to the listening public. The membership of the committee was representative and able.[5] It held numerous meetings and consulted with a wide variety of organizations and interests. It prepared a document which was printed and distributed in advance of the Atlantic City convention of the NAB and which was recognized generally as an important contribution to the development of radio broadcasting in the United States. . . . . The code actually adopted . . . . at the convention . . . . is a totally different thing. . . . . Its objectives seem to be not so much meeting the social obligations set for radio by Mr. Sarnoff as making the acceptance of a code an end in itself. . . . . The proposed code was in two sections which were printed in a pamphlet of twenty pages. . . . . The code which actually emerged . . . . was . . . . printed in eight. . . . . Self-regulation is to be encouraged, but its objective must be public service, not industrial public relations. . . . ."

The reader may find profit in comparing the proposed text on "Controversial Public Issues" with what was evolved in the private rooms of the convention hotel.

Soon N.A.B. felt obliged to issue a *Code Manual* to "clarify" questions raised by the Code. The original, or 1939, *Manual* undertook to describe the preliminary symptoms of "controversy" in the simple terms of a first-aid warning pasted in a medicine-cabinet, so that the most guileless broadcaster might be on his guard. Specific areas of "controversy," such as foreign policy; birth control; the political views of sponsors; the rift in organized labor; "discussion (or dramatization) of labor problems on the air is almost always of a controversial nature"; the "fact that employers, as a rule, are inclined to frown on" stations that "open their facilities to labor"; the existence of "small groups" of educators who were "muddying the waters of possible cooperation" were given special and extended treatment.

From time to time new problems arose and were met by special bulletins from N.A.B. Thus on June 28, 1940, the following appeared:

"Following a thorough discussion of the subject, the Board of Directors, at a meeting in New York held last Saturday, expressed the view that political broadcasts should be limited to speakers, interviews and announcements, and to broadcasts of *bona fide* political meetings or rallies held outside the studio. It was the

[5] That it was. The committee's report was emasculated in private conferences and later on the floor. The fact that advertising men deny any part in this is of no more consequence than the fact that many political bosses never hold public office.

feeling of the Board that stations and networks will find that the best interests of the industry will be served by a broadcasting policy which would bar the following: dramatizations of political issues, either in the form of announcements or programs; studio political 'rallies'; audience participation programs such as the 'man in the street' type; anonymous, simulated and unidentified voices at any time."

In 1942 there arose a thorny problem which the 1939 Code Committee had not foreseen. The Co-operative League of the United States, a consumers' group, announced that it was inaugurating a series of programs entitled "Let's Get Together, Neighbor." Shortly before the program was to have gone on the air as a paid feature over several N.B.C. and C.B.S. stations, the networks backed out. A considerable controversy was stirred up, and the F.C.C. wrote to the networks requesting a full statement. Both replied that such programs in their opinion were controversial in nature, because they proposed a system of marketing which was different from that generally followed in this country and also because the League desired to solicit memberships.[6]

The late Senator George Norris of Nebraska told the Senate that, inasmuch as the movement "represents six or eight million families in the United States," he felt that the networks' refusal of time was "a direct denial of fundamental right." The Senator thereupon introduced a resolution to determine, among other things, "whether the Communications Act of 1934 should be further amended to authorize the Federal Communications Commission to prevent such discrimination."

The instinctive reaction of N.A.B. was expressed by Neville Miller, its president, in the usual "restrained" language:

. . . . "one of the gravest threats to freedom of speech in recent years. It would direct a Senate committee to determine whether a government agency should decide what the people of America should hear and what they should not hear on the radio. If the proposed investigation materializes, you may be sure that all the advocates of bureaucratic control of both radio and the press will be on hand to urge the enactment of a law which would put an end to the American System of Broadcasting."

Having said this, Miller sat down and talked the thing over with N.B.C., C.B.S., and the Co-operative League. At a conference on December 14 and 15, it was decided that the League could take to the air early in 1943. Whereupon, N.A.B. added a new section to its Code:

"Solicitations of memberships in organizations, except where such memberships are incidental to the rendering of commercial services such as in insurance

_____
[6] A C.B.S. press release dated October 7, 1942, put it: ". . . The programs offered by the League were designed to promote a fundamental change in the present system of marketing and distribution. . . . The Columbia Broadcasting System has declined the offer . . . because of [its] long-established policy not to sell time for programs devoted to public controversial issues."

plan either in respect to casualty to life or property, or for membership in the American Red Cross or like organizations engaged in charitable work, are deemed to be unacceptable under the basic theory of the Code, and therefore time should be neither given nor sold for this purpose."

In a separate statement applying specifically to the Co-operative League's bid for time, N.A.B. made certain things clear:

"We believe that the advertising of cooperatives is and has been acceptable under the Code when the programs offered are designed to sell goods, trademarks or services of cooperatives. It is agreed that there is no objection to commercial copy incorporated in a program sponsored by a cooperative enterprise which states that (a) any person can make purchases at cooperatives; (b) membership in cooperatives is open and voluntary; (c) cooperatives are owned by members, each of whom has one vote; (d) profits or savings are returned to member-owners. However, in making such statements no attack is to be made on any other business enterprise or system of distribution. . . . ."

One thing emerged clearly from the incident: the advertising man's enemies were, *ipso facto,* the broadcaster's enemies.[7]

On May 5, 1943, *Variety,* an entertainment trade-journal that has consistently maintained an independently critical attitude toward the broadcasting industry, exploded:

. . . . "The masterminds of the NAB have, in essence and by a single rap of the gavel, served notice on the American people that our broadcasting system is no longer open to any form of commercial solicitation unless it involves something like the transfer of a can of soup or a cake of soap. . . . . Is radio to become an exclusive privilege of the merchant? Is an organization, movement or cause, regardless of how sound or deserving, to be barred from the ears of the American people just because the broadcaster, so unlike the newspaper publisher, prefers to slap down a blanket interdict rather than exercise his powers of discrimination? The amendment puts the thumb on organizations that have become the basic fabric of the economic and social life of the American community. To mention but one: organized labor. . . . ."

However, N.A.B. did not share *Variety's* fears about labor. In a pamphlet issued in 1941 the Association boasted: "So confident are both the AFL and the CIO in the NAB Labor Relations Department that they have agreed never to complain to the FCC about alleged grievances in the handling of labor programs on the air by any station until the NAB Labor Department has been given an opportunity of trying to adjust the difference."

In August, 1943, N.A.B.'s Labor Department apparently passed up such an opportunity. At any rate, Richard T. Frankensteen, vice-president of the United Automobile Workers, wrote in that month to F.C.C. Chairman Fly that a speech made by him over WHKC, the Columbus, Ohio, Mutual

---

[7] A former advertising executive, once prominent in radio, is authority for the statement that N.B.C. and C.B.S. were specifically warned by advertising men to drop the Co-operative "hot potato."

Broadcasting System outlet, had been censored and that the station was following a general policy of censorship against labor spokesmen "not in the public interest."

The U.A.W. petitioned the F.C.C. to hold up the station's renewal application, pending a hearing. This the F.C.C. declined to do, and in May, 1944, it renewed WHKC's license for the usual 3 years. However, 2 months later, it held a hearing, in the course of which the disputants were brought together. In June, 1945, the Commission finally dismissed the proceedings in a memorable order which, in effect, threw the door open to the sale of time for the discussion of public issues.

Meanwhile, the labor volcano was erupting in several other directions. In July, 1943, the U.A.W. sought to buy time over several stations for transcriptions "advocating an orderly postwar reconversion and stabilization program." This occasioned the N.A.B. to get out, on July 23, a *Special Information Bulletin*, which read in part:

"Manifestly any movement to influence public opinion on the subject of the actions of Congress is not 'broadcasts in connection with a political campaign in behalf of or against the candidacy of a legally qualified candidate for nomination or election to public office, or in behalf of or against a public proposal which is subject to ballot.' Therefore broadcasts of this nature should not be classed as political under the Code, nor should they be presented on paid time."

The broadcasters' position was put even more succinctly by Woods of the Blue Network at an F.C.C. hearing late in 1943. As Commissioner Durr recalled his heated exchanges with Woods, the latter took the view that

"anything at all about a labor union is controversial, *prima facie*." Hence Blue felt that it could not sell time to a labor union for any purpose. Woods did not think it was "controversial" within the meaning of the NAB Code when W. J. Cameron, in his intermission commentary during the Ford Symphony Hour, assailed organized labor, the President of the United States or "anyone else Mr. Ford happened not to like." Similarly Woods felt that it was "all right" for a commentator working for a company under federal indictment for allegedly engaging in improper cartel arrangements to defend cartels and attack the Department of Justice. On the other hand, he did not see how he could let a labor union sponsor a symphony, even if the union's name was never mentioned. "Things like that get around, you know." Finally, it was proper for a company devoting its entire output to the government, and therefore having nothing at the moment to sell to the public, to point out over he air how it was helping to win the war; whereas it would be a violation of the Code to permit the men who were working for these companies to tell radio listeners what they were doing, "as that would be controversial."

"The FCC has cancelled the 'controversial issue' clause," wailed *Broadcasting*, the N.A.B.'s unacknowledged "semi-official" organ. Actually, a good many broadcasters were ahead of N.A.B., and even of the F.C.C. As of the summer of 1945, more than three hundred stations, and even

Woods' A.B.C., were providing time for labor discussion, both sustaining and commercial. In August the Code Committee reported out a new and somewhat abbreviated set of Standards which differed little from previous Codes, save that the effort to curb "controversy" had been abandoned—at least in writing.

Variety saw other consequences. In its issue of September 5, 1945, it noted:

"Apparently taking their cue from the revision of the NAB Code permitting sale of time for controversial issues, slanted commercials that have been projected in the last couple of weeks on some of the top-budgeted nighttime network shows sponsored by top industries have created considerable eyebrow raising. Apparently the fear of abuses raised by some broadcasters who opposed revision of the code have been justified on the basis of lobby material against pending legislation in Washington already used in commercial copy. The duPont 'Cavalcade of America' show on NBC managed to get through a plug citing the advantages of international agreements (cartels), while the commercials on the 'Telephone Hour' show on the same net have taken up the cudgels against pending legislation for expansion of rural telephone service." [8]

The N.A.B. has other, less flamboyant functions than the drafting of codes and the citing of instances of government attack upon free speech and "the American way." In and out of its headquarters in Washington many standing committees work ceaselessly to produce that unanimity among broadcasters which thus far has eluded them.

One such committee handles music-copyright problems. The duty of another is to "foster" the increased use of radio as an advertising medium, to which end it maintains "close contacts with advertisers and potential advertisers, and with advertising agencies." A third attends to legal matters, "with particular reference to FCC regulations," and is further charged to "scan all legislative proposals affecting radio in state legislatures and the national Congress, and take appropriate steps with reference thereto."

The functions of various other standing committees are described in the N.A.B. prospectus as being to (1) "maintain contact with departments and schools of journalism in the universities to bring about the establishment of courses of study which will equip people to more effectively write and broadcast radio news"; (2) "encourage more and better listening"; (3) "maintain contact with organized groups who use radio or are interested in its social side, such as women's clubs, religious organizations, labor organizations, civic groups, etc."; (4) study "program trends"; (5) conduct "research in advancing the welfare of the broadcast industry"; (6) handle technical engineering matters; and (7) "study office forms and general office practices." In addition, N.A.B. employs a publicity staff and avails

---

[8] N.B.C. is said to have protested to the advertising agencies over these two "slips," which the New York script-readers thought Hollywood would check and which Hollywood script-readers understood had been passed by New York.

itself of the services of a Co-ordinator of Listener Activity, Mrs. Dorothy Lewis.

What sort of body do the members of N.A.B. want it to be? A trade-association capable of mustering a united front against A.S.C.A.P. and Petrillo? If so, it compares favorably with the American Newspaper Publishers' Association (A.N.P.A.). An agency for the "harnessing" of the energies of women's clubs and others active in listener groups? If so, it compares favorably with the Johnston (formerly Hays) Office. An enforcement arm of the A.N.A. and the A.A.A.A. to project their "moral standards" into the ether? If so, it has done well, for, like the A.N.P.A., it has embraced and virtually canonized the "Golden Rules" of advertising.

Yet to say, as some do, that N.A.B. could never be more than the sum of all these things is to ignore the presence on its membership list, and from time to time in its councils, of station-owners and network executives who believe in things and accomplish things far above the lowest common denominator of the Association. The committee report on the 1939 Code, as distinguished from the Code that was adopted, bore the unmistakable imprint of men who were trying to grapple with a problem which few newspapers and magazines in our time have even touched. These men saw the strength of a formula that sought to avoid a monopoly of the airways for those with the most money to spend on "propaganda." The weakness of their formula was deeply imbedded in the greed and cynicism of a few broadcasters and in the dependence of almost all broadcasters upon national advertising revenue.

To the advertising agencies that pulled the strings, the choice was simple. They did not want "outsiders" bidding for the already overcrowded commercial time. They could see no point in running the risk of losing big business for the sake of accepting the few dollars the unions and cooperatives had to pay, particularly as the union business did not funnel through the agencies, dropping off the usual "full 15 per cent" en route. True, the advertising men could have made these points "informally," without committing the words to paper. They undoubtedly thought exclusion would seem more palatable if they called it a "Code of Ethics."

When Justin Miller, a former justice of the Court of Appeals for the District of Columbia and no relative of his predecessor, took office as president of N.A.B. in September, 1945, he was widely acclaimed as the man to lead the broadcasters back to the concept of self-regulation outlined by Sarnoff. To which he quite properly replied that he would need the solid backing of all broadcasters to accomplish anything, for he was fully conscious of the fact that N.A.B. is no exception to the rule that trade-associations can never be much stronger than their weakest components.

Until the broadcasters get it through their heads that the price they would have to pay for needling politicians into abolishing the very mild form of government regulation that now exists would be public revulsion and a very much more severe form of regulation ultimately; until they show some signs of recognizing that public apathy is not the same thing as public approval and that sending a very pleasant lady around the country is no substitute for prying deeply into the unrealized citizen-needs as well as the surface tastes of listeners; until the N.A.B. devises a way to write a courageous, affirmative code that cannot be nullified by advertising men or flouted with impunity by "bad" broadcasters, codes and presidents are likely to come and go without effecting much change.

Meanwhile, the monotonous references to "free speech" and "the American System" which greet each criticism of broadcasting, however valid and temperate it may be, have exposed the N.A.B. not only to public ridicule but to the very real peril of eventual government excesses, for, as the A.N.P.A. might also discover in time, the American people may react one day, when their support is really needed to defend genuine freedoms, precisely as the shepherds of the fable reacted to the ultimate cry of "Wolf! Wolf!"

Donald Horton

TELEVISION STANDARDS
AND THE ENGINEERING COMPROMISE

In the American radio communication systems, the basic rules and specifications for the design and operation of the technical equipment of broadcasting are established by law for the entire industry. This is a peculiarity
of radio communication which appears to have no counterpart in other
industries. The "Standards of Good Engineering Practice" for various types
of radio transmission, through which technological uniformity is obtained,
are promulgated by the Federal Communications Commission. Television
broadcasting, like other forms of radio transmission, is also subject to a
set of technical standards adopted by the Commission.

Technical (or technological) standardization in the television field
might appear to be of interest only to engineers and broadcasters. It is the
purpose of this paper [1] to show that the subject is worth sociological study
on two counts: first, as a special form of the general social process of
standardization, and second, because of the importance of technological
standardization as a determinant of the social and economic characteristics
of the emergent television medium.

Standardization as a General Social Process

If by standardization we mean a reduction of the range of variation of
social behavior by the establishment of norms or models, and of the per-

Originally presented at a meeting of the Society for Social Research of the University of
Chicago in August, 1949. Published by permission of the author.

[1] At the time of the preparation of this paper there had recently been announced a
series of hearings by the F.C.C., to begin in the Fall of 1949, on Ultra High Frequency
allocations, color television, and related subjects. The paper was intended to suggest
some of the issues and interests that would be represented in the proceedings, and to
place them in a context of sociological analysis. The hearings will have been completed,
and decisions rendered, by the time the present volume is published. Although it might
have made the paper more useful for some purposes to hold it until these decisions could
be reviewed, it was felt that the generality of the present treatment justified its publication in approximately its original form.

missible limits of deviation, then standardization is the universal process through which cultural uniformity is obtained. Codes, customs, laws, rules, ethical and moral norms, are all devices for social-cultural standardization in this general sense, and the processes of codification, enactment of law, adoption of rules, and development of custom and norms are all specific forms of the general process of standardization. Without them the minimum conditions for social life could not be achieved.

In some areas of contemporary life, the need for standardization has been outrunning its accomplishment. A standardization problem exists. The problem arises because on the one hand the units of a society—especially its economic-technical units—tend to become increasingly differentiated, and the inventiveness characteristic of contemporary society constantly produces new devices, practices, procedures, social as well as technological, among the differentiated units. On the other hand, the increasing inter-dependence of these units makes the uniformities necessary for cooperation more important as they become more difficult to obtain. The striving for standardized practices—in statistical records, in forms of contract, in book-keeping and accounting, in commercial and technical terminology, in traffic regulation and a host of other matters—is symptomatic.

Technological Standardization

The problem of standardization has become especially acute in industry in recent years. The rise of mass-production, with its principle of the assembly of interchangeable parts, has increased the trend toward mutual dependence among producing units with respect to materials, equipment, motive power, technical knowledge and technically trained personnel. Yet precisely in the area of technology there is the strongest tendency for invention, protected by the exclusive interests of competing enterprises, to produce incompatible variations in equipment and procedure. The practice of establishing technical standards [2] has developed in response to this dilemma.

Technical standardization is usually accomplished by voluntary agree-ment among the engineers and managers of industry, usually under the auspices of a committee of the appropriate professional organization of engineers. In some cases, standards are developed for a specific industry (e.g., ceramics, electrical equipment); in others, they are intended to be universal (e.g., color standards). The standards of one industry or techno-logical field are adjusted, as far as possible, to be congruent with those of

[2] See: "Standards in Industry," *The Annals*, v. 137, 1928. Martino, Robert A., *Stand-ardization Activities of National Technical and Trade Organizations*, Misc. Publ. M 169, Nat'l Bureau of Standards, U.S. Dep't of Commerce, Washington, 1941. Brady, Robert A., *The Rationalization Movement in German Industry*, Berkeley, Univ. of Calif., 1933.

other fields. The result is a system of integrated standard measures, speci-fications, tolerances, nomenclature, etc. which is constantly being extended into new technological areas, both nationally and internationally.[3] As the system is extended, it is also subject to revision, to keep the standards of technology in adjustment with advances in fundamental science. The standardization process thus represents, at least in aim, the striving of the engineering spirit to impose a rational, scientific order on the industrial system.[4]

Technical Standardization in Television

Standardization in the radio field has the further special feature, men-tioned above, of legal enactment rather than purely voluntary agreement. The intervention of the State, through the F.C.C., introduces political and social considerations that are lacking in the private, voluntary arrangements arrived at by industry and its engineers. Our present purpose is to examine this process and to consider some of its implications for the development of the American television system.

The history of standardization in television is the record of a social effort to establish a new major technological system of communication on an orderly and rational basis. One should not, however, imagine a group of dispassionate and farseeing planners performing this task in the quiet atmosphere of the laboratory. On the contrary, the planning process has involved intense and intricate conflicts. It has continued intermittently more than a decade and has not yet terminated. In this brief account we can give only a highly generalized analysis which reduces the complex historical record of television standardization to the interaction of three social groups,—engineers, entrepreneurs, and representatives of the state. Each of these groups is conceived of as oriented towards characteristic interests and ideal aims, sufficiently exclusive and divergent to make com-promise difficult and its outcome unstable.

THE ENGINEERING INTEREST: The engineer is important in this context

[3] See, for example, the report of the Conference on Unification of Engineering Stand-ards held under the auspices of the Combined Production and Resources Board (of the U.S.A., Great Britain and Canada). The First World War gave force to the standardi-zation movement in its early years by showing the need for uniformity in materials and equipment supplied to the armed forces by different industrial units. The Second World War intensified the need for standardization of the products produced and used inter-changeably among the allied nations. The recent move to standardize the military equip-ment of the nations bound by the Atlantic Pact (*New York Times*, December 20, 1949) is a logical outcome of this development.

[4] The achievement of specific standards no doubt involves difficulties and resistances arising from patent rights, competitive interests, the biases of the engineers themselves in favor of the companies employing them, and the like; but the process has not been studied as a social phenomenon and we have no information on the typical problems of standization or the ways in which they are solved.

not as a supervisor of industrial technology but in his creative role as designer and inventor, adapting theoretical scientific knowledge to practical ends. The engineers who play this role are typically employed in industrial laboratories and their contributions to the development of television have at the same time advanced the economic interests of their employers. But one observes that they have a common professional loyalty to the engineering art—a cultural stream of knowledge and skills, governed by characteristic aims and principles, which exists and grows to some degree independently of the industrial system in which it finds application and support.

The general social aim of the engineer, in his profession, is not so easily identified as the medical researcher's aim to eliminate disease, or the scientist's aim to extend knowledge. Merton has commented on the readiness with which engineers surrender to their business employers the responsibility for social application of their work.[5] But while the engineer has no control over the technological systems he designs and constructs, he appears to find an adequate social aim in what he speaks of as "the advancement of the art." To advance the engineering art is the great social task, national and international in scope, in which he and his professional colleagues are cooperatively engaged. If private interests, for a time, prevent the social application of new technical knowledge, the engineer accepts the fact in the confident belief that nothing is permanently lost. Directly or indirectly, through its immediate or remote effects on other inventions or increments in knowledge, in one country or another, the advance will make its contribution to social welfare.

It may be hypothesized that in every well defined special branch of the engineering art there are more specific objectives in terms of which "advancement of the art" may be measured. In television the goal has been clearly defined: it is to extend vision to a distance by electrical means. The first criterion by which the state of the art is to be judged is therefore the degree to which the view provided by a television image corresponds to what would be observed of the scene directly. By this criterion the image should have as much detail as can ordinarily be resolved by the eye; it should be in natural color; and it should be three dimensional. As long as television lacks these qualities, television engineers will be striving to advance the art towards this goal of the perfect approximation to natural vision.

But this psychological or psychophysical criterion is not adequate for a television *system*. Here the criterion is necessarily social. The ideal television system would, with the maximum economy and efficiency, permit any potential viewer to witness the transmitted event, however distant.

[5] Merton, Robert K., *Social Theory and Social Structure*, Ch. XIII, "The Machine, the Worker and the Engineer." Glencoe, The Free Press, 1949.

As long as there are limitations on this distributional aspect of television there will be continuous inventive effort towards overcoming them. It may be predicted that just as the engineers will persist in their effort to develop television in color and in three dimensions, they will also rest unsatisfied until international television broadcasting is made practicable.

THE ECONOMIC INTEREST: Ideally, then, the interrelated processes of invention and engineering development should continue without pause until such a system is available. But other factors interfere with this ideal progression. The work of the engineer, especially in the field of electronics, is very costly. It is estimated that R.C.A. alone had invested at least ten million dollars in television research and development before the present commercial system was launched in 1941. Parallel with the record of technical advancement in the art is a rapidly cumulative economic investment. This is probably not a linear relationship, but one in which at some point the returns in technical advancement begin to diminish while the rate of investment rises more sharply. For example, in television one measure of the quality of a television image, with respect to the amount of pictorial detail it contains, is the number of horizontal scanning lines of which it is composed. In the period from 1929 to 1939 this number rose, first very rapidly, then more slowly; the problems encountered in attempting to increase the line structure were increasingly complicated and it is highly probable that the cost of developing this feature of television mounted disproportionately.

Sooner or later there arises a demand, on the part of the sponsor of the engineering work, for a commercial application of it. The engineer is then required to produce a practical device or, as in the television case, a practical system of interrelated mechanisms representing the highest current achievement of the art. In order to do this he must make a series of technical compromises because in any state of the art short of the ideal goal it is impossible to maximize all the values of the system simultaneously. For example, television, like the motion picture, depends on the physiological phenomenon of persistence of vision. The "picture" is actually a running dot of light moving so rapidly that the illusion of a continuous image is created. This dot traverses the surface of the viewing screen a specified number of times per second, just as the motion picture is presented at the rate of twenty-four frames per second. Below a certain threshold value of the repetition rate, the average viewer will perceive a disturbing flicker in the image. This threshold varies with the brightness of the image and its size. The higher the repetition rate, generally speaking, the less flicker and the greater the permissible size and brightness of the image. But, on the other hand, if other conditions are equal, the higher the repetition rate, the smaller the number of lines. What is gained in some qualities is lost in another. The ideal system would have all these values maximized. But at any point short of the ideal goal, a technical compromise among these factors has to be worked out.

Since the engineers employed in private industry are not responsible for the commercial development of their inventions, it is up to the business men to decide at what point the available compromise system is ready to be exploited on a scale that will recoup the prior investment in research and establish a profitable business. This question involves social-psychological as well as economic problems. It requires an estimate of the degree to which a compromise technology, short of its theoretical ideal state, is capable of performing a social function, of providing a high enough level of need-satisfaction, relative to competing instruments or services already available.

In the case of television, it was the general consensus of the industry that this point had been reached in 1939-1940, by which time the present black-and-white television picture appeared to be the best compromise that could be developed.

THE POLITICAL INTEREST: In the case of the radio communication systems the interest of the state is represented by the Federal Communications Commission. Its intervention is due, as is well known, to the fact that the radio services operate in the public domain and are thus subject to the federal regulatory power. Much of the work of the Commission is concerned with the licensing of broadcasters, and the regulation of certain aspects of the on-going activities of its licensees. But we shall consider only its role in the establishment of the television system. This role has been centered in the promulgation of rules of Good Engineering Practice or technical standards, and in the allocating of channels. These are two facets of the same problem as the subsequent discussion will indicate.

Television Engineering Standards

The television signal consists of a complex of waves which have interdependent functions. They determine the number of picture elements transmitted per second, synchronize the image in the receiving set with the image in the camera, and coordinate the picture and sound transmissions. A television receiver works only if the receiver and the transmitter are designed to operate with the same number of scanning lines per second, the same plan of interlacing lines, the same synchronizing pulses, and so on. If competitive transmitters operated with different values of these variables, it would be impossible for television to become an effective medium of communication. It was obviously in the public interest to establish the entire television industry on the basis of a single set of technical standards such that any transmitter could be received by any receiving set put on the market by any manufacturer. One of the first tasks of the Commission in relation to television, aside from the granting of licenses for experimental broadcasting, was to promulgate such a set of engineering standards.

It should be observed that the standards published by the Commission have the force of law throughout the television broadcasting field, and they may be changed only through the established mechanism of Commission hearings and the promulgation of new rules. This is in contrast to the standards of industry generally which rest on voluntary agreement. The television standards commit the entire industry to a given technology, and it is no longer possible for any one corporate unit to introduce a more advanced system at the expense of the others, as in the case of the recent abrogation of the accepted standards in the phonograph record field. Theoretically, the Commission could give permission for such a unilateral development, but in practice it does not make decisions affecting so directly the capital investment of the radio and television industries without obtaining consensus among at least the most powerful of them.

It is a fundamental problem of technological standardization that once a standard method or procedure is adopted it tends to become fixed in a matrix of related and dependent practices and the greater the degree to which this occurs, the greater will be the resistance to new, if incompatible, developments. If in addition there is involved a large investment in equipment and other property, the question of obsolescence arises and the resistance to innovation increases. This is, of course, a well known phenomenon. One might add that the resistance to change becomes greater still when there is in question a complete system of interrelated standards, governing an integrated system of apparatus and activities. Such is preeminently the case in radio and television where the standards are of a systemic character, controlling the entire technological level of the communication system from studio to transmitter to home receiving set. Even so, if standards were purely voluntary a well financed, aggressive entrepreneur, controlling a new improvement in technology, might force the industry to revise its standards upwards and write off the obsolescence. But where the standards are supported by political power, and it requires the consent of the most powerful economic interests to change them, such a development is unlikely. Armstrong's long, but finally successful, fight for FM is an example of the difficulties involved.

Standardization in television was therefore a rather momentous event when it was undertaken in 1940 and 1941. The universality of these standards, their systemic character, their legal status, and the fact that an entire mass communication system was to be built on them at the cost of a tremendous investment by industry and the public, meant that once they were adopted a massive wall would have been erected against further technological advances. It was a matter of major concern, therefore, that the best possible engineering compromise be worked out. This was achieved by a remarkable committee of engineers, appointed by the industry at the request of the FCC in 1940. This group, known as the National Television System Committee,[6] performed the heroic task of preparing a full set of standards in the space of four months. The standards were recommended to and adopted by the Commission in 1941. To complete our discussion of the issues involved in this event, the problem of allocation must be referred to.

The Allocation of Communication Channels

Transmission of a radio or television signal having a given frequency can be effective only if the broadcaster has an exclusive right to use that frequency in the geographical area in which the signal is to be received. Otherwise there would be such mutual interference of signals that none would serve for communication. The determination of which frequencies may be used in any community is the process of "allocation" of frequencies. This task is by law vested in the F.C.C. The Commission is responsible for working out an allocation plan that will distribute the available frequencies in an equitable way. In making its allocation plan with respect to a given radio service, such as television, the Commission must take into account the geographical range of transmission, which determines the minimum spatial separation of transmitters operating with the same frequencies; the necessary staggering of assignments in order to avoid the interference that occurs between transmitters operating on adjacent frequencies; the total frequency range in the radio spectrum that may be assigned to a given service, in the face of competition by innumerable radio services for frequency assignments; and the distribution of the available frequencies in some logical relation to the distribution of population and the probable demand for channels by local broadcasters.

We noted above that in television the transmission does not involve a single wave of a given frequency, but a complex of waves having a considerable range of frequency. Such a transmission is said to require a *channel* and the allocation procedure consists of assigning channels of specified frequencies.

In all broadcast services there is a scarcity of available frequencies relative to demand. By 1940 the lower portions of the spectrum were already crowded and the problem of finding space for television was difficult. It was the obligation of the Commission to find the maximum space, that would permit the largest possible number of television channel assign-

[6] Fink, Donald G. (ed.) *Television Standards and Practice:* Selected Papers from the Proceedings of the National Television System Committee and Its Panels. New York, McGraw-Hill Book Company, Inc., 1943.

ments, without at the same time encroaching on other radio services. If too little space were available, there would be not enough channels to satisfy the requirements of the broadcasting industry; there could not be an equitable distribution of service to the communities of the nation; and the resulting system would be characterized by a socially undesirable degree of actual or potential monopoly control of the few available channels. Thus the allocation question has social and political ramifications of great importance.

Now the availability of spectrum space is relative to the width of the channel. The wider the channel for a television transmission, the fewer such channels can be accommodated in a given space. Thus the allocation problem is directly related to an engineering problem, and to the problem of technical standards.

Relation between Allocation and Standards

For the engineers engaged in the standardization effort problems of this kind were presented: the higher the quality of the television picture (in terms of the number of picture elements, and of the number of scanning lines reproduced per second), the greater the width of the required channel. Thus an important issue to be compromised was that of picture quality as against the socio-political requirements of the allocation plan. The alternatives were better pictures, fewer stations, greater monopoly and less equitable distribution of channels to smaller communities and rural areas; or the converse.

The best compromise that could be worked out among these factors was a black and white picture having 525 horizontal lines and a picture repetition rate of thirty frames per second and requiring a channel 6 megacycles (six million cycles) wide. These are the characteristics of the present television medium.

The necessity for such wide channels meant that the entire system would have to operate in a region of the spectrum known as the Very High Frequency or VHF region (54–216 megacycles), characterized by very short waves. Such waves behave more like light waves than like the long waves of AM radio broadcasting, and as a result they are receivable only within a relatively short distance of the transmitter. To maintain picture quality meant a sacrifice with regard to the other criterion of system —distribution distance. One of the major consequences of this sacrifice has been the great cost and difficulty of the current effort to establish national television networks, and the probability of a long delay in the provision of international television service.

THE CONJUNCTURE OF INTERESTS: Thus in 1941, in the work of the National Television System Committee, the engineering, economic and political interests were reconciled in what appeared to be the most practicable working compromise. The acceptance of this compromise involved the assumption on the part of industry that the resultant quality of the television service would be satisfactory to the public; and on the part of the Commission that a satisfactory distribution system could be established. For the engineers it meant standardization at a level far short of the theoretical goal, and the probability that a long period of time would elapse before further advances could be made. In a way, each of these assumptions appears to have been questionable, and the issues of the 1949-50 F.C.C. hearings can be interpreted as the outcome of these faulty assumptions.

In the ideal course of events, the setting of standards would have led to the immediate development of a nationwide mass communication system, involving an investment of perhaps several billion dollars. Such a system once established would have stood for a long time as an immovable obstacle to further basic changes. What actually happened was that, first, the war occurred almost immediately, and the development of the system was postponed until 1947. It was then shortly discovered that the engineering estimates of the distance required between stations to avoid mutual interference were in error. Unexpected interference was occurring; and it became apparent that the allocation scheme was inadequate. This inadequacy was all the greater because the demand on the part of broadcasters for channel assignments was unexpectedly large. The Commission was therefore faced with this dilemma: if it spaced stations more widely in order to prevent interference, fewer stations could be accommodated in the region of the spectrum assigned to this service. Fewer stations would mean a less equitable service to the public, and a greater potential danger of monopoly control. On the other hand to increase the number of channels would require either that other radio services be displaced, at great economic cost, or that new channel space be found higher up in the spectrum. Fortunately, war-time research had advanced the radio art to the point where it is now possible to use for television broadcasting a still higher part of the spectrum known as the Ultra High Frequency region (475–890 megacycles). The Commission's pending allocation scheme calls for the opening up of a series of television channels in this area. The practical consequence of this move is that in some geographical regions television will operate with one range of frequencies, and in others with frequencies of a different order. The television sets usable in the one region will not be usable in the other except by means of a special converter. In still other geographical areas a set able to receive both types of signals will be required. Before putting this allocation scheme into effect, the Commission will have to establish engineering standards for the ultra high frequency service. In this way the standardization issue enters the hearing.

A second issue is that of color. The issue has a long and complex history which we cannot now review. In brief, the possibility of television in natural color, which is one of the ideal conditions of the television art, was not yet fully within reach at the time of the original standards compromise. However, wartime research in the field of electronics made possible the development of a successful system of color television by 1946, so that, in effect, when the industry was launched in 1947, the technical system was already theoretically obsolete (in terms of the state of advancement of the art). The industry, however, rejected efforts to have color television standards adopted; but meanwhile the public interest in color has increased, as a result of the controversy, and of public demonstrations of the color system; and at the present time there is agitation in Congress for a review, at the forthcoming hearing, of the state of the art, with a view to the adoption of color television standards, and the provision of a color television service. If the demand for color is evidence of dissatisfaction with the quality of the present black and white image, it would appear that the other major assumption of the television compromise, i.e., that the standards adopted would provide a satisfactory service, was also in error. It has developed, therefore, that a major technical innovation, which might have been damned up behind the wall of investment in the broadcasting system for a very long period of time may actually break through in the present special circumstances.

In addition to the problems of allocation, of standards for ultra high frequency transmission, and of standards for color television, the Commission is also concerned with several other matters of considerable importance, such as standards and assignments for theatre television, and the proposed method of broadcasting television signals from airborne transmitters. These issues, however, will not be discussed. They do not appear to alter in any significant way the analysis given above.

Conclusion

Standardization of a complete technological system, at the very onset of its development, is an unprecedented occurrence. Here standardization is transformed from a method of regulating and giving uniformity in current industrial practice into an act of socio-economic planning in which the technical structure of an entire industry is determined in advance. The fact that this is also to be a highly influential medium of mass communication has added to the gravity of the decisions to be made. This peculiar feature of the television case arises from the fact that radio and television operate in the public domain, subject to federal regulation. And television is the first major communications industry in this field (if we except FM) to arise, *de novo*, since the regulatory power was established. It may be that new industries arising in other fields, especially those to be built to utilize atomic power, will be established on a similar foundation of advance planning and standardization.

If this should be the case, a study of the planning process in television, and in other situations where planning is done on a smaller scale, may be an important sociological task. Perhaps one of the chief problems will be to determine the conditions of error in such planning, and to what extent social science could help to prevent such errors from occurring.

Governmental Relations

Because of the problems of social control and social policy involved, there has developed a body of literature on the governmental relations of the mass media. Most of the studies deal with some particular aspect of the relationship with special emphasis on the question of what the relationship should be. However, the literature does contain a comprehensive analysis of government as party to the mass communication process, and excerpts have been taken from Chafee's work which takes a broad perspective on the problem, including social and political factors as well as legal ones. This is followed by a selection from an intensive historical analysis of the factors underlying the establishment of a broadcasting monopoly in Britain, in which Coase documents the influence of the governmental bureaucracy on the decision. Finally, part of a famous report by the Federal Communications Commission is included as an example of a governmental agency's own statement of the evaluative factors to be taken into consideration in its regulatory activities.

Zechariah Chafee

GOVERNMENT AND MASS COMMUNICATIONS

Besides the recent legal events to which I have just called attention, there are more deep-seated causes for grave anxiety about the future of the freedom of the press. Modern democratic society is in the greatest crisis of its history, because new conditions have been rapidly created by a technical civilization. The issue is whether the old ideal of a free society can be maintained against the hazards presented by these new conditions. Men are constantly called upon to learn over again how to live together. It is a hard task. When unprecedented disputes and difficulties confront them, they repeatedly turn for help to the government, as the recognized umpire. All the traditional liberties are subjected to novel strains, and freedom of the press cannot escape. Many problems of democracy extending far outside the range of this book are bound to influence mass communications. I propose to examine five general factors in the United States which have an indirect but strong tendency to increase governmental control over the distribution of news and opinions.

1. *The growth in functions, range of activities, and interventions of government generally.*—Technical instruments make for a more complete control of many social activities by the government, more particularly in order to redress disproportions and injustices created in the economic process. The same instruments make for a state control of public opinion. To put the point more broadly, the government has got into the habit of intervening in most other businesses, so why should it keep its hands off communications businesses? Why should the tendency toward collectivism stop when it is a question of regulating newspapers?

The physical facilities of communication are essential. Unless these are adequate, any program of free communication will fail. With the growing complexity of these facilities it is harder to keep them open. It did not matter how many packet ships or carrier pigeons brought news of Napc-

Reprinted from *Government and Mass Communications* (1947), pp. 10-21; 773-81, by permission of the author and the publisher. (Copyright, 1947, by the University of Chicago Press.)

leon's battles—they did not interfere with each other. International radio circuits would. The government is not concerned if a new journal sets up its presses next door to an established organ. It steps in immediately when a new broadcasting station overlaps a used frequency.

It is true that what has just been said primarily concerns governmental encouragement of the flow of traffic rather than interference therewith. Yet it does have some tendency to increase restrictions as well. The three functions of government in relation to mass communications, described at the start of this chapter, are not separated by high barriers. Whatever makes the government more active in one respect about communications opens opportunities for further activity in other respects. Officials will think more and more about the press and other news agencies. For example, the Federal Communications Commission is mainly occupied with keeping the channels open, but, in so doing, it has been confronted with delicate problems of awarding frequencies to A or B with some attention to the content of their programs. "If A is happy, B is not," and B runs the risk of being put off the air for what he says. Thus far the Commission has suppressed virtually nothing, but the risk remains. Furthermore, if some action by the government happens to affect a newspaper or other communications enterprise adversely, people are likely to suspect that the officials are getting even with their critics, whether or not any such design exists. Admirers of Ralph Ingersoll firmly believed that he was drafted in the hope of wrecking *PM;* and the government's suit to open the channels of the Associated Press was supposed to be due to the hostility of the administration toward the editorial policies of the *Chicago Tribune.* Later I shall consider how the government can best promote communications or participate in them without penalizing persons of adverse views, but at the moment I wish to stress that all governmental activities in the field are in a sense interwoven.

In many subjects the complexity of the pertinent facts increases. Equal access to the facts becomes more and more difficult. The power of governments over the sources of information tends to grow. Hence the misuse of this power by governments becomes a more and more serious danger. Governments withhold one part of the facts and use the other for sales talk. This tendency is fostered by general worship of efficient salesmanship. Hence we observe an increasing amount of government activity in the field of what is called "propaganda," viz., the creation by government of various kinds of information and publicity, thus emphasizing and stimulating public interest and response in certain directions at the expense of other interests and ideas. Even when completely devoid of such intentions to falsify and propagandize, governments must make increasing use of communications. A modern government is an ever greater participant in social and economic affairs. This has created a necessity for more extensive and better intercommunication between it and the public in the interests of both. One gets a homely illustration of this by looking at the numerous kinds of placards on the walls of a post office today. How many subjects would not have been a government concern thirty years ago?

On the other hand, a modern government makes great demands for secrecy. Of course, state secrets are nothing new. Military information was always guarded from the enemy, and bureaucrats have often invoked public safety as a protection from criticism. What is significant is the enormous recent expansion of the subjects which officials are seeking to hide from publication until they give the signal. If persuasion fails to prevent leaks, they are tempted to use threats. The result may be a hush-hush attitude, likely to extend beyond the real public need for silence. This is illustrated by Burleson's postal censorship in the last war. A direct consequence of secrecy in the ordinary press may be great activity of the subsidiary press in disseminating the concealed material, and this is more dangerous than frank discussion in the general press. One may add that Drew Pearson's rumors are a poor substitute for frank official disclosures. Too often we get as gossip what ought to reach us as regular news.

No doubt there are many matters which ought not to be disclosed for a time, but the officials should not have a free hand to determine what those matters are or to lock them up forever. It may be human nature for them to want their mere say-so to be decisive on the need for secrecy, but the possession of such a power would allow them to hoist public safety as an umbrella to cover their own mistakes. Secrecy has other dangers. The controversy over atomic-bomb control shows how the claim of military security may possibly be used to hamper civilians in proper scientific activity, the progress of which depends on public communication in lectures and learned periodicals. In short, official encroachments on freedom of the press will be probable unless the boundary line between secrecy and publicity is very carefully demarcated. And officials must not do the demarcating. That is a job for the representatives of the people in Congress.

Having shown several reasons why the general tendency of government to expand in all directions is likely to reach the field of mass communications, I shall now go on to situations in the country at large which seem likely to encourage that result.

2. *The centralization of economic power resulting from technological developments.*—A technical society makes for the centralization of economic power, and the drift toward monopoly aggravates the problem of obtaining justice. The same technical tendencies make for large-scale enterprises in the field of communications and present us with the problem as to how various sections of the community shall have adequate channels to make their appeal to the conscience and mind of the community. As the instrumentalities increase in quantity and variety, they tend to pass under the control of corporate wealth and like-minded individuals, so that they cease

to express fully the diversified interests of the public. Big concentrations of economic power in other industries are also a danger to free speech because they do or can exert direct and indirect pressure upon newspapers and radio stations in various and subtle ways. Hence the government will be inclined to use compulsion on the press with the intent of promoting freedom. Examples of possible resulting government efforts to keep channels open are Sherman Act suits like that against the Associated Press and regulations by the Federal Communications Commission against the networks or against newspaper control of broadcasting stations.

The principle of freedom of the press was laid down when the press was a means of *individual* expression, comment, and criticism. Now it is an industry for profit, using techniques of mass suggestion and possessing great power. A government is always quicker to exercise control when organizations are involved rather than individuals. Is the old principle of the *Areopagitica* applicable to this new situation?

3. *The effect of social complexity in splitting the community into groups.* —The American community is split into groups, with consequent feelings of ill-treatment and outbreaks of violence. Under such circumstances acrimonious controversy in the press may endanger unity. Hence the government may conceivably prohibit such controversy, or encourage people to pour oil on the troubled waters, or do its own pouring.

This split-up situation has further effects on the press. In a complex pluralistic and dynamic society we must pick one set of group standards; this inevitably increases tension with all the others. Concentration of newspapers and broadcasting stations in the hands of the wealthy group causes inadequate access to less fortunate groups, a peril to justice. The press then fails to satisfy the need for social health through adequate communications in order to relieve the stresses and strains and class antagonisms caused by increasing industrialization. A widespread belief in the unfairness of the media arises. The challenge to the media as they are now operated, which lies behind all other challenges, is the left-wing challenge; that the means of production are owned and controlled by private groups who are not the servants of the people, not ultimately representative of their interests, and therefore do not fit into a coherent concept of public service. Stalin has compared the Soviet press with the American press and claimed the first is "free," the second "not free" because the people of the United States do not have access to paper, presses, etc. This is not only the classical Communist challenge. It is repeated in one form or another on every progressive level. Some social groups aspiring to recognition feel unrecognized, for instance, the Negroes. Other groups of rising economic importance feel that their new importance is not reflected by the media; this is true of organized workers in their various forms of self-articulation and representation. New workers' parties of every shade complain that capitalist control of the media is used to exclude their case from proportionate ("just") public attention. Even governmental bodies are inclined to regard the press as less progressive than the executive instrument of the constitutional authority. They tend to regard the media as not sufficiently tutored in the realities and responsibilities of public management and less co-operative in the business of government than they think they have reason to expect.

When a considerable number of people voice a grievance, they bring pressure on the government to do something on their behalf.

While many new groups have grown in power, one element in the community which possessed a great deal of influence at the time of the First Amendment has ceased to have any political importance—the intellectual élite of clergymen, scholars, lawyers, and plantation owners, which comprised not only Federalists but also Jefferson and numerous associates of his. The prolonged retention of preponderating political power by any aristocracy is objectionable, even by the aristocracy of the mind which Jefferson envisaged; but the absence of a recognized intellectual élite in America today does create dangers, which are the price we pay for free education and the largest electorate in the world. Until the middle of the nineteenth century, most writers wrote for a comparatively small group of well-educated men who formed a coherent body of opinion. The rulers and higher officials were members of this group and so followed its standards of literary freedom unless governmental interests were very seriously threatened. The rest of the community did not read much and did not care what was written. Now nearly everybody does read and care, but the standards are variegated. The lack of a strong united front among serious readers in the face of governmental restrictions on the free flow of ideas is illustrated whenever notable books are banned in Boston.

One other aspect of this division into groups has caused much trouble in recent years and is still a motive of governmental interference with the press. The emergence since 1917 of groups which propose to deny freedom if they succeed prompts the state to deny them freedom so that they will not succeed. The newspapers and pamphlets issued by these groups often attract attention from other special groups, who constantly demand restrictive measures. Farmers are arrayed against the Industrial Workers of the World, patriotic societies against Communists. The appeal of the "solid citizens" for governmental help is hard to resist.

4. *The effects of large-scale communication on quality.*—A technical society tends to supplant additional and organic forms of cohesion with mechanistic and artificial forms of togetherness. When next-door neighbors do not even know each other, there is no formation of neighborhood opinion. The same technical tendencies replace the old process of talking it out with those around you, by mass instruments of communication in which the common interests of a community are reduced to the lowest

common denominator. The Commission was greatly disturbed by the drift toward meaninglessness in the press.

This situation differs from those previously reviewed in that it does not directly impel the government to step in. For example, officials will get more excited about the power of radio networks than about the trivialities of soap opera. The point is that the low level of so much in mass communications will weaken resistance to the government whenever other reasons do lead it to interfere with newspapers or radio or films. When people have come to regard a publication as trash, they do not care much if it is kept from them. They readily forget the underlying issue of the importance of untrammeled discussion. What harm, they think, if something can no longer be published which was never worth publishing anyway. For example, if the Federal Communications Commission should limit the "commercial" element in each broadcast to ten seconds at the start, my first impulse would be to throw up my hat and cheer because I am so sick of the way toothpaste is mixed with toccatas and cosmetics with campaigns. Yet the implications of such a ruling for administrative dictation of contents would be very serious. Contrast the excitement over the banning of *Strange Fruit;* here was something known to be really good.

The maintenance and breadth of freedom depend ultimately on the toleration of private citizens. Hence it is alarming when a recent *Fortune* survey shows that citizens do not place much value on free speech. One reason for this may be that they do not place much value on what would be suppressed.

5. *The growing importance of mass media as agencies for maintaining unity and co-operative understanding.*—The fact that the instrumentalities of communication reach many more people than formerly tends to make the government more solicitous about them. The Tory government around 1800 left the expensive newspapers to say what they pleased but tried to tax Cobbett's two-penny journal out of existence. Freedom of speech worked well when only five thousand people could hear what was being said and a few thousand more would read some book or pamphlet. Will this principle of laissez faire still be allowed to operate when audiences are now to be counted by the million? For example, suppose that television existed in December, 1941, and that an agency was about to send out a transmission of Pearl Harbor during the bombing. Would the government have permitted this? Did liberty of the press then cease to be desirable? The impulse to censor is obviously strengthened by the multiplied distribution of dubious material.

As the war went on, men came to realize that our technical civilization has created a potential world community. Obviously, a community with its citizens widely separated can be held together only by mass communications. This raises the problem as to how instruments of communication can be most responsibly used to further the cause of international comity. As the shrinking of world distances has changed the basis of international relations, it has become increasingly important to safeguard the channels of news for the sake of world peace. This factor has its less idealistic side. A government sees its own interests in security, trade, etc., affected seriously by outward and inward communications and so has a strong reason for censoring or guiding them. Consequently, the United States government is bound to participate in the maintenance and management of cables and international radio circuits.

The value of domestic mass communications to the party in power is also becoming obvious. The totalitarians abroad made systematic use of newspapers, radio, and films. This may conceivably influence American politicians. Huey Long showed what can be done, with his sound trucks and his legislation to bludgeon opposition journals into line. Efforts will be needed to avoid this temptation.

Finally, the belief is growing that freedom of the press is so important to the state that it cannot be irresponsibly exercised. It is conceived to be so closely interwoven with the advance of society that it differs from other freedoms. Although this has been described as the Fascist point of view, it is not wholly remote from the position of many citizens who regard themselves as democratic, except that they want responsibility imposed without governmental compulsion. Indeed, insistence on the need of responsibility in the press is the leading theme of the Commission's general report. When men become very much aware of the importance of communications in modern life and are exploring the deficiencies which prevent their accomplishing what they might, the question is bound to arise: Why should not the governmental power, which is invoked to remove so many current evils, be asked to step in and straighten out this mess too? There are plenty of reasons for a negative answer, of course, but persons who overlook those reasons may easily make an affirmative reply because of the gloomy picture presented by the large amount of irresponsibility which is now exhibited by many agencies of communication.

❂   ❂   ❂

The fact that active governmental participation in mass communications is sometimes advocated as a cure for the diseases of the commercial press naturally increases the resentment of newspapermen. This is not the only reason for a (government) information service, of course. Even if there were perfect private media, a government official still has to make his thoughts clear to the people. But the following position taken by a few rebellious Nieman Fellows, though presumably not typical of newspapermen, especially those toward the top, is shared by many outside critics of the press.

"I am less concerned by possible governmental restrictions than by the failure of the press to restrict itself. Press freedom is in danger because the press does not behave responsibly. Responsibility should go with power. Instead, a kind of Gresham's Law operates in the field of journalism. Just as bad money tends to drive out good, so newspapers with poor ethics tend to drive out papers with better standards. The government should act vigorously to make the newspaper press responsible. The existing libel laws fall short of the need. The best way to offset the misrepresentations of the mass-circulation media is to establish *one* government newspaper, *one* government radio station, and *one* government movie producer. This will enable the government to present its point of view to the public."

These advocates of a government-owned press and the newspaper leaders who are so terrified of its coming both seem to me completely off the road, although in different ditches. As to the first group, government ownership is not a satisfactory remedy for the present shortcomings of the communications industries. The evils of bigness will persist in a big government newspaper, unless indeed it is so unenterprising and dull as to be unread. And, on the other hand, the newspaper leaders who fight all efficient public information because it will give us something like *Pravda* and the British Broadcasting Corporation are either insincere or "fraidy-cats." Given the hostility of Congress toward mild experiments in the information field, the enormous funds required for a national newspaper will not be appropriated in any foreseeable future. It would be more sensible to expect the Federal Theater project of WPA to produce a replica of the Paris Opera House in Washington equipped with teachers of coloratura singing and the ballet. The nearest we ever came to a national domestic channel of mass communications was when President Roosevelt was offered a chance to buy the Blue Network and declined. Something can be said for a municipal radio station like WNYC or for broadcasting at a state university; but, so long as high federal officers find nation-wide hookups on all the networks available, any proposal for sending out much more than time signals and weather reports at the expense of the taxpayers is likely to fall on deaf ears in the Capitol. The notion that OWI would develop into a peacetime octopus seems to me ridiculous. If its Domestic Branch was open to blame, this was not because it was continually seeking new worlds to conquer but on the ground of undue caution for fear of what Congress might do. Its denunciators in high press circles have got so excited that they have mistaken Caspar Milquetoast for Boris Karloff.

There is much more basis for the fear that the government will work through the private press with propaganda and careful concealment of official weakness, although the demand for plate-glass objectivity comes with rather a bad grace from some newspapermen who are past masters at shaping facts to suit their own policies. An improvement in the accuracy and fairness of the regular press is likely to be paralleled in the performance of government publicity experts, who have often got their preliminary experience in work for newspapers, broadcasters, etc. As I said about the defects of the communications industries, it is mainly a question of raising professional standards. Not that we want to encourage devious practices in government just because the private media indulge in them, but the fact that some persons do wrong is not a conclusive reason for denying other persons the opportunity to do right in ways which the country badly needs. If Congress were more sympathetic to information services, as I have suggested, the past or potential publicity programs of specific agencies could be examined in relation to their honesty and abstention from objectionable propaganda. Bad actors could be denied funds and public-spirited performers encouraged. This is not a problem to be solved by sweeping formulas.

A final objection to further publicity is that it will add to what is now enormous in bulk. For example, the *New York Times* now gets twenty-one pounds of government handouts every day in Washington and ten pounds more at its home office. One is appalled by the prospect of more tonnage per annum—"of making many books there is no end; and much study is a weariness of the flesh." Certainly greater quantity can be justified only by distinctly higher quality. This was stressed by one member of our Commission, although he was strongly in favor of information services:

"Some of the fear of the official mind on the part of members of the communications industries is unnatural. One point, however, we must allow them. They may not know how to use the influence of the press for all it is worth, but they will certainly be justified if they are preventing narrower or even more confused controls from affecting it. If their case is that their present system does tend to enrich, the case against them must be in the name of a system which will even more patently enrich as well as regulate. A merely negative approach, such as we have had too often from government information services, will only confirm these representatives of the press in their argument. It suggests for one thing a great improvement in the government's sense of the news media, which is capable of creating a greater trust in its advice and co-operation, particularly abroad. One of the keys to the freedom of the press may be, in fact, a reexamination of government information services, with the possibility of a 'free' public agency supplying an intelligence and information service to the press outside it, under an authority which is guaranteed to be free from political dictation."

The supporters of government information are between the devil and the deep sea. If the information is poorly contrived, we do not want it. If it is well contrived, it arouses the jealousy of Congress and the press. Still, as between the two alternatives, the choice is obvious.

In spite of all the objections, we are plainly going to have a good deal of government information of some sort or other. To say nothing more of press conferences and departmental handouts, the extent of its participation in mass communications is impressively evidenced by the following list (compiled in 1945), which shows twenty-eight federal agencies engaged in the production or use of motion pictures: Department of Agriculture; Alien Property Custodian (enemy-owned or controlled films in United States at outbreak of war); Bureau of the Budget (accounting of government film expenditures); Civil Service Commission (library of visual aids material for training officers in different agencies); Coast Guard; Department of Commerce; Office of Education (films for training war workers); Office of Inter-American Affairs; Department of the Interior; Department of Justice (films for federal penal institutions); Department of Labor; Library of Congress; Marine Corps; Maritime Commission; National Archives; Department of the Navy; Office of Price Administration; Public Health Service; Social Security Board; Department of State; Office of Strategic Services; Tennessee Valley Authority; Department of the Treasury (war-bond drives); Veterans Administration; Department of War; Office of War Information (Domestic and Overseas Branches); War Manpower Commission; War Production Board.

The list also gives six international or semigovernmental bodies which operate films in connection with our government; American Council on Education; American Red Cross; Combined Production and Resources Board (allocation of film supplies among United States, United Kingdom, and Canada); Pan American Union (clearing-house and Sunday film shows); United Nations Central Training Film Library; United Nations Relief and Rehabilitation Administration.

Granted, then, that there is to be such a thing as governmental information service in peace, what are to be its nature and functions? This leads to at least two further questions, which I shall not attempt to answer, but which are so important that they ought to be stated.

First, should there be a centralized service something like OWI, although with more vision than its Domestic Branch possessed, or should we merely have several mutually independent services attached to different agencies as at present? Our Commission received conflicting views on this difficult problem. On one side was the experienced newspaperman whom I have already quoted as favoring only "consolidation up to the Cabinet level." His objection to an over-all service was: "It is skating on thin ice to depend on the standards of the men involved. If all information goes through one person, the situation is very dangerous." On the other hand, an equally experienced newspaperman, who had also worked for the government, said:

"If the public is to get a clear, coherent, and comprehensive story of the operation of the bureaus, a centralized agency is necessary. There is assumed, of course, a reasonable degree of honesty in this agency. I disagree with [the preceding informant's] idea of governmental handouts at the department level. Without a centralized information agency, the reports given out by the various agencies that would come out in such reports are not altogether a fair representation of the facts. Often they are small parts of a big story, or are in fact personal feuds and rivalries rather than disagreements on policy. Reporters have often been used as instruments in personal rivalries, for example in the War Production Board. This practice is tempting to subordinate officials. The ordinary channels do not give a fair picture of how the government is operating, because peace, harmony, and brotherly love are not news as a rule; a fight is. Experience does not bear out the view that public airing of disputes expedites decisions. It serves the public interest to have the various departments reach agreements on the facts and the policy to be adopted before making them too public. Perhaps the revelation of the differences among officials serves as a check on bureaucracy, but the press will find out about these anyway without having them stressed by segregated information services of the agencies involved in a controversy. A related point is that a colorful figure in an agency may receive wide publicity, while his successor may do much better work in a quiet way and receive no attention from the reporters.

"The clearance function of a centralized agency is useful even in peace, but (unlike wartime) probably no great harm is done if there is no such agency. The result of its absence is not the withholding of the truth, but rather partial and incomplete information. An example of the way a centralized information agency would contribute to the clarification of the public mind is provided by the trouble that arose in connection with food stories during the war. Apart from such predictions of starvation as Louis Bromfield's, two or three government departments had adopted divergent views—on the basis of scattered data extrapolated in different directions. Eventually it was agreed that the Bureau of Agricultural Economics was more likely to be right than any other agency dealing with food, and the situation became much clearer."

This last point in favor of centralization has much weight. One can think of many nation-wide peacetime problems such as housing, inflation, unemployment, the attraction of venture capital to new businesses—to name only a few—which concern several different agencies. The segregated information bureau of a single agency does not see the problem as a whole. A pooling of knowledge and imagination is essential in order to make citizens understand the problem and the remedies which the government is undertaking.

On the other hand, there are objections to extreme centralization which have not yet been mentioned. An over-all information service lacks expertness in any one field, and yet this is indispensable if the law and the practical situation are to be satisfactorily explained. In this connection it is rather significant that Mr. Grierson spoke of the work of bureaucrats in the Canadian information service, whereas our Commission was told that the work of OFF and OWI did not affect the bureaus at all. "The information officers were not bureaucrats. The bureaucracy played a *nil* part in the information operations of the United States government." It may have been pleasant to avoid a hated word which would have increased the bombardment against OWI, and yet I surmise that the active participation of the officials of numerous permanent Canadian agencies in the projects of their unified information service had a good deal to do with its success as compared with the Domestic Branch of OWI.

Moreover, even if Congress should unexpectedly consent to a centralized information service, there would still have to be separate publicity groups in many federal agencies. This is proved by the fact that the existence of OWI during the war did not relieve the Office of Price Administration from issuing much explanatory matter about its regulations and aims. It is inconceivable that the establishment of a centralized service in peace would enable the Department of Agriculture to stop distributing bulletins to farmers. No doubt, more co-ordination of the separate information services is practicable and desirable, but I doubt whether they ought to be merged into any all-embracing office.

If a centralized information service of any sort is established, it will naturally be closely related to the President. It is interesting that Elmer Davis, in his final report to the President, recommended that if there is ever again a domestic OWI, it should be under the direction of the President's press secretary, who could blend White House publicity with all other publicity and guarantee that it really expressed the will of the head of the Administration.

My own feeling is that this question of many services versus one service does not need to be solved now. *Solvitur in ambulando.* If the separate services can be made increasingly fruitful and if they develop a desirable amount of co-ordination, questions of more unification or less will be worked out by the men participating and members of Congress, where (so I hope) the question will receive more light and less heat than in the past.

Second, should an information service merely distribute what is commonly known as news, or should it also deal with "pre-news," that is, questions of principle and decision—the considerations on which policy is based? The broader scope has much more effect on national morale. Accordingly, the Office of Facts and Figures charged itself with an obligation to provide the people of the country with whatever information it thought relevant to decisions on questions of principle. It felt no particular responsibility for getting out military communiqués with which it had had nothing to do. The American newspapers, being unfriendly, took the position that its only responsibility domestically was to get communiqués out promptly. This view was accepted by its successor, OWI, which evidently considered it had no duty to provide the people of this country with information relative to important decisions—questions of principle and policy. The problem in the war was whether the government was to perform the neuter and sterilized task of getting military communiqués out at 11:30 instead of 11:45, or whether its job was to enable a free people to govern themselves. Corresponding alternatives will be presented during peace. Of course, great masses of pure facts will always have to be distributed, for instance, crop reports. Whether more than this be practicable under present conditions is not for me to say, but much more than facts is needed by us citizens if we are to become conscious that we are partners and not just passengers in the difficult enterprise of government.

R. H. Coase

THE ORIGIN OF THE MONOPOLY
OF BROADCASTING IN GREAT BRITAIN

It is broadly true to say that the establishment of the broadcasting service in Great Britain as a monopoly was the result of Post Office policy. The attainment of the monopoly was no doubt made easier by the necessity for some agreement as between the radio manufacturers on the question of patents and by the fact that the manufacturers' main interest was not in the operation of a broadcasting service but in the sale of receiving sets. But the obvious desire of the Post Office for a single company was decisive. There can be no question that if the Post Office had wanted to bring about competing broadcasting systems, it would have been possible to do so. Although the two groups may, at the end of their long negotiations, have preferred to have a combined system, they would have been willing to operate independently if the Post Office had wanted them to do so. I shall therefore examine in this section the basis of Post Office policy towards broadcasting and attempt to discover the reasons which led to favour a monopoly.

The Post Office derived its powers to control wireless telephony in the early 1920's from the Wireless Telegraphy Act of 1904. In this Act it is provided that in order to operate apparatus either for transmitting or receiving wireless signals, it was necessary to have a licence and also that this licence may be in a form and with conditions determined by the Postmaster General.

At first, the Post Office thought of wireless telephony, as did others, as simply a new method of transmitting messages and therefore as requiring co-ordination with other means of communication and particularly with wireless telegraphy. Thus, the Postmaster General in an answer to a parliamentary question on wireless telephony on April 20th, 1920, said: "I am giving every possible facility for its further development, but its progress

Reprinted from *Economica*, Vol. XLV (August, 1947), pp. 205-10, by permission of the author and the publisher. (Copyright, 1947.)

must be co-ordinated with that of wireless telegraphy." And later in the same year, in the answer in which the Postmaster General alluded to the suspension of the Marconi Company experiments in broadcasting, he goes on to add: "Experiments are, however, being made to test the practicability of using high-speed wireless telegraphy for news and commercial services, and promising results have been obtained." Much the same attitude was shown in 1921.

That wireless telephony was considered to have only limited uses and therefore to be of no particular importance, would itself be sufficient to explain the Post Office's lack of encouragement to experiments in broadcasting. But there is, I believe, another factor which should be taken into account. The allocation of wavelength was the responsibility of the Wireless Sub-Committee of the Imperial Communications Committee. On this Committee there were three Service representatives, one Post Office representative and the representatives of certain other Departments. It was, therefore, a Committee on which the Services were strongly represented. Now we know that it was with reluctance that the Services agreed to wavelengths of 325 to 450 metres being allocated to broadcasting (and then only with restrictions on the hours of service). It seems clear that their opposition would have been very much stronger at an earlier date. The Post Office would have had to exert considerable pressure on the Service Departments—and this they were probably unwilling to do.

But in the Spring of 1922 came the applications from the manufacturers. These had been influenced by events in the United States. But so, too, was the Post Office. Mr. F. J. Brown, Assistant Secretary of the Post Office, had spent the winter of 1921–22 in the United States; he had taken a great interest in broadcasting developments, had discussed the subject with many of the leading authorities in the United States and had attended some of the meetings of Mr. Hoover's first Radio Conference. In the United States at that time there was no effective regulation of the number of broadcasting stations. It seems that the only regulation was of the wavelength on which stations could broadcast—and the only wavelength then allowed was, for most stations, 360 metres. The need for some regulation of the number of stations was evident; and Mr. F. J. Brown was impressed by this as well as by the great strides broadcasting was making in the United States.

The way in which this question was treated in Great Britain led some to conclude that a monopoly was needed in order to prevent interference. Consider the following argument taken from a speech in the House of Commons by Mr. Kellaway, the Postmaster General. ". . . it would be impossible to have a large number of firms broadcasting. It would result in a sort of chaos, only in a much more aggravated form than that which has arisen in the United States of America, and which has compelled the

United States, or the Department over which Mr. Hoover presides, and who is responsible for broadcasting, to do what we are now doing at the beginning, that is, proceed to lay down very drastic regulations, indeed, for the control of wireless broadcasting.

"It was, therefore, necessary that the firms should come together, if the thing was to be efficiently done. You could not have 24 firms broadcasting in this country. There was not room . . . . and it was suggested to them that, for the purpose of broadcasting information, whatever it might be, they should form themselves, if possible, into one group, one company."

Mr. Kellaway does not say that it is necessary to have a monopoly in order that there should not be interference; but the wording would be very liable to cause the incautious listener to imagine that this was so. Certainly many at this time seem to have been confused by the way the problem was presented. For example, a witness before the Sykes Committee having said "It is arguable that there must be one central Broadcasting Authority," was immediately answered by Lord Burnham in the following words: "It is not a fact; already it is common knowledge; that in America the want of regulation has meant very chaotic conditions." And there are many other examples.

But we cannot, of course, assume that the Post Office officials shared this view. It was obvious to them that the possibility of interference made necessary not a monopoly but a limitation in the number of broadcasting stations. Why then was it Post Office policy to bring about a monopoly? Mr. E. H. Shaughnessy, who was Engineer in charge of the Wireless Section of the Post Office, was asked, when giving evidence to the Sykes Committee, about the necessity for a monopoly in transmission. He first referred to the problem of the Marconi Company's patents. But he went on to say that "if they were prepared to licence people, then you would have a very large number of firms asking for permission probably, and some of them might be sufficiently wealthy to put up decent stations—most of them would not—you would have a very great difficulty in acquiescing, you could not acquiesce in all demands. And then you would have the difficulty of selecting the firms which the Post Office thought were most suitable for the job, and whatever selection is made by the Post Office, the Post Office would be accused of favouring certain firms. So that the solution of the problem seemed to be to make all those firms get together to form one Company for the purpose of doing the broadcasting." There can be little doubt that here we have the main reason which led the Post Office to favour a monopoly. The difficulty of selection if there was not a monopoly must have been in the minds of Post Office officials for some time. It was this problem, as we have seen, which caused the Post Office early in 1921 to prefer to deal with an application from the Wireless Society of London rather than with one from the Marconi Company.

Captain G. R. Loring, the Post Office representative, then said: "We cannot give the Marconi Company preferential treatment over any other firm, so that if they asked for permission . . . . half a dozen other companies could come along, and we should have to give them similar permission, whereas if the Wireless Society were to apply it would make it much easier for us." This point of view was reaffirmed when, in April, 1923, the *Daily Express* applied to the Post Office for a broadcasting licence. Of this, Mr. F. J. Brown said: "The answer which the Postmaster General caused to be sent to this application was this. That he did not want to give facilities to one particular newspaper or organization which he could not give to other newspapers and organizations and he asked the *Daily Express* how they would propose to meet that difficulty."

There can be no question that there was a very real danger of creating monopolistic conditions in other fields if broadcasting licences were granted to particular firms. The nature of this danger was made evident when the Marconi Company, in April, 1922, proposed to set up broadcasting stations. And Mr. F. J. Brown has said: "It was . . . contrary to the policy of the British Government to grant a monopoly of broadcasting to one, or even to two or three, manufacturing firms, as this would place them in a superior position to their competitors for pushing the sale of their goods." This aspect of the question seems to have been constantly in the mind of the Post Office. A large number of the modifications to the draft scheme which were put forward by the Postmaster General during the course of the negotiations seem to have had as their aim the protection of the interests of the smaller firms.

But it so happens that the plan for independent operation by the two groups which was evolved in the course of the negotiations was one which avoided this particular difficulty. All radio manufacturers would have been free to join one or other of the groups; none could have been penalised by the existence of independent broadcasting companies. Yet the Post Office still preferred that there should be a monopoly. The reason is fairly clear. There would still have remained the problem of the allocation of wavelengths and districts between the two groups. And the Post Office could not have avoided responsibility for the solution of these difficult problems. And there is also reason to suppose that the Post Office considered that it would be more economical to have one company instead of two or more.

I have described the arguments which led the Post Office to favour a monopolistic broadcasting organization. The Post Office did not itself wish to operate the broadcasting service. Consequently the only solution was to attempt to establish a single broadcasting company. But the problem to which a monopoly was seen as a solution by the Post Office was one of Civil Service administration. The view that a monopoly in broadcasting was better for the listener was to come later.

Federal Communications Commission

PUBLIC SERVICE RESPONSIBILITY OF BROADCAST LICENSEES: SOME ASPECTS OF "PUBLIC INTEREST" IN PROGRAM SERVICE

Federal Communications Commission must determine, with respect to each application granted or denied or renewed, whether or not the program service proposed is "in the public interest, convenience, and necessity."

The Federal Radio Commission was faced with this problem from the very beginning, and in 1928 it laid down a broad definition which may still be cited in part:

"Broadcasting stations are licensed to serve the public and not for purpose of furthering the private or selfish interests of individuals or groups of individuals. The standard of public interest, convenience, or necessity means nothing if it does not mean this . . . The emphasis should be on the *receiving* of service and the standard of public interest, convenience, or necessity should be construed accordingly. . . . The *entire* listening public within the service area of a station or of a group of stations in one community, is entitled to service from that station or stations. . . . In a sense a broadcasting station may be regarded as a sort of mouthpiece on the air for the community it serves, over which its public events of general interest, its political campaigns, its election results, its athletic contests, its orchestras and artists, and discussion of its public issues may be broadcast. If . . . *the station performs its duty in furnishing a well rounded program, the rights of the community* have been achieved." (In re Great Lakes Broadcasting Co., FRC. Docket No. 4900; cf. 3rd Annual Report of the F.R.C., pp. 32-36.)

Commission policy with respect to public interest determinations is for the most part set by opinion in particular cases. (See, for example, cases indexed under "Program Service" in Volumes 1 through 9 of the Commission's Decisions.) A useful purpose is served, however, by oc-

Excerpted with minor editorial adaptations from the report of the Federal Communications Commission, *Public Service Responsibility of Broadcast Licensees,* March 7, 1946.

casional overall reviews of Commission policy. This Part will discuss four major issues currently involved in the application of the "public interest" standard to program service policy; namely, (A) the carrying of sustaining programs, (B) the carrying of local live programs, (C) the carrying of programs devoted to public discussion, and (D) the elimination of commercial advertising excesses.

A. THE CARRYING OF SUSTAINING PROGRAMS: The commercial program, paid for and in many instances also selected, written, casted, and produced by advertisers and advertising agencies, is the staple fare of American listening. More than half of all broadcast time is devoted to commercial programs; the most popular programs on the air are commercial. The evidence is overwhelming that the popularity of American broadcasting as we know it is based in no small part upon its commercial programs.

Nevertheless, since the early days of broadcasting, broadcasters and the Commission alike have recognized that sustaining programs also play an integral and irreplaceable part in the American system of broadcasting. The sustaining program has five distinctive and outstanding functions.

1. To secure for the station or network a means by which in the overall structure of its program service, it can achieve a *balanced* interpretation of public needs.
2. To provide programs which by their very nature may not be sponsored with propriety.
3. To provide programs for significant minority tastes and interests.
4. To provide programs devoted to the needs and purposes of nonprofit organizations.
5. To provide a field for experiment in new types of programs, secure from the restrictions that obtain with reference to programs in which the advertiser's interest in selling goods predominates.

❉   ❉   ❉

B. THE CARRYING OF LOCAL LIVE PROGRAMS: All or substantially all programs currently broadcast are of four kinds: (1) network programs, including programs furnished to a station by telephone circuit from another station; (2) recorded (including transcribed) programs; (3) wire programs (chiefly wire news, syndicated to many stations by telegraph or teletype and read off the wire by a local announcer); and (4) local live programs, including remote broadcasts.

Network Programs. The merit of network programs is universally recognized; indeed, the Commission's Chain Broadcasting Regulations 3.101 and 3.102 were designed in considerable part to insure a freer flow of network programs to the listener. In January 1945, approximately 47.9% of all the time of standard broadcast stations was devoted to network programs.

Transcriptions. The transcribed or recorded program has not had similar recognition. As early as 1922, the Department of Commerce by regulation prohibited the playing of phonograph records by stations having the better (Class B) channel assignments except in emergencies or to fill in between program periods; and later in the year it amended the regulation to prohibit even such use of records by Class B stations. Through the years the phonograph record, and to a lesser extent the transcription, have been considered inferior program sources.

No good reason appears, however, for not recognizing today the significant role which the transcription and the record, like the network, can play in radio programming.

In January, 1945, approximately 32.3% of all the time of standard broadcast stations was devoted to transcriptions and recordings.

Wire Programs. The wire service, by which spot news and sometimes also other program texts are telegraphically distributed to stations, has in recent years assumed a role of increasing importance. By means of wire service for news and other texts of a timely nature, plus transcriptions for programs of less urgent timeliness, the unaffiliated station can very nearly achieve the breadth of service attained through network affiliation. No statistics are currently available concerning the proportion of time devoted to wire service programs.

Local Live Programs. There remains for discussion the local live program, for which also, no precise statistics are available. It is known, however, that in January, 1945, approximately 19.7% of all the time of standard broadcast stations was devoted to local live *and* wire service programs; and that during the best listening hours from 6 to 11 P.M., approximately 15.7% of all the time was devoted to these two classes of programs combined.

In granting and renewing licenses, the Commission has given repeated and explicit recognition to the need for adequate reflection in programs of local interests, activities and talent. Assurances by the applicant that "local talent will be available," that there will be "a reasonable portion of time for programs which include religious, educational, and civic matters"; that "time will be devoted to local news at frequent intervals, to market reports, agricultural topics and to various civic and political activities that occur in the city" have contributed to favorable decision on many applications. As the Commission noted in its *Supplemental Report on Chain Broadcasting* (1941):

"It has been the consistent intention of the Commission to assure that an adequate amount of time *during the good listening hours* shall be made available to meet the needs of the community in terms of public expression and of local interest. If these regulations do not accomplish this objective, the subject will be given further consideration."

The networks themselves have recognized the importance of local live programs. Under date of October 9, 1944, the National Broadcasting Company, when requesting the Commission to amend Chain Broadcasting Regulation 3.104, stated:

"Over the years our affiliated stations have been producing highly important local programs in these three open hours of the morning segment. From 8 a.m. to 10 a.m. N.Y.T., most of the stations have developed variety or 'morning clock' programs which have met popular acceptance. These periods are not only profitable to the individual station but are sought for use by civic, patriotic and religious groups for special appeals because of their local listening audience appeal. Likewise, from 12 noon to 1 p.m., they have developed highly important news farm programs or other local interest shows. *To interfere with local program schedules of many years' standing would deprive our stations of their full opportunity to render a desirable local public service.*"

The Commission's reply, released December 20, 1944, as Mimeograph No. 79574, stated in part:

"One purpose of Regulation 3.104 was to leave 14 of the 35 evening hours in each week free of network option, *in order to foster the development of local programs*[1] . . . The Commission . . . concurs fully in your statement that interference with local programs which have met with public acceptance and which are sought for use by local civic, patriotic and religious groups, local church services, and other highly important local program schedules of years' standing is to be avoided."

The courts have also supported the position taken by the Commission that the interests of the whole listening public require that provision be made for local program service. Where the record showed that of the two stations already functioning in an area, one carried 50 percent network programs and the other 85 percent, the court stated: "In view of this situation it is not difficult to see why the Commission decided that public interest would be served by the construction of a local non-network station."[2]

❋   ❋   ❋

While parallels between broadcast stations and newspapers must be approached with caution, their common elements with respect to local interest may be significant. The local newspaper achieves world-wide news

[1] The failure of Regulation 3.104 to achieve this purpose is illustrated by the eight charts, presented elsewhere in the report, showing many stations which carried no non-network programs whatever during the evening hours on the two days analyzed.

[2] *Great Western Broadcasting Association, Inc.* v. *F.C.C.,* 94 Fed. (2nd) 244,248. In the KHMO case, the court ordered the Commission to issue a license to an applicant for a local station in an area where three stations were already operating, none of which gave genuine local service. The court expressed approval of the Commission's findings in similar cases, that "under the direct provisions of the statute the *rights of the citizens to enjoy local broadcasting privileges were being denied.*" (*Courier Post Broadcasting Co.* v. *F.C.C.,* 104 F [2] 213,218).

coverage through the great press associations, taps the country's foremost writers and cartoonists through the feature syndicates, and from the picture services procures photographs from everywhere in abundant quantity. But the local newspaper editor, faced with such abundant incoming material, does not therefore discharge his local reporters and photographers, nor does he seek to reproduce locally the New York *Times* or *Daily News*. He appreciates the keen interest in local material and makes the most of that material—especially on the front page. The hours from 6 to 11 P.M. are the "front page" of the broadcast station. The statistics of local programming during these hours, or generally, are not impressive.

❖   ❖   ❖

C. DISCUSSION OF PUBLIC ISSUES: American broadcasters have always recognized that broadcasting is not merely a means of entertainment but also an unequaled medium for the dissemination of news, information, and opinion, and for the discussion of public issues. Radio's role in broadcasting the election returns of November 1920 is one of which broadcasters are justly proud; and during the quarter of a century which has since elapsed, broadcasting has continued to include news, information, opinion and public discussion in its regular budget of program material.

Especially in recent years, such information programs as news and news commentaries have achieved a popularity exceeding the popularity of any other single type of program. The war, of course, tremendously increased listener interest in such programs; but if broadcasters face the crucial problems of the post-war era with skill, fairness, and courage, there is no reason why broadcasting cannot play as important a role in our democracy hereafter as it has achieved during the war years.

The use of broadcasting as an instrument for the dissemination of news, ideas, and opinions raises a multitude of problems of a complex and sometimes delicate nature, which do not arise in connection with purely entertainment programs. A few such problems may be briefly noted, without any attempt to present an exhaustive list:

(1) Shall time for the presentation of one point of view on a public issue be sold, or shall all such presentations of points of view be on sustaining time only?

(2) If presentations of points of view are to be limited only to sustaining time, what measures can be taken to insure that adequate sustaining time during good listening hours is made available for such presentations, and that such time is equitably distributed?

(3) If time is also on occasion to be sold for presentation of a point of view, what precautions are necessary to insure that the most time shall not gravitate to the side prepared to spend the most money?

(4) Are forums, town meetings, and round-table type broadcasts, in

which two or more points of view are aired together, intrinsically superior to the separate presentation of points of view at various times?

(5) Should such programs be sponsored?

(6) What measures will insure that such programs be indeed fair and well-balanced among opposing points of view?

(7) Should locally originated discussion programs in which residents of a community can themselves discuss issues of local, national, or international importance be encouraged, and if so how?

(8) How can unbiased presentation of the news be achieved?

(9) Should news be sponsored, and if so, to what extent should the advertiser influence or control the presentation of the news?

(10) How and by whom should commentators be selected?

(11) Should commentators be forbidden, permitted, or encouraged to express their own personal opinions?

(12) Is a denial of free speech involved when a commentator is discharged or his program discontinued because something which he has said has offended (a) the advertiser, (b) the station, (c) a minority of his listeners, or (d) a majority of his listeners?

(13) What provisions, over and above Section 315 of the Communications Acts of 1934,[3] are necessary or desirable in connection with the operation of broadcast stations during a political campaign?

(14) Does a station operate in the public interest which charges a higher rate for political broadcasts than for commercial programs?

(15) The Federal Communications Commission is forbidden by law to censor broadcasts. Should station licensees have the absolute right of censorship, or should their review of broadcasts be limited to protection against libel, dissemination of criminal matter, etc.?

(16) Should broadcasters be relieved of responsibility for libel with respect to broadcasts over which they exercise no control?

(17) Should the "right to reply" to broadcasts be afforded; and if so, to whom should the right be afforded, and under what circumstances?

(18) When a station refuses time on the air requested for the discussion of public issues should it be required to state in writing its reasons for refusal? Should it be required to maintain a record of all such requests for time, and of the disposal made of them?

(19) What measures can be taken to open broadcasting to types of informational programs which contravene the interests of large adver-

---

[3] "Sec. 315. If any licensee shall permit any person who is a legally qualified candidate for any public office to use a broadcasting station, he shall afford equal opportunities to all other such candidates for that office in the use of such broadcasting station, and the Commission shall make rules and regulations to carry this provision into effect: *Provided,* That such licensee shall have no power of censorship over the material broadcast under the provisions of this section. No obligation is hereby imposed upon any licensee to allow the use of its station by any such candidate."

tisers—for example, news of the reports and decisions of the Federal Trade Commission concerning unfair advertising; reports of the American Medical Association concerning the effects of cigarette-smoking; temperance broadcasts; etc.?

These are only a few of the many questions which are raised in complaints to the Commission from day to day. The future of American broadcasting as an instrument of democracy depends in no small part upon the establishment of sound solutions of such problems, and on the fair and impartial application of general solutions to particular cases.

Under the Communications Act, primary responsibility for solving these and similar issues rests upon the licensees of broadcast stations themselves. Probably no other type of problem in the entire broadcasting industry is as important, or requires of the broadcaster a greater sense of objectivity, responsibility, and fair play.

While primary responsibility in such matters rests with the individual broadcaster, the Commission is required by the statute to review periodically the station's operation, in order to determine whether the station has in fact been operated in the public interest. Certainly, the establishment of sound station policy with respect to news, information, and the discussion of public issues is a major factor in operation in the public interest.

The Commission has never laid down, and does not now propose to lay down, any categorical answers to such questions as those raised above. Rather than enunciating general policies, the Commission reaches decisions on such matters in the crucible of particular cases.[4]

One matter of primary concern, however, can be met by an over-all statement of policy, and must be met as part of the general problem of over-all program balance. This is the question of the *quantity* of time which should be made available for the discussion of public issues.

The problems involved in making time available for the discussion of public issues are admittedly complex. Any vigorous presentation of a point of view will of necessity annoy or offend at least some listeners. There may be a temptation, accordingly, for broadcasters to avoid as much as possible any discussion over their stations, and to limit their broadcasts to entertainment programs which offend no one.

To operate in this manner, obviously, is to thwart the effectiveness of broadcasting in a democracy.

✿   ✿   ✿

The carrying of any particular public discussion, of course, is a problem for the individual broadcaster. But the public interest clearly requires

---

[4] See, for example, the *Mayflower* case, 8 F.C.C. 333 and *United Broadcasting Company* (WHKC) case, decided June 26, 1945.

that an adequate amount of time be made available for the discussion of public issues; and the Commission, in determining whether a station has served the public interest, will take into consideration the amount of time which has been or will be devoted to the discussion of public issues.

Summary and Conclusions—Proposals for Future Commission Policy

A. ROLE OF THE PUBLIC: Primary responsibility for the American system of broadcasting rests with the licensee of broadcast stations, including the network organizations. It is to the stations and networks rather than to federal regulation that listeners must primarily turn for improved standards of program service. The Commission, as the licensing agency established by Congress, has a responsibility to consider overall program service in its public interest determinations, but affirmative improvement of program service must be the result primarily of other forces.

One such force is self-regulation by the industry itself, through its trade associations.

Licensees acting individually can also do much to raise program service standards, and some progress has indeed been made. Here and there across the country, some stations have evidenced an increased awareness of the importance of sustaining programs, live programs, and discussion programs. Other stations have eliminated from their own program service the middle commercial, the transcribed commercial, the piling up of commercials, etc. This trend toward self-improvement, if continued, may further buttress the industry against the rising tide of informed and responsible criticism.

Forces outside the broadcasting industry similarly have a role in improved program service. There is need, for example, for professional radio critics, who will play in this field the role which literary and dramatic critics have long assumed in the older forms of artistic expression. It is, indeed, a curious instance of the time lag in our adjustment to changed circumstances that while plays and concerts performed to comparatively small audiences in the "legitimate" theater or concert hall are regularly reviewed in the press, radio's best productions performed before an audience of millions receive only occasional and limited critical consideration. *Publicity* for radio programs is useful, but limited in the function it performs. Responsible criticism can do much more than mere promotion; it can raise the standards of public appreciation and stimulate the free and unfettered development of radio as a new medium of artistic expression. The independent radio critic, assuming the same role long occupied by the dramatic critic and the literary critic, can bring to bear an objective judgment on questions of good taste and of artistic merit which lie outside the purview of this commission. The reviews and critiques published weekly in *Variety* afford an illustration of the role that independent criticism can play; newspapers and periodicals might well consider the institution of similar independent critiques for the general public.

Radio listener councils can do much to improve the quality of program service. Such councils, notably in Cleveland, Ohio, and Madison, Wisconsin, have already shown the possibilities of independent listener organization. First, they can provide a much needed channel through which listeners can convey to broadcasters the wishes of the vast but not generally articulate radio audience. Second, listener councils can engage in much needed research concerning public tastes and attitudes. Third, listener councils can check on the failure of network affiliates to carry outstanding network sustaining programs, and on the local programs substituted for outstanding network sustaining programs. Fourth, they can serve to publicize and to promote outstanding programs—especially sustaining programs which at present suffer a serious handicap for lack of the vast promotional enterprise which goes to publicize many commercial programs. Other useful functions would also no doubt result from an increase in the number and an extension of the range of activities of listener councils, cooperating with the broadcasting industry but speaking solely for the interest of listeners themselves.

Colleges and universities, some of them already active in the field, have a like distinctive role to play. Together with the public schools, they have it in their power to raise a new generation of listeners with higher standards and expectations of what radio can offer.

In radio workshops, knowledge may be acquired of the techniques of radio production. There are already many examples, of students graduating from such work who have found their way into the industry, carrying with them standards and conceptions of radio's role, as well as talents, by which radio service cannot fail to be enriched.

Even more important, however, is the role of colleges and universities in the field of radio research. There is room for a vast expansion of studies of the commercial, artistic and social aspects of radio. The cultural aspects of radio's influence provide in themselves a vast and fascinating field of research.

It is hoped that the facts emerging from this report and the recommendations which follow will be of interest to the groups mentioned. With them rather than with the Commission rests much of the hope for improved broadcasting quality.

B. Role of the Commission: While much of the responsibility for improved program service lies with the broadcasting industry and with the public, the Commission has a statutory responsibility for the public interest, of which it cannot divest itself. The Commission's experience with the detailed review of broadcast renewal applications since April, 1945, together with the facts set forth in this report, indicate some current trends in broadcasting which, with reference to licensing procedure, require its particular attention.

In issuing and in renewing the licenses of broadcast stations the Commission proposes to give particular consideration to four program service factors relevant to the public interest. There are: (1) the carrying of sustaining programs, including network sustaining programs, with particular reference to the retention by licensees of a proper discretion and responsibility for maintaining a well-balanced program structure; (2) the carrying of local live programs; (3) the carrying of programs devoted to the discussion of public issues; and (4) the elimination of advertising excesses.

(1) *Sustaining Programs.* The carrying of sustaining programs has always been deemed one aspect of broadcast operation in the public interest. Sustaining programs perform a five-fold function in (a) maintaining an overall program balance, (b) providing time for programs inappropriate for sponsorship, (c) providing time for programs serving particular minority tastes and interests, (d) providing time for non-profit organizations—religious, civic, agricultural, labor, education, etc., and (e) providing time for experiment and for unfettered artistic self-expression.

Accordingly, the Commission concludes that one standard of operation in the public interest is a reasonable proportion of time devoted to sustaining programs.

Moreover, if sustaining programs are to perform their traditional functions in the American system of broadcasting, they must be broadcast at hours when the public is awake and listening. The time devoted to sustaining programs, accordingly, should be reasonably distributed among the various segments of the broadcast day.

For reasons set forth, the Commission in considering overall program balance, will also take note of network sustaining programs available to but not carried by a station, and of the programs which the station substitutes therefor.

(2) *Local Live Programs.* The Commission has always placed a marked emphasis, and in some cases perhaps an undue emphasis, on the carrying of local live programs as a standard of public interest. The development of network, transcription, and wire news services is such that no sound public interest appears to be served by continuing to stress local live programs exclusively at the expense of these other categories. Nevertheless, reasonable provision for local self-expression still remains an essential function of a station's operation and will continue to be so regarded by the Commission. In particular, public interest requires that such programs should not be crowded out of the best listening hours.

(3) *Programs devoted to the discussion of public issues.* The crucial need for discussion programs, at the local, national, and international

levels alike is universally realized. Accordingly, the carrying of such programs in reasonable sufficiency, and during good listening hours, is a factor
to be considered in any finding of public interest.

(4) *Advertising excesses.* The evidence set forth above warrants the
conclusion that some stations during some or many portions of the broadcast day have engaged in advertising excesses which are incompatible with
their public responsibilities, and which threaten the good name of broadcasting itself.

As the broadcasting industry itself has insisted, the public interest
clearly requires that the amount of time devoted to advertising matter shall
bear a reasonable relationship to the amount of time devoted to programs.
Accordingly, in its application forms the Commission will request the applicant to state how much time he proposes to devote to advertising matter
in any one hour.

This by itself will not, of course, result in the elimination of some of the
particular excesses described. This is a matter in which self-regulation by
the industry may properly be sought and indeed expected. The Commission
has no desire to concern itself with the particular length, content, or irri-
tating qualities of particular commercial plugs.

6

COMMUNICATION CONTENT

Analysis of Media Content

For many research problems in communications it is necessary to describe the contents of the mass media in a rigorous fashion. For this purpose students in the field have developed the technique of content analysis—the *objective, systematic, and quantitative* analysis of symbol materials. The uses of content analysis in the study of the communication process are many and varied: they include the investigation of cultural patterns, the prediction of events, the identification of the communicator's intentions, the application of communication standards, and the description of responses to communications. (A full discussion of these and other uses of content analysis, together with a discussion of technical problems, may be found in Berelson and Lazarsfeld, cited in the bibliography).

No attempt has been made here to represent adequately the literature on the techniques of content analysis. However, the essay by Lasswell, a pioneer in this field, does deal with the central methodological question in the treatment of communication content. This item may be considered in conjunction with the article by Kris and Leites, which describes broad trends in political propaganda without the use of refined or precise measurement. The use of content analysis to document cultural trends is illustrated in the selection from Lowenthal's study of biographies. The character of certain types of communication content often makes it impossible or undesirable to proceed with completely quantified methods. In such cases, the empirical objective can often be attained through a careful blending of measurement and interpretation, as illustrated in Asheim's comparative study of two media.

Harold D. Lasswell

WHY BE QUANTITATIVE?

The point of view of this book is that the study of politics can be advanced by the quantitative analysis of political discourse. Why be quantitative? In reply, it is perhaps appropriate to bring out the limitations of qualitative analysis in terms of the work of the present writer.

At the end of World War I, research on politically significant communication was almost entirely qualitative, consisting in the discovery and illustration of propaganda themes and their use. When the present writer described the propaganda of World War I in *Propaganda Technique in the World War* (1927)[1] he took note of certain common themes running through the propaganda of all belligerent powers. The themes were:

The enemy is a menace.
(German militarism threatens us all.)
We are protective.
(We protect ourselves and others.)
The enemy is obstructive.
(They block our future aims.)
We are helpful.
(We aid in the achievement of positive goals.)
The enemy is immoral and insolent.
(They violate legal and moral standards and they hold everyone else in contempt.)
We are moral and appreciative.
(We conform to moral and legal standards and we respect others.)
The enemy will be defeated.
We will win.

Reprinted from *Language of Politics* (1949), pp. 40-52, by permission of the author and the publisher. (Copyright, 1949, by The Policy Sciences Foundation.)
[1] Kegan Paul, London, and Knopf, New York, 1927; reprinted by Peter Smith, New York, 1938.

265

The book was organized to show the form taken by these themes when domestic, allied or enemy audiences were addressed. The chapter on "The Illusion of Victory" showed what was told the home audience on the themes, "The enemy will be defeated," "We will win." The chapter on "Satanism" described how the self was presented as "moral" and "appreciative" while the enemy was "immoral" and "insolent." The "menacing" and "obstructive" rôle of the enemy and our own "protective" and "helpful" activity were illustrated in the chapter on "War Guilt and War Aims." Special attention was paid to "preserving friendship" (of allies and neutrals) and "demoralizing the enemy." Each chapter was composed of excerpts selected chiefly from the propaganda of the United States, Great Britain, Germany and France.

Although none of the criteria which guided the choice of quotations is stated in the book, it is obvious that some selections were made because they clearly stated a theme or developed a theme in detail. No doubt these criteria justified the citation of the extended account of alleged Entente violations of international law which had been compiled by Dr. Ernst Müller-Meiningen (pp. 85-86). In some cases, the wide dissemination of the material was no doubt a selective factor, notably in the case of *J'accuse!*, an exposé of Germany by Richard Grelling (p. 54). Sometimes the eminence of the speaker appears to have been the deciding factor, as with the Bryce report on alleged atrocities perpetrated by the Germans in Belgium (p. 19). In certain instances, the excerpt was a sample of what was distributed by (or to) a professional, vocation, educational or other special group (pp. 70 ff.).

No evidence is given in the book that all the material studied by the author was examined with the same degree of care. We are not informed whether the author actually read or glanced through all the copies of the principal mass-circulation newspapers, periodicals, books and pamphlets of Germany and other countries; or whether he read British, French and American material as fully as German.

Of course, the study did not purport to be an exhaustive history of propaganda during the war. It was called an essay in technique, and the hope was expressed that it would have some influence in directing professional historians toward the study of propaganda, and that the scheme of classification would prove helpful in the organization of future research. The book was to some extent successful in both objectives. Research on war propaganda, as indeed on every phase of propaganda, went forward with vigor, many monographs growing out of the original essay or attributing some degree of influence to it.[2]

Among the most comprehensive books on the propaganda of World

[2] See Ralph Haswell Lutz, "Studies of War Propaganda, 1914-33," *Journal of Modern History*, 5: 496-516 (December, 1933).

War II was those of Hans Thimme, *Weltkrieg ohne Waffen* (1932) [3], and George G. Bruntz, *Allied Propaganda and the Collapse of the German Empire in 1918* (1938) [4]. Both historians explored archives of newspaper, magazine and other source material, the first relying chiefly upon the Reich archives and the second utilizing the Hoover War Library at Stanford University.

Whenever the propaganda message was described, the method adopted by these writers was similar to that of *Propaganda Technique in the World War*. Excerpts were chosen to illustrate what was circulated to different publics and what themes were used. The authors left unspecified their criteria of choice, although these were obviously similar to those of the earlier work. In many respects these monographs are more satisfactory than the first book, since the authors made use of new source material, and employed to advantage the accumulated results of historical scholarship on the relative importance of persons, channels and symbols in the war.

The results, however, can not be accepted as in all respects satisfactory; many relevant questions remain unanswered. Can we assume that a scholar read his sources with the same degree of care throughout this research? Did he allow his eye to travel over the thousands upon thousands of pages of parliamentary debates, newspapers, magazines and other sources listed in his bibliography or notes? Or did he use a sampling system, scanning some pages superficially, though concentrating upon certain periods? Was the sampling system for the *Frankfurter Zeitung*, if one was employed, comparable with the one for the *Manchester Guardian?* Were the leaflets chosen simply because they were conveniently available to the scholar, or were they genuinely representative of the most widely circulated propaganda leaflets?

The very fact that such questions can be raised at all points to a certain lack of method in presenting and conducting research on the history of war propaganda. In all of the books to which reference has been made no explicit justification was given of most of the excerpts chosen to illustrate a specific theme, to characterize the content of any particular channel, or to describe the propaganda directed toward or reaching any given audience. It is impossible to determine from the final report whether the same number or a comparable number of mass circulation media were read for France as for England or Germany, or whether publications were explored with the same degree of intensity at all dates, or whether certain dates were singled out for intensive note-taking.

The limitations of these monographs are apparent when anyone undertakes to follow a particular theme through various periods, channels and

---

[3] Cotta'sche Buchhandlung Nachfolger, Stuttgart and Berlin.
[4] Stanford University Press, Stanford.

audiences. We know that every belligerent used "war aim" propaganda. But suppose we want to find the degree of emphasis laid upon war aims from period to period. Or assume that we ask how they differed when presented to the upper, middle or lower classes of the home population, or to neutral, ally or enemy. Was the war aim propaganda more prominent in the magazines than in the pamphlets, or the reverse? The same questions apply to every theme.

To some extent, historians of war propaganda have sought to reduce ambiguity by multiplying the number of subperiods described within the whole period. Walter Zimmerman studied the English press from the time of Sarajevo to the entry of England into the war, selecting thirty daily newspapers, eight Sunday papers, nine weeklies, four monthlies and two quarterlies, intending to cover all the important regional and social groups in Great Britain.[5] Even in this period, however, we can not be certain of the criteria used in selecting quotations. It is obvious that Zimmerman does not summarize all thirty daily papers every day, but we are left in the dark about why he quotes one paper one day or week and omits it the next time. Even if we assume that his judgment is good, it is permissible to ask if such arbitrary selection procedures create a properly balanced picture, or whether they result in special pleading based, if not on deliberate deception, then on unconscious bias.

The same problem remains in the detailed monograph by Friederike Recktenwald, in which she restricts herself to a single set of themes having to do with British war aims.[6] Miss Recktenwald divides the course of the war into subperiods, and reproduces or summarizes material from the British press having to do with war aims. Although this procedure gives us a plausible indication of the relative amount of attention paid to war aims at different times, not all reasonable doubts are allayed. She follows no consistent scheme of reporting. During any given subperiod only a few quotations may be reproduced; yet this may not invariably mean that there was less war-aim news or diminished editorial prominence. It may signify no more than that what was said is less interesting to the historian because the style is less vivid and quotable. We can not rely upon Miss Recktenwald's excerpts to be true samples of the total stream of news and comment reaching the British public, or even of any particular newspaper, or group of newspapers. The moment we ask clear questions that call for reliable bases of comparison, the arbitrary and dubious character of the monograph is apparent.

It is possible, however, to find studies of great technical excellence.

[5] *Die Englische Presse zum Ausbruch des Weltkrieges,* Verlag "Hochschule und Ausland," Charlottenburg, 1928.
[6] *Kriegsziele und öffentliche Meinung Englands, 1914-16,* W. Köhlhammer, Stuttgart, 1929.

In matters of systematic definition and historic detail, we can go back half a century to *A Study of Public Opinion and Lord Beaconsfield, 1875-1880,* by George Carslake Thompson (1886).[7] At the beginning of that remarkable work, a series of terms for the analysis of public opinion is carefully defined. These terms are consistently applied throughout the two fact-stuffed volumes. One part of the analytical scheme names the standards applied by the British public on foreign policy questions. Among the standards were "international law," "interest," "morality," and "taste." Thompson pointed out that such standards were applied according to the public's conception of England's rôle in relation to other nations, and that these ranged all the way from "England as an island" to "England as a European or Asiatic great power."

In applying these standards and conceptions, Thompson distinguished certain broad motives—"sentimental" or "diplomatic"—that were operating among the members of the British public in their basic orientation toward foreign policy. At any given time—for instance, at the outbreak of war between Russia and Turkey—these standards, conceptions and motivations (public "notions") were fused into public "views." The views of the British public in 1876 were classified as "Anti-Turkism," "Anti-war," "Order," "Legalism," "Anti-Russianism and Philo-Turkism." Such views in turn were related to corresponding policies. In this way, "Anti-Turkism" was bracketed with "emancipation," "Anti-war" with "isolation." The book described each successive phase of England's reaction to the war between Russia and Turkey, and copiously illustrated every move by excerpts from a list of publications.

Thompson's treatise is noteworthy for the unification of carefully defined abstractions with exhaustive data from the sources. Nevertheless, the outcome of all the admirable intelligence and industry that went into this treatise does not yield maximum results, because of a basic failure: the problem of sampling, recording and summarizing sources was not resolved. Hence, the entire foundation of the work rests on shaky ground. Thompson divides the five years with which he deals into subperiods, according to some predominant characteristic. One such subperiod is the "incubation period, third phase," from the opening of the Parliamentary Session of 1876 to the Servian declaration of war. This is followed by the "atrocity period," which in turn is divided into several parts. For each subperiod, Thompson narrates the stream of events and selects from the sources the quotations that impress him as important not only because they are conspicuous, but because they bear some relationship to his systematic scheme of analysis (standards, conceptions, motivations, views and policies). However, the critical reader is still justified in remaining skeptical of the representativeness of the quotations. He can not be sure why they impressed the

7 Macmillan, London, 2 vols., 1886.

author when he was reading and making notes on the sources, or organizing his chapters. An excerpt may be the only one that appeared in a given newspaper or magazine on the same subject during the period; or, on the contrary, it may be only one among a tremendous gush of news and editorial items. Thompson does not tell us. The fundamental operation—of source handling—remained highly arbitrary.

If the excellence of the Thompson study lies in system and rich detail, a few recent publications rank above it in the sampling of sources. D. F. Willcox (1900) [8] classified the contents of a single issue of 240 newspapers according to topic (by column inches). Later A. A. Tenney, Jr., at Columbia University, interested a number of students in space measurement and initiated investigations of immediate value to world politics. Julian L. Woodward examined the foreign news published in 40 American morning newspapers and improved the technical state of the subject by showing the effect of different sampling methods upon the result. In general, he found that a small number of issues distributed throughout the year were enough to give a reliable picture of the amount of attention usually given by an American morning newspaper to foreign news (at least during a non-crisis period). [9]

In general, these investigations were not expressly related to political science. They were made by statisticians interested in having something to count, or sociologists who were exploring the general social process. The senior author of the present work undertook to direct research toward the use of objective procedures in gathering the data pertinent to political hypotheses. Schuyler Foster, for example, examined the treatment given European war news in the New York *Times* during definite periods before our participation in the war of 1914-18. He summarized his results in tabular and graphical form, and showed that the crisis that led immediately to our entry into the war was the final one in a series of crises of ever-increasing intensity. He measured these fluctuations by recording the frequency with which different kinds of news or editorial comment were made about the war or America's relation to it. The use of quantitative methods gave precision to part of the history of America's mobilization for war, and opened up a series of question about the relation between the ups and downs in the New York *Times* and corresponding fluctuations in New York newspapers reaching different social groups, and in newspapers published in cities of different sizes throughout the country. [10]

[8] "The American Newspaper," *Annals of the American Academy of Political and Social Science*, 16: 56-92 (1900).

[9] *Foreign News in American Morning Newspapers*, Columbia University Press, New York, 1930.

[10] "How America Became Belligerent: A Quantitative Study of War-News, 1914-17," *American Journal of Sociology*, 40: 464-76 (January, 1935). See also studies sum-

More exact methods give us a means of clarifying certain categories that have been at the root of many past evils in the work of historians and social scientists. For a century, controversy has raged over the relative weight of "material" and "ideological" factors in the social and political process. This controversy has been sterile of scientific results, though the propaganda resonance of "dialectical materialism" has been enormous.

Insofar as sterility can be attributed to technical factors in the domain of scholarship, the significant factor is failure to deal adequately with "ideological" elements. The usual account of how material and ideological factors interact upon one another leaves the process in a cloud of mystery. It is as though you put people in an environment called material—and presto!—their ideas change in a predictable way; and if they do not, the failure is ascribed to an ideological lag of some kind. But the relations, though assumed, are not demonstrated. So far as the material dimensions are concerned, operational methods have been worked out to describe them; not so with the ideological. We are amply equipped to describe such "material" changes as fluctuations in output or amount of machinery employed in production; but we can not match this part of the description with equally precise ways of describing the ideological. The result is that the historical and social sciences have been making comparisons between patterns, only a few of which are handled with precision. The other dimensions remain wholly qualitative, impressionistic and conjectural.[11]

We have undertaken to clear up some of the confusion that has long beset the analysis of "environment" by introducing basic distinctions: the first between the "attention frame" and "surroundings," and the second between the "media frame" and the "non-media frame." The attention frame or "milieu" is the part of an environment reaching the focus of attention of a person or group; the surroundings do not reach the focus. The media frame is composed of the signs coming to the focus of attention (the press which is actually read, for instance). The non-media frame includes the features of an environment that, although not signs, reach attention, such as conspicuous buildings, or persons. Whether any given set of surrounding does affect the structure of attention is to be settled by observing the phenomena, not by assumption.

The fundamental nature of these relations is evident when we reflect upon the requirements for a scientific explanation of response. Two sets of factors are involved: the environment and predispositions. R (response) is a function, in the mathematical sense, of E (environment) and P (pre-

marized in Quincy Wright, A Study of War, University of Chicago Press, Chicago, 2 vols., 1942. Note especially Chapter XXX.

[11] See Harold D. Lasswell, "Communications Research and Politics," in Print Radio, and Film in a Democracy, edited by Douglas Waples, University of Chicago, Chicago, 1942, pp. 101-117.

disposition); and we have shown that the part of the environment immediately affecting response is what comes to the focus of attention (the attention frame). Information about surroundings is pertinent only to the degree to which it can be shown that the surroundings determine attention. In deciding whether any feature of the environment comes to the focus, it is necessary to demonstrate that a minimum (the threshold level) has been elicited. We do not consider that radio programs which are blacked out by static have come to the attention of an audience. A threshold level has not been reached. (The threshold is not part of the R in the formula of explanation used above; only changes above the threshold are called "effects"—response to what is brought into the attention field.)

The procedures of "content analysis" of communication are appropriate to the problem of describing the structure of attention in quantitative terms.[12] Before entering upon technicalities, it may be pointed out that quantitative ways of describing attention serve many practical, as well as scientific, purposes. *Anticipating the enemy* is one of the most crucial and tantalizing problems in the conduct of war. The intelligence branch of every staff or operations agency is matching wits with the enemy. The job is to out-guess the enemy, to foretell his military, diplomatic, economic and propaganda moves before he makes them, and to estimate where attack would do him the most harm. A principal source of information is what the enemy disseminates in his media of communication.

The Global War introduced a new source of information about the enemy—radio broadcasts under his supervision. When the enemy speaks to his home population, it is possible to listen in. We overhear what the enemy says to his allies, to neutrals and to his enemies. At the outbreak of the Global War, belligerent governments set monitors to work, listening, recording and summarizing the output of enemy and enemy-controlled stations. In Great Britain a group connected with the British Broadcasting Corporation subjected this enormous body of material to systematic examination and began forecasting Nazi policy. These estimates have since been restudied.[13] The same procedures have also been applied to the press

[12] For a review of the research situation at the outbreak of the war (1939), consult Douglas Waples, Bernard Berelson, and Franklyn R. Bradshaw *What Reading Does to People*, University of Chicago Press, Chicago, 1940. More recent developments are noted in Harold D. Lasswell, "Content Analysis," in Bruce L. Smith, Harold D. Lasswell and Ralph D. Casey, *Propaganda, Communication and Public Opinion*, Princeton University Press, Princeton, 1946. (Modified from *Document* II, Experimental Division for the Study of Wartime Communications, Library of Congress, 1942.)

[13] Ernst Kris, Hans Speier and Associates, *German Radio Propaganda; Report on Home Broadcasts During the War*, Oxford University Press, New York, 1944. See also *Propaganda by Short Wave*, edited by Harwood L. Childs and John B. Whitton, Princeton University Press, Princeton, 1942; and the valuable essay by Charles Siepmann, *Radio in Wartime*, Oxford University Press, Oxford, 1942. A survey of the situation in 1939 is by Thomas Grandin, *The Political Use of Radio*, Geneva Research Centre, Geneva, 1939; for a later period, Arno Huth *Radio Today; The Present State of Broadcasting in the*

and to every other channel of communication. The full plan of the enemy often appears only when the entire stream of communication is interpreted as a whole.

As we improve our methods of describing public attention and response, our results become more useful for another practical purpose—the *detecting of political propaganda*. During World War II, the U. S. Department of Justice employed objective propaganda analysis to expose and prosecute enemy agents, like the Transocean Information Service (Nazi-controlled) and "native Fascists." The Federal Communications Commission described in Court the Axis themes recognized by experts who monitored and analyzed short-wave broadcasts emanating from Germany, Japan and Italy. Objective procedures had been applied in discovering these themes. Objective procedures were also used to analyze the periodicals published by the defendants, and to reveal the parallels between them and the themes disseminated by Axis propagandists.[14]

Quite apart from the use of legal action, it is important that members of the public be informed of the behavior of those with access to the channels of communication. In deciding how much we can rely upon a given newspaper, it is important to know if that newspaper ceases to attack Russia when Germany and Russia sign a non-aggression pact, and then returns to the attack as soon as Germany and Russia fall apart. Under these conditions, we have grounds for inferring a pro-German propaganda policy. By studying the news, editorial and feature material in a medium of communication under known German control, we can check on this inference. We may find that the two media distribute praise and blame in the same way among public leaders and the political parties; and that they take the same stand on domestic and foreign issues. If so, our inference is strengthened that the channel is dominated by pro-German policies.[15]

World, Geneva Research Centre, Geneva, 1942. Concerning the news and documentary film, the most penetrating inquiry to date, is by Siegfried Kracauer, *Propaganda and the Nazi War Film,* Museum of Modern Art Film Library, New York, 1942.

[14] *United States of America* vs. *William Dudley Pelley* (and others), tried in the U. S. District Court for the Southern District of Indiana, Indianapolis Division, summer, 1942; conviction affirmed on appeal to the U. S. Circuit Court of Appeals, Southern Circuit, October Term, 1942. A writ of certiorari denied by the U. S. Supreme Court. Government witnesses included Harold N. Graves, Jr., of the Federal Communications Commission, and Harold D. Lasswell.

[15] The historians of literature have relied upon quantitative analysis as one of the chief means at their disposal in the many "detection" problems that confront them. They must detect corrupt texts, decide among competing attributions of authorship, arrive at the true order in which works were composed, determine the sources relied upon by the author and the influences affecting authorship. As Yule points out, the technique of word-counting goes back many centuries, at least to the "Masoretes," who, after the destruction of the Jewish state, A.D. 70, devoted themselves to preserving the text of the Bible and the correct manner of pronunciation. It is curious to see that, despite the ease and amount of word-counting, first-class statisticians have only begun to concern themselves with the problems involved—notably G. Udny Yule, *The Statistical Study of*

In the preceding paragraphs, we have said that policy may be served by objective procedures used to anticipate the enemy and to detect propaganda. Also, as scientific knowledge increases, the possibility of control improves; hence, a third contribution of objective research to policy is *skill*.[16] Skill is the most economical utilization of available means to attain a goal. Appraisals of skill are among the most difficult judgments to establish on a convincing basis, since they depend upon exhaustive knowledge of concrete circumstances and of scientific relations. To say that A is more skillful than B in a given situation is to allow for all factors being "equal." It is not easy to demonstrate that the two sets of environing and predispos-

Literary Vocabulary, Cambridge University Press, Cambridge, Eng., 1944. Although word-counting is involved in the study of communication, not all quantitative procedures are necessarily "content analysis." This term can legitimately be applied only when "counts" are undertaken with reference to a general theory of the communication process. In this sense, "content analysis" is quite recent.

The literary historians have occasionally been stimulated by the methods of crytography, and they have also made direct contributions to the subject. One example of the influence of this art is Edith Rickert, long associated with J. M. Manly in Chaucerian research, who worked in the "Black Chamber" during World War I, and subsequently devised new ways of studying style: *New Methods for the Study of Literature*, University of Chicago Press, Chicago, 1926. A brief example of differences in the handling of political material by different authors is revealed by a simple study of Scipio's alleged speech to the mutineers in 206 B.C. In Polybius "The speech contains 520 words, in which pronouns or verbal forms of the first person singular occur 14 times—i.e., once in every 37 words. In Livy the speech occupies about 1025 words, and there are no less than 64 occurrences of *ego* or *meus* or verbs in the first person singular—i.e., one word in every 16—a frequency of more than double." (R. S. Conway, *The Portrait of a Roman Gentleman, from Livy*, Bull. of the John Rylands Library, Manchester, 7 (1922-23: 8-22.)

An absorbing mystery story has been written in which detection depends upon content analysis and engineering: Brett Rutledge (pseud. of Elliott Paul), *The Death of Lord Haw Haw*, Random House, New York, 1940. On certain problems see Wladimir Eliasberg, "Linguistics and Political Criminology," *Journal of Criminal Psychopathology*, 5 (1944): 769-774.

[16] Hypotheses or assumptions about skill have been stated or implied in quantitative studies of many channels of expression. Special attention has been given to oratory, from this point of view, and especially to such quantifiable characteristics as length of sentence. The language of Rufus Choate so greatly impressed his contemporaries that the chief justice of the highest court in Massachusetts, Joseph Neilson, was among those who gave it special study (*Memoirs of Rufus Choate*, Houghton, Mifflin, 1884). Choate was given to long sentences, averaging no fewer than 37 words in one of his most famous cases. Nearly an eighth of all his sentences, in this instance, contained more than 80 words. Consult John W. Black, "Rufus Choate," in *A History and Criticism of American Public Address*, prepared under the auspices of The National Association of Teachers of Speech, William Norwood Brigance, Editor, McGraw-Hill, New York, 1943. Vol. 1, pp. 455-456. More technical investigations are conducted by modern specialists on public speaking. Howard L. Runion, for example, concentrated on fifty speeches by Woodrow Wilson, and counted many features, including the use of figures of speech. (Unpublished dissertation, University of Wisconsin, 1932. For more detail see Dayton David McKean, "Woodrow Wilson," in *op. cit.* Vol. 2, pp. 968-992, Brigance, editor.) It is perhaps unnecessary to remark that studies of classical orators are researches into the style of classical historians. See, for instance, Grover Cleveland Kenyan, *Antithesis in the Speeches of Greek Historians*, University of Chicago Libraries, Chicago 1941.

ing factors are strictly comparable. The simple fact that the Nazis won out in Germany against the Socialists and other parties does not necessarily warrant the conclusion that the Nazis were more skillful propagandists than their antagonists. Or the failure of the French to hold out against the Germans longer in 1940 was not necessarily because French propagandists were lacking in skill. The "skill" factor can be separated from the others only when a very comprehensive view can be gained of the context. Did the responsible heads of state choose the most suitable personnel to conduct propaganda operations? Were the most effective symbols chosen? The most useful media? In each case, the question must be answered with reference to alternatives available in the original situation.

That content analysis has a direct bearing on the evaluation of skill is evident, since such methods introduce a degree of precise description at many points in the propaganda process. Directives can be described in detail; so, too, can material released through the propaganda agencies and disseminated through various media controlled by, or beyond the control of, the propagandist. Indeed, as we pointed out in our analysis of the attention factor in world politics,[17] every link in the chain of communication can be described when suitable methods are used; quantitative procedures reduce the margin of uncertainty in the basic data. (There is, of course, no implication that non-quantitative methods should be dropped. On the contrary, there is need of more systematic theory and of more luminous "hunches" if the full potentialities of precision are to be realized in practice. As the history of quantification shows [in economics, for instance], there is never-ending, fruitful interplay between theory, hunch, impression and precision.)

A fourth contribution relates not to policy as a whole, but to the special objectives of humane politics. The aim of humane politics is a commonwealth in which the dignity of man is accepted in theory and fact. Whatever *improves our understanding of attitude* is a potential instrument of humane politics. Up to the present, physical science has not provided us with means of penetrating the skull of a human being and directly reading off his experiences. Hence, we are compelled to rely upon indirect means of piercing the wall that separates us from him. Words provide us with clues, but we hesitate to take all phrases at their face value. Apart from deliberate duplicity, langauge has shortcomings as a vehicle for the transmission of thought and feeling. It is important to recognize that we obtain insight into the world of the other person when we are fully acquainted with what has come to his attention. Certainly the world of the country boy is full of the sights and smells and sounds of nature. The city boy, on

[17] See Harold D. Lasswell in Lyman Bryson (ed.) *The Communication of Ideas,* Harper's, New York, 1948, Chapters IV and XV.

the other hand, lives in a labyrinth of streets, buildings, vehicles and crowds. A Chinese youth of good family has his ancestors continually thrust upon his notice; an American youth may vaguely recall his grand-parents. The son of an English ruling family may be reared on the anec-dotes of centuries of imperial history, while the son of an American busi-ness man recalls that there was a Revolution and that Bunker Hill had something to do with it.

The dominant political symbols of an epoch provide part of the common experience of millions of men. There is some fascination in the thought of how many human beings are bound together by a thread no more sub-stantial than the resonance of a name or the clang of a slogan. In war, men suffer pain, hunger, sorrow; the specific source of pain, the specific sensa-tion of one's specific object of sorrow, may be very private. In contrast, the key symbol enters directly into the focus of all men and provides an element of common experience.[18]

It is obvious that a complete survey of mass attention will go far beyond the press, the broadcast or the film. It will cover every medium of mass communication. Further, a complete survey would concentrate upon the

[18] The use of key symbols in Quantitative analysis of compaarative literature is exemplified by Josephine Miles, "Some Major Poetic Words," *Essays and Studies* (by members of the Department of English, University of California), University of Cali-fornia Publications in English, Vol. XIV, University of California Press, Berkeley and Los Angeles, 1943, pp. 233-239. ". . . the trend of change through five hundred years of main consistencies may be justly observed, and may be summarized in these three ways: First, in terms of parts of speech, it may be said that all the verbs to be stressed by more than one poet were established by Donne or sooner; the adjectives, by Burns, or sooner; the last noun, not until Poe, Second, in terms of new subject matter, the direction is clear from *making* to *thinking*, from *good* and *great* to *high* and *sweet* and *wild*, and from *heaven* and man to *soul* and *heart*, to *eye* and *hand*, and then to *day*, *sun*, *dream*, *night*; it is the direction from action to thought, and from conceived to sensed. Third, in terms of contrast between first and last, the prevailing strength of the three main words, *man*, *love*, and *see*, stands out, mainly the simple verbs are lost, and *heart*, *day*, and *night* are the fresher forces. These three views, as we have seen, add up strongly to one: the view of a general stability in the language of major English poetry, tempered by the shift, gradual in all save Collins, from action and concept toward feel-ing and sensing."

Expertly conducted studies in expressive media other than literature can throw a light on the changing outlook of peoples. The ruling classes of Delft, for instance, early retired from the brewing industry to live upon investments in the East India Company, and remained retired generation after generation. As they shrank from all forms of com-mercial activity, no other outgoing mode of life attracted them. Max Eisler has been able to demonstrate a remarkable parallel between Delft's paintings and the quietism of Delft life. First, they found landscapes too breezy and, withdrawing indoors, bought church interiors. Presently these seemed too expansive, and they took to cozy home interiors. Vermeer was the culminating artist in this development, and we see in his paintings the citizens of Delft in unvarying sunshine lounging at table, staring at their reflections in a mirror, or at their jewels; sometimes they have passed from lethargy to sleep. And in these paintings the walls are seen coming closer and closer. Year by year, the world of the Delft rentiers grows narrower and narrower, though always in perpetual sunshine (Max Eisler, *Alt-Delft*, Vienna, 1923. Put in perspective by Miriam Beard, *A History of the Business Man*, Macmillan, New York, 1938, p. 306.)

most active decision-makers, disclosing the milieu of the heads of states, the chiefs of staff, diplomats and all other groups. An exhaustive inventory would describe the entire intelligence process.[19]

Why, then, be quantitative about communication? Because of the scientific and policy gains that can come of it. The social process is one of *collaboration* and *communication;* and quantitative methods have already demonstrated their usefulness in dealing with the former. Further understanding and control depend upon equalizing our skill in relation to both.

[19] Special studies eventually to be made public have been completed by some of our associates in the World Attention Survey: Professor Richard Burks, Wayne University; Dr. Heinz H. F. Eulau; Dr. Bruno Foa, formerly University of Turin; Doris Lewis; Dean James J. Robbins, American University; Professor David N. Rowe, Yale University; Professor Douglas Waples, University of Chicago.

Ernst Kris and Nathan Leites

TRENDS IN
TWENTIETH CENTURY PROPAGANDA

In speaking of propaganda, we refer to the political sphere and not to promotional activities in general. We define acts of propaganda, in agreement with H. D. Lasswell [1] as attempts to influence attitudes of large numbers of people on controversial issues of relevance to a group. Propaganda is thus distinguished from education which deals with non-controversial issues. Moreover, not all treatments of controversial issues of relevance to a group fall under the definition; they are not propaganda if they aim at the clarification of issues rather than at the changing of attitudes.

In the following, we deal mainly with propaganda by agents of government and exclusively with propaganda using the channels of mass communication, i.e., principally print, radio and film.

However, neither the potentialities of any one medium, nor the variety of promotional devices used by all will be discussed here. We are concerned with the place of propaganda in Western civilization. Our general hypothesis is that responses to political propaganda in the Western world have considerably changed during the last decades; and that these changes are related to trends in the sociopsychological conditions of life in the twentieth century.

We shall not be able to offer conclusive proof for the points we wish to make. We do not know of the existence of data comprehensive and reliable enough to demonstrate in quantitative terms broad hypotheses about changes in responses to propaganda. We start out from changes in content and style of propaganda, assuming that they reflect the propagandist's expectation as to the response of his audience. The propagandist may be mis-

Reprinted from *Psychoanalysis and the Social Sciences*, Vol. I (1947), pp. 393-409, by permission of the authors and the publisher. (Copyright, 1947, by the International Universities Press.)

[1] Lasswell, H. D. *Propaganda Techniques in the World War*, New York, Alfred A. Knopf, 1927. Smith, B. L., Lasswell, H. D. and Casey, R. D. *Propaganda, Communication, and Public Opinion*, Princeton Univ. Press, 1946.

taken in his expectations, but finally he will be informed to some extent about his audiences' response, and adapt his output, within limit, to their predispositions.

We choose two situations in which propaganda was directed towards comparable objectives: the two World Wars.

Wartime propaganda is enacted in a situation with strictly limited goals. Under whatever conditions, the objective of propagandists in wartime is to maximize social participation among members of their own group and to minimize participation among members of the enemy group. Social participation is characterized by concern for the objectives of the group, the sharing of its activities, and the preparedness to accept deprivations on its behalf. High "participation" is therefore identical with high "morale." Its psychological dynamics are mutual identifications among group members, and identification of individual members with leaders or leading ideals of the group, strong cathexis of the goal set by the group, and decreased cathexis of the self; processes that at least in part are preconscious and unconscious. Low participation may manifest itself in two ways: first, participation may be shifted partly or totally from one group to another. In this case, one may speak of a split in participation. Second, low participation may manifest itself as a withdrawal of individuals from the political sphere; in this case, we speak of privatization [2] (H. Speier and M. Otis).[3]

The psychological dynamics of a split in participation are obvious; one set of identifications and objectives has been replaced by another. The only dynamic change consists in the fact that, as a rule, the old group has not lost its cathexis, but has become the target of hostility.

The dynamics of privatization are more complex: withdrawal of cathexes from the group of its objectives leads to a process comparable to, but not identical with a narcissistic regression. Concern with the self becomes dominant. Since the striving for individual indulgence is maximized, the individual becomes exceedingly vulnerable to deprivation.

Modern warfare is distinguished from older types of warfare by the fact that it affects larger numbers of individuals. In total war "nations at arms" oppose each other with all their resources. Hence participation becomes increasingly important. To the extent that preparedness for war infringes upon life in peace, the problem continues to exist in peacetime.

Participation of whole nations was more essential during World War I

[2] Two kinds of decreased participation in the direction of privatization can be distinguished: first, a decrease of active attitudes towards the political sphere, in favor of passive or merely adjusting attitudes; in this case, one must speak of a decrease of attitudinal participation; second, a decrease of the actual sharing in political action; in this case, one might speak of a decrease of behavioral participation.

[3] Speier, H. and Otis, M. "German Radio Propaganda to France during the Battle of France," in: *Radio Research*, 1942/43 eds. P. F. Lazarsfeld and F. N. Stanton, New York, Duell, Sloan & Pearce, 1944, pp. 208-247.

than during any previous war; and yet it was somewhat less essential than during World War II; the first World War, especially at its onset, was "less total" than the second. On the other hand, the media of mass communication were less developed; radio and film had hardly been tested. Three areas of difference between the propagandas of the two wars seem particularly relevant in our context:

1. Propaganda during the second World War exhibited, on the whole, a higher degree of sobriety than propaganda during World War I; the incidence of highly emotionalized terms was probably lower.

2. Propaganda during the second World War was, on the whole, less moralistic than propaganda during the first World War; the incidence of preference statements as against fact statements was probably lower.

3. Propaganda during the second World War tended to put a moderate ceiling on grosser divergences from presently or subsequently ascertainable facts, divergences that were more frequent in propaganda during the first World War. Also, propaganda during the second World War tended to give fuller information about relevant events than propaganda during World War I.

In summarizing the psychological aspects of these differences, we might say that propaganda appeals were less frequently directed to id and superego, more prominently to the ego.

In this respect, these areas of difference are representative of others. At least two qualifications to the points mentioned above are essential: first, most of the differences we stress became ever clearer the longer the scond World War lasted; second, they were more accentuated in the propaganda of the Western democracies than in that of Germany and Russia.[4]

The use of emotionalized language was, at the outset of World War II, almost completely absent in British propaganda. When, in the autumn of 1939, Mr. Churchill, then First Lord of the Admiralty, referred to the Nazis as "Huns," thus using the stereotype current during World War I, he was publicly rebuked. Basically, that attitude persisted throughout the war in Britain and the United States. "We don't want to be driven into hate" was the tenor of opinion. There were modifications of this attitude: in the United States in regard to Japan, in Britain after the severe onslaught of bombing. However, hate campaigns remained largely unacceptable. In Germany, a similar attitude persisted: attempts of German propaganda to brandish the bombing of German cities by British and later by American planes as barbarism, to speak of the crews of these planes as "night pirates" and of German raids against Britain as retaliatory largely failed to arouse indignant hate.

The waning power of *moral* argumentation in propaganda is best illustrated

---

[4] In the following, we shall in the main limit ourselves to examples from American, British and German propaganda, and some data on response; information on reactions of Russian and Japanese audiences is not accessible.

by the fact that one of the predominant themes of propaganda during World War I played no comparable part in World War II. The theme "Our cause is right; theirs is wrong" was secondary in the propaganda of the Western powers; its part in German propaganda was limited; only in Russian propaganda was its role presumably comparable to that it had played in World War I propaganda. In the democratic countries and in Germany, the moral argumentation was replaced by one in terms of indulgence and deprivation (profit or loss): "We are winning; they are losing"; and: "These will be the blessings of victory; these the calamities of defeat." There is evidence indicating that both in the democracies and in Germany this type of appeal was eminently successful. In other words: success of propaganda was dependent on the transformation of superego appeals into appeals to the ego.[5]

The third area of difference, the increased concern for some agreement between the content of propaganda and ascertainable facts, and the increased concern for detailed information was to some considerable extent related to technological change. Thus, during the first World War, the German people were never explicitly (and implicitly only much later) informed about the German defeat in the battle of the Marne in September 1914. A similar reticence during the second World War would not have proved expedient, since in spite of coercive measures, allied radio transmissions were widely listened to by Germans. However, technological progress was not the only reason for the change. The concern with credibility had increased, independently of the technology of communication. The tendency to check statements of one's own against those of enemy governments existed both in Germany and in the democracies; while it was limited in Germany, it was widely spread in Britain and the United States.

The differences of propaganda during World Wars I and II are epitomized in the treatment of a theme related to all three areas discussed—enemy atrocities. As far as we know, only Russian propaganda on German atrocities, and German propaganda on Russian atrocities gave to this theme about the same importance in World War II that all propagandists had given it during World War I. But German reports on allied atrocities were rather timid, if compared to the inventiveness of German propaganda in other areas; and German propaganda about Soviet atrocities was largely designed to create fear and defensive combativeness rather than hate and indignation. In the democracies, however, the "playing down" of reports on enemy atrocities was a guiding principle of propaganda, at least until 1945. While during World War I, allied propagandists did not refrain from exaggerating and even inventing atrocities, uncontestable evidence of enemy atrocities was, for a long time, withheld during World War II. It is needless to say that the atrocities to which this documentation referred and which, at the end of the war and after the war became manifest to the soldiers of armies traversing Europe, were of a kind totally different in horror from anything the world of the earlier twentieth century had known.

[5] Masserman, J. H. *Principles of Dynamic Psychiatry*, Philadelphia, W. B. Saunders, 1946. He makes a similar point (p. 219). He speaks of "resonance with personal incentives."

The purposeful reticence of the democratic governments becomes thereby even more significant.

No adequate understanding of these propaganda trends is possible, unless we take two closely related trends in the predispositions of the public into account. Our thesis is that the differences between the propaganda styles during both World Wars are largely due to the rising tendencies towards *distrust* and *privatization*—tendencies that we believe to have existed in the Western democracies as well as in Germany.

Distrust is directed primarily against the propagandist and the authority he represents, secondarily also against the "suggestibility" of the "propagandee." [6]

The first mentioned manifestation of distrust can be traced back to the last war. Propaganda operated then on a new level of technological perfection; the latent possibilities of the mass communication media became suddenly manifest; in all belligerent countries, outbursts of enthusiasm for war occurred. Propagandists, like children playing with a new toy, charged their messages with many manufactured contents. After the war, they reported on their own achievements—sometimes exaggerating the extent to which they had distorted events. These reports helped to create the aura of secret power that ever since has surrounded propagandists. In Britain and the United States, some of this prestige was transferred from the propagandist to the public relations counsel; some of the men who had successfully worked in government agencies became pioneers of modern advertising. Beliefs in the power of propaganda led to a phobia of political persuasion: propaganda became "a bad name," an influence against which the common man had to guard himself.

The political and economic failures of the postwar era, the futility of the idealistic appeals which had helped to conclude the first World War, reinforced this distrust. Its spread and influence on the political scene, however, was sharply different in different areas. In Germany, the distrust of propaganda was manipulated by the nationalist, and later, the national-socialist movement. Propaganda was identified with those allied propaganda efforts that had accompanied German defeat.[7] While distrust was directed against one side, nationalist and national socialist propaganda could operate more freely under the guise of anti-propaganda. In the Western democracies, the propaganda phobia rose during the Great Depression. It became a lasting attitude both in the United States and possibly to a lesser degree, in the United Kingdom; and it took years of experience to discover a propaganda style that would at least not provoke distrust. While the disdain of propaganda had been initiated by the upper strata, it was during the second World War more intense with lower socio-economic groups.

At this point, it becomes essential to supplement our analysis of the distrust of propaganda by a discussion of contemporary privatization ten-

[6] Kris, E. "The Danger of Propaganda," *American Imago*, 2, 1941, pp. 1-42. Kris, E. "Some Problems of War Propaganda." A Note on Propaganda, Old and New, *Psychoanalytic Quarterly*, 2, 1943, pp. 381-99.

[7] For the question of the actual contribution of propaganda to this defeat and generally for the question of the limited influence of propaganda on warfare, see Kris, E., Speier, H. and Associates, *German Radio Propaganda*, New York, Oxford Univ. Press, 1944.

dencies. Many motivations contribute to such tendencies. Some of them are not taken up here.[8]

Individuals in the mass societies of the twentieth century are to an ever increasing extent involved in public affairs; it becomes increasingly difficult to ignore them. But "ordinary" individuals have ever less the feeling that they can *understand* or *influence* the very events upon which their life and happiness is known to depend.[9] At the same time, leaders in both totalitarian and democratic societies claim that decisions ultimately rest upon the common man's consent, and that the information supplied to him fully enables him to evaluate the situation. The contrast between these claims and the common man's experience extends to many areas. Thus in economic life ever more depends upon state interference. But, on the other hand, people increasingly regard economic policy as a province in which the professional specialist is paramount and the common man incompetent. The increasing "statification" of economic life has been accompanied by a rising mass reputation of scientific economics as a specialty. The emotional charges of simple economic formulae such as "free enterprise" or "socialization of the means of production" seem to have decreased (one might speak, at least in certain areas, of the silent breakdown of "capitalism" and "socialism" as ideologies). While the economic specialist is to fulfill the most urgent demand of the common man, that for security of employment, the distance between him and his beneficiary grows; he becomes part of a powerful elite, upon which the common man looks with a distrust rooted in dependency.

This is but one instance of the experience of disparity—of insight as well as power—between the common man and the various political organizations into which he is integrated. That disparity counteracts the feeling of power which accompanies the manipulation of increasingly effective machinery, whether of production or destruction: the common man is usually acutely aware of the fact that the "button" he is "pushing" belongs to an apparatus far out of the reach of any unorganized individual.

This feeling of disparity greatly affects the common man's attitude to foreign policy. The potential proximity of total war produces situations that not only seem inherently incomprehensible, but that he, the common man, feels cannot be made comprehensible to him by his government. "Security considerations," he infers, are the reason why the "real dope" is kept away from him. Thus the distance between the common man and the policy maker has grown to such an extent that awe and distrust support each other.

The common man feels impotent in a world where specialized skills control events that at any moment may transform his life. That feeling of impotence bestows upon political facts something of the solidity of natural events, like weather or hurricane, that come and go. Two attitudes result from this feeling: First, one does not inquire into the causation of the events thus viewed; second, one does not inquire into their morality.[10]

[8] For instance, we do not propose to discuss how privatization is related to changes in values.

[9] Mannheim, K. *Man and Society in an Age of Transition*, K. Paul, Trench, Trubner & Co., London, 1940. Kecskemeti, P. and Leites, N. *Some Psychological Hypotheses on Nazi Germany*, Washington, D.C. Library of Congress, 1945 (multigraphed).

[10] American soldiers during the second World War were frequently explicitly opposed to discussions of its causation: going into its pre-history was frequently regarded as futile and somewhat "out of this world."

The feeling that politics as such is outside the reach of morals is an extreme form of this attitude. Probably moral indignation as a reaction to political events has been declining since the turn of the century. One may compare the intense reactions to injustice against individuals under comparatively stable social conditions—the Dreyfus affair, the cases of Ferrer, Nurse Cavell, Sacco and Vanzetti— with the limited reactions to Nazi terror and extermination practices as they gradually became notorious. In the case of the Nazis, public reaction went through a sequence of frank disbelief, reserved doubt, short lived shock and subsequent indifference.

The psychological dynamics operating the interplay of distrust and privatization can now be formulated more sharply. We here distinguish in the continuum of distrusteful attitudes, two cases: One we call critical distrust; the other projective distrust.[11] In the child's development, the former arose not independently from the latter. Critical distrust facilitates adjustment to reality and independence; it is at the foundation of scientific thought, and is an essential incentive in the battle against what Freud called the prohibition of thinking in the individual. Critical distrust has gained a decisive importance in modern society, since technology has played havoc with many kinds of magic. Projective distrust, on the other hand, is derived ultimately from ambivalence; it is an expression of hostility, in which aggressive tendencies against others, frequently against authority, are perceived as tendencies of others, frequently as attitudes of authority.

We allude to these complex questions only in order to round off our argumentation: in the world of the twentieth century, the exercise of critical distrust by the common man meets with many obstacles; it is at the same time increasingly stimulated and increasingly frustrated. He therefore regressively turns to projective distrust: He fears, suspects and hates what he cannot understand and master.

Privatization is, amongst other things, a result of the hostility between the individual and the leadership of the group: We mentioned that it is comparable to what is known as a narcissistic regression. In order to maintain this attitude in which self-interest predominates over group interest— the self in this case may include "primary" groups such as the family— projective distrust is set into operation. Scepticism becomes the guarantor of privatization: scepticism here acts as a defense. If the individual, for instance, were to accept available evidence on atrocities, his emotional involvement in politics might rise; he might hate or experience enthusiasm. Thus privatization could not be maintained. The propagandist's concern in wartime is therefore to reduce such scepticism.

[11] We do not propose here to discuss in detail their genetic interrelation, nor their pathological manifestations, especially in obsessional neuroses and paranoid syndromes. (See H. Deutsch's classical expositions. "Zur Psychologie des Misstrauens," *Imago*, 7, 1921, pp. 71-83.) A fuller treatment would also have to consider the question of retaliatory and self-punitive distrust.

That concern, we said, was more clearly expressed in the democracies than in Germany or Russia. In order fully to understand this difference, we turn to a more detailed discussion of the relationship between propagandist and "propagandee." Every propaganda acts occurs in such a relationship; in the case of propaganda by agents of governments, it is the relationship between the individual and his government.

We discuss this relationship in regard to two types of political organization: the totalitarian state with the charismatic leader and democracy. In both cases, the propagandists speak for the leaders, who are the chief propagandists. In both cases, propaganda presupposes, and attempts to strengthen identifications of the propagandees with the propagandists. These identifications, however, have a different character under the two regimes.

In a totalitarian state these identifications concern, to a large extent, id and superego functions. These identifications facilitate the gratifying completion of impulses, as superego functions have been projected upon the propagandist, and as he is idealized in an archaic sense: omnipotence, ominscience and infallibility are attributed to him.

In democratic states, the corresponding identifications concern, to a large extent, ego functions which are delegated to the propagandist. Amongst these functions, the scrutiny of the existing situation and the anticipation of the future are of predominant importance. While the propagandee relies upon the propagandist for the fulfillment of these functions, he retains a critical attitude in relation to him.

Superego and ego identifications, of course, constantly interact. The distribution of their intensities, however, is clearly dependent upon the institutionalized relationship between propagandist and propagandee. In this sense, we may say that the one is typical of totalitarian, the other of democratic propaganda relations.

That difference is reflected in the devices of propaganda. Totalitarian propaganda tries to sway the audience into participation; its preferred setting is the visible leader talking to the masses; it is modeled after the relations between the hypnotist and his medium. Democratic propaganda gives weight to insight as basis for participation; it is to a greater extent modeled after the principles of guidance or education.

The nature of the two propaganda situations accounts for the fact that for each of the two kinds of propagandists different goals are difficult to reach. The totalitarian propagandist finds it arduous to stimulate initiative among his followers. When German propaganda was faced with the task of stimulating cooperative action "from below" among the citizens of bombed towns, that difficulty became apparent: the devices then adopted were plain imitations of the techniques of British propagandists in a similar situation. Democratic propagandists meet a comparable difficulty when faced with the task of manifestly denying information on reasons for government action, that is, of demanding implicit trust for a limited time. The impasse in which allied leadership found itself when faced with a public demand for the opening of a second front, especially in 1943, is an example.

The two types of propagandists react to the impact of distrust and privatization in different ways; these tendencies show a different incidence under the two political orders. In a totalitarian state, privatization grows with deprivation. Then the latent cleavage of the totalitarian state becomes manifest, the cleavage between the faithful, from whose ranks elite and sub-elite are recruited, and the indifferent, who are controlled by the faithful. Their mounting privatization renders this control more difficult. Superego identifications cease to function with ever more individuals, and finally they function only with the fanatics. When that situation crystallized in Germany with the approach of defeat, two devices were adopted: First, a gradual revision of propaganda policy. Appeals to superego identifications became less and less important and increased weight was given to the stimulation of fear: ego interests should now motivate continued allegiance. But this did not prevent further privatization. Thus the central method of all totalitarian social control was applied ever more consistently: violence. In its last phases, Nazi propaganda hardly fulfilled the purpose of gaining participation in the present; building the Nazi myth, it addressed its appeals to future generations.

Democratic propaganda is better equipped to deal with the tendency towards privatization, since it puts greater emphasis on the creation of insight. Its appeals are better in tune with a high level of distrust. In totalitarian regimes, there is a polarization between the politicized and the privatized, which is, however, difficult to perceive from the outside. In democratic states, tendencies towards privatization are clearly perceptible but their distribution within the society is less clear cut.

There are periods when this tendency decreases: in America after Pearl Harbor, in Britain after May 1940. While enthusiasm was kept at a low level, determination prevailed and sacrifice was willingly sustained.

What was the part of the propagandist in such situations? It may be illustrated by turning to one specific situation, in which democratic propaganda reached its greatest success.

We refer to Churchill's propaganda feat during the spring of 1940. The series of speeches he made in May, June and July of 1940 are remembered for the singular depth of feeling and the heroic quality of language. But these qualities were only accessories to the major political impact of these speeches. Their function was a threefold one—to warn Britain of the danger, to clarify its extent, and to indicate how everyone could help to meet it. In order to illustrate this point, we refer to one topic only: the announcement of the Battle of Britain.

The first intimation was made on May 12th, three days after Churchill's appointment, when the Battle of Flanders had not yet reached its climax. After having described the battles on all fronts, Churchill added that "many preparations had to be made at home." On May 19th, after the surrender of Holland, and during the climax of the Belgian battles, he devoted well over one-third of his speech to announcing "that after this . . . there will come the battle for our island." And after demanding full mobilization of production, he gave for the first time the "box score": he reported that the R.A.F. had been downing three to four enemy planes for each of their own. This, he inferred, was the basis of any hope. On June 4th, in his famous speech after Dunkirk, the theme was taken up anew and an elaborate account of the chances of the fighter force in a battle over the homeland was given. Churchill went into technical details; at a time when France seemed still vigorously to resist, he acquainted the British people with the chances of their survival. While the enemy had broken through the allied front with a few thousand armored vehicles, he forecast the future by saying: "May it not also be that the course of civilization itself will be defended by the skill and devotion of a few thousand airmen. And while he discussed the necessity of ever increasing production, he spoke at this time of imminent defeat of "the great British armies of the later years of war."

In the later speeches of that unforgettable spring, he elaborated on the subject. Every one could understand how his own behavior was related to the total situation, and how this situation was structured; how supplies were needed for the repair and construction of fighter planes, and how in this matter every detail, even the smallest one, could contribute to the final result. All this information was released well in advance of any German attack.

Thus Churchill had not only given the "warning signal" and mobilized "emergency reactions." His detailed analysis of the situation also contributed to the prevention of an inexpediently large and rapid increase in anxiety: unknown danger was transformed into a danger known in kind and extent. He fulfilled those functions of leadership that can be compared to those fulfilled in the life of the individual by the organization of the ego.[12] At the same time, Churchill offered his own courage as a model: "If you behave as I do, you will behave right." He not only spoke of Britain's "finest hour" but was careful to add that in this hour "every man and woman had their chance."

The propagandist thus seems to fulfill a double function: first that of structuring the situation so that it can be anticipated and understood, and second, that of offering himself as a model.

It is essential to understand the difference between the democratic leader who functions as a model and the charismatic leader.[13] The latter offers himself as an object that replaces superego functions in the individual. The model function of leadership implies that in identifying with the leader, the individual will best serve the ideals he shares with him. But the understanding of the situation is a precondition for such moral participation.

The general problem which we here finally approach concerns the relation between ego and superego functions. One might tentatively formulate the hypothesis that in a situation in which the ego functions smoothly, the

[12] Kris, E. "Danger and Morale," American Journal of Orthopsychiatry, 14, 1944, pp. 147-155.
[13] Redl, F. "Group Education and Leadership," Psychiatry, 5, 1942, pp. 573-596.

tension between ego and superego is apt to be low. In fact, we find in the study of superego formation in the child some evidence in support of such a formulation.[14] However, other evidence is contradictory. Frequently, successful ego performance is accompanied by intense conflicts between ego and superego. We therefore reject this formulation and substitute another: unsuccessful ego functions endanger the positive relationship between ego and superego. They tend to encourage regressive trends. Individuals who feel impotent in the face of a world they do not understand, and are distrustful of those who should act as their guides, tend to revert to patterns of behavior known from childhood, in which an increase of hostility against the adults and many neurotic or delinquent mechanisms may develop. The incidence of such maladjustments may increase in a society in which privatization tendencies have become dominant.[15]

Little can be said here about what conclusions can be drawn for the future of democratic propaganda from these considerations. They clearly point to the desirability of sharp and wide increases of insight into events in the world at large among the citizens. Briefly, the trend towards distrust and privatization among the audience of the propagandist should be turned into a trend towards increase of insight. That trend would find a parallel in changes of related techniques: psycho-therapy and education, largely under the influence of psychoanalysis, have substituted or are substituting insight for pressure. If the appropriate education, on a vast enough scale and at a rapid enough rate is not provided for, the distrust and privatization of the masses may become a fertile soil for totalitarian management.

[14] Friedlander, K. "Formation of the Antisocial Character," *The Psycho-Analytic Study of the Child*, New York, International Universities Press, I, 1945, pp. 189-204.

[15] We here note that the traditional discussion of the applicability of "individual" psychological hypotheses to "social" events lacks substance, since events dealt with in the empirical analysis of human affairs, "psychological" or "sociological," occur in individuals. We deal with frequencies of incidence.

Leo Lowenthal

BIOGRAPHIES
IN POPULAR MAGAZINES

The following study is concerned with the content analysis of biographies, a literary topic which has inundated the book market for the last three decades, and has for some time been a regular feature of popular magazines. Surprisingly enough, not very much attention has been paid to this phenomenon, none whatever to biographies appearing in magazines, and little to those published in book form.[1]

It started before the first World War, but the main onrush came shortly afterwards. The popular biography was one of the most conspicuous newcomers in the realm of print since the introduction of the short story. The circulation of books by Emil Ludwig,[2] André Maurois, Lytton Strachey, Stefan Zweig, etc., reached a figure in the millions, and with each new publication, the number of languages into which they were translated grew. Even if it were only a passing literary fad, one would still have to explain why this fashion has had such longevity and is more and

Reprinted from *Radio Research, 1942-43* (1943), pp. 507-520, by permission of the author. (Copyright, 1943, by Paul Lazarsfeld and Frank Stanton.)

[1] Edward H. O'Neill, *A History of American Biography*, University of Pennsylvania Press, 1935. His remarks on pp. 179 ff. on the period since 1919 as the "most prolific one in American history for biographical writing," are quoted by Helen McGill Hughes, *News and the Human Interest Story*, University of Chicago Press, 1940, p. 285 f. The book by William S. Gray and Ruth Munroe, *The Reading Interests and Habits of Adults*, Macmillan, New York, 1930, which analyzes readers' figures for boods and magazines, does not even introduce the category of biographies in its tables on the contents of magazines, and applies it only once for books in a sample analysis of readers in Hyde Park, Chicago. The only comment the authors have to offer is: "There is some tendency to prefer biographies and poetry, especially in moderate doses to other types of reading except fiction" (p. 154). Finally, I want to quote as a witness in this case of scientific negligence, Donald A. Stouffer, *The Art of Biography in Eighteenth Century England*, Princeton University Press, 1941, who in his excellent and very thorough study says: "Biography as a branch of literature has been too long neglected" (p. 3).

[2] Up to the spring of 1939, 3.1 million copies of his books were sold: 1.2 million in Germany, 1.1 million in the U.S., 0.8 million elsewhere. (Cf. Emil Ludwig, *Traduction des Œuvres*, Moscia, 1939, p. 2.)

more becoming a regular feature in the most diversified media of publications.

Who's Who, once known as a title of a specialized dictionary for editors and advertisers, has nowadays become the outspoken or implied question in innumerable popular contexts. The interest in individuals has become a kind of mass gossip. The majority of weeklies and monthlies, and many dailies too, publish at least one life story or a fragment of one in each issue; theatre programs present abridged biographies of all the actors; the more sophisticated periodicals, such as *The New Republic* or *Harper's,* offer short accounts of the main intellectual achievements of their contributors; and a glance into the popular corners of the book trade, including drug store counters, will invariably fall on biographies. All this forces the conclusion that there must be a social need seeking gratification by this type of literature.

One way to find out would be to study the readers' reactions, to explore by means of various interviewing techniques what they are looking for, what they think about the biographical jungle. But it seems to be rather premature to collect and to evaluate such solicited response until more is known about the content structure itself.

As an experiment in content analysis, a year's publication of *The Saturday Evening Post (SEP)* and of *Collier's* for the period from April 1940 to March 1941 was covered.[3] It is regrettable that a complete investigation could not be made for the most recent material, but samples taken at random from magazines under investigation showed that no basic change in the selection or content structure has occurred since this country's entry into the war.[4]

Before entering into a discussion of our material we shall briefly look into the fate of the biographical feature during the past decades.

Production—Yesterday

Biographical sections have not always been a standing feature in these periodicals. If we turn back the pages we find distinct differences in the number of articles as well as in the selection of people treated.

Table I gives a survey of the professional distribution of the "heroes" in biographies between 1901 and 1941.[5]

[3] It should not be inferred that the results as presented here are without much change applicable to all other magazines which present general and diversified topics. From a few selections taken from less widely circulated and more expensive magazines, ranging from *The New Yorker* to the dollar-a-copy *Fortune,* it seems very likely that the biographies presented there differ in their average content structure and therefore in their social and psychological implications from these lower-priced popular periodicals. The difference in contents corresponds to a difference in readership.

[4] Cf. footnote 11 of this article.

[5] For the collection of data prior to 1940 the writer is indebted to Miss Miriam Wexner.

Table I indicates clearly a tremendous increase in biographies as time goes on. The average figure of biographies in 1941 is almost four times as high as at the beginning of the century. The biography has nowadays become a regular weekly feature. Just to illustrate how relatively small the number of biographies was forty years ago: in 52 issues of the *SEP* of 1901-02 we find altogether twenty-one biographies as compared with

TABLE I—Distribution of Biographies According to Professions in "Saturday Evening Post" and "Collier's" for Selected Years Between 1901-1941

	1901-1914 (5 Sample Yrs.)		1922-1930 (6 Sample Yrs.)		1930-1934 (4 Years)		1940-1941 (1 Year)	
	No.	%	No.	%	No.	%	No.	%
Political life	81	46	112	28	95	31	31	25
Business and professional	49	28	72	18	42	14	25	20
Entertainment	47	26	211	54	169	55	69	55
Total number	177	100	395	100	306	100	125	100
Yearly average of biographies	36		66		77		125	

not less than fifty-seven in 1940-41. The smallness of the earlier figure in comparison to the present day is emphasized by the fact that non-fictional contributions at that time far outnumbered the fiction material. A fair average of distribution in the past would be about three fictional and eight non-fictional contributions; today we never find more than twice as many non-fictional as fictional contributions and in the majority of cases even fewer.

We put the subjects of the biographies in three groups: the spheres of political life, of business and professions, and of entertainment (the latter in the broadest sense of the word). Looking at our table we find for the time before World War I very high interest in political figures and an almost equal distribution of business and professional men, on the one hand, and of entertainers on the other. This picture changes completely after the war. The figures from political life have been cut by 40 per cent; the business and professional men have lost 30 per cent of their personnel while the entertainers have gained 50 per cent. This numerical relation seems to be rather constant from 1922 up to the present day. If we reformulate our professional distribution by leaving out the figures from political life we see even more clearly the considerable decrease of people from the serious and important professions and a corresponding increase of entertainers. The social impact of this change comes to the fore strikingly if we analyze the composition of the entertainers. This can be seen from Table II.

While at the beginning of the century three quarters of the entertainers were serious artists and writers, we find that this class of people is reduced by half twenty years later and tends to disappear almost completely at present.

TABLE II—Proportion of Biographies of Entertainers from the Realm of Serious Arts [a] in "SEP" and "Collier's" for Selected Years Between 1901-1941

(In Per Cent of Total Biographies of Entertainers in Each Period)

Period	Proportion Entertainers from Serious Arts	Total No. Entertainers
1901-1914 (5 sample yrs.)	77	47
1922-1930 (6 sample yrs.)	38	211
1930-1934 (4 yrs.)	29	169
1940-1941 (1 yr.)	9	69

[a] This group includes literature, fine arts, music, dance, theater.

As an instance of the selection of biographies typical of the first decade of the century, it is notable that out of the twenty-one biographies of the *SEP* 1901-02, eleven came from the political sphere, seven from the business and professions, and three from entertainment and sport. The people in the political group are numerically prominent until before Election Day in the various years: candidates for high office, i.e., the President or senators; the Secretary of the Treasury; an eminent State governor. In the business world, we are introduced to J. P. Morgan, the banker; his partner, George W. Perkins; James J. Hill, the railroad president. In the professions, we find one of the pioneers in aviation; the inventor of the torpedo; a famous Negro educator; an immigrant scientist. Among the entertainers there is an opera singer, Emma Calvé; a poet, Eugene Field; a popular fiction writer, F. Marion Crawford.

If we look at such a selection of people we find that it represents a fair cross-section of socially important occupations. Still, in 1922 the picture is more similar to the professional distribution quoted above than to the one which is characteristic of the present day magazines. If we take, for example, *Collier's* of 1922 we find in a total of 20 biographies only two entertainers, but eight business and professional men and ten politicians. Leaving out the latter ones, we find among others: Clarence C. Little, the progressive President of the University of Maine; Leonard P. Ayres, the very-outspoken Vice-President of the Cleveland Trust Company; Director-General of the United States Railroad Administration, James C. Davis; President of the New York Central Railroad, A. H. Smith; and the City Planner, John Nolen. From the entertainment field, we have a short résumé of the stage comedian, Joe Cook (incidentally, by Franklin P. Adams), and an autobiographical sketch by Charlie Chaplin.

We might say that a large proportion of the heroes in both samples are idols of production, that they stem from the productive life, from industry, business, and natural sciences. There is not a single hero from the world of sports and the few artists and entertainers either do not belong to the sphere of cheap or mass entertainment or represent a serious attitude toward their art as in the case of Chaplin.[6] The first quarter of the century cherishes biography in terms of an open-minded liberal society which really wants to know something about its own figures on the decisive social, commercial, and cultural fronts. Even in the late Twenties, when jazz composers and the sports people are admitted to the inner circle of biographical heroes, their biographies are written almost exclusively to supplement the reader's knowledge of the technical requirements and accomplishments of their respective fields.[7] These people, then, are treated as an embellishment of the national scene, not yet as something that in itself represents a special phenomenon which demands almost undivided attention.

We should like to quote from two stories which seem to be characteristic of this past epoch. In a sketch of Theodore Roosevelt, the following comment is made in connection with the assassination of McKinley: "We, who give such chances of success to all that it is possible for a young man to go as a laborer into the steel business and before he has reached his mature prime become, through his own industry and talent, the president of a vast steel association—we, who make this possible as no country has ever made it possible, have been stabbed in the back by anarchy." [8]

This unbroken confidence in the opportunities open to every individual serves as the *leitmotiv* of the biographies. To a very great extent they are to be looked upon as examples of success which can be imitated. These life stories are really intended to be educational models. They are written—at least ideologically—for someone who the next day may try to emulate the man whom he has just envied.

A biography seems to be the means by which an average person is able to reconcile his interest in the important trends of history and in the per-

---

[6] We have omitted from our discussion and our figures a number of very short biographical features which amounted to little more than anecdotes. These were published fairly regularly by the SEP until the late Twenties under the headings "Unknown Captains of Industry," "Wall Street Men," sometimes called "Bulls and Bears," "Who's Who and Why," "Workingman's Wife," "Literary Folk."

[7] See, for instance, the SEP, September 19, 1925, where the auto-racer,, Barney Oldfield, tells a reporter details of his racing experiences and of the mechanics of racing and automobiles; September 26, 1925, in which the vaudeville actress, Elsie Janis, comments on her imitation acts and also gives details of her techniques. The same holds true for the biography of the band leader, Sousa, in the SEP, October 31, 1925, and of the radio announcer, Graham McNamee, May 1, 1926; after a few remarks about his own life and career, McNamee goes on to discuss the technical aspects of radio and his experiences in radio with famous people.

[8] *Saturday Evening Post*, October 12, 1901.

sonal lives of other people. In the past, and especially before the first World War, the popular biography lived in an optimistic atmosphere where understanding of historical processes and interest in successful people seemed to integrate pleasantly into one harmonious endeavor: "We know now that the men of trade and commerce and finance are the real builders of freedom, science, and art—and we watch them and study them accordingly. . . . Of course, Mr. Perkins is a 'self-made man.' Who that has ever made a career was not?" [9] This may be taken as a classical formulation for a period of "rugged individualism" in which there is neither the time nor the desire to stimulate a closer interest in the organizers and organization of leisure time, but which is characterized by eagerness and confidence that the social ladder may be scaled on a mass basis.[10]

Consumption—Today

When we turn to our present day sample we face an assortment of people which is both qualitatively and quantitatively removed from the standards of the past.

Only two decades ago people from the realm of entertainment played a very negligible role in the biographical material. They form now, numerically, the first group. While we have not found a single figure from the world of sports in our earlier samples given above, we find them now close to the top of favorite selections. The proportion of people from political life and from business and professions, both representing the "serious side," has declined from 74 to 45 per cent of the total.

Let us examine the group of people representing non-political aspects of life. 69 are from the world of entertainment and sport; 25 from that

---

[9] *Saturday Evening Post*, June 28, 1902.

[10] Here and there we find a casual remark on the function of biographies as models for individual imitation. Cf., for instance, Mandel Sherman, "Book Selection and Self Therapy," in *The Practice of Book Selection*, edited by Louis R. Wilson, University of Chicago Press, 1939, p. 172. "In 1890 a book appeared entitled *Acres of Diamonds*, by Russell H. Conwell. This book dealt especially with the problems of attaining success in life. The author attempted to encourage the reader by giving examples of the struggles and triumphs of noted successful men and women. This pattern of encouraging the reader by citing examples of great men has continued, and in recent years a number of books have appeared in which most of the content dealt with case histories of noted individuals. Some psychologists have suggested that interest in autobiographies and biographies has arisen in part from the attempts of the readers to compare their own lives with those about whom they read, and thus to seek encouragement from the evidence of the struggles of successful people."

Helen M. Hughes in her suggestive study has not avoided the tendency to settle the problem of biographies by rather simplified psychological formulae. By quoting generously O'Neill, Bernarr MacFadden, and André Maurois, she points to the differences of the more commemorative and eulogistic elements in earlier biographies and the "anxious groping for certainty of people who live in times of rapid change," which is supposed to be connected with the present interest in biography.

which we called before the "serious side." Almost half of the 25 belong to some kind of communications professions: there are ten newspapermen and radio commentators. Of the remaining 15 business and professional people, there are a pair of munitions traders, Athanasiades and Juan March; Dr. Brinkley, a quack doctor; and Mr. Angas, judged by many as a dubious financial expert; Pittsburgh Phil, a horse race gambler in the "grand style"; Mrs. D'Arcy Grant, a woman sailor, and Jo Carstairs, the owner of an island resort; the Varian brothers, inventors of gadgets, and Mr. Taylor, an inventor of fool-proof sports devices; Howard Johnson, a roadside restaurant genius; Jinx Falkenburg, at that time a professional model; and finally, Dr. Peabody, a retired rector of a swanky society prep school.

The "serious" people are not so serious after all. In fact there are only nine who might be looked upon as rather important or characteristic figures of the industrial, commercial, or professional activities, and six of these are newspapermen or radio commentators.

We called the heroes of the past "idols of production": we feel entitled to call the present day magazine heroes "idols of consumption." Indeed, almost every one of them is directly, or indirectly, related to the sphere of leisure time: either he does not belong to vocations which serve society's basic needs (e.g., the heroes of the world of entertainment and sport), or he amounts, more or less, to a caricature of a socially productive agent. If we add to the group of the 69 people from the entertainment and sports world the ten newspaper and radio men, the professional model, the inventor of sports devices, the quack doctor, the horse race gambler, the inventors of gadgets, the owner of the island resort, and the restaurant chain owners, we see 87 of all 94 non-political heroes directly active in the consumers' world.

Of the eight figures who cannot exactly be classified as connected with consumption, not more than three—namely, the automobile producer, Sloan; the engineer and industrialist, Stout; and the air line czar, Smith—are important or characteristic functionaries in the world of production. The two armament magnates, the female freight boat skipper, the prep school head, and the doubtful market prophet remind us of the standardized protagonists in mystery novels and related fictional merchandise: people with a more or less normal and typical personal and vocational background who would bore us to death if we did not discover that behind the "average" front lurks a "human interest" situation.

By substituting such a classification according to spheres of activity for the cruder one according to professions, we are now prepared to present the vocational stratifications of our heroes in a new form. It is shown in Table III for the *SEP* and *Collier's* of 1940-41.

If a student in some very distant future should use popular magazines of 1941 as a source of information as to what figures the American public looked to in the first stages of the greatest crisis since the birth of the Union, he would come to a grotesque result. While the industrial and professional endeavors are geared to a maximum of speed and efficiency, the idols of the masses are not, as they were in the past, the leading names in the battle of production, but the headliners of the movies, the ball parks, and the night clubs. While we found that around 1900 and even around 1920 the vocational distribution of magazine heroes was a rather accurate

TABLE III—The Heroes and Their Spheres

	Number of Stories	Per Cent
Sphere of production	3	2
Sphere of consumption	91	73
Entertainers and sports figures	69	55
Newspaper and radio figures	10	8
Agents of consumers' goods	5	4
Topics of light fiction	7	6
Sphere of politics	31	25
Total	125	100

reflection of the nation's living trends, we observe that today the hero-selection corresponds to needs quite different from those of genuine information. They seem to lead to a dream world of the masses who no longer are capable or willing to conceive of biographies primarily as a means of orientation and education. They receive information not about the agents and methods of social production but about the agents and methods of social and individual consumption. During the leisure in which they read, they read almost exclusively about people who are directly, or indirectly, providing for the reader's leisure time. The vocational set-up of the dramatis personae is organized as if the social production process were either completely exterminated or tacitly understood, and needed no further interpretation. Instead, the leisure time period seems to be the new social riddle on which extensive reading and studying has to be done.[11]

The human incorporation of all the social agencies taking care of society as a unity of consumers represents a literary type which is turned out as a

[11] It will be very important to check later how far the present war situation has confirmed, changed, or even reversed the trend. A few casual observations on the present-day situation may be mentioned.

The New York Times "Magazine" on July 12, 1942, published an article "Wallace Warns Against 'New Isolationism.'" The Vice-President of the United States is photographed playing tennis. The caption for the picture reads "Mr. Wallace's Serve." This picture and its caption are a very revealing symbol. The word "serve" does not refer to social usefulness, but to a feature in the Vice-President's private life.

This remark can be supplemented by quoting a few issues of the SEP and Collier's, picked at random from their publications during the summer of 1942. While everywhere else in this study we have limited ourselves to the analysis of strictly biographical contributions, we should like, by quoting some of the topics of the entire issues which we have chosen for this year, to emphasize the over-all importance of the spheres of con-

standardized article, marketed by a tremendous business, and consumed by another mass institution, the nation's magazine reading public. Thus biography lives as a mass element among the other elements of mass literature.

Our discovery of a common professional physiognomy in all of these portraits encouraged us to guess that what is true of the selection of people will also be true of the selection of what is said about these people. This hypothesis has been quite justified, as we propose to demonstrate in the following pages. Our content analysis not only revealed impressive regularities in the occurrence, omission, and treatment of certain topics, but also showed that these regularities may be interpreted in terms of the very same category of consumption which was the key to the selection of the biographical subjects. Consumption is a thread running through every aspect of these stories. The characteristics which we have observed in the literary style of the author, in his presentation of personal relations, of professions and personalities, can all be integrated around the concept of the consumer.

For classification of the stories' contents, we decided on a four-fold scheme. First there are what one might call the sociological aspects of the man: his relations to other people, the pattern of his daily life, his relation to the world in which he lives. Second, his psychology: what the nature of his development has been and the structure of his personality. Third, his history: what his encounter with the world has been like—the object world which he has mastered or failed to master. Fourth, the evaluation of these data which the author more or less consciously conveys by his choice of language. Granted that this scheme is somewhat arbitrary, we think our division of subject matter has resulted in a fairly efficient worksheet, especially when we consider the backward state of content analysis of this type.

sumption. Not only has the selection of heroes for biographies not changed since America's active participation in the war, but many other of the non-fictional articles are also still concerned with consumers' interests.

Of the ten non-fictional articles in the *SEP*, August 8, 1942, five are connected with the consumers' world: a serial on Hollywood agents; a report on a hometown circus; a report on roadside restaurants; an analysis of women as book readers; and an essay on the horse and buggy. In an issue one week later, August 15, 1942, there is a report on the International Correspondence School; the continuation of the serial on the Hollywood agents; and a biography on the radio idol, Kate Smith. Or let us look at *Collier's*, which as a whole, devotes a much higher percentage of articles to war topics than the *SEP*. Out of nine articles in the issue of July 4, 1942, five belong to the consumers' world. There is again one on the horse and buggy, another one on a baseball hero, a third one on an Army comedian, a fourth one on a Broadway producer, and finally, one on budget buffets. Three weeks later, on July 25, out of ten articles, again five belong to the same category.

In other words, out of 37 articles found in four issues of two leading popular magazines during the present crisis, not less than 17 treat the gustatory and entertainment features of the average citizen.

There appears to be some cause for concern in the fact that so much of the fare presented to the reading public during the times immediately preceding the war and during the war itself is almost completely divorced from important social issues.

As we studied our stories, we looked almost in vain for such vital subjects as the man's relations to politics or to social problems in general. Our category of sociology reduces itself to the *private lives* of the heroes. Similarly, our category of psychology was found to contain mainly a static image of a human being to whom a number of things happen, culminating in a success which seems to be none of his doing. This whole section becomes merged with our category of history which is primarily concerned with success data, too, and then takes on the character of a catalogue of *"just Facts."* When we survey the material on how authors evaluate their subjects, what stands out most clearly is the biographers' preoccupation with justifying their hero by means of undiscriminating *superlatives* while still interpreting him in terms which bring him as close as possible to the level of the average man.

Lester Asheim

FROM BOOK TO FILM

Every year the people of the United States contribute several billion paid admissions to film theaters throughout the country. Every year at least fifty percent of the movies which this vast audience pushes to the highest box-office success are film adaptations of widely-read novels. If important changes occur in the film adaptations of those books, the implications of those changes are of great interest.

What kinds of things are lost and gained by those who see the film as a substitute for reading the book? Do the changes fall into discernible patterns which may provide insights into the intent of the producers of the film, and into the effects upon its audience? Do the changes affect the materials so vitally that our "popular culture" is of a different order of things from the traditional cultural heritage of the "intellectual"? Or are the changes merely form changes which do not alter the ultimate message conveyed, the problems presented, or the insights provided?

In one form or another, these questions have been asked many times, but most previous approaches to them have been highly impressionistic. Literary and esthetic standards have been applied, not with objective rigor, but on the basis of personal reference, snap judgment, isolated instance, and random impression. Yet the fact that the film as a form of narrative reaches a far greater audience than does the novel [1] makes the evaluation of the social and cultural implications of alterations in the content of film adaptations a matter of great concern to anyone interested in art, or in society.

Reprinted from *From Book to Film*, unpublished Ph.D. dissertation, Graduate Library School, University of Chicago (1949), by permission of the author.

[1] According to Paul Lazarsfeld and Patricia Kendall (*Radio Listening in America*, New York: Prentice-Hall, Inc., 1948, pp. 2-3), 61 per cent of a representative cross section of the adult population had seen one or more movies in the previous month; 26 per cent had read at least one book during the month. Since the peak of movie attendance is at about age 19, and the sample used reached no respondents under age 21, the figures for movie attendance may be taken as conservative.

The study from which this material is abstracted [2] is an attempt to devise a method for making an objective and quantitative comparison of the manifest content of twenty-four classic and "standard" novels and the corresponding twenty-four films based upon them, to ascertain more scientifically than heretofore exactly what happens when a book is adapted to the screen. The method chosen to provide a tool for measuring the difference between the treatment accorded the same thematic material in two different media was that of comparative content analysis.

The Analysis Procedure

The main analysis procedure consisted broadly of three steps: (1) viewing the film; (2) reading the book; (3) comparing the book with the script. The film was viewed first in order that no preconceptions be brought to the film which would hamper the complete objectivity of the analysis of manifest content. As the film was run, the analyst took notes on the beginning and ending of each scene, the content of the scene, and the transition from one scene to another. Immediately following the viewing of the film a complete outline of it was made from the notes, expanding them from memory. The book was then read, and notations made wherever a scene, a line of dialogue, or a piece of action was recognized as the basis of some corresponding scene, dialogue, or action in the film.

During the reading, all characters not in the film were noted, and all changes that could be identified were jotted down, while the book-page-number notation was made opposite the portion to which it related on the outline of the film mentioned above. When the reading of the book was completed, the script was checked: first, against the outline of the film to correct the script against its release form, and then against each page of the book which had been noted upon the film outline. In this way it was possible to check each line of dialogue word for word, to note to what extent the action was retained or altered, and to compare setting descriptions with those in the novel. These notations of omission, addition, or alteration form the raw data of the investigation.

The Tables of "Carry-Over"

As an introduction to the material in broad terms, a table was prepared for each book-film pair to show relative proportion of space devoted to each of its major aspects in the original novel and in its corresponding film script. The tables were constructed to show, in parallel columns, the pro-

[2] Lester Asheim, *From Book to Film*. (Unpublished doctoral dissertation, University of Chicago, 1949.)

portion of the total pagination of book and of script which is devoted to each of the component parts of the whole.

The following table is representative of the twenty-four which appear in the completed study, and indicates the way in which—even in these general terms—a purely quantitative analysis of content can be useful to point up patterns in so heterogeneous and subtle a process as adaption of novels to a new medium of expression.

TABLE I—The Adventures of Huckleberry Finn

| | Percentage[3] | |
Content Aspects	Book	Film
The story of Huck and Jim	37%	44%
The story of Huck and the two swindlers	29	38
The incidents involving Tom Sawyer	27	..
Incidental adventures and characterization of Huck	14	9
The story of Huck and Pap	8	11
Pure description	8	2
The story of Huck, the widow Douglas, and Miss Watson	2	11

The two main plot lines of the book are retained as the main ones in the film, while the third most important sequence, in which Tom Sawyer is the dominant figure, is completely omitted. The two other aspects which are expanded by the film—those dealing with Pap, and with the Widow Douglas and Miss Watson—are related to the main story of Huck and Jim. Incidental adventures which are irrelevant to the main plot lines are reduced. In place of the Tom Sawyer material, a completely new sequence is added to the Huck-Jim story, accounting in part for its greater proportionate length in the film. A more unified construction results from these changes, which places primary emphasis upon the title character and eliminates material which would divert attention to others.

The figures in these 24 tables—called the tables of carry-over—represent a rough, quantitative gauge of the degree of fidelity with which each film carries over the material from the book, in terms of the amount of space devoted to each aspect in each medium. From these figures, the accompanying list of the films in descending order of their fidelity to the novel (Table II) was constructed in the following manner. For each book-film in the sample, the deviations between the book and the film on each item were taken (if the film devotes 24 percent of its length to the development of a plot line to which the book devotes 35 percent of its length, the deviation is 11) and the sum of these deviations was expressed as a percentage of the total content of both. This figure provides a gross indicator of the comparative degree of fidelity in carry-over; one hundred

[3] Each column represents more than 100 per cent because a book or script page may contribute to more than one aspect of the whole at a single time.

would represent a completely new film play in which no material from the novel was carried over at all, while zero would represent a completely literal transference to the screen without deviation of any kind.

While an impressionistic ranking of the titles reveals essentially the same order of titles by fidelity (the two order arrangements represent a rank order correlation of .83), the mathematical method provides a sharper and less subjective arrangement, and corrects for certain instances (see *Les Miserables,* for instance) where the faithful retention of those incidents which do appear in the film tends to obscure the amount of omission which characterizes the script.

TABLE II—The Twenty-Four Films Ranked in Ascending Order of Their Percent of Deviation from the Original Novel

Rank	Impressionistic Ranking[4]	Film	Per Cent of Deviation
1	2	Pride and Prejudice	11
2	1	The Magnificent Ambersons	13
3	7.5	Alice Adams	14
4	10	David Copperfield	17
5	4	A Tale of Two Cities	18
6.5	6	Tom Sawyer	21
6.5	7.5	Victory	21
8.5	5	The Grapes of Wrath	24
8.5	16	Of Human Bondage	24
11	3	The Light That Failed	25
11	9	Jane Eyre	25
11	11	For Whom the Bell Tolls	25
13.5	21	Huckleberry Finn	27
13.5	22	I Married a Doctor (Main Street)	27
15.5	12	Wuthering Heights	30
15.5	17	In This Our Life	30
17	13.5	The Good Earth	34
18	13.5	Anna Karenina	36
19	18	The Virginian	42
20	15	Les Miserables	44
21.5	19	The Sea Wolf	48
21.5	20	Kitty Foyle	48
23	23	Dr. Jekyll and Mr. Hyde	55
24	24	The House of the Seven Gables	62

The Presentation and Interpretation of the Data

In effect, these "Tables of Carry-Over" are like the panoramic shot which sets the scene. The next section of the study serves the function of a "close-up," which clarifies the details within the broader picture. To present the data in the most economical and meaningful way, the quantitative analysis was combined with an analysis in terms of presumed intent and effect. The mere description of changes is in itself a complex problem;

[4] Rank order assigned by the writer on an impressionistic basis prior to the determination of the per cent deviation rank.

when coupled with the interpretation of the change, its complexity is accordingly increased.

Even so commonplace a concept as that of the "inevitable happy ending" raises questions of definitions and, in the end, yields much more revealing information concerning the film and its audience than the cliché that "the film must always end in a clinch." Table III lists the twenty-four titles, and indicates by "B" for book and "F" for film, the kind of ending which is provided in each version. "Happy" as used here relates to an ending which provides the main protagonist with the goal he has been seeking throughout the story, while "unhappy" relates to an ending in which the leading character fails, completely or in the main, to achieve his goal.

TABLE III—Comparison of Book and Film Endings [5] in "Happy-Unhappy" Terms

Book-Film	Happy	Unhappy
Alice Adams	F	B
Anna Karenina		BF
David Copperfield	BF	
Dr. Jekyll and Mr. Hyde		BF
For Whom the Bell Tolls		BF
The Good Earth		BF
The Grapes of Wrath	(F)	(B)
The House of the Seven Gables	BF	
Huckleberry Finn	BF	
Main Street (I Married a Doctor)	F	(B)
In This Our Life	F	B
Jane Eyre	BF	
Kitty Foyle	F	(B)
The Light That Failed		BF
The Magnificent Ambersons	BF	
Les Miserables	BF	
Of Human Bondage	BF	
Pride and Prejudice	BF	
The Sea Wolf	BF	
A Tale of Two Cities	(BF)	(BF)
Tom Sawyer	BF	
Victory	F	B
The Virginian	BF	
Wuthering Heights	(BF)	(BF)

Parentheses enclosing a "B" or "F" indicate that the exact nature of the ending designated is explained more fully in the text.

Eighteen of the film versions retain the *same kind* of ending as the books upon which they are based: eleven of them are happy; five, unhappy; and two (*A Tale of Two Cities* and *Wuthering Heights*) a combination happy-unhappy, in that the goal is achieved but the main protagonist dies. Three of the films, while retaining the *type* of ending which

[5] Endings are compared on the basis of plot lines common to both book and film. Thus the "happy" ending of the Levin story which ends the book, *Anna Karenina*, is not considered, but only the "unhappy" ending of the Anna story, common to both.

occurs in the book, alter the details of the action. *The House of the Seven Gables* has a happy ending in both book and film, but the latter adds love interest which the former does not possess. *The Good Earth* ends unhappily in both versions, but the film alters the emphasis to concentrate mainly on the death of O-Lan as an affirmation of Wang's devotion to the land and his love of his wife. The film version of *The Sea Wolf*, through a general alteration in the entire plot structure, presents a happy ending which differs in most of its details from the equally happy ending of the book.

"Happy" and "unhappy" are not, however, completely adequate terms with which to describe the situation which obtains as the story closes. Since our definition may require that an ending be described as happy although both hero and heroine die *(Wuthering Heights)*, the "affirmative" and "negative" terminology of Fritz Lang is probably more suitable:

I think the audience's apparent preference for happy resolutions is more accurately described as a preference for *affirmative* resolutions, as a desire to see dramatised the rightness of its ideals and the *eventual* achievement of its hopes. The death of a hero if he dies for an acceptable ideal is not a tragedy. The death of a protagonist, if he dies because he lives counter to an ideal, is affirmative.[6]

In the light of these terms, it is seen that *although unhappy endings are retained by the films in many cases, in no case are negative endings retained* (Table IV). Thus, the happiness or unhappiness of the endings is not really the important factor in relation to the film maker's view of entertainment. Of the thirteen unhappy endings which occur in the novels in the sample, seven are retained in the film version. The popular belief that "the movies always have to have a happy ending" is not substantiated by the sample films, although it is true that the happy ending is more typical of moving pictures than it is of standard fiction in general.

An unhappy ending may be retained so long as it does not call into question the certainties and assurances with which the audience sustains itself. Although more than half of the "unhappy" endings are retained in the sample films, none of them keeps the note of indecision, frustration, hopelessness, or despair which marks seven of the novels. In every instance, action is rearranged or rewritten to provide hope and consolation, a sense of pattern and meaning, and a note of affirmation.

Additional Generalizations from the Findings

Upon the basis of similarly intensive analysis for all of the twenty-four films in the sample, certain generalization may be made about what happens to a novel when it reaches the screen. Naturally, certain obvious

[6] "Happily Ever After," *The Penguin Film Review* V (January, 1948, p. 28. (Italics are Mr. Lang's.)

findings result: the nature of the medium inevitably forces the translation of the verbal form of the novel into the visual form of the film; requirements of length almost invariably force a condensation of the material of the novel for film purposes; the more active sequences from the novel are the ones most frequently used for the film version; the importance of the

TABLE IV—Comparison of Book and Film Endings in "Affirmative-Negative" Terms

Book-Film	Affirmative	Negative
Alice Adams	F (B)	(B)
Anna Karenina	BF*	
David Copperfield	BF	
Dr. Jekyll and Mr. Hyde	BF*	
For Whom the Bell Tolls	B (F)*	
The Good Earth	F*	B
The Grapes of Wrath	F (B)	(B)
The House of the Seven Gables	BF	
Huckleberry Finn	BF	
Main Street (I Married a Doctor)	F (B)	(B)
In This Our Life	F (B)	(B)
Jane Eyre	BF	
Kitty Foyle	F (B)	(B)
The Light That Failed	BF*	
The Magnificent Ambersons	BF	
Les Miserables	BF	
Of Human Bondage	BF	
Pride and Prejudice	BF	
The Sea Wolf	BF	
A Tale of Two Cities	BF*	
Tom Sawyer	BF	
Victory	F	B
The Virginian	BF	
Wuthering Heights	BF*	

Parentheses enclosing a "B" or "F" indicate that the exact nature of the ending designated is explained more fully in the text.
* Indicates films which have an "unhappy" ending by the definition used in Table III.

romantic love story is stressed to a greater extent in the film than in the novel; etc.

Certain of the other findings, a few of which are quoted below, can not so readily be determined by an impressionistic recall of films seen, and some of them emphatically contradict frequently-voiced generalizations about what the movies "always" do to favorite books. The findings, however, are based upon a rigorous collection of factual data which gives them a degree of reliability difficult to refute.

From the evidence of the twenty-four films analyzed, it would appear that in general:

(1) *Despite the emphasis on action, description (translated into pictorial scenes which serve the descriptive function) is not lost in the transition of the novel from page to film.* In 54 percent of the films, as great a proportion or more of the total length of the film is devoted to descriptive

scenes as is devoted to descriptive passages in the novels from which the films are derived.

(2) *Normal chronological sequence is followed more closely in the film than in the novel.* Whereas seven of the novels begin in the middle of the action and then pick up background later, only two of the film versions follow this sequence of events, and one of these puts the recapitulation of background in straight chronological order once it has begun the "flashback."

(3) *While action is increased in the film adaptations, the proportion of violence, brutality, and sadism is reduced in comparison to their incidence in the novels.* Seven of the films in the sample invent scenes of violent action which are not in the original novel, but in five of these cases many other instances of violence are eliminated, so that the total effect even in these films is one of reduction rather than increase in violence. Of seventeen novels which contain scenes of violence of one kind or another, only three of the film versions increase the incidence of violence, whereas twelve reduce it, and two retain it in identical proportion to the whole. While the vividness of filmic presentation may be greater, in terms of manifest content the films present less violence than do the novels.

(4) *The title of the original novel is almost always retained by the film version even when many changes occur in the adaptation.* The popular belief that the movies invariably alter a serious title to something titillating like "Purple Passion" is not borne out by the sample films. In only one instance out of the twenty-four is there a change of title from the popular short title of the novel.

Certain cautions are necessary concerning the general application of the findings. It probably goes without saying that the nature of the original novel itself determines many of the changes required; the universe of the novel is so heterogeneous that the analysis of a small sample, while a valid technique for determining what changes occurred in the chosen films, is not a reliable method for predicting in minute detail what *specific* changes will occur in another sample of book-films. It may be stated with reasonable assurance, however, that the *pattern* of changes will be repeated in any sample of film adaptation, and the implications of that pattern merit continued study and evaluation.

Popular Culture

The extensive development of the mass media over the past half century has had important effects not only upon the social and political life of the country but upon its cultural life as well. The media have created the largest and most varied audience for commercially produced communications that has ever existed. In doing so, every medium has developed a body of content with wide popular appeal and cultural influence—the daytime serial and dramatic sketch on the radio, the feature film, the short story in the popular magazine, the human interest story in the newspaper, best sellers and light fiction in the book field.

The large amount of exposure to such materials cannot help but affect the level of taste of the American audience. The effect of radio's popularization of serious music is discussed in the article by Adorno which centers upon aesthetic considerations. The historical development of human interest stories, analyzed in sociological terms which relate the communication material to the social trends of its period, is the subject of the essay by Hughes. Finally, Riesman and Denney address themselves to the central question of whether the emphasis upon entertainment in the mass media diverts the audience from an interest in basic political problems and thus contributes to a mass apathy toward public concerns.

T. W. Adorno

A SOCIAL CRITIQUE OF
RADIO MUSIC

Some would approach the problem of radio by formulating questions of this type: If we confront such and such a sector of the population with such and such a type of music, what reactions may we expect? How can these reactions be measured and expressed statistically? Or: How many sectors of the population have been brought into contact with music and how do they respond to it?

What intention lies behind such questions? This approach falls into two major operations:

(a) We subject some groups to a number of different treatments and see how they react to each.

(b) We select and recommend the procedure which produces the effect we desire.

The aim itself, the tool by which we achieve it, and the persons upon whom it works are generally taken for granted in this procedure. The guiding interest behind such investigations is basically one of *administrative* technique: how to manipulate the masses. The pattern is that of market analysis even if it appears to be completely remote from any selling purpose. It might be research of an *exploitive* character, i.e. guided by the desire to induce as large a section of the population as possible to buy a certain commodity. Or it may be what Paul F. Lazarsfeld calls *benevolent* administrative research, putting questions such as, "How can we bring good music to as large a number of listeners as possible?"

I would like to suggest an approach that is antagonistic to exploitive and at least supplementary to benevolent administrative research. It abandons the form of question indicated by a sentence like: How can we, under given conditions, best further certain aims? On the contrary, this approach in some cases questions the aims and in all cases the successful accom-

Reprinted from *The Kenyon Review,* Vol. VII (1945), pp. 208-217, by permission of the author and the publisher. (Copyright, 1945, by Kenyon College.)

plishment of these aims under the given conditions. Let us examine the question: how can good music be conveyed to the largest possible audience?

What is "good music"? Is it just the music which is given out and accepted as "good" according to current standards, say the programs of the Toscanini concerts? We cannot pass it as "good" simply on the basis of the names of great composers or performers, that is, by social convention. Furthermore, is the goodness of music invariant, or is it something that may change in the course of history with the technique at our disposal? For instance, let us take it for granted—as I do—that Beethoven really is good music. Is it not possible that this music, by the very problems it sets for itself, is far away from our own situation? That by constant repetition it has deteriorated so much that it has ceased to be the living force it was and has become a museum piece which no longer possesses the power to speak to the millions to whom it is brought? Or, even if this is not so, and if Beethoven in a musically young country like America is still as fresh as on the first day, is radio actually an adequate means of communication? Does a symphony played on the air remain a symphony? Are the changes it undergoes by wireless transmission merely slight and negligible modifications or do those changes affect the very essence of the music? Are not the stations in such a case bringing the masses in contact with something totally different from what it is supposed to be, thus also exercising an influence quite different from the one intended? And as to the large numbers of people who listen to "good music": *how* do they listen to it? Do they listen to a Beethoven symphony in a concentrated mood? Can they do so even if they want to? Is there not a strong likelihood that they listen to it as they would to a Tchaikovsky symphony, that is to say, simply listen to some neat tunes or exciting harmonic stimuli? Or do they listen to it as they do to jazz, waiting in the introduction of the finale of Brahms' First Symphony for the solo of the French horn, as they would for Benny Goodman's solo clarinet chorus? Would not such a type of listening make the high cultural ideal of bringing good music to large numbers of people altogether illusory?

These questions have arisen out of the consideration of so simple a phrase as "bringing good music to as large an audience as possible." None of these or similar questions can be wholly solved in terms of even the most benevolent research of the administrative type. One should not study the attitude of listeners, without considering how far these attitudes reflect broader social behavior patterns and, even more, how far they are conditioned by the structure of society as a whole. This leads directly to the problem of a social critique of radio music, that of discovering its social position and function. We first state certain axioms.

(a) We live in a society of commodities—that is, a society in which production of goods is taking place, not primarily to satisfy human wants and needs, but for profit. Human needs are satisfied only incidentally, as it were. This basic condition of production affects the form of the product as well as the human inter-relationships.

(b) In our commodity society there exists a general trend toward a heavy concentration of capital which makes for a shrinking of the free market in favor of monopolized mass production of standardized goods; this holds true particularly of the communications industry.

(c) The more the difficulties of contemporary society increase as it seeks its own continuance, the stronger becomes the general tendency to maintain, by all means available, the existing conditions of power and property relations against the threats which they themselves breed. Whereas on the one hand standardization necessarily follows from the conditions of contemporary economy, it becomes, on the other hand, one of the means of preserving a commodity society at a stage in which, according to the level of the productive forces, it has already lost its justification.

(d) Since in our society the forces of production are highly developed, and, at the same time, the relations of production fetter those productive forces, it is full of antagonisms. These antagonisms are not limited to the economic sphere where they are universally recognized, but dominate also the cultural sphere where they are less easily recognized.

How did music become, as our first axiom asserts it to be, a commodity? After music lost its feudal protectors during the latter part of the 18th Century it had to go to the market. The market left its imprint on it either because it was manufactured with a view to its selling chances, or because it was produced in conscious and violent reaction against the market requirements. What seems significant, however, in the present situation, and what is certainly deeply connected with the trend to standardization and mass production, is that *today the commodity character of music tends radically to alter it.* Bach in his day was considered, and considered himself, an artisan, although his music functioned as art. Today music is considered ethereal and sublime, although it actually functions as a commodity. Today the terms ethereal and sublime have become trademarks. Music has become a means instead of an end, a fetish. That is to say, music has ceased to be a human force and is consumed like other consumers' goods. This produces "commodity listening," a listening whose ideal it is to dispense as far as possible with any effort on the part of the recipient—even if such an effort on the part of the recipient is the necessary condition of grasping the sense of the music. It is the ideal of Aunt Jemima's ready-mix for pancakes extended to the field of music. The listener suspends all intellectual activity when dealing with music and is content with consuming and evaluating its gustatory qualities—just as if the music which tasted best were also the best music possible.

Famous master violins may serve as a drastic illustration of musical fetishism. Whereas only the expert is able to distinguish a "Strad" from a good modern fiddle, and whereas he is often least preoccupied with the tone quality of the fiddles, the layman, induced to treat these instruments as commodities, gives them a disproportionate attention and even a sort of adoration. One radio company went so far as to arrange a cycle of broadcasts looking, not primarily to the music played, nor even to the performance, but to what might be called an acoustic exhibition of famous instruments such as Paganini's violin and Chopin's piano. This shows how far the commodity attitude in radio music goes, though under a cloak of culture and erudition.

Our second axiom—increasing standardization—is bound up with the commodity character of music. There is, first of all, the haunting similarity between most musical programs, except for the few non-conformist stations which use recorded material of serious music; and also the standardization of orchestral performance, despite the musical trademark of an individual orchestra. And there is, above all, that whole sphere of music whose life-blood is standardization: popular music, jazz, be it hot, sweet, or hybrid.

The third point of our social critique of radio concerns its ideological effect. Radio music's ideological tendencies realize themselves regardless of the intent of radio functionaries. There need be nothing intentionally malicious in the maintenance of vested interests. Nonetheless, music under present radio auspices serves to keep listeners from criticizing social realities; in short, it has a soporific effect upon social consciousness. The illusion is furthered that the best is just good enough for the man in the street. The ruined farmer is consoled by the radio-instilled belief that Toscanini is playing for him and for him alone, and that an order of things that allows him to hear Toscanini compensates for low market prices for farm products; even though he is ploughing cotton under, radio is giving him culture. Radio music is calling back to its broad bosom all the prodigal sons and daughters whom the harsh father has expelled from the door. In this respect radio music offers a new function not inherent in music as an art—the function of creating smugness and self-satisfaction.

The last group of problems in a social critique of radio would be those pertaining to social antagonisms. While radio marks a tremendous technical advance, it has proved an impetus to progress neither in music itself nor in musical listening. Radio is an essentially new technique of musical reproduction. But it does not broadcast, to any considerable extent, serious modern music. It limits itself to music created under pre-radio conditions. Nor has it, itself, thus far evoked any music really adequate to its technical conditions.

The most important antagonisms arise in the field of so-called musical mass-culture. Does the mass distribution of music really mean a rise of musical culture? Are the masses actually brought into contact with the kind of music which, from broader social considerations, may be regarded as desirable? Are the masses really participating in music culture or are they merely forced consumers of musical commodities? What is the role that music actually, not verbally, plays for them?

Under the aegis of radio there has set in a retrogression of listening. In spite of and even because of the quantitative increase in musical delivery, the psychological effects of this listening are very much akin to those of the motion picture and sport spectatoritis which promotes a retrogressive and sometimes even infantile type of person. "Retrogressive" is meant here in a psychological and not a purely musical sense.

An illustration: A symphony of the Beethoven type, so-called classical, is one of the most highly integrated musical forms. The whole is everything; the part, that is to say, what the layman calls the melody, is relatively unimportant. Retrogressive listening to a symphony is listening which, instead of grasping that whole, dwells upon those melodies, just as if the symphony were structurally the same as a ballad. There exists today a tendency to listen to Beethoven's Fifth as if it were a set of quotations from Beethoven's Fifth. We have developed a larger framework of concepts such as atomistic listening and quotation listening, which lead us to the hypothesis that something like a musical children's language is taking shape.

As today a much larger number of people listen to music than in pre-radio days, it is difficult to compare today's mass-listening with what could be called the elite listening of the past. Even if we restrict ourselves, however, to select groups of today's listeners (say, those who listen to the Philharmonics in New York and Boston), one suspects that the Philharmonic listener of today listens in radio terms. A clear indication is the relation to serious advanced modern music. In the Wagnerian period, the elite listener was eager follow the most daring musical exploits. Today the corresponding group is the firmest bulwark against musical progress and feels happy only if it is fed Beethoven's Seventh Symphony again and again.

In analyzing the fan mail of an educational station in a rural section in the Middle West, which has been emphasizing serious music at regular hours with a highly skilled and resourceful announcer, one is struck by the apparent enthusiasm of the listeners' reception, by the vast response, and by the belief in the highly progressive social function that this program was fulfilling. I have read all of those letters and cards very carefully. They are exuberant indeed. But they are enthusiastic in a manner that makes one feel uncomfortable. It is what might be called standardized enthusiasm. The communications are almost literally identical: "Dear X, Your Music Shop is swell. It widens my musical horizon and gives me an ever deeper feeling for the profound qualities of our great music. I can no longer bear the trashy jazz which we usually have to listen to. Continue with your grand work and let us have more of it." No musical item was mentioned, no specific reference to any particular feature was made, no criticism was offered, although the programs were amateurish and planless.

It would do little good to explain these standard responses by reference to the difficulty in verbalizing musical experience: for anybody who has had profound musical experiences and finds it hard to verbalize them may stammer and use awkward expressions, but he would be reluctant, even if he knew no other, to cloak them in rubber stamp phrases. I am forced to another explanation. The listeners were strongly under the spell of the announcer as the personified voice of radio as a social institution, and they responded to his call to prove one's cultural level and education by appreciating this good music. But they actually failed to achieve that very appreciation which stamped them as cultured. They took refuge in repeating, often literally, the announcer's speeches in behalf of culture. Their behavior might be compared with that of the fanatical radio listener entering a bakery and asking for "that delicious, golden crispy Bond Bread."

Another study led to a similar observation. A number of high school boys were subjected to an experiment concerning the role of "plugging" in achieving popularity for popular music. They identified, first, those songs played most frequently on the air during a given period—that is, those songs rating highest according to the *Variety* figures—with those they regarded as the most popular ones according to general opinion. Further, they identified those songs which they regarded as most popular with those they happened to like themselves. Here it is particularly opportune to make clear the approach of a social critique. If we took such a case in isolation, it might appear that radio, by a kind of Darwinian process of selection, actually plays most frequently those songs that are best liked by the people and is, therefore, fulfilling their demands. We know, however, from another section of our study, that the "plugging" of songs does not follow the response they elicit but the vested interests of song publishers. The identification of the successful with the most frequently played is thus an illusion—an illusion, to be sure, that may become an operating social force and in turn really make the much-played a success: because through such an identification the listeners follow what they believe to be the crowd and thus come to constitute one.

The standardization of production in this field, as in most others, goes so far that the listener virtually has no choice. Products are forced upon him. His freedom has ceased to exist. This process, however, if it were to work openly and undisguised, would promote a resistance which could easily endanger the whole system. The less the listener has to choose, the more is he made to believe that he has a choice: and the more the whole machine functions only for the sake of profit, the more must he be convinced that it is functioning for him and his sake only or, as it is put, as a public service. In radio we can witness today something very similar to those comic and paradoxical forms of competition between gasolines which do not differ in anything but their names. The consumer is unwilling to recognize that he is totally dependent, and he likes to preserve the illusion of private initiative and free choice. Thus standardization in radio produces its veil of pseudo-individualism. It is this veil which enforces upon us scepticism with regard to any first-hand information from listeners. We must try to understand them better than they understand themselves. This brings us easily into conflict with common sense notions, such as "giving the people what they want."

This raises the question of controls and safeguards against biased imagination. Music is not a realm of subjective tastes and relative values, except to those who do not want to undergo the discipline of the subject matter. As soon as one enters the field of musical technology and structure, the arbitrariness of evaluation vanishes, and we are faced with decisions about right and wrong and true and false. I should like to give some examples of what I call musico-technological control of sociological interpretation. I mentioned above the social tendency toward a pseudo-individualism to hide the increase of standardization. This tendency in today's mass-produced music can be expressed in precise technical terms. Musical analysis can furnish us with plenty of materials which manifest, so far as rhythmical patterns, sound combinations, melodic and harmonic structures are concerned, that even apparently divergent schools of popular music, such as Sweet and Swing, are essentially the same. It can further be shown that their differences have no bearing on the musical essence itself. It can be shown that each band has assumed certain mannerisms with no musical function and no other purpose than to make it easier for the listener to recognize the particular band—such as, say, the musically nonsensical staccati with which Guy Lombardo likes to end certain legato phrases.

And now an example from the field of serious music. If we analyze a score of a Beethoven symphony in terms of all the thematic and dynamic interrelationships defined in the music, develop the necessary conditions of fulfilling its prescriptions by a performance, and then analyze the extent to which these prescriptions can be realized by radio, the proposition that symphonic music and the radio are incompatible becomes concretely defined and, so to speak, measurable. Here again the formulation of research problems is affected by our critical outlook. I suspect that people listen to serious music largely in terms of entertainment. Our technical analysis allows us to formulate this suspicion in exact terms. Studies on the Radio Voice have shown that with regard to such categories as the prevalence of sound colors, emphasis on detail, the isolation of the main tune, and similar features, a symphony on the air becomes a piece of entertainment.

Consequently it would be absurd to maintain that it could be received by the listeners as anything but entertainment. Entertainment may have its uses, but a recognition of radio music as such would shatter the listeners' artificially fostered belief that they are dealing with the world's greatest music.

Helen MacGill Hughes

HUMAN INTEREST STORIES
AND DEMOCRACY

Charles Merz, speculating on the state of the Union, once remarked that it is doubtful whether anything really unifies the country like its murders. Like so many outrageous and undocumented assertions, particularly the more cynical ones, this statement is probably the simple truth. He refers, of course, to murders as made public in the newspapers, and so, eventually, to something that Cooley has commented upon: that the press, by acquainting people with each others' lives, has implemented the democracy.[1] Like other liberals, Cooley looked upon the newspaper as an indispensable condition of government by the people. But, paradoxically, it is not the political news that informs people about one another. It is the revelations of private life and those inconsequential items that in the newspaper office are known as human interest stories. Now historians of the press maintain that it was this type of "copy" that, in America, made newspaper reading a universal habit. And so the question arises, Does the personal news which characterizes the popular newspaper play a part in welding the American democracy? The question is all the more pertinent because the forms of the totalitarian state which are threatening democratic structures are invariably opposed to this aspect of journalism.

From its beginning in the penny dailies of a century ago, the popular press has envisaged its reader as a plain man of brief schooling who, as Mencken says, "misses the hard words."[2] As soon as newspapermen recognized that the great difference between the educated and others lies in

Reprinted from *The Public Opinion Quarterly*, Vol. I (April, 1937), pp. 73-83, by permission of the author and the publisher. (Copyright, 1937, by Princeton University Press.)

[1] Cooley, C. H., *Social Organization* (New York: Scribner's, 1929), pp. 177-8.

[2] Mencken, H. L., *The American Language* (New York: Knopf, 1919), pp. 185-6. The common failure to understand abstract words is well exhibited in chapter 1 of Wembridge, E., *Life Among the Lowbrows* (Boston: Houghton Mifflin, 1931).
"A song-writer," says Sigmund Spaeth, "would hardly dare to use *whom* in a sentence. . . . 'Who are you with tonight?' sounds both proper and provocative and the

vocabulary, they found it possible to tell substantially the same news in such a way that the uneducated comprehended and enjoyed it.

The conversion of news into stories told in the language of the street, but "written up" like fiction, brought new classes of readers, described by Whitelaw Reid as "men who can't read or at least had not been habitual and regular readers of the high-priced daily newspapers." [3] Day and Bennett, editors of the first penny papers, the *New York Sun* and the *New York Herald,* referred to their readers of the 1830's as "artisans and mechanics," "the man of labor," and "the small merchant." The Yellow Press in the 'nineties delved into other new strata of readers when it enlisted women and immigrants, the former by love stories and department store advertisements, the latter by pictures and words of one syllable. All this time, and continuing into the present, cities were growing by draining population from the rural regions, so there have always been new recruits to be enrolled as metropolitan newspaper readers.[4] For the first time these classes were brought imaginatively into the orbit of city and ultimately national life. For them the newspaper offers a view of a magical world. A working girl who read Hearst's *New York Evening Journal* once wrote:

> It is very exciting to read of a girl who has disappeared from home, no one knowing where she has gone and in about three days a description of the girl will appear in the *Journal* and the way the detectives disguise themselves and go in search for this wayward girl. . . . Take for example the strange disappearance of Miss Dorothy Arnold, this is a case that I have followed up ever since I first saw its appearance in the *Journal* and I expect to follow it to its end. I am very anxious to know where Miss Arnold is and whether she has become the bride of Mr. George Griscom. The way I hope it will end is where she will return to her parents and they will welcome her with open heart and hands.[5]

To just such literate but unsophisticated city-dwellers—the demos [6]—the newspaper was a collection of stories. Reading matter like the *Journal's*

song could not possibly have achieved popularity with the burden of a 'whom' on its neck."—*The Facts of Life in Popular Song* (New York: McGraw-Hill, 1935), p. 24.

[3] "Recent Changes in the Press," *American and English Studies* (New York: Scribner's, 1913), Vol, 11, pp. 297-8. Reid was speaking of the year 1901.

[4] *True Story Magazine* regards itself as the spokesman of country people, transplanted to the city. Promotion material depicts the reader as a woman who, in her home town knew all the neighbors, but who lives now in a small city flat and knows no one. *Vide* advertisement, *Chicago Tribune,* April 22, 1930.

[5] Symposium on "The American Newspaper," *Collier's Weekly,* September 2, 1911, p. 22.

[6] *Demos* is not an economic term like *proletariat.* Sumner divides the *classes,* who initiate custom, from the *masses* who conserve it. (*Folkways,* Ginn, 1906, p. 45). Redfield distinguishes the tribal *folk* that sings folk-songs from the city *demos* that buys jazz songs (*Tepoztlan,* University of Chicago Press, 1930, p. 6). The American demos is not purely urban. Blumer describes the *mass,* referring to those of all classes who follow fashions, murder stories, land booms, etc., and so take part in mass behavior ("Molding of Mass Behavior Through the Motion Picture," *Publications of the American Socio-*

makes them readers and establishes the reading habit. To do so it must, it seems, have the character of a fairy tale. It transports the reader into another world, but, like the Negro folk-play, *Green Pastures,* it conceives the new world invariably in terms of the known. Sophisticated literature has at all times explored people and places that are unfamiliar and intriguing but there is always the familiar core of private sentiments, ambitions, and passions that humanizes even the bizarre and the outlandish. But *popular* literature, though it revolves about that small circle of personal vicissitudes, is realistic; the scenes of action hardly venture further than the reader's curiosity.[7]

The newspaper's stories reflected the popular mind, that is to say the way the demos thought about the things that came within its comprehension. Like the movies and *Saturday Evening Post* fiction they frequently turned out to be stories of young love and its trials.[8] But within this range of experience known to the demos, the stories were the medium for presenting the unfamiliar and strange. For the human interest story invaded a succession of areas of life for its settings. To that extent the penny press and later the Yellow Press contributed to the education of simple-minded people in some of the facts of contemporary social life. In this the cheap press was joined by the dime novel, the story weekly and the confession magazine. The great growth of the popular newspaper in the last century accompanied by the urbanization of the demos, whose burgeoning curiosity about the world was the beginning of sophistication. The interesting thing is that such a mission was far from the publisher's intention: it all came about as an irrelevant and unforeseen effect of the compulsion put upon the reporter to provide attractive copy in order to sell the paper.

Before the penny press, the newspapers confined their news to business and politics. Benjamin Day unconventionally hunted news in the police court. The *Sun's* intriguing accounts of vicious, violent, and uproarious life as it paraded before minor magistrates in the night sessions were, for thousands of obscure citizens, hitherto without a newspaper, the first impressions of the city to supplement their own direct experiences of sight

logical Society, 1935, p. 116). In this discussion of popular literature the demos means the readers—at first artisans, then immigrants, then women—who find in the newspaper the enjoyment that others find in books.

[7] A *True Story Magazine* advertisement, discussing the question: "How does a group of people first acquire its reading habit?" answers that it is through "simple stories, simply told, of people like the readers themselves; stories with the same problems that the readers themselves are constantly meeting."—Macfadden advertisement in the *New York Times,* December 3 and 18, 1935.

[8] According to Colonel Joy of the Hays organization, "the best movie story concerns a man and a maid who are going some place, encounter difficulties, overcome them, and are rewarded."—Pew, M., "Shop Talk at Thirty," *Editor and Publisher,* March 12, 1932, p. 46.

and hearing. Day's discovery that mechanics and artisans could be readily interested in them is initially responsible for the fact that present-day trials have become public circuses and criminals public characters.

Day's competitor, James Gordon Bennett, was shrewd enough to appreciate the fact that the size of New York prevented the oral circulation of news that everyone would find worth telling if he knew of it, and he announced in his *Herald*:[9]

We shall give a correct picture of the world—in Wall Street—in the Exchange —in the Post Office—at the Theaters—in the Opera—in short, wherever human nature or real life best displays its freaks and vagaries.

The "collector of news" was employed to write up incidents of the city streets and tell New Yorkers about each other. The doings of the rich, for one thing, had become a subject of excited speculation among the poor. On this interest Bennett founded an important innovation, society news. He sent reporters to balls and banquets, printed a list of guests (designated tantalizingly by the first and last letters of their names) and told what they wore. Later on, Hearst reported fashionable functions on a heroic scale, giving as much as five pages to the Bradley-Martin masquerade, copiously illustrated by staff artists.[10]

Then there developed an interest in the contrary direction; the middle-class and the wealthy became curious about the poor. This was evinced in the vogue of slumming parties and of books like Jake Riis's *How the Other Half Lives*. Hearst's *Sunday Journal* ran illustrated sketches by Stephen Crane of his experiences in the Tenderloin. New York was dotted with little worlds like Chinatown, the Bowery, Little Italy, and other exotic neighborhoods which were a perpetual source of wonder for those on the outside.[11] A great volume of "feature stuff" brought the life of the immigrant and the poor into the newspaper. At this time, too, "Annie Laurie" (Winifred Black) was engaged to write accounts of women's lives and she produced features on such subjects as *The Strange Things Women Do For Love*, that were not police court news, but simply a commentary on the newer and freer careers that young women in particular were pursuing in the city. The shop girl who had inspired some of O. Henry's short stories, the business girl, and the "bachelor girl" began to exist for newspaper readers. For purposes of the newspaper the city became a laboratory for the concoction of stories.

[9] May 11, 1835.
[10] An account of the repercussions of this publicity appears in Brown, H. C., *Brownstone Fronts and Saratoga Trunks* (New York: Dutton, 1935), pp. 330 ff.
[11] Sightseeing bus conductors in New York have discovered that what middle-aged country visitors want is a version of the Bowery that was true forty years ago, but not true now. They hope to see the dives of the "sinful city" as the earlier legends in popular literature depicted it—Berger, M., "O. Henry Returns to His Bagdad," *New York Times Magazine*, November 24, 1935.

These new departures were accompanied by a change in the balance of power in the editorial rooms, for when the newspaper office became the admitting ward for anything at all that the readers found interesting, local news, which the older papers had almost ignored, became actually more important than any other. Writing in 1879, Whitelaw Reid of the *Tribune* prophesied that city, national, and world news would be revalued in accordance with their relative interest for the reader, and that "the City Department may then cease to be the place where raw beginners wreak their will." [12] His astuteness as a prophet is acknowledged in a more modern pronouncement: "A dog fight in Champa Street is better than a war abroad." [13] What was called the City Desk now represents the largest department in a newspaper's organization. "The trend unmistakably in New York," writes Stanley Walker, "is toward complete coverage. . . . The space devoted to local news in most New York papers has increased 50 per cent in the last fifteen years." [14]

Dog fights, lovesick girls and masked balls—"the interesting" rather than "the important," to use Hearst's distinction—provoke spontaneous comment and the newspaper did no more than make their area of diffusion wider. The knowledge of the city that it disseminated corresponded to what the readers found acceptable. And on this gossipy level the newspaper made a beginning of creating those conditions of close communication whose absence denies the city the social cohesion that the village possesses.

For sixty years the penny papers contented themselves with an orbit of news-coverage that surveyed with a fair measure of completeness, the small daily world of "the mechanic and the man of labor." The news the *Sun* enumerated in 1882 as causing temporary increases in circulation was of Presidential and civic elections, the last days of walking matches, great fires, and hangings in or near the city.[15] It was Hearst who took his readers out of the State of New York and caused them to move imaginatively in a larger sphere.

A despatch was sent from Havana reporting that a seventeen-year-old Cuban girl, Evangelina Cisneros, was to be imprisoned for twenty years off the African coast for a political offense. Hearst seized upon it, exclaiming to his editor, Chamberlain, "We can make a national issue of this case. It will do more to open the eyes of the country to Spanish cruelty and oppression than a thousand editorials or political speeches." This unknown girl's misfortune, because of its human interest, caught the readers' imagination

---

[12] "Practical Issues in a Newspaper Office," *American and English Studies* (New York: Scribner's, 1913) Vol. II, p. 256.

[13] Credited to Bonfils and Tammen of the *Denver Post*, whose office is on Champa Street.—Walker, S., *City Editor* (New York: Stokes, 1934), p. 87.

[14] *Ibid.*, pp. 45-6 and 52-6. Fifteen years ago a New York morning paper might have 40 local items; now it has 100, some illustrated.

[15] O'Brien, F. M., *The Story of "The Sun"* (New York: Doran, 1918), pp. 324-5.

and it did become a national issue in a more profound sense than any prior question between the United States and Spain. The *Journal* ·launched a crusade to free her. Petitions with thousands of signatures, at first from such notable women as Julia Ward Howe and the widow of Jefferson Davis, and then from any woman who wanted to sign, were sent to the Pope and the Queen-Regent of Spain. The *Journal* gave more than two pages a day to the campaign, heading them: "The Whole Country Rising to the Rescue: More than Ten Thousand Women Petition for the Release of Miss Cisneros." As the *Journal's* readers saw it, the Cisneros case was one of monstrous persecution that any human being would naturally want to prevent. To their simple thinking the question of the invasion of Spanish jurisdiction did not exist. The diplomatic game has its own set of conventions; they are not those of plain people.

That a small local incident became public business was an unplanned effect of newspaper competition. Hearst had just bought the *New York Journal* and was trying desperately to seize for it the market of Pultizer's *New York World*. During the Spanish-American War which soon followed, the two papers vied with each other not so much in reporting as in exploiting the news as a means to ensnare buyers. The streamer headline came into regular use for the first time. Its purpose was to force attention upon the inflammatory reports which soon earned them the name, the Yellow Press. To Pulizer the war brought "an opportunity," as he put it, "to test the effect on circulation." [16] To readers of the Yellow Press it appeared as a thrilling, but at the same time a simplified affair; complicated issues like the sugar market and the location of naval bases were not discussed—no one would enjoy reading that. The campaign was made personal and epic. The *Journal* referred to the Spanish commander of Cuba as "Butcher" Weyler. A private comment of the Spanish Ambassador was headlined "The Worst Insult to the United States in its History." The next day the withdrawal of the Ambassador was announced as "*Journal's* Letter Gets De Lome His Walking Papers." [17] Later came the news: "Spain Refuses to Apologize." This went on for weeks until war was finally declared.

The diplomatic gestures were, of course, reported in all newspapers, but the Yellow Press construed events in terms of the recognizable and informal rules of a street fight. They indulged in the habit of making categorical moral distinctions and calling names that unsophisticated people—and others—fall into in trying to picture the relations between nation and nation.[18] As Godkin of the sober *New York Post* complained, they treated

[16] Seitz, D., *Joseph Pulitzer: His Life and Letters* (New York: Simon and Schuster, 1924), p. 238.

[17] February 9, 1898.

[18] "In sophisticated people participation (in a drama) may not be in the fate of the hero, but in the fate of the whole idea to which hero and villain are essential. . . . In popular representation the handles for identification are almost always marked. You

the war like a prize-fight and begot "in hundreds of thousands of the class that enjoys prize-fights an eager desire to read about it." Famous editorial writer that he was, Godkin found it hard to believe that real political power—which, as Merriam has recently said, lies in a "definite common pattern of impulse" [19]—is exerted, not by the editorial but by interesting news. Whether there is truth or not in the legend that Hearst made it, this war at all events was wrested from the hands of diplomats. It became popular in the sense that the people entered into it enthusiastically and that they identified themselves wholly with it. The Yellow Press, by its jingo patriotism and its conversion of the news into dramatic concepts, led the attention of the demos from the local scene to the world of international relations. It also created *national* heroes and villains.

The popular newspaper continued the informal education of the demos into the formidable fields of business and science. Here again the familiar gave the entrée to the unknown and, because the commonest object of spontaneous interest is man himself, all copy tended to take the form of personal stories. Business news appeared in the guise of success stories. As expounded to him by politicians and soapbox haranguers, men of power and property are likely to strike the common man as predatory monsters called "The Milk Trust" or "The Traction Interests," and so, among the masses who have no business affairs of their own and no interest in the routine news of business and finance, any understanding there is of the difficulties, the temptations, and the triumphs of merchants and financiers will come from the reading of a personal revelation. For there the *man* is recognized and perhaps forgiven; the *magnate* is feared and hated, envied, or simply disregarded.[20]

One of the best instances of a concentration of general attention on a technical matter occurred when the *New York Sun* put human interest into a report of the convention of the Sanitary Conference of American Republics. The news that Dr. C. W. Stiles had identified the hookworm as the mysterious destroyer of southern "white trash" was facetiously headed

know who the hero is at once. And no work promises to be easily popular where the marking is not definite and the choice clear, . . . a fact which bears heavily on the character of news."—Lippmann, W., *Public Opinion* (New York: Harcourt Brace, 1922), pp. 162-3.

[19] Merriam, C. E., *Political Power: Its Composition and Incidence* (New York: McGraw-Hill, 1935), p. 7.

[20] Perceiving this, J. P. Morgan's advisers permitted wide circulation of a photograph, taken during the Senate hearing on munitions, that showed him talking with a circus midget who had climbed into his lap. The Senators wanted the picture destroyed.—*Vide* Walker, *op. cit.*, p. 106.

When the steel magnates of the country had a banquet years ago, a reporter put human interest into the news by reciting the menu of extravagant foreign dishes, followed by what each actually ate. One had a little gruel; another had prunes and milk; in short, all were elderly sick men, denied the plain man's luxury of enjoying a full meal.

"Germ of Laziness Found?" [21] The account below it was sober enough, but the reference to a universal human failing caught immediate attention and gave rise to innumerable jokes and cartoons. Yet the effect of the hubbub was, as Mark Sullivan put it, "to make Stiles the target for newspaper and stage humorists the world over; next, the object of scorn and vituperation in all the region south of the Potomac River and east of the Mississippi; and finally, years later, one of the heroes of medical science in his generation." [22]

All this time newspapermen were making the more obviously personal crises—elopements, murders, bereavements—the occasion for laying bare some obscure individual's inmost thoughts. The popular press enlivened *everything*. As its scope enlarged,[23] it led the demos through the human interest in a personal story toward an acquaintanceship with a simplified and trivialized, but none the less a wider world. The newspaper implemented this knowledge in perhaps the only possible way. Just what is the effect of this expansion of understanding which the newspaper expedites is a question newspapermen never ask, because it is beyond them. And social philosophers do not ask it because it is beneath them.

It is a matter of common observation that a "big story" in the newspapers becomes, as Northcliffe put it, the talking-point for the day. The Leopold-Loeb trial, one suspects, brought homosexuality into common conversation; the romance of King Edward and Mrs. Simpson animated the subject of morganatic marriage. And, as Merz said of murder, it gives the nation a set of facts on which to test its moral values.[24] Letters like these below are a symptom of general speculation:

Brooklyn: If any person went through a Hell on earth, that person was Mary Nolan. She has been treated cruelly and needs a helping hand. May she be successful in staging her comeback. She deserves all the success in the world.—Well Wisher.

Bronx: I have read with interest the story of Mary Nolan's life. From my experience as a social worker I have concluded that she is more sinned against than sinning. Why is it always made so difficult for a woman to stage a comeback? This "Mr. X" is probably living in security and respectability. Mary Nolan's only chance is to take the public into her confidence. When will the double standard of morality give the woman a fair chance? Through Mary Nolan's story, the *Mirror* has given society a great indictment.—Helen E. Martin, President Bronx Civic Study Club.[25]

[21] December 5, 1902.

[22] *Our Times: Pre-War America* (New York: Scribner's, 1930), Vol. II, p. 293.

[23] This is reflected in a growth in staff. The first penny papers had an editor, police reporter, and local news collector. But the present Hearst papers nearly equal the coverage of standard dailies, using press franchises and a variety of reporters, correspondents, department editors, and columnists.

[24] *The Great American Bandwagon* (New York: John Day, 1928), p. 71.

[25] These appeared, following a completely commonplace and unexceptional news story, in Hearst's *New York Mirror* (a tabloid), November 25, 1933.

Moral speculations are not evoked by news of court procedure; they take form on the reading of an intimate story that shows what the impact of law and convention means as a private experience. A popular literature of true stories, by making the local and the remote world human, may be a substitute on an extended scale for those intimate encounters of direct perception which are the basis of any understanding men have of each other. But this, in the end, puts the reader in the position of a confidant. The difference that intimacy makes in passing judgment is expressed in the aphorism: What's the Constitution between friends? It seems to be always the difference between impersonal news of the external facts and this popular literature that reveals the inner experience, that the *news* raises practical questions of ways and means with the appropriate code taken for granted, but *literature,* like all art, exhibits the inhumanity of doctrine, law, and custom. For literature does more than provoke a plea for exceptional treatment. It induces reverie about oneself and the remote, rather than the immediate objectives of one's own career, and it questions the traditional premises of social life.[26] And since the readers read the news as a pastime and rarely feel called upon to intervene, reverie is free to venture beyond the mores.

Such painful cogitation is the particular burden of uprooted people. Greenhorn immigrants, women entering a freer life, and recent arrivals from the country,[27] in becoming incorporated with the life that extends beyond the local community, are confronted with conflicting patterns of behavior and suffer miseries and uncertainties that are new and, it may seem, incurable. They experience cultural divergencies internally as private moral dilemmas. Indeed, in periods of rapid change, like the present, doubts assail all classes of people and become epidemic. "It is a chief use of social institutions," writes Cooley, "to make up our minds for us, and when in time of confusion they fail to do this, there is more mind-work than most of us are capable of."[28] True and contemporary analogues in the news are at once a comfort and a definition, for human interest stories dramatize for them the opposition between the "right," the legitimate, and the doctrinaire on the one hand, and the "human" on the other.[29] Their protests against the mores may be restated as an aspect of social change of which

[26] Blumer, H., *op. cit.*, pp. 115-27. Blumer holds the movies invoke reverie that is an attack on the mores, since it reaffirms the basic human values in a novel ("newsy") setting. This could be well taken to describe the human interest story.

[27] *True Story* promotion material, picturing the reader as a lonely newcomer to the city continues: "Do you wonder that these people turn to *True Story Magazine* for parallels of their own experience? For some yardstick to measure by in this changing order of a world that is never at rest?"—Advertisement in *Chicago Tribune,* April 22, 1930. The Voice of Experience, a radio counsellor on "Your Personal Problems," reports that the most popular of his ten-cent booklets is the one on the inferiority complex.

[28] *Life and the Student* (New York: Knopf, 1927), p. 219.

[29] The attitude of the tabloid *New York Daily News,* when a Democratic boss made

their own mobility is an expression. The vogue of confessional literature among the demos and of biography among sophisticates may signalize the dissolution of local culture and the emergence of a more inclusive consciousness.

One wonders whether a popular literature of true stories is not perhaps a phenomenon of change *in a free society*. The democratic state, as Hobhouse noted, rests more and more on the personality of its citizens. But under an oppressive and autocratic rule, like the totalitarian state, the citizen may not be his own moral judge. Nor is the press free to be interesting when dedicated to the service of the state. Dictators strive to make discipline absolute by contracting the sympathies and they are suspicious of human interest in newspapers because they fear the unconstrained speculation to which it gives rise.

his son a State Supreme Court Justice was: "What could be more natural than for a father to give his son the break?"—Walker, *op. cit.*, p. 70.

David Riesman and Reuel Denney

DO THE MASS MEDIA "ESCAPE" FROM POLITICS?

Hollywood's discovery of the Negro problem had given the studios a new cycle, and distributors a tough problem: How would the South take to films denouncing racial prejudice? . . . Having already played nine profitable weeks in Manhattan, *Home of the Brave* opened in Dallas and Houston . . . In Dallas, the Negro elevator operator tried to sum up overheard opinion: "Well, I'll tell you, 99 per cent of the people say it's educational, the other 1 per cent say it's good."—*Time,* July 18, 1949.

Critics of the mass media on the whole seem to suppose that the media foster political apathy; that they permit and encourage the audience to "escape" from the political and other realities of life; that, by a kind of Gresham's Law, they drive out the hard money of politics with the soft money of mass entertainment. How can Washington, it is sometimes asked, compete for the consumer's leisure with Hollywood and Broadway?

The position of the critics usually rests on an unspoken assumption of scarcity—that leisure is so limited that time taken, for instance, by comic reading, is taken *from* politics. But, except perhaps on farms, most people have ample time for both. Underneath this criticism, there may be concealed a Puritanical dislike for leisure, a feeling that people ought to occupy their (unfortunately) free time with civic affairs and other serious matters. Or there is the neo-Puritan hygienic feeling that people ought to be "doing something," no matter what, so long as it is not sitting in a movie—a vitamin conscious view of life. This outlook represents a failure to realize that people can afford to "waste" both time and other resources. Instead of pleasurable waste, however, we are apt to use our greatly increased leisure, made possible by material abundance, to go in search of a number of serious agendas, many disguised as "having fun."

Reprinted from *The Changing American Character,* to be published in 1950 by the Yale University Press, under the auspices of the Yale University Committee on National Policy. The research on which the volume is based was financed by the Carnegie Corporation.

In any case, it seems to us that the much-criticized media, especially the press, have maintained a surprisingly responsible attitude towards politics. Even tabloids print political headlines and, often, newspictures on the cover—not comics. Old Indignant Hearst likes to print "the Chief's" editorials, rather than cheesecake, on page one. Local radio stations that are little more than relays for disk-jockeys build their self-esteem (and please the FCC) by presenting news "every hour on the hour," though in fact many in their audience who like commercials may not care for newscasts. Likewise, newsreels usually begin with shots of some political personage or event, postponing Lew Lehr or the fashion show to the end of the reel. Thus, many of the agencies of mass communications give political news a larger play than might be dictated by strict considerations of market research. In this way the media help maintain the prestige of politics as a presumed interest on the part of their audience—even are the very channels that give politics priority.[1]

One reason for this is the desire of those who work for the mass media to do what is right, or considered to be right by those to whom they look for leadership. Just as publishers, under various rationalizations of good will want to publish prestige books even though they may lose money on them, so newspapermen and broadcasters want to raise themselves above "the lowest common denominator" without fully exploring the potential financial profitability of the latter. The movie king who speaks for "mere" entertainment feels on the defensive with the bold producer of *Home of the Brave*.

This is one way of saying that men in the communications industry are much less cynical than they sometimes seem to be; or that their cynicism, even if much displayed, often covers a repressed idealism. They express this far less in their concern for the reactions of their audiences than in their concern for the reactions of the intellectual and taste strata around and "above" them. And these strata are often contemptuous of popular culture. They denounce "Hollywood" or bestsellers in the same tones with which one might attack the worst social cruelties and stupidities. These critics have influence even though their attitude may be a bit like that of the Vermont lady who, in one of our interviews, said she saw only French movies. It later turned out that she had seen one in her life.

Doubtless, a hierarchy among the different kinds of entertainment has always existed. But whereas the hierarchy in earlier days was based, at least to some extent, on criteria of artistry, the hierarchy today seems to be based somewhat more on topic than on mode of treatment. As the

---

[1] Cf. Paul Lazarsfeld and Robert K. Merton, "Mass Communication, Popular Taste and Organized Social Action," in Lyman Bryson, ed., *The Communication of Ideas* (New York: Harper & Bros., 1948), p. 95, on the "status-conferral" function of the media.

audience itself is asked to move on a constantly uptilting gradient of topic and taste, from the comics of childhood to the commentators of adulthood, so the makers of the media, in their own combination of social mobility and ethical uplift, are always impatient to get to the point where, in addition to entertaining, they are, in terms of topic, educating and improving. As the slicks are more high-class than the pulps, so politics is more high-class than sex. The sports writer wants to become a political columnist; the night-club broadcaster moves over, first into political chit-chat, then into political fire; many a newspaper publisher who begins as a "no-nonsense" businessman ends up as a bit of a political moralizer. Just as the new rich are "educated" to philanthropy by their associates, so the new entrants into the mass media are educated away from the "low" commercial motives to ones of more prestige.

It seems, therefore, that the mass media, among their highly complex and ambiguous effects, do help prop up the prestige of the political sphere in the United States, and that, within this sphere, they have the effect of favoring the older, more responsible, more moralizing and uplifting political styles. However, if we are to assess the total impact of the media, we have to register partial agreement—though for different reasons—with the critics of the media. That is, we have to recognize that this politicizing effect is a residue effect, more true of the press than of the movies and radio, more true of a few magazines and newspapers than of the press as a whole. We may partially sum up our opinion of the political influence of the media by observing that the moral and intellectual aims of the media-men have very little of their intended effect. Rather, the needs of the audience and the needs of the media combine to promote a style of viewing politics with evaporated emotion which we may call "tolerance." The demands of this style detach people from political relatedness of an emotional sort, even when, and often especially when, they are filled up with political information, injunctions and interpretations by the media.

Perhaps the most important reason for this is that we Americans resort to the media today with a desperate eagerness to learn the proper responses to make in our social groups—including political responses in those groups where it is fashionable to talk politics. Increasingly, we turn to the media to learn how to handle ourselves in tenuous webs of social relations. Hence, what is said in the media about politics, no matter how stern and responsible the tone, is taken by many in the audience as a signal that tells how "the others" regard and consume politics—and not as a signal orienting the reader himself in politics. This focus on the others is one source of the audience's effort to train itself to regard politics with "tolerance," since this is the appropriate response we Americans must make if we are to be good fellows—and we must make this sort of response even if "the others" happen to be intolerant, angry men.

Most of the writers and broadcasters, moreover, are not angry but tolerant men. Indeed, since the chief strategy of the media as tutors of consumption is to introduce and rationalize changes, enrichments, or discontinuities in conventional tastes and styles, the media have a stake in tolerance: they cannot afford to have people committed to a taste or an opinion that they may want to change tomorrow. But the most powerful factor making for the tolerant slant is probably the sheer size of the audience. The media are subject to a variety of pressures brought by groups seeking protection from attack; and these pressures are internalized in the very structure of large media management and distribution. The larger the scope of the medium, the more likely is it to be produced in a large metropolitan center, where the pressures toward tolerance are greatest. While more free from the pressure of advertisers and that of local cranks than are small-town editors and broadcasters, and often considerably more daring in general, the big-city media with a city-wide or nation-wide audience cannot help but be aware of those attitudes that may offend their complex constituencies.

In the case of the press, for example, whereas the early nineteenth-century editor could gamble on a crusade that might bring him both a libel suit and a circulation, the twentieth-century publisher often cannot afford to let his editor gamble even on an increased circulation. For his managers have guaranteed his circulation to the advertisers, have planned his newsprint supply, and have committed him to Newspaper Guild contracts and distributive relationships long in advance.

Furthermore, as the audience becomes more diffuse in class or age terms, the writer or broadcaster becomes less able to pitch what he has to say in any tone of obloquy based on intimate knowledge of a specific audience. In general, the larger the audience of the medium, the more it is apt to be produced and consumed in a mood of self-censorship and piety. This is not to deny that there are those who have been trained to associate piety and tolerance with the "official" culture but react violently against it—as is demonstrated by their loyalty to those older captains, or newer columnistic commissars, of press and radio who capitalize on their own intolerance and their own appearance of impiety.

Undoubtedly, one reason for this attraction, which in many cases probably encourages columnists to intensify their search for a "tough" approach and even vulgaristic force of style, is that the other forms of popular culture today seldom provide the unequivocal emotional escapes that they provided for many in the nineteenth century. "Escape" is a slippery word, of course, and so is "entertainment"; we must always ask: escape from what and to what? In the nineteenth century, many people were secure enough in their work and their social relations to be able to afford, in their limited leisure time, a certain amount of escape. Some of this did, indeed, take political form, as in the case of torchlight parades. Today, however, people's anxieties about their social relations lead them to use the older escapes, such as fiction and drama, as well as the newer ones such as radio, to find out how to handle exigent personal problems. Increasingly, the topics dealt with in novels and magazine fiction, in radio drama, and in A-budget movies, come from the possibilities faced by people in everyday life. The middle-class American today is more likely to meet in his personal life the same kind of problems acted out or actually faced by a Frank Sinatra or a Joan Crawford than of dreaming of the impossible, as the 19th century audience did when, aided by fiction, it dreamt of waking up as the utterly improbable D'Artagnan or Cinderella. While the lower-class American can still escape, to a degree, into the sheer fantasy of comics and Westerns—though these vehicles, too, become increasingly problem-filled and, in that sense, educative—the middle-class man finds not only that he has abandoned older topics of fantasy but, more important, that what once might have been termed a fantasy— let us say, a dream of sexual romance or a Bahama vacation—is now only one jump away from being real. The audience that seems to seek entertainment finds itself projected instead into its daily social realities. And, since politics is less "real" than this, the consumption of political vituperation may become more than ever an escape, rationalized by its high, media-based prestige.

For the audience, this shift in the forms of its "escape" testifies, as we have said, to its anxieties in the handling of people and, generally, in the solution of problems presented, not in work, but in the leisure and consumption side of life. For the media, the shift is mainly a reflection of audience demand. But, beyond audience demand, the men who work for the media are great believers in what they call "realism"—for much of the same sort of reasons that they are believers in being politically responsible. Yet what Americans seem to us to need, in their politics as in their personal life, is greater scope for fantasy.

Lassalle spoke of the "damned wantlessness" of the poor, but we Americans, despite our wealth, also exhibit wantlessness in the political packages we now conceive, manufacture, and distribute. The result is a political scene of unimaginative dullness, to which people attach themselves either because of ideas of proper consumership or because of the impious excitement held out, like an alluring movie ad, by the residual indignants who have rejected the convention of tolerance. An increased diet of political moralizing and dutiful editorializing will scarcely liberate our presently impoverished political fantasy. Nor are we likely to liberate it by increasing the time allotted to Dinah Shore or Mel Torme. Nevertheless, we have the feeling that if the media encouraged, and if its audience could permit itself, more genuine escape, "away from it all," we would become stronger psychically, and more ready to undertake an awakening of political imagination and commitment.

By going on with our present course of media performance and media criticism, we make it possible for the media to continue to uphold the prestige of the political even when, as for much of our life at present, the political is devoid of substantial content—for one thing, because this very lack of content could only be glimpsed from the less "realistic," more imaginative and fantasy-oriented outlook. The direct impact of the media on political decision may easily become as thin as the impact of the House of Lords on popular opinion in Britain. The serious press refuses to face this situation, and, rather than seeking to explore new emotional currents in American life, it strenuously seeks to present to the "Commons" of the media—the radio, movies, and pulps—a hand-me-down agenda of political debate. Thus, the sources in popular art and culture from which eventual political creation may flow are partially dammed up by false prestige considerations and by the displaced guilts and ethical urges shared by those who control the media and those who, in turn, look to them for a bill of cultural fare.

Given these many ambiguities of intention and effect, of immediate effect and long-run effect, what are the media to do? It is helpful to recognize that what the media do is usually less important than the moods and needs of the audience. And we really know very little about this audience structure: we have looked too much for the messages the media bear and too little for the ways in which the audience actively participates and shapes its experience of the media. The probabilities are, however, that the media, in their direct, message-bearing impact, are likely to do less either to help or hurt the audience than the controllers of the media and their critics like to think. This alone should save us—to borrow a fine phrase from Justice Holmes—from looking either for panaceas or for sudden ruin as the result of any messages or group of messages the media may carry. Awareness of this fact may then permit both the controllers and the critics of the media to reorient their attention. They are free, much freer than they realize, to attend to the medium itself, rather than to the message it purveys or is believed to purvey. The movie producer or critic who is concerned mainly with messages, for instance of ethnic tolerance, may actually despise the movies as an art form. The editorialiser or social scientist who is concerned only with arousing the electorate may hate the English language because it has become for him a mere tool. The broadcaster who wants to expiate for his big salary and sponsors by slipping in a crack against business may have little respect for the aesthetic resources of his medium.

As we have seen, the men who work in radio, film, and fiction tend to give politics, as the press and its uplifters see it, a prestige denied to art, and especially the popular art of the media themselves. There is pathos in this for their personal lives, since it leads them to unwarranted contempt for their own craft. There is irony in this for American politics, since it seems to us that a country which produced artistically first-class movies, papers, and broadcasts—no matter what the topic, and, indeed, subordinating the whole question of topic—would be, politically as well as culturally, a livelier and happier land. Good mass media artists are quite as important, and perhaps even scarcer, than responsible, anti-escapist commentators.

7

COMMUNICATION AUDIENCES

The American Audience

The field of audience research includes not only those studies aiming at accurate description of the audience to various media, channels, or items of communication. In addition, it deals with the factors responsible for the types of communication exposure which do exist as well as with the motivations for seeing, reading, and listening. As in the case of public opinion measurement, there is a considerable body of literature on the technical aspects of audience research; and as in that case, we have not attempted to represent such technical matters here.

The first selection on audience research presents on overview of the field by one of the major research figures in it. In this selection, Lazarsfeld links the problems of audience research with the general field of social psychology. This is followed by Waples' report on his study of the effects of accessibility upon communication exposure, a study which highlights the importance of this factor in determining exposure. Finally, there is the detailed case study by Herzog of the audience for the radio daytime serial; through a series of comparisons of listeners and non-listeners, she attempts to analyze the motives for exposure to this type of material.

Paul F. Lazarsfeld

AUDIENCE RESEARCH

The efforts to determine how many people read a magazine or how many listen to a radio program are historically linked with applied psychology. The first systematic readership survey was done by George Gallup when he was teaching psychology in Iowa and the first systematic work in radio measurement was carried out by two Ohio psychologists, Lumley and Stanton. Since then, more and more precise methods of measurement have been developed and a large mass of substantive results has been accumulated. It would be safe to say that there is now hardly an area of social behavior for which we have more copious and more exact information.[1]

It is worth while to reflect for a moment on the reasons why so much attention is given to a topic which does not seem of too great general importance. The explanation lies in the curious economic structure of the communications industry, which must serve two masters while other industries serve only one. If a soap manufacturer wants to make a profit he has to be sure that people buy his soap. If a broadcaster wants to make money he has to be sure that people listen to his programs, but he must also prove this fact to the soap manufacturer or the latter will not advertise over his station. Added to this is the fact that strong competition between the various media makes it doubly necessary to prove the size of the audience by a variety of very fine measurements. (In line with general practice this paper applies the term audience to radio, magazines, and newspapers, as well as to movies.)

Detailed consideration cannot be given here to problems of measurement, but one case might serve to show the complexity of the field. The earliest measurement figures available for magazines were provided by the Audit Bureau of Circulation (ABC). The ABC is co-operative venture

Reprinted from "Communication Research," in *Current Trends in Social Psychology* (1949), pp. 233-48, by permission of the author and the publisher. (Copyright, 1949, by the University of Pittsburgh Press.)

[1] Blankenship, A. B., editor, *How to Conduct Consumer and Opinion Research*, New York, Harper's, 1946.

which established complicated machinery to obtain reliable statistics on the number of copies each issue of a magazine sells. After some time it became apparent that mere circulation figures were not sufficient because one magazine was being read by a number of people. Ways were devised, therefore, to count the number of readers instead of the number of copies sold, and magazines were then grouped according to the number of readers they have per copy. But now the question arose of what a reader is. Is a person who just glances at a copy to be classed as a reader, or one who reads five items, or fifteen items, in an issue? It became necessary to find out which items and how many items in an issue people have read. This in turn led to further methodological difficulties. If a magazine, for instance, carried a serial story in several installments, how could one be sure that the people who were interviewed did not confuse one installment with another? Special "confusion tests" were developed to examine this factor of memory.

In this respect radio research had a special advantage. The memory factor could be eliminated by inserting a mechanical device in the radio set which would record the stations to which the radio was tuned. At the present time, magazine researchers are experimenting with chemicals by which one could measure the amount of time a magazine was open at a particular page and thereby exposed to light. There is, however, even a further difficulty which arises. It may be that people are more influenced by the advertising in a magazine if it is strongly identified with the magazine content. Therefore, one must discover the type of content and the balance of content which people prefer.

A similar development took place in research in the other mass media. It requires a two-term course to teach and discuss all the techniques of audience measurement. In the present discussion we shall be mainly interested in the findings which these audience surveys have brought about rather than in the technical problems of measurement. Efforts will be made to organize the research results around such generalizations as might be of interest to a social psychologist, or as might require his helpful interpretation or indicate new areas of research to him.

The criteria of classification of the audiences of the various media can be roughly divided into three parts. One is based on what is usually called *primary* characteristics, such as sex, age, education, and economic level. The second group might be called *psychological* characteristics which are based on scores of personality tests, or attitudes on a variety of issues, and the like. Finally, people can be classified by their other *"communication habits"* and by this means we can compare, for instance, the reading habits of people with their listening habits.

Primary Characteristics of Various Audiences

One must distinguish between the printed media and the spectator media. Obviously the audience of the former need a certain amount of reading skill, but practically everyone can be part of a radio or movie audience. We would expect, therefore, to find rather sharp correlations between magazine reading and formal education. Varying somewhat according to the types of questions asked, it can be said that about two-thirds of the population read magazines with some regularity. The following table shows how this frequency varies among three educational levels.[2]

TABLE I—Proportion of Magazine Readers in Three Educational Groups as Reported by Two Studies (NORC Survey and Magazine Audience Bureau)

	NORC	MAB
College	86%	92%
High School	68	85
Less Than High School	43	48

Other studies have used more specific indices, such as the number and types of magazines read, with education always playing the expected dominant role.

When radio entered the scene, many educators took the optimistic view that this situation might be corrected with the new medium. All the people who, due to social circumstances, could not acquire much formal reading skill, would now quench their thirst for knowledge by listening to educational radio programs. This expectation was not fulfilled. All subsequent research studies have shown that listening to serious programs is also highly related to education. The following table is based on a survey in which

TABLE II—Proportion of Respondents Picking the Two Types of Programs among Their Favorites

	Public Affairs		Classical Music	
	1945	1947	1945	1947
College	55%	63%	54%	54%
High School	40	43	32	27
Less Than High School	33	35	21	22

people were asked to select their favorite radio programs from a long list. Taking public affairs discussions and classical music as the most typical representatives of serious programs we can see here how the popularity

[2] Lazarsfeld, Paul, and Wynant, R., "Magazines in 90 Cities: Who Reads What," *Public Opinion Quarterly*, 1937, 4: 29-41.

of such fare increases with increased education. To indicate the reliability of these results, two national NORC samples taken at two different times are reported.

At least two lines of interpretation seem indicated. People with little formal education lack reading skill but they probably also do not have what might be called "conception skill"; they are not likely to be found in the audience for serious subject matter even if listening alone is required. In regard to classical music an added sociological element may be involved. In the so-called higher economic strata respect for good music and similar matter is imbued with prestige; there are pressures and rewards operating to make people listen to, and perhaps in the end to like, good music. The same is not true for the less educated low-income groups.

Obviously, this field is open for the social psychologist to develop more refined interpretations. Deviant cases would be one important avenue of further study. There are many people who do not follow the trend and in spite of little formal education are very much interested in serious radio programs. Only a very few beginnings in studying these exceptions have been made thus far and a detailed examination would be very desirable.

This matter is of considerable cultural importance. Documentary films and serious radio programs could do a great deal to raise the cultural level of a country if people could become more interested in them. But we must determine how we can overcome the resistance of just those groups which are most recalcitrant and which the educators most want to reach. We cannot do like the early Tudor king who, wanting his subjects to read one of his theoretical tracts, made arrangements with the Catholic Church to grant indulgences to the readers. Today psychological research must somehow deal with the problem of reaching the lower educated strata through the use of the new forms of mass education which the spectator media have developed.

While the relation between education and communication habits is probably more significant socially, the role of age is statistically more spectacular. Wherever it is possible to classify an item as light entertainment, studies show that its audience will be heavily drawn from the younger age groups. The following table provides two examples of age differentials in

TABLE III—Proportion of People for Whom Popular Music is a Favorite Radio Program and Who Go to the Movies at Least Once a Week

	Popular Music		Movie Attendance	
Age	1945	1947	1945	1947
21-29	72%	62%	48%	39%
30-39	50	52	28	25
40-49	41	47	27	21
50+	22	26	13	23

audiences of such light fare. The first two columns give the proportion in each age group which chooses popular music' as one of its favorite types of radio program. The third column represents the proportion claiming at least once-a-week movie attendance. The data are from the two NORC surveys mentioned above.

It is probable that something akin to "vitality" plays a part in the younger age group's preference for popular music. When it comes to movies, another factor—that of the generally different type of social life indulged in by different age groups—must be added.

Additional findings corroborate the age differential still further. All studies show a clear negative correlation between youth and interest in public affairs, young people being less concerned. The results of magazine research have not been compiled in a manner that makes for easy comparison, but again all the indications seem to be that, with increased age, interest tends to shift from lighter fiction to heavier nonfiction subject-matter.

Whatever the explanation of these differentials, we have here again an area where the results of communication research can be of concrete value to the social psychologist. There are few data available to him as highly related to age as these, and his investigation of various age-phases might be greatly enhanced by their incorporation.

A third primary characteristic, the difference between men and women, is also of significance. In the case of all media, women show considerably less interest in public affairs. Women in the main read fiction in magazines while men are much more inclined to read nonfictional material. Women, of course, also provide the vast majority of the daytime radio audience. As a result, radio during the day has developed a large supply of programs especially addressed to women, such as daytime serials, woman commentators, and home economics programs. It is interesting to speculate on the possibility that daytime radio tends to reinforce the difference in the interests of men and women which the social and economic structure of our society has developed.[3]

One further primary characteristic has been studied in considerable detail, the difference between urban and rural dwellers. For many years, Professor Whan of Manhattan College, Kansas, and Professor Summers of Ohio State University have made periodic surveys in a number of Midwestern states in which they compare radio listening habits of farmers and urbanites. Unfortunately the results have not been summarized for general

[3] The Advertising Research Foundation, *The Continuing Study of Newspaper Reading*, 1945. *Life*, "Continuing Study of Magazine Audiences," Reports, 6 and 8. Beville, H. M., Jr., "The ABCD's of Radio Audiences," *Public Opinion Quarterly*, 1940, 4: 195-206. Lazarsfeld, Paul, "Audience Research in the Movie Field," *The Annals of the American Academy of Political and Social Science*, 1947.

publication but the authors' reports are available to students especially interested in this aspect of the problem.

Personality Characteristics

On several occasions efforts have been made to determine the relation of personality characteristics to communication patterns, and this again is an area capable of great expansion by the psychologist. The study of daytime serial audiences is an example of the interesting beginning that has been made. About half of the women at home during the day are avid fans of these descriptions of people in everyday life eternally getting into trouble, getting out of trouble, and immediately getting into trouble again. The other half of the available female audience dislike these programs as much as their friends are absorbed by them. Great efforts have been made to discover what psychological differences exist between those who do and those who do not listen to the serials. Are the fans more introverted and therefore more likely to live in a world of fantasy rather than of fact? Are they much more frustrated, more dissatisfied with their life? Are they less attractive and therefore more isolated socially? At one time or another every conceivable personality test has been applied to these two types of women. The results so far have been disappointing, but this does not mean that eventually a valid psychological explanation will not be found.

A similar effort was made at the time when the Orson Welles' broadcast on the invasion from Mars drove thousands of people into panic and flight from their homes.[4] Listeners who became frightened were compared with listeners who had the presence of mind to check and who found that the story of the invasion was merely a dramatic play. Thematic apperception tests were given to the two groups of listeners following the hypothesis that the degree of general excitability would be related to the two types of reaction. Again the results were negative, but again it is not a closed chapter.

Nearest to a finding of passable caliber emerged from a comparison of women who do and do not listen to the radio while at home in the morning. In one study the women who did not listen while they did their housework stated quite definitely that "it is difficult to do two things at one time," revealing that they had so-called "one-track minds." Obviously it requires further investigation to state clearly what the psychological characteristics of such mentalities are.

In general, there seems to be practically no correlation between personality characteristics and communication habits, and it is necessary to

[4] Cantril, H., Gaudet, H., and Herzog, H., *Invasion from Mars*, Princeton, Princeton, University Press, 1940.

speculate on this fact. It might well be that the notion of "interest" is less of a psychological category than we usually assume. Perhaps what a person is interested in does not depend on his personality but on his position in the social system. People are interested in the things which the groups to which they belong believe to be worth while. Group stratification in our society is along economic, educational, sex, and age lines; so perhaps it is not surprising that these *primary* characteristics are related to a greater degree to communication habits than are personality traits.

There are additional factors which help explain this low relationship of communication habits and personality traits. In all the fields that have been touched by communication research the self-selection of audiences plays a considerable role. People with political convictions read the newspapers that correspond to their opinions. People with hobbies read the sections of the newspaper which report on these hobbies most fully. This seemingly trivial observation becomes more interesting as we add to it certain corollary findings which can be gleaned from a variety of studies. It has been found, for instance, that people are inclined to read the same news items in newspapers which they have already heard discussed on the radio. In general, they do not look for information on new topics in magazines but for more information on topics with which they are already acquainted. When a magazine or radio program occasionally has the purpose of telling of the contributions of a specific minority to American culture, a large proportion of the audience usually consists of the minority which is being praised. The audience to which the content is being directed and which presumably needs conversion is largely missing.[5]

If we accept the overwhelming evidence of the self-selectiveness and circular reinforcement of audiences we may go a step further to indicate an important element in this selection. In the further examination of such data the student is struck by a strong projective factor in audience behavior. When people are asked to name their favorite movie stars, the majority of men mention actors and the majority of women select actresses. Detailed studies of the readers of magazine stories have shown a distinct conformity between the content of the story and the structure of the audience. If the story is set in a small town more people coming from small towns will read it. The average age of readers varies markedly and is parallel to the age of the hero. Pictures of men in printed media are more often noticed by men, while women are more likely to look at pictures of women.

In general, then, people look not for new experiences in the mass media but for a repetition and an elaboration of their old experiences into which they can more easily project themselves. If we assume then that the types

[5] Lazarsfeld, Paul, *Radio and the Printed Page*, New York, Duell, Sloan and Pearce, 1940.

of experience they have had are determined more by their social roles and context rather than by their psychological traits, it is not surprising that we find primary characteristics so dominant in the correlations which communications research has unearthed.

It should be noticed, however, that this general consideration calls for refinement by the social psychologist. For one thing, not even these correlations are very high and the exceptions deserve a great deal of consideration. It would not be difficult to pick out people who prefer subject matter which complements rather than projects their own experiences. How do such supplementary interests develop, and in what type of people do they occur? There are numerous people who lack formal education, who live in very uninspiring environments, and who still are awakened through some medium of mass communication to develop strong educational interests of their own. A detailed study of the exceptions to all the findings reported here, if guided by available knowledge and general theoretical consideration, should greatly advance the field which the communications researchers have recently opened up.

In the second place, the problem has not been solved when we say that the social role rather than the psychological characteristics of individuals determine their communication habits. This is an oversimplification of the matter, since the fact remains that individuals partly select their social roles. The interaction between what we have distinguished as primary and psychological characteristics is another part of the field where the social psychologist could be of help.

Interrelation between Various Kinds of Audience Behavior

It is not surprising that people who do not read magazines also do not read books, for reading skill is required in both activities. But even if education and similar factors are kept constant, many marked relationships remain. A list of examples would read as follows:

People who listen to news commentators on the radio are also more likely to read news magazines and, in smaller towns, to subscribe to the Sunday edition of metropolitan newspapers.

People who read the more serious type of magazine are also more likely to listen to the more serious type of radio program.

Women who listen a great deal to the radio during the day also listen more during the evening.

Women who are interested in the "true fiction" type of magazine are also more interested in daytime serials and prefer the romantic type of movies.

People who never go to the movies at all are also likely to listen less to the radio.

If a book has been turned into a movie the people who have read the book are more likely to see the movie and vice versa.

Some of these findings might sound obvious, but a rather important generalization can be derived from them. On mere speculative grounds one might assume that the mass media have to compete for audiences. If a person listens continuously to radio news his interest might be satisfied and he would not be available as a reader of a news magazine. But as an over-all fact, the opposite seems to prevail. One medium benefits by the interests which another medium stimulates. This mutually compensatory character of the mass media has a number of interesting social implications which have occasionally been discussed in the literature.[6]

From a psychological point of view the examples just given suggest strongly the application of factor analysis to communication behavior. A few preliminary studies make it appear quite likely that a number of basic factors could be found. One is likely to be a rather general element related to whether a person is more interested in individualized activities or more inclined to matters requiring mass participation. Another is the factor of general "seriousness," which determines whether a person is mainly interested in fiction material or is inclined to read and listen to such things as public affairs, popular science, biography, and so on. In radio there seems to be the tendency for those who are interested in music not to be interested in verbal programs, and vice versa. All this, however, is still very much a matter of speculation, because unfortunately little work has yet been done.[7]

One might, in this context, include also the relation between supply and demand in the mass media. It is by no means true that people have definite desires and pick out what they "need" from the available supply of programs, magazines, and so on. It seems rather that the supply itself *creates* the demand. There exist interesting findings, for instance, on the importance of availability of the communication in determining the size of its audience. In one study, Waples ascertained what books students were interested in and then put the less desired ones within easy reach in the dormitory, while the books which the students had designated as more attractive were placed at some distance. In general, the student tended to read the books which were easily available.[8]

Similar observations have been made by broadcasters. Every radio program has a certain "rating" indicating the proportion of radio sets that are tuned in to it. A similar rating can be derived for a certain time spot: the proportion of radio sets which are tuned in at a given hour of the day.

[6] Beville, H. M., Jr., "The Challenge of the New Media-Television, F. M., and Facsimile," *Journalism Quarterly*, 1948, 25: 3-11.

[7] Robinson, W. S., "Preliminary Report on Factors in Radio Listening," *Journal of Applied Psychology*, 1939, 23.

[8] Waples, D., and Tyler, R. W., *What People Want to Read About: A Study of Group Interests and a Survey of Problems in Adult Reading*, Chicago, American Library Association and the University of Chicago Press.

In a stable radio schedule it is of course not possible to unravel what part in a specific rating is played by the attraction of the program as against the role of daily listening habits. But sometimes a program is transferred to another time and then the change in rating can be used to weigh the importance of the two factors. The general finding is that on the average the time spot is more important than the content of the program itself, although there are some notable exceptions. Social psychologists might find such data worthy of their more careful attention.

Altogether, in fact, social psychologists might find it worth while to give more attention to the statistical data which the radio industry can offer in this respect. It is possible, for instance, to take a certain program type such as the quiz program and count the number of hours weekly such programs are offered. We also know the approximate number of people who listen to them. By a time-series analysis one could study how change in supply and change in extent of listening are related. In some preliminary calculations, Rashevsky has come to expect a certain regularity of changes in supply and demand which seems to be justified by the facts.[9]

The whole topic is of special importance for one who is interested in using the mass media for mass education. The argument against more serious movies and broadcasts is usually that people don't want them. The counterargument is that if more of them were available more people would develop an interest in them. In England there is more listening to serious programs than in America. Is this due to a national difference or to the fact that the British broadcasting system provides serious programs more systematically? If the latter is the case, then an important social question can be raised. Could we get in this country a more serious level of listening if the broadcasters considered "raising the level of taste" one of their responsibilities? The social scientist could provide important data by systematic experimentation.

It was mentioned before that lower educated people do not like to listen to serious programs even if all efforts are made by dramatizations and other techniques to make them easily understandable. Suppose under some pretext we were to pay lower educated subjects to listen to a list of such programs for three months. After this experimental period was over, we could watch to see how many would keep on listening to some of these programs of their own free will. If after overcoming their initial resistance, the people who need radio education most would really acquire a taste for it, an important argument would be made in favor of those who desire a more serious program schedule.

[9] Rashevsky, N., *Mathematical Theory of Human Relations.* Mathematical Biophysics Monograph No. 3, Principia Press, Bloomington, Indiana.

Douglas Waples

THE RELATION OF SUBJECT INTEREST
TO ACTUAL READING

The relationship between actual reading and the subjects of most interest was studied with reference to a population of employees of a Chicago textile factory and the students of the University of Chicago. Four types of data were obtained from the factory workers, namely, ratings of subjects for reading interest, checks to show what newspaper items had been read, diaries to record magazine reading, and lists of books read during two periods of two weeks each. Two types of data were obtained from the college groups: ratings on subject interest and checks on a list of non-fiction books to show which had been read. Data on book-reading were obtained from college students because returns from the factory workers on book-reading were inadequate.

Such data make it possible to compare the subjects of most interest to these groups with the subjects most and least read about in newspapers, magazines, and books—all three, or with the subjects read about in each type of publication separately. The comparisons also show how much material on the various subjects each type of publication contains.

Amount of reading.—The relative amounts of reading on particular subjects will be shown later in connection with the readers' interests in the subjects. At this point, Table I is presented to show the gross amounts of reading reported by each sex in each type of publication for the two periods studied.

These figures agree closely with the reports of previous investigators. The reader will note that about 90 per cent of the total reading by these factory workers is confined to the daily press. The remaining 10 per cent is divided between magazine reading and book-reading. The men read more in books and the women more in magazines. In all sources combined, the men read more than the women.

Reprinted from *The Library Quarterly*, Vol. II (1932), pp. 54-58, 65-70, by permission of the author and the Graduate Library School, University of Chicago.

The table is important if only to show the necessity for studying reading in newspapers and magazines in any attempt to describe the reading of the industrial population. Reading studies, based on library records and other data restricted largely to books, may be wholly misleading.

TABLE I—Average Number of Thousand Words Read per Week by Factory Workers in Different Sources

(August, 1930, and March, 1931)

Source	Men	Percentage of Total	Women	Percentage of Total
Non-fiction books				
1930	5	...	6	...
1931	14	...	(No non-fiction)	...
Both	19	6.4	6	2.9
Non-fiction magazine articles				
1930	5	...	7	...
1931	3	...	8	...
Both	8	2.7	15	7.1
Newspapers				
1930	91	...	24	...
1931	178	...	165	...
Both	269	90.9	189	90.0
Total reading				
1930	101	...	37	...
1931	195	...	173	...
Both	296	100	210	100

Reading versus interests.—The relation between the subject interests and the actual reading of the factory groups is most clearly and accurately conveyed by the coefficients of correlation contained in the first column of Table II. For the non-statistical reader it may be remarked that the closer a correlation is to 1.00, the closer the correspondence of actual reading with reading interest.

TABLE II—Relationships Between Subject Interests and Actual Reading, Shown by Coefficients of Correlation

	r	P.E.
Factory women:		
Newspaper reading versus subject interest	.003	.062
Magazine reading versus subject interest	.251	.058
Composite reading versus subject interest	.025	.062
Subject interest (August, 1930) versus subject interest (March, 1931). $r = .80 \pm .022$		
Factory men:		
Newspaper reading versus subject interest	.131	.061
Magazine reading versus subject interest	.049	.062
Composite reading versus subject interest	.136	.061
Subject interest (August, 1930) versus subject interest (March, 1931). $r = .81 \pm .021$		

It will be noted that the coefficients in the table are with one exception either zero or nearly zero. This means that there is only a very slight tendency for the factory workers to read more on the subjects of most interest than on the subjects of least interest. The exception is the correlation between magazine reading and subjects of interest to the factory women. It appears that women find more material on subjects of interest to them in the magazines they read than either women or men find in any other type of reading. Yet even in magazines the women's subject interests are expressed only to a very slight degree.

Newspaper reading, space, and subject interest.—It has already been shown in Table I that newspapers constitute 90 per cent of the reading by these groups and in Table II that what is read about in newspapers has only a chance relationship to the subject of most interest ($r = .003$ for the women and .131 for the men). Yet the relationship between actual reading on different subjects and space devoted to the subjects is marked. For men the correlation is .857 and for women .800. Evidently the men's reading is slightly more influenced by relative space than the women's. It is therefore important to know the relation between the amount of space given to the various subjects and the relative appeal of the subjects to the given readers. This relationship, as one might expect, is low. The correlations between space and subject interest are, for men, .173; and for women, − .018.

The relative amount of space given to the subjects in which the factory workers had previously expressed their reading interests was determined by counting the column inches devoted to each subject in each of the morning and evening newspapers read by the group during the two days of the test. The results of this count show that only four of the twenty-three most interesting subjects receive as much as fifty column inches in both issues of the newspapers examined. Another twelve of the twenty-three most interesting subjects received less than fifty column inches. Another four received less than five column inches. The remaining three did not appear at all.

Yet the four most interesting subjects that receive fifty inches or more are all among the subjects which the men read most about in the newspapers. Only one subject of major interest to women received fifty inches, but this one is among the subjects also most read about by women. Thus, *the most interesting subjects are all among the subjects most read about when they receive considerable space.*

How much reading is done on *uninteresting* subjects that receive large amounts of space? Of the 117 subjects on which interest ratings were obtained, only 20 received as much as fifty inches, or enough space in the two issues of the six papers to be conspicuous. Of the 20 subjects, 18 occur among the 23 subjects on which most newspaper reading is done by men and 15 occur among the 23 subjects on which women read most. Of the 18 subjects most read about by men, 8 have less than average interest and 10 have more than average interest. Of the 15 subjects most read about by women, 9 have less than average interest and only 6 have more than average interest.

It thus appears that both men and women read on any subject that receives large space. This is consistent with what anyone knows from his personal experience in reading newspapers; because they are unavoidable one reads or skims the items that receive large amounts of space with small regard to the subjects treated.

Returns on a check-list of book titles were obtained from twenty odd groups of students on the University of Chicago campus. The groups were formed with reference to sex, college year, field of specialization for senior college and graduate students, and other differences such as intelligence, parents' schooling, race, place of residence, and scholastic standing. An entirely typical group, for the present illustration, is a group composed of Freshmen girls. This group is properly sampled by the 71 individuals making returns, since, when the 71 scores for subject interest are divided at random and the two halves are correlated, the coefficient is $.90 \pm .012$. The reliability coefficient of the scores on actual reading, similarly obtained, is $.758 \pm .048$.

When the subject scores of the Freshmen girls were compared with the scores for actual reading, the result was much the same as for the factory workers; there was no more relationship than might result from mere chance. In fact, for the Freshmen girls, there is a slight tendency to do more reading in non-fiction books on uninteresting subjects than on interesting subjects, since the coefficient of correlation is negative $(r = -.117)$.

To see what effect on this relationship might be due to differences in the "readability" of the books, the list of 124 titles was reduced by omitting those that are written in a style that is technical, or difficult for any other reason. The number of titles thus omitted was 74, reducing the list to 50 titles attractively written and reducing the number of subjects from 62 to 34. When the interest scores on the 34 subjects were correlated with the reading scores based on the attractively written books, the coefficient rose from $-.117$ to $+.334$. The important influence of "readability" upon the relation of subject interest and actual reading is thus apparent. When the books are equally readable, more reading is done on the subjects of most interest.

While the relationship between subject interest and actual reading in non-fiction books is positive and significant when differences in "readability" are minimized, a coefficient of .334 is still a long way from perfect correspondence. That is to say, the difference between this coefficient and the highest one our reliabilities would permit (about .80) shows clearly the presence of other variable factors in the situation.

One such factor that can safely be assumed on the basis of data presented is accessibility. This we have seen to be highly influential in its effects upon reading in newspapers and magazines. We do not know the relative accessibility to the given students of the books on the non-fiction check-list. If we did, we could determine the correspondence between subject interest and book-reading when the readers' selection is confined to books that are both readable and accessible. Data are being collected to this end which should certainly establish a closer correspondence between subject interest and actual reading than .334, the relationship which exists when the books actually read differ widely in their accessibility to the group as a whole.

The foregoing evidence on student reading in non-fiction books thus supports the assumptions made at the outset to explain the consistency of data on book-reading and the data on reading in newspapers and magazines as related to subject interest. The relationship is scant because attractively written material on the preferred subjects is not readily accessible to the readers.

Taken as a whole, the contents of these tables support the general finding that no significantly positive relationship exists between the subjects of most interest and the subjects on which the industrial groups do most reading. The interpretations supplied in this paper, however, go beyond this fact to conditions that help to explain it. They suggest very plainly what every librarian knows, namely, (1) that accessibility, whether represented by space in the given newspapers, or selection of magazines, or availability of books, is perhaps the most important single influence upon actual reading, except for readers in highly specialized fields who will take any amount of trouble to obtain an important reference; (2) that "readability" is the next important influence, and (3) that accessibility and readability in combination virtually determine what the general reader reads.

What every librarian does not know, and what has probably not been demonstrated before in equally objective terms, is that so small a proportion of the "readable" printed matter available to the American citizen is concerned with the particular questions upon which he most wants to read. It is altogether probable that this condition applies to the half of the total adult population that has been estimated to read little but newspapers. If so, the publisher, librarian, book dealer, or teacher who brings interesting and trustworthy reading on the desired subjects within easy reach of the multitude will deserve well of his country. The possibilities of this achievement obviously depend upon such further studies as may furnish group standards for "readability" and "accessibility" that the publisher and librarian may put to practical use.

Herta Herzog

WHAT DO WE REALLY KNOW
ABOUT DAY-TIME SERIAL LISTENERS?

This is the day of mass audiences. And commanding one of the largest of these is the radio daytime serial. At least twenty million women in this country keep a regular rendezvous with these serials. Small wonder, then, that this type of program has been the occasion for heated, though not always illuminating, discussion. If only because such a large sector of our population is devoted to the daytime serial, it receives and requires detailed study.

From the standpoint of social research, we should like to know the effects of these serials upon the women who have for years listened to them regularly. And yet, we should not expect a simple conclusive result. Unlike a single concerted campaign, with effects which can be measured by modern devices of social research, the putative influences of the serial have developed through slow accretions. Consequently, they are difficult to determine. Only by piecing together a variety of materials through a process of continued observation and careful interpretation can we trace these effects.

Three sources of information must be examined before we can consider the effects of daytime serials. We must first obtain systematic knowledge of their content. This cannot be learned through incidental listening. Indeed, not even the writing or production of these serials necessarily equips one to discern the peculiar character and structure of these programs. This cannot, so to speak, be perceived by the naked eye. A content analysis, such as that reported by Rudolf Arnheim,[1] is an initial step toward better perception. Even more exacting studies of variations in type are required.

A second approach is the comparative study of listeners and non-lis-

Reprinted from *Radio Research*, 1942-43 (1943), pp. 3-23, by permission of the author and the copyright holders. (Copyright, 1943, by Paul Lazarsfeld and Frank Stanton.)

[1] Arnheim, Rudolph, "The World of the Daytime Serial," *Radio Research, 1942-43*, pp. 34-85.

teners: a type of analysis which is often heir to fallacies. Consider, for example, the studies which demonstrate that delinquent children go to the movies more frequently than non-delinquents. Which is cause and which effect? Yet such comparisons are indispensable for a fuller understanding of the problem.

And thirdly, a close study of listeners themselves brings us nearer to our goal. What satisfactions do listeners say they derive from daytime serials? As psychologists, what is our judgment on these assertions? Do their remarks, interpreted in terms of general psychological knowledge, enable us to explain their devotion to the serials?

In addition to content analyses, then, we wish to examine the structure of the audience and the gratifications derived from daytime serials. This article is devoted to a survey of current knowledge about these listeners.

As a guide for our analyses, we advance the following speculations on likely differences between listeners and non-listeners to daytime serials.

(1) It might well be that women who are somewhat isolated from their community spend more time listening to daytime serials. For one reason or another, they might have difficulties in establishing and maintaining relations with other people. Or, possibly, they may not be acceptable to various social groups. In either case, they might turn more frequently to the enjoyment of serial dramas.

(2) It is also possible that the intellectual range of listeners is not as broad as that of non-listeners. By reason of their upbringing and limited experience, listeners might be unfamiliar with or have fewer opportunities for alternative ways of spending their time. Their interests might be less varied. Thus, having perceived little scope for enjoyment in their immediate environment, they may find in the daytime serials vicarious experiences and interests which they cannot provide for themselves.

(3) Since most serials deal with the experiences of "people like yourselves," they might be especially attractive to those whose interest is mainly directed toward personal problems. Presumably, then, listeners should manifest less awareness of and interest in such public affairs as current events and politics than non-listeners.

(4) Listeners might also be women beset with anxieties and frustrations. The serial might provide solace and compensation for women whose wishes and expectations outran their achievements.

(5) Finally, the listeners and non-listeners might be distinguished by their preference for listening to the radio in general. Perhaps listening to daytime serials is merely a special case of general habituation to a source of so many forms of entertainment.

Other lines of speculation could be developed. But the foregoing can be tested, at least to some extent. Moreover, these five hypothetical factors are obviously not independent. Personality characteristics can account for differences in social participation. Variations in intellectual range can lead to preferences for particular media of communication. Furthermore, several of these factors might simultaneously play a role.

If speculation is to give way to controlled inquiry, if fancy is to defer to fact, we must turn to the available evidence in this field. Our main source material consists of four studies. A nation-wide study, conducted among non-farm women, and study of a cross-section of the Iowa population, furnish precise information on the extent to which women listen to daytime serials. These surveys include data bearing on some of the five hypotheses we have developed. We are fortunate in being able to draw upon a third study conducted among a cross-section of Erie County, Ohio, even though it was directed toward quite different problems. Among the questions asked of respondents in this study were their radio program preferences; consequently, we can discriminate between women who included daytime serials among their favorite programs and those who did not. This enables us to utilize for our present purposes a considerable amount of other information concerning the "listeners" and "non-listeners" is this sample. The fourth study, based on interviews with women in Syracuse, Memphis and Minneapolis, is entirely devoted to material pertinent to our immediate problem. However, the sample in this three-city investigation is so small that only very large differences in attributes of listeners and non-listeners can be considered reliable.

The interweaving of data from these four studies [2] extends our knowledge of daytime serial listeners considerably beyond any previous level and provides a secure basis for further research in this field.

Social Participation

The data at hand do not support the prevalent opinion that daytime serial listeners are more isolated socially than non-listeners. This is evident, for example, from the answers of the 5,325 women in the Iowa study to the following questions:

> How many times (during last two weeks) have you attended church or gone to church affairs?
> How many times (during last two weeks) have you attended other meetings or social gatherings?

[2] The nation-wide study was undertaken under the direction of the Office of Radio Research; the figures are quoted with the permission of Blackett-Sample-Hummert. The Iowa survey was conducted by the Office of Radio Research in co-operation with Prof. F. L. Whan of the University of Wichita, Kansas. The Erie County data are taken from a larger study conducted jointly by the Office of Radio Research and Elmo Roper, Inc. The three-city study was undertaken by the Columbia Broadcasting System and the data are quoted with their permission.

A summary of their answers is recorded in Table I which also includes data on the frequency of motion picture attendance.

TABLE I—Median Number of Participations Reported by Listeners and Non-listeners to Daytime Serials in Iowa

	Median Number of Attendances	
	Listeners*	Non-listeners
Church affairs (during last 2 weeks)	1.54	1.62
Other social gatherings (during last 2 weeks)	0.58	0.74
Movies (during last 4 weeks)	0.58	0.51
Total number of cases	2,545	2,780

* In this and the following tables "listeners" refers to women who listen to daytime serials; "non-listeners" refers to women who do not listen to daytime serials.

These data do not yield significant differences in the frequency of social participation of listeners and non-listeners. This result is corroborated by information on the membership of 300 of the Ohio county women in clubs, lodges or other such organizations. Forty-six per cent of the listeners and 47 per cent of the non-listeners belonged to organizations of this type. Only a small fraction of the total sample participated in discussion- and reading-groups; listeners and non-listeners were represented among these in equal proportions.

The extent of social participation becomes especially significant in time of war. Consequently, a question on their civilian defense activities was asked of women in the three-city study. A third of the women reported participation in such activities and again the percentage was similar for listeners and non-listeners.

Of course, it is possible that social relations have a different psychological significance for listeners than for non-listeners. Or perhaps they participate differently: the listeners may, for example, be less disposed toward leadership in various associations. But questions of this order are more directly related to other aspects of our analysis. So far as *extent* of social participation is concerned, we can conclude, with some assurance, that there is no vacuum in the lives of listeners for which they compensate by turning to daytime serial dramas.

Range of Intellectual Interests

There is more justification for our conjecture on the scope of listeners' intellectual interests. Several indices suggest that the daytime serial listener is somewhat less equipped than the non-listener to provide a wide range of intellectual experiences.

To begin with, there is a definite difference in the extent of formal education. The data show that the proportion of listeners among women who continued their education beyond high school is only about two-thirds of that among women who have not advanced beyond elementary school. Moreover, all four surveys indicate that it is formal education which is pertinent in this regard and not low income (associated with little education) or a relatively younger age-distribution (associated with more formal education).

A glimpse into the same psychological context of limited intellectual interests of listeners is provided by comparing the size of communities in which listeners and non-listeners live. There are about one and a half as many listeners among farm women as among women living in metropolitan areas, with smaller cities intermediate. The larger cities provide a greater variety of entertainment and their populations are, by and large, more aware of a wider range of entertainment and hobbies.[3]

In contrast, listeners and non-listeners do not differ materially in the amount of their reading. Three of our studies which included questions on the number of books, magazines and newspapers read are in complete agreement on that score. Moreover, a specific inquiry in the Ohio county study revealed that listeners and non-listeners utilized the public library to the same extent.

However, there are differences in the type of reading characteristic of listeners and non-listeners. Only the three-city study includes information on the types of books preferred by the two categories of women. One statistically significant difference emerges from this information: listeners more frequently prefer mystery novels and do not prefer historical novels as often as non-listeners.

The 5,325 women interviewed in Iowa provide instructive details on magazine preferences. Most of the magazines read by a very high proportion of the total sample of women are as often read by listeners as by non-listeners. This is true, for example, of *McCall's* or the *Ladies' Home Journal* or the *Woman's Home Companion*, all of which were read by more than 1,000 of the approximately 5,000 women in the sample. It holds also for magazines with a somewhat smaller number of readers in the sample (500-1,000), such as *Good Housekeeping, Better Homes and Gardens, Collier's, Life* or *Look*.[4]

[3] If we compare women on the same economic level who own and who do not own telephones, we find that there is somewhat more reference to serial listening in non-telephone homes. It is probably justified to take telephone ownership as a further index of sophistication. The result, incidentally, is also useful for better evaluation of program ratings. If there is more serial listening in non-telephone homes, most current ratings would underestimate the size of audiences of this type of program.

[4] Of the most popular magazines in the sample, only the *Reader's Digest* appears to be somewhat of an exception. Among its better-educated readers the proportion of serial story listeners is below the average (39 per cent against an average of 46 per cent listeners among women with a high school education or more). For the altogether fewer,

However, some interesting differences between listeners and non-listeners are apparent in the case of several magazines with more restricted circulation among the total Iowa sample. Table II lists magazines, the readers of which listen to daytime serials well above or below the average of all Iowa women.

This table permits us to draw several conclusions. If a magazine is especially preferred by daytime serial listeners, it is one of two types: either its content is notably similar to that of the serial (the "true story") or it centers about home life.

The magazines whose readers listen to daytime serials far less frequently than the average, are all of a more sophisticated or cosmopolitan type, as can be seen from the lower part of Table II.[5]

TABLE II—Magazines with the Highest and the Lowest Proportion of Daytime Serial Listeners among Their Iowa Readers

	Proportion Listening to Daytime Serials	Total No. of Cases
Total sample	48%	5,325
True Confessions	67	82
True Story	66	201
Household	57	416
Parents' Magazine	55	118
Time	33	177
Vogue	31	32
Harper's Magazine	29	52
Mademoiselle	28	74
New Yorker	25	20

However, the data reported in Table II must be viewed in their proper context. None of the magazines listed in this table is widely read by the women in the Iowa sample; consequently, these differences do not in fact

poorly educated readers of the *Digest*, the proportion of serial listeners corresponds to the average among less-educated women.

[5] The results of Table II have been tested to see whether education introduces a spurious element. The appeal of the magazines mentioned is likely to vary for women on different educational levels. The readers of *Household*, for instance, or of *True Story* are likely to be less educated than those of *Harper's*, or the *New Yorker*. Thus it is possible that the high proportion of serial listeners in the first, and the low proportion in the second group of magazines of Table II is due merely to the greater proportion of serial listeners among less-educated women and does not reflect a different appeal for serial and non-serial listeners of comparable education. The proportion of serial listeners in the first group of magazines is above the average for both better- and less-educated women. In the second group of sophisticated magazines, the proportion of less-educated readers is negligible to start with. But even if we study only the better-educated we find that the proportion of serial listeners among the readers of these magazines is below the average proportion of serial listeners among the better-educated women in the total sample.

bulk large in the entire pattern of reading habits of listeners and non-listeners.

Why are women with little formal education more disposed to listen to daytime serials? Partly, we think, because these serials provide the more naive individual with a much-desired, though vicarious, contact with human affairs which the more sophisticated person obtains at first hand through her wider range of experience. Moreover, the serials which abound in arrays of stereotyped characters and situations are less likely to satisfy those who have more discriminating perspectives. Whether the radio serials will serve as a type of psychological mass-education or as stultifying tales of chance, love and illogic depends on their future content. They are undoubtedly a major form of entertainment for the less-educated segment of American women.

Concern with Public Affairs

We can now anticipate to some extent the comparative interest of listeners and non-listeners in current events and politics. Since concern with public affairs is in part a matter of general intellectual interests, we should expect to find that listeners are somewhat laggard in this respect. Yet this tendency should not be marked, for listeners and non-listeners do not differ in the extent of social participation and this too is an aspect of concern with public affairs. In point of fact, our data support these inferences.

Our first index of concern with public affairs is the degree of interest in news programs. Several studies include data on favorite radio programs and from these we can establish the comparative frequency with which listeners and non-listeners include news programs in this preferred category. Table III summarizes our findings in three studies.

TABLE III—Proportion of Listeners and Non-listeners to Daytime Serials Who Mention News Programs among Their Favorite Radio Programs

	Total Number of Women Interviewed	Proportion Mentioning News Programs Among Favorites	
Source		Listeners %	Non-listener %
Nationwide non-farm	4,991	31.7	36.4
Ohio county cross-section	1,500	56.1	54.0
Iowa State cross-section	5,325	79.1	81.0

Listeners and non-listeners do not differ materially or consistently so far as interest in news programs is concerned.[6] This finding is supported by the

---

[6] Differences in the proportions of news-program listeners in the three surveys are largely a result of differences in interviewing techniques. In the Iowa study, respondents

use of another standard index of interest in current events: the reading of out-of-town newspapers.[7] In the Ohio county study, listeners and non-listeners report the same proportion of out-of-town papers in their total newspaper inventory.

The Ohio county material was collected during the presidential campaign of 1940 with the specific purpose of gauging current attitudes toward that political event. Consequently, it provides a substantial basis for the study of listeners' interest in public affairs. Voting in a national election has always been considered a sign of civic consciousness. Table IV shows the proportion of women who, at different phases of the presidential campaign, did not expect to vote and the proportion who actually did not vote.

TABLE IV—Proportion of Listeners and Non-listeners to Daytime Serials in an Ohio County Who Were Prospective and Actual Non-voters at Three Different Interview Periods

| | | Proportion of "Non-Voters" Among: | |
Date of Interview	Total Number of Women Interviewed[8]	Listeners %	Non-listeners %
May 1940	1,500	20.5	18.6
October 1940	600	25.6	20.1
Election Day	300	31.7	18.2

Let us first center the discussion on the women's vote-intention in May, six months before the election and in October, just a few weeks before it. We see that the differences between the two groups of respondents is small and statistically quite insignificant. So far as general interest in the election is concerned, the daytime serial listeners do not lag much behind their non-listener counterparts. Further evidence, of a more introspective nature, bears on this point. Respondents were asked to gauge their own interest in the election. Again, the proportion of non-listeners who claimed "a great

were asked to check *five* types of favorite programs, thus making the frequency of any one type higher than in the other surveys (where respondents were free to check as many as they wished). In the Ohio county study, respondents mentioned an average of three favorite types of program. In the nation-wide survey, the average was only two programs and consequently the frequency with which any one type was mentioned is least. For present purposes, these variations are irrelevant; we are solely concerned with the comparison of figures for listeners and non-listeners *in each survey*.

[7] See P. F. Lazarsfeld, "The Daily Newspaper and Its Competitors," *The Annals of the American Academy of Political and Social Science*, January, 1942, p. 32.

[8] A word of explanation is necessary to account for the fact that different numbers of women are quoted in the text for the Ohio cross-section. The original total of 1,500 women in this sample was carefully divided into five well-matched subgroups of 300 each. Most of these women were re-interviewed at least once during the study, some of them several times. According to the general plan of the study, the number of interviews was different at different phases. The careful matching of the subgroups, however, makes even the smaller groups an unusually good cross-section of the total population in this Ohio county.

deal of interest" is not significantly larger than that of listeners to daytime serials.[9]

When it comes to actual voting, however, we find a larger and statistically significant difference: considerably fewer serial listeners go to the polls (see third line, Table IV). It is not unlikely that psychological factors play more of a role in this connection than a lack of concern with public affairs. Consider certain apposite data. In examining the magazine reading-practices of listeners, we noted that they evidenced more interest in journals dealing with home life. This may reflect a concern with their own personal problems. Much the same preoccupation with private affairs is found among Ohio county listeners. Though they evidence as much general interest as non-listeners in public affairs, they are less active in pursuing these interests. An inventory of activities of the Ohio sample during the presidential campaign indicates that daytime serial listeners less often participated actively in political campaigns to help elect their own candidates. The interpretation of the marked difference in actual voting of listeners and non-listeners should therefore be left pending until we know something more of the personality characteristics of listeners. Before turning to this subject, a general remark is in order.

This study of civic and political activities of women respondents has significant implications, in view of the concern with which political scientists have viewed the comparative indifference to voting exhibited by women in this country. Since women who have for years listened regularly to daytime serials do not show a better voting record—indeed, it may be somewhat worse—than non-listeners of similar formal education, it is evident that these programs have neglected a great public service. By emphasizing, during the pre-election period, the obligation of every American woman to go to the polls, the daytime serials could undoubtedly make a valuable public contribution.[10]

Personality Characteristics

We should preface with a caveat our analysis of two sets of data bearing on characteristic personality traits of listeners. The quantitative measurement of personality traits is still very much in its infancy. All material in this area of research must be viewed with considerable caution.

[9] The table on interest corresponding to Table IV on voting above, reads as follows:

Date of Interview	Total number of women interviewed	Proportion of women expressing "a great deal" of interest in the election	
		Listeners	Non-listeners
May 1940	1,500	20.1%	25.5%
October 1940	600	29.2	34.2

[10] Rudolf Arnheim shows that the serials are inclined to picture government problems in a rather bad light, cf. *op. cit.*

In the Ohio county study, a group of women were repeatedly interviewed by the same persons. After they came to know the interviewees fairly well, the interviewers rated them in terms of a five-point rating scale of personality traits.

An example will serve to clarify the procedure. The rating scale on "assurance" identified the highest level in the following terms: "Extremely sure of self; positive; emphatic; determined; convinced she is absolutely right." The midpoint was described as "Average; moderate conviction but not too positive"; and the lowest level as "Very hesitant, unassured, manner seems to lack conviction; little confidence in own ideas."

The ratings by interviewers were classified separately for listeners and non-listeners, yielding the results reported in Table V.

TABLE V—Distribution of Listeners and Non-listeners to Daytime Serials along a Five-point Scale Rating the Degree of Their Assurance

Degree of Assurance	Listeners %	Non-listeners %
1. (Highest degree)	6.5	4.6
2.	5.6	18.3
3. (Average)	44.0	45.0
4.	32.7	24.5
5. (Lowest degree)	11.2	7.6
Total per cent	100.0	100.0
Total number of cases	107	131

It is evident that there are relatively more non-listeners in the high-assurance sector of the scale. The conventional statistical basis for measuring such a relationship is termed a bi-serial correlation (r), which is similar to a correlation coefficient. If r were equal to zero, it would indicate no relationship between listening and self-assurance. If it were plus 1, it would express the highest degree of positive relationship, indicating that all non-listeners are very sure of themselves and all listeners diffident.

The bi-serial r for our data is .16, which indicates a slight relationship between non-listening and self-assurance. In other words, our interviewers estimated that listeners were somewhat more diffident than non-listeners.[11]

Three other traits, rated in the same fashion, are of interest for our purposes. One of these, "energy," had a bi-serial correlation of .16 with listening to daytime dramas. "Talkativeness," another of these, was found with equal frequency among listeners and non-listeners, the bi-serial correlation being .04. In view of some observations to be made later in this article, it is interesting that the third trait, "emotionality," also showed no relationship

[11] It should be remembered that the interviewers had no interest in and hardly any recollection of the respondents' program preferences. The entire study centered around political subject matter, and the rating scales were filled in about three months after the women had been asked for their program preferences.

with listening, at least on the basis of interviewers' estimates. The lowest degree of emotionality was characterized as "Keen, well-poised, self-controlled, cool-headed; reasoning type"; and the highest degree as "Very emotional, excitable, hot-blooded, high-strung, impatient, volatile; expresses feelings very freely." The bi-serial correlation between emotionality and listening was .02.

These data, then, indicate little difference, if any, between listeners and non-listeners with respect to psychological traits estimated by interviewers who knew the respondents well. The two groups of women do not differ in outward signs of emotionality, but the daytime serial listeners appear to be very slightly less energetic and self-assured.[12]

This largely negative result is corroborated at one point by the way the women feel about themselves. A question which had proved quite revealing in previous studies was used in the Iowa survey.[13] Each of the 5,325 women was asked: "Do you think that you worry more, less or the same as compared with other women?" The results are summarized in the following table:

TABLE VI—Extent of "Worrying" among Listeners and Non-listeners to Daytime Serials

	Listeners %	Non-listeners %
Worries more	15.1	13.8
Worries the same	49.6	44.5
Worries less	21.3	21.8
Don't know	12.4	15.2
Refused to answer	1.6	4.7
Total per cent	100.0	100.0
Total number of cases	2,545	2,780

We see that listeners and non-listeners do not differ significantly in their appraisal of the extent to which they worry. The limited data of the three-city study yielded the same result. The question is probably of greater diagnostic value than its apparent simplicity would suggest. And the results which it affords, though they manifestly require further confirmation, are clear-cut. Listeners to daytime serials are apparently no more beset by anxieties than are women who do not listen to these programs. More detailed investigation of the personality characteristics of listeners and non-listeners is clearly one of the most important lines for future research in this field. It may prove useful to set forth suggestions for such research.

The range and types of outlets and means of relaxation prevalent among

---

[12] The correlations for these two traits are just twice their standard errors.

[13] See for instance, Cantril, Gaudet and Herzog, *The Invasion from Mars*. Princeton University Press, 1939.

listeners and non-listeners should be clarified.[14] Inquiries concerning the frequency of church attendance, participation in social gatherings and movie attendance are obviously only the crudest beginnings of research on personal interests and social participation. For one thing, they all refer to conventional social activities of a rather passive nature. Quite different findings might result from inquiries into hobbies, friendships, interests, etc. Moreover, it is not simply a matter of present activities but also of aspirations. How would the respondent prefer to spend her leisure time? Questions of the following type might be fruitful in this regard: "If you had more time, what would you like to do with it? Would you do the things you are doing now but in a more leisurely and effective way; or is there something else you would prefer to do?"

The emotional structure of daytime serial listeners, with particular respect to the extent and major areas of frustration, requires further investigation. Had the Iowa survey followed the question on anxiety by another on the types of problems with which respondents are preoccupied, it is altogether possible that definite differences between listeners and non-listeners would have been discovered. Further aspects of anxiety should be examined in this connection. What types of anxiety are exhibited? Do respondents worry in a relatively subdued, controlled fashion or do they surrender to acute neurotic anxieties? Information on the scope of goals and the disparity between goals and accomplishments is also needed. This could be elicited by questions of the following type: "What three things are you most proud of? What three things would you most like to have?" The specific areas of frustration could be ascertained by questions of this kind: "Do you feel that for the most part other people have been kind, indifferent or unfriendly to you? Do you feel that your family has been advancing, stagnating or declining? In what ways, if any, would you like your husband or children to be different from what they are?" These questions are deliberately undefined in some respects, to provide scope for personal projections by the respondent. The degree and type of anxieties could be more elaborately measured by such psychological tests as the psycho-neurotic inventory or the so-called projection tests. In addition to determination of respondents' problems it will be necessary to discover as well the means which they have for coping with them. Are they resigned to their situation, or do they suppose that "problems will settle themselves," or do they actively seek definite solutions? How do they go about it? What are their main sources of guidance and advice?

Obviously, materials of this type can be interpreted only after the primary characteristics of respondents have been controlled. In this connec-

[14] For suggestions on the types of characteristics to be studied among daytime serial listeners, the writer is indebted to Dr. Rosalind Gould.

tion, we should note a peculiar role played by formal education. In some of our data, it appeared that differences between listeners and non-listeners are somewhat more marked among well-educated than among less-educated women. If a woman listens extensively to daytime serials although her education gives her access to a wider range of alternative experiences, then she exhibits the "typical" characteristics of the serial listener in a more pronounced fashion than the listener with relatively little education. This indicates that comparisons of the personality characteristic of listeners and non-listeners might fruitfully begin with better-educated women.

Media of Communication: Preferences and Practices

The most conspicuous differences between listeners and non-listeners appears in their general attitude toward radio. On this point the evidence is ample. Of course, daytime serial addicts listen to the radio considerably more during the day than non-listeners to daytime serials. However, the same pattern of amount of listening is also true for the evening. After the serial devotee has listened to numerous stories during the day, she continues to listen 2.43 hours during an average weekday evening whereas the woman who does not listen to daytime serials spends only 2.15 hours during the evening with the radio. Serial devotees indicate that they can be found listening to the radio at 10:00 P.M. an average of four evenings a week; non-listeners report only half as many late evenings at the radio.

Even more marked are differences of the two groups with respect to general preferences for various media of communication. In the Ohio county study, women were asked: "Where do you think you will get most of your information about issues and candidates in the coming presidential election?" The following table compares the answers of listeners and non-listeners interviewed in October 1940.

TABLE VII—Source of Political Information for Listeners and Non-listeners to Daytime Serials

Source of Information on Election	Listeners %	Non-listeners %
Radio	40.2	33.3
Newspapers and magazines	32.4	41.7
Friends and relatives	25.4	22.0
Public speakers and newsreels	2.0	3.0
Total per cent	100.0	100.0
Total number of cases	299	363

For the listeners, the radio is more important than newspapers, the contrary being true for non-listeners.

At this point we should examine the possibility that our analysis is misleading. It is well known from other studies that women with little educa-

tion are more likely to turn to the radio than to the newspaper for information and entertainment.[15] As we have seen that less-educated women are
also more likely to listen to daytime serials, the preceding table might simply record the spurious effect of education which could account both for
serial listening and for media preference. A more detailed analysis, however, shows that this is not the case. The preference for radio as a source
of information is greater for daytime serial listeners on all levels of education.

This finding is further corroborated by the three-city study. Not only do
serial listeners prefer the radio to newspapers as a source of news, but they
are also less critical of radio in many other respects than are women who
do not listen to serials. The most conspicuous result along these lines is so
marked that it becomes statistically significant, although this part of the
study deals with only 212 women. Respondents were asked to agree or disagree with the following statement: "Too many commercials are in bad
taste, speak of stomach disorders, decaying teeth and other distasteful subjects." Sixty-eight per cent of the non-listeners endorsed this statement in
contrast to only 37 per cent of the serial listeners.

This general radio-mindedness of daytime serial listeners reconciles two
final items of information which might otherwise have seemed contradictory. There are two university radio stations in Iowa which broadcast rather
"highbrow" programs. The difference in intellectual range of listeners and
non-listeners would lead us to expect the former to be considerably less
interested in these educational stations. In fact, the difference is negligible
(31 per cent of serial listeners and 34 per cent of non-listeners tune in these
stations). Apparently if it is the radio which presents somewhat alien subject matter, the daytime serial listeners are willing to accept it. On the other
hand, when asked to indicate the parts of the newspaper which they read,
serial listeners express less interest in editorial and current news items, even
though, as we have seen, they are as interested as non-listeners in such news
when it comes to them over the radio. In any appraisal of serial listeners,
then, their radio-mindedness must be considered a major factor.

[15] See P. F. Lazarsfeld, *Radio and the Printed Page*, Duell, Sloan and Pearce, New
York, 1941, Chapters I and IV.

International Communication

Recent technological advances, particularly in radio, have greatly expanded the scope of international communication to mass audiences. Hitherto, consideration of this field was often limited to wartime propaganda designed directly for military objectives. Now, however, because of the technical capacity to communicate across international boundaries, entire populations are considered to be appropriate audiences for international communications and almost all nations are undertaking to wage psychological peacefare as well as warfare. The objective of "peoples speaking to peoples" is not always met; usually it is governments speaking to peoples and on occasion even governments speaking to governments through public channels.

Because of the potentiality of international communication to preserve peace and to build a world community, more and more attention is being given to the technical, political, psychological, and ethical problems involved in informing and persuading audiences which are foreign to the communicating agency. A substantive review of the role which international communications play on the world scene is presented in the essay by Angell. Diagnosis and prescription is Speier's contribution—diagnosis of American psychological warfare policies during World War II and, based upon that, prescription for more effective operation in the future.

Robert C. Angell

INTERNATIONAL COMMUNICATION AND
THE WORLD SOCIETY

My task is, I take it, to scrutinize the far-flung process of international communication with a view to determining whether or not it is contributing,
or may contribute, to the growth of consensus among the peoples of the
world. Implicit in such a statement of the task is a definition of communication that is at variance with the word's original meaning—to make
things common. We shall here mean by it merely the passing of ideas
from one mind to another. The receiving mind may not accept the ideas,
and even the originating mind may not believe them. One further explanation should be made. I have not dealt with communication that takes place
within the boundaries of one nation but which refers to the people of another nation, though admitting its great importance. It seems to me that
the inclusion of this in the scope of international communication would so
broaden the problem as to rob this paper of all unity of conception and
treatment.

I shall hardly touch upon the movement of people from country to
country. This, of course, is actually one form of communication. During the
war it was a very important one, because large numbers of men spent
long periods away from home among strangers. But in peacetime the bulk
of contacts of this kind are made by two groups of persons: businessmen
and tourists. The contacts in both cases are fleeting and segmental. Since
the visitors from abroad do not stay long enough to settle down into a life-
routine, they frequently show all the instability and impulsiveness that sociologists characterize as *anomie*. They neither make friends with natives
nor win their admiration. Exchange of students and professors is a different
matter. Long residence and involvement in a way of life shared by natives

produce real fellowship. But such exchange goes on in such small measure at present as to be a very minor factor in the general situation.

Though most of us undoubtedly believe that the volume of international communication is increasing year by year, we cannot assume that to be the case. The difficulties of measuring the volume of communication across national borders are, however, very great. For some media we can obtain statistics; for others, we cannot. The discussion will proceed in terms of six channels of communication under two main heads. Point-to-point communication includes mail, on the one hand, and cable and radiotelegraph messages, on the other. International telephone traffic is not large enough to be significant. Under mass communication I will include wire and wireless press dispatches, short-wave broadcasting, moving pictures, and magazines and books. Most of the trends that I will give are for the United States alone. It seemed impossible to assemble world-wide data at this time. I do not make the assumption that the trends for the United States are typical of the world, but I do assume that we know enough about the peculiar position of the United States in the world to be able to make rough corrections and thus arrive at some conception of global trends.

The figures on foreign mail for selected years show very clearly that point-to-point communication of this type is closely related to the movement of persons. It is evident that immigrants into a country continue to write relatives and friends in the homeland for years after their migration. But, as the tide of immigration slows up and then ceases, as happened about 1930, there is a direct reflection of this process in the dispatch of foreign mail. Just before the recent war it is evident that the lessening number of immigrant letters was being offset by a rising trend, probably in commercial correspondence. The peak war figure (1945) again shows the importance of the movement of persons, this time members of our armed services; and the decline in 1946 reflects their return home in large numbers. Whether these men made friendships abroad that will keep our mail communication higher than it was before the war for some time to come is an interesting question to which we cannot give an answer.

Since mail communication is so closely tied to migration, the world trends in mail communication may be estimated from a consideration of population movements around the globe. The declining birth rates in Europe in the twentieth century have slowed down the outward movement of population that was so marked until World War I. The flight of refugees before Hitler and the forced movements of peoples incident to the war and its aftermath are not likely to give rise to extensive mail communication for the simple reason that those who have migrated have left few of their own kind behind. In other parts of the world I am not aware that there has been any sharp variation in trends. My conclusion would therefore be that person-to-person mail communication throughout the world is declining somewhat but that this is offset in part by increasing business correspondence.

No one series of data can give the picture with respect to cable and wireless or radiotelegraph communication for the United States because of the differing ways in which the data have been gathered. There can be no doubt that, so far as the United States is concerned, there is a constantly increasing flow of messages of this kind to and from the remainder of the world. And there is no reason to suppose that we are unrepresentative of the global situation in this regard. Because we industrialized earlier than most parts of the world, it can be argued that the trend of recent decades in the United States understates rather than overstates the world trend.

From a consideration of the data so far adduced it would appear that the decline in mail communication is probably not being offset by the increase in cable and radiotelegraph communication. Though the latter was growing rapidly just before World War II, only about one two-hundredth as many words were being transmitted this way as by mail (assuming the average letter to contain three hundred words). In the absence of counter-evidence, we must assume that the world will tend to revert to something like this pre-war situation.

Point-to-point communication is, however, probably going to be only a minor factor in the development of the world society. Although sociologists are impressed by the superiority for purposes of social integration of the intimate type of communication that is represented by personal letters, it is obviously the mass agencies of communication that, because of their tremendous reach, hold the greatest hope for world understanding.

The best index I have been able to discover of international newspaper communication is the foreign press traffic transmitted by American companies engaged in the cable and radio telegraph businesses. These figures show a great increase from the period of the twenties to the period of the late thirties and early forties. There can be not the slightest doubt that, so far as the world situation is reflected by press messages to and from the United States, newspapers have been constantly improving their foreign coverage. Though our press is undoubtedly able to afford greater coverage than the press of other nations, there is no reason to suppose that the trend shown is not a world-wide one.

International short-wave broadcasting was developed in the thirties by European countries and by Japan. Before Pearl Harbor the United States did very little in this field. There were then seven "licensees" operating transmitters a few hours a week, but only one of them had been able to obtain a subsidy sufficient to cover costs.[1] All this changed very rapidly with our entry into the war. We soon caught up with the European countries, and ultimately we surpassed them. The war peak was reached in

[1] Llewellyn White and Robert D. Leigh, *Peoples Speaking to Peoples* (1946), p. 43.

1944. The Russians were then beaming more than 90 hours of broadcasting a day in 37 languages through 15 short-wave transmitters.[2] In the same year Great Britain was transmitting almost 110 hours a day in 39 languages, and the United States more than 153 hours in 34 languages.[3] All three have reduced these schedules considerably since the war but are still maintaining a level infinitely higher than before the war. Russia is now operating short-wave transmitters 42 hours a day in 30 languages, the British Broadcasting Corporation, 88 hours in 46 languages, and "The Voice of the U.S.A.," 57 hours in 25 languages over 36 transmitters.[4] Our broadcasts are sponsored by the Office of International Information and Cultural Affairs of the State Department. At the moment it appears certain that Congress will greatly reduce our national effort in this field.

I have been unable to obtain statistical data on the international exchange of films. Until the early thirties it seems clear that almost all traffic was outward from the United States and that the foreign market was very profitable to Hollywood. With the advent of the sound picture, language barriers became more important. The competition between American and foreign films became keener outside the United States. British films were the only ones that could invade the American market. In the late thirties somewhat more than two hundred foreign-produced films were shown in this country yearly,[5] while between 35 and 40 per cent of the world revenue for film rentals was received from outside the United States by American distributors.[6] At the present time foreign nations are trying to build up their own moving-picture industries and are forcing their own exhibitors to keep a certain ratio between domestic films and the importations from Hollywood.

Although magazines and books are not such pervasive agencies of mass communication as the newspaper, the radio, and the moving picture, they cannot be ignored. It makes little difference whether such printed matter is in the original language or translated, whether shipped abroad or produced abroad. The main point is that the indigenous culture of one country is communicated to another. World interchange of books has been going on for centuries. There is every reason to believe that there has been a steady acceleration of the process. Although American book publishers have sold a very small percentage of their product abroad, many pirated editions in other languages have been issued. European publishers have been far ahead of ours in cultivating foreign markets. With respect to

[2] *New York Times*, April 27, 1947.

[3] *Education on the Air: 16th Yearbook of the Institute for Education by Radio, 1945*, p. 40.

[4] *New York Times*, April 27, 1947.

[5] See *President's Annual Report to the Motion Picture Producers and Distributors of America*, various years.

[6] *Ibid*, March 30, 1942, p. 53.

magazines, on the other hand, we have been the most successful. *Reader's Digest* publishes seven foreign-language editions, and *Time* and *Newsweek* publish English editions in foreign countries. It is said that in a few parts of the world *Reader's Digest* outcirculates any domestic magazine. Because of the expense of magazines and books, several countries including our own have set up library and reading-room facilities in large cities abroad. We have seventy-five of these in forty-five foreign countries, and it is estimated that they serve three and one-half million readers a year.[7] This seems to indicate that there are large numbers of persons abroad to which every nation can cater by supplying them with accurate information about its own people and with representative examples of their creative writing.

The immediate future may see some important changes in the amount of international mass communication. Radiotelegraph, which is fast replacing cables, is likely to be used increasingly for multiple-address broadcasting. Britain and Russia are showing the way in this field. By this technique news can be beamed to all the press-receiving stations over a wide area in a single transmission. It is now mechanically possible for any publication in the world to receive 100,000 words of foreign news daily. With respect to short-wave radio, we may expect that other European countries and the oriental nations will enter the field in competition with Russia, Britain, the United States, and France. If we drastically cut down our efforts of this kind, we shall be taking a course that others probably will not follow. In the field of motion pictures, the future may not see a greater number of films crossing national borders, but the chances are that there will be more exchange among nations and less domination by Hollywood. There will be more interaction. Probably the same may be said for magazines and books. Our book-publishing industry awakened to our backwardness in cultivating foreign markets and for a time operated the United States International Book Association. It is likely that the success of our magazines in invading foreign territory will stimulate competition from other nations. There is also a real likelihood that truly international magazines will emerge, drawing on contributors from all over the world, and publishing in different languages.

Thus far we have been concerned merely with the amount of communication flowing from one nation to another. But quantity is not nearly so important as quality or content. If most of what is passing back and forth is on subjects unimportant for international good will, or if it is warped to the degree that no good purpose is served by its transmission, then quantity is of no significance whatever. Before one can deal with the crucial question of quality, it seems necessary to formulate a theory of international

[7] Ferdinand Kuhn, "Letting the Whole World Know," *Survey Graphic*, XXXV (December, 1946), 493.

communication. If our aim is to achieve peace among nations, we should ask ourselves what, under existing conditions, are the essential functions of such communication.

It seems to me that the basic need is to communicate the way of life of different peoples to one another so as to achieve three objectives: (1) an appreciation of the common human qualities underlying cultural differences; (2) an understanding of the central values of other cultures; and (3) a realization that the different value systems of the world's peoples are each compatible with the universal human qualities even when not compatible with each other. The achievement of these three objectives would not insure world peace, since many of us who understood how the Nazis got that way still felt we had to go to war with them. But appreciation of the fact that the different cultures have at least a common basis in human nature (and many pairs of cultures have more than that) would give all peoples more tolerance toward one another and more hope that incompatible value systems could gradually be modified.

My whole argument rests upon the existence of what I have called common human qualities. This idea was developed some forty years ago by Charles Horton Cooley, under the concept of human nature. He said:

"By human nature, I suppose, we may understand those sentiments and impulses that are human in being superior to those of the lower animals, and also in the sense that they belong to mankind at large, and not to any particular race or time. It means, particularly, sympathy and the innumerable sentiments into which sympathy enters, such as love, resentment, ambition, vanity, hero-worship, and the feeling of social right and wrong.

"Human nature in this sense is justly regarded as a comparatively permanent element in society. Always and everywhere men seek honor and dread ridicule, defer to public opinion, cherish their goods and their children, and admire courage, generosity, and success. It is always safe to assume that people are and have been human . . .

"There is no better proof of this generic likeness of human nature than in the ease and joy with which the modern man makes himself at home in literature depicting the most remote and varied phases of life—in Homer, in the Nibelung tales, in the Hebrew Scriptures, in the legends of the American Indians, in stories of frontier life, of soldiers and sailors, of criminals and tramps, and so on. The more penetratingly any phase of human life is studied the more an essential likeness to ourselves is revealed.

". . . The view here maintained is that human nature is not something existing separately in the individual, but a *group-nature or primary phase of society*, a relatively simple and general condition of the social mind. It is something more, on the one hand, than the mere instinct that is born in us—though that enters into it—and something less, on the other, than the more elaborate development of ideas and sentiments that makes up institutions. It is the nature that is developed and expressed in those simple, face-to-face groups that are somewhat alike in all societies, groups of the family, the playground, and the neighborhood. In the essential similarity of these is to be found the basis, in experience, for similar ideas and sentiments in the human mind. In these, everywhere, human nature comes into existence. Man does not have it at birth; he cannot acquire it except through fellowship, and it decays in isolation." [8]

We may, I think, take it as a principle that, the more adequately communication conveys to the people of one country the human qualities, similar to their own, of people of other countries, the greater the chance of co-operation among nations. In the long run world peace can rest upon nothing less than a sense of fellowship among the members of the human species. World political organization must be based upon a world moral order, and that moral order can develop only as peoples come to feel that they are fundamentally similar enough to have common objectives.

Appreciation of the human nature of the peoples of other countries requires the visualization of them in intimate association, since it is there that human nature is developed and most clearly manifests itself. The communication must be so vivid as to make American parents realize, for instance, that the loyalty of African natives to their family circles is very similar to our own.

So far as the second objective is concerned, the need is merely that the central values of other peoples be clearly understood. I emphasize values because, following Toynbee [9] and many other writers, I regard the value system as the core of any culture and its most important feature so far as relation to other cultures is concerned. I do not think that it is very important to communicate instrumental aspects of culture because it is not necessary that they be accommodated to each other. If we can come to some *rapprochement* with Russian communism, for instance, is it of slight moment whether we eat the same dishes or make automobiles in the same way, or even realize that we do not.

One might suppose that the third objective follows from the other two—that those who have been convinced of a universal human nature and have been informed regarding the cultural values of other peoples will conclude that the values of these peoples stem in some way from human nature. With this supposition I do not agree. We are likely to grant the fundamental humanity of other peoples, but we are likely to believe, unless the contrary is demonstrated to us, that they have been fooled into accepting cultural values which, in the last analysis, are incompatible with human nature. We do not give them credit for the same consistency between

[8] *Social Organization* (1909), p. 28 *et passim*.
[9] Arnold J. Toynbee, *A Study of History* (New York: Oxford University Press, 1946).

values and human nature that we assume to be axiomatic for ourselves. It is essential, therefore, that this relationship in foreign cultures be communicated. This is a most difficult task, since it involves the whole theory of life involved in each of these other cultures. This theory cannot be grasped through Sunday supplement simplifications, but only through mastery of moral, philosophical, or religious thinkers.

Adequate communication means the making of things truly common. In relation to any of our three objectives, this requires the transmission of the facts as available to an unbiased observer on the scene to those in other lands for whom such facts are important for the maintenance of peace. With any such criterion in mind world communication today is woefully deficient.

In the first place, little passes from culture to culture that leads to an appreciation of our common human nature. In wartime there is positive propaganda to undermine any such idea. Japanese and German inhumanity is treated, not merely as a part of their attitude toward out-groups, but as an ever present aspect of character. In peacetime things are better. There is little negative propaganda of this kind, but there is likewise little positive communication. Occasionally, a newsreel shows family life in some foreign land in an appealing light; more rarely a short-wave broadcast or a magazine article may emphasize the human-nature traits possessed by men of other nations. But most of us who really appreciate how fundamentally similar men are throughout the world have probably been influenced by either prolonged residence abroad, intimate correspondence, or great novels and plays. As already indicated, it is likely that the amount of intimate correspondence across national borders is decreasing. We may hope that the exchange of students and professors will soon show a sharp increase. The growing popularity of cheap editions of good foreign novels is a hopeful trend. If Dostoievski, Victor Hugo, and our own Thoreau were to become available at low cost in all countries, the common human nature which underlies cultural differences would be better appreciated. Documentary moving pictures are a new medium from which we may expect much also. As far as international radiobroadcasting is concerned, there is no reason why each country should not frame its programs with the specific objective, among others, of showing to the world the essential humanity of its own people.

Our norm for adequate communication is even less well met in the field of cultural values. It is not that there are not broad crisscrossing streams of communication; it is that they are mostly biased. Newspapers, magazines, radio, and the movies all play important communicative roles, but they do a remarkably poor job of conveying the true cultural values of one society to others. The breakdown can take place at any stage in the process: before formulation of the matter to be communicated, either by selection or by distortion; during the passage from one country to another, by censorship either as it leaves or enters; and after arrival in the country of destination, again by selection or distortion.

Newspapers find their problem much more aggravated today than before World War I. Then there was a fairly free flow of news around the globe. News services had their correspondents all over the world, and they transmitted their messages in the main without hindrance. The importance of censorship with propaganda was learned, however, during the first war —a lesson that was acted upon more effectively by Goebbels than by anyone else. Today there are many nations where correspondents are not allowed to travel freely, and where all that they write is subject to censorship. But adequate communication is not distorted only by such repressive measures. Our own news services are likely to send abroad a disproportionate number of sensational items, thus misrepresenting us to foreign peoples.

The same countries that control the overflow of news also control its inflow. Fearful of what certain items may do to domestic morale, they carefully screen what goes into the newspapers and see to it that distortion is employed when that seems expedient. Even the so-called "free countries" like the United States and Britain do not allow foreign radiotelegraph companies to maintain reception facilities within their borders.

It has been suggested in a report to the Commission on Freedom of the Press that newspapers need to form syndicates across national frontiers to supply signed background and interpretive articles concerning events abroad.[10] At present only a few large papers can afford to have men stationed abroad to provide such service.

Magazines and books probably give a much truer exposition of foreign cultures and their central values than do newspapers. The books and articles of native authors who make sound interpretations of their own culture are frequently translated and pass successfully into foreign markets. The United States is now trying to obtain this result in another way—by publishing a Russian-language magazine, *Amerika*, for Russian consumption. Another variation is for writers to make prolonged visits in foreign countries and then to portray for their countrymen the essence of the other cultures. Goethe interpreted Italy to the Germans; Lord Bryce, the United States to Britain; and Pearl Buck, China to the United States.

Short-wave broadcasting is much less reliable from the standpoint of intercultural understanding. Nations have used this medium as a weapon in the war of propaganda. One reason for this is that radio reception is hard to prevent. Material that would have no chance of appearing in a foreign magazine or newspaper or on foreign moving-picture screens may be put on the air with considerable likelihood that it will reach its mark. Countermeasures are not very effective. "Jamming" is likely to be resented

[10] White and Leigh, *op. cit.*, pp. 87-88.

by the citizens of the nation attempting it, and forbidding citizens to listen to foreign broadcasts is likely to whet their curiosity. A second reason that short-wave transmissions have often been propagandistic in tone is that they are not money-making enterprises. Since the state has to subsidize them, the government quite naturally regards them as a tool of foreign policy.

To the degree that a nation regards short-wave broadcasting as a means of penetrating the defenses of other nations, it will represent its own cultural values in such a way as to have the desired effect upon those at whom the programs are beamed. Whether the attempt is to convince the listeners of the magnanimity of the sponsoring nation or of its ruthless power, the probability is in either case that a true picture of national values and national aspirations is not given. People cannot rely upon their radio receivers to give them anything but a biased version of the essence of other cultures. One way of rectifying this distortion would be for nations to enter into agreements to exchange broadcasts over each other's facilities. Each could then hold the other to something closely corresponding to the truth.

Because of censorship in the receiving country, moving pictures are almost never allowed to exaggerate the virtues of the originating nation. Of course, such censorship sometimes prevents the showing of even a truthful picture. But perhaps the greatest reason for an unfavorable impression is that a nation does not always put its best foot forward in its films. That is certainly the case with many of our Hollywood movies. I was once seriously asked by a London detective whether it was safe to be on the streets of Chicago at night without a gun. R. H. Heindel found that 583 out of 1,000 British school children obtained more of their ideas about the United States from the moving pictures than from any other source; and that 705 believed that our pictures give a true impression of American life.[11] What an opinion of us they must have! It has remained for a British Member of Parliament, Robert Boothby, to put the thing in a nutshell: "Anyone who suggests that the American films portray the American way of living is an enemy of the United States."[12] We can perhaps hope that foreign competition will force us to make better pictures, thus saving us from our own self-depreciation.

If present communication channels are pitifully inadequate in giving a clear and accurate conception of the central values of foreign cultures, they are a fortiori so in giving an appreciation of the connection between the values of other cultures and human nature. However much each nation realizes that it is to its interest to try to persuade foreigners of the humane basis of its own system of values, it seems to believe quite as

[11] "American Attitudes of British School Children," School and Society, XLVI (December 25, 1937), 838-40.

[12] Quoted in Ruth A. Inglis, Freedom of the Movies (1947), p. 4.

strongly that it must prevent others from persuading its own people of the corresponding fact. Hence we resist the propagation of Marxism just as Russia resists the propagation of the principles of our Bill of Rights. It is only a very rare book, like Professor Northrop's *The Meeting of East and West*, which gets the problem squarely before the people of the world. It seems visionary to hope that many persons in every nation can be brought to understand that the various value systems of the world are like separate stalks growing from the same root, but only this would seem sufficient to initiate the accommodation process that could produce a world moral order.

The picture that I have painted of communication in the world today is bleak indeed. Yet I would not leave the impression that there are no hopeful features in the situation. I will mention three.

In the first place, unbiased communication cannot altogether be prevented in the modern world. Literacy is growing by leaps and bounds, and a literate person may ferret out the truth even against great obstacles. The late war has brought millions of people into close contact with foreigners, and some of these contacts will be continued. The differentiation of classes in all the great states creates communities of interest across national boundaries that give rise to communication. We have a Communist party; perhaps there is still in Russia a group with capitalist sympathies. Finally, even the most seclusive society has to send abroad political and economic representatives, some of whom will bring back truths about the outside world.

Second, no nation can afford to isolate itself in the modern world because it will be technologically outdistanced if it does so. The attempt will be made by some countries to accept scientific and technological advances while excluding all political, moral, and religious influences. This attempt can hardly be a complete success. Modern radios will bring in distant broadcasts; modern techniques of industrial management imply democratic principles.

The third hopeful circumstance that I see involves perhaps a little wishful thinking. It is my belief that there is a growing sense of professional ethics in the communication field. I believe that there is more sober self-control by newspapers and news services, more realization on the part of moving-picture producers of their international responsibilities, more inclination on the part of governments to make their short-wave broadcasts as accurate as they would like to have those of other countries. In short, I think that I see a trend toward honest communication. UNESCO has been founded to promote such a trend, and its first year's projects seem intelligently conceived to this end.

The shortcomings of world communication today are so many and the signs of future improvement are so few that many believe that the chances for world peace would be greater if we cut off communication between nations altogether, or at least eliminated the most propagandistic media.

This is indeed a doctrine of despair. It is a doctrine I find repellent, but I agree that we are in a real dilemma. Free communication may make for sharpened conflicts; but we can never hope to get to one world without communication. The whole problem is one of world morality. Communication needs to be governed by international moral standards. Paradoxically, such standards can only develop through communication. While they are a-building we take a grave risk. It is, in General Eisenhower's phrase, a calculated risk, and probably the greatest one in history. But we must take it. We must hope that adequate moral controls will develop faster than misuse of world communications.

The only practical suggestions I have to offer are by no means new or original. It may be worth while, however, to gather them together into a unified program that we Americans might, as a beginning, seek to carry out in this country:

1. Encourage further study of the international communications problem. Nothing is more important than to bridge the cultural chasms between nations; yet we are profoundly ignorant of how to go about it.

2. Increase the flow of international communication. We should maintain our war-made contacts throughout the world and work to reduce barriers like high postal rates and communications charges, tariffs, quota restrictions, and censorship.

3. Foster a greater sense of international responsibility among those performing communications functions. Our press and our motion pictures have often done a disservice to the cause of international understanding by misrepresenting this country to foreigners.

4. Foster particularly the exchange of creative works of literature, both fiction and nonfiction. These works leave a deeper impression than other forms of distance communication. They enable us really to put ourselves in other peoples' positions.

5. Foster exchange of students, professors, and other professional men. There is no link with foreign lands quite so strong as this one.

6. Support UNESCO. Through this organization we may hope that the efforts of Americans can be integrated with those of other nationalities to achieve a vital world community.

This is a far-reaching program. It will not be effectuated without a great deal of work on the part of a great many people. But ours is a time that calls for a superhuman effort to avert interhuman tragedy.

Hans Speier

THE FUTURE OF
PSYCHOLOGICAL WARFARE

In the two world wars American psychological warfare was improvised after the outbreak of hostilities and conducted according to hit-or-miss methods. No peacetime agency existed which had preserved and developed pertinent skills and knowledge in this field, trained expert personnel, or engaged in appropriate research and planning.

Psychological warfare was regarded as an operation requiring no planning, training, and research. During the past two world wars its direction was entrusted largely to men with experience in furnishing news, opinions, advertisements, and entertainment to the home population, and their skills appeared to be adequate.

As the nation demobilized its armed strength after the wars, expenditures for purposes of psychological warfare were not curtailed in proportion to the reduction of the total funds appropriated for defense but were, as a matter of course, reduced to nil. At present hardly a skeleton organization for planning and research in psychological warfare exists, and the legacy of experience accumulated during the last war in both tactical and strategic propaganda is being dissipated by negligence. There is also an almost complete lack of accurate studies of the effectiveness of the various propaganda measures and devices used against the enemy in the second world war. During a war, enemy response to propaganda cannot be studied adequately. Only after the termination of hostilities can research, based on classified data, interviews and captured enemy sources, attempt to strike a balance between ignorance and such enthusiastic claims as Captain Ellis M. Zacharias' book [1] contains. In the prevailing circumstances we are as

Reprinted from *The Public Opinion Quarterly*, Vol. XII (Spring, 1948), pp. 5-18, by permission of the author and the publisher. (Copyright, 1948, by Princeton University Press.)

[1] *Secret Missions*, New York: Putnam's Sons, 1946.—In the absence of response analyses there will always be a tendency, as there was after the first world war, to judge the effect of propaganda on the basis of its content or volume, of sweeping opinions by well

deficient in our knowledge of the effectiveness of propaganda as we were during the war about the best way of conducting it.

The absence of peacetime preparation for wartime propaganda led to weaknesses in both the organization and conduct of psychological warfare in the last war, as is well known to those who had a part in it. Many of its weaknesses resulted from imperfect coordination of the improvised propaganda agencies and their various branches, from the lack of adequate standards in the recruitment of personnel, and from imperfect coordination of the propaganda offices with the established authorities that made political and military decisions.[2] But even within the limits set by these deficiencies the possibilities of psychological warfare were not fully exploited because they were not fully explored. The propaganda agencies could spare neither time nor talent for that purpose. Other government agencies, whose cooperation would have been vital, were not interested. Most available academic studies were retrospective, and centered around the psychological aspects of the problem without regard to its political implications.

One of the resulting shortcomings of American propaganda during the last war was the lack of political planning beyond the news of the week. The dissemination of news was regarded as the primary task. It is significant that even the term "psychological warfare" was used only by the military in designating their propaganda units, whereas the civilian agencies did not officially spread propaganda, but "information and the truth." To illustrate, the *Report on the Activities of the Office of War Information in the European Theater of Operations during the Calendar Year 1944* went so far as to deny categorically that the OWI was engaged in any attempt at persuasion. The OWI "does not try," said the Report, "to persuade people to like the United States; it tries to help people to understand the United States, on the assumption that the more the truth about America is known, the more the nature of American civilization is understood, the better for all concerned."[3]

---

known persons (including enemy leaders), and of events preceded by certain propaganda activities.

[2] Although the awareness of propaganda possibilities was stronger in the Third Reich than in the United States during the second world war, and although propaganda policy was on the whole more closely coordinated with general policy, several dramatic instances of imperfect coordination have come to light from Nazi sources as well. Policy directives for the domestic press were not fully coordinated with those for the radio, because Goebbels' Under-Secretary, Dr. Dietrich, used his direct responsibility to Hitler as Press Chief of the Reich Government to protect his independence from Goebbels. Hitler's and Dietrich's famous announcements of October, 1941, that the war in the East had been won by Germany were made without consultation of Goebbels, who regarded these announcements as the biggest propaganda blunder of the war. Goebbels learned subsequently from Hitler that the announcements were made to exert pressure upon Japan to enter the war. (Cf. Rudolf Semmler, *Goebbels—The Man Next to Hitler,* London: John Westhouse Ltd., 1947, pp. 54 ff., 111 ff.)

[3] Within the OWI insistence on truth was often justified as a policy for maintaining

The most important news during the war was "produced" in battle and by statesmen or their ghost writers. The propagandists had virtually no influence on these productions; they functioned as wholesale and retail agents in the news business. Consequently, their prestige within the government was low and their influence limited. On the whole, this unproductive, distributive function was willingly accepted. Major propaganda policies depended upon general policies that were oriented toward speedy military victory rather than toward a desirable distribution of political power after victory. The propagandists felt happy about scoops and good news, and they did not really know how to deal with bad news. Some of them, particularly those overseas, made efforts to plan within the limits of the decisions which they were permitted to make and the materials which were available to them, but for the most part no effective preparations could be made at this level for dealing with alternative courses of events.

Let us assume that the invasion of France had failed. American psychological warfare would have had nothing to work with but General Eisenhower's brief statement which, as was subsequently revealed, he had personally prepared for that contingency. Or take President Roosevelt's announcement of the war aim of unconditional surrender. Without doubting the political need for adopting this war aim,[4] its psychological repercussions could be foreseen to be considerable, so considerable indeed that it would have been worthwhile exploring them in advance. The desirable effects on the Soviet leaders and on the resistance elements in occupied Europe could have been maximized; the undesirable effect on the Germans could have been minimized without sacrifice of principle.[5] Such exploration would have required less care than is usually given to the preparation of a public speech by a presidential candidate, but it would indeed have presupposed both closer cooperation between the President and the directors of political warfare and recognition of the nature and function of war propaganda.

In the past two world wars the United States could afford to improvise psychological warfare. Victory was virtually certain when the United States entered the war on the side of Great Britain and Russia. The psychological effect of the initial American defeats was reduced to that of temporary setbacks by the successful Soviet resistance to the German armies, the lack of any real fear that the American homeland would be invaded or bombed, and by general confidence in the eventual decisiveness of the national war

"credibility" of output, although in public utterances moral rather than expedient justifications were put forth.

[4] Cf. Hans Speier, "War Aims in Political Warfare," in *Social Research*, vol. XII, no. 2, May, 1945.

[5] There is an illuminating discussion of the impact of "unconditional surrender" on American propaganda in the forthcoming book by Wallace Carroll, *Persuade or Perish*, New York: Houghton Mifflin Company.

potential. The offensive against the "morale" of the enemy was waged primarily by bombs both in Germany and Japan.[6] The material superiority of the Allies made it unnecessary to examine exhaustively what support political warfare might be able .to give to the military effort.

The United States cannot afford to persist in its indifference toward political and psychological warfare trusting that it will be able to rely on improvisation once more, if it should be impossible to avoid war. The conditions permitting improvisation during the last two world wars will not recur in the event of another war. It is unsound to presume that the American armed forces will in all circumstances be able to inflict defeat upon any aggressor or alliance of aggressors without the aid of adequately prepared political warfare, conducted on the basis of obtainable knowledge and coordinated planning. The time has come for examining our beliefs in the efficacy of traditional democratic information policies. Can they still be based on the assumption that dissemination of knowledge and news enables man to reason rightly and that anyone who reasons rightly will necessarily act rightly?[7]

Must We Be on the Defensive in Psychological Warfare?

A new American attitude toward psychological warfare has been expressed in the Report of the President's Advisory Commission on Universal Training of May 29, 1947. In dealing with many facets of national security, the Report relates the discussion of universal military training to a survey of "The World Situation and the Preservation of Peace" (Part II), the "Nature of Possible Future Warfare" (Part III), and the "Essentials of an Integrated National Security Program" (Part IV). It calls attention to the importance of a coordinated intelligence service, an integrated and effective program of scientific research and development, the "vital matter" of

[6] At Casablanca it was decided by British and American leaders to enlarge the attack against Germany not only in order to destroy or dislocate the German military, economic, and industrial system but also with the objective of "undermining the morale of the German people to the point where their capacity for armed resistance is fatally weakened." In accordance with this decision, by the end of the war the total tonnage of bombs dropped on German cities was almost twice as large as that dropped on manufacturing targets.

[7] E. H. Carr, in The Twenty Years' Crisis 1919-39 (New York: Macmillan, 1942, p. 34), mentions these assumptions as two of the three convictions underlying 19th century optimism, the third being that the pursuit of the Good is a matter of right reasoning. While the foreign policy of the United States in the 20th century has been influenced by these convictions less than Mr. Carr will have us believe, there can be little doubt that the international information policy of the United States can still be explained largely in terms of these convictions. While general policy concerns itself with what is to be done, information policy deals with that which is to be said about what has been and is to be done. Information policy therefore reflects the principles of general policy, and not only its compromises with reality.

industrial mobilization and stockpiling, the function of the regular armed forces and the need for unified command. Finally, it urges action to fill the "tremendous gaps in the availability of comprehensive and adequate medical care and education to all of the American people." In so comprehensive a survey by so distinguished a group of advisers the appraisal of psychological warfare and its bearing on national security merits close study.

Above all, the Commission has been more strongly impressed by the need for defensive measures to maintain the morale of the American people in a future war than by the desirability of preparing in peacetime for measures to break the enemy's morale. One might be inclined to regard this defensive orientation as a reflection of American interest in peace and in resistance to changes of the post-war distribution of power. On closer analysis it appears, however, that the Report dimly expresses sentiments which are still more significant. To the traditional American view of propaganda as something evil there has been added an as yet not wholly articulate doubt regarding the power of persuasion through the dissemination of "the truth."

The Commission recommends, to be sure, a "foreign information service," so that the "advocates of rival ideologies" be thwarted in their sedulous attempt "to sow distrust of our actions and our form of government through a program of studied misrepresentation." "Truth," the Report says, "is our greatest ally in defeating this campaign." Considering the Report as a whole, however, the traditional American confidence in "truth" as a weapon in international conflict appears to be shaken: this confidence no longer extends to a future war, but only to the present post- or pre-war period.

One might say the Commission concerned itself with the technical possibilities of violence rather than with the political change in the post-war distribution of power.[8] While it stresses that psychological warfare will assume increased importance in a future war, it appears to derive this expectation from the improvement of offensive weapons. Now historical experience suggests that the specific historical form of propaganda is not a function of armament, but like the specific historical form of war as a whole, is a trait of the civilization in which it occurs. In particular, the nature of wartime propaganda depends on the extent of mass participation

---

[8] While it lists and discusses seven "general factors" likely to affect the nature of future war and to alter past concepts of defense, such as the increased destructiveness of offensive weapons, atomic, bacteriological and chemical, it mentions the decisive political factor only in passing and in an inconspicuous clause: ". . . all that we have learned about the tempo and universality of war in the predictable future convinces us that we will need more trained men more quickly than we did in World War II, when the sacrifices of our allies bought us the time necessary to convert civilians into soldiers, sailors and airmen."

in war, on the tension between warring nations, and on their respective political systems, popular beliefs, and ideologies.

It might be argued that a nation which would resort to, say, bacteriological warfare against an enemy can also be expected to use all available psychological weapons. Yet it must be remembered that the most deadly weapons may be employed in order to spread terror among enemy civilians, but at the same time restraint may be exercised in inciting revolution against the enemy government because of cherished anti- or counter-revolutionary ideals. In view of certain moral traditions and political beliefs that may prevail in a belligerent country, efficiency in destruction cannot be regarded as sufficient basis for determining the scope or intensity of psychological warfare.

If the Commission had merely stressed that modern weapons of destruction may undermine the morale of the civilian population, paralyze its will to fight or work and disrupt order, it would have pointed at the vulnerability of all governments and nations in modern war. Instead, the Commission regards American democracy as especially vulnerable to psychological warfare and fifth column activities.[9] It holds it "possible that subversive elements within the domestic population might constitute a sufficiently large and well armed group to constitute a quasi-military force." In another instance, the success of the enemy's non-military warfare is inadvertently conceded in advance. "When the time for attack arrived, the enemy's primary purpose would be to immobilize us militarily, industrially, and politically through the force of his initial assault and the effectiveness of his fifth column." Note that the Commission does not speak of activity but of effectiveness.

The Commission urges strong defense measures to reduce this danger. It envisages the possible need for imposing martial law "to guard against defeatism, demoralization and disorder." It fails to recommend, however, any measures which would enable the United States to take the offensive in political and psychological warfare. This surrender of initiative to the enemy is all the more noteworthy in view of the fact that in the field of military warfare the Commission adheres to the old maxim that the strongest form of defense is counter-attack. Were the members of the Commission convinced that the United States cannot but leave the political initiative in times of war to the enemy, cannot retaliate and need therefore not think about the preparation of attack? Or were they persuaded that

[9] These dangers are painted in colors as dark as those commonly used in depicting the threat to national security by the "preplacement of atomic or biological weapons," which in the words of the President's Air Policy Commission "may soon become a major military problem." See also, Bernard Brodie in *The Absolute Weapon*, New York: Harcourt, 1946, and Ansley Coale, *The Problem of Reducing the Vulnerability to Atomic Bombs*, Princeton: Princeton University Press, 1947.

in a future war the lethal effect of American military weapons will be such as to render concern with political and moral persuasion unnecessary?

Psychological Warfare as a Subject for Moral Indignation

The Commission is indignant about the methods of psychological warfare which it expects the enemy to use. Atomic, bacteriological, and other attacks are discussed in the Report as possibilities which the nation must realistically face without any show of such indignation. Similarly sober and realistic is the discussion of a possible surprise attack against the United States (in defiance of international law). Only when considering the enemy's psychological warfare is a strongly moralistic language adopted, so that one gains the startling impression that the Commission had stronger moral feelings on foreign radio broadcasts than on the subject of atomic or bacteriological warfare. Says the Report, "Without cohesive machinery for restoring order, conditions of near anarchy and demoralization would prevail in the bomb-torn areas. . . . Reinforcing the internal efforts to sow disunity and defeatism, there would be broadcast warnings by the enemy that failure to surrender at once would be the signal for even more formidable attacks, promises of a 'just' peace, and all the other tricks in the arsenal of corrupt psychological warfare." [10]

Let us disregard the question as to whether or not it is historically sound and politically wise to state publicly that the loyalty of the citizens may falter when the nation is fighting for its life. The point of particular interest in the quoted passage is the unqualified assumption that a future enemy could not possibly offer a just peace to the United States in good faith; any such conjectural offer is dismissed as trickery. The enemy is defined in advance as a "total enemy" [11] with whom it will be impossible and undesirable to come to terms. Apparently, only the exploitation of total victory or total defeat is held to be realistic. To put it differently, the Commission disregarded the possibility that diplomacy may play a role in a future war. Historical experience suggests, however, that it is precisely in an absolute war to the finish against such a total enemy that a nation feels itself justified to use all conceivable "tricks" of deception and trickery, without restraint by any scruples which help limit the conduct of war. The advance denunciation of the enemy as an absolute enemy enhances the chance that when

---

[10] Compare this moralistic tone with the language used by the President's Air Policy Commission in its discussion of the possible use of biological weapons: "Mankind has not indulged in biological warfare on a large scale so far; but the biological sciences are evolving so rapidly that it is impossible to predict the future. The nations might be foolish enough to try it out."

[11] Cf. Hans Speier, "The Social Types of War," *American Journal of Sociology*, vol. XLVI, 1941, pp. 445-454.

the time comes all psychological warfare measures will be taken against that enemy which promise success, whether they are "corrupt" or not. At the same time, the peacetime denunciation of such measures as being tricks and "corrupt" militates against the effective preparation of political and psychological warfare.

The Commission may not have found it necessary to consider at length the probable duration of a future all-out global war. The Report fails in any case to state that such war may be an exhaustive, long-drawn-out struggle. It is indeed as difficult to imagine its termination until the last chance of retaliation and resistance to occupation has vanished, as it is not to expect its ideological heat to be more intense than that of the last war. On the other hand, the very destructiveness of full-scale global war may promote attempts to effect changes in the world balance of power by methods of political penetration in certain limited areas and by selected military means. The present international scene is indeed more easily intelligible as a pattern of minor wars waged to avoid as yet a major one, than in terms of peace threatened by the possibility of war.

Generally speaking, any war can be terminated by sufficient superiority of force, but since the ultimate end of war, whatever its length and character, is the establishment of a more desirable peace rather than victory, the idea of such peace must guide grand strategy. If psychological warfare is merely defensive and not grounded in specific political ideas—i.e., means to the end of desirable peace—, the stage is set for reducing it to tricks and information. One can only wish that a future enemy of the United States will confine himself to tricks and to information in his propaganda.

Tactical Propaganda

During hostilities, the ultimate aim of political warfare against the enemy consists in causing him to take such actions as stop, waste, or reduce his war efforts. Propaganda directed at the enemy is ineffective if it merely succeeds in changing attitudes and opinions. In fact, it may be said to be not only ineffective but sometimes harmful, since the skillful counter-propagandist on the enemy side may advertise its practical futility to his domestic audience as proof of high morale at home, as an indication of enemy blundering, and as a spur to continued resistance.[12]

If response by action is the objective of political warfare and the test of its success, propaganda must be directed with a clear understanding of what kind of action is both practical and politically desirable. The condi-

---

[12] After November 9, 1944, the anniversary of the German revolution at the end of the first world war, Goebbels celebrated the stability of the German home front, saying that it had bravely withstood the alleged Anglo-American agitation for a revolt against the Hitler regime.

tions of success differ for tactical and strategic propaganda. Tactical propaganda is primarily directed at enemy soldiers in direct support of military actions on the field of battle. Strategic propaganda aims primarily at enemy civilians and soldiers behind the front.

Enemy soldiers at the front can under certain conditions cease fighting and desert or surrender. The means used to achieve this end vary, but all of them are related to the expectation that man prefers life to death if other motivations do not intervene and that he will, in certain circumstances, act according to this preference.[13]

The considerable experience obtained during the last war in conducting tactical propaganda, and the appraisals of its effectiveness, need careful study. It is well known, for example, that apart from all other factors influencing the response to tactical propaganda its success depends on the clear demonstration of the feasibility (rather than desirability) of surrender. Our knowledge of such elements as the optimum timing of tactical propaganda and of the varied motives of resistance to it is as yet quite imperfect. Little is known about response to tactical propaganda in relation to the national background, the combat situation, and the nature, size, and cohesion of the group under attack. Equally important for a reduction of our ignorance in this field is the systematic exploration of the possible use of tactical propaganda against such categories of enemy combatants as are engaged in fighting on the sea and in the air, as well as on land. Since tactical propaganda must be based upon sound psychological principles, research in combat propaganda should also utilize the greatly increased insight into the causes of combat fatigue which has been gained during the last war.[14]

As to strategic propaganda, the pivotal point of analysis must be the fact that enemy civilians and soldiers behind the front lines cannot respond to propaganda by acts of surrender or desertion. There is no physical line for them to cross. Tactical propaganda is in a position to offer a reward— safety; strategic propaganda can offer only continued and increased deprivation. While tactical propaganda presents an alternative to the risk of getting killed on the field of battle, successful strategic propaganda adds to the risk of getting killed—i.e., in air raids—that of getting caught by the home police. The eccentricity of strategic propaganda resides in the paradox that it augments the chance of survival for enemy civilians to the extent that it is unsuccessful.

The ultimate aim of strategic propaganda cannot be surrender but is subversion, i.e., action of the enemy population or elements of it against

[13] Concerning the difficulties of surrender, cf. Milton Shulman, *Defeat in the West*, New York: Dutton and Company, 1948.

[14] Cf. particularly the studies by R. R. Grinker and J. P. Spiegel, *Men under Stress*, Philadelphia: Blakiston, 1945; and S. L. A. Marshall, *Men against Fire*, Washington: *The Infantry Journal*, and New York: William Morrow, 1947.

their government.[15] All other actions, or failures to act against the enemy, which strategic propaganda may try to induce are either derivatives of political acts of subversion (malingering, slowing down, "griping," etc.) or non-political substitutes for subversive activities, such as privatization or panic. If subversion is defined as action against one's own government (taking the place of action against the enemy) or as hostile dissociation through action from one's own collective self, privatization may be defined as action for one's own private self based upon estrangement from political life.[16] Pragmatically quite important are the derivatives of privatization or panic, i.e., the less dramatic actions or failures to act which are associated with malaise, anxiety, hopelessness, confusion, distrust, etc.; they reduce the enemy's war effort through waste.

In order to be successful, subversion propaganda must attempt by all means at its disposal to maximize motivations for sacrificial actions. It must try to inspire belief in moral and political ideas that are worth the sacrifice. In addition, it must be based on a realistic appraisal of the feasibility and risks of subversive activity in the enemy country.

"Missionary" subversion propaganda. Strategic subversion propaganda presupposes not only the ability but also the authorization of the propagandist to engage in revolutionary talk. Authorization for such talk will appear to be most sincere if the regime itself is revolutionary, or represents at least the political and moral ideas in the name of which its propagandists advocate hostile actions by the recipients of propaganda against their own regime. In this case, the propagandist may be said to have a sense of mission. French propaganda during the war following the French Revolution against the royalist alliance massed against France was *missionary* subversion propaganda. So was the propaganda of Soviet Russia against Germany in the first world war.

"Cynical" subversion propaganda. There is also cynical propaganda for subversion, which has the exclusive purpose of weakening the enemy war effort, but which has no disposition or intention to regard and treat the rebels as friends. In this case the sense of mission is lost and moral conviction is replaced by a more or less skilful technique of feigning. Goebbels

---

[15] No consideration is given here to propaganda directed at the enemy government as over against the governed, because the effective direct mode of communicating with the enemy government is diplomatic negotiation in times of war as well as peace. Similarly, no reference is made here to (tactical and strategic) deception propaganda, a few historical cases of which await close analysis.

[16] Cf. Hans Speier and Margaret Otis, "German Radio Propaganda to France during the Battle of France," in *Radio Research 1942-1943*, edited by Paul F. Lazarsfeld and Frank Stanton, New York: Duell, Sloan and Pearce, 1944, p. 208-246, and Ernst Kris and Nathan Leites, "Trends in Twentieth Century Propaganda," in *Psychoanalysis and the Social Sciences,* ed. by Geza Roheim, New York: International Universities Press, 1948.

used Torgler, an imprisoned German communist, to tell the Russians that Stalin had betrayed the communist cause.

"Moralistic" and "judicious" subversion propaganda. Two intermediate types of subversion propaganda, which are neither missionary nor cynical, may be called respectively *moralistic* and *judicious*. Moralistic subversion propaganda attempts to incite subversive activities by stressing their moral glory, but withholds the identification of the propagandist with the subversive cause. Moralistic propaganda presents subversion either pointedly as an exclusive moral obligation of the enemy population or points out that the response to it will determine the political treatment of the enemy after his defeat. American propaganda to Germany and Austria during the second world war contained elements of this type of strategic propaganda.

British propaganda during the first world war exhorting the minorities in the Austro-Hungarian Empire to rise against Austria and claim their independence illustrates the meaning of judicious subversion propaganda. It presupposes rational political judgment of what particular form and direction of seditious activity on the enemy side would be in the political interest of the executing groups as well as the advocating power. Thus judicious subversion propaganda rests on appraisal of politically parallel, but not necessarily morally identical, interests.

As has been indicated, freedom to conduct subversion propaganda and freedom to choose among its various types exists only within the limits set by the moral traditions and political institutions of the belligerent countries. Propagandists of a counter-revolutionary country may feign missionary and judicious propaganda, if they put their minds to it, but the manipulatory disposition and the moral indifference required for that purpose are likely to produce traces of callousness and cynicism in other phases of their work. And these traces betray the insincerity of the propaganda for subversion. Even if the Nazis had been twice as skillful as they were in their propaganda for a new order in Europe, they would still have revealed their true nature by their ecstatic reports of the carnage that took place during the Battle of Britain.

One should not overestimate the possibilities of dissimulation in propaganda. Nor should the study of propaganda techniques be regarded as the most important preparation for offensive political warfare. Such study cannot lead to an appreciation of propaganda in the past or in the future, if it is not enlightened by an understanding of the specific historical situation in which propaganda is conducted, of the political conflict between the belligerents, the character and strength of their moral beliefs and the domestic distribution of power in the countries concerned. This means that a productive study of strategic propaganda in the future must be as specific as strategic military planning. It cannot neglect the moral geography of future conflict and cannot be conducted without regard to the policy aims of specific countries.

It has been observed that with the exception of the Soviet output, "propaganda during the Second World War was on the whole less moralistic than propaganda during the First World War." [17] Furthermore, the staggering progress made in the development of means of destruction and the disillusioning discrepancy between the sweeping moral claims of the victors in the second world war and their halting performance in establishing jointly a solid peace have promoted the continued spread of nihilism in wide areas and strata of the population in the West. These developments invite the prediction that distrust of propaganda will grow in general and that American strategic propaganda in a future war will put a still lower ceiling on moral ideas. In particular, such moral ideas as would inspire faith and sacrificial subversive action on the part of the enemy, may be extremely scarce. Instead of missionary subversion propaganda, an increased effort to achieve privatization and the derivatives of privatization which are associated with anxiety and confusion may be expected. Without direction to the contrary, an exploitation of the devastating effects of super-weapons may well be the activity which American propagandists will feel most competent to undertake. In additional, the moralistic, i.e., non-missionary type of subversion propaganda, may be regarded by them as useful, particularly in addressing satellite countries.

In case of a war between the United States and the Soviet Union, however, the ideological conflict between East and West would be extremely great. The Soviet Union would probably wage missionary subversive propaganda both against "monopoly-capitalism" and, particularly in the Far East, against the United States as an exploiter of colored races. The Soviets would merely have to intensify what they are doing at present. The domestic policy of the Soviet Government would not necessarily lend credibility to their missionary appeal. There will be many recipients of their propaganda, however, who will contrast the Soviet ideal of liberation with their immediate experiences and grievances instead of comparing it with the remote Soviet reality.

The United States, too, can wage sincere political subversion propaganda against the dictatorial Soviet regime, particularly in the political realm. It is quite doubtful, however, whether such efforts at subversion and the Western idea of political freedom would be capable of piercing the armor of Russian nationalism and communist indoctrination. At best, the paramount question to be answered in specific political terms, would be: "Freedom for what?" It is a grave question. Would it be possible to answer it under the stress of absolute war?

Planning and preparation for strategic propaganda in a future war

[17] Kris and Leites, *op. cit.*, p. 295.

must begin now. It must concentrate on a realistic exploration of the possibilities of judicious propaganda and its political aims so as to avoid the
danger of cynicism, the wastefulness of moralistic chatter, the naive reliance
on psychological tricks and over-confidence in the effect of good news
which material superiority is expected to produce.

The coordination of political, military, socio-psychological, and technical
thought which such planning requires will also illuminate the need for the
administrative coordination which psychological warfare lacked in the
second world war, and without which it may well be impotent in the event
of a third world war.

8

COMMUNICATION EFFECTS

The effects of communication are many and diverse. They may be short-range or long-run. They may be manifest or latent. They may be strong or weak. They may derive from any number of aspects of the communication content. They may be considered as psychological or political or economic or sociological. They may operate upon opinions, values, information levels, skills, taste, behavior.

Because of the variety and the complexity of the effects of communications, this topic probably represents the most neglected area in communication research. Most studies have dealt with short-run effects upon opinion because the available research methods have seemed most applicable to this problem. However, there is developing a set of procedures which constitutes some advance toward the objective of rigorous, systematic research in this field.

The first selection is taken from Charters' summary of the Payne Fund investigations of the effects of motion pictures upon children. This review indicates various techniques which were employed in the parent study: before-and-after attitude testing, educational testing, analysis of personal documents and case histories, physiological measurement. The article by Shils and Janowitz illustrates the application of case study analysis to the problem of the impact of formal propaganda under critical conditions, and especially in comparison with the effectiveness of primary group contacts. The next selection, from Warner and Henry's analysis of the psychological role of daytime serials for lower middle class housewives, is one of the few illustrations of the application of projective tests to the problems of communication research; it may be that such methods will provide an answer to the problem of analyzing communication effects at the "deeper" levels of personality. Then follows an example of careful experimental study of communication effects taken from a series of studies by Hovland and associates which now stand as the fullest and most refined investigations of their type. Finally, the article by Berelson is intended to represent a

395

movement to systematize the contributions of empirical studies to the end of developing what might be called a theory of communication; this article attempts to set up an analytic model in terms of which empirical findings can be usefully organized.

W. W. *Charters*

MOTION PICTURES AND YOUTH

DEVELOPING ATTITUDES: Because a close relationship between the attitude of an individual and his actions may be assumed, the study of the effect of motion pictures upon the attitude of children toward important social values is central in importance.

Peterson and Thurstone by the use of different techniques isolated the influence of specific pictures upon groups of children while keeping constant the factors of community standards, habits of children, school influence, home training, and the like. They assumed that these had not materially influenced the children in the brief period between their first and second tests of attitudes; the factor that had changed during the period was exposure to a specific film.

These investigators used eleven highly sensitive instruments to discover changes in attitude toward or against the following eight social objects: the Germans (a scale and a paired comparison), war (two scales), crime, prohibition, the Chinese, capital punishment, the punishment of criminals (two scales), and the Negro. The instruments were scales which consisted of approximately thirty statements each expressing an attitude toward an object. These statements varied in intensity of position from one extreme of attitude against the object to the other extreme of attitude in favor of the object. The statements were weighted according to techniques described in the study [1] and a total score was computed for each individual to express his attitude toward an object.

The scales were given to high-school children shortly before a picture was seen and the position of the group upon the scale was computed. The picture (which in all cases the children had not seen before) was shown and approximately the day after the showing the scale was given again.

Reprinted from *Motion Pictures and Youth* (1933), pp. 18-25; 35-43, by permission of the author and the publisher. (Copyright, 1933, by Macmillan Co.)

[1] *Motion Pictures and the Social Attitudes of Children*, by Ruth C. Peterson and L. L. Thurstone.

The new position of the groups was computed and the resulting change in position noted. In some cases the scale was again checked by some of the groups after two and one-half, five, eight, and nineteen months had elapsed to determine the permanence of the changes which were noted the day after the showing of the picture.

Approximately 4,000 individuals participated in the study as subjects. Most of the subjects were junior and senior high-school students. The exceptions were three in number. In one study 246 college students were used and in another about 100 fourth- and fifth-grade children checked the scale while in three other studies sixth-grade children were included with the junior and senior high-school students. The children were located in the schools of small towns in the neighborhood of Chicago and at Mooseheart, the children's home supported by the Loyal Order of Moose. Small towns were chosen primarily because of the ease of selecting pictures which had not been seen by the children.

Thirteen pictures were selected which met three criteria: they definitely pertained to the issues to be studied, they were free enough from objectionable matter so that high-school principals could be asked to send their students to see them, and they were sufficiently recent to eliminate distractions caused by fashions or photography. Between 600 and 800 pictures of all kinds were reviewed and from them the thirteen used in the studies were selected. This selection represents an attempt to secure films which would in the judgment of the reviewers be likely to produce a noticeable change in attitude if changes were produced by any pictures. All, however, were well-known films. The titles and issues were: "Four Sons" (on the Germans and war); "Street of Chance" (gambling); "Hide Out" (prohibition); "Son of the Gods" (the Chinese); "Welcome Danger" (the Chinese); "The Valiant" (capital punishment); "Journey's End" (war); "All Quiet on the Western Front" (war); "The Criminal Code" (punishment of criminals); "Alibi" (punishment of criminals); "The Birth of a Nation" (the Negro); "Big House" (punishment of criminals); and "Numbered Men" (punishment of criminals).

The outstanding contribution of the study is the establishment of the fact that the attitude of children toward a social value can be measurably changed by one exposure to a picture. An outstanding picture of potency in its influence upon attitude was "Son of the Gods," a picture selected because it was thought to be favorable to the Chinese. Prior to the showing of the picture the mean attitude of a population of 182 children from grades 9 to 12 inclusive stood at 6.72 on a scale in which the extreme positions were approximately 3.5 at the favorable end of the scale and 9.5 at the unfavorable end. After the children had seen the picture the mean shifted 1.22 steps in a favorable direction from 6.72 to 5.50 and this difference was 17.5 times the probable error of the differences. The shift in attitude is "very striking." "The Birth of a Nation" was shown to 434 children of grades 6 to 12 inclusive. Prior to the showing the mean position of this population was 7.41 with extremes of approximately 2.5 at the unfavorable end of the scale to approximately 9.5 at the favorable end. After exposure to the picture the position shifted in an unfavorable direction to 5.93 with a difference of 1.48, which was 25.5 times the probable error of the differences. This was the largest shift obtained in the studies. "All Quiet on the Western Front" produced in 214 junior and senior high-school students a shift against war 14.98 times the probable error of the differences and "The Criminal Code" a shift against the punishment of criminals 12.2 times the probable error of the difference with 246 college students and 11.7 times against the same issue with 276 high-school students. These were the outstanding cases. Significant results were obtained, also, from the showing of "Four Sons" upon attitude toward the Germans, "Welcome Danger," "The Valiant," and "All Quiet on the Western Front." Statistically important changes did not result from single showings of "Four Sons" upon the attitude toward war, of "Hide Out" toward prohibition, of "Journey's End," with one group, toward war, and "Alibi," "Big House," and "Numbered Men" toward the punishment of criminals. In all of these cases but one the differences, however, were in the expected direction. In "Street of Chance" the investigators expected to discover a change of attitude favorable to gambling but a significant change against gambling was recorded.

The range of influence of the motion picture is sensibly broadened by a second fact which these attitude studies have discovered. The investigators found that the effect of pictures upon attitude is cumulative. They demonstrated the fact that two pictures are more powerful than one and three are more potent than two. At Mooseheart, when "Big House" was shown to 138 junior and senior high-school children and "Numbered Men" to another group of 168, neither produced a statistically significant shift in attitude toward the punishment of criminals. When both pictures were seen by a group the change became significant. The shift was then 3.0 times the probable error of the differences. When to these two exposures was added exposure to a third film on the same subject, "The Criminal Code," the shift was still greater and amounted to 6.7 times the probable error.

Again at Mooseheart "Journey's End" and "All Quiet on the Western Front" were shown separately and in combination. These pictures had individual potency. "Journey's End" alone caused a shift of 5.07 times the probable error against war and "All Quiet on the Western Front" produced one of 6.07 times in the same direction. When the former was followed by the latter the shift was increased to 8.07 times the probable error and when the latter was followed by the former the amount of change was increased to 8.26 times.

This pair of studies indicates a significant hypothesis, namely, that even though one picture related to a social issue may not significantly affect the attitude of an individual or a group, continued exposure to pictures of similar character will in the end produce a measurable change of attitude. What the range and limits of such influence may be we do not know. Whether or not it is true in this area that the repetitions of exposure would increase indefinitely is a subject worthy of investigation. Whether or not there is a threshold of personal sensitivity in children above which many pictures do not rise in power and influence we can not say. But it is worth while to know that under the conditions of these studies at least, the cumulative effect of pictures upon attitudes is unmistakably indicated.

To these two leads into the influence of motion pictures upon attitudes Peterson and Thurstone have added a third. They have shown that the shifts created by exposure to a film have substantial permanence. In six localities the attitude scales were repeated at varying intervals and changes in average positions of the groups were computed. The case of the high school at Geneva, Illinois, is typical. Before seeing the film, "Son of the Gods," the children's position on a scale of attitude toward the Chinese was 6.61 and promptly after seeing the film it was 5.19—a shift in favor of the Chinese. Five months after seeing the film there was a recession to 5.72 toward the original position of 5.19 and nineteen months later the position was 5.76. That is to say, the effect of the film had not worn off in a year and a half. In none of the six localities was the recession complete except in one. At Paxton, Illinois, the original position was 4.34 on the scale of attitude toward war before exposure to the film, "All Quiet on the Western Front." After viewing the picture the group shifted to 3.74, indicating a less favorable attitude toward war. Eight months later the position had changed to 4.64 which is more favorable to war than was the original attitude. Probably other influences had played upon the children during these eight months. In all other cases residual traces of the exposure were in evidence at the end of periods of two and one-half, four, six, or eight months.

The principle of permanence is indicated by these investigations. One cannot say that the effects of pictures disappear rapidly. And this position is supported in numerous cases reported by Blumer from the movie autobiographies of his subjects, where hundreds of memories of the influence of specific pictures are related in later years by adults. In other cases Blumer's autobiographers, however, attest to the short-lived influence of movies upon conduct.

This trio of conclusions has great significance for education. We can conclude on the basis of fact that single pictures may produce a change in attitude, that the influence of pictures is cumulative, and that their effects are substantially permanent. This is the second link in the chain of evidence.

How to interpret the social significance of these changes is an interesting consideration. One clue is given in the scores upon the scales. For instance, to select one of the more powerful films, before the picture "Son of the Gods" was shown there were individuals in the group at one extreme position of unfavorableness marked 9.5 upon the scale—meaning roughly: "There are no refined or cultured Chinese," "I don't see how any one could ever like the Chinese," or "There is nothing about the Chinese that I like or admire." Six steps to the other extreme in this group were those who held: "I like the Chinese" and "I'd like to know more Chinese people." The mode of the group and the average were slightly unfavorable at 6.72, which is slightly beyond the neutral point of 6 and toward the unfavorable end. The mode (the most common position taken by the individuals in the group) was: "I have no particular love nor hate for the Chinese." After the picture was shown the same spread of six units was in evidence, from 3.5 to 9.5, but there were fewer children at 9.5 and more at 3.5. The change was 1.22 indicating a shift of about 20 per cent of the distance between the positions of the most extreme and the least extreme individuals in the group. The mode had shifted from neutrality to a point between "The Chinese are pretty decent" and "Chinese parents are unusually devoted to their children."

* * *

INFLUENCING CONDUCT: Conduct is a product of many factors. Of these factors the preceding investigations have explored four. We may assume the obvious position that information is a factor in behavior: what one knows determines in part what one does. We may also assume that attitudes toward social objects affect conduct: if one is friendly toward an objective of action in a situation he will be influenced to build one behavior pattern; if unfriendly, to build another. It may also be fairly assumed that experiences which are accompanied by excitement and emotion have a more powerful effect upon conduct than do those which are placid and uninteresting. Likewise, we may assume that fatigue expressed either by increased or decreased sleep motility results in producing a tone of behavior by which conduct patterns are affected. We have seen that motion pictures have an influence upon all of these factors.

We were able to check the validity of these assumptions, which square with common sense, by a mass of evidence from the studies of Blumer and his associates. Here it was possible to secure hundreds of cases in which the information and attitudes acquired in the movies were directly operative in the conduct of children.

Blumer, Thrasher, and their associates [2] supplemented the foregoing indirect studies of conduct by investigating the direct relationships existing between movies and conduct. Blumer used an autobiography technique, supplemented by interviews, accounts of conversations, and questionnaires. His major study was based upon the case reports of 634 students in two universities, 481 college and junior-college students in four colleges, 583 high-school students, 67 office workers, and 58 factory workers. After studying many biographies written without specific directions and discovering the patterns into which they unconsciously fell, he formulated a few questions to guide the writers as follows: trace the history of your interest in the movies; describe how motion pictures have affected your emotions and your moods; write fully about what you have imitated from the movies; describe your experience with pictures of love and romance; write fully about any ambitions and temptations you have gotten from the movies. Unusual care was taken to preserve the anonymity of the writers. Interviews were held with 81 university students who had previously written autobiographies and 54 high-school students who had not. Careful accounts of conversations were secured from several fraternities, several sororities, and girls' groups and from several cliques of high-school boys and girls, from conversations of high-school boys and girls at parties, and from boys' gangs, play groups, office girls, and factory workers. Direct questionnaires were administered to 1,200 children in the fifth and sixth grades of 12 public schools in Chicago distributed between schools in high, medium, and low delinquency areas. One set of questionnaires was filled out by a special school for truants and boys with behavior problems. Direct observations were made of children while in attendance at small neighborhood theaters.

From these sources a huge mass of materials was collected. The materials were analyzed to discover trends and significant facts. The main use of the material "has been to show and illuminate the different kinds of ways in which motion pictures touch the lives of young people." Experiences which recurred with a high rate of frequency in the separate documents were selected and samples of each type were presented in the report.

Obviously the validity of personal reports is an issue that has a bearing upon the conclusions of the investigators. Upon this question Blumer took all known precautions against error and presents the following facts about the safeguards which they threw around the investigations: (1) Machinery was set up to demonstrate in an obvious manner the anonymity of the written accounts. (2) The utmost care and attention were devoted to gaining full coöperation from the students in securing their frank, honest, and unexaggerated statements. (3) The interviews held six months after the auto-

---

[2] *Movies and Conduct*, by Herbert Blumer; *Movies, Delinquency, and Crime*, by Herbert Blumer and Philip M. Hauser; *Boys, Movies, and City Streets*, by Paul G. Cressey and Frederick M. Thrasher.

biographies were written were used in the cases of some 60 students with their consent but without this previous knowledge as a check against agreement between the content of the written report and the substance of the interview; no discrepancy of importance was discovered. (4) The accounts were checked for internal consistency and some twenty which showed contradiction were discarded. (5) Conversations were checked against the written reports. (6) Individuals were asked to write only about those experiences which they recalled vividly.

The chief means of checking the character of the experiences given in the written documents was "in the comparison of document with document. The accounts were written independently by students in different schools and localities. . . . The comparison of large numbers of documents coming from different groups of people with no knowledge of each other made it possible to ascertain the general run of experiences. The contents of documents coming from different sources yielded substantially the same general kind of experiences."

In short the validity of the report is determined by the care taken to secure valid materials and by the mass and consistency of testimony bearing upon significant issues. This mass and consistency protects the validity of the conclusions.

Foremost among the contributions of these reports is the elaboration of the phenomenon of "emotional possession" which is characteristic of the experience of children before the motion-picture screen. Watching in the dark of the theater, the young child sits in the presence of reality when he observes the actors perform and the plot of the drama unfold. He sees the actions of people living in a real world—not of actors playing a make-believe rôle. His emotions are aroused in ways that have been described. He forgets his surroundings. He loses ordinary control of his feelings, his actions, and his thoughts. He identifies himself with the plot and loses himself in the picture. His "emotional condition may get such a strong grip on him that even his efforts to rid himself of it by reasoning with himself may prove of little avail." He is possessed by the drama.

The intensity of child experience in viewing pictures cannot be fully appreciated by adults. To adults the picture is good or bad, the acting satisfactory or unsatisfactory, the singing up to or not up to standard. To them a picture is just a picture. They may recall memories of thrills they used to have but the memories are pale in comparison to the actual experience. They get a more vivid impression of this excitement by watching a theater full of children as a thrilling drama unreels. They see the symptoms of keen emotion. But even in the presence of these manifestations they miss the depth and intensity of the child's experience.

Several factors contribute to emotional possession. The actions and the setting are concrete. When in the fairy story the child is told that the prince led his troops into battle he has to provide his own imagery; but in the picture he sees the charming prince at the head of a band of "real" men. Every significant visual image is provided before his eyes in the motion picture. He does not have to translate the words in which the story is conveyed. He sees machines; he does not hear about them. He visits the islands of the southern seas in a real ship; he does not have to listen to a narrator describe the scenes in words alone. The motion picture tells a very concrete and simple tale in a fashion which makes the story easy to grasp.

Emotional possession is also caused by the dramatic forms of the picture. One of the objectives of drama is to arouse the emotions. Indeed, the weakness of many "teaching films" is the absence of dramatic elements—often necessarily omitted because of the nature of the content to be taught. But in the commercial movies and in teaching films of action, the dramatic flow of the story stirs the emotions and produces that intensity of experience which Blumer calls "emotional possession."

A third factor which contributes its influence to this condition is the attractiveness of the pictures—beautiful and thrilling scenes, interesting people, attractive persons moving on the stage, stimulating color, expert lighting, and the like. The child wants to be a part of such a bit of life. He does not pull back from the experience; he hurls himself into it.

All of these factors and probably others produce a condition that is favorable to certain types of learning. This is the quality of authority. Children accept as true, correct, proper, right what they see on the screen. They have little knowledge. The people on the screen are confidence-producing. Everything works to build up a magnificent and impressive world. Holaday and Stoddard found the children accepting both fact and error as fact. Blumer indicates the power of movie patterns upon conduct. The authority of the screen may account for some of the striking change of attitude of children found by Peterson and Thurstone.

All of these considerations lead inevitably to the increasing strength of the conclusion that the motion picture is an extremely powerful medium of education.

A second conclusion drawn from the report is that the range of influence of movies is very wide. Blumer found in studying two thousand children what every parent knows about his own child—that the movies dominate the patterns of play of children in a wide variety of forms. He presents scores of cases to show that the world of phantasy of young children and adolescents and of both sexes is ruled by movie subjects. Dozens of cases are presented to show the effects of the movies in stimulating emotions of fright, sorrow, love, and "excitement." Cases are presented to illustrate how the movies give children techniques of action in situations which are of interest to them ranging from the trivial techniques of the playground to disturbing cues for the delinquent. And most far-reaching of all he indicates how they stir powerful ambitions, good and bad; develop permanent ideals, high and low; and crystallize the framework of life careers. In most unexpected quarters the influence of the movies is discovered in the reports of Blumer and Thrasher and their associates.

A third concept which supplements emotional possession and range of influence is the guidance concept which grows out of the preceding paragraph. Children are born into a world of which they know nothing. They are little individualists who have laboriously to learn how to fit into social groups. They possess impulses, instincts, wishes, desires, which drive them on to seek experience, adventure, and satisfaction. They are avidly interested in everything that seems to them to be able to provide what they want.

Yet they know so little and are so anxious to learn. They seek information, stimulation, and guidance in every direction. They are often confused, frequently maladjusted, and sometimes without confidence. In this situation the motion picture seems to be a godsend to them. While they are being entertained they are being shown in attractive and authoritative fashion what to do. They are guided in one direction or another as they absorb rightly or wrongly this idea or that one. Sometimes the guidance is good, at other times it is bad. Sometimes it lies in a direction opposed to the teachings of the home or the school; at other times it reinforces them. But always the motion picture is potentially a powerfully influential director. Not the only guide which leads them, to be sure: the community, chums and playmates, the home, the school, the church, the newspapers, all are used by these omnivorous seekers after the kinds of experience they want. But among them the motion picture possesses potency so substantial that society must not fail to understand and see that it is used beneficently in the guidance of children.

One means of helping the child to dominate his movie experiences rather than be possessed emotionally by them is a fourth product of these investigations. It is possible to increase control of movie experiences by developing what Ruckmick calls adult discount and Blumer describes as emotional detachment. Blumer describes one interesting series of cases to show the stages of growth of this maturer attitude. Certain fourth graders showed in the most undisguised fashion a great interest in serial thrillers and particularly in one. They talked freely and spoke with frank enthusiasm. The sixth graders were reluctant to talk. They admitted interest yet felt some shame at their interest in a "childish" picture. Their attitude was one of affected sophistication. The attitude of the eighth graders was, however, one of spontaneous and frank disapproval, dislike, and disgust at serials. The steps were three in number, frank approval, affected sophistication, and mature disapproval.

Three methods of developing adult discount or emotional detachment are mentioned by Blumer. The one most commonly present in the evolution of children's attitudes is the response to the attitude of slighly older groups or the "sophisticated" members of one's own group—as just indicated. The child is quick to put away childish things when his group frowns upon them as childish and he enjoys exhibiting superiority and sophistication. In later years and with wider experience adult discount may be produced by a second factor: the conviction that the pictures are not true to life. "In real life things aren't that way." This is a normal method of developing sophistication. The third method is to give children instruction about the movies. Sometimes Blumer found that talks with parents, or suggestions that "this is only make believe" from older people, helped the children to develop emotional detachment. Particularly, however, detachment comes with learning how pictures are made, how effects are secured, what to look for in pictures, what makes pictures artistically good or bad. Dale's appreciation study contributes to this end.

In summary of the direct influences of motion pictures on conduct: they owe their power over children chiefly to the factor of emotional possession; the range of influence of commercial movies is very wide; the motion picture because of its potency in many directions plays a substantial and significant rôle in the informal guidance of children; and the influence of pictures can be controlled in considerable measure by the development of emotional detachment and the application of an adult discount. In producing this intelligent attitude toward the movies, instruction in motion-picture criticism and appreciation provides a promising lead.

With this section, we have concluded a description of the studies which essayed to measure the influence of the motion picture as such. We see that as an instrument of education it has unusual power to impart information, to influence specific attitudes toward objects of social value, to affect emotions either in gross or in microscopic proportions, to affect health in a minor degree through sleep disturbance, and to affect profoundly the patterns of conduct of children.

Edward A. Shils and Morris Janowitz

COHESION AND DISINTEGRATION IN
THE WEHRMACHT IN WORLD WAR II

(Introductory Note: The analysis of the German army as a social group from which the following selection was drawn emphasized the crucial importance of primary group organization in the maintenance of fighting effectiveness and morale. It appears that the immediately present agents and symbols of authority—junior officers, NCO's, and conceptions of soldierly honor—were effective because of their consistency with the personality system of the individual soldier. The excerpt which has been reprinted deals with the effectiveness of more remote or secondary symbols, in German military morale: on the one hand, those of indoctrination by the Nazis, and, on the other hand, the propaganda appeals employed by the Allied Expeditionary Forces in Europe.)

Strategic aspects of the war. For the mass of the German Army, the strategic phases of the war were viewed apathetically. The ignorance of the German troops about important military events, even on their own front, was partly a result of the poverty of information about the actual course of the war—itself a part of Nazi policy.[1] But the deliberate management of ignorance need not always result in such far-reaching indifference as the German soldiers showed. Deliberately maintained ignorance would have resulted in a flood of rumors, had the German soldiers been more eager to know about the strategic phases of the war. As it was, there were very few rumors on the subject—merely apathy. Three weeks after the fall of the city of Aachen, there were still many prisoners being taken in the adjoining area who did not know that the city had fallen. For at least a week after the beginning of von Rundstedt's counter-offensive, most of the troops

Reprinted from *The Public Opinion Quarterly*, Vol. XII (1948), pp. 300-306; 308-315, by permission of the authors and the publisher. (Copyright, 1948, by Princeton University Press.)
[1] Nazi propagandists, with their hyperpolitical orientation, tended to overestimate the German soldier's responsiveness to politics.

on the northern hinge of the bulge did not know that the offensive was taking place and were not much interested when they were told after capture. Of 140 Ps/W taken between December 23-24, 1944, only 35 per cent had heard of the counter-offensive and only 7 per cent said that they thought it significant.[2]

Some exception to this extensive strategic indifference existed with respect to the Eastern front. Although the German soldiers were extremely ignorant of the state of affairs on that front and made little attempt to reduce their ignorance, still the question of Russians was so emotionally charged, so much the source of anxiety, that it is quite likely that fear of the Russians did play a role in strengthening resistance. National Socialist propaganda had long worked on the traditional repugnance and fear of the German towards the Russian. The experience of the German soldiers in Russia in 1941 and 1942 increased this repugnance by direct perception of the primitive life of the Russian villager. But probably more important was the projection onto the Russians of the guilt feelings generated by the ruthless brutality of the Germans in Russia during the occupation period. The shudder of horror which frequently accompanied a German soldier's remarks about Russia was a result of all these factors. These attitudes influenced German resistance in the West through the shift of soldiers from East to West and the consequent diffusion of their attitudes among their comrades. They also took effect by making soldiers worry about what would happen to their families if the Russians entered Germany. Of course, it should also be mentioned that this fear of the Russians also made some German soldiers welcome a speedier collapse on the Western front in the hope that a larger part of Germany would fall under Anglo-American control.

Before the actual occupation, only a small minority expressed fear of the consequences of an Anglo-American occupation. The continuing monthly opinion poll conducted by the Psychological Warfare Branch, mentioned elsewhere, never showed more than 20 per cent of the prisoners answering "yes" to the question, "Do you believe that revenge will be taken against the population after the war?" Those who feared retribution were confirmed Nazis. Yet the general absence of fear of revenge did not cause a diminution of German resistance.

Neither did expectations about the outcome of the war play a great role in the integration or disintegration of the German Army. The statistics regarding German soldier opinion cited below show that pessimism as to final triumph was quite compatible with excellence in fighting behavior. The far greater effectiveness of considerations of self-preservation, and their vast

---

[2] The fact that the High Command made no attempt to explain away the defeat of the counter-offensive may have been due, among other things, to its conviction of the irrelevance of strategic consideration in the morale of the ordinary soldier.

preponderance over interest in the outcome of the war and the strategic situation, is shown by German prisoner recall of the contents of Allied propaganda leaflets (see Table I). In the last two months of 1944 and the first two months of 1945, not less than 59 per cent of the sample of prisoners taken each month recalled references to the preservation of the individual, and the figure rose to 76 per cent in February of 1945. On the other hand, the proportion of prisoners recalling references to the total strategic situation of the war and the prospect of the outcome of the war seldom

**TABLE I—Tabulation of Allied Leaflet Propaganda Themes
Remembered by German Ps/W**

	Dec. 15-31 1944	Jan. 1-15 1945	Jan. 15-31 1945	Feb. 1-15 1945
Number of Ps/W	60	83	99	135
Themes and appeals remembered:				
a. Promise of good treatment as Ps/W and self-preservation through surrender	63%	65%	59%	76%
b. Military news	15	17	19	30
c. Strategical hopelessness of Germany's position	13	12	25	26
d. Hopelessness of a local tactical situation	3	1	7	7
e. Political attacks on German leaders	7	5	4	8
f. Bombing of German cities	2	8	6	...
g. Allied Military Government	7	3	..	...
h. Appeals to civilians	5	4	2	...

(The percentages add up to more than 100% since some Ps/W remembered more than one topic. Only Ps/W remembering at least one theme were included in this tabulation.)

amounted to more than 20 per cent, while references to political subjects seldom amounted to more than 10 per cent. The general tendency was not to think about the outcome of the war unless forced to do so by direct interrogation. Even pessimism was counter-balanced by the reassurances provided by identification with a strong and benevolent Führer, by identification with good officers, and by the psychological support of a closely integrated primary group.

The ethics of war and patriotism. Quite consistently, ethical aspects of the war did not trouble the German soldier much. When pressed by Allied interrogators, Ps/W said that Germany had been forced to fight for its life. There were very few German soldiers who said that Germany had been morally wrong to attack Poland, or Russia. Most of them thought that if anything had been wrong about the war, it was largely in the realm of technical decisions. The decision to extirpate the Jews had been too drastic not because of its immorality but because it united the world against Germany. The declaration of war against the Soviet Union was wrong only because it created a two-front war. But these were all arguments which had to be forced from the Ps/W. Left to themselves, they seldom mentioned them.

The assumption underlying these arguments was that the strong national state is a good in itself. But it was not, in fact, the highest good for any but the "hard core." In September 1944, for example, only 5 per cent of a sample of 634 Ps/W said that they were worried about anything other than personal or familial problems, while in the very same survey, more than half of the Ps/W said they believed that Germany was losing the war or that they were at best uncertain of the war's outcome. In brief, fear for Germany's future as a nation does not seem to have been very important in the ordinary soldier's outlook and in motivating his combat behavior. As a matter of fact, as the war became more and more patently a threat to the persistence of the German national state, the narcissism of the German soldier increased correspondingly, so that the idea of national survival did not become an object of widespread preoccupation even when it might have been expected to become so.[3]

Ethical-religious scruples seem to have played an equally small role. Although there were a few interesting cases of Roman Catholic deserters, Roman Catholics (except Austrians, Czechs and Polish nationals) do not seem to have deserted disproportionately. Prisoners seldom expressed remorse for Nazi atrocities, and practically no case was noted of a desertion because of moral repugnance against Nazi atrocities.

Political ideals. The significance of political ideals, of symbols of political systems, was rather pronounced in the case of the "hard core" minority of fervent Nazis in the German Army. Their desire for discipline under a strong leader made them enthusiasts for the totalitarian political system. Their passionate aggressiveness also promoted projective tendencies which facilitated their acceptance of the Nazi picture of an innocent and harmless Germany encircled by the dark, threatening cloud of Bolsheviks, Jews, Negroes, etc., and perpetually in danger from inner enemies as well. But for most of the German soldiers, the political system of National Socialism was of little interest.

The *system* was indeed of very slight concern to German civilians also, even though dissatisfaction increased to a high pitch towards the end of the war. Soldiers on the whole were out of touch with the operation of the Party on the home front. Hence the political system impinged little on their consciousness. Thus, for example, of 53 potential and actual deserters in the Mediterranean theater, only one alleged political grounds for his action. The irrelevance of party politics to effective soldiering has already been

[3] The proposition often asserted during the war that the Allies' refusal to promise a "soft peace" to the Germans was prolonging the war, i.e., that German military resistance was motivated by fear of what the Allies would do to Germany in event of its defeat, scarcely finds support in the fact that in October 1944, when the German front was stiffening, 74 per cent of a sample of 345 Ps/W said they did not expect revenge to be taken against the German population after the war.

treated above: here we need only repeat the statement of a German soldier, "Nazism begins ten miles behind the front line."

Nor did the soldiers react in any noticeable way to the various attempts to Nazify the army. When the Nazi Party salute was introduced in 1944, it was accepted as just one more army order, about equal in significance to an order requiring the carrying of gas masks. The introduction of the *National Socialistische Führungsoffiziere* (Guidance, or Indoctrination Officer), usually known as the NSFO, was regarded apathetically or as a joke. The contempt for the NSFO was derived not from his Nazi connection but from his status as an "outsider" who was not a real soldier. The especially Nazified Waffen SS divisions were never the object of hostility on the part of the ordinary soldier, even when the responsibility for atrocities was attributed to them. On the contrary, the Waffen SS was highly esteemed, not as a Nazi formation, but for its excellent fighting capacity. Wehrmacht soldiers always felt safer when there was a Waffen SS unit on their flank.

Devotion to Hitler. In contrast to the utterly apolitical attitude of the German infantry soldier towards almost all secondary symbols, an intense and personal devotion to Adolph Hitler was maintained in the German Army throughout the war. There could be little doubt that a high degree of identification with the Führer was an important factor in prolonging German resistance. Despite fluctuations in expectations as to the outcome of the war the trust in Hitler remained at a very high level even after the beginning of the serious reverses in France and Germany. In monthly opinion polls of German Ps/W opinion from D-Day until January 1945, in all but two samples over 60 per cent expressed confidence in Hitler,[4] and confidence in January was nearly as high as it was in the preceding June. During this same period considerably more than half of the German soldiers in seven out of eight polls said they believed that it was impossible for the German Army to defeat the Allies in France. Only when the German Army began to break up in the face of overwhelming Allied fire power and deep, communications-cutting penetrations, did confidence in Hitler fall to the unprecedentedly low level of 30 per cent. Even when defeatism was rising to the point at which only one-tenth of the prisoners taken as of March 1945 believed that the Germans had any change of success, still a third retained confidence in Hitler.[5]

Belief in the good intentions of the Führer, in his eminent moral qualities, in his devotion and contributions to the well-being of the German people, continued on an even higher level. This strong attachment grew in

---

[4] See Gurfein, M. I., and Janowitz, Morris, "Trends in Wehrmacht Morale," *The Public Opinion Quarterly*, Vol. 10, No. 1 (1946), p. 78.

[5] Much of the reduction of trust in Hitler which occurred in this final period was simply a diminution in esteem for Hitler's technical skill as a strategist and as a diplomat.

large part from the feeling of strength and protection which the German
soldier got from his conception of the Führer personality.

For older men, who had lived through the unemployment of the closing
years of the Weimar Republic and who experienced the joy of being rein-
stated in gainful employment by Nazi full-employment policies, Hitler was
above all the man who had provided economic security. This attitude extended even to left wing soldiers of this generation, who denounced the
National Socialist political system, but found occasion to say a good word
for Hitler as a man who had restored order and work in Germany. For
men of the generation between 22-35, who had first experienced Hitler's
charisma in the struggles to establish their manliness during late adoles-
cence, Hitler was the prototype of strength and masculinity. For the
younger Nazi fanatics, he was a father substitute, providing the vigilant
discipline and the repression of dangerous impulses both in the individual
and in the social environment; for them he had the additional merit of
legitimating revolt against the family and traditional restraints.

Prisoners spoke of Hitler with enthusiasm, and even those who expressed
regret over the difficulties which his policies had brought on Germany by
engendering a two-front war and by allowing the Jews to be persecuted
so fiercely as to arouse world hatred—even these men retained their warm
esteem for his good intentions. They found it necessary to exculpate him
in some way by attributing his errors to dishonest advisors who kept the
truth from him, or to certain technical difficulties in his strategic doctrines
which did not in any way reflect on his fundamental moral greatness or
nobility.

It was difficult for German soldiers, as long as they had this attitude
toward Hitler, to rebel mentally against the war. Time after time, prisoners
who were asked why Hitler continued the war when they themselves admitted it was so obviously lost, said he wouldn't continue the war and waste
lives if he did not have a good, even though undisclosed, strategic reason
for doing so, or if he didn't have the resources to realize his ends. Nazis as
well as non-Nazi answered in this way. Or else they would say, "the Führer
has never deceived us," or, "he must have a good reason for doing what he
does."

There was obviously a fear of rendering an independent judgment of
events among the German soldiers and a desire for some strong leader to
assume the responsibility for determining their fate. American and British
soldiers often complained that the complexity of the army organization and
strategy was so great and their own particular part was so small that they
could not see the role of their personal missions. Their failure to see the
connection made them miserable because it reduced their sense of personal
autonomy. In the German Army, on the other hand, there was no difficulty

for soldiers who were used throughout their lives to having other persons determine their objectives for them.

It is also possible that the very high devotion to Hitler under conditions of great stress was in part a reaction formation growing from a hostility against lesser authorities, which emerged as the weakness of these authorities became more manifest. In the last year of the war, hostility and contempt on the part of the German soldiers toward Nazi Party functionaries and toward Nazi Party leaders below Hitler (particularly Goebbels and Goering) was increasing. After the *Putsch* of July 20, hostility toward senior Wehrmacht officers also increased somewhat, although it never reached the levels of hostility displayed by civilians against local civilian Party officials and leaders. It is possible, therefore, that guilt created in ambivalent personalities by giving expression, even though verbally, to hostility against subordinate agents of authority, had to be alleviated by reaffirmed belief in the central and highest authority.

Weakening of the Hitler symbol. As the integral pattern of defense was broken down, however, and as danger to physical survival increased, devotion to Hitler deteriorated. The tendency to attribute virtue to the strong and immorality to the weak took hold increasingly, and while it did not lead to a complete rejection of Hitler, it reached a higher point than at any other stage in the history of National Socialism. The announcement of Hitler's death met an incapacity to respond on the part of many soldiers. There seemed to be no willingness to question the truth of the report, but the great upsurge of preoccupation with physical survival as a result of disintegration of the military primary group, the loss of contact with junior officers and the greatly intensified threat of destruction, caused a deadening of the power to respond to this event. For the vast horde of dishevelled, dirty, bewildered prisoners, who were being taken in the last weeks of the war, Hitler was of slight importance alongside the problem of their own biological survival and the welfare of their families. For the small minority who still had sufficient energy to occupy themselves with "larger problems," the news of Hitler's death released a sort of amorphous resentment against the fallen leader whose weakness and immorality had been proven by the failure of his strategy. But even here, the resentment was not expressed in explicit denunciations of Hitler's character or personality. The emphasis was all on technical deficiencies and weaknesses.

The explanation of the deterioration and final—though probably only temporary—hostility toward Hitler may in part be sought in the average German soldier's ambivalence toward the symbols of authority. This psychological mechanism, which also helps to explain the lack of a significant resistance movement inside Germany, enables us to understand the curve of Hitler's fame among the German people. Hitler, the father symbol, was loved for his power and his great accomplishments and hated for his oppressiveness, but the latter sentiment was repressed. While he remained strong it was psychologically expedient—as well as politically expedient—to identify with Hitler and to displace hostility on to weaker minority groups and foreigners. But once Hitler's authority had been undermined, the German soldiers rejected it and tended to express their hostility by projecting their own weakness on to him.

Thus the only important secondary symbol in motiviating the behavior of the German soldiers during the recent war also lost its efficacy when the primary group relations of comradeliness, solidarity and subordination to junior officers broke down, and with it the superego of the individual, on which the effective functioning of the primary group depends.[6]

Propaganda themes. The most striking aspect of Nazi indoctrination of their own men during combat was the employment of negative appeals and counter-propaganda, which attempted less to reply directly to the substance of our claims than to explain the reasons why the Allies were using propaganda.

The Nazis frankly believed that they could employ our propaganda efforts as a point of departure for strengthening the unpolitical resolve of their men. They had the legend of the effectiveness of Allied propaganda in World War I as a warning from which to "conclude" that if the Germans failed to be tricked by propaganda this time, success was assured. A typical instance of this attitude was contained in a captured order order issued by the Officer in Command of the garrison of Boulogne on September 11, 1944, in which he appealed to his men not to be misled by Allied propaganda. The German order claimed that the propaganda attack in the form of leaflets was in itself an expression of the weakness of the Allied offensive, which was in desperate need of the port for communications. During the same period, an NSF (political officer) issued an elaborate statement in which he reminded the garrison at Le Havre that the "enemy resorts to propaganda as a weapon which he used in the last stages of the first world war," in order to point out that German victory depended on the determination of the German soldier to resist Allied propaganda.

In the fall and winter of 1944, the campaign to counteract Allied propaganda by "exposing" it was intensified and elaborated. (This method had the obvious advantage that direct refutations of Allied claims could largely be avoided.) *Mitteilung für die Truppe* (October 1944), a newspaper for

---

[6] The mixture of apathy and resentment against Hitler persisted through the first part of the demobilization period following the end of the war, but as life began to reorganize and to take on new meaning and the attitudes toward authority, which sustain and are sustained by the routines of daily life, revived, esteem for Hitler also began to revive. It is likely to revive still further and to assume a prominent place in German life once more, if the new elite which is being created under the Allied occupation shows weakness and lack of decisiveness and self-confidence.

officer indoctrination, reviewed the major weapons in the "poison offensive." They included: attacks against the Party and its predominant leaders ("this is not surprising as the enemy will, of course, attack those institutions which give us our greatest strength"); appeals to the Austrians to separate themselves from the Germans ("the time when we were split up in small states was the time of our greatest weakness"); sympathy with the poor German women who work in hellish factories ("the institution must be a good one, otherwise the enemy would not attack it").

Other themes "exposed" in leaflets were: the enemy attempts to separate the leaders from the people ("Just as the Kaiser was blamed in 1918, it now is Hitler who is supposed to be responsible"); the enemy admits his own losses in an exaggerated way in order to obtain the reputation of veracity and to lie all the more at the opportune moment.

Even earlier in the Western campaign, the Germans followed the policy of stamping Allied leaflets with the imprint, "Hostile Propaganda," and then allowing them to circulate in limited numbers. This was being carried out at the same time that mutually contradictory orders for the complete destruction of all enemy propaganda were being issued. The explanation, in part, is that the Nazis realized that it would be impossible to suppress the flood of Allied leaflets, and therefore sought to clearly label them as such and to employ them as a point of departure for counter-propaganda.

The procedure of overstamping Allied leaflets was linked with follow-up indoctrination talks. Such indoctrination lectures, which were conducted by the Nazi NSFO's, became towards the end of the war one of the main vehicles of Nazi indoctrination of their own troops. Ps/W claimed, although it was probably not entirely correct, that they usually slept through such sessions, or at least paid little attention, until the closing *Sieg Heil* was sounded. At this late date in the war, emphasis on oral propaganda was made necessary by the marked disruption of communications. Radio listening at the front was almost non-existent due to the lack of equipment; when in reserve, troops listened more frequently. Newspapers were distributed only with great difficulty. More important were the leaflets which were either dropped by air on their own troops or distributed through command channels.

"Strength through fear." Major lines of the negative approach employed by these leaflets in indoctrination talks, in the rumors circulated by NSF officers, stressed "strength through fear," particularly fear of Russia and the general consequences of complete destruction that would follow defeat.

Because of the German soldier's concern about the welfare of his family living inside Germany, Nazi agencies were constantly issuing statements about the successful evacuation of German civilians to the east bank of the Rhine.

Equally stressed in the strength through fear theme were retaliation threats against the families of deserters, mistreatment of prisoners of war in Anglo-American prison camps, and the ultimate fate of prisoners. The phrase *Sieg oder Sibirien* (Victory or Siberia) was emphasized and much material was released to prove that the Anglo-Americans planned to turn over their prisoners to the Russians. When the U.S. Army stopped shipping German Ps/W to the United States, Nazi propaganda officers spread the rumor among German soldiers "that the way to Siberia is shorter from France than from the United States."

Statements by Ps/W revealed that shortly before the Rundstedt counter-attack, speeches by NSFO's were increased. One of the main subjects seems to have been weapons. In retrospect, the intent of the directives under which they were working was obvious. Attempts were made to explain the absence of the Luftwaffe, while the arrival in the near future of new and better weapons was guaranteed.

Psychological preparation for the December counter-offensive was built around the Rundstedt order of the day that "everything is at stake." Exhortations were backed up with exaggerated statements by unit commanders that large amounts of men and material were to be employed. Immediately thereafter, official statements were issued that significant penetrations had been achieved; special editions of troop papers were prepared announcing that 40,000 Americans had been killed.

Such announcements received little attention among the troops actually engaged in the counter-offensive because of the obvious difficulties in disseminating propaganda to fighting troops.

Nevertheless, after the failure of the counter-attack, the Nazis felt called upon to formulate a plausible line to explain the sum total result of that military effort, especially for those who felt that better military judgment would have resulted in a purely defensive strategy against Russia. On January 25, *Front und Heimat* announced that the December offensive had smashed the plan for a simultaneous onslaught: "The East can hold only if the West does too. . . . Every fighting man in the West knows that the Anglo-Americans are doing all they can, although belatedly, to start the assault on the Fortress Germany. Our task in the West now is to postpone that time as long as possible and to guard the back of our Armies in the East."

Despite the obvious limitations on the efficacy of propaganda during March and April 1945, the Nazis continued to the very end to keep up their propaganda efforts. Due to the confusion within the ranks of the Wehrmacht and the resulting difficulties of dissemination, the task devolved almost wholly on the NSFO's who spent much of their time reading to the troops the most recent orders governing desertion. Leaflets called largely on the Landser's military spirit to carry on. One even demanded that he remain silent (*zu schweigen*). The Nazis taxed their fancy to create rumors as the last means of bolstering morale. Here a favorite technique for stimulating favorable rumors was for CO's to read to their men "classified" documents from official sources which contained promises of secret weapons or discussed the great losses being inflicted upon the Allies.

The Impact of Allied Propaganda on Wehrmacht Solidarity

The system of controls which the social structure of the Wehrmacht exercised over its individual members greatly reduced those areas in which symbolic appeals of the Allies could work. But the millions of leaflets which were dropped weekly and the "round-the-clock" broadcasts to the German troops certainly did not fail to produce some reactions.

The very first German Ps/W who were interrogated directly on their reactions to Allied propaganda soon revealed a stereotyped range of answers which could be predicted from their degree of Nazification. The fanatical Nazi claimed, "No German would believe anything the enemy has to say," while an extreme attitude of acceptance was typified by a confirmed anti-Nazi who pleaded with his captors: "Now is the moment to flood the troops with leaflets. You have no idea of the effect sober and effective leaflets have on retreating troops." But these extreme reactions of soldiers were of low frequency; Nazi soldiers might admit the truth of our leaflets but usually would not accept their conclusions and implications.

The fundamentally indifferent reaction to Allied propaganda was most interestingly shown in an intensive study of 150 Ps/W captured in October 1944 of whom 65 per cent had seen our leaflets and for the most part professed that they believed their contents. This was a group which had fought very obstinately, and the number of active deserters, if any, was extremely small. Some forty of these Ps/W offered extended comments as to what they meant when they said they believed the contents of Allied leaflets.

Five stated outright that they believed the messages and that the leaflets assisted them and their comrades to surrender.

Seven declared they believed the leaflets, but were powerless to do anything about appeals to surrender.

Eight stated that they believed the contents, but nevertheless as soldiers and decent individuals would never think of deserting.

Twenty-two declared that events justified belief in the leaflets, but they clearly implied that this had been of little importance in their battle experiences.

In Normandy, where the relatively small front was blanketed with printed material, up to 90 per cent of the Ps/W reported that they had read Allied leaflets, yet this period was characterized by very high German morale and stiff resistance.

Throughout the Western campaign, with the exception of periods of extremely bad weather or when the front was fluid, the cumulative percentage of exposure ranged between 60 and 80 per cent. (This cumulative percentage of exposure was based on statements by Ps/W that they had seen leaflets sometime while fighting on the Western front after D-Day. A few samples indicated that penetration during any single month covered about 20 per cent of the prisoners.) Radio listening among combat troops was confined to a minute fraction due to the lack of equipment; rear troops listened more frequently. In the case of both leaflets and radio it was found that there was widespread but desultory comment on the propaganda, much of which comment distorted the actual contents.

Not only was there wide penetration by Allied leaflets and newssheets, but German soldiers frequently circulated them extensively among their comrades. A readership study of *Nachrichten für die Truppe,* a daily newssheet published by the Allied Psychological Warfare Division, showed that each copy which was picked up had an average readership of between four and five soldiers—a figure which is extremely large in view of the conditions of combat life. Not only were leaflets widely circulated, but it became a widespread practice for soldiers to carry Allied leaflets on their person, especially the "safe conduct pass" leaflets which bore a statement by General Eisenhower guaranteeing the bearer swift and safe conduct through Allied lines and the protection of the Geneva convention. There is evidence that in certain sectors of the front, German soldiers even organized black-market trading in Allied propaganda materials.

It is relevant to discuss here the differences in effectiveness between tactical and strategic propaganda. By tactical propaganda, we refer to propaganda which seeks to promise immediate results in the tactical situation. The clearest example of this type of propaganda is afforded by "cross the lines" loudspeaker broadcasts, which sometimes facilitated immediate capture of the prisoners of war—not by propaganda in the ordinary sense, but by giving instructions on how to surrender safely, once the wish to surrender was present.

No sufficiently accurate estimate is available of the total number of prisoners captured by the use of such techniques, but signal successes involving hundreds of isolated troops in the Normandy campaign have been credited to psychological warfare combat teams. Even more successful were the loud-speaker-carrying tanks employed in the Rhine River offensive, when the first signs of weakening resistance were encountered. For example, the Fourth Armored Division reported that its psychological warfare unit captured over 500 prisoners in a four-day dash from the Kyll River to the Rhine. Firsthand investigation of these loudspeaker missions, and interrogation of prisoners captured under such circumstances, establish that Allied propaganda was effective in describing the tactical situation to totally isolated and helpless soldiers and in arranging an Allied cease fire and thereby presenting an assurance to the German soldier of a safe surrender. The successful targets for such broadcasts were groups where solidarity and ability to function as a unit were largely destroyed. Leaflets especially written for specific sectors and dropped on pin point targets by fighter-bombs were used instead of loudspeakers where larger units were cut off. This method proved less successful, since the units to which they were addressed were usually better integrated and the necessary cease fire conditions could not be arranged.

Less spectacular, but more extensive, was strategic propaganda. Allied directives called for emphasis on four themes in this type of propaganda: (1) Ideological attacks on the Nazi Party and Germany's war aims, (2) the strategical hopelessness of Germany's military and economic position, (3) the justness of the United Nations war aims and their unity and determination to carry them out (unconditional surrender, although made known to the troops, was never stressed), (4) promises of good treatment to prisoners of war, with appeals to self-preservation through surrender.

Although it is extremely difficult, especially in view of the lack of essential data, to assess the efficacy of these various themes, some tentative clues might be seen in the answers given to the key attitude questions in the monthly Psychological Warfare opinion poll of captured German soldiers.[7] Thus, there was no significant decline in attachment to Nazi ideólogy until February and March 1945. In other words, propaganda attacks on Nazi ideology seem to have been of little avail, and attachment to secondary symbols, e.g., Hitler, declined only when the smaller military units began to break up under very heavy pressure.

Since the German soldier was quite ignorant of military news on other fronts, it was believed that a great deal of printed material should contain factual reports of the military situation, stressing the strategical hopelessness of the German position. As a result, the third most frequently recalled items of our propaganda were the military news reports. It seems reasonable to believe that the emphasis on these subjects did contribute to the development of defeatist sentiment.

Despite the vast amount of space devoted to ideological attacks on German leaders, only about five per cent of the Ps/W mentioned this topic—a fact which supported the contention as to the general failure of ideological or secondary appeals. Finally, the presentation of the justness of our war aims was carried out in such a way as to avoid stressing the unconditional surrender aspects of our intentions, while emphasizing postwar peace intentions and organizational efforts; much was made of United Nations unity. All this fell on deaf ears, for of this material only a small minority of Ps/W (about 5 per cent) recalled specific statements about military government plans for the German occupation.

[7] Cf. Gurfein, M. I., and Janowitz, Morris, *op. cit.*

As has been pointed out previously, the themes which were most successful, at least in attracting attention and remaining fixed in the memory, were those promising good treatment as prisoners of war. In other words, propaganda referring to immediate concrete situations and problems seems to have been most effective in some respects.

The single leaflet most effective in communicating the promise of good treatment was the "safe conduct pass." Significantly, it was usually printed on the back of leaflets which contained no elaborate propaganda appeals except those of self-preservation. The rank and file tended to be favorably disposed to its official language and legal, document-like character. In one sector where General Eisenhower's signature was left off the leaflet, doubt was cast on its authenticity.

Belief in the veracity of this appeal was no doubt based on the attitude that the British and the Americans were respectable law-abiding soldiers who would treat their captives according to international law. As a result of this predisposition and the wide use of the safe conduct leaflets, as well as our actual practices in treating prisoners well, the German soldier came to have no fear of capture by British or American troops. The most that can be claimed for this lack of fear was that it many have decreased or undercut any tendency to fight to the death; it produced no active opposition to continued hostilities.

As an extension of the safe-conduct approach, leaflets were prepared instructing non-commissioned officers in detailed procedures by which their men could safely be removed from battle so as to avoid our fire and at the same time avoid evacuation by the German field police. If the Germans could not be induced to withdraw from combat actively, Allied propaganda appealed to them to hide in cellars. This in fact became a favorite technique of surrender, since it avoided the need of facing the conscience-twinging desertion problem.

As a result of psychological warfare research, a series of leaflets was prepared whose attack was aimed at primary group organization in the German Army, without recourse to ideological symbols. Group organization depended on the acceptance of immediate leadership and mutual trust. Therefore this series of leaflets sought to stimulate group discussion among the men and to bring into their focus of attention concerns which would loosen solidarity. One leaflet declared, "Do not take our (the Allies) word for it; ask your comrade; find out how he feels." Thereupon followed a series of questions on personal concerns, family problems, tactical consideration and supply problems. Discussion of these problems was expected to increase anxiety. It was assumed that to the degree that the soldier found that he was not isolated in his opinion, to that degree he would be strengthened in his resolve to end hostilities, for himself at least.

Conclusion

At the beginning of the second world war, many publicists and specialists in propaganda attributed almost supreme importance to psychological warfare operations. The legendary success of Allied propaganda against the German Army at the end of the first world war and the tremendous expansion of the advertising and mass communications industries in the ensuing two decades had convinced many people that human behavior could be extensively manipulated by mass communications. They tended furthermore to stress that military morale was to a great extent a function of the belief in the rightness of the "larger" cause which was at issue in the war; good soldiers were therefore those who clearly understood the political and moral implications of what was at stake. They explained the striking successes of the German Army in the early phases of the war by the "ideological possession" of the German soldiers, and they accordingly thought that propaganda attacking doctrinal conceptions would be defeating this army.

Studies of the German Army's morale and fighting effectiveness made during the last three years of the war throw considerable doubt on these hypotheses. The solidarity of the German Army was discovered by these studies—which left much to be desired from the standpoint of scientific rigor—to be based only very indirectly and very partially on political convictions or broader ethical beliefs. Where conditions were such as to allow primary group life to function smoothly, and where the primary group developed a high degree of cohesion, morale was high and resistance effective or at least very determined, regardless in the main of the political attitudes of the soldiers. The conditions of primary group life were related to spatial proximity, the capacity for intimate communication, the provision of paternal protectiveness by NCO's and junior officers, and the gratification of certain personality needs, e.g., manliness, by the military organization and its activities. The larger structure of the army served to maintain morale through the provision of the framework in which potentially individuating physical threats were kept at a minimum—through the organization of supplies and through adequate strategic dispositions.

The behavior of the German Army demonstrated that the focus of attention and concern beyond one's immediate face-to-face social circles might be slight indeed and still not interfere with the achievement of a high degree of military effectiveness. It also showed that attempts to modify behavior by means of symbols referring to events or values outside the focus of attention and concern would be given an indifferent response by the vast majority of the German soldiers. This was almost equally true under conditions of primary group integrity and under conditions of extreme primary group disintegration. In the former, primary needs were met adequately through the gratifications provided by the other members of the group; in the latter, the individual had regressed to a narcissistic state in which symbols referring to the outer world were irrelevant to his first concern—"saving his own skin."

At moments of primary group disintegration, a particular kind of propaganda less hortatory or analytical, but addressing the intensified desire to survive and describing the precise procedures by which physical survival could be achieved, was likely to facilitate further disintegration. Furthermore, in some cases aspects of the environment towards which the soldier might hitherto have been emotionally indifferent were defined for him by prolonged exposure to propaganda under conditions of disintegration. Some of these wider aspects, e.g., particular strategic consideration, then tended to be taken into account in his motivation and he was more likely to implement his defeatist mood by surrender than he would have been without exposure to propaganda.

It seems necessary, therefore, to reconsider the potentialities of propaganda in the context of all the other variables which influence behavior. The erroneous views concerning the omnipotence of propaganda must be given up and their place must be taken by much more differentiated views as to the possibilities of certain kinds of propaganda under different sets of conditions.

It must be recognized that on the moral plane most men are members of the larger society by virtue of identifications which are mediated through the human beings with whom they are in personal relationships. Many are bound into the larger society only by primary group identifications. Only a small proportion possessing special training or rather particular kinds of personalities are capable of giving a preponderant share of their attention and concern to the symbols of the larger world. The conditions under which these different groups will respond to propaganda will differ, as will also the type of propaganda to which they will respond.

W. Lloyd Warner and William E. Henry

THE RADIO DAY-TIME SERIAL:
A SYMBOLIC ANALYSIS

Hypotheses and Methods of Study: The influence of the radio on contemporary America is incalculable; it has penetrated into every aspect of our private and public life. It is said to be responsible for weakening or strengthening some of our basic social institutions, yet little is known about these important matters, few disinterested studies have been made of them to ascertain what radio is as a social form and as a medium of mass communication. Even less is known of what its various programs are as symbol systems and how they affect their audience. Frequently articles and editorials in the public press and popular journals express the bias of competing mass media or the "superior attitudes" of those who disapprove of contemporary mass literature and folk drama.

In its short existence the radio has developed several highly formalized types of entertainment; one of the most popular of these is the "soap opera," or daytime serial, a form of "folk" literature that appeals to over twenty million American women.[1]

Despite the attacks in the public press and of several leading psychiatrists in scientific journals on the daytime serial because of its supposed harmful effects on its audience, our present study discovered little or nothing to confirm their results. It should be said now that we found the representative programs we selected functioned very much like a folk tale, expressing the hopes and fears of its female audience and on the whole contributed to the integration of their lives into the world in which they lived. To come to such conclusions we had to learn what the daytime serial is as a symbol system, and how its symbols functioned in the public and private lives of the women who listened. We shall devote the remainder

Reprinted from *Genetic Psychology Monographs*, 37 (1948), pp. 7-13; 55-64, by permission of the authors and the publisher. (Copyright, 1948, by The Journal Press.)
[1] There are approximately 40 of these programs carried primarily by NBC and CBS.

of our paper to our conclusions and describing the methods used to obtain them.

Before the intensive study was begun the writers listened to most of the current daytime serials and learned that they could be divided into symbolic types. One of the most important, from the point of view of number of problems aired and size of audience, was what we have called the Family Type. Here the family provides the dramatic persons in the play and the center of the drama is a woman, usually the wife and mother to other important figures in the play. We decided to select one of the more popular serials of this type for our study. The Big Sister program was chosen because it has one of the largest audiences among daytime serials.

The conceptual scheme used in this analysis is a combination of the theories and methods of those psychological disciplines which study the emotions, beliefs, and motivations making up the internal life of the individual and the research methods which study the society that largely dominates the lives of individuals. When the behavior of the group and the private lives of the individuals composing the group are understood, then exact statements and predictions can be made about the behavior of these individuals when they compose a radio audience.[2]

The daytime serials, like many other dramas, is primarily a verbal symbol system which stimulates its audience as individuals and as members of society. Drama is always "an idealized representation of human life—of character, emotion, action—under forms manifest to the sense." The individuals composing the audience have, as members of society, a common body of understanding through which they interpret what they see and hear in terms of the customary symbolic behavior making up the common life of America. But each individual in the audience has a whole body of emotions and unconscious feelings and ideas which the serial must also satisfy. These emotionally charged private symbols, combined with those customarily used by all members of the group, are always present in every radio audience. Therefore, to understand how a daytime serial functions and how it is used by its audience, we need to know the symbolic content of the serial and how its symbols stimulate the women both as members of society and as individuals with private worlds and private fantasies.

In the light of the above basic formulations and to get useful and reliable answers from our investigations we asked the questions which follow in the next paragraph. When we were satisfied that the questions were sufficiently pointed and comprehensive, we then designed the research instruments and field techniques for getting the evidence necessary and sufficient to answer them. The answers constitute the conclusions of this paper.

The questions are:

[2] Warner, W. L. "The Society, the Individual and His Mental Disorders," *American Journal of Psychiatry*, 1937, 44, 275-84.

1. What is the symbolic content of the Big Sister program?

2. What are the social characteristics of its audience?

3. What are the overt and covert psychological characteristics of its audience?

4. How does the Big Sister program, as a symbolic system, stimulate the women (a) overtly, as members of American society and (b) covertly and privately, as separate individuals? Or, to ask this question another way, what does it mean to them, and how does the Big Sister program function in the public and private lives of the listening audience?

5. Is its influence positive or negative—that is, does it assist the women who listen to adjust to the external realities of American society and aid them in making emotional adjustments within themselves and thereby contribute positively to their lives, or does it stimulate them non-adaptively and contribute to their inner emotional maladjustment and disorient their external relations with their families in general?

If it is the former it means that the program helps guide and direct their anxieties and wishes into channels of thought and feeling that are normal and adaptive. If it is the latter, it means that the program contributes to neurotic anxiety and reduces the listener's effective relations with herself and with those about her.

Since it has been used in most varied contexts the term, symbol, must be defined before we give it further use. For the person who is interpreting it, a symbol is, in common sense terms, something which stands for something else. A symbol, or symbol system, directs one's attention to some other object. It organizes, records, and communicates our thoughts and feelings about ourselves and the world around us. To all human beings who interpret symbols, the relation between the symbol and that for which it stands is its *meaning*.[3] For symbols to be of significance (have meaning) it is necessary for the individual to have learned by previous experience how to interpret what he perceives. This experience is largely socially conditioned.[4]

Each society has symbolic systems which are, generally, ways of looking at and evaluating the world and its people. In fact, the society in which an individual participates is, in large part, a web of symbolic relations which control and organize the individual's thinking, feeling, and acting.[5]

[3] Ogden, C. K., and Richards, I. A. *The Meaning of Meaning*. New York: Harcourt Brace, 1927.

[4] Mead, G. H. *Mind, Self, and Society*. Chicago: University of Chicago Press, 1946. Freud, Sigmund. *New Introductory Lectures on Psychoanalysis*. New York: Garden City Publishing, 1933.

[5] Durkheim, Emile. *Elementary Forms of the Religious Life*. (Trans. J. W. Swain.) New York: Macmillan, 1926. Warner, W. L. *A Black Civilization*. New York: Harper, 1937. Warner, W. L. and Lunt, P. S. *The Social Life of a Modern Community*. New Haven: Yale University Press, 1941.

In this system the individual is an organism motivated by socio-biologica drives.[6] To survive as a normal being the individual must organize hi biological nature into a social self and participate with a minimum o conflict with others in the society while trying for a maximum of satisfac tion in discharging his energies. To be normal and adaptive this satisfactior must be achieved both for him and for his society.

Every individual in a given culture uses symbols in two ways: (a) pub licly when his values and concepts conform to group norms (the worc c-a-t refers to and means an object in which there is general agreement) and (b) privately when his own set of private meanings gives special sig nificance to the symbols and the things for which they stand.[7] Essentially the difference between public and private meanings of symbols is the difference between Emile Durkheim's "collective representation" and Sigmund Freud's concept of "dream work" and "content of the unconscious."

Therefore, to learn what a symbol system such as the daytime serial means, it is necessary to find out what the overt and public significance is and what the private and covert significance is to the individual.

Five research instruments were used: [8] (a) the Thematic Apperception Test (modified); (b) the Verbal Projective, a story technique which we constructed on the basis of the Big Sister plots; (c) directed interviews at the radio during the Big Sister program; (d) non-directed interviews; and (e) a schedule of social characteristics.

Ordinary interviewing, with the use of other appropriate instruments, is sufficient to understand the public symbol. But special techniques and instruments are necessary for getting at latent and private meanings. The

[6] Miller, N. E., and Dollard, J. Social Learning and Imitation. New Haven: Yale University Press, 1941.

[7] Durkheim, Emile. op. cit. Durkheim, Emile. Le Suicide. Paris: Alcan, 1930. Durkheim, Emile. Division of Labor in Society. (Trans. Simpson.) New York: Macmillan, 1933. Soap Opera, Fortune, 1946, 33, No. 3, p. 119.

[8] The research organized for our present purposes was based on the work that has been done in the study of American communities, and the social and psychological personality studies now being done by the Committee on Human Development and the Committee on Human Relations in Industry at the University of Chicago. To help us to get inside the unconscious and emotional lives of the individuals who were the subjects of these studies, the inner private life of the individual as well as his outer and public life is examined by a variety of scientific techniques running all the way from social anthropology through the standard psychological and socio-psychological procedures, through the use of projective techniques such as the Rorschach and the Thematic Apperception Test. The Research on Indian Education of the Office of Indian Affairs and the Committee on Human Development illustrate this methodology. Present studies of personality development of mid-western children now under way are continuing this approach in our own society. Henry, W. E. "The Thematic Apperception Technique in the Study of Culture-Personality Relations," Genetic Psychology Monograph, 1947, 35, 3-135. Leighton, D. and Kluckhohn, C. The Children of the People. Cambridge: Harvard University Press, 1947. MacGregor, G. Warriors Without Weapons. Chicago: University of Chicago Press, 1946. Thompson, L. and Joseph, A. The Hopi Way. Chicago: University of Chicago Press, 1945.

projective techniques were developed for the purposes of doing this quickly and economically. As L. K. Frank[9] says, projective techniques were created

to induce the individual to reveal his way of organizing experience by giving him a field (objects, materials, experiences) with relatively little structure and cultural patterning so that the personality can project upon that plastic field his way of seeing life, his meanings, significances, patterns, and especially his feelings. Thus we elicit a projection of the individual's *private world* because he has to organize the field, interpret the material and react effectively to it.

We used the Thematic Apperception Test[10] to study the personality of each listener. A large literature has been developed around this test and the analytical procedures for its interpretation. These cards have been used over a great variety of research situations, and the normal and abnormal types of responses to them studied. The subject is asked to tell a story about each card, in which he says what has happened, what is happening, and what the outcome of the picture will be. It has been found that the personalities and social situations of the respondents are projected into the stories they tell. The responses tell the research about the interpersonal relations of the subject, permitting integration of the results with the accompanying social analysis and with the subject's responses to the Big Sister Verbal Projective test.

The standard Thematic Apperception Test was modified for this study. Rather than administer the entire series of pictures to all subjects, a selection of 10 from the whole set was made. These 10 were selected according to the following criteria: (a) Our analysis of the daytime serial and our hypotheses as to the nature of this group of listeners suggested that certain psychological and social problems were of greater relevance than others. Therefore, an effort was made to secure data that were directly relevant to the hypotheses advanced. (b) Previous experience with the Thematic Apperception Test suggested that certain pictures were apt to give material directly relevant to our problem. Therefore, only those pictures were selected which gave promise of giving appropriate data. The method of analysis and the principles of interpretation used in this study were developed in previous researches of the Committee on Human Development of the University of Chicago and the Research on Indian Education. This method is described in Henry.[11]

[9] Frank, L. K. "Projective Methods for the Study of Personality," *Journal of Psychology*, 1939, 8, pp. 389-413.
[10] Murray, H. A. *Explorations in Personality*. New York: Oxford University Press, 1938. *Thematic Apperception Test*. Cambridge: Harvard University Press, Murray, H. A., et al. "Techniques for a Systematic Investigation of Fantasy," *Journal of Psychology*, 1937, 3, pp. 115-143.
[11] Henry, W. E. "The Thematic Apperception Technique in the Study of Culture-Personality Relations." *Genetic Psychology Monograph*, 1947, 35, 3-135.

The Verbal Projective test, fashioned from the characters and plot situation of the Big Sister program, was constructed and pre-tested with habitual listeners to the Big Sister program to make sure it was acceptable to them as being true to what is expected by listeners to the program. It is composed of a short summary of the plot of Big Sister and five stories. The characters of Ruth Wayne (Big Sister) and her husband, Dr. John Wayne, in this test were given the names used on the radio. The other characters were composites of similar characters in the script. They were given different names from those used on the radio.[12] The use of the Waynes' names and the new names for the other characters made it possible for us to tell our subjects that we were testing "future plots that might be used" and thereby stimulate them to greater imaginative efforts and reduce their tendency to feel that we were testing our memories of past sequences.

At the conclusion of the Big Sister test, the interviewee was asked to go through her answers to each of the stories for further amplification and clarification. She was then asked to tell what she thought each of the characters looks like. From this procedure we obtained pictorial stereotypes of the good and bad women who make up the plot of Big Sister. These stereotypes acted as checks on the verbal stories told by the respondents. This procedure was of considerable benefit to our analysis. The subjects were finally asked: What do you think will happen to them in the future? Do you have any other suggestions for future plots? Would you mind if some day I returned while you were actually listening to the program?

A small number of women were interviewed while they were listening to the Big Sister program to make sure that the responses we were getting to our test compared to the responses the same women gave to the Big Sister program. While the number was small, this procedure, when coupled with the pre-testing program and with the spontaneous responses of the subjects who often said that the characters in the stories were "just like those in Big Sister," increased our confidence that our instrument was reliable and our results valid.

To give us further insight, certain critical cases were further interviewed by the non-directed method. When the women told about their own personal and family problems (for which we interviewed) we obtained further checks on (a) the validity of our results from the other instruments, and (b) more knowledge about their private lives and how the program fitted into their basic emotional and social needs. The projective techniques stimulate the women to tell about their own private

[12] The character of Christine in our Verbal Projective is a combination of Diane and Hope in recent episodes. The character of Billy is Neddy, and Tom is Frank in these same episodes.

problems, and this procedure moves easily over to interviewing them directly on their own real situations.

A social schedule was constructed to obtain data on the family, the women's status in the family, occupation of husband, principal source of income, the house type, neighborhood lived in, education, daytime serial listening, and general radio listening.

Field workers were trained in the use of several instruments.[13] When in the field their procedure was, first, to collect information for the schedule of social characteristics; next, to record the reactions of the Big Sister Verbal Projective; and finally, to administer the Thematic Apperception Test. In a few cases the subject was then thoroughly interviewed, and in other cases she was reinterviewed during the Big Sister broadcast.

✷   ✷   ✷

The Social and Psychological Functions of the Big Sister Program: The problems involved in analyzing "the meaning of meaning" are exceedingly complex and often perplexing to those who give this area of human mental life their attention. For us, the meaning of a symbol lies in how it is used by the interpreter,[14] by those who exhibit it to others for interpretation, and by its functions in our culture.[15] We have seen that the meanings of the Big Sister Program as a symbol system fit into each of these categories of meaning.

To return to the development of our argument, we have shown that the women publicly and privately identify with the symbols of the Big Sister Program, for the characters and their actions, as a system of cultural symbols, express the values and ideas common to the restrictive confines of the family where the women who listen live their lives.

The outside world for the women of the level of the Common Man is not highly rewarding or an easy place for them to be. They must constantly try to maintain peaceful and well ordered relations within their families or they endanger their security. They must continue to do this while they struggle to make economic ends meet with the modest help of their husbands' salaries and wages. They feel the pressure of the surround-

---

[13] The writers wish to take this opportunity to thank the members of the field staff for their aid in the gathering of data. The staff were all mature graduate students from the Departments of Anthropology and Sociology, the Committee on Human Development, and the Committee on Human Relations in Industry, of the University of Chicago. Mr. Warner and Mr. Henry fashioned the instruments, directed the field research, and analyzed the results.

[14] Ogden, C. K. and Richards, I. A. *The Meaning of Meaning*. New York: Harcourt Brace, 1927. "Soap Opera," *Fortune*, 1946, 33, No. 3, 119. Henry, W. E. "The Thematic Apperception Technique in the Study of Culture-Personality Relations." *Genetic Psychology Monograph*, 1947, 35, 3-135.

[15] Durkheim, Emile. *Elementary Forms of the Religious Life*. (Trans. J. W. Swain.) New York: Macmillan, 1926. Warner, W. L. *A Black Civilization*. New York: Harper, 1937.

ing environment and know the need of restraining their actions within the limits of what their economy permits and within the moral confines of the traditional roles of women and mothers as they are defined by the conventions of the level of the Common Man.

The comparatively free courting period when love and sex are dominant is past. Adaption then meant the prudent use of sex symbols and sex sentiments to achieve the goal of winning a mate. At this earlier period in their lives, society positively affirmed and approved of such impulsive behavior. Now—married and often mothers—their social and economic tasks become the dominant motifs of their existence; and impulse behavior, while present, is treated as of secondary importance and, if allowed to take a dominant place in their activities, as wicked or absurd.

The marriage relation permits sex expression within its limits; but the obligations and duties assigned to women by our society in their roles of wives and mothers, and the realities of being a housewife, reduce this once dominant theme in the life of the young woman to a secondary and restricted one in the activities of the mature married woman. To make such an adjustment from a period of freedom to a period of constraint is not easy. To these women, Ruth is a symbol of a socially superior woman who has done this successfully, who is still attractive, and still a "nice person to know." Christine, on the other hand, is a mature woman who continues long after youth to make egoistic impulse demands and is roundly condemned by those who listen. It is interesting to speculate on the intensity of listener hostility that would develop should the Christines of the Big Sister story be rewarded for their impulse demands and, should this happen, to wonder how long the radio listeners would continue to be loyal to the program. The Ruths of our culture, symbols of sublimated impulse life and figures of social and economic reality, must be rewarded and triumph; and the Christines, symbols of uncontrolled emotion and ego satisfaction, must always fail, for therein lie hope and confidence for those who listen to daytime serials and, it is not too much to say, for our culture. The women of the level of the Common Man carry the heavy load of tradition and convention wherein are stored our most treasured beliefs and valued sentiments. It is no accident that these women are rigidly trained and under constant constraint, for our cultural stability and the continuance of our way of life are greatly dependent upon them.

The career women of our contrast group have achieved greater inward as well as outward autonomy.[16] They have greater inward autonomy in their attitudes towards themselves and the world around them, and this is expressed in the conceptualization of their own world as well as their view of the characters of the Big Sister serial. On the other hand, the wives

16 Piaget, J. The Language and Thought of the Child. New York: Harcourt Brace, 1932. Piaget, J., The Moral Judgment of the Child. New York: Harcourt Brace, 1932.

of the level of the Common Man grow up in a family where they are largely dependent and subordinate to their parents; they marry and form a new family where their actions continue bound by the family system and they are subordinate as wives to their husbands. The only period in their lives when they had personal freedom and autonomy was the brief time before marriage when they were sufficiently mature to be courted, while making their decisions about wedlock. The private worlds of these women accordingly reflect their subordination, limitations, and the strict routines of their daily lives.

The women of the contrast group, while showing greater intellectual and imaginative freedom, are more likely to have a higher rate of neurosis, and it is probable that the reveries of many of them will be filled with symbolic themes that are non-adaptive and frequently escapist. This seems true because such women have been trained by the ordinary routines common in American child-rearing and, as persons, are not as well prepared as men to live in a career world which is still traditionally male, where taking chances and initiating action are frequently part of the daily routine. There are no separate routines as yet to help career women solve their personal problems and quiet their anxieties. In this respect the housewife is much better off.

The women in the listener group, although troubled and perplexed by the world around them, probably show less neurotic incidence because they have reduced the area of their interest and narrowed the field of their emotional expression. This contraction has permitted them to adjust to the daily problems of taking an administrative and responsible role within the limits of the family where their personal and emotional power is dominant. This dominance, however, is not absolute; it can only be forceful and certain as long as a woman obeys the code which underlies all family systems and which controls their narrowly limited self-initiated action. Such personal power can only be retained when the woman—by action if not by thought—recognizes her subordinate role in the total society and accepts her economic dependence on the husband as well as subordination to him as a male and the greater limitation of her freedom in the world outside the family. The average American woman of the lower-middle class participates comparatively little outside her family. The church, which reinforces by its absolute dicta the same principles of self-control and limitation of action for women, is her principal area of action. The associations to which she belongs are of the auxiliary and fraternal type.[17] The Yankee City analysis of such association shows that they are elaborations of the family structure, and women who participate in them do so primarily by extending their family roles of wives and mothers. In other words, the

[17] Warner, W. L., and Lunt, P. S. *The Social Life of A Modern Community*. New Haven: Yale University Press, 1945.

wives of the Common Man level of American society live in a well-knit social system. Its critics may or may not like it; but it is a system functioning and well balanced, and as such it does solve problems for those who are in it. Its conventions are a way of life which limits the freedom of action but supplies people with a code that is well labeled with directing signs to guide them through, and help them avoid, conflict.

Successful adaptation depends on a rigorous training period to learn how to live this highly controlled role so that the inner person corresponds with the outer demands of the social system. Successful adaptation for personalities formed to fit into such a tightly-knit system demands that the social system itself continually and effectively reinforce their determination to live up to the moral values of their group and maintain confidence in themselves and the things for which they stand.

The principal sources of such stimuli are their contacts with other people, the church, and associations, and several forms of entertainment. We have spoken previously about the church and the effect of the family and other institutions on the inner life and outward behavior of these women. For the lower-middle class woman, the radio and the daytime serial, in the field of entertainment, occupy a unique place. They are always available, of immediate access, and—above all—*in the home of the housewife.* They are part of her familiar and daily surroundings, where she lives with her family, and the center of events for her group. The characters and plot of the Big Sister program, and daytime serials generally, possess the home of the woman as their stage. While she goes about her household tasks and while she thinks about her relations with others and her family, she listens to her program. Reality and fantasy easily blend together. Some of our responses show that the women have the radio going constantly, and give or withdraw their attention without being aware of so doing.

One of the most important functions of Big Sister and similar programs now becomes abundantly clear. The most striking difference between the responses to the T.A.T. pictures, which give the personality structures and organized attitudes of the listeners, and the responses to the Verbal Projectives, which show how listening to the Big Sister program affects its audience, is that the outcomes of the stories, both to the specific stories and to the general outcome of the plot, were far more positive than the outcomes to the T.A.T. pictures. True, the outcomes to the stories still expressed the difficulties of adjustment of interpersonal relations within the context of the family, thereby exhibiting real, not neurotic, anxiety about their own affairs; but the listeners had confidence in the future and believed that Ruth's moral strength and social astuteness would solve all problems.

The listeners' anxieties, shown in their T.A.T. responses, express their own difficulties in adjusting to their way of life. Their responses to what will happen to the characters in the Big Sister program show their awareness of the difficulties of normal adjustment to life's realities; but the effect of the Big Sister program is to direct their hopes into confident and optimistic channels. Eighty-five per cent of the responses of the women to the question, "What do you think will happen to them in the future?" were positive and optimistic ("Ruth and John will succeed" and other good outcomes); whereas only 15 per cent were pessimistic ("Ruth and John will fail to solve their problems," or "Nothing good will happen"). The outcomes of the five stories have a similar tone to them. A confident theme runs throughout the predictions for the future. In all of them there is an underlying assumption that this is a moral universe where evil is punished and virtue is rewarded.

The evidence on all these symbolic points and on the social and psychological functions of the program is vivid and clear. The women respect and admire Ruth, all of them identify with her, and, therefore, in varying degrees, imitate her. It was important for us to know what their conception of her is. As we have said, Ruth to them is the perfect wife. She is a person who keeps adaptive control over herself, whose impulse life is sublimated, and whose moral code is strict and outlook on life highly regulated. Her outward appearance, her clothes, her physical traits are symbols of what they consider her reality to be. The answers to the question of her appearance almost unanimously agreed on these points. Christine's outward appearance symbolized what her personality is to her listeners. She is a symbol of explicitly condemned but implicitly accepted impulse life. Her dress expresses her sexuality; Ruth's, her character and moral worth.

Christine is always viewed in all respects as the antagonist of Ruth, thereby pitting impulse against character and moral restraint. According to the attitudes of the listeners, Christine—instead of being a "normal" woman—makes strong and uncontrolled sex and emotional demands, and she uses them as a weapon for her own egoistic purposes and, accordingly, is forever being punished. Uncontrolled impulse life is thereby condemned, but at the same time there is an implicit approval of it. The attitude towards this character is always ambivalent. She must always lose to Ruth and be condemned for what she does; yet there is sufficient identification with her emotional experiences to give the women vicarious satisfaction in what Christine does.

Ruth's anxieties are about the affairs of those around her—the people who make up her family or who are of critical importance to it. She is never without anxiety and never will be; but she is always the problem-solver. She straightens out difficulties for the interpersonal world in which she has her existence and relies on her own normal anxieties to maintain her own and others' security. She and her audience look forward to her future with confidence because Ruth's moral strength and social intelligence are sufficiently powerful to conquer all the obstacles that constantly appear in her world—a world like that of her listeners which is filled with perplexity. The difference between the problems of Ruth and her listeners is that her personal problems are always major, the audience's rarely so; but they always need moral strength and social astuteness in meeting their minor crises or their own difficulties, may become major. Furthermore, the petty difficulties of the women, seemingly insignificant, are now dramatized and become significant and important; and the women who experience these difficulties feel themselves to be significant people.

The Big Sister program thus acts constructively in the lives of the women and functions for them very much as did the morality plays of former times. The dramatis personnae, in act and symbol, express the conflicting forces of good and evil. The audience happily identifies with the Devil as well as God's angels but forever demands the Devil be punished for what he does. Thus emotions are released adaptively, beliefs are socially oriented, and the values of the group are reaffirmed in the experiences of the audience.

*   *   *

SUMMARY OF FINDINGS: This pilot research on the responses of the audience and the effect of this serial on its listeners yielded a number of important conclusions which are stated here in the form of a series of interconnected propositions:

A. The Program Functions to Identify the Audience with the Characters in the Plot.
  1. The Big Sister serial is a drama which functions to express the hopes and fears of its audience.
  a. Its basic themes portray these anxieties and hopes.
  b. The themes are symbolically expressed in the plot and action through the personalities of the characters.
  c. The audience, identifying with the plot and characters of Big Sister, relate their own personal problems to those of the play.
  2. The program is a drama of the middle-class family.
  a. "Everything in the world" is centered within the focus of an upper-middle class family (Big Sister's). Consequently, social realities outside the family are secondary and enter only reflected in the structure and action of the family.
  3. As conceived by the listeners, the program expresses the psychological realities of their place in life, for it states the traditional symbolic themes of family life they have learned from our culture. This statement means that for most listeners:

  a. The present characters motivate the plot and their motives are plausible.
  b. New themes can only be added (to this serial and others like it) if they conform to the basic one of the drama.
  c. Social and economic situations (the realism of social science) can only be developed in a very secondary way, never as basic to the story.

B. The Symbolic Content of the Program is Definite and Clearly Defined.
  1. The characters in the Big Sister program are men and women of the upper-middle class and, for the great majority of the audience (those from the Common Man level of America, 65 per cent of our population), this is essentially an emulatory device where the behavior and morals of the heroine are copied by the listeners because she is of higher status and because she expresses the moral ideals of the listeners.
  2. The basic and primary theme is that good and noble women who are wives and mothers are invincible within their own arena of life, the American family. Men, who are superordinate elsewhere, are subordinate and dependent on the wisdom of the wife. This primary theme always triumphs over the secondary theme which runs counter to it, that family ties can be broken and woman's security threatened chiefly by the loss of the husband to other women, and, quite secondarily and obliquely, by death. From the point of view of middle-class culture to which most of the listeners to Big Sister belong, these themes are expressions of social reality.
  3. The basic themes of the Big Sister program express the spartan, restrictive virtues of American middle-class morality; the good, well-disciplined woman who is the mother (sexless) of all living is praised and rewarded.

C. The Majority of the Women Who Listen Have the Social Characteristics of the Common Man Level of American Society.
  1. The women who listen, being normally distributed through the several socio-economic levels of our society, belong in most cases to the Common Man social level.[18] At this social level ordinarily:
  a. The woman is economically dependent upon the moderate salary or wage of her husband.
  b. The world beyond the family is largely outside her sphere of action, but it threatens her society.

[18] Wilder, F. F. *Radio's Daytime Serial.* (Pamphlet.) New York: Columbia Broadcasting System, 1945.

c. Her security, as well as that of her dependent children, depends upon her husband.

d. The moral code is more rigid and strict, particularly for women, than at the top and bottom social levels.

e. Adaptation and real anxiety about it are morally phrased, for the behavior of the woman must be highly prescribed and closely regulated or she will lose her position as wife and mother and, thereby, her security.

f. Because her economic position and her larger social situation are dependent upon others (particularly a male) and beyond her control, anxiety develops. Also, with the decreasing role of the housewife in this society, she often questions her utility and, consequently, worries about being a good wife and mother.

(The above, *a* through *f*, were first learned from previous community and personality researches on American women but were further strengthened and confirmed by this research.)

D. The Big Sister Program Has Specified Psychological Functions That Were Expressed in the Responses of the Women Studied.

1. The Big Sister program arouses normal and adaptive anxiety in the women who listen.

2. The Big Sister program directly and indirectly condemns neurotic and non-adaptive anxiety.

3. This program provides moral beliefs, values, and techniques, for solving emotional and interpersonal problems for its audience and makes them feel they are learning while they listen (thus: "I find the program is educational").

4. It directs the private reveries and fantasies of the listeners into socially approved channels of action.

5. The Big Sister program increases the women's sense of security in a world they feel is often threatening by:

a. Reaffirming the basic security of the marriage ties (John's and Ruth's).

b. Accentuating the basic security of the position of the husband (John Wayne is a successful physician).

c. "Demonstrating" that those who behave properly and stay away from wrong-doing exercise moral control over those who do not.

d. Showing that wrong behavior is punished.

6. The Big Sister program, in dramatizing the significance of the wife's role in basic human affairs, increases the woman's feeling of importance by showing that the family is of the highest importance and that she has control over the vicissitudes of family life.

7. It thereby decreases their feeling of futility and makes them feel essential and wanted.

8. The women aspire to, and measure themselves by, identification with Ruth, the heroine; however, the identification is not with Ruth alone, but with the whole program and the other characters in the plot. This permits sublimated impulse satisfaction by the listeners, first, unconsciously identifying with the bad woman and, later, consciously punishing her through the action of the plot.

9. Unregulated impulse life is condemned since it is always connected with characters who are condemned and never related to those who are approved.

E. The Program Has Specific Social Functions (as Expressed in the Responses of the Women Studied).

1. The primary social function of the program (how it works) is to strengthen and stabilize the basic social structure of our society, the family. It so functions by dramatizing family crises and the ideals and values involved, as they are understood and felt by the women who listen, and by making the good wife (Ruth) the center of action and power.

2. Our society, by offering a choice to women between being housewives or career women (usually professional), frequently creates a dilemma for them: The career woman's role is attractive because it is usually of higher status than the occupation of the Common Man level and offers more moral and emotional freedom. On the other hand, such a role is often frightening, demands hard work, ability to buck the system, and the capacity for self-initiated action. Most of the life of such women is outside the family. The Big Sister program plays up to the importance of the role of the wife and therefore obliquely depreciates the role (career women) the ordinary listener has avoided, or not been able to take. It helps resolve any conflict she may have within her for not choosing the other role (that once might have been open to her) and reinforces her present position.

F. Evaluation of the Psychological and Social Effects of the Program Can be Made.

1. Essentially the Big Sister drama is a contemporary minor morality play which expresses, as did the morality plays of ancient times, the feelings and beliefs of its audience by use of idealized symbols of good and evil and of things feared and hoped for (the characters and their actions). It differs from the morality play of earlier times primarily because modern culture is secularized, whereas our earlier society was dominated by sacred beliefs and values.

Carl I. Hovland, Arthur A. Lumsdaine and Fred D. Sheffield

SHORT-TIME AND LONG-TIME EFFECTS
OF AN ORIENTATION FILM

In connection with the use of the orientation films, the question arose as to how well the effects of the film were retained over a long period of time. The practical significance of this question lay in judging the need for later supplementary material covering the same ground as the films. In the experiments with orientation films presented earlier, the effects were determined at time intervals ranging from four to seven days after the film showings. In the present study, effects were determined at two time intervals after the film showing, one at five days and another at nine weeks. The primary objective of the study was to discover the extent to which the "short-time" (five-day) effects endure, as evidenced by the extent to which they were still present after a nine-week interval had elapsed.

The phrasing of the practical question to be answered by the study carries the implication that a decrement in effects is to be expected after a lapse of time. A more general question is to ask what is the influence of passage of time on the effects produced by the film. From this standpoint one need not anticipate only decrements with time; rather, in some cases the effect of time may be to enhance the initial effects of the film. Thus, some of the effects of the film may be "sleepers" that do not occur immediately but require a lapse of time before the full effect is evidenced. It should be realized, of course, that in making a controlled-variation study of the influence of time, it is not time per se that is the variable under study but rather the events which occur during the lapse of time.

The film used in this study was "The Battle of Britain." This film was chosen partly because its initial effects, as determined from a previous study, were relatively large, providing a better base for measuring retention than would be the case with a film having small initial effects.

Reprinted from *Experiments in Mass Communications* (1949), pp. 182-190; 197-200, by permission of the authors and the publisher. (Copyright, 1949, by Princeton University Press.)

The before-after experimental design was used. The "before" Questionnaire was given to ten Infantry Replacement Training Companies during the first week of the study (April 1943). During the second week, the film was shown to five of the ten companies. The other five companies were controls and did not see the film during the study. Five days after the film showings, three of the film companies and three of the control companies were given the "after" questionnaire. These six companies were used to determine the *short-time* effects of the film. The remaining four companies (two controls and two experimental) were used nine weeks after the film showings to determine the *long-time* effects of the film. A nine-week interval was used because it was the longest period during which the companies would retain the same personnel. The experimental design is outlined below.

WEEK OF STUDY	SHORT-TIME GROUPS		LONG-TIME GROUPS	
	Experimental (3 Companies)	Control (3 Companies)	Experimental (2 Companies)	Control (2 Companies)
First Week	"Before" Questionnaire	"Before" Questionnaire	"Before" Questionnaire	"Before" Questionnaire
Second Week	Film Showing	....	Film Showing	....
Third Week	"After" Questionnaire	"After" Questionnaire	....	....
Eleventh Week	....	....	"After" Questionnaire	"After" Questionnaire

It will be observed in the experimental design that the same sample of men was not used at the two different times after the film. A design involving a short-time and long-time measure on the same men was avoided on the grounds that the first "after" measure might affect the results obtained on the second. It must also be observed that more men were used in the short-time measurement of effects than the long-time measurement. The reason for this was that an incidental purpose of the study was to make a more detailed analysis of the short-time effects of the film than was possible with the after-only procedure that had been used at the first camp at which "The Battle of Britain" had been studied. To get a sizable number of cases for this analysis, the greater number of men were concentrated in the short-time measurement.

After the equating of the film and control groups, the resultant samples were 900 for the short-time effects (450 film and 450 control) and 500 for the long-time effects (250 film and 250 control).

Results with Fact-Quiz Items

The results for the ten fact-quiz items (which were included only in the "after" questionnaire) are shown in Table I. The items in the table are arranged in descending order of magnitude of *short-time* effect.

TABLE I—Short-Time and Long-Time Effects of "The Battle of Britain" on Fact-Quiz Questions

Fact-Quiz Items	Control	Short-Time Film	Diff.	Control	Long-Time Film	Diff.	Difference (Long-Time Minus Short-Time)
1. RAF not destroyed on ground because kept planes at edge of fields	23%	80%	57%	21%	53%	32%	−25%
2. First targets of Luftwaffe were ports and ships	13	58	45	13	20	7	−38
3. Luftwaffe ten times as large as the RAF	24	56	32	19	33	14	−18
4. Nazi plan was to destroy RAF, then invade England	30	58	28	26	40	14	−14
5. British Navy could not operate in channel because of danger of air attacks	41	60	19	37	44	7	−12
6. After fall of France British could equip only one modern division	5	21	16	3	8	5	−11
7. Famous statement "Never . . . was so much owed by so many to so few" referred to the RAF	23	34	11	17	28	11	0
8. Goering the head of the German Force	58	65	7	51	58	7	0
9. "Luftwaffe" the name of the German Air Force	66	72	6	65	70	5	−1
10. Germans lost about 2000 planes in the Battle of Britain	49	54	5	49	58	9	+4
Mean	33.2%	55.8%	22.6%	30.1%	41.2%	11.1%	−11.5%

It can be seen in Table I that all of the items showed a decrement with passage of time except some of the items with very small short-time effects. The long-time mean score on the fact quiz was slightly less than half as great as that obtained in the short-time measurement. Thus retention was about 50 per cent after nine weeks. If the results in Table I are recomputed excluding the last three items, where the obtained "effects" are of questionable reliability, the means are 29.7 per cent and 12.9 per cent for short-time and long-time effects, respectively, giving a retention value of 12.9 divided by 29.7 or 43 per cent.

Results with Opinion Items

In contrast with the foregoing findings for fact-quiz items, the results for opinion items did not show an overall decrement during the interval of nine weeks. Instead, some items showed the expected decrement while others showed reliable increment, with a mean effect that was slightly greater for the long-time measurement than for the short-time. For the entire group of opinion items used in the after questionnaire, the range was from a decrement of −17% to an increment of +14%, with a mean of +1.9%.[1] The variance of the differences between the short-time and the long-time "effects" was 40.3%. By contrast, when the groups were compared before the film showing, the range of the second-order differences was only from −7% to +7% with a variance of 14.6%.

Comparison of Short-Time and Long-Time Effects on Individual Opinion Items Showing a Reliable Effect at Either Time Interval

The foregoing comparisons were based upon all opinion items included in the questionnaire and therefore included many items for which no reliable effect of the film was demonstrated. Of special interest are the items which individually exhibited reliable effects of the film. In Table II the results at the two time intervals are shown for the 15 opinion items for which a reliable effect was obtained at either or both of the two time intervals.

The criterion of reliability used for the selection of items in Table II required a 10 per cent difference between film and control after the film showing. In terms of the empirical distributions of film-minus-control differences before the film, a difference of 10 per cent was beyond the 1 per cent level of confidence at either time interval. (The standard deviations of the distributions of "before" difference between film and control were 2.7 per cent and 3.5 per cent, respectively, for the short-time and long-time groups.) In the table the content is indicated for each of the 15 items, as well as the film and control percentages for each time interval. The items are arranged in descending order of magnitude of *short-time* effect.

As can be seen from Table II the average for the 15 items was about the same for short-time and long-time effects, with a slight advantage (2.4 per cent) in favor of the long-time effects.

However, Table II brings out clearly the fact that the near equality of the averages is a balance of some effects that were larger in the short-time measurement and others that were larger in the long-time measurement rather than approximate equality of individual effects at the two time intervals. This trend is perhaps somewhat exaggerated in Table II owing to the selection of effects that met the criterion of 10 per cent at either time interval. Thus borderline instances that just barely met the criterion at only one of the time intervals would be expected to regress somewhat in a replication of the experiment.

These findings are of considerable significance both from the standpoint

[1] This included all opinion items except those involving ranking of enemy and allied strength and two questions about branch of service that could not be scored individually.

**TABLE II—Short-Time and Long-Time Effects of "The Battle of Britain"
on Significantly Affected Opinion Questions**

Content of Opinion Item	Control	Short-Time Film	Diff.	Control	Long-Time Film	Diff.	Difference (Long-Time Minus Short-Time)
1. RAF gave Nazis first real defeat	21%	45%	24%	20%	27%	7%	−17%
2. RAF most important in preventing German conquest of England	54	78	24	46	69	23	−1
3. Nazi invasion attempt failed because of determined resistance of British	51	71	20	54	68	14	−6
4. Battle of Britain was a real invasion attempt	32	46	14	30	40	10	−4
5. England's refusal to surrender saved U.S. cities from bombing	62	74	12	67	74	7	−5
6. RAF has done about the best job of fighting in the war	49	60	11	42	45	3	−8
7. British more democratic than before Battle of Britain	55	65	10	59	62	3	−7
8. American workers in war plants should not work longer hours	48	52	4	42	54	12	8
9. America and Allies can still lose the war (disagree)	34	37	3	35	48	13	10
10. We would be fighting on American soil if Britain had not held off Nazis	52	55	3	50	62	12	9
11. British are doing their fair share of the fighting	71	73	2	61	77	16	14
12. Better just to defend U.S. rather than going overseas to fight	83	84	1	79	90	11	10
13. If England had been conquered the U.S. would have been attacked next	23	24	1	22	32	10	9
14. The war will probably end in less than one year	11	10	−1	12	22	10	11
15. The British not to blame for America's having to get into the war	56	54	−2	44	55	11	13
Mean	46.8%	55.2%	8.4%	44.2%	55.0%	10.8%	2.4%

of methodology of research on educational films and from the standpoint of theory as to the effects of educational programs on attitudes. Methodologically, they raise the problem as to the point in time at which effects of a film or other educational device are to be measured. From the standpoint of theory they raise the possibility of "sleeper" effects in the case of opinions and the implications of such effects for theory of attitude or opinion changes. From the standpoint either of educational film research or of the use of educational films it would be very desirable to know how generally this finding holds for documentary films of this type and also to know what factors determine whether the effects will show a loss or a gain with time. Unfortunately, studies of long-time effects were not made on any of the other orientation films, so no evidence can be given as to the generality of the results.

An analogy may be drawn between the findings reported here and the finding in studies of retention that "substance" is better retained than verbatim learning.[2] Thus the general ideas in a passage of verbal material are retained with little loss over periods in which memory for the actual wording has dropped markedly. In the present study retention for opinions—which correspond to the substance—averaged better than 100 per cent whereas memory for detailed facts dropped to only half of its initial value.

However, this analogy is somewhat superficial in view of the fact that the average for opinions was a mixture of some gains and losses on particular items of "substance" (if opinions can be regarded as "substance"). In this connection it may be pointed out that another familiar phenomenon in learning studies—the phenomenon of "reminiscence," in which more rather than less of the original content is recalled after a lapse of time—is more frequently found in the case of substance material than in the case of detailed verbal content.[3] Thus the present results may be regarded as a mixture of the greater retention of general ideas plus "reminiscence" for part of the material.

One hypothesis as to the source of the "sleeper" effects involving a purely methodological artifact was checked but was not supported by the data. This hypothesis was that the before-after procedure may cause a "consistency reaction" which would occur when the two questionnaires are close together in time but which could not be present for two questionnaires separated by an interval as long as eleven weeks. (The possibility of a "consistency reaction" is discussed in Appendix C of *Experiments in Mass Communication* along with other methodological aspects of the before-after procedure.) The effect of the "consistency reaction," if present, would be a tendency for the respondent, having given a particular answer to a question on one occasion, to give the same answer when questioned in a similar context a short time later. Hence the true magnitude of the change effected by the film would not be revealed at the short-time interval. Since some of the questions in the present study were asked only in the "after" questionnaire and others both before and after, it was possible to

[2] Cofer, C. N. "A Comparison of Logical and Verbatim Learning of Prose Passages of Different Lengths." *Amer. J. Psychol.*, 1941, 54, 1-20.

[3] English, H. B., Wellborn, E. L., and Killian, C. D. "Studies in Substance Memorization." *J. gen. Psychol.*, 1934, 11, 233-60. See also Buxton, C. E. " 'Reminiscence' in the Studies of Professor English and His Associates." *Psychol. Rev.*, 1942, 49, 494-504.

check whether after-only questions show the normal forgetting decrement with time and only the before-after questions show an increment. This finding would be expected if the "consistency reaction" were reduced where an 11-week interval is allowed between before and after tests.

However, no significant relation was found between whether the question was an after-only or a before-after question and whether it showed a decrement or an increment with time. In Table II the after-only questions were numbers 2, 7, 8, 11, 14, and 15. Of these six after-only items, it can be seen that two showed a decrement and four showed an increment in effects as a function of time. Of the remaining nine questions, asked both before and after, five showed a decrement and four showed an increment. Thus while the hypothetical "consistency reaction" may have functioned to some extent to reduce the size of the decrement, the data do not at all support it as the factor responsible for the delayed or augmented effects. As can be seen in Table III the results are in the opposite direction from the prediction of the consistency hypothesis. (The apparent difference in retention of the after-only items is not significant.)

TABLE III—Mean Effect (Film % Minus Control %)

	Short-Time	Long-Time
For six after-only items	6.2%	12.5%
For nine before-after items	9.9	9.7

❋   ❋   ❋

Other Hypotheses

A number of other hypotheses may be advanced suggesting possible factors contributing to the increments on some of the opinion items. These hypotheses could not be checked in the present experiment but they are presented below because they may provide useful areas for future study.

1. *Forgetting of an initially discounted source.* One hypothesis that could explain the results would be that some of the themes of the presentation were initially accepted and others were initially discounted as having a biased source. According to this hypothesis, forgetting is the rule but the *source* of an item of information is more quickly forgotten than the material presented. Thus the men might have retained a feeling that the British did well in the war long after they have forgotten about seeing the film, "The Battle of Britain." The factors involved in this hypothesis would be maximized in situations where the content was very well presented but where the source was suspect, so that the main factor preventing an attitude change is nonacceptance of the trustworthiness of the source. In this case, what is remembered and what is believed may be kept separate at

first, but if the content "sticks" after the source is forgotten, it may no longer be discounted. Content would of course be subject to some forgetting, so that the net result would be a decrement of effect with passage of time for those contents which are *immediately* accepted contents, but an increment of effect for those contents for which forgetting of the suspected source proceeded more rapidly than forgetting of the content.

2. *Delayed interpretation in a relevant context.* Another hypothesis is that while forgetting of content is the rule, the implications of the initially learned content may not be apparent to the audience at the outset but may become more clear later when the material learned in the film becomes relevant to some new experience. Thus the film, "The Battle of Britain" showed the defeat of the Luftwaffe by the much smaller RAF and the frustration of the Nazi plans for the capitulation of Britain. Initial effects on fact-quiz and attitude items indicated that this content was learned. However, the film in no way presented the idea that the Nazi military machine was weak or that their strategy and tactics were inferior, and nothing in the initial effects indicated that this was a conclusion immediately drawn by the men as a result of seeing the film. However, if the men were later forced to consider the implications of these facts as to the likelihood that the Nazis could defeat the Allies, they might conclude that if the Germans could not defeat little Britain they have little chance of winning the war, as in the delayed effect on item number 14 in Table II.

An expectation from this second hypothesis is that material directly related to the content of the film would tend to show a decrement with time in correspondence with the forgetting curve, whereas increments would occur only for indirect implications of the content that could be initiated at a later time while a fair amount of the content was still retained. However, a differentiation between direct and indirect implications is one which it was not feasible to make clearly with these films.

3. *Conversion of details into attitudes.* A third hypothesis to account for the results involved a possible factor that would, if it actually functions, be of more general significance for theory concerning attitude formation. According to this hypothesis, forgetting is accompanied by loss of specificity of content—the details drop out and the "general idea" that is retained is in a more generalizable form, so that the individual has a greater tendency to go beyond the facts initially learned. In this sense attitudes are to a certain extent "general ideas" that lack specificity and generalize more broadly than is justified by the evidence.

An example of the interpretation from this hypothesis in the case of the film, "The Battle of Britain," would be that initially the men learned specific facts about the performance of the British, particularly the RAF, during the Battle of Britain, but as the specific facts were forgotten all that was remembered was that the British had performed well in the war. In this form the "general idea" applies to all British rather than just the RAF and to the entire war rather than just the Luftwaffe attack on England. Any opinions that dealt with specific contents would show a decrement with time, whereas those dealing with generalizations beyond the evidence would show an increment with time.

Delayed Effects on Orientation Objectives

One final question raised by the findings in this comparison of long-time and short-time effects of an orientation film is the extent to which delayed effects were found in the orientation objectives of the film. This is a question of methodological importance in the evaluation of an educational program designed to affect attitudes, because the evaluation may provide a different answer depending on the point in time at which the program is evaluated. The findings in the present study indicate a real possibility that at least in the case of the film, "The Battle of Britain," greater effects on orientation attitudes were obtained after a nine-week lapse of time than after only five days. The relevant findings are presented below.

The orientation objective most relevant to the film was that of increasing confidence in our ally, Britain. While many items about Britain were included to test the effects of the film, only six items were used for the specific purpose of determining general orientation attitudes toward Britain. The short-time and long-time effects for these items are shown in Table IV. The effects are measured as differences between before-after changes for all questions used in both questionnaires.

Results on other standard orientation items not specific to opinions

TABLE IV—Effects on the Orientation Objective of Increasing Men's Confidence in the British

Content of Item	Effect of Film	
	Short-Time Effect	Long-Time Effect
British are doing all they can to help in the war	7%	3%
British will try to work out a just peace after the war	9	7
British are taking it easy in hope that U.S. will win the war for them (disagree)	2	9
British are doing their fair share of the fighting	2	16
British will fight on to the end (rather than seek a separate peace)	1	4
British are to blame for America's entry into war (disagree)	−2	11
Mean	3.2%	8.3%

of the British are shown in Table V. These items are of lesser relevance to the film than the above items concerning Britain as an ally. Specific contents of individual items are not shown; only the general area of the items is given. In the case of each area, however, the results given are the averages for all of the standard items used in that area.

TABLE V—Effects on Generalized Orientation Objectives

	Average Effect of Film	
Content of Area	Short-Time	Long-Time
The U.S. had to fight—war was unavoidable (3 items)	0.3%	6.0%
Resentment against the enemy (2 items)	−2.0	5.0
Confidence in home support (4 items)	−1.0	2.0
Willingness to serve (2 items)	1.5	0.5
Mean	0.5%	3.4%

In both Tables IV and V the mean effect is larger at the long-time interval. This indicates that a greater effect of the film in achieving its orientation objectives was present after nine weeks than after one week. However, the results are not highly consistent from item to item in Table IV nor from area to area in Table V. In neither case is the result reliable at the 5 per cent level if we treat the questions used as a sample from the population of relevant items.

While inconclusive, the results have a bearing on two important problems: (1) they support the hypothesis that changes in opinions of a general rather than specific nature may show increasing effects with lapse of time, and (2) they focus attention on the methodological problem of selecting the point in time at which measurements should be made after a presentation in order to detect its full effects. At the outset of the present studies it was more or less assumed that deterioration of effects with time would be the rule; it now appears that this assumption is not warranted in the case of opinions of a general nature.

Bernard Berelson

COMMUNICATIONS AND PUBLIC OPINION

Of the importance of this topic it is hardly necessary to speak. If the defenses of peace and prosperity, not to mention other desirable political conditions, are to be constructed in men's minds, then the critical position of communication and public opinion for that defense is evident. What is not so evident, perhaps, is why social scientists have given so little systematic attention to problems of the formation of public opinion with special reference to the role of the media of communication in that process. It was not evident to a "classical" writer on public opinion twenty-five years ago,[1] and it may be even less so today.

In any case, the field of interest is now developing and the line of development is reasonably clear. The political scientist's concern with political parties was generalized to a concern with the role of pressure groups in political life. The concern with pressure groups led directly into concern with propaganda, and that into concern with public opinion and the effect of propaganda upon it. At about this time, technicians began to develop scientific instruments by which to measure public opinion; a new medium of communication with great potentialities for popular influence came vigorously upon the scene; in a series of presidential elections people voted strongly for one candidate while their newspapers voted strongly for his opponent; and a World War made more visible as well as more urgent the battle for men's minds. Thus the background of academic interest was prepared just when dramatic events highlighted the urgency of the problem and when technical developments provided means for at least some solutions. As a result, interest in communication and public opinion is now at an all-time high.

The purpose of this paper is to discuss the relationship between communication and public opinion. "Discuss" here means to report on some

Reprinted from *Communications in Modern Society*, edited by Wilbur Schramm (1948), pp. 168-85, by permission of the author and the publisher. (Copyright, 1948, University of Illinois Press.)

[1] Walter Lippmann, *Public Opinion*, Harcourt Brace, 1922, p. 243.

(illustrative) research findings in the area and to propose relevant (and again illustrative) hypotheses for investigation. By communication is meant the transmission of symbols via the major media of mass communication—radio, newspaper, film, magazine, book—and the major medium of private communication—personal conversation. By public opinion is meant people's response (that is, approval, disapproval, or indifference) to controversial political and social issues of general attention, such as international relations, domestic policy, election candidates, ethnic relations.

The paper is organized into two parts because the relationship between communication and public opinion is twofold. The first section deals with the effect of public opinion upon communication and the second with the effect of communication upon public opinion. The second section is traditional, and there is more to say about it; the first is usually neglected.

Effect of Public Opinion upon Communication

This problem is usually neglected in analyses of the relationship because it is not so obvious as the other and perhaps because it is more difficult to study. The problem deals with the extent to which, and the ways in which, communication content is determined to harmonize with the actual or presumed opinions of the actual or potential audience. It is clear that one factor, among others, that conditions what the media of communications say on social and political issues is the desire or expectation of the readers-listeners-seers to be told certain things and not others. The reporter or commentator or editor or producer may know or may think he knows "what his public wants" on a given issue, and to the extent that such knowledge affects what he communicates, to that extent public opinion becomes a determinant of communications. This aspect of the relationship between communication and public opinion is not always admitted, or even recognized, because of the immorality of suggesting that anything but "truth" or "justice" contributes to the character of communication content.[2] However, everyone knows that communication channels of various kinds tell people what they want to hear. In such cases, public opinion sets limits upon the nature of what is typically communicated.

This determination (or really, partial determination, since this is of course not the only factor responsible for communication content any more than communication content is the only factor responsible for public opinion) can operate in two ways, once the communication channel (newspaper, magazine, political writer, radio commentator, and so forth) has

[2] However, some circles frankly acknowledge the power of the public to participate thus indirectly in the construction of communication content. This position is usually rationalized in terms of the presumed democratic ethic in which "the public is entitled to what it wants."

attracted to itself a distinguishable audience. The two ways are themselves interrelated and can coexist. First, it can operate through conscious and deliberate and calculated manipulation of the content in order to coincide with the dominant audience opinion. Sometimes this operates by rule of thumb, as when someone on the production line in the communication process decides that "our public won't take this, or won't like it." Sometimes it operates through elaborate machinery organized precisely for the purpose, as when thousands of research dollars and hours are spent in finding out what kinds of people the audience is composed of and what kinds of opinions they hold on controversial issues. Whether the decision to conform to audience predispositions is taken on the front line or in the front office is for the moment immaterial; so is the question of why it happens, e.g., the desire or need for constant and large audiences for economic reasons. The important point is that overt consideration of audience opinion does (help to) shape the social and political content of the mass media. Everyone recalls the story of the foreign correspondent who cabled a thoroughgoing analysis of a relatively obscure Hungarian crisis to the home office only to be told: "We do not think it advisable to print it because it does not reflect Midwestern opinion on this point." [3]

The other method by which public opinion can affect communications is implicit, through the sincere and more or less nonconscious correspondence of ideology between producers and consumers. The two groups often see the world through the same colored glasses. The correspondence is achieved through a two-way process: the audience selects the communications which it finds most congenial and the producers select people with "the right viewpoint" to prepare communications for other people with "the right viewpoint." Although this latter process also occurs through deliberate decision,[4] it also happens through the most laudable and honest motives that people of the same general persuasion as their audience are found in influential positions in particular communication agencies. This is all the more true in specialized enterprises like trade papers or magazines like *Fortune* or *The Nation*. In such cases, producers react to new issues and events like the modal members of their audience; and their communications fit audience predispositions, not through a process of tailoring, but through correspondence in outlook. "The daily re-election of the editor" serves to make the editor quite sensitive to the wishes of the electors. Here again the economic necessity to hold an audience and the political desire to do so are relevant factors, as well as the "correctness" of outlook. The point is that the nature of one's audience places certain limits upon what one can say to it—and still have an audience. The need of the audience is

[3] Leo Rosten, *The Washington Correspondents*, Harcourt Brace, 1937, p. 231.
[4] See Rosten, *op. cit.*, for examples.

not only to be informed but also to be satisfied, and the latter is sometimes evaluated more highly than the former.

It is important to take account of this direction in the flow of influence between communication and public opinion in order to appreciate the reciprocal nature of that influence, i.e., to recognize that it is not all a one-way process. It is also important to note that the total effect of this reciprocal process is probably to stabilize and "conservatize" opinion since ideologies are constantly in process of reinforcement thereby. The over-all picture, then, is that of like begetting like begetting like.

The Effect of Communication on Public Opinion

But the effect of communication on public opinion needs to be examined much more closely and directly than that. To speak roughly, in the 1920's propaganda was considered all-powerful—"it got us into the war"— and thus communication was thought to determine public opinion practically by itself. In the 1930's the Roosevelt campaigns "proved" that the newspaper had lost its influence and that a "golden voice" on the radio could sway men in almost any direction. Now, in the 1940's, a body of empirical research is accumulating which provides some refined knowledge about the effect of communication on public opinion and promises to provide a good deal more in the next years.

What has such research contributed to the problem? By and large, do communications influence public opinion? By and large, of course, the answer is yes. But by-and-large questions and answers are not sufficient for a scientific theory of communication and public opinion. The proper answer to the general question, the answer which constitutes a useful formulation for research purposes, is this:

> Some kinds of *communication* on some kinds of *issues*,
> brought to the attention of some kinds of *people* under
> some kinds of *conditions*, have some kinds of *effects*.

This formulation identifies five central factors (or rather groups of factors) which are involved in the process, and it is the interrelationship of these variables which represents the subject matter of theory in this field. At present, students can fill out only part of the total picture—a small part— but the development of major variables and the formulation of hypotheses and generalizations concerning them are steps in the right direction. Theoretical integration in any full sense is not as yet possible, but descriptions of some ways in which these factors operate can be usefully made. Each set of factors will be discussed illustratively (*not* completely) in an effort to demonstrate how each of them conditions the total effect of communication on public opinion and thus contributes to the formulation of a general theory.

KINDS OF COMMUNICATION: The effectiveness of communications as an influence upon public opinion varies with the nature of the communication.

First let us deal with the effect of certain media characteristics. The more personal the media, the more effective it is in converting opinions. This means (other things being equal) that personal conversation is more effective than a radio speech, and that a radio speech is more effective than a newspaper account of it. The greater the amount of "personalism" the communication act contains, the more effective it presumably is. Recent analyses have confirmed the critical importance in opinion formation of personal contact between the individual and his fellows. The individual's opinions are formed in the context of his formal and informal group associations. College students become more liberal in political opinion over the period of their college attendance largely through the influence of the liberality of the college community, that is, the older students and the instructional staff.[5] Intensive case studies of current opinion toward the USSR held by adult men reveal the powerful influence of personal contacts: "The need to conform in one's opinion to the opinions of one's associates and of members of favored groups is an important motivational factor." [6] This effect operated in two ways: directly through the process of conformity as such and indirectly through the sharing of common values and information. The formation of political opinion during a presidential campaign was dependent upon personal influence to a large extent; the political homogeneity of social groups was strikingly high. "In comparison with the formal media of communication, personal relationships are potentially more influential for two reasons: their coverage is greater and they have certain psychological advantages over the formal media." [7] Personal contacts are more casual and nonpurposive than the formal media, they are more flexible in countering resistance, they can provide more desirable rewards for compliance, they offer reliance and trust in an intimate source, and they can persuade without convincing.[8]

The greater effectiveness of radio over newspapers derives to some extent from its greater "personalism." The radio speaks "to you" more than the newspaper does; it more closely approximates a personal conversation and can thus be more persuasive. The listener can "get a feel" of the

[5] Theodore M. Newcomb, *Personality and Social Change: Attitude Formation in a Student Community*, Dryden Press, 1943.

[6] Mahlon Brewster Smith, *Functional and Descriptive Analysis of Public Opinion*. Doctoral dissertation, Harvard University, 1947, p. 500.

[7] Paul Lazarsfeld, Bernard Berelson, and Hazel Gaudet, *The People's Choice: How the Voter Makes up His Mind in a Presidential Campaign*, Duell, Sloan and Pearce, New York, 1944, p. 150.

[8] For a full discussion of these factors, see chapter 16 of *The People's Choice*.

speaker's personality, and this is often more effective a factor making for conversion of opinion than the content of the argument itself. The dominant characteristic which enabled Kate Smith to sell nearly $40,000,000 worth of war bonds in one day was the listener's image and evaluation of her personality established over a period of time.[9] In other areas, too, the (radio) personality of such influencers of public opinion as Raymond Gram Swing or Gabriel Heatter or Franklin Delano Roosevelt contributes to their influence.

This discussion of the role of personal contact in opinion formation would not be complete without mention of the relationship between personal conversation and the formal media of communication. This relationship introduces the notion of the "opinion leader" or "opinion transmitter" who takes material from the formal media and passes it on, with or without distortion or affect, to associates who do not use the formal media so frequently in the particular area of concern. There are such people in all social groups and for all social topics, from politics to sports and fashions. This "two-step flow of communication" has been identified and is currently being studied intensively.[10] The concept is of central importance for the formation of a general theory of communication and public opinion.

Within a medium of communication, the particular channels specialized to the subject's predispositions are more effective in converting his opinion than the generalized channels. "The specialized magazine already has a foot in the door, so to speak, because it is accepted by the reader as a reliable spokesman for some cause or group in which he is greatly interested and with which he identifies himself. The general magazine tries to speak to everyone at once and as a result is less able to aim its shots directly at a particular target. . . . In Erie County in 1940, *The Farm Journal* was mentioned as a concrete influence upon changes in vote intention as frequently as *Collier's*, despite their great difference in circulation, and the Townsend publication as frequently as *Life* or *The Saturday Evening Post*." [11] Similarly farm programs on the air are probably more effective in influencing farmers' opinions than general radio programs dealing with the same issues.[12] Although there is little direct evidence on this point, it is at least a plausible hypothesis that the specialized communication, per unit of exposure, is more effective in promoting opinion changes than the gen-

[9] Robert K. Merton with the assistance of Marjorie Fiske and Alberta Curtis, *Mass Persuasion; the Social Psychology of a War Bond Drive*. Harper and Brothers, New York, 1946.

[10] See *The People's Choice*, pp. 49-51 and pp. 151-52; and the forthcoming study of the flow of influence among women in a midwestern community by Paul Lazarsfeld and C. Wright Mills.

[11] Lazarsfeld, Berelson, and Gaudet, *The People's Choice*, pp. 135-36.

[12] Some indirect evidence for this is available in William S. Robinson, "Radio Comes to the Farmer" in Lazarsfeld and Stanton, editors, *Radio Research, 1941*, Duell, Sloan and Pearce, New York, 1941, pp. 224-94.

eralized communication. In a sense, then, this is an obstacle to the homo-genizing influence of the mass channels in the mass media.

These are a few ways in which distinctions among the media them-selves are involved in the effect of communication upon opinion. What about communication content? Obviously it has a central position in this process. Perhaps the primary distinction in communication content as a factor affecting public opinion is the most primitive, namely, the distinction between the reportorial content and the editorial or interpretive content. Too often discussions of the general problem of the effect of communica-tions upon public opinion is restricted to the latter kind of content. Yet the former is probably more effective in converting opinion. The events re-ported through the media presumably change more minds—or solidify more —than the comments of editorial writers, columnists, and commentators. "It was Sherman and Sheridan, and not Greeley and Raymond, who had elected him (Lincoln in 1864)." [13] And again, "Opinion is generally de-termined more by events than by words—unless those words are them-selves interpreted as an 'event'." [14] In addition events tend to solidify opin-ion changes produced by words, changes which otherwise would be short-lived; and the *fait accompli* event crystallizes opinion in favor of the event even though words had not previously been able to do so. [15] Thus the reportorial content of the media is probably more influential than the interpretive.

However, it is necessary to make two remarks here. First, the distinction between "events" and "words" is not easy to make. Is a major speech by the President of the United States an "event" or just "propaganda"? Or a report issued by a pressure group? Or an investigation by a Congressional committee? Or a tour of inspection? What about "propaganda of the deed"? Although the distinction is useful, the borderline is not always crystal-clear. And secondly, many events exercise influence not in and of themselves, but with active assistance from "words." Thus, for example, the relatively sharp changes in opinion on the interventionist-isolationist issue which occurred at the time of the fall of France in June, 1940, are often attributed to the event itself. However, it must be recognized that this event was strongly interpreted in one way (i.e., pro-interventionism) by most newspapers and radio commentators and by the pronouncements of the national administration. What if most communication channels and the official administration had taken another view of the event? At the least one might suppose that the effect of "the event" would have been different. More recently, the event represented by people's experience in the meat

[13] Frank Luther Mott, "Newspapers in Presidential Campaigns," *Public Opinion Quarterly*, Vol. VIII, 1944, p. 354.

[14] Hadley Cantril, "The Use of Trends," in Cantril, editor, *Gauging Public Opinion*, Princeton, 1944, p. 226.

[15] See Cantril, *op. cit.*, pp. 227-28, for examples.

crisis in the fall of 1946 was sometimes credited with the Republican congressional victory at that time. Yet it must be remembered that the communication media gave that event a dominant interpretation (i.e., anti-administration) even though another was possible. In short, the interrelationship of "events" and "words" must be recognized in this connection. The fact is that the communication media are most effective when their reportorial and interpretive contents are in congruence.

Finally, to illustrate this aspect of the process, there is the hypothesis that emotional content of the media is more effective in converting opinions than rational content. There is some evidence for this. Votes for a Socialist candidate were increased more by "emotional" leaflets than by "rational" ones.[16] The highly effective bond broadcasts by Kate Smith even omitted two "rational" themes in favor of emphasis upon various "emotional" ones.[17] In the case of this distinction, of course, the need is not so much to test the finding as to refine it, especially for different population groups.

KINDS OF ISSUES: The effectiveness of communications as an influence upon public opinion varies with the nature of the issue.

Communication content is more effective in influencing public opinion on new or unstructured issues, i.e., those not particularly correlated with existing attitude clusters. The closer the opinion situation is to the *tabula resa*, the easier it is for the communication media to write their own ticket. "Verbal statements and outlines of courses of action have maximum importance when opinion is unstructured. . . ."[18] Again, with reference to opinion toward the USSR: "The object of the attitude is remote, the facts are ambiguous, and a person may fashion his own picture of Russia or fall in with the prevailing stereotypes"[19]—which are provided predominantly by the formal media.

Communication content is more effective in influencing opinion on peripheral issues than on crucial issues. That is, it is easier for the media to shape opinion on what to do about local courts than what to do about organized labor; and it is probably easier for them to shape opinion toward organized labor than on ethnic relations. The "relevance-quotient" or "intensity-quotient" of the issue is inversely correlated with the capacity of communication content to change minds.

Finally, communications are probably more effective in influencing opinion on "personalities" than on "issues." In the first place, Americans are an individualistic people. They like to have heroes; and the communications

[16] George W. Hartmann, "A Field Experiment on the Comparative Effectiveness of 'Emotional' and 'Rational' Political Leaflets in Determining Election Results," *Journal of Abnormal and Social Psychology*, Vol. XXXI, 1936, pp. 99-114.

[17] See Merton *op. cit.*, Chapter III: "The Bond Appeals: A Thematic Analysis," pp. 45-69.

[18] Cantril, "The Use of Trends," in Cantril, editor, *Gauging Public Opinion*, p. 226.

[19] Smith, *op. cit.*, p. 195.

media do their best to supply heroes of various kinds to various groups in the population.[20] Secondly, Americans do not like to believe that there are deep-cutting political issues which have the potentiality of "class-ifying" the public so that they tend to resist the acceptance or even the recognition of some basic issues. As a result, the media probably can sway more people with "personality" arguments than with "issue" arguments.[21]

KINDS OF PEOPLE: The effectiveness of communications as an influence upon public opinion varies with the nature of the people.

In the first place, varying proportions of people simply do not read or see or listen to the different media. So far as direct effect of the media is concerned (and omitting considerations of indirect effects through such a process as opinion leadership), two-thirds of the adult population is not influenced by books, about one-half is not influenced by motion pictures, and so on. Direct effects of the media upon public opinion can be exercised only upon that part of public which attends to the different media (and to different parts of them)—and that rules out distinguishable groups at the outset.

On one side of the coin is the distinction between peripheral and central issues; on the other side is the distinction between strong and weak predispositions. The stronger predispositions are on the issue, the more difficult it is for the media to convert opinions. Strong predispositions "compel" an opinion which the media only helps to rationalize and reinforce; in recent presidential elections very few people of high income, rural residence, and Protestant religion were *converted* to a Republican vote by the media of communication. Strong predispositions make for greater interest in the issue, an earlier decision on it, and fewer changes afterwards. All this is clear enough. What may or may not be so clear, however, is that the strongly predisposed on an issue actually manage not only to avoid contrary communication material, so that it just does not come to their attention, but also that they manage to misunderstand the material (which objectively is straightforward) when confronted by it. This has been particularly demonstrated in connection with communication material on ethnic relations, a topic on which predispositions run strong. Prejudiced people find several ways in which to evade the message of pro-tolerance propaganda: they avoid the intended identifications, they invalidate the message, they change the frame of reference, they "just don't get it." [22]

[20] For an example see Leo Lowenthal, "Biographies in Popular Magazines," pp. 507-48, in Lazarsfeld and Stanton, editors, *Radio Research, 1942-1943*, Duell, Sloan and Pearce, New York, 1944.

[21] For a specific instance in which this was the case, see Bernard Berelson, "The Effects of Print upon Public Opinion," in Waples, editor, *Print, Radio and Film in a Democracy*, University of Chicago Press, 1942, pp. 55-56.

[22] Eunice Cooper and Marie Jahoda, "The Evasion of Propaganda: How Prejudiced People Respond to Anti-prejudice Propaganda," *Journal of Psychology*, Vol. XXIII, 1947, pp. 15-25.

The less informed people are on an issue, the more susceptible they are to opinion conversion through the influence of the communication media. This means that the less informed are more mercurial in their opinions; the base of data upon which stable opinion is more securely founded [23] is simply absent for them, and the media (or more frequently, personal contacts) can more readily move them in different directions. "The compulsion of (media-supplied and other) stereotypes is great, particularly for persons with meager informational backgrounds." [24]

KINDS OF CONDITIONS: The effectiveness of communications as an influence upon public opinion varies with the nature of the conditions.

Many mass communications on controversial issues in this country have to make their way in a competitive situation, i.e., under conditions in which alternative proposals are also available in the media. In some areas, such as the desirability of professing religious beliefs, this is not true: there is a virtual pro-religious monopoly on conmunications available to large audiences in America today. But it is the case in most areas of political and social concern, although here too various minority groups, e.g., the Communists, feel that their point of view is not given fair or proper attention in the mass media. It is necessary to recognize that the effect of communications upon public opinion must usually be exercised in this context of competing communication content and not in a context of monopoly. This is of central importance: communication has effects upon converting opinion under conditions of monopoly which are much greater than its effects under conditions of competition (even though that competition might be quite uneven). However, the effectiveness of formal communications is not unlimited; there are suggestions that the virtual monopoly exercised by the Nazis over communication content did not succeed in converting some large groups of Germans to their political philosophy.

That is one point—the greater but not absolute effectiveness of communication monopoly. Another deals with the problem of "balance" within competition. What does "balance" mean in the mass media? Does it mean a fifty-fifty division between pro and anti content? What is a "fair" distribution of attention to the different sides on a public controversy? One approach to this matter is to consider what might be called "functional balance" in the media, i.e., the proportionate distribution of content which enables partisans on an issue to read or see or listen to their own side with reasonably equal facility. This does not necessitate an automatic fifty-fifty division of the content. In one presidential campaign, for example, the Republicans and Democrats in a community read and heard their own side

[23] Cantril, "The Use of Trends," op. cit., p. 229.
[24] Smith, op. cit., p. 195. In this connection, see also Herbert Hyman and Paul Sheatsley, "Some Reasons Why Information Campaigns Fail," Public Opinion Quarterly, Vol. XI, 1947, pp. 412-23.

about equally, even though there was about a two-to-one disproportion of content favoring the Republicans.[25] In any case, the effect of the communication media upon public opinion is a function of the degree of competition on the issue within the media.

Another condition of communication exposure which affects opinion conversions is the purposiveness or non-purposiveness of the exposure. There is some slight evidence to suggest that non-purposive (or accidental) reading and listening is more effective in changing opinions than purposive (or deliberate).[26] In the first place, people see and hear more congenial material through deliberate communication exposure, and accidental reading and listening is more likely to bring diverse viewpoints to their attention. Secondly, in such exposure defenses against new ideas are presumably weaker because preconceptions are not so pervasively present. Finally, there may be other psychological advantages centering around the gratification of "overhearing" something "not meant for you," a consideration that also weakens the resistance to "propaganda" (since "it would not be propaganda if it wasn't intended for you"). This factor of accidental-and-deliberate communication exposure corresponds to the factor of indirect-and-direct communication content, and the same hypothesis probably holds.[27] Direct content attacks the issue head-on (e.g., an article urging fairer treatment of the Negroes). Indirect content takes the roundabout approach (e.g., a story about Negro children without direct reference to the problem of race relations). The indirect content is more effective in converting opinions for much the same reasons which apply to accidental exposure.

KINDS OF EFFECTS: Finally, the media of communication have different kinds of effects upon public opinion.

First, a distinction should be made between the effect of the media upon the holding of certain opinions rather than others and their effect upon the holding of political opinions at all. Most attention has been given to the former problem, but the latter—the problem of the creation and maintenance of political interest or political apathy—is of considerable importance. The media have a major influence in producing an interest in public affairs by constantly bringing them to people's attention in a context of presumed citizenly concern. The more the media stress a political

---

[25] Lazarsfeld, Berelson, and Gaudet, *The People's Choice*, Chapters XIII and XIV, pp. 110-36.

[26] Based upon an unpublished manuscript by Paul F. Lazarsfeld.

[27] For recent discussions of other conditions affecting this relationship, see Samuel Flowerman, "Mass Propaganda in the War Against Bigotry," *Journal of Abnormal and Social Psychology*, Vol. XLII, 1947, pp. 429-39; and Ernst Kris and Nathan Leites, "Trends in 20th Century Propaganda," in *Psychoanalysis and the Social Sciences*, International University Press, 1947, pp. 393-409.

issue, the less indecision there is on the issue among the general public.[28] At the same time, however, the communication media may also be promoting in actuality, but without intention, a sense of political apathy among some of its audience. This can occur in at least two ways.

In the first place, it is at least a plausible hypothesis that the attractive substance and easy accessibility of the entertainment or recreational or diversionary content of the mass media operate to minimize political interest for some groups in the population. Comedians, dramatic sketches, and popular music on the air; light fiction of the adventure, mystery, or romantic variety in magazines and books; comics and comic strips; feature films of "straight entertainment"—such "non-serious" content of the media may well serve to divert attention from political affairs directly and also to re-create the audience so that it is under less compulsion to "face up" to the general political problems which confront it and which shape its life. This is said with complete recognition of the psychological relief provided by such communication materials for many people; at the same time, their effect in lowering political interest and attention seems equally clear.

Secondly, the media may increase political apathy simply through presentation of the magnitude, the diversity, and the complexity of the political issues on which the responsible citizen is supposed to be informed. Some readers and listeners, conscious of their inability to become informed other than superficially on more than a few public problems, retreat from the whole area. How can one know what should be done about the Palestine partition, about inflation, about the Greek guerrillas and the Chinese communists, about race relations in the United States, about the cold war with the USSR, about labor-management relations generally or the latest strike specifically, about "free enterprise" or "planning," about the atom— all at the same time? The media atmosphere of public responsibility for public actions may thus become a boomerang: the more the public is enjoined to exercise its duty to become an "informed citizenry," the less it feels able to do so. And, overwhelmed by the presentation of issues and problems of a public nature, part of the audience may withdraw into the relative security of their private problems and their private lives.

In any discussion of the effect of the media upon the *kinds* of political opinions held by people, an initial distinction should be made between long-run and short-run effects. The importance of the former is inversely related to the research attention which has been given them. The fact that it is easier to study short-run changes in attitudes produced by the communication media—not that that is easy!—should not divert attention from the pervasive, subtle, and durable effects of the media over long periods of time. For example, motion pictures undoubtedly affect the po-

[28] Berelson, *op. cit.*, p. 53.

litical attention of their audiences over the long run by strengthening certain "basic" values in terms of which political issues are later decided. The influence is remote and indirect, but it is nonetheless present and active. Or again, the communication media affect public opinion over the long run by providing a set of definitions for key political terms (of an affective nature) which come to be accepted through lack of adequate challenge. Thus, "freedom" in this country has mainly been defined in the media in terms of the absence of governmental intervention; and when the value of "freedom" is invoked in a political argument, it usually carries this meaning into the attitudinal battle. Other definitions are possible, but not so current. When it is suggested that "freedom of the press" be defined in terms of the ability of various population groups to secure the kind of communication they want (or someone thinks they should have) rather than in terms of governmental control, the proposal is confronted by the established definition—established through repetition over a long period of time.

Now for the short-run effects of the media upon opinion. Most is known about this area of the general problem, but not much is known. At the least, distinctions should be made among the various kinds of effects which the communication media can have upon public opinion. Usually the term "effect" includes only the conversion of opinions (i.e., changes away from a predispositional position or prior attitudes), but the (more frequent) reinforcement and activation effects should not be overlooked. The media are extremely effective in providing partisans with the deference and the rationalizations needed to maintain their position (i.e., reinforcement): "If the press follows a tenacious policy during an economic crisis, it may be able to retard or prevent shifts from one major party to another." [29] And they are also effective in bringing to visibility people's latent attitudes (i.e., activation).[30]

More than that, the media are effective in structuring political issues for their audiences. For example, there is a tendency for partisans on each side of a controversial matter to agree with their own side's argument in the order in which those arguments are emphasized in mass communications. Thus, the media set the political stage, so to speak, for the ensuing debate. In addition, there is some evidence that private discussions of political matters take their cue from the media's presentation of the issues; people talk politics along the lines laid down in the media.[31]

Finally, one thing must be made quite clear in this discussion of the effects of the media upon public opinion. That is that effects upon the

[29] Harold F. Gosnell, *Machine Politics: Chicago Model,* University of Chicago Press, 1937, p. 181.

[30] For a fuller description of these effects, see Lazarsfeld, Berelson, and Gaudet, *The People's Choice,* Chapters VIII-X.

[31] For documentation of these points, see Berelson, *op. cit.*

audience do not follow directly from and in correspondence with the intent of the communicator or the content of the communication. The predispositions of the reader or listener are deeply involved in the situation, and may operate to block or modify the intended effect or even to set up a boomerang effect. This has been found time and again in studies of the effectiveness of materials promoting tolerance toward ethnic groups, on which topic predisposition run strong.[32] In another context—and under relatively favorable conditions—Communist propaganda provided a catharsis for its subjects, inefficiently for its own objectives, because its themes directly countered strong feelings of individualism and nationalism held by the audience.[33]

Conclusion

This brief discussion of communication and public opinion has indicated the reciprocal effects of the two major factors upon one another, and has presented a categorization in terms of which the effects of communication upon public opinion can usefully be investigated. In this latter analysis, five sets of variables were identified: communications, issues, people, conditions, effects.

The interrelationships of these variables constitute the subject-matter of a scientific theory in this field. For example, illustrative hypothesis can be suggested which deal with these interrelationships:

The more specialized the media (communication), the greater reinforcement (effect).

The greater the competition in a communication system (conditions), the greater reinforcement (effect).

The "deeper" the predispositional affect toward the issue (people), the more effective the indirect content (communication) in converting opinion (effect).

And so on, within the formulation: some kinds of communication on some kinds of issues, brought to the attention of some kinds of people under some kinds of conditions, have some kinds of effects.

It is hypotheses of this sort that should be systematically explored as the next step in research in this field. Whatever the method of investigation (and some of these are better than others)—historical (Mott), trend analysis (Cantril), statistical correlation of ecological and voting data (Gosnell), case study (Smith), opinion survey and analysis (Cottrell),[34] experi-

[32] For example, see Cooper and Jahoda, *op. cit.*
[33] Harold D. Lasswell and Dorothy Blumenstock, *World Revolutionary Propaganda: A Chicago Study*, Knopf, 1939. Section V: "The Influence of Propaganda," pp. 247-358.
[34] Leonard Cottrell, *American Opinion on World Affairs in the Atomic Age*, Princeton University Press, 1948.

mental (I. and E. Division),[35] panel (Lazarsfeld, Berelson, and Gaudet)—this sort of propositional organization should be considered as the framework of study. In this way, a scientific theory of communications and public opinion can be developed for the enrichment not only of the field of communications research generally, but for social science as well.

[35] Information and Education Division, U.S. War Department, "The Effects of Presenting 'One Side' vs. 'Both Sides' in Changing Opinions on a Controversial Subject," in Theodore Newcomb and Eugene Hartley, eds., *Readings in Social Psychology*, Holt, 1947, pp. 566-79.

9

PUBLIC OPINION, COMMUNICATION, AND DEMOCRATIC OBJECTIVES

Since the problems of public opinion and communication are concerned with the "marketplace of ideas" in the democratic society, questions of social and political values cannot and should not be neglected. The problems of social control, political processes, and social objectives are interlarded with considerations of the proper conduct of the communication media as well as with considerations of the state and quality of public opinion upon basic issues. Communication research can not only contribute to knowledge on the best means of realizing social values and objectives; it can also be guided in its selection of problems by value considerations.

This is strikingly illustrated in the selection from Merton's case study of an instance of mass persuasion which points up the moral implications of objective research findings. Some of the major insights of research to date are brought to bear in Lasswell's attempt to construct standards and criteria for a healthy democratic public opinion.

With the conviction that the matter of communication and public opinion is too important to be left to the researchers, men of good will have recently devoted themselves, in the U.S. and in Britain, to the problems of the communication media. From these two bodies—the Commission on the Freedom of the Press in this country and the Royal Commission on the Press in Britain—have come definite statements of the standards of performance by which the press should be evaluated. It is on this note that our collection ends.

Robert K. Merton

MASS PERSUASION:
THE MORAL DIMENSION

Our primary concern with the social psychology of mass persuasion should not obscure its moral dimension. The technician or practitioner in mass opinion and his academic counterpart, the student of social psychology, cannot escape the moral issues which permeate propaganda as a means of social control. The character of these moral issues differs somewhat for the practitioner and the investigator, but in both cases the issues themselves are inescapable.

The practitioner in propaganda is at once confronted by a dilemma: he must either forego the use of certain techniques of persuasion which will help him obtain the immediate end-in-view or violate prevailing moral codes. He must choose between being a less than fully effective technician and a scrupulous human being or an effective technician and a less than scrupulous human being. The pressure of the immediate objective tends to push him toward the first of these alternatives.[1] For when effective mass persuasion is sought, and when "effectiveness" is measured solely by the number of people who can be brought to the desired action or the desired frame of mind, then the choice of techniques of persuasion will be governed by a narrowly technical and amoral criterion. And this criterion exacts a price of the prevailing morality, for it expresses a manipulative attitude toward man and society. It inevitably pushes toward the use of whatsoever techniques "work."

The sense of power that accrues to manipulators of mass opinion, it would appear, does not always compensate for the correlative sense of guilt. The conflict may lead them to a flight into cynicism. Or it may lead to uneasy efforts to exonerate themselves from moral responsibility for the use of manipulative techniques by helplessly declaring, to themselves and to all who will listen, that "unfortunately, that's the way the world is. Peo-

Reprinted from *Mass Persuasion* (1947), pp. 185-189, by permission of the author and the publisher. (Copyright, 1947, by Harper & Bros.)

[1] R. K. Merton, "Social Structure and Anomie," *Amer. Soc. Review*, 1938, 3, 672-82.

ple are moved by emotions, by fear and hope and anxiety, and not by information or knowledge." It may be pointed out that complex situations must be simplified for mass publics and, in the course of simplification, much that is relevant must be omitted. Or, to take the concrete case we have been examining, it may be argued that the definition of war bonds as a device for curbing inflation is too cold and too remote and too difficult a conception to be effective in mass persuasion. It is preferable to focus on the sacred and sentimental aspects of war bonds, for this "copy slant" brings "results."

Like most half-truths, the notion that leaders of mass opinion must traffic in sentiment has a specious cogency. Values *are* rooted in sentiment and values *are* ineluctably linked with action. But the whole-truth extends beyond this observation. Appeals to sentiment within the context of relevant information and knowledge are basically different from appeals to sentiment which blur and obscure this knowledge. Mass persuasion is not manipulative when it provides access to the pertinent facts; it is manipulative when the appeal to sentiment is used to the exclusion of pertinent information.

The technician, then, must decide whether or not to use certain techniques which though possibly "effective" violate his own sentiments and moral codes. He must decide whether or not he should devise techniques for exploiting mass anxieties, for using sentimental appeals in place of information, for masking private purpose in the guise of common purpose.[2] He faces the moral problem of choosing not only among social ends but also among propaganda means.

Although less conspicuous and less commonly admitted, a comparable problem confronts the social scientist investigating mass opinion. He may adopt the standpoint of the positivist, proclaim the ethical neutrality of science, insist upon his exclusive concern with the advancement of knowledge, explain that science deals only with the discovery of uniformities and not with ends and assert that in his role as a detached and dispassionate scientist, he has no traffic with values. He may, in short, affirm an occupa-

---

[2] During the war, imagination triumphed over conscience among advertisers who "ingeniously" related their products to the war effort. Radio commercials were not immune from this technique. A commercial dentist, for example, suggests that a victory smile helps boost morale and that we can have that smile by purchasing our dentures from him. So, too, a clothing manufacturer reminds listeners that morale is a precious asset in time of war and that smart clothes, more particularly Selfridge Lane Clothes, give a man confidence and courage. Even ice cream becomes essential to the war effort. "Expecting your boys back from an army camp? Give them JL Ice Cream. They get good food in the army and it's your job to give them the same at home." And a manufacturer of cosmetics becomes solicitous about the imbalance in the sex ratio resulting from the war. "Fewer men around because of the war? Competition keen? Keep your skin smooth. Keep attractive for the boys in the service when they come marching home." Office of Radio Research, *Broadcasting the War*, Bur. Intelligence, OWI, 1943, p. 37.

tional philosophy which appears to absolve him of any responsibility for the use to which his discoveries in methods of mass persuasion may be put. With its specious and delusory distinction between "ends" and "means" and its insistence that the intrusion of social values into the work of scientists makes for special pleading, this philosophy fails to note that the investigator's social values do influence his choice and definition of problems. The investigator may naïvely suppose that he is engaged in the value-free activity of research, whereas in fact he may simply have so defined his research problems that the results will be of use to one group in the society, and not to others. His very choice and definition of a problem reflects his tacit values.

To illustrate: the "value-free" investigator of propaganda proceeds to the well-established mode of scientific formulations, and states his findings: "*If* these techniques of persuasion are used, *then* there will be (with a stated degree of probability) a given proportion of people persuaded to take the desired action." Here, then, is a formulation in the honored and successful tradition of science—apparently free of values. The investigator takes no moral stand. He merely reports his findings, and these, if they are valid, can be used by any interested group, liberal or reactionary, democratic or fascistic, idealistic or power-hungry. But this comfortable solution of a moral problem by the abdication of moral responsibility happens to be no solution at all, for it overlooks the crux of the problem: the initial formulation of the scientific investigation has been conditioned by the implied values of the scientist.

Thus, had the investigator been oriented toward such democratic values as respect for the dignity of the individual, he would have framed his scientific problem differently. He would not only have asked which techniques of persuasion produce the *immediate result* of moving a given proportion of people to action, but also, what are the *further, more remote* but not necessarily less significant, *effects* of these techniques upon the individual personality and the society? He would be, in short, sensitized to certain questions stemming from his democratic values which would otherwise be readily overlooked. For example he would ask, Does the unelaborated appeal to sentiment which displaces the information pertinent to assessing this sentiment blunt the critical capacities of listeners? What are the effects upon the personality of being subjected to virtual terrorization by advertisements which threaten the individual with social ostracism unless he uses the advertised defense against halitosis or B.O.? Or, more relevantly, what are the effects, in addition to increasing the sale of bonds, of terrorizing the parents of boys in military service by the threat that only through their purchase of war bonds can they ensure the safety of their sons and their ultimate return home? Do certain types of war bond drives by celebrities do more to pyramid their reputations as patriots than to further the sale of bonds which would otherwise not have been purchased? No single advertising or propaganda campaign may significantly affect the psychological stability of those subjected to it. But a society subjected ceaselessly to a flow of "effective" half-truths and the exploitation of mass anxieties may all the sooner lose that mutuality of confidence and reciprocal trust so essential to a stable social structure. A "morally neutral" investigation of propaganda will be less likely than an inquiry stemming from democratic values to address itself to such questions.

The issue has been drawn in its most general terms by John Dewey: "Certainly nothing can justify or condemn means except ends, results. But we have to include consequences impartially. . . . It is wilful folly to fasten upon some single end or consequence which is liked, and permit the view of that to blot from perception all other undesired and undesirable consequences." [3] If this study has one major implication for the understanding of mass persuasion, it consists in this recognition of the intimate interrelation of technique and morality.

[3] John Dewey, *Human Nature and Conduct* (New York: Henry Holt & Co., 1922), pp. 228-229. *Cf.* R. K. Merton, "The Unanticipated Consequences of Purposive Social Action," *American Sociological Review*, 1936, 1, 894-904.

Harold D. Lasswell

DEMOCRACY THROUGH
PUBLIC OPINION

Public Opinion in the Public Interest

Democratic government in America was achieved as a by-product of the expansion of society on this continent. Americans have come to cherish the by-product and to take thought about the ways and means of preserving and perfecting democracy throughout the future course of American history. We know that in many parts of the world the reaction against democracy is outspoken and energetic; yet among all who share the traditions of America, the problem is not *whether* democracy ought to live, but *how*. One factor in democratic survival is the reiteration of faith in the practice of justice by majority rule. But the survival of democratic government depends upon many other acts as well; to the repetition of the permanent goals and methods of democracy there must be joined the discovery of popular and consistent measures of public policy.

We know that the level of democratic attainment depends upon public opinion, and that opinion, like democratic government itself, is a social variable of ever-shifting scope, direction, and intensity of expression. When opinion sustains the ends and means of democratic government, public opinion is in the public interest. For this purpose we must examine the basic characteristics of public opinion in general, and then single out the variables upon which it significantly relies.

In order to distinguish public opinion from the official acts of government, we may call the acts of government the *dominant* opinion of the community. "Government by public opinion" means government in which there is a high degree of correspondence between dominant opinion and majority opinion through any selected period of time. The community is acting as a public when it makes debatable demands for collective action, even

Reprinted from *Democracy Through Public Opinion* (1941), pp. 20-22, 84-93, by permission of the author and the publisher. (Copyright, 1941, by Chi Omega Fraternity.)

when the acts of government do not coincide with majority or plurality opinion.

A distinction must be made between the community acting as a public and as a crowd. Whenever a topic is beyond debate, the community no longer acts as a public. Public indignation against the assassin of a beloved public figure is not public opinion; it is an expression of community sentiment. Whatever is defended with life and honor and without hesitation is not of the world of opinion, but of right and wrong.

Though the border line between the debatable and the non-debatable is sometimes vague and indistinct, the facts are clear in many situations. There are counties where no white man has ever voted a Republican ticket, and there are counties where a respectable Democrat is a contradiction in terms. Inside these tight local communities there is no public opinion about party membership. The matter is undebatable.

For many purposes it is convenient to distinguish between active and latent public opinion. Public opinion is active when opinions are being expressed, latent when there is no expression. When anyone says that there is latent public opinion in favor of busses, he means that he is predicting that public opinion would be so and so were the issue raised. There is a parallel distinction with regard to community sentiment. Sentiment is active when expressed, latent when unexpressed; statements about latency are predictions.

Just what social effects can be expected from public opinion? These are conveniently divisible into three: adjustment, catharsis, and violence. Public opinion culminates in adjustment when an abiding change in social practice occurs as when a city changes its form of government as a result of public discussion. But often there are no determinable changes in social practice. All that happens is that people who advocate and argue have an opportunity to express their emotions: this is catharsis. The third possible outcome of controversy is somewhat ominous. If the level of insecurity is high—owing perhaps to economic breakdown—opinion may not become unified in time on behalf of measures for the alleviation of distress, or for the restoration of sounder conditions. Insecurity may continue to pile up; the flame of propaganda burns ever more brightly on behalf of every conceivable proposal; yet nothing but frustration results. Young and old grow disillusioned with the processes of democratic discussion, and hotspurs demand action, even violence. Public opinion has intensified the level of discontent and contributed to the severity of social crisis. Controversy has become a prelude to violence.

It is evident that the public interest is not served when controversy leads to the frustrations that feed eventual violence. Public opinion in the public interest must serve the two ends of adjustment and catharsis.

One basic characteristic of public opinion is that it is tightly bound up with private opinion. Indeed, it may be useful to remind ourselves of the never-ending chain of private and collective acts. There is a dynamic connection between what is thought and felt in private and what is said and done in intimate circles and in public. We are often under the illusion that if we have a thought in private it has nothing to do with the fate of society. We may tell ourselves that all politics are corrupt and that an honest man will stay out. It is significant, and even ominous, if we have such an idea. It probably means that scores or even millions of our fellow citizens are entertaining similar thoughts. What we come to think and feel is intimately bound up with the collective processes in which we find ourselves. A private moment of thought may provide us with the justification for making many important subsequent decisions. Our private resolve may stiffen our determination to refrain from running for office, or from contributing to the support of a research bureau devoted to the discovery of the facts about public finance. What we think affects what we do, and what we do in turn affects what we think.

Our private thoughts often become our intimate communications, and exercise an obvious effect upon others. We may advise our son to stay out of public affairs and to mind his own business, and this advice may be given by thousands of other fathers to their sons. Fathers throughout society may be telling their sons that only crooks and crackpots go into politics, and if they have influence with their sons, such fathers have contributed to the anti-democratic current. The person who objects to the "futility" of public discussion may not think that he is an enemy of democracy. But his attitude may fortify the attitudes of others. The prestige of public careers dwindles down; confidence is undermined in the possibility of talent and integrity in the service of the community. For years this may make no appreciable difference. Then a crisis may arise, fostered possibly by war or by a breakdown of economic life. Like subtle poison democratic defeatism has spread its destructive influence, and under stress, there comes explicit admiration for autocracy. "Dictators get things done; democrats talk."

❈   ❈   ❈

Democracy Needs a New Way to Talk

Let us grant the possibility that democratic methods may be improved. Our means of locomotion have not frozen in the horse and buggy era, and our modes of collective deliberation may be susceptible to improvement.

Indeed, there has been a current of candid self-criticism among the champions of democracy, and this dissatisfaction has already led to some exceptionally stimulating experiments. The problem, in general, is to minimize the distorting effects of undisciplined emotion, and to maximate the quest of truth and clarity.

The method of "debate" has been under fire. We are told that debates degenerate into dog fights. A debater is, by popular definition, a gladiator. He is a battler, not a truth seeker. His mind is made up in advance that his prestige depends on winning the argument, not on aiding truth. The traditional attitude of the debater is not compatible with the firm, yet modest, presentation of a probable, hence somewhat doubtful, picture of the future. The tentative exploration of new insight does not fit the battle mind. Deference goes to the master of artifice, including the specialist on vociferous simulations of sincerity.

Criticism of debate has prepared the way for alternative plans of public discussion. The leading idea is to reduce the irreconcilability that is inseparable from the popular notion of debate. Participants in the discussion do not enter distinctly labeled "yes-men" and "no-men." Under these circumstances the deference of the individual does not depend quite so much upon pugilistic cunning. He can take the attitude of one who is genuinely interested in the pursuit of sound public policy. This means that he can make concessions in the interest of truth without suffering personal humiliation. Participants do not enter a "ring"; they share an hour of inquiry. They do not need to rationalize every sentence by insisting upon its consistency with the position affirmed at the outset. The situation is redefined in the minds of participants and spectators: it is "discussion," not "argument"; it is "inquiry," not "controversy"; it is "symposium," not "debate." Positions are not arbitrarily limited to two. It is implied that there are many positions between "emphatically yes" and "emphatically no" that can be rationally taken. Everyone is invited to search for the position along the continuum that best corresponds to his views and preferences.

Another tendency in modern experimentation is to enlarge the part played by the audience. This is implied in the "forum" movement, which undertakes to reduce the passivity of those who listen to what is said by the principal speakers. Audience members are encouraged to ask questions, state views and express opinions. Many Americans are trained to passivity in public by the "sermon." The sermon is a unilateral pronouncement in a situation highly charged with ceremonial values. It would be a scandal to break into a sermon and to challenge the preacher. In more ways than one the traditional attitude of the sermonizer is summarized in the advice of the old parson to the young one: "I tell them I'm going to tell them; I tell them; I tell him I am telling them; I tell them I've told them." "Telling them" is what the preacher does.

The American political "rally" is a situation in which the speeches are secular sermons. The speakers do not expect to disagree with one another, and they do not expect to be disagreed with by the audience. Members of the audience may participate by shouts and cheers, not by discussion. Congregations and party mass meetings do not debate difference. They celebrate unity. In the English scene the pattern of heckling does not add to the intellectual calibre of what takes place. The heckler may intervene at any time, and the object of the game is to embarrass the speaker. In defense the speaker develops quick repartee, and the mock battle is highly prized public entertainment. The institution of heckling is of no importance for democracy, except possibly to perpetuate some wit and many bad manners. It is sometimes suggested that the dynamic attitude of the audience carries over into the spheres of public life, and aids in the perpetuation of democratic initiative and self-respect. But this suggestion has never been confirmed.

For many years American young people interested in public affairs were trained in a style of public discussion that excluded the audience and exaggerated the battle psychology of the participants. This was the "debate." "Affirmative" and "negative" teams were pitted against one another in a rigid routine of principal speech and brief rebuttal. There were three "Honorable Judges" who selected the winner by secret ballot. The "Ladies and Gentlemen" of the audience were trusted no further than their cheers could reach. They were not supposed to intervene with question, view or opinion. And if their minds were affected in any way by the proceedings, there was no official way of determining the fact.

The pattern of academic debate was devised in the shadow of judicial rather than legislative example. Court judges are supposed to apply strict rules to what comes before them, and some of the reality of the court was preserved in the debate. But the unreality of the procedure is apparent. Decisions on public policy are governed by no fixed body of rules. There were no rules on public policy that the debate judges could possibly apply. Indeed, they were supposed to overlook personal preferences on public issues and to judge the contestants exclusively on points of technique. Emphasis was kept on the aggrandizement of the individual rather than upon the purposes to be served by discussions of public policy. The academic debate was not strictly comparable with court, congress, or any known situation in mature life. It was entirely an individualistic performance in which vague rules of persuasiveness were applied for the glory of the contestant.

The academic pattern of debate flourished for years before it met rebuff. In recent years many variations have been introduced into the conduct of college and high school discussion of public questions. Some debating leagues have discarded the judge system and substituted votes by the audience. Since the audience is less equipped to evaluate the skillfulness of the performance, the idea of judging the expertness of the debaters has often been abandoned entirely. The audience is frankly asked to vote its preferences on the topic under discussion. The "debate" has dissolved into a forum.

Forums have grown increasingly popular in these troubled times; yet they cannot be regarded as wholly successful instruments of democracy. The curse of informality is discursiveness; hence discussion may breed a sense of frustration where pride of achievement is wanted. By fostering confusion, forums may actually contribute to the level of anxiety, and the sense of futility that lowers the prestige of good talk.

The infirmities of informality are well known. Issues are often left vaguely defined. The discussion may proceed in disorderly, hit-and-miss fashion, so that no clear line of tactical or strategical march is discernible. Disproportionate opportunities may be seized by "cranks" and "crackpots" who "sound off" in a manner that outrages the sentiments of all who hold moderate views.

It is quite proper to emphasize the catharsis function of public controversy. Few institutions are more symbolic of free discussion than "Hyde Park Corner" in London, where a medley of discordant speakers ply their hearers with nostrums of every description.

The conspicuous place of the "Hyde Park" tradition has somewhat cast in the shadow another characteristic feature of public discussion in Great Britain, which is the disciplined rigor of procedure in the House of Commons. All manner of safeguards have grown up whose function is to minimize the distorting effect of irrelevant passion upon the course of deliberations. There is dignity and seriousness in the House debate, and intemperate outbursts or mere shouting contests are kept at a minimum by the customs of the House, and the vigilance of "Mr. Speaker." Foreign commentators upon the Mother of Parliaments have been uniformly appreciative of the variety and the practicability of the several expedients that minimize the resort to irrelevance. A. Lawrence Lowell, among others, wisely chose from the observation of British experience many examples of technical means of keeping the focus of attention upon the matter in hand.

After all, questions of public policy are singularly fraught with significance of life and death, and it is altogether appropriate that they should be considered in an atmosphere of dignity and responsibility. Society is rich in alternative means of boisterous or insolent catharsis—this, indeed, is one of the chief functions of many forms of public amusement. Since democracy reveres self-discipline, it can hope to spread among its citizens a keen sense of when *not* to join in public discussion. It is always appropriate to insist upon clarification of the obscure, or to contribute significant fact and neglected interpretation. But the Quaker meeting is a more appropriate model for the consideration of grave public questions than Hyde Park.

Are there feasible ways of perfecting the existing patterns of discussion

—not only in the government, but in private business and professional associations as well?

Let us explore a little more closely the frailties of existing procedure. The root of the difficulty is the word problem. Respect for talk does not depend upon hearing talk that you agree with. It depends upon hearing talk disciplined by methods that you can respect. If we do not need to agree, we certainly cannot afford to confuse. We do need to clarify.

Existing methods of debate and symposium do not deal successfully with the flow of words. They allow words to contribute to public confusion, not clarification. We know that uncertainty cannot be removed from our thinking about the world. But confusion can. Confusion occurs when alternatives are not clearly seen.

We need methods of introducing discipline into the handling of language in public discussion. There is no excuse for impenetrable barrages of language at the start of public discussion. As it is, we begin by allowing advocates to talk a great deal at the start, and by the time they have piled assertion upon assertion, issues are confused, tempers are ruffled and the battle is on. Talk in public ceases to be a quest for sound public policy and disintegrates into a fight; or in eagerness to maintain the emotional equanimity of the discussion, views and opinions are given friendly but unclarified hospitality.

Perhaps we can clarify public discussion by adopting a new pattern. If so, we need to provide for a new function. Someone should be charged with the responsibility for clarifying what is said. The job of the clarifier would be to make words make sense.

How would the clarifier work? He would ask questions of each contributor to the discussion. Suppose that Mr. A has spoken for five minutes in favor of more taxes on the lesser income groups. Mr. B has spoken against the proposal. The clarifier would try to disclose to the audience just how A and B view the results of what they propose. Mr. A, let us assume, says that everybody will feel more responsible if he pays taxes. Mr. B retorts that in fact the people with the lowest incomes pay the most taxes, but Mr. A does not think they are responsible. The clarifier would have to find out what is meant by "paying taxes" and by "responsibility." Both men may agree that the lower income groups pay the most taxes. Mr. A may want to be understood as saying that the "irresponsibility" of the poorer people comes from the invisibility of the burden that bears on them. He may predict that the lower income groups will become more active for efficiency in government, and against more expenditures for relief, if they understand that they bear much of the community load. The clarifier can find out if Mr. B agrees with this picture of the probable outcome of direct taxes on the low income groups. And so on. The clarifier will not take sides. He will not express personal preferences. He will perform a strictly technical function. He will ask the questions that every member of the audience would ask if he were able to think of them promptly and ask them consecutively. Before audience participation, the situation will be clarified to a point where relevant contributions can be distinctly recognized.

The very name "clarifier" is an important symbol of how public discussion can work. Talk in public should pursue the common end of clarifying the ends and means of public policy. The clarifier differs from the judge, who applies a body of legal rules to the words presented before him. He differs from the "chairman," who looks simply to the rules of order. The clarifier is not a "moderator," if by the moderator we mean one who tries to keep the discussion advancing toward clarity, but who holds his own intervention within modest bounds.

There is no exact counterpart of the clarifier now functioning in our civilization, although the function is often performed by men who operate under different names. The task of clarifier is sometimes performed by the interrogator at committee hearings. Senator LaFollette, for example, has often kept after the witness until he has brought out what the witness intends to say, and how it is related to other testimony. Judges frequently perform the clarifying role, but they operate in other situations than general discussion of public policy. Moderators of meetings strive to keep discussion on the track. But usually they are untrained in word analysis, and are intimidated from playing a too active part in what is said.[1]

If the role of the clarifier is itself to be made clear, it must be embodied in personalities of certain characteristics. The clarifier must be alert and informed; and he must be capable of arousing confidence that he sincerely wants clarity.

The idea of the clarifier can be extended to all occasions where there is collective discussion, public or not. Every committee meeting can make use of the clarifier. Meetings of boards of directors, boards of trustees, cabinets, commissions, administrative councils, executive committees, advisory boards, conciliation committees; all depend for their successful issue upon the skillful use of the mind. They rely upon discussion, and their

---

[1] Could the "clarifier" be given a better name? There are several terms that deserve careful consideration before usage is finally crystallized around the clarifier. We might speak of the "examiner." But since school days most of us feel that examiners are out to test memory and skill, not to co-operate in new discovery. The clarifier aids in the process of creative thought. He is not an inventory man. If we called the clarifier "Mr. Quiz" we should collect all of the false connotations of the examiner. The "questioner" or "asker" is descriptive. These words emphasize the fact that questions are asked, and imply nothing about the purpose. The "enquirer" is full of friendly associations in the popular mind. Yet there is no implication of special expertness in the "enquirer." He has a sound intention, devoid of technique. The "clarifier" can be launched under auspices which convey an idea of competence in word analysis. The word "investigator" is too rich in gum-shoe connotations; and the "inquisitor" is definitely hostile, like the "prosecutor."

processes can be improved by a specialist who performs the clarifying function.

As a specialist on thinking in collective situations, the clarifier can enlarge his experience of the ways and means of successful discussion. There is, at present, no adequate body of knowledge about this vital process. One of the many difficult questions is how far to encourage, or to discourage, the use of definitions in discussion.

The clarifier not only needs to decide when to encourage definitions, but when to permit the making of any logical distinction whatsoever. Dozens of logical points can be scored with regard to any stream of communication; the clarifier cannot be blind to them, but equally he cannot be blind to other values which are involved in the total act of communication. Discussion may be turned aside from the solution of pressing questions, while participants "quibble" about points of consistency, generality, or economy of statement. The general problem of the clarifier is to find how much talk about logic enables the stream of talk to come to intelligent results.

❈   ❈   ❈

World Trend and Public Opinion

What of the future? What can be done by American public opinion to safeguard the basic values of our own society in these turbulent times?

Our opinions about public policy are profoundly affected by the views that we entertain about the future. The probable shape of things to come enters into the calculations of every rational person who does not care to waste his energy on hopeless enterprises. The problem is not to drift with the current, but to navigate the stream, and this calls for the correct anticipation of what lies ahead.

Before leaders of opinion can clarify their neighbors, they must clarify themselves about the connection between democracy in America and the dominant trends of world reality. They must show how America can cope with the problems of the age without losing majority rule in the interest of justice.

No one can wisely be over-optimistic about his success in divining the direction of history. Our eyes are blinded by passion and our ears are split by the noise of war.

However, opinion may be clarified about the primary problems and trends of our time; already there are enough facts to justify the serious consideration of certain major possibilities.

The chief problem of our age, we may suggest, is how to operate a machine society. The advent of the machine has not only revolutionized our ways of making a living; it has heightened the tempo and increased the irregularity of social change. If our habits of operating the machine have led to prosperity they have also induced collapse. If they have fostered world trade, they have also provoked world war. No doubt the fundamental problem of man is how to regularize the tempo of social change in a machine society.

One major trend is toward *job security,* toward full utilization of resources. Drastic experiments have already been undertaken in various parts of the world.

Another major trend in modern states is tightly bound up with the abolition of joblessness, though separable from it. We may speak of it as the psychological abolition of unemployment; i.e., not "work relief" but *security on a respected job.* Where unemployment is psychologically. eliminated, self-respect mounts again.

Yet a third trend of world affairs seems to be toward the *moderation of vast differences in individual income.* The rich resources of our vast American continent are inadequately developed.

Twelve million American families have less than $1,000 a year to buy the products of our farms and factories. When we add the six million single individuals who get less than $1,000 a year we find, that, all told, 54,600,000 Americans must try to live on $1,000 or less each year. This is two-fifths of our entire population. These 54,600,000 men, women and children are equal to the combined population of 36 of our 48 states.

The American people are still a scarcity people, unable to provide abundantly for themselves despite the lavish resources of the continent, the stupendous productivity of the machine, and the optimism of the American tradition.

The three major trends that have been mentioned may be summed up in the three words: Stability, deference, moderation.

In every part of the world these trends are accompanied, facilitated, or held in check by a swarm of local factors.

The presence or absence of secondary features in different nations is determined by local factors of inherited culture and immediate circumstance. The continuation or discontinuation of democracy depends upon such local factors. Where democracy has died, the death is to be attributed to local conditions. Democracy has declined and disappeared under stress in nations where it was poorly rooted; or it has been suppressed by outside force.

The problem of the machine is everywhere; but whether these problems are met by democracy or nondemocracy depends upon local factors.

Where democracy has failed, therefore, many local factors are responsible. When we examine these special conditions in America, we find that the chances of democratic survival are relatively good.

For one thing, democracy is deeply rooted in the life of our society. For another, America has a continuous history of national success. We have not been humiliated in defeat at the end of a desperate foreign war. We need no revenge. Then, too, we are forewarned; there is no need for America to slide unwittingly down the European path through private monopolism to dictatorship. European despotism is an instructive example of what to avoid on this side of the water.

But the general condition of democratic survival is that it meets the needs of the time. It must cope with the problem of the machine. And if our analysis is correct, American democracy will live if it guides national policy in three directions: toward job security, toward security on a respected job, toward moderation of great differences in individual income.

Public opinion is already informed, to some extent, of practicable means of coping with the problems of a machine society. The significant alternatives already have spokesmen; and the spokesmen may well become more expert in their task of clarification.

In a sense public opinion in America has been confused by the very uniqueness of the position occupied by this nation in the twentieth century. Alone among the major continents, America has been free to face the basic issues of the new century, free from the paralyzing dissensions of the recent past. To all intents and purposes the North American continent is a unified community, unified in the possession of stupendous natural resources, and in access to a single market. In contrast to Europe, our continent has long been united. We attained a great measure of internal union, democracy and peace in the nineteenth century.

Other continents stayed in the nineteenth century; they carried over into the twentieth century the internal conflicts that they were unable to overcome in the nineteenth. The continents of Europe, Asia and Africa were torn apart by contending states that fed on ancient animosities of space, class, race, and creed. America, on the other hand, faced the twentieth century with unity of aspiration in a rich and spacious continent. The American continental economy rests on a peaceful and united market.

There is nothing so abstruse about these matters that they cannot be clarified to Americans. They are already dimly understood, but there is need of greater clarity.

In particular, there is need of clarity about the position of America in the total historical process of our time. By perceiving the trends of the time, democracy can live and grow. Such basic clarity is an instrument of self-respect; men and women who are not clear about the part they play in the historical drama in which they move cannot entirely respect their own intelligence, hence they cannot wholly respect themselves.

We know that clarity is no "once and for all" achievement; and it is not to be confounded with the compulsive repetition of respected words. Clarity is a provisional picture of where events are going, and of what can be done under the circumstances to advance justice.

Leaders of opinion may perceive that we are in an active phase of world revolutionary change. There is nothing unprecedented about this. The civilization of the West moves in great revolutionary waves that appear to spread from definite centers and to continue until they lap the shores of every continent. The story of the West is the story of the rise and spread and restriction of new patterns of thought and deed. Each pattern, though related in detail to the old, is ever new in arrangement of component parts. New ways of talking and doing are forever combining in new ways to alter the tapestry of civilization.

Although most Americans may think of revolution as a violent clash of rowdies in the street, it is not necessarily anything of the kind. A revolution may come silently. Violence often comes, if at all, when the revolution is already well advanced. New methods of production create new ways of making a living, and new groups come into existence. Persons who belong to new groups gradually take on new ways of thinking, feeling, acting. They focus their attention upon different aspects of reality than their neighbors, and their attitudes are subtly transformed as a result. Private and collective attitudes are no longer what they were; the basis has been laid for new currents in public and private opinion.

That the machine society is a skill society is inadequately understood by public opinion. Yet certain basic figures about the population of countries like the United States and Great Britain are informative in this regard. There has been an enormous increase in the white-collar skill group in recent decades. If we take 1870 as a base and compute the relative increase, we find that clerical and other salaried employees have expanded something like sixfold in relation to other groups in the last sixty years. If we look at the brain workers, we find that they have increased about threefold relative to the total population during the same sixty-year period.

Other groupings of the population confirm the same conclusion: the machine society is a skill society. The professional skill group, together with the better paid clerical, commercial, managerial, "working on their own account" groups, constituted 35 per cent of the occupied population in 1870. In 1930 the figure was 44 per cent. In England these groups account for one third of the occupied population. The occupational groups constituting the "middle classes" have doubled in England since the war. In the same period the lesser white-collar groups have increased threefold. (Figures are from Alvin Hansen, T. M. Sogge, and Colin Clark.)

There are certain psychological consequences of acquiring skill. Skill can be acquired by discipline. The individual must suppress his impulses toward irrelevant activity. He must sacrifice the present for the future. But all men are not born to sacrifice equally. Some men acquire skill easily because they take readily to self-discipline; others find it arduous and repugnant. This is the sacrificial aspect of learning. In return for what the individual gives up in the present, we make promises of future happiness (success). "Strive and succeed" is the pithy motto that sums up the official attitude of our society.

Some of the psychological consequences of the machine society work themselves out in the lives of the non-skill group. The non-skilled, or the possessors of superannuated or non-employed skills, suffer severe blows to their self-esteem. In the machine society deference goes to those who are skilled in technology and in control. This is a gadgeteering age that respects science, invention, control. The machine has cut a great gap between skilled and non-skilled.

American public opinion is shocked by the violence and despotism that has attended the recent revolutions in other continents. We are only too acutely aware of the tragedies of war and civil strife that have disfigured the face of recent history. So grave are these events that no friend of America or of humanity can wish for America to suffer the same sacrifices. We can clearly see that the task of America is to achieve the skill society, free from the distortions and the tragedies that have beset the skill revolution in other continents.

Public opinion can see that America is in a remarkably advantageous position to march toward security on a respected job without giving up the practice of majority rule, and without going through the violent internal crises of other continents. The assets of America are plain to all: a peaceful continental market, with abundant resources conducive to self-sufficiency; a long apprenticeship to the requirements of democratic government; a horrible European example of what to avoid. Above all, perhaps, is a unified middle class outlook. We have traditionally cherished no aristocracy of birth that looks down with contempt upon middle class concern with skill. We respect sacrifice, work, attainment. We are comparatively free from "bums" at the bottom of the social structure who believe that "society owes me a living," or from gilded bums at the top of the social pyramid who expect the same indulgence. Whatever the imperfections, the American people have succeeded in making substantial strides toward a skill democracy in their own continent.

In the future, as in the past, we must take the initiative in safeguarding our sister continent to the South from foreign encroachment. We can strengthen the cultural, economic and strategic bonds that join us in a common destiny and protect this hemisphere from invaders.

Many of our abundant resources of men and material must be poured into the urgent task of military defense of this continent and this hemisphere. Modern wars are conducted on four fronts: military, economic, moral, organizational. Victory depends upon the efficient development of every special instrument, and the proper integration of each in the total operation.

The billions of dollars that are needed for continental security and development can be wisely spent for a balanced program of military, economic, moral and organizational defense.

The emergency affords a remarkable opportunity for the moral defense of America, notably by putting an end to the invidious distinction between those who are employed in government and in private enterprise.

The enemies of America will wage war for the capture of American opinion, and we may safely predict that this campaign will proceed by other measures than frontal attack. They will incite every group against every other group in the nation. In particular, this means ringing the changes upon every conceivable difference of racial, religious, sectional, and economic characteristic. No doubt one of the most insidious jibes will continue to be aimed at "plutocratic democracy."

The best defense against sneers at "pluto-democrats" is not to deserve them. Americans are not jealous of moderately big incomes. Only when bigness verges on monopoly, and when there is hereditary transmission of influence to incompetents, do Americans harbor resentment.

Public opinion can continue to be clarified about the need of social balance and regularity; the vital significance of such basic relationships is increased, not diminished, by crisis.

Throughout this book we have stressed the imperative need of clarity, of clarity about the ends and means of justice through public opinion. Clarity must include insight into the trend of world affairs, and a rational understanding of how democracy *can* survive and develop.

In this connection we have pointed out the trends toward job security, security on a respected job, and moderation of huge differences of individual income. The sacrifice of democracy is not a fundamental trend of the times; democracy can live or die, depending upon local factors. Indeed, democracy is itself one of the longrun requirements of the skill society; it is eclipsed where it comes into irreconcilable conflict with the demand for security on a respected job.

If our analysis is correct, America, almost alone among the continents, *can* meet the needs of the time without giving up the rule of the majority. Public opinion, instructed by failures elsewhere, can demand proper means of harmonizing the use of machines with justice, with man's fundamental craving for self-respect. In America we can achieve democracy through public opinion.

The Commission on Freedom of the Press

THE REQUIREMENTS

If the freedom of the press is freighted with the responsibility of providing the current intelligence needed by a free society, we have to discover what a free society requires. Its requirements in America today are greater in variety, quantity, and quality than those of any previous society in any age. They are the requirements of a self-governing republic of continental size, whose doings have become, within a generation, matters of common concern in new and important ways. Its internal arrangements, from being thought of mainly as matters of private interest and automatic market adjustments, have become affairs of conflict and conscious compromise among organized groups, whose powers appear not to be bounded by "natural law," economic or other. Externally, it has suddenly assumed a leading role in the attempt to establish peaceful relationships among all the states on the globe.

Today our society needs, first, a truthful, comprehensive, and intelligent account of the day's events in a context which gives them meaning; second, a forum for the exchange of comment and criticism; third, a means of projecting the opinions and attitudes of the groups in the society to one another; fourth, a method of presenting and clarifying the goals and values of the society; and, fifth, a way of reaching every member of the society by the currents of information, thought, and feeling which the press supplies.

The Commission has no idea that these five ideal demands can ever be completely met. All of them cannot be met by any one medium; some do not apply at all to a particular unit; nor do all apply with equal relevance to all parts of the communications industry. The Commission does not suppose that these standards will be new to the managers of the press; they are drawn largely from their professions and practices.

Reprinted from *A Free and Responsible Press: Report of the Commission on Freedom of the Press* (1947), pp. 20-29, by permission of the publisher. (Copyright, 1947, by The University of Chicago Press.)

A Truthful, Comprehensive, and Intelligent Account of the Day's Events in a Context which Gives Them Meaning

The first requirement is that the media should be accurate. They should not lie.

Here the first link in the chain of responsibility is the reporter at the source of the news. He must be careful and competent. He must estimate correctly which sources are most authoritative. He must prefer firsthand observation to hearsay. He must know what questions to ask, what things to observe, and which items to report. His employer has the duty of training him to do his work as it ought to be done.

Of equal importance with reportorial accuracy are the identification of fact as fact and opinion as opinion, and their separation, so far as possible. This is necessary all the way from the reporter's file, up through the copy and makeup desks and editorial offices, to the final, published product. The distinction cannot, of course, be made absolute. There is no fact without a context and no factual report which is uncolored by the opinions of the reporter. But modern conditions require greater effort than ever to make the distinction between fact and opinion. In a simpler order of society published accounts of events within the experience of the community could be compared with other sources of information. Today this is usually impossible. The account of an isolated fact, however accurate in itself, may be misleading and, in effect, untrue.

The greatest danger here is in the communication of information internationally. The press now bears a responsibility in all countries, and particularly in democratic countries, where foreign policies are responsive to popular majorities, to report international events in such a way that they can be understood. It is no longer enough to report *the fact* truthfully. It is now necessary to report *the truth about the fact*.

In this country a similar obligation rests upon the press in reporting domestic news. The country has many groups which are partially insulated from one another and which need to be interpreted to one another. Factually correct but substantially untrue accounts of the behavior of members of one of these social islands can intensify the antagonisms of others toward them. A single incident will be accepted as a sample of group action unless the press has given a flow of information and interpretation concerning the relations between two racial groups such as to enable the reader to set a single event in its proper perspective. If it is allowed to pass as a sample of such action, the requirement that the press present an accurate account of the day's events in a context which gives them meaning has not been met.

A Forum for the Exchange of Comment and Criticism

The second requirement means that the great agencies of mass communication should regard themselves as common carriers of public discussion.[1] The units of the press have in varying degrees assumed this function and should assume the responsibilities which go with it, more generally and more explicitly.

It is vital to a free society that an idea should not be stifled by the circumstances of its birth. The press cannot and should not be expected to print everybody's ideas. But the giant units can and should assume the duty of publishing significant ideas contrary to their own, as a matter of objective reporting, distinct from their proper function of advocacy. Their control over the various ways of reaching the ear of America is such that, if they do not publish ideas which differ from their own, those ideas will never reach the ear of America. If that happens, one of the chief reasons for the freedom which these giants claim disappears.

Access to a unit of the press acting as a common carrier is possible in a number of ways, all of which, however, involve selection on the part of the managers of the unit. The individual whose views are not represented on an editorial page may reach an audience through a public statement reported as news, through a letter to the editor, through a statement printed in advertising space, or through a magazine article. But some seekers for space are bound to be disappointed and must resort to pamphlets or such duplicating devices as will spread their ideas to such public as will attend to them.

But all the important viewpoints and interests in the society should be represented in its agencies of mass communication. Those who have these viewpoints and interests cannot count on explaining them to their fellow-citizens through newspapers or radio stations of their own. Even if they could make the necessary investment, they could have no assurance that their publications would be read or their programs heard by the public outside their own adherents. An ideal combination would include general media, inevitably solicitous to present their own views, but setting forth other views fairly. As checks on their fairness, and partial safeguards against ignoring important matters, more specialized media of advocacy have a vital place. In the absence of such a combination the partially insulated groups in society will continue to be insulated. The unchallenged assumptions of each group will continue to harden into prejudice. The mass me-

---

[1] By the use of this analogy the Commission does not intend to suggest that the agencies of communication should be subject to the legal obligations of common carriers, such as compulsory reception of all applicants for space, the regulation of rates, etc.

dium reaches across all groups; through the mass medium they can come to understand one another.

Whether a unit of the press is an advocate or a common carrier, it ought to identify the sources of its facts, opinions, and arguments so that the reader or listener can judge them. Persons who are presented with facts, opinions, and arguments are properly influenced by the general reliability of those who offer them. If the veracity of statements is to be appraised, those who offer them must be known.

Identification of source is necessary to a free society. Democracy, in time of peace, at least, has a justifiable confidence that full and free discussion will strengthen rather than weaken it. But, if the discussion is to have the effect for which democracy hopes, if it is to be really full and free, the names and the characters of the participants must not be hidden from view.

The Projection of a Representative Picture of the Constituent Groups in the Society

This requirement is closely related to the two preceding. People make decisions in large part in terms of favorable or unfavorable images. They relate fact and opinion to stereotypes. Today the motion picture, the radio, the book, the magazine, the newspaper, and the comic strip are principal agents in creating and perpetuating these conventional conceptions. When the images they portray fail to present the social group truly, they tend to pervert judgment.

Such failure may occur indirectly and incidentally. Even if nothing is said about the Chinese in the dialogue of a film, yet if the Chinese appear in a succession of pictures as sinister drug addicts and militarists, an image of China is built which needs to be balanced by another. If the Negro appears in the stories published in magazines of national circulation only as a servant, if children figure constantly in radio dramas as impertinent and ungovernable brats—the image of the Negro and the American child is distorted. The plugging of special color and "hate" words in radio and press dispatches, in advertising copy, in news stories—such words as "ruthless," "confused," "bureaucratic"—performs inevitably the same image-making function.

Responsible performance here simply means that the images repeated and emphasized be such as are in total representative of the social group as it is. The truth about any social group, though it should not exclude its weaknesses and vices, includes also recognition of its values, its aspirations, and its common humanity. The Commission holds to the faith that if people are exposed to the inner truth of the life of a particular group, they will gradually build up respect for and understanding of it.

The Presentation and Clarification of the
Goals and Values of the Society

The press has a similar responsibility with regard to the values and goals of our society as a whole. The mass media, whether or not they wish to do so, blur or clarify these ideals as they report the failings and achievements of every day.[2] The Commission does not call upon the press to sentimentalize, to manipulate the facts for the purpose of painting a rosy picture. The Commission believes in realistic reporting of the events and forces that militate against the attainment of social goals as well as those which work for them. We must recognize, however, that the agencies of mass communication are an educational instrument, perhaps the most powerful there is; and they must assume a responsibility like that of educators in stating and clarifying the ideals toward which the community should strive.

Full Access to the Day's Intelligence

It is obvious that the amount of current information required by the citizens in a modern industrial society is far greater than that required in any earlier day. We do not assume that all citizens at all times will actually use all the material they receive. By necessity or choice large numbers of people voluntarily delegate analysis and decision to leaders whom they trust. Such leadership in our society is freely chosen and constantly changing; it is informal, unofficial, and flexible. Any citizen may at any time assume the power of decision. In this way government is carried on by consent.

But such leadership does not alter the need for the wide distribution of news and opinion. The leaders are not identified; we can inform them only by making information available to everybody.

The five requirements listed in this chapter suggest what our society is entitled to demand of its press. We can now proceed to examine the tools, the structure, and the performance of the press to see how it is meeting these demands.

[2] A striking indication of the continuous need to renew the basic values of our society is given in the recent poll of public opinion by the National Opinion Research Center at Denver, in which one out of every three persons polled did not think the newspapers should be allowed to criticize the American form of government, even in peacetime. Only 57 per cent thought that the Socialist party should be allowed, in peacetime, to publish newspapers in the United States. Another poll revealed that less than a fourth of those questioned had a "reasonably accurate idea" of what the Bill of Rights is. Here is widespread ignorance with regard to the value most cherished by the press—its own freedom—which seems only dimly understood by many of its consumers.

Let us summarize these demands in another way.

The character of the service required of the American press by the American people differs from the service previously demanded, first, in this —that it is essential to the operation of the economy and to the government of the Republic. Second, it is a service of greatly increased responsibilities both as to the quantity and as to the quality of the information required. In terms of quantity, the information about themselves and about their world made available to the American people must be as extensive as the range of their interests and concerns as citizens of a self-governing, industrialized community in the closely integrated modern world. In terms of quality, the information provided must be provided in such a form, and with so scrupulous a regard for the wholeness of the truth and the fairness of its presentation, that the American people may make for themselves, by the exercise of reason and of conscience, the fundamental decisions necessary to the direction of their government and of their lives.

Royal Commission on the Press

THE STANDARD BY WHICH THE PRESS SHOULD BE JUDGED

Any judgment of the performance of the Press will necessarily depend upon the standard from which it is derived. At least three distinct standards appear to us to be relevant, and to be implicit in judgments that are commonly made.

The Press as an Instrument of Information and Instruction

The Press may be judged, first, as the chief agency for instructing the public on the main issues of the day. The importance of this function needs no emphasis.

The democratic form of society demands of its members an active and intelligent participation in the affairs of their community, whether local or national. It assumes that they are sufficiently well informed about the issues of the day to be able to form the broad judgments required by an election, and to maintain between elections the vigilance necessary in those whose governors are their servants and not their masters. More and more it demands also an alert and informed participation not only in purely political processes but also in the efforts of the community to adjust its social and economic life to increasingly complex circumstances. Democratic society, therefore, needs a clear and truthful account of events, of their background and their causes; a forum for discussion and informed criticism; and a means whereby individuals and groups can express a point of view or advocate a cause.

The responsibility for fulfilling these needs unavoidably rests in large measure upon the Press, that is on the newspapers and the periodicals, which are the main source from which information, discussion, and advocacy reach the public. In recent years this function has been shared with the radio; but the impermanence of broadcasting, together with the limita-

Reprinted from *Report of the Royal Commission on the Press, 1947-49*, pp. 100-106.

tions on the quantity and character of controversial material which can be diffused over the air, still leaves the Press in a central position. A useful service is being rendered on a small scale by the factual publications of specialist societies and learned bodies, such as the Royal Institute of International Affairs and the British Society for International Understanding; and a number of newsletters of differing value supply information and comment to subscribers; but any shortcomings of the Press in this field are unlikely to be adequately made good by any other agency.

The Press's Standard for Itself

The second standard of judgment which may be applied to the Press is that enunciated by its own spokesmen. It does not differ very greatly from the first, but is somewhat lower.

The proprietors of newspapers gave some indication of the conception entertained by the Press of the functions of newspapers and the standards proper to them in their replies to one of our questionnaires. The questionnaire asked:

Question 2. What is the proper function of a newspaper? What is the character and extent of its responsibility to the public?

Question 1. Do you agree with the American Commission on Freedom of the Press that those who operate the Press have a duty to give expression to ideas which the processes of free speech have brought to public attention, whether or not they agree with them?

Question. 8. Should a paper be a mouthpiece of a particular set of opinions or should it present several points of view on a given topic?

Question 9. Do you believe that news and opinion should be strictly separated?

Question 10. What do you regard as a reasonable standard of accuracy? Does it include not merely the correctness of the facts stated, but also the statement of all relevant facts?

The commonest reply to the first question was, in effect, "to report news and comment upon it," but there was some elaboration of this. For example, Odhams Press Ltd. wrote:

The chief function of a newspaper is to report current events and interpret them to its readers. It is also an important and proper function of the Press to comment on matters of public interest for the guidance of the public, to inform, educate, entertain and enlighten its readers, and to provide a forum for the expression and exchange of opinion.

The advertising columns of the modern newspapers have an important function as part of the machinery of commerce, and they are used to an increasing degree by Government departments and national corporations for giving information to the public.

A newspaper has a responsibility to the public to report facts as accurately and as fully as the circumstances of publication allow and to be honest in the expression of opinion.

That news and comment should be given fully and fairly was emphasised by others. London Express Newspaper Ltd. wrote:

Editorial staffs freely assume (in our opinion) the following moral obligations to the public:—
(i) that of giving in the newspaper a correct and balanced account of what is happening,
(ii) that of expressing opinions on controversial matters in such a way as to advance, by fair argument, tendencies, purposes, etc., that appear to be desirable.

Co-operative Press Ltd. (which publishes *Reynolds News*) wrote of a newspaper's responsibility "to strive constantly to report fairly and objectively what is significant while expressing its own opinions clearly and forcibly"; and Associated Newspapers Ltd. of responsibility "to publish all the important news with as much detail as space permits." And the Newspaper Society, representing the proprietors of provincial newspapers, wrote:

The proper function of a newspaper is to report fairly, accurately and objectively local and/or national and/or international news, according to its particular field; to provide, when necessary, fair, accurate and objective background information to enable the public to understand news items; to comment upon important subjects; to diagnose, express and lead public opinion and to give expression to this in the form of letters to the editor; and to further any political opinions it may hold.

Some replies referred to the interests of readers as the criterion of what constitutes news. Daily Mirror Newspapers, for example, said:

A newspaper's function is threefold, to publish news (serious or otherwise) of interest to its readers, to publish opinionative articles and readers' letters on current topics, to express its own opinion.

Kemsley Newspapers Ltd., in the course of a long reply, said:

. . . if a newspaper desires to attain importance and stability it must tell its readers what has happened within the compass over which their interests are spread.

and The Observer Ltd. said:

The space allotted to any subject must be influenced by the judgment of the editorial staff, both on the importance of the subject and consequent willingness to read about it, taking into consideration the particular class of reader which their paper serves.

While there was general agreement that a newspaper has a right, and possibly a duty, to formulate and express its own opinions, there was some difference on the question whether, and to what extent, it should publish those of others. It was generally agreed on the one hand that, in the words of Odhams Press Ltd., "there is no obligation on any of the several units of the Press to provide a universal platform" for the propagation of ideas, and on the other that opinions which by reason either of their importance or of their general interest have become news, ought to be reported whether or not the newspapers agree with them. Some undertakings thought that this was as far as a paper was bound to go and that it was under no obligation in ventilating a particular topic to present opinions upon it other than its own. The Observer Ltd. suggested that it was "preferable that newspapers should make their own standpoint clear and explicit . . . than that they should pretend to an impartiality which is delusive"—a point of view expressed in somewhat similar terms by Odhams Press Ltd. and the Co-operative Press Ltd. On the other hand, The Times Publishing Co. Ltd., referring to the duty of the newspaper to give news, said: "Provision of news certainly includes the presentation of current ideas, whether or not the newspaper approves of them, in reported speeches, published correspondence, articles and book reviews"; and Kemsley Newspapers Ltd., referring to feature and news columns as distinct from leading articles, said: "it is better where there are strong cleavages of view to present the differing opinions."

The replies to Question 10 emphasised the importance attached to accuracy. "The only standard of accuracy which we find tolerable," wrote London Express Newspaper Ltd., "is complete accuracy." But this reply and others suggested that accuracy did not always include the statement of all relevant facts: some would of necessity be omitted, either because they were not available at the time of publication, or because there was no space for them. In the main the replies referred to factual accuracy, but the People's Press Printing Society Ltd. (which publishes the *Daily Worker*) remarked: "Accuracy in a newspaper is not only a matter of the correctness of the news that it carries, but of the accuracy with which the newspaper as a whole reflects the significant news of the day."

There was general, and frequently emphatic, agreement that news and opinion should be strictly separated, qualified in some cases only by the suggestion that, especially in newspapers of the present size, some news may be contained in opinion columns, and by reservations for the articles of specialists such as political or industrial correspondents. It was suggested that it was legitimate for special correspondents to report the news and at the same time comment upon it, provided that their articles were distinguishable from straight news reports. Kemsley Newspapers Ltd., one of the undertakings which made this point, added: "Neither in headlines nor in the text should propaganda be allowed to colour news."

The Press as an Industry

The third standard by which the Press may be judged regards the Press less as a public service than as a great industry concerned with the collection and diffusion of news.

The idea of what constitutes news varies from office to office: a paper's standard of news values is one of the most distinctive facets of its personality. There are, however, certain elements common to all conceptions of news. To be news an event must first be interesting to the public, and the public for this purpose means for each paper the people who read that paper, and others like them. Second, and equally important, it must be new, and newness is measured in newspaper offices in terms of minutes. This follows partly from the notion that the public is more interested in what occurred last night than in what occurred yesterday morning, and partly from the fact that a newspaper is created afresh every day. Each issue is designed as something separate and distinct from every other issue and tends inevitably to concentrate on what has occurred since the last was published and to avoid repeating what has already been said.

If news must be both new and interesting, which of the new events occurring every day are held to be of the greatest and most general interest? The replies to a question to this effect in our questionnaire suggest that the answer is: those concerning sport, followed by news about people, news of strange or amusing adventures, tragedies, accidents, and crimes, news, that is, whose sentiment or excitement brings some colour into life. Mr. Francis Williams, an ex-editor of the *Daily Herald,* said: ". . . over the large field of readership of newspapers there is a demand for something bright and interesting, a sort of 'cocktail' before the meal rather than the solid meal"; and a sub-editor on the *Daily Express* added: ". . . we as newspapers are not concerned with what will appear important to posterity. What we have to do is to produce something which will seem, if not important, at least interesting to the man in the street, and to the man in the street the daffodils in Regent's Park are often more important . . . than a massacre in Chungking."

The replies to the questionnaire did not rate interest in public affairs very high, though many undertakings thought that it was increasing, partly as a result of education, but mainly because of the increased impact of politics, and particularly of Government activity, on the lives of ordinary people. The latter point suggests that interest in public affairs is intermittent and varies in intensity with the range of the reader's experience and the relevance to his own affairs of a given event. Explaining the great prominence given in the *Daily Mail* to an announcement of an increase in the price of coal and the paper's comparative lack of interest in the causes of the increase, the editor of the *Daily Mail* said: "I think what would be in the mind of the sub-editor would be this: the public to whom he is selling his newspaper, his readers, are more interested in the fact that the price of coal is going up than that the cost of production is getting more and more difficult." The public's taste in news of public affairs to some extent reflects, or is thought to reflect, its taste in news generally, and the exciting and exceptional features of affairs are considered to have a higher news value than the normal daily events and the background which gives them meaning.

The reader's taste in political news is affected by his own political opinions, especially if they are strong. Members of a political party are naturally more interested in the speeches of their own leaders than in those of the opposing party, and most readers probably prefer news which confirms their own opinions to news which does not. The Co-operative Press Ltd. said in reply to our questionnaire: "If a newspaper does not reflect the limitations and prejudices of at least a considerable section of the public, it will soon cease to exist, for it will find no buyers."

Newspapers are not guided entirely in their conception of news by what the majority wants: most of them feel some obligation to report matters which they believe to be important, even if these interest only a minority. But their judgment, like the reader's, is affected by political opinion. Opponents of the Government will think it important that the public should be informed of the Government's shortcomings, while its supporters will with equal honesty think it more important to inform the public of the Government's achievements.

The Standard to Be Applied

In our view no standard of judgment can be wholly relevant which fails to take some account of the bases both of the first of these standards and of the third. The Press is not purely an agency for the political education of the public, much though democratic society may need such an agency. On the other hand, it cannot be considered purely as an industry: the inescapable fact that it is the main source of information, discussion, and advocacy imposes upon it responsibilities greater than those resting on an industry which does not deal in information and ideas.

The first standard fails to allow for the fact that the primary business of a newspaper undertaking is to sell newspapers. Only by selling newspapers can such an undertaking maintain its existence. Given a free choice people will buy only newspapers which interest them, and a newspaper must consequently either gauge accurately what the public wants and supply it, or persuade the public to accept something different. The latter can be done only slowly and within narrow limits, and while most newspapers do contain material of minority interest, they are bound to cater for the most part for what they believe—on the basis of considerable study—to be the tastes of the majority.

If, however, public demand plays so large a part in determining what a newspaper publishes, it is apparent that a newspaper catering for a mass public will be led to adopt a concept of news nearer to that indicated in paragraphs above than to the clear and truthful account of events and their background and causes which our first standard demands.

The first standard is not, therefore, wholly relevant; but if it is set too high, the third may be set too low. Though a newspaper is a commercial enterprise it does not follow that it need necessarily pursue commercial advantage without limit. A newspaper whose financial position is precarious will, it is true, be compelled to concern itself almost entirely with money-making; but a successful undertaking seldom aims exclusively at profit; it is also interested in its own conception of success, and that conception may include a regard for the responsibilities imposed on the Press by the part which it plays in the life of the community.

The statements of the proprietors assume that the acceptance of certain public responsibilities is compatible with the successful conduct of a newspaper as a commercial undertaking. We believe that a standard by which the Press can reasonably be judged can be based on this assumption; but that the standard enunciated by the Press itself is somewhat idealised in relation to practice and tends to make too little allowance for the fact that the Press is an industry.

It follows from what we have said about public demand that not all newspapers can perform the same degree of public service, or be expected to observe the same standards. How each paper can best tell the public what it ought to know will depend both on the tastes and education of the particular section of the public to which it is addressed and on the character of the paper itself. If a paper's public looks to it almost entirely for entertainment, the amount of serious information it can communicate is small.

There are, however, two essential requirements which in our view newspapers individually and the Press collectively ought to fulfil, and we propose to take these as our own standard of judgment. They form a standard more modest and, we believe, more in accordance with reality than the first and second of the three hypothetical standards which we have discussed, but more in accordance with the aspirations of the Press than the third.

The first of these requirements is that if a newspaper purports to record and discuss public affairs, it should at least record them truthfully. It may express what opinions it pleases—and nothing we may say hereafter is intended to criticise the opinions of any newspaper, or to question its right to express them—but opinions should be advocated without suppressing or distorting the relevant facts. If a paper adheres to a political party it should be plain to the reader that it does so, but from the columns of opinion, not from the colouring given to the news. A paper's politics and those of its readers will inevitably and legitimately affect its judgment of the relative interest of certain items of news, but the news it reports it should report truthfully and without excessive bias. The second requirement is that the number and variety of newspapers should be such that the Press as a whole gives an opportunity for all important points of view to be effectively presented in terms of the varying standards of taste, political opinion, and education among the principal groups of the population.

These two requirements are not stated as alternatives: they are complementary. We recognise that even if they are satisfied, the pre-occupation of the Press with the exceptional, and the limited range of interests of the readers of any paper, must continue to throw the picture of events presented by the Press out of focus; but if the Press gives its readers the means of forming judgments on the problems of most immediate interest to them, that is perhaps as much as need be asked of it at present.

10

METHODS IN PUBLIC OPINION RESEARCH

Problems of Research Design

Analysis of the methodology of public opinion research has produced a voluminous literature during the past fifteen years. Technical advances have been made on most problems. Since there are such a large number of particular technical matters which require and have been given attention by the field, it has been necessary here to present only a set of examples of research methods in public opinion. The articles and excerpts have been selected as illustrative of some of the central aspects involved in the methodology of opinion research. A number of other problems, notably those relating attitude research to communication research (e.g. audience analysis), have been excluded for lack of space.

The problems of public opinion methodology are classified under three headings: problems of research design, problems of data collection, and problems of analysis. The articles included under the first heading are designed to represent issues involved in the formulation of research in three major approaches. Maccoby and Holt discuss the sample survey; Lazarsfeld, the panel technique; Samuel Stouffer, the use of experiments. The approach of Mass Observation, which comes close to the case study method, has been included as a fourth.

As illustrative of problems of data collection, we have included articles on the sources of bias, sample design, and interview construction. Kornhauser's analysis represents a systematic review of the sources of bias in attitude surveys. Hansen and Hauser seek to evaluate the issues involved in the two major approaches to sampling—area sampling and quota control—while Lazarsfeld discusses the advantages and uses of open ended interviews as compared with the more direct and standardized interviewing approach. Among other problems of data collection facing public opinion researchers, for which we have not included articles, are interviewer bias, the non-respondent, use of mail questionnaires, the use of projective tests and group interviews, and techniques for classifying attitude data.

The problems of analysis and reporting of opinion data are crucial if misleading results are to be avoided. Katz formulates a number of rules for the interpretation of survey data, while the Social Science Research Council's report on "The Pre-Election Polls of 1948" analyzes a well known case of error. Finally, the article by Blumer presents the position of a critic of the mode of reasoning involved in public opinion research.

Developing public opinion research methods is a most active branch of social science. Currently, the interest of research groups in substantive problems is producing efforts to refine techniques of sampling, to control interviewer bias, to perfect new methods of scaling and to apply projective tests. There is also considerable interest in modifying procedures so as to make them applicable in foreign areas, especially in the so-called undeveloped countries. The results of these efforts are certain to produce a new body of technique and to render our present approaches out of date.

Eleanor E. Maccoby and Robert R. Holt

HOW SURVEYS ARE MADE

The surveying of public attitudes and opinions during recent years has attracted an increasingly large audience. The "public opinion polls" now share newspaper space with the most omniscient columnists and during pre-election weeks they become front-page news.

To most people, who know about polls only what they read in the newspapers, surveying must appear to be a transparently simple procedure. The questions asked seem obvious enough and the percentages always add to a hundred. They seldom suspect the tortuous and detailed labors which lie behind the neat columns of figures. For many such followers of public opinion the final results are doubtless the only part of the process of surveying that has any interest, but there are others who are not so easily satisfied.

This article is meant for those people, not themselves expert in surveying, whose interest in public opinion includes a curiosity as to how the surveys are made, and perhaps an interest in the possibilities of using the polling procedure in their own organizations or communities. It is not intended as a manual of instructions for beginning pollers; no short article could serve such a purpose adequately. It proposes to describe briefly the major steps that are followed in surveying and to answer thereby some of the common questions as to the techniques which lie behind survey findings.

The first step in any survey, as in any other planned observation, is to define the question which the survey is to answer. The more clearly the objectives of the study are specified, the more likely it is to yield clear-cut results.

Usually the definition of objectives begins with a broad, general statement of the problem and then turns to a listing of all the items of information the survey will gather. The survey director must analyze his problem

Reprinted from *The Journal of Social Issues,* Vol. 2 (1946), pp. 44-56, by permission of the authors and publishers.

499

carefully to make sure that he includes in his study as many of the pertinent aspects of his problem as he can. It is his responsibility to find out as much as he can in this planning stage about the important factors bearing on the subject of the study.

Suppose we consider as an example the problem of conducting a survey on public attitudes toward taxes. It is necessary to define the problem by specifying what varieties of taxes the survey will cover. Attitudes toward federal taxes may be different from attitudes toward state and local taxes, and the survey may deal with all or only some of these. If the survey is to deal with both income taxes and sales taxes, a distinction must be made between them in the detailed plans for the survey. The administration of tax policy would be an important consideration; public reactions to the tax forms, dates and methods of payment should be studied. An effort might be made to find out the extent to which people would be willing to see public services curtailed for the sake of reducing taxes. Full understanding of the attitudes in this area would require data on the level of public information about taxes. Do people know what the tax rates are? Do they know what the money is used for? The survey should also cover the relation, if any, between attitudes toward taxes and other attitudes and personal attributes of the people interviewed. Do attitudes toward taxes differ in different income and education groups? How are they correlated with attitudes toward other governmental activities?

The survey director must consider all these aspects of his problem. It may be that he will not be able to deal with them all, because of limitations of time or money and he will therefore have to limit the scope of the survey. His goal is to specify what aspects of the subject he will cover, and to anticipate exactly what tables he will want in his final report.

While most studies require a single survey of one particular group, this is not always the case. Surveys may be designed in a variety of ways, depending on the objectives of the study. It may be desirable for some purposes to survey two contrasting communities or industrial plants and to compare the two sets of results. In studies where it is important to measure changes or trends in opinions or behavior, a group of people may be selected as respondents and this group may be interviewed several times at specified intervals. When studying cause-and-effect relationships it is sometimes possible to use experimental techniques. To study the effects of a certain motion picture on attitudes, for example, two similar groups might be selected, an "experimental" group who would be shown the film and a "control" group who would not. The influence of the picture on the attitudes of the experimental group could then be studied.

As part of the basic planning of the survey, the survey director must define exactly the group to be covered by the survey. If he is studying the opinions of the American people on a certain issue, the group to be studied (the "universe") will probably be the entire adult population. If he is making a morale survey within a certain factory, the universe might be all the employees in the factory. Or perhaps the survey is to cover only the skilled, semi-skilled and unskilled workers, not the clerical and managerial staff.

When the group to be studied has been decided upon, the next question to be answered is: Can the survey include a contact with each member of the group? In a study of employees' morale, it may be possible to interview every employee. In a nation-wide public opinion survey, however, it is obviously impossible to poll each adult person in the country. More often than not, a survey must be based upon a *sample* of the universe. Some individuals must be selected from the universe in such a way that they will represent all the people in the universe.

The most reliable way to choose the individuals to be included in a sample survey is to use some random method of selection. Selecting at random means using some automatic method of choosing which gives each individual in the group to be studied an equal chance (or at least a *known* chance) of being in the sample. To take a random sample of the members of an organization, for example, one might take every tenth card in the membership file. To decide which card to take as the first case, one might open a book at random and take the last digit of the page number. Experience in survey work has demonstrated that if, instead of selecting at random, a surveyer tries to pick a representative sample by choosing certain people or places that he believes are representative, a biased sample will probably result. When surveys are based on random sampling, the probable size of the sampling error can be computed mathematically. The errors in a sample which has not been selected by random methods cannot be estimated in any precise way.

There are many pitfalls in choosing a random sample, many ways in which bias may creep in and prevent the selection from being truly random. Suppose interviewers have been sent to certain blocks in a city and told to visit every fifth dwelling on each block. In counting dwellings, there is danger that the interviewers will miss alley dwellings, basement apartments, servants' quarters over garages, and other inconspicuous households. It is evident that if this happened the sample would be biased in the direction of having too few people in the lower income groups.

Bias may be created when no attempt is made to include in the sample those people who are hard to find at home. If the interviewers take all their interviews in households where they find someone home the first time they call, it is clear that people who are not home much do not have an equal chance of coming into the sample. It is well known to surveyers that people who stay home a good deal differ as a group from people who do not.

When samples are taken from lists of names there is danger that the list will be incomplete. This was apparently partly responsible for the miscarriage of the *Literary Digest* poll of the 1936 presidential election. The sample used by the *Digest,* purporting to represent all voters, was taken from such sources as lists of telephone subscribers. This meant that people without telephones (on the average from a lower socio-economic level than people with telephones) were not represented adequately. An additional bias was probably introduced by the fact that the poll depended on people mailing in the post-cards which they received. The people who mailed in their cards were probably not comparable to the people who did not.

Bias may also be introduced into a sample by allowing the interviewers freedom in the choice of the people to be interviewed. In some polling operations, interviewers are told the number of interviews to take, and they are told that these interviews must be distributed in certain ways. For example, an interviewer might be instructed to take one-half of his interviews with men, the other half with women; one-tenth with Negroes, nine-tenths with whites; and one-fourth of the interviews from each of four income groups. Aside from these restrictions, the interviewer has freedom of choice, and it is evident that he could follow instructions and still interview only "available" people—waitresses, barbers, policemen, people at railway stations, people who sit on their front porches or stroll in the park, and so on. It is clear that with this procedure, certain groups in the population may be under-represented.

Whenever sampling is done by a system of random selection, the more cases the sample has, the more likely it is to represent the universe well. The reasoning behind this is as follows: Suppose a survey is being done of opinions about foreign affairs. This is a subject on which people with different amounts of education differ markedly, so it is important to have college graduates, high school graduates, grade school graduates, people with some grade school, and people with no formal education at all. If only three cases were chosen, they obviously could not adequately represent these five educational groups. A sample of forty cases might easily, by chance, contain four college graduates, or it might contain none—there is not a very good chance that the true proportion of college graduates (perhaps five percent) would be obtained. The larger the number of cases, however, the better the chances that all the levels of education will be represented in their proper proportions. It might be argued that one should deliberately select the right number of people from each educational level and consider this as a representative group. But it would be representative only with respect to education, and there are many other characteristics which are related to opinions on foreign affairs, some of which would not be known in advance. A large sample randomly selected assures a sample which will be reasonably representative of *all* characteristics of the people in the universe.

When random methods of selection are followed, increasing the number of cases will improve the sample by reducing the sampling error, but mere increase in the number of cases will not correct for a bias in the sample. When a sample is "biased" its errors are not chance errors which tend to cancel each other out but are systematic and create deviations in the same direction. For example, in a survey of income and savings the results would be greatly affected by the inclusion or exclusion of a few millionaires. By chance a sample might contain too many millionaires or too few. If this error was purely a matter of random sampling error, an increase in the number of cases would provide a better chance of getting just the right proportion of millionaires. But suppose millionaires could not be interviewed because the interviewers could not get past the butlers and secretaries, or because the millionaires were out hunting in the Maine woods or tarpon fishing off Florida; then all the errors would operate in the direction of including too few millionaires rather than too many and the sample would be biased. Increasing the number of cases in the sample would not reduce the error, since the same cause of error would affect the new cases and in the same direction.

In deciding how many people will be included in his sample, the survey director is usually influenced by considerations of economy. His purpose is not to use the largest possible sample but rather to use the smallest sample which will give results of acceptable accuracy. Sampling experts have worked out formulae for estimating the sampling error which is involved in samples of different sizes. The survey director chooses, then, a sample size which will have a sampling error small enough for his purposes.

Among the factors which determine the number of cases needed for a sample survey, the following are perhaps the most important:

1. The desired accuracy of the survey results. If the survey director wishes to be reasonably sure that his final figures are accurate within one percent, he must have a larger sample than if he is willing to accept a margin of error of five percent.

2. The variability of the characteristic to be measured. It would take more cases to sample for a variable like income, which has a wide range and many different values, than to sample for variables like age or sex.

3. The desired breakdowns of the findings. Fewer cases are needed in a national survey, for example, if the findings are to be used only as national estimates than if they are to be broken down by state or region. In the latter case, it would be necessary to have enough cases in each state or region to represent it separately, while for national figures alone this would not be necessary.

When the objectives of a survey call for a national sample, it is seldom possible to select respondents by taking, say, every ten thousandth person in the country. Travel expenses for the interviewers would be too great;

some method must be adopted to reduce the number of communities in which interviews are taken. Usually this is done by first choosing a sample of counties and then selecting a sample of people to be interviewed within these counties. In selecting the counties where interviews will be taken, the survey director can cut down the sampling error by "stratifying" the sample. This means simply that he will arrange all the counties of the country in order according to some characteristic, (such as percent of Negro population), divide these ordered counties into strata (high, medium and low), and select sample counties at random within each stratum, thus making sure that a proper proportion of counties with high, medium and low Negro populations will come into the sample.

The "modes of stratification" which are used are always characteristics which are thought to be related to the subject matter of the survey. It would be possible, for example, to stratify counties according to their average annual rainfall, so that a proper proportion of wet and dry counties would be included in the sample. But, to continue a previous example, if the survey were measuring attitudes toward our foreign policy, the sample would not be improved by this stratification since such attitudes are presumably not related to rainfall. A stratification of the counties according to the average educational level might, however, improve the sample, for if education tends to be related to attitudes toward world affairs then by making sure that the sample contains a proper proportion of counties that are high, medium and low in educational status the chances are increased of obtaining a proper representation of people of different points of view toward foreign affairs.

With these phases of study planning completed, the survey director proceeds to write the questionnaire itself. First he must decide whether he will use any "open" questions, or whether they will all be of the "closed" or "polling" variety. Polling questions, the kind most frequently used in the ordinary Gallup and Fortune polls, are questions such as the following:

"If the election were held today, who would you vote for—Roosevelt or Dewey?
        Roosevelt____   Dewey____   Don't know____

In questions of this sort, the interviewer simply checks the choice which his respondent makes. Polling questions can be more complex than this, of course:

"Which of these comes closest to expressing what you would like to have the U.S. do after the war?" (July, 1945, *Fortune*)
1. Enter into no alliances, and have as little as possible to do with other countries.
2. Depend only on separate alliances with certain countries.
3. Take an active part in an international organization.
4. Don't know.

In using questions like the one above, the interviewer may either read off the alternatives, or he may hand the respondent the list of possible answers and ask him to choose one.

In contrast to these kinds of questions, "open" questions do not present the respondent with fixed alternatives from which he must choose, but ask a general question which the respondent may answer in his own words. The following are examples of open questions: "What do you think will happen to prices of the things you buy in the next year or so?" "Why do you think so?" "As you see it, what is the main thing the U.N. is set up to do?" When questions of this sort are asked, the interviewer must write down each respondent's answer as nearly verbatim as possible, and these answers must be grouped into categories later. When polling questions are used, the interviewer's job is much easier, and the answers are easier to handle in analysis later on.

Polling questions are usually used in surveys to obtain enumerative material, such as age, education, nationality, and the like, or simple statements of fact (Do you own a radio? Are you a registered voter?). They are also frequently used for surveying attitudes if the survey deals with well-understood issues on which people have clear-cut opinions. But in an area where attitudes are complex and confused, there is danger that polling questions will yield misleading results. When open questions are used, people express their views together with any reservations or contingencies which are present in their minds; when they are presented with a polling question and asked to choose one of the alternatives, they may not have an opportunity to express their reservations, unless specific additional questions are asked to bring them out. Polling questions have certain disadvantages, too, when it comes to asking people to make suggestions for improving a situation which they dislike, or to give reasons for their beliefs. If check-lists of alternatives are presented to them, there is the danger of suggesting ideas which were not actually present in their minds. There is also the danger that not all the great variety of possible reasons and suggestions will be included among the poll's alternatives. A common practice in questionnaire construction is to combine polling and open questions. For example, polling questions to which the respondent must answer "Yes" or "No" are often followed by the question "Why do you think so?" and the interviewer then writes down the respondent's reason in the blank provided.

In writing his questionnaire, the survey director must give careful attention to the order in which different topics and particular questions are taken up. The opening questions must be such as to interest the respondent and stimulate his cooperation. The sequence of questions must be orderly, and logical transitions must be made from one topic to another. The context in which a question is asked can have the greatest influence on the answers to it. Likewise the order and number of alternatives can affect the results greatly in a question where the respondent chooses one of a set of alternatives as his answer. To take care of this difficulty, interviewers are sometimes instructed to vary the order in which they present alternatives, or sometimes different forms of the questionnaire are prepared, giving the questions in a different order.

The so-called "funnel" arrangement of questions is often useful. In this procedure, a very general question is followed by one in the same area which is somewhat narrower, and this in turn is followed by a more specific question. This technique permits the respondent to answer the general question spontaneously before any specific aspects of the problem have been suggested to him, but nevertheless pins him down later on specific points. Suppose, for example, that a study is being done on consumers' cooperation with the Government's food conservation program, and the study calls for a table showing how many people are using less bread than they normally would. People may be asked first: "Are you personally doing anything to conserve food?" and if they say they are doing something, they may then be asked "What are you doing?" The answers to these questions will give evidence on what aspects of the food conservation program are upper-most in people's minds, but some people may fail to mention conservation of bread even though they are actually eating less of it. To get specific information, the survey could proceed to a direct question on whether the respondent was conserving bread, and if necessary, could then include questions on the different ways of saving bread.

The task of writing the questions themselves is a difficult one. The writer's first objective must be to make sure that his question is understood. Its wording must be clear and unambiguous, and the words used must be simple enough so that they will be understood by the least educated of the respondents. There are certain regional variations in the use of words which the writer must keep in mind if his question is not to mean different things in different parts of the country. In addition the writer must avoid referring to particular ideas, policies, recent events, or personalities, unless he has some assurance that the respondents will be familiar with them. It is hardly necessary to point out that, in order to be understood, a question must be reasonably brief. If a question contains two or three long sentences, the respondent will often forget what the first part of the question was before he gives his answer, so that he actually responds only to the last few words of the question.

Each question should have a single focus. If it contains several ideas, it is impossible to tell what part of the question the respondent's answer refers to. For example, the question "Do you think a man would be wise to put his money into real estate and securities these days?" is poorly worded, for one man might answer "Yes" when he believes that real estate is a good investment and securities a poor investment, while another man's "Yes" might signify approval of securities but not of real estate.

The writer of questions must keep in mind the fact that the use of prestige words or other emotionally-toned words may materially affect the responses to a question.[1] It is well known, for example, that attaching a prestige name such as Roosevelt's to a policy proposed in a question will increase the proportion of respondents who express approval of the policy. Similarly, it is almost certain that more people would say "Yes" to: "Do you think the United States should send food to the starving people in Europe?" than would agree if the word "starving" were omitted.

The survey director must be careful in the use of emotionally-toned words, but there are occasions in which he may find it desirable to employ them. If he is studying opinions about sending food to Europe, he may deliberately use the word "starving" because many people in Europe are, in fact, starving, and because the publicity on the food crisis appeals to people on the grounds that they must help starving people. To omit the word, then, might be to underestimate the number who would be willing to share American food under the conditions actually prevailing. Furthermore, the survey director sometimes finds it desirable to include an emotionally-toned question with the specific purpose of finding out how many people hold their opinions so firmly that they cannot be swayed by devices of this kind.

The question of the effect of emotional "loading" on the answers to a question leads to the more general problem of bias in questions. The point is often raised: Do the answers obtained in a survey represent the "true" attitudes which people have, or have the attitudes been distorted by a "leading" question? In survey research, every attitude must be studied through the answers to questions, and no answer is free from the influence carried by the wording of the question which was used. Every question is "leading," in the sense that it at least specifies the subject-matter about which the respondent is being asked to talk.

For these reasons it is important that each survey finding be interpreted in the light of the particular question which was used. Findings must not be loosely generalized to cover whole areas of opinion. Particularly when a study deals with attitudes which are complex, it is important to ask a battery of questions bearing upon different aspects of the problem, so as to achieve a "well defined context for interpretation."

Although the problems of question-wording need to be emphasized, the survey director in writing his questionnaire can take comfort from the fact that in many cases small differences in question-wording produce relatively little change in public response. Especially when the questions are about facts which are well known to the respondents, it is surprisingly difficult to affect the answers much by context, question order, or the wording of the questions.

[1] Cantril, H., *Gauging Public Opinion*, Princeton, Princeton Univ. Press, 1944, Chapter II.

It is important to give every question a test run before using it. Often questions which appear satisfactory when they are written turn out to be too difficult or ambiguous, or they unexpectedly set off irrelevant trains of thought on the part of the respondents. Questions can be tested for defects of this sort by trying them out on a representative group of people. The answers given on the pretest are taken down in full, and the respondents are asked to explain what they mean by their answers. This procedure enables the survey director to detect questions which are being misunderstood. Often several forms of a question must be tried out before the best wording is found. In the pretest, variations in question order may also be tried out, until a smooth sequence is achieved.

The pretest permits the survey director to check the answers he is getting against the objectives of the survey, to see whether the kind of information being assembled will solve the problems that underlie the survey. Questions must be discarded if it is found that they merely sound interesting but do not contribute anything to the objectives.

The survey director must make sure that his interviewers are well trained before they begin work, and arrange for their supervision throughout the interviewing process. Poor interviewing can ruin a survey even though the planning and questionnaire construction have been well done.

The calibre of interviewers needed to do the job depends, of course, on the complexity of the subject, whether polling or open questions are used, and on the amount of freedom which the interviewers will be allowed in the interviewing situation. A certain amount of judgment on the part of the interviewer is *always* required. Respondents frequently make replies which are not answers to the questions at all. In these cases the interviewer must recognize this and repeat the question. Interviewing can never be completely mechanical, if for no other reason than that the interviewer must learn ways to gain the cooperation of the respondent before he can begin the formal interview. For intensive interviewing, in which the interviewer is allowed to adapt his questions to the individual case to some extent, a high degree of skill and training is required. For most surveys interviewers must be personable, intelligent, and tactful.

Perhaps the most important basic principle an interviewing staff must be taught is not to influence the answers of the people being interviewed. This means that they must learn to avoid expressing disapproval or approval of anything the respondent says. When they have some latitude in the rewording of questions they must ask them in a non-directive way. For example, it should become habitual to ask "Are you working now?" instead of "You're not working now, are you?" Similarly, in using open questions in which a respondent gives reasons for his opinion, the interviewer must learn to stimulate discussion without slanting it. He may try to get the person to express himself more fully by the use of such questions as "Why do you think so?" and "Just how do you mean that?" but must avoid suggestive questions such as: "Is that because of the high cost of living?"

The quality of a survey can always be improved by devoting a good deal of attention to training the interviewers on the specific subject-matter of the survey. There are almost always certain terms which need to be very clearly defined in the interviewers' minds. For example, if an interviewer must check whether or not the respondent is employed, he must learn to know how to classify people who are employed part-time. If he is to include only farmers in the survey, he must have the term "farmer" defined so that he will know whether or not to talk to nurserymen, seasonal farm laborers, small farmers who work part time in the city, and so on.

When the interview schedules have been filled out and sent in to a central office, the survey director must tabulate the answers in some way so that the survey results will be summarized and easily understood. The simplest way would be to go through the schedules and tally the answers to each question, so that a count would be obtained. This system is not very convenient for comparisons of groups within the sample, however. To find out how men compare with women on a certain question, it would be necessary to divide the schedules into two groups for men and women, and tally separately. If a count by income groups were desired, a new grouping of the schedules and a new tally would be required.

For large-scale operations where internal comparisons will be needed, it is usually found to be most convenient in the long run to record the answers on punch-cards. Different answers are numbered (or "coded"); each respondent has a separate card, and on this card are punched the numbers which represent his answers to all the questions. After the punching has been done, the process of counting the different answers is greatly simplified, for the sorting and counting machines will sort the cards into any desired groups and count the answers automatically.

Coding is a fairly simple job when the respondent has been presented with a group of alternatives from which he must choose; each of the alternatives can be given a number, and the cards may be punched immediately from the questionnaires which have been filled out. When full narrative answers are given to open questions, however, coding is more difficult. Suppose, for example, that people have been asked to give their reasons for their opinions on a certain issue. A great variety of reasons will be given, and the reasons will be worded in many different ways. These reasons must be grouped into a limited number of categories, and each category must be numbered for purposes of punching on the cards.

It is the responsibility of the survey director to present his findings in such a way as to prevent unsophisticated readers from coming to unjustified conclusions. The problem of misinterpretation of findings very often arises when two percentages are being compared, as in the table below:[1]

Attitude toward continuation
of price ceilings:

	March, 1945	March, 1946
Favorable	68%	74%
Unfavorable	25%	23%
Don't know	7%	3%
	100%	100%

The question is, has there been a real change in attitudes toward price ceilings? Assume for the moment that the survey reporting these findings had a small sample with a sampling error of five percentage points. Under these circumstances, it is quite possible that the true percentage favoring continuation of price ceilings during the two years is, say, 72 percent, that there has been no change in this percentage, but that the two figures which were obtained differed from 72 percent because of random sampling error. A large increase would be needed before one could feel confident that a real change in sentiment has occurred. On the other hand, if the survey were based on a large number of cases, and had a sampling error of only one percentage point, the difference between the percentages shown above could be relied on as showing a real difference, not just a chance one. There are statistical formulae by which the survey director can compute the probable range of error of his percentages, and he must test his differences for reliability before presenting them in his report.

In presenting his findings, it is also the responsibility of the director to caution his readers against generalizing the findings to a different population from the one measured by the survey. If the survey is based upon a sample of midwestern farmers, this fact should be emphasized, so that the reader will not assume that the results apply to all the farmers of the nation.

As has been pointed out earlier, each answer must be interpreted in the light of the particular question asked. Answers to one question cannot be taken to represent attitudes toward other aspects of a broad field of attitudes. For example, if most people say Britain ought to pay for the food which we send to her, it should not be concluded that the majority would recommend withholding food if Britain cannot pay. The survey director must not only avoid drawing unwarranted conclusions himself, but he must caution his readers against doing so. He cannot, of course, prevent misuse of the findings by unscrupulous readers, but he can minimize their misuse by well-intentioned people who will avoid pitfalls if they are only pointed out.

[1] This table does not represent actual survey findings, but is simply included here for illustrative purposes.

Paul F. Lazarsfeld

THE USE OF PANELS
IN SOCIAL RESEARCH

The following remarks are designed to draw attention to a fairly recent development in social research. In its bare essentials, the type of study to be discussed consists of repeated interviews made with the same group of persons. The people participating as subjects in such studies are commonly known as panel members and the whole procedure has become widely known under the name of panel technique.

There are two main types of research problems to which the panel technique is likely to be applied. If the effect of some specific event or series of events is to be studied, then we have the first type of situation in which the panel technique may be used. In one such case, a sample of voters in an Ohio county was kept under observation for six months during the 1940 Presidential campaign, the purpose being to study what effect the propaganda of the two parties had upon the way people made up their minds.[1] In another case, the American Association for the United Nations wanted to find out the best way of getting Americans more interested in the progress of U.N. activities. A sample of persons in a mid-West city of about 800,000 was interviewed about their attitudes towards the United Nations and the actions of the United States in foreign affairs. An intensive informational campaign was conducted by this organization and after the campaign was over the same sample was interviewed again.[2] In a similar way, advertising agencies sometimes use panels to study the effectiveness of their promotional efforts.[3]

The other main type of panel study is somewhat more difficult to describe because no major findings are yet available in the literature. In

Reprinted from *The Proceedings of the American Philosophical Society*, Vol. 92 (November, 1948), pp. 405-410, by permission of the author and publisher. (Copyright, 1948, by American Philosophical Society.)

[1] Lazarsfeld, P. F., B. Berelson, and H. Gaudet, *The people's choice*, N. Y., Duell, Sloan and Pearce, 1944.

[2] National Opinion Research Center, Report No. 37a, Cincinnati Looks Again.

[3] Root, A. R., and A. C. Welch, The continuing consumer study: a basic method for the engineering of advertising, *Jour. Marketing* 7, July 1942.

a society as complex and changing as our own, the individual is continually placed in a situation where he must reconcile the different and variant elements of his experience. A Quaker who is a convinced pacifist sees the country endangered by an enemy. How will he resolve the conflict between his pacifism and his patriotism? A convinced Communist sees the Soviet Union making moves which he considers imperialistic. How will he reconcile his party loyalty and his intellectual judgment on a specific political issue? But we don't need to remain in the area of big issues to look for problems of this kind. In everyday life almost everyone is continuously under cross-pressures of some kind. People belong to different social groups which may have conflicting interests. The individual must make all sorts of choices among his needs, desires, and situational demands, some of which are relatively important, others relatively insignificant.

The study of people under cross pressure is one of the major concerns of social science today. In going through recent social science literature one often comes across statements of the following sort, "In getting higher education the English Catholic must choose between ethnic affiliation and religion; he generally chooses to study with his Protestant ethnic fellows at McGill University. . . ."[4] The application of the panel technique to problems of this sort allows a greater degree of analytical precision. It would allow us to state, for example, the proportion of English Catholics who go to McGill for their higher education and the proportion who go to Catholic institutions, and to compare intensively those who resolve the conflict between their ethnic affiliation and their religion in one way with those who resolve this conflict in another.

The understanding of what actually transpires in such situations will make for tremendous gains in the understanding of social change. The application of the panel technique to this area of social science interest will be one of its major contributions. By keeping sets of people under repeated observation, we can register the changes they make in their attitudes, affiliations, habits, and expectations. We can learn which of the various attitudes, affiliations, etc., are more basic and hence more constant and which are more superficial and changeable. We hope to determine, if elements change, which element in a psychological or social situation is the more dominant one controlling the changes in the other factors.

The outstanding example of such a study is that undertaken by Theodore Newcomb of the students of a "progressive" college attended by the daughters of well-to-do families. The faculty of this college was quite liberal but the background of the girls quite conservative. For four years the investigators observed the various ways in which one group of girls resolved this conflict.[5]

[4] Hughes, E. C. *French Canada in transition*, 86, Univ. of Chicago Press, 1943.

[5] Newcomb, T., *Personality and social change*, N. Y., Dryden Press, 1942.

The reader who is somewhat acquainted with social science literature will at this point raise a justified question especially with reference to the first type of study. If we want to know the effect of a political campaign or a similiar event, why do we have to reinterview the same people? Couldn't we interview one group of respondents before the event and a similar one after the event. By comparing the two, the argument runs, we would get a fairly good idea as to the influence which the event had. Numerous examples of this kind come to mind. Many of us have seen public opinion polls taken, for instance, before and after the President made a major public announcement. If people think better of him after the speech then we are sure the speech was a success. Poll data are available which show that the attitude of the average American to the Russians improved every time they were victorious in a battle during the war and slumped every time the Russians, after the war, made a move against one of their neighboring countries. This type of study is undoubtedly of very great value and is usually called a trend study.[6]

It is important to consider the differences between such trend studies and the panel technique. A considerable amount of additional information is obtained by reinterviewing the same people. The most important difference is our ability to single out in a panel study exactly who are the people who change. Once singled out, the changers can be subjected to more intensive study to determine the psychological and social-psychological elements which operated to produce the changes in question. A trend study may show us the net impact of events on opinion. A panel study can allow us to single out the individuals who changed their opinion in the course of the repeated interviewing, to probe for the psychological meaning of the event, and the role played by the various mass media of communication in the change. By interviewing the same people at least twice, we can answer questions such as the following: Are people more likely to change when they are very interested in an event and follow it in great detail; or when they are only slightly concerned and know of it only in a casual way? Some preliminary evidence seems to show that the latter is more likely to be the case. There are many proverbs which claim that men are more apt to shift than women and many others which claim the exact opposite. The panel technique permits us to say whether men or women are more likely to shift their opinions. Incidentally, the results so far do not seem to point to any sex differences.

The study of actual changes often leads to unexpected results. At the time that Senator Black was appointed a judge of the Supreme Court, he was accused of having been at one time a member of the Ku Klux Klan. It happens that there is some information available on who was affected

[6] Bruner, Jerome S., *Mandate from the people*, N. Y., Duell, Sloan and Pearce, 1944; Cantril, Hadley, *Gauging public opinion*, Princeton Univ. Press, 1944.

by this allegation which suddenly threatened to change the image of a liberal into that of a reactionary. Although Senator Black received about the same amount of approval before and after the allegation, a kind of game of musical chairs took place. Jews and Catholics turned against him while about an equivalent number of Protestants were more in favor of his appointment than before the storm broke.[7]

The last example points to a second value of the panel technique. Trend studies often indicate that an event has not brought about any net change in opinion. But it might very well be that underneath this apparent constancy, there is a great amount of shifting of positions which can only be found out if the same people and their attitudes are traced over a period of time. At the beginning of the present 1948 presidential campaign, there is some indication of a new development in American politics. As long as Roosevelt was alive, there was a strong feeling in the population that the Democratic Party was the party of the common man whereas the Republicans represented more the interests of the wealthier sections of the population. There are indications that this appraisal of the two parties has changed somewhat and that voters, especially among the working class, are less sure than before which of the two parties represents their interests better.

Suppose that one further development takes place (for which there is no evidence but which we bring in to make our example more dramatic); some sections of the business community might feel that their interest in an active recovery program in Europe is better served by a Democratic administration. Then we might have at this moment an internal shift in the social stratification of the two parties which might go beyond any net change in both which polls or the election might show up. Such a social restratification of the major parties has taken place several times in the political history of the country. The historian looking back over this period many decades hence will not miss such a development. But if we want to know and understand it at the time it happens, we have to make studies of repeated interviews with the same people.

This is not the place to go further into detail on the comparison of panel and trend studies.[8] We shall turn rather to the other type of panel study in order to show briefly some of its considerably more complex technical aspects. The following table (table 1) exemplifies some of the technical difficulties. It is taken from a small group of people who were interviewed twice during a presidential election. Each respondent was asked two questions: How he intended to vote and whether he felt that the Republican candidate if elected would make a good President. Because

[7] Lazarsfeld, P. F., The change of opinion during a political discussion. *Jour. Ap. Psychol.* 23: 131-147, 1939.

[8] Interested readers will find such a discussion and concrete examples in chapter 10, The panel, in *Say it with figures*, H. Zeisel, N. Y., Harpers, 1946.

both questions were each answered on two different occasions by each respondent we have four pieces of information about each member of the panel. Table 1 classifies these replies first according to whether they were

TABLE I

| First Interview | Second Interview | | | | |
	Dem. Ag.	Dem. For	Rep. Ag.	Rep. For	Totals
Dem. Against	68	2	1	1	72
Dem. For	11	12	0	1	24
Rep. Against	1	0	23	11	35
Rep. For	2	1	3	129	135
Total	82	15	27	142	266

obtained at the first interview or at the second. For each interview we can then sub-classify the respondents into four groups: those who wanted to vote Democratic and who were also personally opposed to the Republican candidate; those who wanted to vote Democratic but personally respected the opposing candidate; those with Republican vote intentions who, however, disapproved of their party's candidate; and, those with Republican vote intentions who also approved of the candidate.

All the information which can be obtained from two questions and two interviews with the same respondents can be represented in the following type of table.

Let us first look at the last column. Most Democrats are against the person of the Republican candidate and most Republicans are for him. But 59 of the 266 respondents have a kind of personal attachment. Twenty-four Democrats think that the opposing candidate is all right while 35 Republicans, although they intend to vote for their party, obviously wish that another candidate had been put up.

Now let us look at the bottom row of figures which come from the second interview. The number of people with such detached views has decreased. Obviously, what the campaign has done is to intensify partisan feeling. Only 15 Democrats now have a good word to say about the Republican candidate and only 27 Republicans have any doubts left about him.

But that is not all that we would like to know from this table. How do people reconcile their vote intention and their opinion on a specific issue? Do the Democrats who like the opposing candidate shift to him or do they remain Democrats and start to see him in a darker light? The answer is given in the second row of our table. There is only one case of the former, but 11 cases of the latter type. And it so happens that similar figures prevail for the Republicans. Let us look at the third row where we find the respondents who at the first interview intended to vote Republican but didn't like their candidate. One of them switched to the

Democrats but 11 now feel better towards their candidate. In this one case there is no doubt that more people adjust their cross-pressures in a one-sided direction. If their party loyalties are in conflict with a specific opinion of their own they are rather more likely to maintain their party loyalties and change their opinion.

This is of course just one example from which no general conclusion should be drawn. But it shows the type of problem and the type of procedures which derive from the use of the panel technique. Just for the record it might be mentioned that the statistical analysis of tables like the preceding one is quite difficult and proper procedures are still in the process of development. It can easily be seen how many more problems would arise if we had more than two interviews and more than two questionnaire items to deal with.

Besides the difficulties in analysis discussed above, there is one other drawback of the panel technique. There is a danger that we may change our respondent's attitude by the very fact that we reinterview them repeatedly. In some cases the danger is obvious. Suppose, for example, we interview people during a vaccination campaign. If we repeatedly ask people whether they have been vaccinated, our interviewers will probably act as reminders and speed up the success of the campaign in our panel beyond the performance of the population at large. In this case, then, the results of our study will be quite misleading. It could of course happen that our interviewers antagonize the respondents and as a result they might be less likely to get vaccinated. In other cases the panel bias is not likely to be marked. If interest in an election is high and everyone talks about it, the fact that a respondent has been asked about his vote intentions is not going to influence him very much. In any case this is a matter for concrete study. We cannot tell in advance when bias is likely to exist or not.

Actually, a few such studies of bias have been made. The technique used is fairly simple. At the time the panel is picked out a second group of respondents known as a "control group" is set up as closely matched to the panel as possible. This second group, however, is not interviewed until the whole panel study nears its end. At the time the last interview is made with the panel, the control group is also interviewed. From a statistical point of view the two groups were originally alike and should therefore at the end of the study show the same distribution of attitudes were it not that the panel group was interviewed repeatedly. Whatever significant differences show up between the two groups can be attributed to the effect of the panel bias.

Two examples should give an idea of how much work there is still to be done in this direction. During a presidential campaign it was found that the distribution of opinions in the panel was no different than in the control group. But the panel made up its mind somewhat quicker. Under the impact of the repeated interviews the "Don't Knows" in the end were less numerous in the panel than in the control group. This is a very encouraging result. On the other hand it was found that if people were repeatedly interviewed about their newspaper reading habits the panel group was likely to do more newspaper reading than the control group. The reappearance of the interviewer obviously stimulated the reading interests of the panel members. There was some indication, however, that approximately from the third interview on this effect became less and less marked. It might very well be that if the panel had gone on longer, the panel bias would have disappeared in the end.

TABLE II

		2nd Interview		
		Yes	No	Totals
1st Interview	Yes	50	50	100
	No	50	850	900
Totals—		100	900	1000

TABLE III

		2nd Interview		
		Yes	No	Totals
1st Interview	Yes	400	100	500
	No	100	400	500
Totals—		500	500	1000

There are many operational problems involved in panel studies just as in any other large-scale research operation. How can we get people to participate in a panel and to stick to it? How do we substitute for unavoidable losses? Is it sometimes possible to correspond with panel members by mail rather than to make personal contacts? Should we handle a panel as the American Senate is handled, always substituting part of it by new members?

Finally, there are a number of serious statistical problems to be dealt with. They all center around the concept of turnover. The following two tables exemplify the problem. They each represent one question on which people have been interviewed twice.

In the first question (table 2) 100 people changed their minds one way or another. On the second question (table 3) 200 people did so. One might feel that the turnover on the second question is therefore greater. But one must consider that many fewer people said "Yes" to the first question at the time of the first interview. One therefore cannot expect as many people to change as in the second case. It might be more advisable to compute the turnover as percentage of the people who said "Yes" both times. This would give a turnover of 200 per cent for the first and 50 per cent for the second table and now we would have to say that the first question has the larger turnover. There are obviously still many other ways in which turnover can be described. What index we can use to describe best the turnover in such tables is a very vexing problem, especially because most all of the statistical treatment of panel data goes back to this one point. But this is not the place to deal with such technical matters at length. It is preferable to end up with some more general theoretical considerations which will show the place panel studies are likely to hold in the social sciences in the coming years.

Basically, what we do in a panel study is relate information obtained at one time to information obtained at a subsequent time. We are in the center of what has come to be called dynamic social research. We study changes and we want to explain these changes. We know who changed and we have information on people prior to their change. Explaining the change necessarily means to relate this previous information to the subsequent change. Everything will depend therefore upon how ingenious we are in deciding what information we should gather at different time periods. To exemplify the problem more clearly, let us assume that we are dealing with a panel of people who are about to move into a public housing project where Negroes and white will live together.[9] If we center our attention on the whites then we know in advance that some of them will get along with their Negro fellow tenants and some will not. Some will improve their ability to get along with people of other races and some will not. What information should we collect from all these prospective tenants prior to the time they move into the housing project to help us explain what shifts in racial attitudes will take place?

We will obviously want to know their race attitudes prior to their entrance into the housing project. But it will also be important to know their *expectations*. It may turn out that the greater their initial uneasiness the more will they be pleasantly surprised be reality. On the other hand we know that some people have a hard time experiencing "reality," and if they enter a situation with apprehension they behave nervously and start trouble. Some sort of index of psychological flexibility is needed.

Pieces of information about the psychological predisposition of the respondents have been called *intervening variables* because they intervene, as it were, between the individual's reaction and the situation in which he is placed.[10] In the example given above, where a group of individuals are about to enter a public housing project, we have people who will be subject to the same external experience. They will, however, react differently. Between the external situation and the individual response there intervene certain psychological and social characteristics which channel the response in an individually characteristic fashion. Social psychologists in recent years have developed out of their experience many hypotheses as to which intervening variables are of importance. We talk of a persons' *level of aspiration* or of a person's *expectations*, indicating that we consider that such information will be of value in interpreting

[9] An especially rich source for such explanatory variables will be found in a housing study organized by the Lavanburg Foundation under the direction of Robert K. Merton.

[10] The interested reader will find a thoroughgoing discussion of important intervening variables in Sherif, M., *An outline of social psychology*, N. Y., Harpers, 1948.

how the individuals will react to the situations in which they are placed.

The important intervening variables have to be ascertained before expected changes take place. To follow through with the examples given above, we should know as much as we can about the panel members before they move into the inter-racial housing project. Once they have been living there it is too late to look for such information, for we can never know then whether what we have found has not already been influenced by their new experience. This is, of course, exactly where the importance of the panel technique lies. We periodically study people's attitudes, expectations, and aspirations. We find out what has happened to them between interviews: what they read, with whom they talked, what external events impressed them, etc. Both the situational factors and the intervening variables change continuously. Our analysis would weave back and forth from these two series of data, expressing, in one case, reaction to the situation as a function of some psychological predisposition, and, in another, the psychological predisposition as a function of the changing situation. We would want to know how people's expectations affect the way they react to changes in their environment; and how the environment experienced changes their hopes and concerns.

On more than one occasion it has been said that one of the difficulties which impede the progress of social science is the fact that we cannot experiment with human beings in the same way that the agricultural station experiments with animals and plants. It should not be overlooked, however, that life itself is in a very real sense a continuous series of experiments. In the course of time, almost everything conceivable and sometimes things previously inconceivable happen to one group of persons or another. Although many of these events are, as yet, unpredictable, some events, fortunately for our purpose, occur with sufficient regularity or frequency so that if we know just what sort of persons will be subject to them, we can observe the various ways in which they will respond. Panel studies are conducted, usually, on the impact of events of a given predictable regularity such as voting in a presidential election, exposure to certain advertising, etc. If we find the right statistical technique we will be able to interrelate "stimulus, predisposition, and response" and with time and experience our hope is to understand, predict, and control human behavior more successfully.

Samuel A. Stouffer

SOME OBSERVATIONS
ON STUDY DESIGN

To alter the folkways, social science itself must take the initiative. We must be clear in our own minds what proof consists of, and we must, if possible, provide dramatic examples of the advantages of relying on something more than plausibility. And the heart of our problem lies in study design *in advance*, such that the evidence is not capable of a dozen alternative interpretations.

Basically, I think it is essential that we always keep in mind the model of a controlled experiment, even if in practice we may have to deviate from an ideal model. Take the simple accompanying diagram.

	Before	After	After — Before
Experimental group	x_1	x_2	$d = x_2 - x_1$
Control group	x_1'	x_2'	$d' = x_2' - x_1'$

The test of whether a difference d is attributable to what we think it is attributable to is whether d is significantly larger than d'.

We used this model over and over again during the war to measure the effectiveness of orientation films in changing soldiers' attitudes. These experiences are described in Volume III of our *Studies in Social Psychology in World War II*.[1]

One of the troubles with using this careful design was that the effectiveness of a single film when thus measured turned out to be so slight. If, instead of using the complete experimental design, we simply took an

Reprinted from *The American Journal of Sociology*, Vol. 55 (January 1950), pp. 356-59, by permission of the author and publisher (Copyright, 1950, by The University of Chicago Press.)

[1] Carl I. Hovland, Arthur A. Lumsdaine, and Fred D. Sheffield, *Experiments in Mass Communication* (Princeton: Princeton University Press, 1949).

unselected sample of men and compared the attitudes of those who said they had seen a film with those who said they had not, we got much more impressive differences. This was more rewarding to us, too, for the management wanted to believe the films were powerful medicine. The gimmick was the selective fallibility of memory. Men who correctly remembered seeing the films were likely to be those most sensitized to their message. Men who were bored or indifferent may have actually seen them but slept through them or just forgot.

Most of the time we are not able or not patient enough to design studies containing all four cells as in the diagram above. Sometimes we have only the top two cells, as in the accompanying diagram. In this

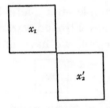

situation we have two observations of the same individuals or groups taken at different times. This is often a very useful design. In the army, for example, we would take a group of recruits, ascertain their attitudes, and restudy the same men later. From this we could tell whose attitudes changed and in what direction (it was almost always for the worse, which did not endear us to the army!). But exactly what factors in the early training period were most responsible for deterioration of attitudes could only be inferred indirectly.

The panel study is usually more informative than a more frequent design, which might be pictured thus:

$$x_1$$

$$x_2'$$

Here at one point in time we have one sample, and at a later point in time we have another sample. We observe that our measure, say, the mean, is greater for the recent sample than for the earlier one. But we are precluded from observing which men or what type of men shifted. Moreover, there is always the disturbing possibility that the populations in our two samples were initially different; hence the differences might not be attributable to conditions taking place in the time interval between the two observations. Thus we would study a group of soldiers in the United States and later ask the same questions of a group of soldiers overseas. Having matched the two groups of men carefully by branch of service, length of time in the army, rank, etc., we hoped that the results of the study would approximate what would be found if the same men could have been studied twice. But this could be no more than a hope. Some important factors could not be adequately controlled, for example, physical conditions. Men who went overseas were initially in better shape on the average than men who had been kept behind; but, if the follow-up study was in the tropics, there was a chance that unfavorable climate already had begun to take its toll. And so it went. How much men overseas changed called for a panel study as a minimum if we were to have much confidence in the findings.

A very common attempt to get the results of a controlled experiment

without paying the price is with the design that might be as shown in the accompanying diagram. This is usually what we get with correlation analysis. We have two or more groups of men whom we study at the same point in time. Thus we have men in the infantry and men in the air corps and compare their attitudes. How much of the difference between x'_1 and x_1 we can attribute to experience in a given branch of service and how much is a function of attributes of the men selected for each branch we cannot know assuredly. True, we can try to rule out various possibilities by matching; we can compare men from the two branches with the same age and education, for example. But there is all too often a wide-open gate through which other uncontrolled variables can march.

Sometimes, believe it or not, we have only one cell:

When this happens, we do not know much of anything. But we can still fill pages of social science journals with "brilliant analysis" if we use plausible conjecture in supplying missing cells from our imagination. Thus we may find that the adolescent today has wild ideas and conclude that society is going to the dogs. We fill in the dotted cell representing our own yesterdays with hypothetical data, where x_1 represents us and x_2 our

offspring. The tragicomic part is that most of the public, including, I fear, many social scienitsts, are so acculturated that they ask for no better data.

I do not intend to disparage all research not conforming to the canons of the controlled experiment. I think that we will see more of full experimental design in sociology and social psychology in the future than in the past. But I am well aware of the practical difficulties of its execution, and I know that there are numberless important situations in which it is not feasible at all. What I am arguing for is awareness of the limitations of a design in which crucial cells are missing.

Sometimes by forethought and patchwork we can get approximations which are useful if we are careful to avoid overinterpretation. Let me cite an example:

In Europe during the war the army tested the idea of putting an entire platoon of Negro soldiers into a white infantry outfit. This was done in several companies. The Negroes fought beside white soldiers. After several months we were asked to find out what the white troops thought about the innovation. We found that only 7 per cent of the white soldiers in companies with Negro platoons said that they disliked the idea very much, whereas 62 per cent of the white soldiers in divisions without Negro troops said they would dislike the idea very much if it were tried in their outfits. We have:

	Before	After
Experimental		7%
Control		62%

Now, were these white soldiers who fought beside Negroes men who were naturally more favorable to Negroes than the cross-section of white infantrymen? We did not think so, since, for example, they contained about the same proportion of southerners. The point was of some importance, however, if we were to make the inference that actual experience with Negroes reduced hostility from 62 to 7 per cent. As a second-best substitute, we asked the white soldiers in companies with Negro platoons if they could recall how they felt when the innovation was first proposed. It happens that 67 per cent said they were initially opposed to the idea. Thus we could tentatively fill in a missing cell and conclude that, under the conditions obtaining, there probably had been a marked change in attitude.

Even if this had been a perfectly controlled experiment, there was still plenty of chance to draw erroneous inferences. The conclusions apply only to situations closely approximating those of the study. It happens, for example, that the Negroes involved were men who volunteered to leave rear-area jobs for combat duty. If other Negroes had been involved, the situation might have been different. Moreover, they had white officers. One army colonel who saw this study and whom I expected to ridicule it because he usually opposed innovations, surprised me by offering congratulations. "This proves," he said, "what I have been arguing in all my thirty years in the army—that niggers will do all right if you give 'em white officers!" Moreover, the study applied only to combat experience. Other studies would be needed to justify extending the findings to non-combat or garrison duty. In other words, one lone study, however well designed, can be a very dangerous thing if it is exploited beyond its immediate implications.

Now experiments take time and money, and there is no use denying that we in social science cannot be as prodigal with the replications as the biologist who can run a hundred experiments simultaneously by growing plants in all kinds of soils and conditions. The relative ease of experimentation in much—not all—of natural science goes far to account for the difference in quality of proof demanded by physical and biological sciences, on the one hand, and social scientists, on the other.

Though we cannot always design neat experiments when we want to, we can at least keep the experimental model in front of our eyes and behave cautiously when we fill in missing cells with dotted lines. But there is a further and even more important operation we can perform in the interest of economy. That lies in our choice of the initial problem.

J. G. Ferraby

PLANNING
A MASS-OBSERVATION INVESTIGATION

Mass-Observation uses techniques which are related to the poll technique but differ from it in many respects.[1] The way in which these techniques are applied can be illustrated by a description of the steps in planning one of our recent investigations, just recently published in book form under the title *Britain and Her Birth-rate*. The investigation aimed at finding out the real reasons why the birth rate was falling and at throwing light on possible ways of stemming the fall.

Methods available to Mass-Observation are as follows:

1. *Direct interviewing.*—Normally, open-end questions are used; but alternative-answer questions are occasionally included.

2. *Informal interviewing.*—The contact is told that the interviewer is investigating public opinion. The subject is often introduced by a pre-determined question; but, once the initial question has been asked, the interviewer is free to interpose further remarks in order to keep the contact talking and to probe further into the views expressed. The interviewer is given a general instruction not to ask leading questions, but no other limitation is placed on the questions and remarks which may be used for probing.

3. *Indirect interviewing.*—The same as informal interviewing, except that the contact is not told that an investigation of public opinion is taking place. This involves first getting into conversation with the contact, then leading the conversation around to the subject of the interview.

Reprinted from American Journal of Sociology, Vol. 51, (July 1945), pp. 1-6, by permission of the author and publisher. (Copyright, 1945, by The University of Chicago Press.)

[1] Mass-Observation was founded by Tom Harrisson and Charles Madge in 1937 to study the society in which we live. A great deal of its work is concerned with public opinion, and its methods differ in several respects from those most used in America. The present article is a digest of only part of the findings of a recent survey, published under the title *Britain and Her Birth-rate* by John Murray, London, in 1945. The author of this article has worked with Mass-Observation for a number of years.

4. *Observation.*—Observing scenes, events, and behavior; recording overheard comments.

5. *The National Panel of Voluntary Observers.*—This panel is peculiar to Mass-Observation. It consists of interested individuals who send in written reports in answer to a monthly directive. Other activities include the keeping of diaries, collection of material for our War Library, making occasional special reports, etc. The panel is drawn from all walks of life but is not a cross-section of the public, being better educated and more intelligent than the average. It provides comments which are more detailed and franker than those obtained by interviewing.

In planning our birth-rate investigation, the point from which we started was that the investigation should be concerned with the family; and it soon resolved itself into an investigation of factors bearing upon the size of the family. We prefer not to have our terms of reference too specifically determined before the start of the investigation, since it nearly always happens either that the original problem is found to be so closely related to others that it cannot very well be investigated apart from them or that the problem is so complex that it cannot be covered in its entirety. The previous investigation in the "Change" series ("The Journey Home") started by being exclusively about demobilization; but before it was completed, it was found necessary to include a considerable amount of material on general attitudes to postwar conditions and the postwar world. In the family investigation the reverse was the case. It very quickly became clear that the field was so vast that it would not be possible to deal with more than a few aspects of it, and it was soon decided to concentrate on the reasons why women do not have more children than they do. The name "family investigation" stuck, however, and it is in this way that we refer to the investigation in this article.

The first step in any investigation is to reconnoiter the field, this being done by means of informal and indirect interviews. Which to use depends largely on the social sanctions attached to the subject. If the subject is one concerning which people are likely to be chary about giving frank views to a stranger, the more tortuous indirect method is necessary; if the subject is one which does not strike any very deep chord informal interviews are likely to be sufficient; but it is often necessary to try both in order to determine the type of reaction.

In the family investigation we had expected that there would be a good deal of resistance to frank discussion, and we had even considered it possible that the greater part of the investigation might have to be done by indirect methods; but in actual fact it was quickly found that women were quite willing to discuss the matter openly.

Having obtained some preliminary interviews, in this way it is possible to see what aspects of the problem interest people most. It will probably then be necessary to obtain some more indirect or informal interviews on particular problems. When these have been collected, the time has come to take stock of the position.

.The first question to be answered is: What methods do we expect to make use of? It having become clear that results could be expected from direct interviewing, it was decided to center the family investigation around a questionnaire. Problems of the questionnaire are dealt with later. Informal and indirect interviews, had, for the time being, played their part, although they were to be used again later. There remains observation and the panel.

The chief way in which observation was used in this survey was in following up individual families. Visits were paid to the mothers and then to the married daughters. One family consisted of a mother and thirteen children, several of the daughters having married. The observation showed both the way in which membership of a large family had affected the attitude of the daughters toward children and the different ways in which women from an identical background reacted. Indirect interviews were obtained with these women, as well as observations of them; and this material proved very valuable in interpreting the results of the questionnaire. The observational reports showed the life led by women having some of the more frequently found attitudes to the problems investigated. A second family gave equally valuable data, particularly in showing how subjective are such matters as "too much work" and "not enough money." It is not possible in an article such as this to detail the observational methods used or the results obtained; but we ourselves feel that without these observations the survey would have been far less adequate and the interpretation of the results far more a matter of guesswork.

There are very few investigations in which it is not possible to use the panel, in one way or another. The family investigation seemed particularly suited to it. We decided to ask members of the panel to report on several things. What did they think determined the number of children people had? What did they think prevented people from having more children? What was the history of their own family (if they had one), and how were their decisions formed on the number of children to have? What did they think about contraceptives? Were these efficient or not? Some of the questions we asked were designed to get information on matters which could scarcely be dealt with by interviews; some filled in gaps we did not expect to cover by interviews, although this would have been possible. All were phrased in a way which would encourage the members of the panel to let themselves go and to answer at length.

There is one drawback to the use of the panel which is unavoidable. It it not possible to try out questions before putting them in the monthly directive; and, consequently, it is not always possible to ask questions which the replies show later would have been best. In the present investigation several questions were asked which eventually, when the scope of the investigation had been narrowed down, were not required. But this difficulty is counterbalanced by the fact that, once the question has been asked, it is in the files permanently. We frequently find that there is a considerable amount of material in our files relevant to a new investigation, which has been collected in a quite different context. More rarely diaries can be used as illustrative material, and it was hoped this would be possible in the family investigation; but examination of some of the diaries failed to produce anything of value.

After having decided what methods are suited to the particular investigation, the places in which the investigation is to be carried out are settled. Mass-Observation rarely undertakes a national survey. To apply Mass-Observation methods on a national scale would be a very costly proceeding even if it were possible. Untrained part-time investigators are not suitable for the more intensive type of survey, and we work exclusively with full-time or trained part-time investigators. Interviewing with open-end questions takes longer than with alternative-answer questions, so that a smaller sample is used than by the polls—rarely more than one thousand. Moreover, a national poll must necessarily be somewhat superficial, and on theoretical grounds we consider more profitable in most cases to carry out the investigation intensively over a limited area rather than superficially over a wider area.

The normal procedure is to carry out the greater part of the investigation in one region, usually London, and to supplement this by one or more smaller investigations in contrasting regions. This was the plan followed for the family survey. Using gross reproduction rates, seven London boroughs were chosen, three of which had high gross reproduction rates, three of which had low ones, and one of which was intermediate. As a contrast to London, a country town with an intermediate gross reproduction rate was chosen, and two hundred interviews were carried out there. For practical purposes we find a check sample of two hundred quite sufficient. If there is a qualitative difference in the reaction, two hundred interviews are sufficient to determine it. Regional numerical differences are not of great importance unless they are very large, in which case even two hundred interviews would locate them; for Mass-Observation aims at giving a picture of the real attitudes of the people, and the human mind cannot grasp the significance of differences of frequency of the order of 5 per cent.

It might have been a greater contrast if the check interviews had been carried out in villages, but this was not practicable. In villages everyone knows about everyone else's affairs, and on so intimate a subject as the size of the family no reliance could be placed on the answers obtained, since people would not dare to be frank. In towns the same repression does not exist, as was demonstrated by the number of women who admitted to a totally strange interviewer that they got married because they had to.

After deciding on the regions to be investigated, the next point to be settled is the nature of the sample. Sometimes the standard stratification of sex, age, and economic group is found to be adequate, although Mass-Observation uses a socioeconomic grouping equivalent to class rather than a purely economic one, on the grounds that to do anything else is to sacrifice the substance for the shadow where general opinion is concerned. But often this is felt not to be the most adequate stratification. In the family survey it seemed likely that education was of more importance than either class or economic standing, since class was to some extent covered by the contrast between boroughs of high and those of low fertility. A careful check was kept on the education distribution as the survey proceeded, and investigators were warned of any discrepancy between the estimated education distribution for the borough and the distribution of the sample.

The plan with regard to sex and age changed as the survey proceeded. The original plan was to ask everyone the same basic questionnaire, with groups of questions as alternatives for the different ages and sexes. But reflection upon preliminary results made it clear that women of child-bearing age were by far the most important group. For simple people the problem was a hypothetical one, and it seemed obvious from their replies that their opinions were likely to bear little relation to their action when they married and had to face the prob'em in reality. Older people might have settled views on the matter, but their opinions could only have an indirect effect on the birth rate. It seemed possible that married men might provide material of importance, but preliminary results showed that their interest in the subject was less vital than that of married women. It was decided, therefore, to concentrate entirely on married women of child-bearing age, arbitrarily fixed at twenty to forty-five.

On a subject like childbearing, age within even this limited group seemed vital. Consideration, however, showed that more decisive than age was the length of time the contact had been married. The groups decided upon were, therefore, those married for up to five years (roughly speaking, the war period), those married from five to ten years, and those married over ten years. Figures were not available for the proportion of women who should come in each group, but every effort was made to see that the sample in each area contained the same proportion of each group.

The result of this procedure was to fix groups for stratification which did not correspond to any available data for the areas investigated. This is in accordance with Mass-Observation's principle that exact accuracy of figures should be sacrificed if, by so doing, more meaningful material can be obtained. But in this particular survey the lack of data was extreme; and, furthermore, there was another difficulty—the place where a woman of childbearing age is to be found at a given time of day in wartime is largely dependent on the number of young children she has. If she has six children under fourteen, she is fairly certain to be at home; if she has none, she is fairly certain to be at work; if she has one or two, she may perhaps be found in the street: if she has no children, she may well not be at home even in the evening. We did not feel, therefore, that it was practicable to obtain a sample which was a cross-section of each borough in the very important respects of size of family and occupation of the mother.

For these reasons we decided not to attempt to produce figures for the total number of women of childbearing age holding various points of view. Instead, we aimed at comparing the attitudes of different groups. The main sample was concerned only with women who could be found at home or in the street during the day; and a check sample of women working in a factory was obtained on a similar principle to the regional check sample. Where there were no great regional, occupational, age, or other group differences, it would be reasonable to suppose that the figures obtained were valid for all women; but the chief purpose of the investigation became to compare the views of the different groups. Consequently, the investigation became more concerned with causative factors and less with reporting the situation as a static sociological record.

The next stage is the construction of the questionnaire. This is done in a way very similar to the construction of a poll questionnaire. It is based, however, on the preliminary indirect and informal interviews as well as on the investigator's idea of what points need investigating. Since the questions are open-end ones, it is much easier to judge whether a question is satisfactory than when the experience ˙of reliable interviewers is the only criterion. The nature of even a few verbatim replies from different types of contacts is usually sufficient to make clear deficiencies in the wording of a question. Often it is not so much that the wording of the question is wrong as that the question does not hit the high spot of interest, and a related question on a slightly different issue is found more informative. *

In the family questionnaire the biggest difficulty was to determine the relative importance of various possible factors which might make people want more children. The preliminary interviews made it fairly clear which these were; the chief purpose of the questionnaire was to find out their relative importance and the reasons for their importance. But the possibility of a change in wants was far too subtle for easy investigation; people found it difficult enough to say how many children they wanted now without the added difficulty of projecting their desires into an imaginary future.

Eventually it was decided not to make any attempt to establish the likely magnitude of such things as improved housing conditions, domestic help, family allowances, etc., but simply to ask similar questions about all of them and compare the answers. The style of question used was: "Do you think that, if you could live in the sort of house you like, that would make a difference in the number of children you would like to have?" The number of people saying that this would make a difference gives very little indication of the number who would actually have another child if housing conditions were improved; but the figures for several questions of a similar type are comparable, and the replies of the different groups are comparable, and that was all we needed to find out.

Often in the course of a questionnaire, points arise which seem to repay further investigation, and the family survey was no exception to this rule. We were surprised at the number of women who appeared not able to have as many children as they wanted; the evidence from the questionnaire, however, was not entirely conclusive. We therefore collected a small number of long, informal interviews with older women having completed families; and these confirmed the indications of the questionnaire, providing valuable illustrative material. In another context, fear of childbirth appeared not to be a frequent deterrent, but a very powerful one when it existed, and its intensity was also illustrated by collecting informal interviews.

In describing the various stages in the planning of the family survey it it has been treated as though each stage was quite distinct, one being concluded before the next was started. In practice, decisions concerning one stage vitally affect the succeeding stages, and there is no set order in which different aspects are considered. Regions to be covered are affected by the way in which the sample is to be stratified; the content of the questionnaire affects the stratification of the sample, and so on. The above outline is intended only to indicate the type of solution which Mass-Observation uses for the various problems which affect all surveys.

Such a description would not be complete without a note on the manner in which our surveys are written up, since the whole procedure aims at producing material which can be used in the way to be described. Figures do not form the main part of the report; in the present survey most of the figures are given in an appendix. The basis of the report is the verbatim comments made by the contacts, whether obtained by direct, informal, or indirect methods or from the written replies of the national panel. In this particular survey they also included letters written to a doctor who had spoken over the radio on the subject, letters to which we were allowed access. The report describes the various attitudes found with ample quotations of these verbatim comments and draws conclusions as it goes along. We believe that, since we are in closer contact with the original material than the readers of the report, it is part of our duty in writing the report to indicate the conclusions to which, in our opinion, it leads. Everyone who tries, not only to present a report on public opinion, but also to interpret it, will quickly see how essential a part of the material the actual comments of the contact are. They bring dead figures to life and make the abstract concrete. Without unlimited financial support, it is necessary to sacrifice either a degree of numerical accuracy or a degree of accuracy in interpreting the figures obtained. We believe that in most cases the interpretation of results is more important.

Problems of Data Collection

Arthur Kornhauser

THE PROBLEM OF BIAS
IN OPINION RESEARCH

The term "bias" is used to cover a multitude of opinion research sins. Considerable current attention is devoted to specific practical problems at the procedural level—biased questions, interviewer bias, sampling bias, respondents' bias; and beyond this, one encounters vague and general condemnations of biased research. But remarkably little discussion has been focused upon the problem of bias at high levels, the bias of those who control the studies.

As long as bias, like evil, remains an amorphous something to be "against" or, alternatively, as long as it is identified as a series of technical operating faults in the field, we who are responsible for the research conveniently evade the disturbing issue of our own biases and how they affect our research. At times, with unbecoming psychological naivete, we even hide behind indignant declarations about our personal honesty and professional integrity, as if that were an answer. By avoiding the problem, we fail to sensitize ourselves to the manifestations of our own biases and consequently neglect to set up safe-guards and correctives. It is more comfortable to concentrate on improving our foot soldiers than our headquarters staff—that is, ourselves.

The purpose of this paper is to offer a sketchy analysis of the problem and to urge more lively attention to it. The objective is clarification, to the end that all of us in opinion research will face up to the issues and do what we can to find remedies. No one of us can be complacent on this score. Variegated beams and motes are pretty well distributed among our respective eyes. The problem constitutes a major challenge to the vigorous young profession of opinion surveying. For if opinion "facts" depend on the particular polling agency hired to gather them, the buyers and users of opinion research will soon raise most embarrassing questions.

Reprinted from *The International Journal of Opinion and Attitude Research*, Vol. 1 (1947), pp. 1-13, by permission of the author and publisher.

Opinion studies must guard against becoming competitive tools of sales-manship and propaganda instead of scientific research instruments.

If we are to deal with the central and distinctive questions of research bias, the first necessity is to cut through the confusion of accidental and secondary characteristics which cluster about the term. The core issue, stated most simply, is this. Do the inclinations or prepossessions of those responsible for an opinion survey lead to results and conclusions that are one-sided, untrue, or misleading in reference to what they purport to describe? If so, bias is present—and is to be further analyzed and, if possible, "cured." If the essential relationship specified is not present, that is if there are not subjective leanings which produce a corresponding twist of results, then the case is not one of "bias" even though other serious types of error may be in evidence.

The judgment that given research is or is not biased is always a diffi-cult one; in most cases the evidence remains inconclusive. But the prob-lem is no less important because the answer is not sharply black and white.

There is need for thorough detailing of criteria and procedures for judg-ing bias but we shall make no attempt to perform that formidable task in this paper. Certain guiding considerations must suffice. Two elements are always involved: (a) the detection of flaws which mean that opinions under study are misrepresented and (b) interpretation which ascribes these errors to predispositions or desires of the researcher (whether or not he is aware of their biasing influence).

The judgment that material is one-sided, untrue, or misrepresentative contrasts it with an "authentic" picture that presents all that is relevant and important within the context of the particular purposes and uses of the results. The comparison is made partly by noting departures from other parallel information that stands up better under critical scrutiny; partly by testing audiences exposed to the results to see whether they do, in fact, draw erroneous conclusions; partly by rigorous logical analysis that exposes the weaknesses and one-sided implications of method, results, and manner of presentation.

If one has independent evidence about the research man's attitudes, tendencies, and research behavior, the inference as to bias may be more confidently made. Where many lines of evidence concerning the research and the researcher dovetail consistently, one's judgment is reenforced; he concludes that "everything points to bias." Even without confirmatory evidence regarding the subjective inclinations that went into the research, if enough signs in the procedure and report point cumulatively to "slant-ing" of the material in a constant direction, we can *assume* the subjective bias.

Where sufficient corroboration is lacking or where evidence is meager and conflicting, judgment must be suspended. It is important to emphasize that no *objective* technique can yield a final answer. All we can do is keep ourselves alert to whatever looks like biased procedure and results, in our own work and that of others, and take what steps we can to minimize such errors.

The foregoing general formulation of top-level bias may be clarified by contrasting it with several untenable conceptions that are frequently advanced.

In the first place, it will not do to view the problem in absolutist or perfectionist terms. This easily leads to the position that since our attitudes and desires are operating constantly in everything we do, bias is bound to exist in *all* observation and *all* interpretation. Everyone is biased. It can't be avoided.

The obvious answer is that the mere existence of personal inclinations does not mean their inevitable expression in any given research behavior. One has other conflicting and inhibiting values as well. We can set up checks and safeguards against letting our own partisan tendencies lead to differential results in favor of "our side." We can learn to "lean over backwards." Moreover, it is apparent that the operation of biases is not an "all or nothing" matter, as this argument suggests. The practical aim is to reduce the distorting influence to a minimum, not to attain perfection.

A special (and specious) case of this view that sees bias everywhere is the contention that in addressing a question to a person—any question about any topic—one is guiding the individual's thinking and response in a definite direction, that is "*biasing*" it. Asking him what magazines he reads, by this argument, reflects a bias against newspapers and radio since they are not brought to his attention. Clearly this is stretching the definition of "bias" beyond a point of possible usefulness. To be sure, asking about one of the media and not the others *may* indicate bias—but that must be judged with reference to the purposes and use of the inquiry. The essence of the problem lies in distinguishing between those instances in which the directiveness of the questioning does and does not lead to false conclusions. A study purporting to compare magazines can scarcely give misleading results through omitting mention of other media. However, if the problem is to tell an advertiser how he can best reach certain households with his message, obviously the cards are stacked by asking about certain media and not others. Our concern here is simply to warn against the confusion that calls *all* "directing of attention" a process of "biasing."

Another fallacy is contained in the argument that if the research director is *honest*, if he has high regard for professional standards, these motivations guarantee freedom from bias (identified with dishonesty) in his work. Unfortunately for this simple ethical dismissal of the problem, most of our biases sneak in unobserved and without declaring themselves. They are not acts of recognized dishonesty. They adopt many disguises and rely upon the convenient blind-spots and ready rationalizations that keep our moral sentries from detecting them.

According to another conception, research bias is made to cover a wide assortment of technical deficiencies more or less regardless of their source. Thus a "biased sample" usually means a faulty or unrepresentative sample, whether this is due to incompetence or to subjective preferences—and whether the errors are introduced in planning the sample, in instructing interviewers, or in the failure of the interviewers to follow orders.

Two important distinctions are called for here. The first is that between low quality research and biased research. Opinion studies (and the constituent procedures) may be admirably free from bias and yet be poor in quality and untrustworthy. Likewise they may be biased and yet manifest, otherwise, high technical proficiency. Problems of inadequate knowledge and skill and problems of conscious or unconscious slanting of procedures need to be perceived and tackled separately. To keep the distinction clear, it is suggested that we use the terms "sampling *error*," "interviewer *error*," etc., save where we definitely mean "bias" in the sense of *purposive* slanting (either intentionally or "unconsciously").

The second distinction is that between biases at lower levels and those at the top. A biased or dishonest interviewer or statistician constitutes no genuine problem of "research bias," as we are using the term. The errors he introduces are usually evidences rather of technical imperfections at higher levels in the selection, training, and supervision of personnel. However, these processes of selection, training, etc., may also express and implement top-level bias. In that case, the serious problem does have to do with the higher-ups. They are using their agents (again, wittingly or unwittingly) to slant results just as they might otherwise use loaded questions or deceptive samples.

Anyone in touch with opinion research activities over the years has inevitably encountered numerous examples of what we are calling "top-level bias." Most of us can readily testify, if we care to do so, even against our own past slips.

"Off the record," there is more than a little scepticism regarding each new set of research results published by partisan clients—whether cigarette and dentifrice manufacturers, magazines, radio networks, or political groups. It is remarkable how commonly the research conclusions support the sponsor's position and supply him with sales ammunition. Quite apart from partisan sponsorship, however, opinion inquiries are in constant danger of leaning one way or another under the influence of social valuations and predispositions of the research organization and the inescapable social pressures playing upon it. It never ceases to be astonishing how easily, in all good conscience, we adopt those procedures and overlook those errors which conspire to produce results congenial to our own beliefs and our clients' expectations.

It is worth considering the different forms these expressions of bias take, in order to note at what points the research director must be especially on guard against their intrusion.

It is scarcely necessary to state that different opinion research organizations differ enormously in the quality of their work, including prominently differences in the success with which they reduce the play of bias. This paper is in no sense an indictment of opinion research agencies, singly or collectively. A number of them are fully alive to the dangers discussed here and are doing their utmost to minimize bias in their work.

1. *Bias in Choice of Subject Matter for Polls:* In an earlier paper we summarized certain evidence on the one-sided leanings of polls dealing with labor issues.[1] An examination of 155 questions published by leading polling agencies from 1940 to 1945 revealed that only 8 dealt with favorable features of unionism while 81 were concerned with faults and proposed restrictions. Not a single question was aimed at such an important topic, for example, as whether labor disputes are fairly treated in newspaper and radio.

Similar bias in selection of issues tends to occur in other fields where strong sentiments prevail at "upper" levels. For example, how much attention, relatively, is given to fascism and the threat from the right as compared to that devoted to communism and the threat from the left? How commonly do polls on attitudes toward advertising go beyond the question whether the ads are noticed, whether they are annoying, how much they increase the price of a cake of soap if at all, whether advertised products are superior, etc., to dig into such unpalatable topics as whether the ads whip up desires beyond people's ability to satisfy them, whether they foster false values, and in general, what their larger effects on character are, considered within a broad social and human frame of reference instead of adhering to the businessman's viewpoint?

Opinion research in regard to minority groups seems rarely to focus questions on *economic* and *religious* influences supporting prejudice; such questions might well yield results embarrassing to powerful individuals and groups. Hence we do not ask questions, for example, to get at comparative feelings about seeing mass resentments and aggressions channeled against racial, religious, and nationality groups rather than against wealth and special privilege.

2. *Bias in Study Design and Procedure:* In selecting research methods, one is prone to accept procedures that promise acceptable results and to adopt rigorous standards leading to more ready rejection of techniques likely to produce unwelcome material. Suppose the research assignment is to compare the value of several magazines as advertising media. In one

---

[1] "Are Public Opinion Polls Fair to Organized Labor?" *Public Opinion Quarterly,* Winter 1946-47, pp. 484-500. This article contains a number of illustrations of the different types of bias discussed in the next few pages.

case the client is publisher of an outstandingly popular magazine; in another case he is owner of a magazine well down the list according to circulation figures. Will not the research man typically emphasize accurate readership counts in the first case and, with equally scientific arguments, turn to other measures for the second client—such as the high social status of readers, the trust they express in the publication, the amount of time the average reader devotes to it, and so on. Two different pictures are thus obtained, not *contradictory* but *partial*. Whether one approves of the differential procedure or not, it seems difficult to deny the presence of "bias."

Instances of sampling and interviewing bias should likewise be noted at this point. For example, a survey on infringements of civil rights conducted among white people only is certain to conceal the true gravity of the problem. A survey of social attitudes, limited to women at home during the day and without callbacks to reach those who are out, can be expected to secure an unduly traditional and uncritical picture since better educated, socially and professionally active women are likely to be under-represented. Such errors are relevant to the present discussion insofar as they are consciously or unconsciously purposive.

Our procedures often serve to obtain "illustrative evidence" for conclusions held in advance rather than constituting fair *tests* of our tentative answers. If one has the conviction, for example, that anti-Semitism is an expression of over-aggressive, pathological personalities he readily designs a study based on interviews with known violent anti-Semites and the comparison of their personality patterns and attitudes with those of persons known to be passive, indifferent, or friendly toward Jews. The results are pretty well assured. An adequate test would demand the examination of additional groups consisting of persons aggressively and violently active in other directions—say Communists, passionate anti-Catholics, anti-alcohol crusaders, etc. Otherwise conclusions associating aggressive qualities with anti-Semitism are imposed by the design of the study.

3. *Bias in Question Wording and Sequence:* Unfair or loaded phrasing of questions is the most commonly noted manifestation of bias in opinion polling. The more extreme forms of question bias are now generally avoided. Less pronounced slanting, however, insinuates itself into many surveys.

A good illustration is furnished by two polls conducted in the United States a year or two ago on the topic of governmental health insurance and medical care. Different questions were asked in the two surveys and markedly different conclusions emerged, the one set indicating much greater popular approval of a federal health program than the other. The contrasting conclusions, it happened, coincided with the opposed positions of the two medical groups that sponsored the studies.

Not less interesting than this last fact is the observation that a research director for one of the surveying agencies, in a scientific article dealing with the discordant results, fails to mention the relationship of results to sponsor's views. The reader is given no hint that the results came out "right" for each of the propaganda groups.[2]

A few examples taken from recent published polls will illustrate other instances of questions in which it seems probable that bias is evidenced.

"Which do you think is better Americanism: (a) every man should accept the responsibility for getting his own job and a living, or (b) the government should see to it that every man has a job and a living?"

Several biasing elements can be noted here. The attractive moral quality of the expression "every man should accept the responsibility" is contrasted with the harsh words "government should see to it." This difference is accented by introducing the "Americanism" context. Moreover, asking the question in terms of Americanism may cause some respondents to express not their personal preference between (a) and (b) but a judgment as to which accords better with generally accepted views (but perhaps not the respondent's) of Americanism. Finally, the question imposes a fictitious choice by omitting a most important and realistic alternative to (a) and (b), namely: (c) every man should accept the responsibility for getting his own job *under conditions where the government sees that every one has the opportunity to work.* (As asked, the question showed 76% for "a" and 18% for "b"; even at the lowest income level, 58% said "a" against 32% "b". A comparable Fortune Survey question asked: "Do you think the government should provide for all people who have no other means of obtaining a living?" Working people voted 73% "yes", in contrast to the above 18% or 32%.)

"Do you think that the manufacture of atomic bombs should be continued, or that it is necessary to prohibit it for all countries, by international agreement?"

This question, recently used in a Mexican opinion poll, found 66% for prohibiting manufacture of bombs against 26% for continuing. It is a reasonably safe assumption that many of the majority group were expressing a general sentiment in favor of avoiding atomic war. Looked at afterward, however, their responses seem also to be votes to stop current manufacture of bombs—that is, to compel the *United States* to discontinue manufacturing bombs *now*. Therein lies the bias. The question must mislead certain respondents into a simple humanitarian reply while at the same time smuggling in an implication unrecognized and unexamined by most of these people. (Interesting in this connection is the fact that the 66% drops to 51% for professional people; presumably they are more aware of the hidden implications.) The result is obtained by omitting salient features

[2] Stanley L. Payne, "Some Opinion Research Principles Developed Through Studies of Social Medicine," *Public Opinion Quarterly,* Vol. 10, 1946-47, pp. 93-98.

of the issue—that only the U. S. is manufacturing bombs, that serious doubt exists whether completely effective international control can be instituted, and that *when* the manufacture is discontinued is of the essence of the problem. To avoid bias, it is necessary that these points be brought out in a series of questions.

Two further examples are these:

"Would you describe Russia as a peace-loving nation, willing to fight only if she has to defend herself, or as an aggressive nation that would start a war to get something she wants?"

Clearly this dichotomy does not exhaust the possibilities. By omitting intermediate and qualified alternatives and by wording the extremes as they are worded, the question naturally induces large numbers to choose the "aggressive" answer.

"Here is a list of different systems of government operating in the world today. Which form of government do you think most of the people in Russia, Spain, Germany, France, would choose today if they could vote freely for what they wanted?
Form of government that would be chosen:

> Communistic
> Democratic
> Fascist
> Socialistic
> Monarchy
> Don't know

It is hardly necessary to point to the alarming bias involved in offering "democratic" and "socialistic" as alternative responses.

4. *Bias in Interpretation and Reporting:* An interesting recent illustration in the labor opinion field is an article reporting workers' responses to questions on the Taft-Hartley law.[3] A majority of the respondents expressed opposition to the law but a majority also voted *in favor* of each of ten leading provisions of the law when these were asked about separately. The conclusion is drawn that workers have been propagandized into being against the law without their understanding what they are against; they vote *for* the actual content of the law (the ten points) when the "bad" over-all label is removed. The bias in this presentation consists in its offering a simple one-sided interpretation and ignoring two important difficulties. The neglected considerations are these: (a) Single simple questions on separate parts of the law do not, and cannot, approach an adequate summary of the issues. The law is long and complicated. Its provisions would require detailed explanation before the respondent could understand what he is voting on. The ten questions that were asked are deceptively innocent. (b) The results are presented as if they prove that

[3] Claude Robinson, "The Strange Case of the Taft-Hartley Law," *Look*, September 30, 1947, pp. 68-71.

respondents are guilty of self-contradiction, by being *for* the parts of the law but *against* the whole. This overlooks the elementary logical point that different persons can be opposed to the law as a whole for different specific reasons—some being against provision "x", others against "y", "z", etc. The crucial question is how many persons are against the law and yet in favor of *all ten* points asked in the separate items. This could easily be determined and stated in one sentence. It seems fair to interpret its omission as an instance of bias.

Another type of bias in the analysis and reporting of results appears in the use of misleading cross-tabulations. This frequently takes the form of relating social-political opinions to respondents' *education* in a way that indicates, for example, that Republican views on an issue are approved by the better educated people—by implication, because they are better qualified thinkers. A "fair" presentation would have to show the relationship also to *economic* status. The imputed influence of education may disappear when the relation is analyzed within groups homogeneous in respect to economic position.

A similar illustration is that of a survey report that tabulates working people's responses indicative of dissatisfaction, hostility toward employers, etc., according to membership in A. F. of L. unions, CIO unions, independent unions, and no unions. The greater dissatisfaction and antagonism thus associated with the CIO is easily subject to misinterpretation which the report fails adequately to warn against. The correlation may stem in considerable part from differences between CIO members and others in respect to types of occupations, levels of skill, and perhaps age and other factors.

Another form of bias consists of failure to warn readers that the sample of respondents is specially selected or non-representative in a manner that pushes the findings in one direction. This fault occurs notably often in the case where only a fraction of the total sample answers a question, either because others are unable to respond or because replies to preceding questions make this question inappropriate for them. Percentages of those who do answer may be highly deceptive as a consequence, since they constitute a specially informed or specially oriented group. Omission of clear explanations regarding such partial samples easily leads to misinterpretation, whether caused deliberately or through "purposive inadvertence."

Bias may similarly manifest itself in the simple choice of one rather than another method of statistical presentation. If groups are compared by means of an attitude scale, for example, on which each person receives a total score based on a number of questions, the divergence or contrast between groups may be made to appear large by reporting only the difference in *average scores* for the groups. Contrariwise, if the report leans toward minimizing the differences, it neglects averages and instead stresses the percentage of overlapping among individuals in the groups. The same difference in emphasis characterizes alternative ways of reporting correlation figures and other statistical measures. In all such cases, the more adequately the statistical material is reported, the less the danger that it will be misleading. The different summary figures are not *alternatives;* where misunderstanding may occur, *both* averages and percentage overlap (or measures of scatter) are needed.

The remedy for bias is certainly not to be found by denying its existence nor by each of us resolving to abandon his biases. The course of wisdom is rather to take note of the biasing tendencies and influences and to set up conditions and procedures calculated to offset and minimize them. Research bias consists not in *having* inclinations but in letting them affect our research results.

The biases that insinuate themselves into our research express the value systems and inclinations that are integral parts of our personalities. They reflect the cultural influences and conditioning pressures that constitute inescapable features of our lives. For convenience, we shall divide the biases into three classes: personal biases determined by relationship to the client, other personal biases, and "common" or group-membership biases.

Bias that grows out of the client-researcher relation ranges from direct inclination to serve the client's interests in proving a case or securing sales ammunition to subtle deviations in research planning, such as unwittingly accepting his viewpoint or "facts" without sufficient check. Pressures toward this type of bias are particularly marked in advertising and marketing research but they are likewise not too hard to locate in other branches of the opinion research industry. They need to be recognized and guarded against in university studies and in research for non-profit organizations as well as in commercial activities.

It should be noted that the research man who insists that his role is that of a "disinterested" technician and that as such he simply accepts the research assignment as it comes, is especially vulnerable. He easily accepts the client's values and frame of reference along with his problem —and his cash. What he likes to picture as his simple preoccupation with the "facts" turns out to be concern with *particular* facts, selectively viewed from a *particular* standpoint, and seen through *particular* glasses of peculiar and unexamined optical properties. In social research, to be "above" concern for biasing values is to succumb to them.

It must be emphasized that clients are by no means always special pleaders. Very often they want opinion studies to give them unvarnished, authentic knowledge. In this case, the chief danger of bias in the client relationship may arise from an urge to produce unjustifiably positive, definitive results that will impress the client—and lead to further assignments. At times, also, the aim is to come out with conclusions that will win the goodwill of *other* clients.

Quite apart from relations with clients, however, many additional biasing factors are bound to characterize the individual research man and his organization. Each of us has his peculiar, unanalyzed emotional preferences, aversions, blind-spots. For example, strong personal pride and ambitions can readily predispose one to accept or overemphasize questionable evidence that happens to support a view to which he has previously committed himself. Or the research man is swayed by his determination to make his research promote certain policy decisions that he personally favors. Or he over-reaches in efforts to obtain distinctive and spectacular findings. Or he consistently leans in a conservative or a radical direction in his research.

A third set of biases consists of those shared by large groups with which the researcher identifies. Probably the most prominent of these are "class" feelings and national loyalties. But radical and religious prejudices also play a part, as do political party affiliations, regional and occupational ties, and many other group membership influences. No one of us escapes his cultural background, the current climate of opinion, and his present associates. These factors inevitably influence the research we do—the issues we choose to inquire into, the kinds of evidence we consider important, the frames of reference within which we formulate our questions and interpret our results.

Certainly it must not be overlooked that we also have personal ideals, loyalties and group pressures that exert opposing influences to the free play of "biases." Our devotion to "fair play," untrammeled pursuit of scientific truth, maintenance of high professional standards, personal integrity —these contribute powerful forces to hold our biases in check.

The problem is to harness the positive impulses to effective measures of prevention. The constant threat imposed by our biases need not cause despair; the challenge is to achieve impartial results by successfully meeting the threat. In my opinion, this achievement will require much greater attention to the problem than it currently receives.

Morris H. Hansen and Philip M. Hauser

AREA SAMPLING—SOME PRINCIPLES
OF SAMPLE DESIGN

In the following an attempt is made to indicate the types of situations in which one method of sampling is to be preferred over another and to describe the principles on which area sampling is based. In this discussion of sampling methods, we shall consider only the discrepancies between the results obtainable from a complete enumeration of the population under consideration and the estimates made from a sample. Errors of interviewing and other errors arising in survey results that are present in a complete enumeration as much as in a sample enumeration may be either more or less important than sampling errors. We shall confine our remarks here to errors arising because only a sample is covered instead of taking a complete census of a finite population.

The science of sampling design involves: (1) looking at the resources available, the restrictions within which one must work, the mathematical and statistical tools available, the accumulated knowledge of certain characteristics of the populations to be sampled; and (2) putting these together to arrive at the optimum design for the purpose at hand. Ordinarily, there are many alternatives of sample designs, and an understanding of alternative designs and an analysis of their efficiency is necessary if a wise choice is to be made.

The over-all criterion that should be applied in choosing a sampling design is to so design the sample that it will yield the desired information with the reliability required at a minimum cost; or, conversely, that at a fixed cost it will yield estimates of the statistics desired with the maximum reliability possible. Various restrictions and limitations may necessarily be imposed upon the design other than mere cost restrictions. In wartime those restrictions have to do with the number of interviewers with cars and with gasoline rationing, as well as with the ordinary restrictions on time, personnel, etc.

Reprinted from *The Public Opinion Quarterly*, Vol. 9 (Summer 1945), pp. 183-93, by permission of the authors and publisher. (Copyright, 1945, by Princeton University Press.)

A second criterion that a sample design should meet (at least if one is to make important decisions on the basis of the sample results) is that the reliability of the sample results should be susceptible of measurement. Methods of sample selection and estimation are available for which the risk of errors in the sample estimates can be measured and controlled. If such methods are used, as the size of the sample is increased, the expected discrepancies between the estimated value from the sample and the true value (i.e., the value that would be obtained from a complete census) will decrease. With such methods one can know the risk taken that the error due to sampling will exceed a specified amount. This risk (i.e., the risk that the error will exceed any specified amount) can be made as small as desired by taking a sample of adequate size.

An essential feature of such sampling methods is that each element of the population being sampled (housewives, voters, or whoever is being interviewed) has a chance of being included in the sample and, moreover, that that chance or probability is known. The knowledge of the probability of inclusion of various elements of the population makes it possible to apply appropriate weights to the sample results so as to yield "consistent" or "unbiased" estimates, or other estimates for which the risk of error can be measured and controlled.[1]

On the assumption that the above criteria should govern in the selection of a sample design, we are ready to consider the relative merits of the "quota" method, which is commonly used in opinion and market surveys, and the "area sampling" method.

The quota method in its essence involves: (1) the choice of selected characteristics of the population to be sampled, which are used as "controls"; (2) the determination of the proportion of the population possessing the characteristics selected as "controls"; and (3) the fixing of quotas for enumerators who select respondents so that the population interviewed contains the proportion of each class as determined in (2).

These specifications cannot provide sample estimates for which the risk of error can be measured because they do not provide for the selection of persons in a way that permits knowing the probabilities of selection. Errors in the setting of quotas may introduce unknown differences in the probabilities of selection of persons for inclusion in the sample. Moreover, because of the latitude permitted the enumerator in selection of respondents, it is less probable, for example, that the sample will include a housewife without children who works away from home than a woman with children who does her own housework, even though each may be in

---

[1] Here the words "consistent" and "unbiased" are used technically, and have a mathematical definition. See J. Neyman, "Lectures and Conferences on Mathematical Statistics," *Graduate School of the U.S. Department of Agriculture*, Washington 25, D.C., 1938, p. 131; and R. A. Fisher, "Statistical Methods for Research Workers," 6th edition, p. 12, *Oliver and Boyd* (1936), Edinburgh.

the same "control" group. Because the probabilities of inclusion in the sample of various classes of elements are unknown, the estimates frequently made of sampling error of quota sample results, supposedly based on sampling theory, usually are erroneous. A fuller treatment of the difficulties and limitations of the widely known and used quota method is given elsewhere.[2]

Area sampling eliminates dependence on the assignment of quotas that may be more or less seriously in error, and does not permit the interviewer discretion in the choice of the individuals to be included in the sample. With appropriate methods of designating areas for coverage in the sample, the probabilities of inclusion of the various elements of the population are known, and consequently the reliability of results from the sample can be measured and controlled. Area sampling, of course, is not the only method that produces such results, but it is frequently an effective method.

To illustrate how and why area sampling works, suppose we are interested in sampling for certain characteristics of the population in a city. For example, we may want to know the total number of persons in certain broad occupational groups, and the number within each of these occupational groups who have a particular opinion, read a specified magazine, or are in a certain income class.

To estimate the total number of persons having the various characteristics mentioned above, we might proceed by first making an up-to-date list containing the name of every person, or, at considerably less expense, identifying every address or household, in the area to be surveyed, and then selecting a sample from this listing. Through taking a random sample from such listings of individuals or of households (interviewing all persons within the selected households if households are sampled), we could, with an adequate size of sample, obtain an excellent cross-section of the people in the city for any problem. This procedure would lead to highly reliable sample results, but frequently it is not practical for a number of reasons—the principal one being that preparing a listing would cost too much. Moreover, even where a complete pre-listing is already available, it may be too costly to interview the widely scattered sample that would be obtained by sampling individuals (or households) at random from such a listing. One method of getting a reduction in cost over sampling individuals from a pre-listing is to use an area sampling method in which the individuals interviewed are clustered into a selected set of sample areas.

In "area sampling" the entire area in which the population to be

    [2] Philip M. Hauser and Morris H. Hansen, "On Sampling in Market Surveys," *The Journal of Marketing,* July 1944; and Alfred N. Watson, "Measuring the New Market," *Printers' Ink,* June 2, 1944, vol. 207, No. 9, pp. 17-20.

covered is located is subdivided into smaller areas, and each individual in the population is associated with one and only one such small area— for example, the particular small area in which he resides. Neither the names nor numbers of persons residing in the areas need be known in advance. A sample of these small areas is drawn, and all or a sub-sample of the population residing in the selected areas is covered in the survey.

A simple illustration will show that if a complete list of areas is available and a random selection of a sample of areas is made, and if the population of these sample areas is completely enumerated, then the chances (or probabilities) of being included are the same for each individual in the population. Moreover, on the average, the population surveyed within such a sample will reveal precisely the characteristics of the entire population from which the sample was drawn. A sample can be made as reliable a cross-section as desired, for any characteristics whatever, by merely increasing the size of the sample. Thus, if the population is changing in character, a random cross-section of small areas will reveal those shifts.

Suppose, for illustration, that we wish to draw a sample out of a universe of five blocks, and that everyone living in the selected blocks will be interviewed. We shall assume certain values for each block for the total number of votes for a specified candidate, as is shown below, although the illustration will work in the same way whatever values are assumed for the total vote or for any other characteristic.

Block No.	Votes for a Specified Candidate
1	4
2	6
3	2
4	6
5	1
Total	19

Each of the possible samples that will be obtained in drawing at random a sample of two blocks is listed below, together with the estimated total number of votes for the specified candidates from each sample. In unrestricted random sampling of blocks each of these possible samples will have the same probability of being selected. The estimated totals shown are obtained by computing the average number per block from the sample, and multiplying this sample average by the known total number of blocks in the population. The results for each possible sample are as follows:

Sample Consisting of Blocks	Total Votes for the Specified Candidate Enumerated in the Sample	Estimated Total Votes for the Specified Candidate
1 and 2	10	25.0
1 and 3	6	15.0
1 and 4	10	25.0
1 and 5	5	12.5
2 and 3	8	20.0
2 and 4	12	30.0
2 and 5	7	17.5
3 and 4	7	20.0
3 and 5	3	7.5
4 and 5	7	17.5
Total		190.00
Average estimate		19.00
Standard deviation of sample estimates		6.25

Notice, first, that each block appears in four out of ten possible samples of two that can be drawn. Therefore, the probability that an individual living in Block 1 will be included in the sample is .4, and the same is true of an individual living in any one of the other blocks, even though the number of persons in each block may be different. Note, also, that on the average, the estimates from the samples of voters for the specified candidate agree exactly with the actual number of votes for the specified candidate in this population. Furthermore, it is to be observed that the standard deviation of all possible estimates from the sample is equal to 6.25, which is exactly what is given by the formula for the average error of a sample of two blocks, based on statistical theory.[3]

Of course in any real problem the number of blocks will be considerably larger, more efficient methods of estimation may be available, and the sampling variance formula may be considerably more complicated. However, the above example will suffice to illustrate that with area sampling the probabilities of an individual being drawn into the sample can be fixed in advance of the actual enumeration, and that when this is so, and appropriate estimating procedures are used, it is possible to measure the average or standard error of the sample estimate.

The formula for the standard error shows that as the size of the sample increases, the standard deviation of the sample estimate decreases. This fact takes on more meaning for more realistic populations where the number of blocks in the population is very large. Under such circumstances,

[3] The standard error of the estimate from the sample, $\sigma_{\bar{x}}^1$, is equal to $\sigma \, M \, \sqrt{\dfrac{M - m}{(M - 1)m}}$, where σ is the standard deviation between the 5 original blocks of the characteristic being estimated, M is the total number of blocks in the population, and m is the number of blocks included in the sample.

the average error of a sample may be made very small by drawing a fairly large number of blocks, even though the number in the sample consists of a very small proportion of the blocks in the population. We have over-simplified the case here to simplify the illustration, but the principles are just as applicable to more complicated cases.

It is to be emphasized that many modifications in the area method may be introduced that would make effective use of available information concerning the areas being sampled. A very important variation in design is the introduction of a method of subsampling, in which two or more levels of sampling are used. For example, a national population sample may involve the selection of a sample of fairly large areas such as cities or counties, and then of a sample of smaller areas within each; or a sample for a city may involve the selection of a sample of blocks, and the subsampling of addresses or dwelling units from the selected blocks. How-ever, if the subsampling approach is to conform with the criteria of good sampling outlined earlier in this paper, purposive or judgment methods of selecting the units to be included in the sample are excluded.[4]

In evaluating the alternative designs that are possible, many statistical or mathematical tools are available for guiding one to the selection of an efficient method.[5] To illustrate, suppose one is considering taking a sample of blocks in a city, and then preparing a listing of all of the people in the sampled blocks and interviewing every k-th individual on the list. The reliability of the final estimate from such a sample will depend both upon the number of blocks in the sample and the average number of interviews within each block. It is fairly obvious that if all persons were interviewed within, say twenty selected blocks, the sample result might be highly erratic, depending on the particular twenty blocks in the sample. However, if one-tenth of the persons were interviewed in each of 200 blocks, a much better cross section of the city would be obtained and a more reliable sample estimate could be made with the same number of interviews. But

[4] For an illustration of the application of an area subsampling design to obtain a national sample see "The Labor Force Bulletin," No. 5, *Bureau of the Census*, Washington, November 1944.

[5] Morris H. Hansen and William N. Hurwitz, "A New Sample of the Population," *Bureau of the Census*, Washington, Sept. 1944; also, "On the Theory of Sampling from Finite Populations," *Annals of Mathematical Statistics*, vol. XIV (1943), pp. 333-362; and "Relative Efficiencies of Various Sampling Units in Population Inquiries," *Journal American Statistical Association*, vol. 37 (1942), pp. 89-94. J. Neyman, "On the Two Different Aspects of the Representative Method; a Method of Stratified Sampling and the Method of Purposive Selection," *Journal Royal Statistical Society*, New Series, vol. 97 (1934), pp. 558-606; also, "Contribution to the Theory of Sampling Human Populations," *Journal American Statistical Association*, vol. 35 (1938), pp. 101-116. W. G. Cochran, "The Use of Analysis of Variance in Enumeration by Sampling," *Journal American Statistical Association*, vol. 34 (1939), pp. 492-510; also, "Sampling Theory when the Sampling Units are of Unequal Sizes," *Journal American Statistical Association*, vol. 37 (1942) pp. 199-212. P. C. Mahalanobis, "A Sample Survey of the Acreage under Jute in Bengal," *Sankhya*, vol. 4 (1940), pp. 511-530.

if each of 200 blocks must be completely listed before selecting the persons for interview, and if the sample is scattered over 200 instead of twenty blocks, the cost of the survey is increased both by the cost of pre-listing and of more travel. Statistical theory is available to aid in the resolution of this conflict between cost and sampling reliability, and to guide one to an efficient design for a given cost.

The efficiency of area sampling can be increased through the effective use of good maps and of the available data for small areas.[6] For reasonably large-scale survey operations, it may pay to invest in maps which make possible the clear delineation of very small clusters of households and thereby eliminate or reduce the amount of pre-listing necessary. However, if detailed maps for defining very small areas are not available and it is necessary to pre-list whole blocks or moderately large selected rural areas, the cost of pre-listing need not be particularly significant where surveys are to be taken repetitively, since the cost of designating a sample of areas and of listing the dwelling units within the sample areas can be spread over a considerable number of surveys. In some Census experiences in which pre-listing is used and subsamples are drawn from these listings for repetitive surveys, the cost over a year's time of pre-listing actually amounts to less than ten percent of the total survey cost.

It has sometimes been stated that area sampling methods are practicable for the government with mass surveys and extensive resources but are not adaptable to private research organizations on a limited budget. It is clear from the above, that at least the cost of actually selecting the sample need not be a highly significant factor in the total cost of such surveys—and that if this method is more costly than other less rigorous methods it is primarily because of the cost of interviewing within the designated sample households rather than because of the cost of locating the households in which interviews are to be made. Actually, the interviewing cost may be considerably affected by the necessity for call-backs or other steps taken to insure that the pre-designated person or household is interviewed; and procedures are available for making call-backs on only a sample of those not at home on first visit that will yield unbiased sample results.[7] It is ordinarily true, however, that in practice no reasonable number of call-backs can insure an interview with *all* persons designated for interview— and that a small bias may necessarily remain in the estimate due to the non-interviews that remain. An important distinction between area sam-

[6] For discussion of available data for small areas, and of detailed maps see Morris H. Hansen and W. Edwards Deming, "On Some Census Aids to Sampling," *Journal American Statistical Association*, vol. 38 (1943), pp. 353-357; and Morris H. Hansen, "Census to Sample Population Growth," *Domestic Commerce*, vol. 32, No. 11 (1944), p. 6.

[7] "Working Plan for Annual Census of Lumber Produced in 1943" published by the *Forest Service of the Department of Agriculture* in the fall of 1943. William N. Hurwitz extended the theory of double sampling to cover this problem.

pling methods and quota sampling methods lies in the treatment of non-interviews. The quota method, by ignoring the problem, has all of the biases without pointing up the magnitude of this source of error. The area method points up this source of error and makes it possible to correct for it (through calling back to interview all or a sample of the original non-interviews) if the proportion of non-interviews is high. The maximum error attributable to this factor can be kept very small and the maximum bounds of error coming from this cause can be measured.

There should be little question that the efficiency of a sample design should be evaluated in terms of *reliability of results* obtained per dollar of cost, *rather than in terms of the number of interviews* obtained per dollar. Through the use of the principles of sampling described or referred to above, one is aided in the selection of a sampling method which produces results of maximum reliability per dollar expended. However, these principles lead only to choices between alternative designs that conform with the criteria of good sampling, we have assumed. Therefore, they provide a guide only in choosing between those designs for which it is possible to measure the expected sampling error and the sources of the contribution to it, and thus, through proper adjustment in design, to minimize the sampling error per dollar expended.

Since statistical theory is not available for measuring the reliability of sample results obtained by the quota method, this method is automatically excluded from consideration if the criteria of sample design outlined above are to be followed. Thus, although the facts could not be established, it could happen that a quota sampling method would in a particular situation yield more reliable results per dollar than the optimum method chosen through the application of the criteria and sampling theory we have considered. How, then is one to know which to use? A possible answer to this question is the following. If it is important that results of specified reliability be obtained, and if there is a fairly heavy loss involved if the wrong action or decision is taken as a consequence of having depended on results that actually turn out to have larger errors than are considered tolerable, then quota sampling cannot safely be employed, and area sampling or some other method for which the risk of error can be controlled should be used. On the other hand, if conditions are such that only fairly rough estimates are required from the sample, and important decisions do not hinge on the result, then only a small sample is required, or the price to be paid for using a sample whose accuracy can be measured may not be justified. Under these conditions it may be that the biases of the quota method (or of the area method used without call-backs, or of other low-cost methods) will be considerably less important than the errors resulting from the small size of the sample, and thus such methods may produce results of sufficient reliability more economically than would more rigorous alternative methods. It would, of course, be wasteful to pay for assurance of greater reliability in the results than is necessary. However, it appears reasonable to believe that in most instances in which a fairly precise estimate is desired and for which, therefore, a fairly large sample is used, that the possible biases of quota sampling may be sufficiently serious as to make that method considerably less efficient in terms of reliability of results per dollar than the appropriate area sampling methods.

We believe that the question of what criteria should be applied in determining the most appropriate sampling method for a specific purpose is deserving of more extensive attention and consideration than it has yet received.

Paul F. Lazarsfeld

THE CONTROVERSY OVER DETAILED INTERVIEWS—
AN ,OFFER FOR NEGOTIATION

If two people vigorously disagree on whether something is blue or green, the chances are that the object is composed of both colors and that for some reason the two contestants are either unable or unwilling to see more than the one. If in methodological discussions, competent workers assume vehemently opposite positions, it is generally a good time for someone to enter the scene and suggest that the parties are both right and wrong.

Two articles in the PUBLIC OPINION QUARTERLY (Summer, 1943) provide one of the many indications that such a situation has come about in the public opinion field. A representative of the Division of Program Surveys in the Department of Agriculture reports on large-scale research work, the core of which is an interviewing technique "intended to draw full intensive discussions" and using "various non-directive means of stimulating full discussion in the interviewing situation."[1] Preceding this report is an article by a well-known psychologist who dubs this technique "depth interview" and describes it in rather uncomplimentary terms. One of his conclusions is that "there is little or no evidence to support the tacit assumption that the so-called depth interview yields more valid responses from people than do other types."[2] For him, simple "yes-no" questions, used judiciously, are sufficient.

The matter is important from more than a scientific point of view. Applied social research is a new venture. Only yesterday did the government begin large-scale studies in public opinion. The market and consumer studies which are now finding acceptance in many industries are likewise all of recent date. Managers in business as well as in public ad-

Reprinted with editorial adaptations from *The Public Opinion Quarterly,* Vol. 8 (Spring 1944), pp. 38-60, by permission of the author and publisher. (Copyright, 1944, by Princeton University Press.)

[1] Hans E. Skott, "Attitude Research in the Department of Agriculture," *Public Opinion Quarterly,* 1943, 7, 280-292.

[2] Henry C. Link, "An Experiment in Depth Interviewing," *Public Opinion Quarterly,* 1943, 7, 267-279.

ministration are faced with sharply contending factions among research professionals. Should they succumb to skepticism or discouragement and fail to give this new branch of the social sciences the opportunity to prove itself, then development might be seriously retarded. It therefore seems justified to present the problem to a larger public with an earnest effort toward impartiality.

Employing a neutral terminology, we shall allude to our subject as the "open-ended interview." The term serves to describe a crucial aspect of this type of interviewing—the fact that "open-ended interviews" do not set fixed answers in terms of which a respondent must reply. Eventually a more animated expression may be desirable. (To save space we shall abbreviate the term and refer to it hereafter as OI.) Rather than asking for a definition it would be better if the reader visualizes the situation in which an OI occurs. In the interview situation the interviewer by an appropriate introduction attempts to establish the best possible rapport between himself and the respondent because he is aware that he may have to interview the respondent an hour or longer. He then proceeds to ask one of the ten or fifteen questions which have been assigned to him by the central office. Sometimes the respondent himself immediately plunges into great detail, and the interviewer simply permits him to continue. If the first answer is brief, however, the interviewer is instructed to "probe." There are quite a number of devices for eliciting detailed, free response. Mere silence will sometimes induce the respondent to elaborate. Or, the interviewer may just repeat the respondent's own words with an appropriate inflection. Asking for examples will often prove helpful. Then again questions such as the following are used: "How did you happen to notice it? What makes you think so? How did you feel about it before? Do most of your friends have the same opinion?" The trained OI field worker has the goal of his inquiry clearly imprinted in his mind, but he adapts his inquiry to the concrete situation between the interviewee and himself.

If properly conducted, such an OI will result in a detailed document which covers the whole area under investigation, including the interviewer's observations of the respondent's reactions and background.

The OI is suggested by its proponents in opposition to what one might term the "straight poll question." The latter gives the respondent the occasion to answer only "Yes," "No," "Don't know," or to make a choice among a small number of listed possible answers. Between these two extremes there are, of course, several steps. Actually there is hardly a poll where there is not some freedom left for the respondent to express himself in his own way. It is not necessary here to discuss where the straight poll question ends and the OI begins. For all practical purposes the distinction is clear enough.

The Six Main Functions of the OI Technique

1. *Clarifying the meaning of a respondent's answer:* Before asking him whether war profits should be limited, we have to find out what the respondent thinks the word "profit" means. Some people talk of the total income of a company as profit, others believe it is the difference between wholesale and retail prices, still others are of the opinion that war profits are the difference between pre-war and war earnings. By discussing the general subject matter with him we are very likely to obtain a fairly clear picture of what would be equivalent to his *private definition* of these terms. One frequently underestimates the number of terms which seem obvious to the interviewer but which are ambiguous or even unknown to the lower educated section of the population.

In other cases it is not so much the meaning of words as the *implication of an opinion* which has to be clarified. If a respondent is in favor of reducing taxes, does he know that as a result many government services will have to be reduced? If he is in favor of free speech, does he realize that such freedom must also pertain to people who may express opinions that are very distasteful to him?

If respondents are asked to voice their thoughts on a course of action, it is important to know against what *alternative possibilities* they had weighed their choice. A respondent is for the continuation of the Dies Committee: has he weighed that against the possibility that the Department of Justice can adequately handle the problem of subversive activities, or did he feel that if the Dies Committee does not do so, no one else will? Another respondent is for government regulation of business: does he prefer this to completely free enterprise, or has he considered the different ways by which an individual business man be regulated through his own trade organizations?

Finally, the OI permits a respondent to clarify his opinion by introducing *qualifications*. He is in favor of rationing if it is administered fairly for everyone. He is in favor of married women getting defense jobs if it has been made sure that there are no unemployed men left. The respondent might not volunteer such qualifications if the interview is a too hurried one.

2. *Singling out the decisive aspects of an opinion:* If we deal with attitudes toward rather complex objects, we often want to know the *decisive aspects* by which a respondent is guided. Take the opinion on *candidates* for public office. At this moment, for example, the Republicans in some mid-western states prefer Dewey to Willkie as Presidential nominee. What does Dewey stand for in the eyes of these people? Party Loyalty? Isolationism? Administrative ability? Gang-busting? Here again the OI would proceed in characteristic fashion. What has the respondent heard

about the two candidates? What does he think would happen if Dewey were to become President? And so on. In the end we should be able to distinguish groups for which Dewey means quite different things, and fruitful statistical comparisons on a number of social characteristics could be carried through.

Similar possibilities can come up when people are called upon to judge *concrete situations.* They do or do not like the working conditions in their plants. If the answer is in the negative, what features do they especially dislike? In order to get a reasonable idea of people's complaints a rather detailed discussion is necessary; the OI is a good device for this purpose. Other examples of such procedure can easily be found: to what does the respondent attribute rising prices? Or the increase in juvenile delinquency?

Here belong also some recent efforts in the field of *communications* research. People like or dislike a film or a radio program. Through detailed discussions it is possible to bring out quite clearly which elements in the production make for the audience's reaction.[3]

The singling out of decisive aspects also pertains to *issues.* If respondents are against sending lend-lease supplies to Russia, it is important to know what about such a policy they dislike. Do they disapprove of Russian communism, or do they think that the Russians do not need the supplies, or do they feel that other parts of the world war panorama are more important? Here, again, the OI would not only ask for an opinion on the basic issues but would probe the respondents for further details.

3. *What has influenced an opinion:* If people approve of an issue or vote for a candidate (or buy a product), it is useful to divide the determining factors of such action into three main groups: the *decisive features* of the object in question, which account for its being chosen; the *predispositions* of the respondents, which make them act one way or another; and the *influences which are brought to bear upon them,* especially those which mediate between them and the object of their choice.[5] The use of the OI to investigate the first group has just been discussed. The quest for predispositions (attitude, motives) will be dealt with under points four and five. We now consider the use of the OI in the search for *influences.*

The typical research situation here is one wherein we try to assess the importance of a certain event. Let us turn, for example, to people who

[3] P. F. Lazarsfeld and R. K. Merton, "Studies in Radio and Film Propaganda," *Transactions of the New York Academy of Sciences,* Series II, 1943, 6, No. 2, 58-79.

[4] It should be emphasized that the question "why" is useful also for the other purposes which will be discussed in the remaining four points. This is easily understood if one considers that the word has hardly any meaning in itself. It is about equivalent to saying that the respondent should talk some more. "Why" is a good start, but it seldom leads to a constructive end if it is not followed by specific questions directed toward what the interviewer really wants to know.

[5] Paul Lazarsfeld, "The Art of Asking Why," *National Marketing Review,* 1, 1935, 32-43.

bought bonds after listening to Kate Smith or who started storing potatoes after a government campaign to this effect had been started or who improved their production records after a system of music-while-you-work had been introduced in a plant. A well-conducted OI should provide enough information so that the causal role of the exposure can be appraised. The rules for such interviews have been rather well worked out.[6]

4. *Determining complex attitude patterns:* A fourth group of applications comes into play when we turn to the *classification of rather complex attitude patterns*. If we want to ascertain how active people are in their war participation or how disturbed they are by current food shortages, the OI actually discusses such subject matters with the respondents, getting their recent experiences and reactions. The purpose is to make an adequate classification of the material so obtained. Further assumptions come easily to mind. People can be classified according to how satisfied they are with local handling of the draft situation, according to the ways they adjust to the lack of gasoline, according to their satisfaction or dissatisfaction with the amount of information they get on the war, etc. This procedure is singularly characteristic of Rensis Likert's work in the Department of Agriculture.[7]

If it is used to assess the extent to which respondents are concerned with a certain problem and how intensely they feel about it, this approach assumes special importance. Two respondents might give the same answer to a simple opinion poll question. For the one, however, it is an important issue on which he has spent much thought, whereas the other may have formed his opinion spontaneously as the poll investigator asked him about it. The possible perfunctory nature of replies to public opinion polls has been the object of much criticism. Those who feel strongly in favor of the OI emphasize that right at this point such a danger is obviated—the danger that poll results will be misleading because they do not take into account intensity of feeling or amount of concern.

This role of the OI does not necessarily terminate with a one-dimensional rating scale of, say, intensity of feeling. The OI is suitable for more complex ratings as well. In a study of people's reactions to changes in food habits, sponsored by the National Research Council, the interviewers were instructed to "watch carefully for all offhand comments to one of the following frames of reference: Money, Health, Taste, Status."[8] The procedure

---

[6] Paul Lazarsfeld, "Evaluating the Effectiveness of Advertising by Direct Interviews," *Journal of Consulting Psychology,* July-August, 1941.

[7] Likert's work is mainly done for Government agencies and therefore cannot be quoted at the present time. The present paper owes much to discussions with him and some of his associates, especially Bill Gold. (Editor's note: Since the original publication of this article a number of articles on the methodology of this research group have been published, for example, see Maccoby, E. & Holt, R., "How Surveys Are Made," in this volume.)

[8] Kurt Lewin, "Forces Behind Food Habits and Methods of Change," *The Problem of Changing Food Habits,* Bulletin of the National Research Council, Number 108, October 1943.

was to talk with people about current food shortages, the adjustments they had made, and the points at which they experienced difficulties. From their discussion it was possible to classify them into four groups according to which of the four contexts they spontaneously stressed. The study found, for example, that high-income groups refer to health twice as often as money, whereas in low-income groups money is the frame of reference three times more frequently than is health.

Finally we have what is known as the "gratification study." In an analysis of the gratification people get from the Professor Quiz programs, for example, a variety of appeals could be distinguished. Some listeners are very much intrigued by the competitive element of the contest; others like to test their own knowledge; still others hope to learn something from the questions posed on the program.[9] We could not expect the untrained respondent to explain clearly the psychological complexities of his interest or his reaction. It is not even likely that he would classify himself accurately if we let him choose among different possibilities. Again the OI is needed to provide the necessary information for the trained analyst. Its practical use lies in the following direction: If we know what attitudes are statistically dominant we can either strengthen the "appeal" elements in the program which are likely to get an enlarged audience; or we can try to change these attitudes if, for some ulterior reason, we consider the prevailing distribution unsatisfactory.

Such studies have also been made in the public opinion field; for example, in analyzing the gratification people get out of writing letters to senators.[10]

5. *Motivational interpretations:* Ratings, attitude types, and gratification lists are only the beginning of a conceptual line which ends in studies based on *broad motivational interpretations.* We cannot hope here to present systematically the ways in which psychologists distinguish between the different kinds of "drives" according to their range, depth, or the specificity of their relations to the world of objects.[11] The picture would not be complete, nevertheless, if we were to omit a mention of the use of the OI technique for the purpose of understanding people's reactions in such conceptual contexts.

The OI collects a variety of impressions, experiences and sidelines which the respondent offers when he is asked to discuss a given topic. The man who does the study then makes a kind of psychological construction. He creates a picture of some basic motivation of which all these details are, so to speak, manifestations.

---

[9] Herta Herzog, "On Borrowed Experience," *Studies in Philosophy and Social Science,* 1941.

[10] R. Wyant and H. Herzog, "Voting Via the Senate Mailbag," this *Quarterly,* 1941, 5, 590-624.

[11] Gordon W. Allport, "Attitudes," *Handbook of Social Psychology* (ed. C. Murchison), Worcester: Clark University Press, 1935, 798-844.

Consider an example. In studying certain groups of unemployed one makes a variety of observations: they walk slowly, they lose interest in public affairs, do not keep track of their time, express opinions only with hesitation, stop looking for jobs—in short, they can best be understood as discouraged, resigned beings whose psychological living space has been severely contracted. On the basis of this conceptualization we would not expect them, e.g., to join revolutionary movements which require initiative. If, on the other hand, we are interested in retaining whatever morale they do have left, we would reject the idea of a straight dole in favor of work relief which would keep them psychologically "on the go."

There is only a rather short step from this example to the kind of OI studies which we want to discuss. For a number of reasons most of them have been done in the field of advertising.

People who talk about their shoe purchases often mention how embarrassing it is to expose one's feet in stockings, how one is virtually a prisoner in the hands of the salesman, etc. They are also likely to point out that such-and-such a salesman was friendly, or that they do like stores where the customers are not seated too near each other. The study director finally forms the hypothesis that the shoe-buying situation is one likely to evoke a feeling of inferiority. To alleviate this feeling and thus lead to a larger and more satisfied patronage, a number of obvious suggestions can be made for the training of salesmen and the arrangement of the store.

To discuss this use of OI's in a short space is impossible, especially since its logic has not yet been thought through very well. The social scientist who tries to clarify such analysis faces a conflict between two goals to which he is equally devoted. On the one hand, these interpretations serve to integrate a host of details as well as make us aware of new ones which we might otherwise overlook; often they are very brilliant. On the other hand, they violate our need for verification because by their very nature they can never be proved but only made plausible. It is no coincidence that in the two examples given above we have added to each interpretation some practical advice derived from it. What such motivational analysis does is to see past experiences as parts of some psychological drive which can be reactivated by related material, be it propaganda or institutional devices.[12]

6. *Clarifying statistical relationships:* In the five areas outlined so far the OI was the point of departure for all subsequent analysis. Now finally we have to deal with studies where statistical results are available and where the OI serves to *interpret and refine statistical inter-relationships.* The procedure could be called the analysis of deviate cases.

When, for instance, the panic was studied which followed the famous broadcast on the "Invasion From Mars," it was found that people on a lower educational level were most likely to believe in the occurrence of the great

[12] Rhoda Metraux, "Qualitative Attitude Analysis—A Technique for the Study of Verbal Behavior," *The Problem of Changing Food Habits,* Bulletin of the National Research Council, No. 108, October 1943.

catastrophe.[13] Yet some lower-educated people were not frightened at all. When these deviate cases were subject to an OI, many turned out to be mechanics or people who had mechanical hobbies; they were accustomed to checking up on things, a habit the "regular" people had acquired by a successful formal education. On the other hand, quite a number of well-educated people were frightened. When an OI was made with them, the following was sometimes found: During the broadcast they had been in special social situations where it was not clear who should take the initiative of checking up; the lack of social structure impeded purposeful action, and everyone got panicky.

Another example can be taken from unemployment studies. In general it is found that the more amicable the relations in a family prior to the depression, the more firmly would the family stand the impact of unemployment. Again we can inspect deviate cases. A couple fights constantly before the depression, but after the husband becomes unemployed, they get along better. A detailed interview reveals the probability that here the husband wanted to be submissive and the wife dominant, but folkways prevented them from accepting this inverse role. Unemployment, then, enforces a social situation here which is psychologically adequate. Or, a good marriage breaks down surprisingly quickly as a result of the husband's unemployment. A specification of the case shows that the man's sexual habits are rather vulnerable and become disorganized under the blow of the loss of his job.[14]

The general pattern of these studies proceeds from an empirical correlation which is usually not very high. We take cases which do not follow the majority pattern and try to gain an impression or to account for their irregularity. The political scientist is used to such procedure.[15] He knows, for instance, that the more poor people and Catholics live in a given precinct of a big city, the more Democratic votes he can expect. But here is a precinct which qualifies on both scores, and still it went Republican. What accounts for this deviation? Is the Democratic machine inefficient? Has a special local grievance developed? Was there a recent influx of people with different political tradition? This is quite analogous to what we are trying to do when we are faced with individual cases which went statistically out of line. With the help of the OI we try to discover new factors which, if properly introduced, would improve our multiple correlation.

---

[13] Hadley Cantril, Herta Herzog, and Hazel Gaudet, *Invasion from Mars*. Princeton: Princeton University Press, 1939.

[14] Mirra Komarovsky, *The Unemployed Man and His Family*. New York: Institute of Social Research, 1940.

[15] Harold F. Gosnell, *Getting out the Vote*. Chicago: Chicago University Press, 1927.

The Issue Becomes a Problem

The six areas just outlined could be looked at in two ways. For one, they represent desirable goals for public opinion research. We need more detailed knowledge as to what the answers of our respondents mean, on what specific points their opinions are based, in what larger motivational contexts they belong, etc. At the same time, the different applications of the OI also imply criticism to the effect that one straight poll question will hardly ever reach any of these goals successfully.

One can agree with this criticism without concluding that the OI technique is the only remedy. If this paper were written for a psychological journal, for instance, the course of our discussion from here on would be prescribed. We should have to compare results obtained by straight poll questions with those collected by OI's and decide which are preferable according to some adequate criteria. The present analysis, however, falls under the heading of "Research Policy." The research administrator has to make decisions as to the most desirable procedures long before we have provided all the necessary data on the comparative merits of different research methods.

What line of argument would one take in such a situation? No one can close his eyes to the shortcomings of many of the current opinion-poll practices. Having begun with the simple problem of predicting elections, they use, very often, a greatly oversimplified approach for the gauging of attitudes toward complex issues. We shall also agree that a well-conducted OI gives us a fascinating wealth of information on the attitude of a single respondent. When it comes to the statistical analysis of many OI's, the matter is already not so simple. It is in the nature of this technique that just the most valuable details of one OI become difficult to compare with the answers obtained in another interview. It can safely be said that the proponents of the OI technique have made much more progress in the conduct of the interviews than in their statistical analysis.

But even if the OI technique were not to have methodological troubles of its own, it would still be open to one very serious objection. It is necessarily an expensive and slow procedure and, as a result, studies which are made for practical purposes will always be based on a small number of cases. It is inconceivable at this moment that an agency would have the resources or the time to make many thousands of OI's on one subject. This is a decisive drawback. True, a surprisingly small number of cases is needed for a fairly correct estimate of how many Republicans there are in a community or how many people save their fat and grease. But do we want to stop here? Don't we want to know in which social groups some of those activities are more frequent than in others? Aren't we trying to account for the reasons why some people do a thing and others do not? And how can this be done except by careful cross-tabulation of one part of our data against other parts? And for this, a much larger number of cases is needed.

In other words, the OI technique, even if it were perfect in itself, places us in a dilemma. By laying all the stress on the detailed description of the single respondent's attitude, it forces us into relatively small numbers of interviews. This in turn handicaps another important progress in public opinion research: the progress which consists of comparing carefully the distribution of opinions in different sub-groups of the population and relating a given opinion to the personal characteristics and to other attitudes of the respondent.

From the standpoint of research policy, therefore, which is the standpoint taken in this paper, the whole problem comes to this. Is there not some way to use all the good ideas which the proponents of the OI technique have and still to develop methods which are more objective, more manageable on a mass basis—which, in short, give us sufficient material to do a thorough analysis of the factors which make for a given distribution of public opinion?

Under these aspects we shall go once more through the six areas discussed above. In each case we shall look for procedures which combine the administrative advantages of the straight poll question with the psychological advantages of the OI. Quite frankly we want to "eat our cake and have it, too." All folklore notwithstanding, research progress consists in the art of doing things which at first seem incompatible. As we proceed, it will turn out that these compromise techniques do not make the OI superfluous but give it a new and, as we feel, more valuable place in the whole scheme of public opinion research.

To bring out more clearly our trend of thought, we begin with a little scheme. To the left we have our six areas; to the right we have short names for the procedures which would overcome some of the shortcomings of the straight poll question and still be more formalized and manageable on a mass basis than the OI.

Current Applications of the OI Techniques	*Possible Objective Alternatives for the OI*
1. Clarifying the meaning of a respondent's answer	1. Interlocking system of poll questions
2. Singling out the decisive aspects of an opinion	2. Check lists
3. Discerning influences	3. None
4. Determining complex attitude patterns	4. Scales and typologies
5. Interpreting motivation	5. Projective tests
6. Clarifying statistical relationships	6. None

It is to the short description and evaluation of the right side of the scheme that we now turn.

1. *Clarifying meaning by the use of interlocking poll questions:* In the first area we dealt with the clarification of the respondent's opinion. Did he know the significance of what he was talking about? In the course of an OI, by making the respondent elaborate in more detail, we will find out. But after all, the number of possible variations is not so great; it is often possible to get by explicit questions all the material we can use for comparative analysis of many interview returns.

Consider the following two cases. Studenski has pointed out that when people are asked whether they want lower taxes, most of them will say "yes."[16] After having asked this general question, however, he then asked a series of specific questions on whether the government should discontinue relief, work projects, expenses for national defense, expenses for schools, police, etc. Respondents who wanted taxes reduced but services maintained had obviously, to say the least, an inconsistent attitude toward the problem.[17] In a different context, Kornhauser has pointed out the shortcomings of the question: Should Congress pass a law forbidding strikes in war industries or should war workers have the right to go on strike? Obviously there are other devices, such as an improved arbitration system or the endowment of union leaders with some semi-public power to keep their members from striking. By offering a whole set of such alternatives it is undoubtedly possible to get a much clearer picture of the respondent's real attitude.

In this and many similar examples the technique used consists of an *interlocking system of poll questions,* each of which is very simple but which through proper cross-tabulation permits the separation of respondents according to the extent to which they see the implications of their opinion.

Although we cannot go into details here, we have studied dozens of pertinent cases and are satisfied that for any given topic it is always possible to find an appropriate system of interlocking questions. The right procedure consists of beginning the study with a considerable number of very detailed OI's. These should come from different parts of the country and should serve to develop the structure of the problem. Experience

[16] Paul Studenski, "How Polls Can Mislead," *Harpers Magazine,* December 1939.

[17] This is the technique which Henry Link used in a more recent study ("An Experiment in Depth Interviewing," this *Quarterly,* 1943, 7, 267-279). He first obtained a broad commitment on world participation for the post-war period from his respondents; then he asked a series of definite questions: for the sake of America's participation in world affairs, what would people be willing to accept? A standing army? Higher taxes? A lower standard of living? Etc. As a device to clarify the implications of people's opinions this is an appropriate procedure, but it is very confusing if it is suggested as a substitute for or even an improvement on the OI in all areas. It is precisely the purpose of the present paper to provide a general scheme, so that in discussing "depth interviews" *each participant can point to the specific sector of the entire field he has in mind.*

shows that after one to three hundred such reports have been studied, very few new factors come up. At this point we can begin to develop a set of specific questions centering around the main attitude and bringing out its implications and qualifications. There is no reason why we should not ask specifically (by the use of ordinary poll questions) what knowledge and experience the respondent has in this field; what his opinions are in related fields; whether he does or does not expect certain things to happen; whether he has ever thought of the problem, or whether he cannot make up his mind about it, and so on.

Here we come across a very characteristic relationship between the OI and more formalized methods in opinion research. The OI serves as a source of observation and of ideas from which sets of precise poll questions can be derived which will be more manageable in the field and more susceptible to statistical analysis. On one occasion the useful suggestion was made that the special job of *converter* should be developed: that people should specialize in studying OI's and seeing how they could be converted into systems of interlocking questions.

2. *Using check lists to get at the decisive aspects of an opinion:* If we want to know what people like about a candidate or what bothers them about the present rationing system, we can make a list of the probable answers and ask the respondents which answer fits their case.

The advantages and disadvantages of *check lists* have been repeatedly discussed. *The minimum requirement* is that they contain an *exhaustive list of all the possibilities,* for it is known that items not mentioned in a check list are less likely to be mentioned by the respondents. But even a good check list has certain dangers. If people are asked what wish they would make if they had a magic ring, they seldom mention "being very bright," because they do not think of intelligence as something that can be wished for. If, however, they get a check list of possible wishes which includes "intelligence," they are more likely to pick it. *The less concrete the topic is, the more will the check list influence the answers.*

As long as all this is not better explored by comparing the results from large-scale check lists and from the classifications of free answers, it is not possible to make a valid decision. Yet with the help of a careful analysis of OI's it seems logical to assume that exhaustive check lists can be safely constructed—ones which would be as safe as the results of open-ended interviewing. For complex topics the cautious research student will, of course, be hesitant to rely too easily on check lists. When in doubt he will prefer to rely on OI's recorded by conscientious interviewers and classified by sensitive analysts for the study of decisive features.

Again the OI is indispensable in preliminary studies to give one an idea as to what aspects should be considered. If, however, a large number of interviews is to be collected, the interlocking system of questions might be preferable, especially if great effort is made to get an appropriate conversion of preliminary OI's into a system of more precise questions.

3. *Are there other ways of studying what has influenced opinion?*: Whether it is possible to discern influences which are exercised upon people is a controversial question. In more extreme cases such decisions are obviously possible or imposible. If a child goes down to the grocer's "because my mother sent me down," we should consider such a statement as equivalent to a controlled experiment. Putting it rather exaggeratedly: if we set up two groups of well-matched children and had the mothers of the children in one group tell them to go to the grocer's, we should certainly expect to find more children from the "experimental" than from the control group at the grocer's. On the other hand, if a person has committed a crime and we ask him whether that is due to the fact that his parents immigrated to this country, we shall consider whatever he says not very reliable. The command of the mother is much more "discernible" as an influence than the whole background of family life.[18]

Fortunately, in public opinion research we are mostly interested in rather "discernible" influences. Whether people began to salvage paper under the influence of a government campaign or whether a specific pamphlet made them contribute blood to the Red Cross can be discovered fairly well by direct interviewing. For such studies the OI appears to be an important research tool. Thus, it becomes even more urgent to make its use as expert as possible. Sometimes it is not used wisely. Studies of the following kind have been circulated. People who began to can fruit were asked why they did so. Sixty per cent said "because of the campaign," 15% "because it is necessary for the war effort." Here is obviously a meaningless result—for OI or otherwise. Many of the 15% may have learned from the campaign that private canning was a patriotic duty. However, the interviewer was too easily satisfied with the first answer which came to the mind of the respondent instead of asking "Where did you learn that canning is important for the war effort?"[19]

4. *Scales and typologies for the analysis of attitude patterns*: When it comes to the objective correlates for the use of the OI in the classification of complex attitude patterns, we find ourselves in a peculiar situation. The topic has been a favorite one for social-research students; we have discussed "case studies" versus quantitative methods for a decade.[20] An appropriate instance comes from the study which this writer made during

---

[18] E. Smith and E. Suchman, "Do People Know Why They Buy?" *Journal of Applied Psychology*, 1940, 24, 673-684.

[19] We find here a mistake which corresponds to the objection we voiced above against Henry Link's paper. Because he used interlocking questions in one area, he thought that he had shown the uselessness of the OI technique in all other areas. Many of the proponents of the OI, on the other hand, do careful interviewing for the description of attitudes; but when it comes to the discerning of influences, they do bad interviewing and subject their returns to poor classification.

[20] Paul Wallin, *Case Study Methods in the Prediction of Personal Adjustment* (ed., Paul Horst). New York: Social Science Research Council, 1941.

the presidential election of 1940. The task was to appraise how interested people were in the election. Had we used the OI technique, the interviewer would have talked with the respondent and by taking down what he said, by observing his participation in the discussion, he would have formed an opinion on his interest and then noted it in the form of a rating. Instead we asked the respondent three questions: whether he had tried to convince someone of his political ideas; whether he had done anything for the success of his candidate; and whether he was very anxious to see his candidate elected. Each respondent got a definite score according to how he answered the three questions.[21]

But how does such an objective scale compare with the impressionistic ratings obtained from an OI? The problems involved can best be explained by an example.

If in everyday life we call another person timid, we do so because of the way he walks or because of his hesitant speech and sometimes because of cues of which we are not precisely aware ourselves. In each case we use whatever cues the situation offers; they might be quite different from one case to the next. A "timidity rating," on the other hand, would provide us with a list of items on which an interviewer would have to get an observation for every case, if necessary by asking a direct question. The more timidity characteristics on this list applied to the respondents, the higher would be his timidity score. Using such a scale, the interviewer could not make use of incidental observations if they were not included in the list, even if in a special case he had a strong conviction that the respondent was much more timid than his scale value indicated.

All this can be directly applied to our problem. A good OI reproduces the full vividness of an actual observation; but if nothing characteristic happens in the interview situation or if the interviewer misses cues, then we have little on which to base our final classification. With the scale we can count on a definite amount of data, but some of them might be rather artificial and often we must forego valuable observations within our reach. *Thus, a scale because of its rigidity will hardly be as good as an OI under its best conditions but can hardly let us down as much as an OI sometimes does.*

5. *Is there an easy way to get at motivation?* When we discussed broad motivational interpretations, we stressed all the hazards involved in this method. Correspondingly, it is very difficult to find an objective or formalized method for such an approach. *Projective tests* come nearest to it. The general idea of these tests is that people are presented with unstructured

---

[21] If such an interest score was used, it was found that for men the correlation between interest and voting was .20, whereas for women it was .50. Women, if they are not interested, do not vote. Men vote even if they are not interested, probably because they are more subject to social pressure. For a general theory of this score procedure see P. Lazarsfeld and W. Robinson, "Quantification of Case Studies," *Journal of Applied Psychology,* 1940, 24, 831-837.

material. Here is a crying girl; other children are asked to guess why she is crying. Or, an inkblot is shown to some people, as in the Rohrshach test, and they are asked to state what form it signifies to them. It is then assumed that the way people interpret such material, which has no definite meaning of its own, is indicative of what people themselves are concerned with.[22]

Applications to a public-opinion problem can only be invented because, to our knowledge, such studies have never been tried. If one wants to test people's attitudes toward public administration, one might, for instance, tell a short story of a successful public official who was suddenly dismissed. What was the reason? Was he found to be corrupt? Or was he the victim of a political intrigue? Or didn't he agree with the government's policy?

After Pearl Harbor, when so many people were concerned about the weakness of the American Navy, it would not have been easy to ask direct questions on this subject; few people would have cared to give an unpatriotic answer. One might, however, have shown them a series of pictures of battleships varying in degree of technical perfection. Which, in the opinion of the respondent, is an American and which a Japanese battleship? The proportion of people picking out the poor ship as an American model might have been a good index of concern about American armaments.

The psychological assumptions involved in a projective test have yet to be studied exhaustively. The answers are usually quite difficult to classify, and much depends upon the interpretation of the analyst. In the future such techniques may provide a very important tool for public opinion research. For the moment it can hardly be claimed that they are much better formalized than a good OI. If, therefore, one is interested in broad motivational interpretations, a well-conducted OI is probably still the best source for material.

6. *The meaning of statistical relationships.* Nothing has to be added to our discussion of the analysis of deviate cases in the preceding section. Here the OI is in its most legitimate place.

If we now summarize briefly this critical survey of the OI technique, we can make a number of points as to its position in the general scheme of public opinion research.

We saw that the problem is not new. Since the beginning of social research, students have tried to combine the detailed qualitative applications with the advantages of more formalized techniques which could be managed on a mass basis.

We saw, furthermore, that a line along which such an integration could

[22] P. Symonds and W. Samuel, "Projective Methods in the Study of Personality" (Chap. VI of *Psychological Tests and Their Uses*), *Review of Educational Research*, 1941, 11, 80-93.

come about emerges. The OI is indispensable at the beginning of any study where it classifies the structure of a problem in all its details. It is also invaluable at the end of a study for anyone who is not satisfied with the mere recording of the low correlations we usually obtain. Good research consists in weaving back and forth between OI's and the more cut-and-dried procedures.

Problems of Analysis

Daniel Katz

THE INTERPRETATION OF
SURVEY FINDINGS

The results of scientific research are sometimes regarded as pure objective statements of absolute truth devoid of interpretation. But if research findings are to have even scientific meaning, they must be interpreted in terms of the conditions and assumptions of the investigation of which they are the outcome. Merely because an interpretation is not expressly stated in a report does not mean that no inferences are drawn from the presentation of results. In fact the failure to make explicit the assumptions and conditions of the research investigation creates the impression of a finding more universal than the facts justify. Scientific findings must always be considered both in the framework of the particular research study and in relation to similar studies in the same field of knowledge.

The inevitability of interpretation of scientific results imposes the task of criteria and precautions for the evaluation of data. And the role of interpretation takes on new and gigantic proportions in public opinion research. When we study the world of physical facts, our own values do not intrude to color the picture as much as when we make human values the core of our research.

Most polling of public opinion is done by commercial agencies which conduct surveys either for specially interested clients or for newspapers and magazines. Most of the widely publicized poll findings are news services sold to newspapers or magazines. These surveys depend for their existence upon producing news-worthy releases and hence there is some pressure in the direction of the politically-interesting question of the moment rather than toward thorough-going and fundamental research. It must be remembered too that a commercial organization is in business to make money and that the more comprehensive and scientific the study, the higher the cost. It is also true that the poll operator as a business executive is more likely to have the values of his group than the values of the more

Reprinted from *The Journal of Social Issues*, Vol. 2 (1946), pp. 32-43, by permission of the author and publisher.

disinterested academician. That the polling agencies should have their limitations as research organizations is, therefore, to be expected. The surprising fact is that they have yielded so much valuable data both for practical and for scientific purposes.

Even surveys not made for popular consumption are subject to similar influences in that they are conducted for a practical purpose, sometimes by the Government and sometimes by a commercial concern. High research standards can and have been achieved under these conditions, but since so much of the work in public opinion and social science is "applied" rather than "pure" research, the interpretation of findings becomes a crucial problem. The following cautions are suggested, therefore, both to guard against common misinterpretations, about which the "consumer" of facts must be aware, and to point to better research procedures.

The discovery that people's attitudes and opinions can be readily ascertained has led to an indiscriminate attempt to get answers to problems of fact by counting noses. Now when we want to know about people's fears, hopes, aspirations, satisfactions and dissatisfactions, wishes, beliefs and preferences we naturally and justifiably conduct attitude surveys. But when we want to know facts that lie outside of people's subjective feelings, we study the problem directly. It is of some importance, for example, to know how people feel about the treatment of cancer, but public attitudes regarding the efficacy of various treatments cannot be taken as a measure of the actual effectiveness of these treatments.

At this simple level, it is not hard to separate the two problems. What often happens, however, in public opinion research is this: an attempt is made by an interested group to develop a public issue in the press. The real problem is one for factual study and cannot be solved by public debate. But public opinion polls seize upon the issue, conduct a survey, announce how the American people think about the matter and so join the debate.

For example, during the war the problem of absenteeism in war industry was presented in some papers as a crusade against the malingering war worker. The real problem was factual in nature: How much absenteeism was there, what were its causes, how could they be treated to reduce absenteeism? Factual studies were made at this time by industry itself, by the War Manpower Commission, and by OWI. The factual researches indicated that the incidence of absenteeism was exaggerated, that it was due in large measure to the mushrooming of war industry with increased employment of working wives and mothers. The American Institute of Public Opinion, however, disregarding these facts about absenteeism, polled the American public on the question:

"What do you think should be done with workers in war factories who are regularly absent from work without a good excuse?"

The Gallup release to the press reported the answers to this question under a headline stating that the great majority of the American people supported Rickenbacker in his campaign against absenteeism. Both the phrasing of the question and the presentation of the results assumed malingering on the part of war workers—the very problem that called for factual investigation.

Aside from the fact that the American Institute study in its very nature could contribute no evidence on the problem of absenteeism, there is an additional misinterpretation in this particular press release. It assumed that because people are opposed to inexcusable and habitual evil doers, that they were therefore in favor of the Rickenbacker crusade. Gallup treated the question of *what should be done with war workers regularly absent from work without good excuse* as if it had read, *"Do you think that Rickenbacker is correct in assuming that many war workers are regularly absent from work without good excuse?"*.

The main point that needs emphasis is the need of recognizing the difference between people's judgments and the objective facts. There is some danger in substituting opinion-study for factual investigation since it is often easier to poll the man in the street than to conduct a direct and thorough study of the problem. In interpreting survey findings the first caution is not to make people's opinions about objective facts synonymous with the facts themselves. This is not to minimize the importance of people's beliefs and values. The ideas people accept may be of great significance for social action. But it is necessary to distinguish between what people *think* are the facts and what the facts actually are.

Since public opinion polls grew out of forecasting elections, they tend to emphasize the reactions of a cross-section of the nation in most of their studies. In many problems, however, a national cross-section is not the most relevant sample for the hypotheses under investigation. An attitude study of worker morale, for example, needs to be directed at a sample of workers. During the war governmental studies of problems relating to the war effort became more meaningful through the use of special but relevant samples. In checking on popular reaction to the administrative functioning of rationing and price control it was more significant to talk to the person who did the family shopping than to the non-shopper. In getting at reasons for cashing Victory bonds it was important to interview a sample of people who were redeeming their bonds.

Though it is not always practical to set up a special sample for a new study, it is possible to ask the factual questions which will permit the respondents to be divided into the people with direct experience and knowledge and the people not at all involved. Most surveys could be more adequately interpreted if they included in addition to standard factual data such as age, occupation, education and urban-rural status the specific experiential material related to the problem under investigation. When a study is directed at race relations, questions should be asked at the end of the interview about the kind of contacts the respondent has had with members of other racial groups, to find out whether his attitudes are based on second-hand experience or on direct contacts under competitive or cooperative conditions.

In a study of white attitudes toward Negroes NORC reported that 6 out of 10 white persons feel that most Negroes in the United States are being treated fairly. But apparently no attempt was made to get at the basis of these opinions in experience, e.g. whether the respondents had ever known any Negroes, whether they had worked in industry where Negroes had attempted to get jobs, whether they had ever witnessed fair or unfair treatment of Negroes.

The necessity for distinguishing the group with relevant experience is clear in some instances, but there is a borderline area in the matter of informed and uninformed opinion where there is little, if any, direct experience. Both Gallup and Roper often use the filtering question in which respondents are asked if they have heard or know about a specific proposal. Sometimes knowledge is specifically tested and questions are then asked only of the *informed* people. This is a significant advance but it often is not sufficiently exploited. In October of 1945 the American Institute used this filtering question: "Have you heard or read about Sister Kenny or the Kenny method of treating infantile paralysis?" The 52 per cent who answered "Yes" were then asked: "From what you have heard or read do you think it is a good way or a bad way to treat the disease?" The majority who said they had heard of it thought it was a good method. These results have little meaning save as a measure of newspaper treatment of the Kenny method, because the kind of knowledge or experience that people have about the Kenny procedure ,was not explored.

A genuine source of error in interpreting poll returns is to assume that they necessarily represent a crystallized public opinion. The issue posed for people may not constitute a real problem for them, about which they have strong opinions. The tendency is to take any question of present or future political interest and throw it at the public. The issue may be remote from the every-day lives of people; it may have received little public discussion. Hence people have not really made up their minds about it. It is not really an issue as far as they are concerned.

The mistake here stems from a lack of knowledge of the nature of public opinion. A mere collection of expressions of opinion from a national sample does not necessarily constitute public opinion. Because a problem is of practical importance or possible political interest does not mean that there is a public opinion about it. Public opinion arises only after people have either lived through common experiences or have been subject to an educational or propaganda campaign. Only then are they ready to take a stand upon an issue.

One indication of the lack of crystallized public opinion is the percentage of "no opinion" answers. As a matter of fact, the percentage of "no opinion" answers is often an under-representation, because of the premium in the polling procedure on obtaining positive answers. No specific percentage of "no opinion" answers can be set as an absolute index of the lack of crystallization in public thinking but this percentage should always be carefully scrutinized. Other criteria for evaluating the crystallization of opinion include a study of the immediate history of events and of the content of mass media. The following questions, selected from the polls during the past year, suggest an uneven level of opinion-crystallization which is not always taken into account in the public releases on the questions.

"Should the United States Senate approve the United Nations charter for a world organization as adopted at the San Francisco conference?" (July 23, 1945)

Yes	64%
No	3%
No opinion	33%

"At the present time when Congress passes a bill to spend money, the President cannot veto parts of that bill but must accept it in full or veto it. Do you think this should be changed so that the President can veto some items in a bill to spend money without vetoing the entire bill?" (November 15, 1945)

Yes	57%
No	14%
No opinion	29%

"Do you think the secret of making atomic bombs should be put under the control of the new United Nations Security Council, or should the United States keep this secret to itself?" (October 27, 1945)

Put under U.N. control	14%
U.S. should keep control	73%
No opinion	13%

"Should Spain become a member of the United Nations under its present government?" (August 15, 1945)

No	76%
Yes	12%
No opinion	12%

"Do you approve or disapprove of removing all price ceilings now?" (October 23, 1945)

Disapprove	72%
Approve	21%
No opinion	7%

"In the future, do you think every able-bodied young man should be required to take military and naval training for one year?" (November 17, 1945)

Yes	75%
No	21%
No opinion	4%

No single survey finding has much meaning in and of itself. It can be properly interpreted only within a well-defined framework, either one that has been established by the experimental design of the study or one which the respondent has been allowed to establish for himself. Practically, this means that an adequate study must explore a problem thoroughly; it must ask not a single question but a whole series of questions. It must approach the problem from many angles, ask the dependent questions, explore the reasons why, seek the relevant objective background material and personal data. In many cases it must be repeated in time to give trends.

The greatest weakness in opinion research to date has been the failure to set up thorough studies of the problems under consideration. Poll operators will often attempt to cover between 6 and 10 major problems in one questionnaire. A number of issues of high "attention value" will be summarily treated with a single question. Any one of these issues can be appropriately studied only through an integrated survey with many interlocking questions with full exploration of the significant dimensions of the problem. Without a well-constructed framework of hypotheses, survey findings can be interpreted to mean anything and everything.

Too often public opinion polls assume that the complexities of a problem can be met by finding some neutral and unambiguous wording of the single question. Somehow such wording is expected to achieve both adequacy and objectivity of interpretation. Although question wording is important, the assumption that there is some magic by which a single question can be so well phrased with so little suggestive bias that it will furnish adequate and valid answers to a complex problem is naive. The emphasis upon the neutral wording of the single question should be shifted to the adequate experimental design of a well-integrated study. An apparent exception to this generalization is the case where an issue has become so well crystallized through discussion and controversy that almost everyone is ready to take sides for or against, as in a presidential election. Even here the single question has its limitations.

Many errors in the evaluations of findings can be seen in the following specific failures to provide a relevant context for interpretation.

The failure to ask related and dependent questions: In any problem it is essential to ask the related and dependent questions. Unless we know the many qualifications and the range of attitudes, we easily fall into the error of misinterpreting the attitudes of approval or disapproval. People themselves frequently respond with "It depends" when they are confronted with a yes-no type of question. To reflect their attitudes correctly it is necessary to inquire into the dependent circumstances which condition opinion.

Survey findings taken before Pearl Harbor have been interpreted to mean that the American people were precipitated into the war by their government against their will. But Cantril's trend studies clearly show that long before Pearl Harbor the majority of the nation favored warlike measures on our part as long as they stopped short of a declaration of war. People were willing to participate in the war on this basis but their attitude against formal and full participation depended upon no overt attack being made against us. Similarly a number of surveys report that the great majority of the American people are in favor of compulsory military training during peacetime. In many cases, however, this may mean that the individual favors such training if it does not interfere with the vocational or professional education of the trainee, if his own son is not to be taken out of his home at age 17 or 18, if it does not increase taxes, if universal conscription rather than the training of a few technicians is the sounder military preparedness, if the U.N. proves inadequate.

The National Opinion Research Center has demonstrated this point neatly in its release of June 24, 1945. This report reads as follows:

"What the public thinks about peacetime conscription depends in large measure upon the way the problem is presented. A survey just completed by the National Opinion Research Center, University of Denver, shows that 56% of the people of the United States think an annual federal appropriation of two billion dollars would be *better spent on regular education than on military training.* . . .

. . . NORC's interviewing staff talked with a national cross-section of civilian adults in every section of the United States—men and women, young and old, rich and poor, city residents, townspeople, and farmers. All were asked:

"Would you be in favor of or would you be against a law that would require boys to take a year's military training after the war when they become 18 years old?"

Favor military training	72%
Oppose military training	20%
Undecided	8%
	100%

"If the government had two billion dollars a year to spend, would you rather have it spent on a program of better regular education in the schools, or on a program of compulsory military training in the Army or Navy?"

Regular education	56%
Compulsory military training	25%
Neither or both	11%
Undecided	8%
	100%

The range of opinion needs to be represented adequately for proper evaluation of results. The range or degree can be found by providing many alternatives or by asking additional questions. Failure to explore the whole continuum can distort opinion findings. For example, in October 1945 the Psychological Corporation asked this question of a cross-section of the urban and small town population:

"If a man was paid $50 a week for 48 hours work in wartime and he is now working only 40 hours a week, should he still be paid $50?"

On this basis people voted against increasing the hourly rate and the inference was that people favored no raise in wage rates. But the American Institute with more detailed questioning came up with a more adequate answer. Its first question (incidentally stated more objectively than the above phrasing) was:

"Because of loss of overtime, the total weekly pay of many factory workers is less than it was during the war. So that their total weekly pay will be the same as it was during the war, these workers want a 30 per cent increase in their hourly rates. Do you think they should or should not receive this increase?"

Then Gallup went on to ask those opposed to a 30 per cent increase whether or not they would favor a 15 per cent increase of hourly rates. The results showed a clear-cut majority in favor of an increase of either 15 or 30 per cent. In other words by getting a fuller range of answers with an additional question, the meaning of the findings changed.

The range of attitudes can also be explored by the use of an attitude scale which may present four or more alternative positions. Because of the difficulty of people remembering the many alternatives in the attitude scale, the device is commonly used of printing the alternatives on a card which can be handed to the respondent. Roper has employed this technique more extensively than other poll operators. A four-stop attitude scale does not necessarily insure the adequate representation of the range of opinion, but it is an attempt to get away from the over-simplification of issues of the single polling question.

The failure to determine the respondent's own frame of reference: Asking limited and dependent questions makes possible the discovery of the respondent's attitude, but we still may not know enough of his own reasons to be sure of the frame of reference in which he gave his answers. People answering "Yes" to the same question do not necessarily belong in the same category. Their reasons may vary decidedly. For example, a national network recently asked a cross-section of the American people whether or not there should be any government control over news broadcasts over the air. A majority favored control but when they were asked for their reasons it became clear that there was a fundamental difference in basic points of view. One group wanted government control in the interests of military and national security. Another group wanted control not in the interest of censorship but to make sure that private enterprise should not control the sources of information. The two groups, both answering "Yes" to the question, were thinking in such opposed frames of reference that their answers could have been easily misinterpreted if their reasons had not been ascertained. A "reason why" question may often be too direct to get at the frame of reference of the respondent but some procedure, either direct or indirect, is necessary for interpreting the meaning of people's responses.

In general, the open-ended type of question is the basic tool for the determination of the individual's frame of reference. This permits the respondent to answer in terms of his own attitudinal orientation. The dimensions of the problem that seem important to him can thus be discovered. In a large-scale survey it is not necessarily desirable to make all questions open-ended but it is generally wise to retain a few open-ended questions and it is, of course, essential to use such questions extensively in the pretest stage of the questionnaire.

The error of imputing absolute value to a single percentage: The use of single questions in opinion surveys leads to over-generalization from the percentage as *yes* or *no* answers. People are categorized on the basis of their answers to a question and the number of them assigned to a given category determined by the percentage approving one specific question. For example, in the February issue of *Fortune* (1946) the conclusion is reached that 8.8. per cent of the American people are anti-Semites.

To quote:

"Identified as anti-Semites are those respondents to a survey questionnaire who took one or both of two opportunities offered to express hostility to Jews. The questions that elicited the latent hostility of the 8.8 per cent were:
"Are there any organizations or groups of people in this country who you feel might be harmful to the future of the country unless they are curbed?" (If "Yes") Name: (Here 5.1 per cent named Jews)
"Are there any groups of people you think are trying to get ahead at the expense of people like you?" (If "Yes") Name: (Here 6.5 per cent named Jews)
"Once identified, the anti-Semites can be examined by means of their replies to other questions in the same survey."

To infer the absolute amount of anti-Semitism from two questions is a debatable procedure. Merely because 91.2 per cent of the people did not name the Jews on either of the two questions does not establish their complete lack of anti-Semitism. Anti-Semitism is a complex set of attitudes and practices which varies both in intensity and in qualitative aspects. The categorizing of 8 per cent as anti-Semites implies that everyone is either an anti-Semite or not one at all. Obviously, if other types of questions had been used the percentages might have been higher or lower, depending upon the question employed. To say that there is 8.8. per cent of anti-Semites in the United States is to assume that we have a single yardstick to measure this complex attitude and that we know its zero point.

Relative rather than absolute measures are scientifically more justifiable. For example, trend studies in which questions are repeated over a period of time furnish a relative notion of the increase or decrease of sentiment or prejudice. In all fairness to the *Fortune* Survey, it should be stated that it did report relative findings in the trends in anti-Semitism over a period of time.

Another way of presenting relative findings is to compare various groups sampled within the same survey. A good example of this can be seen in the study of German morale made by the U. S. Strategic Bombing Survey of the War Department. The objective was to determine the effect of bombing upon German civilian morale. Since there is no absolute yardstick of morale with a fixed zero point, the study was designed to compare German cities subject to various degrees of bombing on the many dimensions of morale. If relatively more people showed high morale in unbombed than in bombed places, then the finding was meaningful in spite of the lack of an absolute scale. As a matter of fact, in this study the highest morale was found in unbombed communities but there was just as much loss of morale in cities suffering medium bomb tonnage as in heavily bombed cities.

The Misleading Use of "Typical" Cases and "Typical" Comments: Many of the errors described so far are inherent in the usual commercial polling approach to research, but the more scientific work of government agencies and foundations is not without its weaknesses. To enable the administrator to visualize the findings, research results have often quoted "typical" cases and "typical" comments from respondents. These comments and cases make the people whose reactions are being reported living personalities and are a good device for communicating feeling, but they belong more to the literary than the scientific approach. The objection is not so much to the use of case material but to its presentation as typical when no rigorous procedures have been employed to establish the typicality of the quoted material. In fact, the tendency is to select excerpts from interviews which are unusually cogent, colorful and dramatic.

For example, the Surveys Division of OWI and the Division of Program Surveys of the Department of Agriculture both used case materials in presenting their findings to give administrators some feel for the human aspects of the problem. In one study of worker morale in the shipyards, emphasis was placed upon the necessity of a feeling of participation by the shipyard worker himself. One of the older workmen was quoted as follows:

"They used to let more men go on the trial run of the boats. Now they have cut that out and a few of the big shots go and have a party and get drunk. All the men want to get to go on these trips, but they stopped it. The men feel that now. They are usually gone about twelve hours. It would help create a better feeling among the men if they would let them go. We launched a boat Sunday. My foreman, who has worked there 27 years, was there at the launching and he and his wife and baby stood out in the rain to watch it. Those big shots who stood up there under the shelter don't know anything about building a ship. I think those who do the work should get the credit for it and not those big shots who make all those pretty speeches."

Again, in another study, when rent controls were first put into effect during the war, the reaction of those approving it was expressed in the words of a young coppersmith in the Philadelphia navy yards.

"I think it is one of the best moves they ever made here. The rents were going up something terrible. They were taking advantage of the times. They even did it in our own case—trying to soak the guy whose wages had gone up a little. If we didn't have rent control, eventually we'd have to sleep in the park."

It can be argued that these utterances selected for presentation in the final report, though voiced by the articulate few, really represent the feeling of the inarticulate many. But this argument to be tenable must be documented by specific supporting evidence.

The general usage is not to claim explicitly that case materials and comments are typical of all respondents. Quotations are generally presented as expressions of particular people. None the less, the reader will often infer that the dramatic comments presented do typify a whole class of respondents.

SSRC Committee on Analysis of
Pre-Election Polls and Forecasts

THE PRE-ELECTION POLLS
OF 1948

The committee has made a study of available data on the 1948 election forecasts and has come to the following conclusions:

1. The pollsters overreached the capabilities of the public opinion poll as a predicting device in attempting to pick, without qualification, the winner of the 1948 presidential election. They had been led by false assumptions into believing their methods were much more accurate than in fact they are. The election was close. Dewey could have won by carrying Ohio, California, and Illinois which he lost by less than 1 percent of the vote. In such a close election no polls, no advance information of any kind, could have predicted a Truman or Dewey victory with confidence. The failure of the polls was due to neglecting the possibility of a close election and the necessity of measuring preferences very accurately just before the election to determine whether a flat forecast could be made with confidence.

2. The pollsters could have foreseen the possibility of a close contest had they looked more carefully at their data and past errors. They acted in good faith but showed poor judgment in failing to apply in 1948 what they knew about their past errors, and failing to ascertain late campaign shifts.

3. The over-all operation of making election predictions from pre-election polls is a complex one involving eight major steps at each of which error may enter. It is very difficult to unscramble the total error and allocate components of it to these various steps. The evidence indicates that there were two major causes of errors: (a) errors of sampling and interviewing, and (b) errors of forecasting, involving failure to assess the future behavior of undecided voters and to detect shifts of voting intention near the end of the campaign.

4. These sources of error were not new. While Gallup and Crossley

were more successful in picking the winner and his electoral vote in 1940 and 1944 than in 1948, their average errors state by state were at least half as great in the two preceding elections as in 1948. Hence, it is possible that their errors in 1948 were due to much the same causes as those that produced the earlier forecast errors, but if so, these causes operated more strongly. Roper's wide discrepancy in 1948 cannot be explained so readily in terms of factors present in his earlier close estimates of the national vote. It appears to be due to the upsetting of the balance previously maintained among various factors in his polling operations.

5. To improve the accuracy of pre-election poll predictions satisfactorily it is necessary to reduce the error at every step in the over-all polling process. The error at some of the steps, notably sampling and interviewing, could be reduced by using methods now available. But reduction at other steps depends on further basic research in psychological and political behavior.

6. The manner in which the pre-election polls were analyzed, presented and published for public consumption contributed materially to the widespread misinterpretation of the results of the polls and to the great public reaction to their failure to pick the winner. This led to a poor understanding of the lack of accuracy of the polls and of the nature of the errors residing in the polls, with the result that the public placed too much confidence in polls before the 1948 election and too much distrust in them afterwards.

7. The public should draw no inferences from pre-election forecasts that would disparage the accuracy or usefulness of properly conducted sampling surveys in fields in which the response does not involve expression of opinion or intention to act. There are more appropriate methods to check the accuracy of such surveys.

Election forecasts from polls are hazardous. This fact might tempt some polling organizations in the future to limit their political studies to attitudes which cannot be checked up at elections. Thus, they could avoid the spotlight of a public audit of their work. The committee would view such a step with concern, for all possible tests of opinion studies are needed. Election returns are not a direct or even a good test of the adequacy of polling on issues, like the Marshall plan, civil rights, etc. But elections are useful for testing the adequacy of polling methods for estimating the percentage of the vote going to each candidate from various groups in the population. No better test is now known. Even in the case of these estimates, it will not be possible to make election returns a satisfactory test unless pre-election studies and post-election studies are more rigorouly designed so that different types of errors can be partitioned out. The responsibility for working out such designs rests squarely on polling agencies, in cooperation with social scientists.

Apart from their use in election forecasting, opinion polls conducted in relation to elections have great value in giving social science and the public a better understanding of the American democratic process. Such polls do two things: They reveal the voting preferences and voting behavior of different parts of the population, such as men and women, old and young, etc. and they reveal the relation between opinion on important issues and the choice of the candidate for whom the voter casts his ballot. In addition, they reveal the opinions and preferences of those people who do not turn out to vote.

On the basis of its study the committee makes the following recommendations:

1. To improve the accuracy of polls, increased use should be made of the better techniques now available, particularly in sampling and interviewing. Since the reduction of any part of the error greatly increases the chances of a successful forecast, the committee urges that pollers exert every effort to adopt more reliable techniques.

2. Increased attention should be paid to the development of research on each step of the polling operation to attempt to improve methods used in opinion research. This would include research on sampling methods, interviewer bias, concealment of opinions, selection and training of interviewers, etc. Experimental studies of such problems should be planned well in advance of elections. Many of these experiments can be incorporated into regular survey operations and as a part of more general cooperative studies of specific communities.

3. Research should be expanded on the basic sciences, particularly social psychology and political science, which underlie the analysis of voters' behavior. Even if perfect sampling of individuals is employed, we now know too little about voting intentions, factors affecting change in opinion, prestige effects, and similar topics to predict who will translate his opinion into actual voting.

4. In view of the increasing amount of emphasis being placed on public opinion polls, the committee considers it very important for the public to be effectively informed about the limitations of poll results so it can interpret them intelligently. It urges that polling organizations, newspapers and magazines, and social scientists who work with poll results help provide the public with more information about polls, their interpretation and limitations.

5. There should be more effective cooperation between research workers interested in opinion measurement on common problems of methodology, underlying theory, and research design, including more studies of validity and reliability than have been made heretofore. Such cooperation would benefit all parties through the wider dissemination of their findings, and more efficient use of research resources and opportunities for experimentation.

6. More extensive training facilities and opportunities for practical experience under effective supervision should be provided for students who may be interested in research careers in this field, which includes political behavior, psychological research, and opinion measurement and statistical methods.

7. Analysis of the elections is greatly hampered by long delays in the reporting of official returns. The present inadequacies with respect to the collection of election statistics should be remedied by effective organization for rapid and accurate reporting of election statistics at the local, state, and national levels.

The failure of the public opinion polls to predict correctly the outcome of the 1948 presidential election created wide confusion and misgivings about the reliability of the polls. Reactions of the public to the polls ranged from charges of outright fraud to expressions of personal sympathy for the pollsters. Reactions of experts ranged from condemnation for carelessness, unintentional bias, errors of judgment, and use of outmoded techniques, to a determination to make use of this experience to enlarge our knowledge of political behavior and to improve survey methodology.

The Problem of Pre-Election Forecasting

A. *Complexity of the Problem*: Forecasting election returns from pre-election polls is an exceedingly complex and difficult task. It involves two main problems:

First, selecting a sample of persons to be interviewed and ascertaining their voting intentions and political preferences as of the time of interview. Who expects to vote and how does he expect to vote?

Second, forecasting who will actually vote on election day and how they will vote. This requires anticipation of possible shifts from expressed political preference and voting intention between the time of interview and election day. What voters are most likely to change their plans?

B. *Steps Involved in Pre-election Polling and Forecasting*: Each polling organization has its own procedures, but all of them take the following steps:

(1) Design of a plan and instructions for selecting a sample of respondents.

(2) Design of a questionnaire and instructions on interviewing procedure,

(3) Selection of the respondents in the field,

(4) Interviewing the respondents,

(5) Decisions as to which respondents will actually vote,

(6) Decision on what to do about voters who say they are undecided or will not tell how they will vote,.

(7) Processing the data, including adjustments and corrections for trends and other factors,

(8) Interpretation and presentation of results, including the projection of a forecast.

In polling, none of these operations can be performed perfectly. Some error will be made at each step. The total error between a pre-election poll prediction and the actual vote is a combination of the errors entering into these various steps. Some of these errors may cancel out.

A consistently high degree of accuracy of forecasting will be possible only if every step in the process is highly controlled and carefully executed. The committee doubts that such control is possible in the present state of knowledge.

C. *Chances for Successful Prediction*: It is one thing to predict the division of the national popular vote among the presidential candidates and quite another to predict which candidate will be elected. The public has not been interested in the size of the error with which a pre-election poll predicts the percentage of popular votes that a given candidate will receive. It demands that the pre-election poll predict the winner. This is a very severe test, heavily affected by chance in close elections, and is complicated by the electoral college system.

In predicting the winner, the forecast either succeeds in naming the man who is elected or it does not. In forecasting a candidate's percentage of the popular vote, the success of the prediction is a matter of degree. It is usually measured by taking the difference between the percentage forecast for him, and the percentage he actually received.

All three national polls picked the wrong man as winner. They underestimated Truman's percentage of the national vote by 4 to 12 percentage points. Roper made no state forecasts. Crossley and Gallup came within 2 points of the correct state vote in 9 and 3 state respectively and within 4 points in 21 and 17 states respectively. Crossley's greatest errors were −10.8 and +8.2 points, Gallup's −11.5 and +1.7. Gallup did not attempt to forecast in 4 southern states and Crossley in 1.

These state errors can be regarded as the result of two tendencies. The first is a general tendency of the forecasts to underestimate Truman's vote. This is reflected in the *average* of state errors which is −4 or −5 percentage points. The second is the tendency of the errors to vary from state to state around the average error, reflecting special conditions in each state and the effects of chance in the polling and forecasts.

This *error variation* around the *average error* swings from 0 to 8 points in both directions. By itself it is seldom great enough to upset the forecasts except in very close state contests. Even then it tends to balance out in the totaling of the state results. Clearly the *average error*, affecting all states alike, was the more serious source of the failure of the forecast. The problem, therefore, is to seek out the factors that caused it.

The average errors in earlier election forecasts were about 2 points in 1944 and 1940 and 5 to 6 points in 1936.

These average errors of state forecasts all resulted in underestimating the Democratic vote. How long such a tendency could be expected to continue was uncertain. All the presidential polls prior to 1948 had Roosevelt's candidacy as a common factor and it was possible that the new line-up would change the size and direction of the average state error. Moreover, some of the forecasts in intervening congressional elections had overestimated the Democratic vote.

The success of methods of prediction is often tested by comparison with what some simple predicting device would show. As a rule-of-thumb test of election forecasts, an analysis was made of the accuracy that could be attained by merely predicting that the vote in each state will divide exactly as it did in the preceding election. It seems reasonable to expect that polling forecasts should work at least as well as this simple method, over a series of elections, if they are to be of any use. Allowance can be made for the appearance of new parties in 1948 by dealing only with the Republican vote. In the period during which polls have been conducted (1936-48) the accuracy of this simple method of prediction is almost as good as that attained by polling. In periods of rapid political change, however, like 1916-20 and 1928-32, prediction from past elections is very poor. It is to be expected that in such cases polling would be significantly superior to forecasts based on past voting.

Another test can be applied to the performance of the polls in predicting elections. On the basis of average error and error variation found in the polls from 1936 to 1948 one might ask the following question: What are the chances that a poll having such errors would correctly predict the winning presidential candidate in an election having a Democratic victory as close as the 1948 election? The answer to this question is about 1 chance in 4. In elections as close as this when the Republican candidate is the victor, the chances would be about 3 out of 4 that polls with these errors would predict the winner correctly.

From this it appears that the tendency to underestimate the Democratic vote seriously disturbs the chances of success when the Democratic candidate wins a close election. With such a tendency, efforts to reduce the other errors actually decrease the chance of successfully predicting Democratic winners and increase the chances of successfully predicting Republican winners.

Since 1844 there were eight elections so close that the winning candidate had a plurality over his leading opponent of 4 percentage points or less. Forecasting the results of these elections by the methods used in 1948 would have been extremely hazardous though predicting the percentage vote would not necessarily have been more difficult than in other elections.

The Forecasts Compared With Election Results

The latest available returns show a discrepancy of between 4 and 5 percentage points between Crossley's and Gallup's predictions and the actual election results for Truman and Dewey. Roper's error was larger. The predictions and returns for the national election are as follows:

		Percentage of total presidential vote			
	Dewey	Truman	Thurmond	Wallace	Total *
National vote	45.1	49.5	2.4	2.4	99.4
Crossley	49.9	44.8	1.6	3.3	99.6
Gallup	49.5	44.5	2.0	4.0	100.0
Roper	52.2	37.1	5.2	4.3	98.8

* Exclusive of percentages for minor candidates. Gallup percentages calculated on total vote for four principal candidates.

Crossley and Gallup both reported their state-by-state predictions as well as over-all prediction of popular votes. The state-by-state predictions and actual vote will be given in the committee's staff report. Roper released only national averages. Gallup predicted the winning candidate correctly for 30 states (with 323 electoral votes) of 44 states predicted, and Crossley for 32 states (with 353 electoral votes) of 47 states predicted (in two states equal percentages of those polled favored each candidate).

A number of individual city and state polls were analyzed. In general their errors were similar to the state-by-state errors made by Crossley and Gallup. While predictions were made with great accuracy in several instances, there were so many state-by-state predictions made that some predictions will be close just as a matter of chance. Indistinguishable from close predictions due to chance, there may be some that are close due to superior methods.

The following table, based on preliminary election returns, shows the state-by-state errors in predicting the vote for Truman:

Forecast percentage minus election percentage	Number of state errors in Crossley predictions	Number of state errors in Gallup predictions
From —12.0% to —10.1%	2	4
—10.0% to — 8.1%	4	2
— 8.0% to — 6.1%	5	9
— 6.0% to — 4.1%	13	12
— 4.0% to — 2.1%	12	14
— 2.0% to — .1%	7	2
0 % to 1.9%	2	1
2.0% to 3.9%	0	0
4.0% to 5.9%	1	0
6.0% to 7.9%	1	0
Total number of states forecast	47	44

Principal Sources of Error in 1948 Predictions

The total error in the 1948 election predictions is compounded from errors, some of them compensating, enumerated in the eight steps listed in Section III B. It is not possible to measure accurately the various components of the total error. But it is possible, on the basis of the analysis made by the committee, to identify the major sources of error.

The evidence indicates that there were two major causes of errors: (a) errors of sampling and interviewing and (b) errors of forecasting, involving failure to assess the future behavior of undecided voters and to detect shifts near the end of the campaign.

First is the class of errors arising from the sampling and interviewing methods used. Two alternative methods of sampling have been employed in such studies. In the first the individuals to be interviewed are determined in advance by *probability methods*. In the second, the *quota method*, the interviewer is left free, within the restrictions of assigned quotas, to select respondents largely in accordance with his own judgment. This is the method primarily used by the major polling organizations. It is impossible to separate the error introduced by the quotas set from that arising from •the process of selection by the interviewers.

All of the major polling organizations interviewed more people with college education than the actual proportion in the adult population over 21 and too few people with grade school education only. This practice has been defended on the ground that nonvoters are found disproportionally in the classes with little education. If the problem posed were to learn the political preferences on a given day of all individuals over 21 years of age, irrespective of whether or not they would vote, the sampling problem would be theoretically simple. The sample of respondents should be so drawn as to correspond to known characteristics of the total adult population.

But there are only two ways to eliminate potential nonvoters. One way is not to draw them in the sample (as in the case of people known to be under 21). The other way is to eliminate them through screening questions after they are drawn in the sample—questions whose answers will show that the respondent is not likely to vote. The first method is safe only if we know that there is an extremely close association between some objective characteristic (like age under 21) and nonvoting. There is not sufficient factual evidence to justify eliminating a fraction of a group (like part of those with grade school education) when the relationship between the characteristic and nonvoting is far from perfect. This easily could have been one of the most dangerous traps into which the polls fell.

On the other hand, the second method, of eliminating nonvoters through screening questions, also used by the pollsters, is still a primitive procedure in the absence of sound theory and in the absence of experience with which to establish the value of the screening questions. The chief trouble with the quota method is the fact that there is no good procedure for digging into the results to find out what kind of selection the interviewer actually makes—hence the flaws in the several stages of the procedure cannot be clearly separated for analysis. The advantages of the probability method of sampling, advocated by some statisticians, lie primarily in the fact that the errors introduced by selection of respondents by the interviewer can be reduced to a minimum. But with this method, as with the quota method, there is still the difficult problem of screening out the people who will not actually vote.

A second major source of errors in the 1948 election forecasts is to be found in the failure of the polls to detect shifts in voting intentions during the later stages of the campaign. Roper erred by assuming that voting intentions would not change during the campaign, as evidenced by his announcement of September 9. Crossley and Gallup made no attempts to detect the shift in voting intentions in the last two weeks of the campaign. Post-election polls report that about 1 voter in 7 said he made his decision on how to vote within the two weeks preceding the election, and that about 3 out of 4 of these voters said they voted for Truman. Even if one makes allowance for errors in such reports, one must conclude that failure to detect and measure changes of mind about voting during the closing days of the campaign accounts for a considerable part of the total error of the prediction.

The problems of forecasting in 1948 were complicated by the relatively large proportion of voters who were undecided when interviewed. These respondents had to be eliminated as not likely to vote or allocated among the candidates. The number of apparently undecided voters found by the pre-election polls was approximately 15 percent, which is nearly twice as large as that of 1944. This group remained large even after those "leaning" toward one candidate or another were removed.

In general, the "undecided" vote was allocated to the different candidates in accordance with the proportions found among the decided voters or ignored on the assumption that the undecided probably would not vote. The evidence available suggests that a great majority of the "undecided" voters who voted actually voted for Truman and that a better allocation of the "undecided" might have been made from other data available to the pollsters. However, the indications are that defective allocation of the "undecided" vote contributed less than 1.5 percentage points to the overall prediction error. Much more serious may have been the errors due to difficulty of estimating who would vote and who would actually shift allegiance before election.

The error in predicting the actual vote from expressed intention to vote was undoubtedly an important, although not precisely measurable, part of the over-all error of the forecast. The prediction of human behavior from an expression of intent is, in the present state of knowledge, and particularly with the actual methods used, a hazardous venture. This is a central problem for research, which has been largely ignored in pre-election poll predictions. The gap between an expression of intent and actual behavior will continue to be a major source of error in future election forecasts as well as in other attempts to predict human behavior; and in the present state of knowledge, must be recognized as a baffling and unsolved problem imposing serious limitations on opinion poll predictions.

It is a responsibility of social science to contribute much more to knowledge of the contingencies which must be taken into account. Extensive analysis by political scientists and social psychologists of election behavior in 1948 and in other elections is essential to provide more knowledge of how voters act under different circumstances. The poverty of our exact knowledge of how and why people vote in general severely handicaps efforts to predict how they will vote in a particular election.

Interpretation and Presentation

In interpreting the results of the pre-election polls and presenting them to the public, the pollsters went far beyond the bounds of sound reporting of the results of pre-election polls. They attempted the spectacular feat of predicting the winner without qualification. The presentation of the results gave the impression of certainty as to the outcome. The final releases carried very little indication of the limitations of polling and the tendency in past election forecasts to underestimate the Democratic vote. Statements of conditions under which different outcomes of the election might occur were dropped almost completely before the end of the campaign.

The polls also failed to provide the public with sufficient information about the methods of poll operation to permit assessment of the degree of confidence that could be placed in the predictions. The number of cases used, the type of sampling employed, the corrections introduced, and how returns from individuals who did not know for whom they would vote were tabulated, were not discussed adequately. It is recognized that there is pressure from newspaper editors and readers to omit qualifications and "technicalities," but pollsters and social scientists have an important responsibility for educating readers of poll results to evalute them and understand their limitations.

Herbert Blumer

PUBLIC OPINION AND
PUBLIC OPINION POLLING

This paper presents some observations on public opinion and on public opinion polling as currently performed. The observations are not along the line of what seems to be the chief preoccupation of students of public opinion polling, to wit, the internal improvement of their technique. Instead, the observations are designed to invite attention to whether public opinion polling actually deals with public opinion.

The first observations which I wish to make are in the nature of a prelude. They come from a mere logical scrutiny of public opinion polling as an alleged form of scientific investigation. What I note is the inability of public opinion polling to isolate "public opinion" as an abstract or generic concept which could thereby become the focal point for the formation of a system of propositions. It would seem needless to point out that in an avowed scientific enterprise seeking to study a class of empirical items and to develop a series of generalizations about that class it is necessary to identify the class. Such identification enables discrimination between the instances which fall within the class and those which do not. In this manner, the generic character of the object of study becomes delineated. When the generic object of study is distinguishable, it becomes possible to focus study on that object and thus to learn progressively more about the object. In this way the ground is prepared for cumulative generalizations or propositions relative to the generic object of investigation.

As far as I can judge, the current study of public opinion by polling ignores the simple logical point which has just been made. This can be seen through three observations. First, there is no effort, seemingly, to try to identify or to isolate public opinion as an object; we are not given any criteria which characterize or distinguish public opinion and thus

Reprinted from *American Sociological Review*, Vol. 13 (1948), pp. 542-47, by permission of the author and publisher. (Copyright, 1948, by The American Sociological Society.)

we are not able to say that a given empirical instance falls within the class of public opinion and some other empirical instance falls outside of the class of public opinion. Second, there is an absence, as far as I can determine, of using specific studies to test general proposition about public opinion; this suggests that the students are not studying a generic object. This suggestion is supported by the third observation—a paucity, if not a complete absence, of generalizations about public opinion despite the voluminous amount of polling studies of public opinion. It must be concluded, in my judgment, that current public opinion polling has not succeeded in isolating public opinion as a generic object of study.

It may be argued that the isolation of a generic object, especially in the realm of human behavior, is a goal rather than an initial point of departure—and that consequently the present inability to identify public opinion as a generic object is not damning to current public opinion polling. This should be admitted. However, what impresses me is the apparent absence of effort or sincere interest on the part of students of public opinion polling to move in the direction of identifying the object which they are supposedly seeking to study, to record, and to measure. I believe it is fair to say that those trying to study public opinion by polling are so wedded to their technique and so preoccupied with the improvement of their technique that they shunt aside the vital question of whether their technique is suited to the study of what they are ostensibly seeking to study. Their work is largely merely making application of their technique. They are not concerned with independent analysis of the nature of public opinion in order to judge whether the application of their technique fits that nature.

A few words are in order here on an approach that consciously excuses itself from any consideration of such a problem. I refer to the narrow operationalist position that public opinion consists of what public opinion polls poll. Here, curiously, the findings resulting from an operation, or use of an instrument, are regarded as constituting the object of study instead of being some contributory addition to knowledge of the object of study. The operation ceases to be a guided procedure on behalf of an object of inquiry; instead the operation determines intrinsically its own objective. I do not care to consider here the profound logical and psychological difficulties that attend the effort to develop systematic knowledge through a procedure which is not a form of directed inquiry. All that I wish to note is that the results of narrow operationalism, as above specified, merely leave or raise the question of what the results mean. Not having a conceptual point of reference the results are merely disparate findings. It is logically possible, of course, to use such findings to develop a cenceptualization. I fail to see anything being done in this direction by those who subscribe to the narrow operationalist position in the use of public opinion polls. What is logically unpardonable on the part of those who take the narrow operationalist position is for them to hold either wittingly or unwittingly that their investigations are a study of public opinion as this term is conceived in our ordinary discourse. Having rejected as unnecessary the task of characterizing the object of inquiry for the purpose of seeing whether the enquiry is suited to the object of inquiry, it is gratuitous and unwarranted to presume that after all the inquiry is a study of the object which one refuses to characterize. Such a form of trying to eat one's cake and have it too needs no further comment.

The foregoing series of logical observations has been made merely to stress the absence of consideration of a generic object by those engaged in public opinion polling. Apparently, it is by virtue of this absence of consideration that they are obtuse to the functional nature of public opinion in our society and to questions of whether their technique is suited to this functional nature. In this paper I intend to judge the suitability of public opinion polling as a means of studying public opinion. This shall be done from the standpoint of what we know of public opinion in our society.

Admittedly, we do not know a great deal about public opinion. However, we know something. We know enough about public opinion from empirical observations to form a few reasonably reliable judgments about its nature and mode of functioning. In addition, we can make some reasonably secure inferences about the structure and functioning of our society and about collective behavior within our society. This combined body of knowledge derived partly from direct empirical observation and partly from reasonable inference can serve appropriately as means of judging and assessing current public opinion polling as a device for studying public opinion.

Indeed, the features that I wish to note about public opinion and its setting are so obvious and commonplace that I almost blush to call them to the attention of this audience. I would not do so were it not painfully clear that the students of current public opinion polling ignore them either wittingly or unwittingly in their whole research procedure. I shall indicate by number 'the features to be noted.

1.) Public opinion must obviously be recognized as having its setting in a society and as being a function of that society in operation. This means, patently, that public opinion gets its form from the social framework in which it moves, and from the social processes in play in that framework; also that the function and role of public opinion is determined by the part it plays in the operation of the society. If public opinion is to be studied in any realistic sense its depiction must be faithful to its empirical character. I do not wish to be redundant but I find it necessary to say that the empirical character of public opinion is represented by its composition and manner of functioning as a part of a society in operation.

2.) As every sociologist ought to know and as every intelligent layman does know, a society has an organization. It is not a mere aggregation of disparate individuals. A human society is composed of diverse kinds of functional groups. In our American society illustrative instances of functional groups are a corporation, a trade association, a labor union, an ethnic group, a farmers' organization. To a major extent our total collective life is made up of the actions and acts of such groups. These groups are oriented in different directions because of special interests. These groups differ in terms of their strategic position in the society and in terms of opportunities to act. Accordingly, they differ in terms of prestige and power. As functional groups, that is to say as groups acting individually in some corporate or unitary sense, such groups necessarily have to have some organization—some leadership, some policy makers, some individuals who speak on behalf of the group, and some individuals who take the initiative in acting on behalf of the group.

3.) Such functional groups, when they act, have to act through the channels which are available in the society. If the fate of the proposed acts depends on the decisions of individuals or groups who are located at strategic points in the channels of action, then influence and pressure is brought to bear directly or indirectly on such individuals or groups who make the decisions. I take it that this realistic feature of the operation of our American society requires little explication. If an action embodying the interests of a functional group such as a farmers' organization depends for its realization on decisions of Congressmen or a bureau or a set of administrators, then efforts on behalf of that action will seek to influence such Congressmen, bureau, or administrators. Since in every society to some degree, and in our American society to a large degree, there are individuals, committees, boards, legislators, administrators and executives who have to make the decisions affecting the outcome of the actions of functional groups, such key people become the object of direct and indirect influence or pressure.

4. The key individuals referred to who have to make the crucial decisions are almost inevitably confronted with the necessity of *assessing* the various influences, claims, demands, urgings, and pressures that are brought to bear on them. Insofar as they are responsive and responsible they are bound to make such an assessment in the process of arriving at their decisions. Here I want to make the trite remark that in making their assessments these key individuals take into account what they judge to be worthy of being taken into account.

5.) The above points give a crude but essentially realistic picture of certain important ways in which our society operates. The fifth feature I wish to note is that public opinion is formed and expressed in large measure through these ways of societal operation. This point requires a little elaboration. The formation of public opinion occurs as a function of a society in operation. I state the matter in that way to stress that the formation of public opinion does not occur through an interaction of disparate individuals who share equally in the process. Instead the formation of public opinion reflects the functional composition and organization of society. The formation of public opinion occurs in large measure through the interaction of groups. I mean nothing esoteric by this last remark. I merely refer to the common occurrence of the leaders or officials of a functional group taking a stand on behalf of the group with reference to an issue and voicing explicitly or implicitly this stand on behalf of the group. Much of the interaction through which public opinion is formed is through the clash of these group views and positions. In no sense does such a group view imply that it is held in equal manner and in equal degree by all of the members of the group. Many of the members of the group may subscribe to the view without understanding it, many may be indifferent about it, many may share the view only in part, and many may actually not share the view but still not rebel against the representatives of the group who express the view. Nevertheless the view, as indicated, may be introduced into the forum of discussion as the view of the group and may be reacted to as such. To bring out this point in another way, one need merely note that in the more outstanding expressions of view on an issue, the individuals almost always speak either explicitly or implicitly as representatives of groups. I would repeat that in any realistic sense the diversified interaction which gives rise to public opinion is in large measure between functional groups and not merely between disparate individuals.

I think that it is also very clear that in the process of forming public opinion, individuals are not alike in influence nor are groups that are equal numerically in membership alike in influence. This is so evident as not to require elaboration. It is enough merely to point out that differences in prestige, position, and influence that characterize groups and individuals in the functional organizations of a society are brought into play in the formation of public opinion.

The picture of a series of groups and individuals of significantly different influence interacting in the formation of public opinion holds true equally well with reference to the expression of public opinion. By expression of public opinion I mean bringing the public opinion to bear on those who have to act in response to public opinion. This expression is not in the form of a parade or array of the views of disparate individuals, in an open forum. Where the views are voiced in open forum they are likely, as has been indicated, to be in one way or another the expression of group views. But in addition to the voicing of views in the open forum, the expression of public opinion is in the form of direct influence on those who are to act in response to public opinion. Through such means as letters, telegrams, petitions, resolutions, lobbies, delegations, and personal meetings interested groups and individuals bring their views and positions to bear on the key persons who have to make the decisions. I am not concerned with whether such forms of expressing public opinion should occur; I merely wish to emphasize that in any realistic consideration of public opinion it must be recognized that such means of expressing public opinion do occur. A society which has to act will use the channels of action that it has in its structure.

6.) The last feature of public opinion that I wish to note is that in *any realistic sense* public opinion consists of the pattern of the diverse views and positions on the issue *that come to the individuals who have to act in response to the public opinion.* Public opinion which was a mere display, or which was terminal in its very expression, or which never came to the attention of those who have to act on public opinion would be impotent and meaningless as far as affecting the action or operation of society is concerned. Insofar as public opinion is *effective* on societal action it becomes so only by entering into the purview of whoever, like legislators, executives, administrators, and policy makers, have to act on public opinion. To me this proposition is self-evident. If it be granted, the character of public opinion in terms of meaningful operation must be sought in the array of views and positions which enter into the consideration of those who have to take action on public opinion.

It is important to note that the individual who has to act on public opinion has to *assess* the public opinion as it comes to his attention, because of the very fact that this public opinion comes to him in the form of diverse views and usually opposed views. Insofar as he is responsive to public opinion he has to weigh the respective views. How this assessment is made is an obscure matter. But one generalization even though trite, can be made safely, to wit, that the individual takes into account different views only to the extent to which such views count. And views count pretty much on the basis of how the individual judges the "backing" of the views and the implication of the backing. It is in this sense, again, that the organization of the society with its differentiation of prestige and power, enters into the character of public opinion. As was explained above, the key person who has to act on public opinion is usually subject to a variety of presentations, importunities, demands, criticisms, and suggestions that come to him through the various channels in the communicative structure of society. Unless one wishes to conjure in his imagination a very fanciful society he must admit that the servant of public opinion is forced to make an assessment of the expressions of public opinion that come to his attention and that in this assesment consideration is given to expressions only to the extent to which they are judged to "count."

The foregoing six features are, I believe, trite but faithful points about public opinion as it functions in our society. They may serve as a background for the examination of public opinion polling. I may state here that in this discussion I am not concerning myself with the problem of whether the individual opinions one gets through the polling interview are reasonably valid. My discussion, instead, is concerned with the question of the value of poll findings even if one makes the dubious assumption that the individual opinions that are secured are valid.

In my judgment the inherent deficiency of public opinion polling, certainly as currently done, is contained in its sampling procedure. Its current sampling procedure forces a treatment of society as if society were only an aggregation of disparate individuals. Public opinion, in turn, is regarded as being a quantitative distribution of individual opinions. This way of treating society and this way of viewing public opinion must be regarded as markedly unrealistic. The best way I can bring this out is by making continuous reference to the common sense empirical observations of public opinion that were noted previously. We do not know at all whether individuals in the sample represent that portion of structured society that is participating in the formation of public opinion on a given issue. That the sample will catch a number of them, or even a larger number of them, is very likely. But, as far as I am able to determine, there is no way in current public opinion polling to know much about this. Certainly the mere fact that the interviewee either gives or does not give an opinion does not tell you whether he is participating in the formation of public opinion as it is being built up functionally in the society. More important, assuming that the sample catches the individuals who are participating in the formation of the given public opinion, no information is given of their part in this process. One cannot identify from the sample or from the replies of those constituting the sample the social nitch of the individual in that portion of the social structure in which the public opinion is being formed. Such information is not given in the conventional items of age, sex, occupation, economic status, educational attainment or class status. These are rarely the marks of significant functional position in the formation of public opinion on a given issue. We do not know from the conventional kind of sample or from the responses of the interviewee what influence, if any, he has in the formation or expression of public opinion. We do not know whether he has a following or whether he doesn't. We do not know whether or not he is speaking on behalf of a group or groups or whether he even belongs to functional groups interested in the issue. If he does, perchance, express the views of some such functional group, we don't know whether or not that group is busily at work in the channels of society to give vigorous expression to their point of view. We do not even know whether he, as an individual, is translating his opinion into what I have termed previously "effective public opinion."

In short, we know essentially nothing of the individual in the sample with reference to the significance of him or of his opinion in the public opinion that is being built up or which is expressing itself functionally in the operation of society. We do not know whether the individual has the position of an archbishop or an itinerant laborer; whether he belongs to a powerful group taking a vigorous stand on the issue or whether he is a detached recluse with no membership in a functional group; whether he is bringing his opinion to bear in some fashion at strategic points in the operation of society or whether it is isolated and socially impotent. We do not know what role, if any, any individual in the sample plays in the formation of the public opinion on which he is questioned, and we do not know what part, if any, his opinion as given has in the functional public opinion which exists with reference to the issue.

What has just been said with reference to the individual component of the public opinion poll applies collectively to the total findings. The collective findings have no assurance of depicting public opinion on a given issue because these findings ignore the framework and the functional operation of the public opinion. If this is not clear from what has already been said, I would like to point out the enormous difficulty that occurs when one seeks to assess the findings of a public opinion poll in terms of the organization of society with which an administrator, legislator, executive, or similarly placed person has to contend. As I have stated earlier such an individual who is presumably responsive to public opinion has to assess public opinion as it comes to his attention in terms of the functional organization of society to which he is responsive. He has to view that society in terms of groups of divergent influence; in terms of organizations with different degrees of power; in terms of individuals with followings; in terms of indifferent people—all, in other words, in terms of what and who counts in his part of the social world. This type of assessment which is called for in the instance of an organized society in operation is wellnigh impossible to make in the case of the findings of public opinion polls. We are unable to answer such questions as the following: how much power and influence is possessed by those who have the favorable opinion or the unfavorable opinion; who are these people who have the opinion; whom do they represent; how well organized are they; what groups do they belong to that are stirring around on the scene and that are likely to continue to do so; are those people who have the given opinion very much concerned about their opinion; are they going to get busy and do something about it; are they going to get vociferous, militant, and troublesome; are they in the position to influence powerful groups and individuals *who are known;* does the opinion represent a studied policy of significant organizations which will persist and who are likely to remember; is the opinion an ephemeral or momentary view which people will quickly forget? These sample questions show how markedly difficult it is to assess the results of public opinion polling from the standpoint of the things that have to be taken into account in working in an organized society. This difficulty, in turn, signifies that current public opinion polling gives an inaccurate and unrealistic picture of public opinion because of the failure to catch opinions as they are organized and as they operate in a functioning society.

What I have said will appear to many as distinctly invalid on the ground that public opinion polling has *demonstrated* that it can and does detect public opinion faithfully, by virtue of its marked success in predicting election returns. This contention needs to be investigated carefully, particularly since in most circles polling, wherever applied, is regarded as intrinsically valid because of its rather spectacular success in predicting elections. What I think needs to be noted is that the casting of ballots is distinctly an action of separate individuals wherein a ballot cast by one individual has exactly the same weight as a ballot cast by another individual. In this proper sense, and in the sense of real action, voters constitute a population of disparate individuals, each of whom has equal weight to the others. Consequently, the sampling procedure which is based on a population of disparate individuals is eminently suited to securing a picture of what the voting is likely to be. However, to regard the successful use of polling in this area as proof of its automatic validity when applied to an area where people do not act as equally weighted disparate individuals begs the very question under consideration. I would repeat that the formation and expression of public opinion giving rise to effective public opinion is not an action of a population of disparate individuals having equal weight but is a function of a structured society, differentiated into a network of different kinds of groups and individuals having different weight and influence and occupying different strategic positions. Accordingly, to my mind, the success attending polling in the prediction of elections gives no validity to the method as a means of studying, recording or measuring public opinion as it forms and functions in our society.

BIBLIOGRAPHY

General Titles

The Annals of the American Academy of Political and Social Science, *Communication and Social Action*, 250, March 1947.

Lyman Bryson, editor. *The Communication of Ideas*. New York: Harper, 1948.

Paul F. Lazarsfeld, editor. *Radio and the Printed Page*. New York: Duell, Sloan and Pearce, 1940.

Paul F. Lazarsfeld and Frank Stanton, editors. *Radio Research, 1941, Radio Research, 1942-43*. New York: Duell, Sloan and Pearce, 1941, 1944.

Paul F. Lazarsfeld and Frank Stanton, editors. *Communications Research, 1948-49*. New York: Harper, 1949.

Wilbur Schramm, editor. *Communications in Modern Society*. Urbana: University of Illinois, 1948.

Wilbur Schramm, editor. *Mass Communications*. Urbana: University of Illinois, 1949.

Bruce L. Smith, Harold D. Lasswell, and Ralph D. Casey. *Propaganda, Communication, and Public Opinion*. Princeton, New Jersey: Princeton University Press, 1946.

Propaganda and Promotional Activities. Minneapolis, Minnesota: University of Minnesota Press, 1935.

Douglas Waples, editor. *Print, Radio and Film in a Democracy*. Chicago: University of Chicago Press, 1942.

Theory of Public Opinion

Floyd H. Allport. "Toward a Science of Public Opinion," *Public Opinion Quarterly*, 1, January 1937, pp. 7-23.

Norman Angell. *The Public Mind: Its Disorders and Its Exploitation*. London: Douglas, 1926.

Wilhelm Bauer. *Die Öffentliche Meinung in der Weltgeschichte*. Wildpark-Potsdam: Athenaion, 1930.

Wilhelm Bauer. "Public Opinion," *Encyclopedia of the Social Sciences*, 12, pp. 669-74.

James Bryce. *The American Commonwealth*. New York: Macmillan, 1899, pp. 247-54.

Sigmund Freud. *Group Psychology and the Analysis of the Ego*. London: Hogath Press, 1922.

Karl Mannheim. *Ideology and Utopia: An Introduction to the Sociology of Knowledge*. New York: Harcourt, Brace, 1936.

Peter H. Odegard. *The American Public Mind*. New York: Columbia University, 1930.

Kurt Riezler. "What is Public Opinion," *Social Research*, 11, 1944, pp. 397-427.
Hans Speier. "Historical Development of Public Opinion," *American Journal of Sociology*, 55, January 1950, pp. 376-388.
Jean Stoetzel. *Theorie des Opinions*, Paris. Presses Universitaires de France, 1943.
William Graham Sumner. *Folkways: A Study of the Sociological Importance of Usages, Manners, Customs, Mores and Morals*. Boston: Ginn, 1906. Chapters I and V.
Alexis de Tocqueville. *Democracy in America*. New York: Oxford University Press, 1947. Part I, Chs. 9-17.
Ferdinand Tönnies. *Kritik der Öffentlichen Meinung*. Berlin: J. Springer, 1922.
Graham Wallas. *The Great Society*. New York: Macmillan, 1914.
Francis G. Wilson. "Concepts of Public Opinion," *American Political Science Review*, 27, 1933, pp. 371-92.

Formation of Public Opinion

Gabriel Almond. "The Political Attitudes of Wealth," *Journal of Politics*, 8, August 1945, pp. 213-55.
Louis Bean. *Ballot Behavior: A Study of Presidential Elections*. Washington, D.C.: American Council on Public Affairs, 1940.
Louis Bean. *How to Predict Elections*. New York: Knopf, 1948.
Robert T. Bower. "Opinion Research and Historical Interpretation of Elections," *Public Opinion Quarterly*, 12, Fall 1948, pp. 455-69.
Helen Dinerman. "1948 Votes in the Making," *Public Opinion Quarterly*, 12, Winter 1948-49, pp. 586-98.
Leon Festinger. "The Role of Group-belongingness in a Voting Situation," *Human Relations*, 1, 1947, pp. 154-180.
Alfred W. Jones. *Life, Liberty and Property*. Philadelphia: Lippincott, 1941.
Herbert Goldhamer. "Public Opinion and Personality," *American Journal of Sociology*, 55, January 1950, pp. 346-354.
Arthur Kornhauser. "Public Opinion and Social Class," *American Journal of Sociology*, 55, January 1950, pp. 333-45.
Gardner Murphy and Rensis Likert. *Public Opinion and the Individual*. New York: Harper, 1938.
Theodore Newcomb. *Personality and Social Change*. New York: Dryden, 1943.
Muzafer Sherif and Hadley Cantril. *The Psychology of Ego-Involvements, Social Attitudes, and Identifications*. New York: J. Wiley, 1947.
Samuel Stouffer and others. *The American Soldier: Vol. I, Adjustment During Army Life: Vol. II, Combat and Its Aftermath*. Princeton: Princeton University Press, 1949.
U.S. Strategic Bombing Survey. *The Effects of Strategic Bombing on German Morale*. Washington: Government Printing Office, 1947.
U.S. Strategic Bombing Survey. *The Effects of Strategic Bombing on Japanese Morale*. Washington: Government Printing Office, 1947.

Impact of Public Opinion on Public Policy

Gabriel Almond. *The American People and Foreign Policy*. New Haven: Yale Univ. Press, 1950.
Jerome S. Bruner. *Mandate from the People*. New York: Duell, Sloan and Pearce, 1944.

Lewis E. Gleek. "96 Congressmen Make Up Their Minds," *Public Opinion Quarterly*, 4, 1940, pp. 3-24.

Mortin Grodzins. *Americans Betrayed.* Univ. of Chicago Press, 1949. Chapters 2-7, Appendices I and II.

Avery Leiserson. "Opinion Research and the Political Process," *Public Opinion Quarterly*, 13, Spring 1949, pp. 31-38.

Lester Markel, ed. *Public Opinion and Foreign Policy.* New York: Harper, 1949.

"The Public Opinion Polls: Dr. Jekyll or Mr. Hyde," *Public Opinion Quarterly*, 4, June 1940, pp. 212-84.

Lindsay Rogers. *The Pollsters: Public Opinion, Politics and Democratic Leadership.* New York: Knopf, 1949.

David Truman. "Public Opinion Research as a Tool of Public Administration," *Public Administration Review*, 5, 1945, pp. 62-72.

Public Opinion Measurement

(Although no readings in public opinion measurement have been included, a selected bibliography is presented because of the importance of the topic for students.)

Albert Blankenship. *How to Conduct Consumer and Opinion Research.* New York: Harper, 1946.

Hadley Cantril. *Gauging Public Opinion.* Princeton: Princeton University Press, 1947.

John Dollard. "Under What Conditions Do Opinions Predict Behavior?" *Public Opinion Quarterly*, 12, Winter 1948-49, pp. 623-32.

Morris H. Hansen and Philip M. Hauser. "Area Sampling—Some Principles of Sampling Design," *Public Opinion Quarterly*, 9, Summer 1945, pp. 183-193.

Hearings Before the Committee to Investigate Campaign Expenditures. House of Representatives, 78th Congress, 2nd Session, on H. Res. 551, Pt. 12, Washington: Govt. Printing Office, 1945.

Herbert Hyman. "Problems in the Collection of Opinion-Research Data," *American Journal of Sociology*, 55 January 1950, pp. 362-70.

Daniel Katz. "Do Interviewers Bias Polls?" *Public Opinion Quarterly*, 6, Summer 1942, pp. 248-268.

Arthur Kornhauser. "The Problems of Bias in Opinion Research," *International Journal of Opinion and Attitude Research*, 1, December 1947, pp. 1-16.

Arthur Kornhauser. "Are Public Opinion Polls Fair to Organized Labor?" *Public Opinion Quarterly*, 11, Winter 1946-47, pp. 484-500.

Paul F. Lazarsfeld. "The Controversy Over Detailed Interviews—An Offer for Negotiation," *Public Opinion Quarterly*, 8, Spring 1944, pp. 38-60.

Quinn McNemar. "Opinion-Attitude Methodology," *Psychological Bulletin*, 43, July 1946, pp. 289-374.

E. E. Maccoby and R. R. Holt. "How Surveys Are Made," *Journal of Social Issues*, 2, 1946, pp. 45-57.

Frederick Mosteller and others. *The Pre-Election Polls of 1948*, New York: Social Science Research Council, 1949.

Norman Meier and Harold W. Saunders, editors. *The Polls and Public Opinion.* New York: Holt, 1949.

National Opinion Research Center. *Interviewing for N.O.R.C.*, Denver, 1945.

Arnold M. Rose. "Attitude Measurement and the Questionnaire Survey," *The Scientific Monthly*, 68, 1949, pp. 92-101.

Frederick F. Stephan. "History of the Uses of Modern Sampling Procedures," *Journal of the American Statistical Ass'n.,* 43, March 1948, pp. 12-39.

Frederick F. Stephan. "Sampling," *American Journal of Sociology,* 55, January 1950, pp. 371-375.

Frederick F. Stephan. "Sampling in Studies of Opinions, Attitudes and Consumer Wants," *Proceedings of the American Philosophical Society* 92, November 1948, pp. 387-398.

Samuel A. Stouffer and others. *Measurement and Prediction.* Princeton: Princeton University Press, 1950.

Samuel A. Stouffer. "Some Observations on Study Design," *American Journal of Sociology,* 55, January 1950, pp. 355-61.

L. L. Thurstone. "The Measurement of Opinion," *Journal of Abnormal and Social Psychology,* 22, 1928, pp. 415-30.

Theory of Communication

Gordon W. Allport and Leo Postman. *Psychology of Rumor.* New York: Henry Holt, 1947.

Frederick Charles Bartlett. *Political Propaganda.* New York: Macmillan, 1940.

Ernst Kris. "Danger of Propaganda," *American Imago,* 2, 1941, pp. 3-42.

Harold D. Lasswell. "Propaganda," *Encyclopedia of the Social Sciences,* 12, pp. 521-527.

Harold D. Lasswell. "The Triple-Appeal Principle," *American Journal of Sociology,* 37, May 1932, pp. 523-38.

Harold D. Lasswell. "The Strategy of Revolutionary and War Propaganda," in *Public Opinion and World Politics,* edited by Quincy Wright, Chicago: University of Chicago, 1933.

Robert K. Merton. "Introduction to Part III, The Sociology of Knowledge and Mass Communication" in *Social Theory and Social Structure.* Glencoe: Free Press, 1949, pp. 199-216.

Charles Morris. *Signs, Language and Behavior.* New York: Prentice-Hall, 1946.

William Isaac Thomas and Florian Znaniecki. "The Wider Community and the Role of the Press," in *The Polish Peasant in Europe and America.* Boston: Gorham Press, 1920, Vol. IV, pp. 241-271.

Charles K. Ogden and Ivan A. Richards. *The Meaning of Meaning: A Study of the Influence of Language upon Thought and of the Science of Symbolism.* New York: Harcourt, Brace, 1936.

Robert E. Park. "The Natural History of the Newspaper," *American Journal of Sociology,* 22, November 1923, pp. 273-89.

Robert E. Park. "News as a Source of Knowledge," *American Journal of Sociology,* 45, 1940, pp. 669-89.

Claude E. Shannon and Warren Weaver. *A Mathematical Theory of Communication.* Univ. of Illinois Press, 1949.

Norbert Wiener. *Cybernetics, or Control and Communication in the Animal and Machine.* New York: Wiley, 1948. Chapter 8: "Information, Language and Society."

NON-VERBAL COMMUNICATION

Herbert Blumer. "Social Attitudes and Non-Symbolic Interaction," *Journal of Educational Sociology,* 9, 1936, pp. 513-523.

Sebastian de Grazia. "Shostakovich's Seventh Symphony," *Psychiatry*, 6, 1943, pp. 117-22.

David Efron. *Gesture and Environment*. New York: Kings Crown Press, 1941.

Edward Sapir. "Speech as a Personality Trait," *American Journal of Sociology*, 32, May 1927, pp. 892-905.

Hans Speier. "Magic Geography," *Social Research*, 8, September 1941, pp. 310-20.

Communication Media: Structure and Control

HISTORY OF THE COMMUNICATION MEDIA

W. C. Ackerman. "The Dimensions of American Broadcasting," *Public Opinion Quarterly*, 9, Spring, 1945, pp. 1-18.

H. M. Beville, Jr. "The Challenge of the New Media," in *Communication in Modern Society*, edited by Wilbur Schramm. Urbana: University of Illinois, 1948, pp. 126-41.

Lewis Jacobs. *The Rise of the American Film: A Critical History*. New York: Harcourt, Brace, 1939.

Alfred McClung Lee. *The Daily Newspaper in America: The Evolution of a Social Instrument*. New York: Macmillan, 1937.

Lancelot Hogben. *From Cave Painting to Comic Strip: A Kaleidoscope of Human Communication*. New York: Chanticleer Press, 1949.

Frank Luther Mott. *American Journalism: A History of Newspapers in the United States through 250 Years: 1690-1940*. New York: Macmillan, 1941.

Malcolm Willey and Stuart A. Rice. *Communication Agencies and Social Life*. New York and London: McGraw-Hill, 1933, Part III. The Agencies of Mass Impression. Extended in Douglas Waples, "Communications," in *American Journal of Sociology*, 47, May 1942, pp. 907-17.

ORGANIZATION AND MANAGEMENT

Donald Blaisdell. *Economic Power and Political Pressure*. (Temporary National Economic Committee Monograph No. 26). Washington, D.C.: Government Printing Office, 1941.

Neil H. Borden. *The Economic Effects of Advertising*. Chicago: Richard D. Irvin, 1942.

Ralph D. Casey. "Pressure Groups and the Press," in *The Polls and Public Opinion edited by Norman C. Meier and Harold W. Saunders*. New York: Holt, 1949, pp. 124-40.

James T. Farrell. *The Fate of Writing in America*. New York: New Directions, 1946.

Federal Communications Commission. *Report on Chain Broadcasting*. Washington, D.C.: Government Printing Office, 1941.

Mae Huettig. *Economic Control of the Motion Picture Industry*. Philadelphia: University of Pennsylvania, 1944.

Ruth Inglis. *Freedom of the Movies*. Chicago: University of Chicago Press, 1946.

V. O. Key. "The Role and Technique of Pressure Groups," in *Politics, Parties and Pressure Groups*, New York: Crowell, 1942.

Duncan MacDougald, Jr. "The Popular Music Industry," in *Radio Research 1941*, edited by Paul F. Lazarsfeld and Frank K. Stanton, New York: Duell, Sloane and Pearce, 1941, pp. 65-109.

William Miller. *The Book Industry*. New York: Columbia University Press, 1950.

Gunnar Myrdal. *An American Dilemma*. New York: Harper, 1944. Vol. II, Ch. XLII. The Negro Press.

Peter H. Odegard. *Pressure Politics: The Story of the Anti-Saloon League*. New York: Columbia University, 1928.

Robert E. Park. *The Immigrant Press and Its Control*. New York: Harper, 1922, Chapters XV, XVIII.

Political and Economic Planning Group. *Report on the British Press*. London: P.E.P., 1938.

Temporary National Economic Committee. *The Motion Picture Industry—A Pattern of Control* (Monograph No. 43). Washington, D.C.: Government Printing Office, 1941.

Strother H. Walker and Paul Sklar. *Business Finds Its Voice*. New York: Harper, 1938.

Personnel

Theodore Adorno. "Anti-Semitism and Fascist Propaganda," in *Anti-Semitism: A Social Disease*, edited by Ernst Simmel. New York: International Universities Press, 1946, pp. 125-137.

Harold Lasswell. "The Person: Subject and Object of Propaganda," *Annals*, 1935, pp. 187-93.

Leo C. Rosten. *Hollywood*. New York: Harcourt, Brace, 1941. Part II.

Leo C. Rosten. *The Washington Correspondents*. New York: Harcourt, Brace, 1937. Chapters I, V, VI, VIII, IX.

Governmental Relations

Carl Friedrich and Evelyn Sternberg. "Congress and the Control of Radio Broadcasting," *American Political Science Review*, October and December, 1943, pp. 797-818; 1014-26.

Ernst Kris. "Mass Communications Under Totalitarian Governments," *Print, Radio, and Film in a Democracy*, edited by Douglas Waypes. Chicago: University of Chicago, 1942, p. 14-38.

James L. McCamy. *Government Publications for the Citizen*. New York: Columbia University Press, 1949.

James L. McCamy. *Government Publicity: Its Practice in Federal Administration*. Chicago: University of Chicago, 1939, Ch. VIII.

David Riesman. "Civil Liberties in a Period of Transition," in *Public Policy: Yearbook of Harvard Graduate School of Public Administration*, 3, 1942, pp. 33-96.

Thomas P. Robinson. *Radio Networks and the Federal Government*. New York: Columbia University, 1943. Ch. I-V.

Communication Content

Analysis of Media Content

Gordon Allport and Janet M. Faden. "The Psychology of Newspapers: Five Tentative Laws," *Public Opinion Quarterly*, 4, December 1940, pp. 687-703.

Bernard Berelson and Paul Lazarsfeld. *The Analysis of Communication Content*. University of Chicago, Mimeographed, 1948.

Bernard Berelson and Patricia Salter. "Majority-Minority Americans; An Analysis of Magazine Fiction," *Public Opinion Quarterly*, 10, Summer 1946, pp. 168-190.

Hornell Hart. "Changing Social Attitudes and Interests," in *Recent Social Trends in the U.S.* New York: McGraw-Hill, 1934, pp. 382-443.

Susan Kingsbury, Hornell Hart and others. *Newspapers and the News: An Objective Measurement of Ethical and Unethical Behavior by Representative Newspapers.* New York: Putnam's Sons, 1937, Ch. I, II, III.

Siegfried Kracauer. *From Caligari to Hitler.* Princeton: Princeton University Press, 1947.

Siegfried Kracauer. "National Types as Hollywood Presents Them," *Public Opinion Quarterly*, 13, 1949, pp. 53-72.

Ernst Kris and Hans Speier. *German Radio Propaganda.* New York: Oxford University Press, 1944.

Harold Lasswell, Nathan Leites and others. *Language of Politics: Studies in Quantitative Semantics.* New York: Stewart, 1949.

Harold D. Lasswell, *Propaganda Technique in the World War.* New York: Knopf, 1927.

Martha Wolfenstein and Nathan Leites. *Movies: A Psychological Study.* Free Press, 1950.

POPULAR CULTURE

Mortimer Adler. *Art and Prudence.* New York: Longmans, Green, 1937.

Theodore Adorno. "The Radio Symphony: An Experiment in Theory," in *Radio Research, 1941*, pp. 110-139.

Rudolph Arnheim. "The World of the Daytime Serial," in *Radio Research, 1942-43*, edited by Paul F. Lazarsfeld and Frank K. Stanton. New York: Duell Sloane and Pearce, 1943, pp. 507-548.

Lennox Gray. "Communication and the Arts," in *The Communication of Ideas,* edited by Lyman Bryson. New York: Harper, 1948, pp. 119-142.

Patricke Johns-Heine and Hans H. Gerth. "Values in Mass Periodical Fiction, 1921-40," *Public Opinion Quarterly*, 13, Spring, 1949, pp. 95-118.

Paul F. Lazarsfeld and Robert K. Merton. "Mass Communication, Popular Taste and Organized Social Action," in *The Communication of Ideas,* pp. 95-118.

Leo Lowenthal. "Historical Perspectives of Popular Culture," *American Journal of Sociology*, 55, January 1950, pp. 323-332.

Dwight MacDonald. "A Theory of 'Popular Culture'," *Politics* I, February 1944, pp. 20-23.

Edward A. Suchman. "Invitation to Music," in *Radio Research,* 1941, pp. 140-188.

George Orwell. *Dickens, Dali and Others: Studies in Popular Culture.* New York: Reynal and Hitchcock, 1946.

Katherine M. Wolf and Marjorie Fiske. "The Children Talk About Comics," in *Communications Research 1948-49* edited by Paul F. Lazarsfeld and Frank Stanton. New York: Harper, 1949, pp. 3-50.

Communication Audiences

THE AMERICAN AUDIENCE

Bernard Berelson. *The Library's Public.* New York: Columbia University Press, 1949.

Bernard Berelson. "The Public Library, Book Reading, and Political Behavior," *Library Quarterly,* 15, October 1945, pp. 281-299.

H. M. Beville, Jr. "The ABCD's of Radio Audiences," *Public Opinion Quarterly,* 4, June 1940, pp. 195-206.

Paul F. Lazarsfeld and Harry Field. *The People Look at Radio.* Chapel Hill: University of North Carolina Press, 1948.

Paul F. Lazarsfeld and Patricia Kendall. *Radio Listening in America.* New York: Prentice-Hall, 1948.

Robert S. Lynd and Helen M. Lynd. *Middletown in Transition.* New York: Harcourt Brace, 1937. Chapter X.

W. S. Robinson. "Radio Audience Measurement and its Limitations," *Journal of Social Issues,* 3, Summer 1947, pp. 42-60.

Wilbur Schramm and David M. White. "Age, Education, and Economic Status as Factors in Newspaper Reading," *Journalism Quarterly,* June 1949.

Douglas Waples. *People and Print: Social Aspects of Reading in a Depression.* Chicago: University of Chicago Press, 1937.

W. Lloyd Warner and Paul S. Lunt. *The Social Life of a Modern Community.* New Haven: Yale Univ. Press, 1941. Chapter XIX.

Louis R. Wilson. *The Geography of Reading.* Chicago: University of Chicago Press, 1938.

INTERNATIONAL COMMUNICATIONS

George G. Bruntz. *Allied Propaganda and the Collapse of the German Empire in 1918.* Stanford: Stanford University Press, 1938.

Harwood Childs and John B. Whitton. *Propaganda by Short Wave.* Princeton: Princeton University Press, 1942.

Alex Inkeles. "Domestic Broadcasting in the U.S.S.R.," in *Communications Research, 1948-49.* pp. 223-96.

Martin Kriesberg. "Soviet News in the New York Times," *The Public Opinion Quarterly,* 10, Winter 1946-47, pp. 540-64.

Paul F. Lazarsfeld and Genevieve Knupfer. "Communications Research and International Cooperation," in *The Science of Man in the World Crisis,* edited by R. Linton. New York: Columbia University Press, 1945.

Louis Nemzer. "Soviet Friendship Societies," *Public Opinion Quarterly,* 13, Summer 1949, pp. 265-84.

Charles Thompson. *Overseas Information Service of the United States.* Washington: Brookings Institution, 1948.

United Nations Educational, Scientific and Cultural Organizations. *Report of the Commission on Technical Needs in Press, Film, Radio.* Paris, 1948.

Douglas Waples and Harold Lasswell. *National Libraries and Foreign Scholarship.* Chicago: Univ. of Chicago Press, 1936.

L. W. White and Robert D. Leigh. *Peoples Speaking to Peoples.* Chicago: University of Chicago Press, 1946. Ch. I, II, VI.

Communication Effects

Gordon Allport and Hadley Cantril. *The Psychology of Radio.* New York: Harper, 1935.

Hadley Cantril, Hazel Gaudet and Herta Herzog. *Invasion from Mars.* Princeton: Princeton University Press, 1940.

H. F. Gosnell. *Machine Politics: Chicago Model.* Chicago: University of Chicago Press, 1937.

Carl I. Hovland and others. *Experiments on Mass Communications.* Princeton: Princeton University Press, 1949.

Marie Jahoda and Eunice Cooper. "The Evasion of Propaganda: How Prejudiced People Respond to Anti-Prejudice Propaganda," *Journal of Psychology,* 23, 1947, pp. 15-25.

Daniel Katz. "Psychological Barriers to Communication," *The Annals,* 250, March 1947, pp. 17-25.

Joseph T. Klapper. *The Effects of Mass Media: A Report to the Director of the Public Library Inquiry.* New York: Bureau of Applied Social Research, Columbia University, 1949.

Harold D. Lasswell and Dorothy Blumenstock. *World Revolutionary Propaganda.* New York: Knopf, 1939.

Harold D. Lasswell. "Radio as an Instrument of Reducing Personal Insecurity," *Studies in Philosophy and Social Sciences,* 9, 1941.

Frank L. Mott. "Newspapers in Presidential Campaigns," *Public Opinion Quarterly,* 8, Fall 1944, pp. 348-367.

Ruth C. Peterson and L. L. Thurstone. *Motion Pictures and the Social Attitude of Children.* New York: Macmillan, 1933.

William S. Robinson. "Radio Comes to the Farmer," in *Radio Research, 1941,* pp. 224-294.

Douglas Waples, Bernard Berelson and Franklyn Bradshaw. *What Reading Does to People.* Chicago: University of Chicago Press, 1940.

Public Opinion, Communication and Democratic Objectives

Robert J. Blakely. "The Responsibilities of an Editor," in *Communications in Modern Society,* pp. 220-38.

John Dewey. *The Public and Its Problems.* New York: Henry Holt, 1927.

William E. Hocking. *Freedom of the Press: A Framework of Principle.* Chicago: University of Chicago Press, 1947.

Harold D. Lasswell. "Policy and the Intelligence Function: Ideological Intelligence," in *The Analysis of Political Behavior,* New York: Oxford, 1947, pp. 120-32.

Joseph T. Klapper. "Mass Media and the Engineering of Consent," *American Scholar,* 17, October 1948, pp. 419-29.

Talcott Parson. "Propaganda and Social Control," *Psychiatry,* 4, November 1942, pp. 551-72.

Charles Siepmann. *Radio, Television and Society.* Oxford, 1950.

Charles Siepmann. *Radio's Second Chance.* Boston: Little, Brown, 1946.

Louis Wirth. "Consensus and Mass Communication," *American Sociological Review,* 13, February 1948, pp. 1-14.